WHO PAYS STATE AND LOCAL TAXES?

Who Pays State and Local Taxes?

Donald Phares
University of Missouri-St. Louis

Oelgeschlager, Gunn and Hain, Publishers, Inc.
Cambridge, Massachusetts

International Standard Book Number: 0-89946-026-7

Library of Congress Catalog Card Number: 80-15454

Printed in the United States of America

Library of Congress Cataloging in Publication Data

Phares, Donald.
Who pays state and local taxes?

Bibliography: p.
Includes index.
1. Tax incidence – United States. 2. Taxation, State. 3. Local taxation – United States.
I. Title.
HJ2322.A3P46 336.2'94'0973 80-15454
ISBN 0-89946-026-7

To Kathy and 37i: the former for love, the latter for peace of mind.

Contents

List of Tables

List of Figures

Acknowledgments

My gratitude in preparing this book extends to many people. As has become the custom to note, the final responsibility for all errors of omission or commission, of course, must rest squarely on the shoulders of the author; hopefully, they will not be too severe.

Financial assistance from the Ford Foundation combined with a willingness to "let me do my own thing," is greatly appreciated. Particular thanks goes to Jim Kelly of Ford, who was instrumental in the project getting off the ground. I would also like to note my appreciation to the participants in the critics session on this research sponsored by Ford and held in Arlington, Virginia in October 1979. I am grateful for the day's time they gave up, the effort expended in reading an earlier, shorter version of this book, and the many useful criticisms and comments they made. The participants were:

Mr. Robert M. Berne
Graduate School of Public Administration
New York University

Mr. David W. Breneman
The Brookings Institution

Ms. Susan Nelson
The Brookings Institution

Mr. Joseph Pechman
The Brookings Institution

Mr. Andrew Conlin
Professional Staff Member
Sub-Committee on Intergovernmental Relations

Mr. Thomas V. Seessel

Mr. Dennis DeTray
The Rand Corporation

Mr. Joel D. Sherman
Senior Research Manager,
School Finance Study
National Institute of Education

Ms. Carla Edlefson
Citizens' Council for Ohio Schools

Ms. Judith Fernandez
The Rand Corporation

Mr. William A. Gilbert
General Counsel to the Governor
State of Vermont

Ms. Susan Fuhrman
Consultant, The Ford Foundation

Mr. Joseph J. Minarik
The Brookings Institution

Mr. Thomas Vitullo-Martin

Mr. Will Myers
U.S. Advisory Commission on Intergovernmental Relations

Mr. William Wilken,
Senior Researcher, Education Policy Research Institute

At the University of Missouri-St. Louis, I want to thank Jim Laue, Director of the Center for Metropolitan Studies, for the time, environment, and support necessary to bring this project to fruition. No small amount of thanks is also due Sandy Beard and Tib Lanham for typing the seemingly endless drafts of the book. Bruce Welz was also of immense assistance in helping collect much of the data used at various stages in preparing the manuscript. Last, but by no means least, particular appreciation is noted to Dave Skinner. His special talents in getting the computer to cooperate, and at times almost "stand on its head," were absolutely essential to a timely completion of the project and also to the sanity of the author.

Preface

The financial pressures on state and local governments have come squarely into the public limelight. Although at one time only the interested academic or professional was concerned with these mundane matters, this is no longer the case. New York's fiscal trauma in 1975, California's Proposition 13 in 1978, and numerous defaults, near-defaults, and smaller-scale fiscal traumas over this period have all heightened awareness of and anxiety over what goes on in the state and local fisc. Recently, we have witnessed a contagion effect as legislators, politicians, and the media have jumped on the reform, cut, and limit bandwagon. Some form of tax or spending reform legislation has affected nearly every state in the recent few years. In addition, the once staunchly passive taxpayer qua taxpayer has assumed a role as social activist for a variety of reform proposals. Taxpayer groups are pushing for legislation influencing all sorts of state and local financial operations.

One concern common to many interested in or active in state-local tax reform pertains to fairness in taxation or, in slightly more technical parlance, tax equity. They desire to see that the cost of public operations is more fairly apportioned amongst citizens. "Who pays state and local taxes?" thus becomes a crucial question, one that is intimately linked to basic tax policy formulation. Since any change in a given tax system will benefit some more than others, it is more than out of a passing curiosity that the query who bears the burden for state and local spending operations is posed. Concern over taxpayer equity has become a focal element in policy moves to exempt food from the general sales tax, revise the individual income tax, reassess local property taxation, reform the system of school finance, or shift greater financial responsibility to the state and federal governments, to mention but a few areas.

The specific question of who pays state and local taxes is addressed in this book. In order to arm academics, professionals, legislators, the media, and citizen groups with an answer to this question, all taxes in each state are examined in terms of the claim they make on persons at various income levels. This claim or burden that state and local taxes exert on private income is examined both in terms of the quantity of the claim, or its magnitude, and its quality, that is, how it differentially affects low- versus high-income taxpayers. Armed with such detailed information, we have some indication of who pays the cost of state-local operations, how burdensome it is, and who will benefit most from the alteration of an existing tax structure. These data should prove to be a valuable input into a variety of policy issues.[a]

As will become obvious later in the book, the analysis of tax burdens can become an extremely complex, very theoretical subject laden with the strange lexicon, peculiar methodology, and unfamiliar statistical procedures often employed by economists. An attempt has been made to overcome whatever barrier this may impose by presenting the material in as understandable a form as possible, without any sacrifice to the rigor necessary for the results to be useful. Most of the highly theoretical or technical aspects have been simplified or summarized and then referenced for the reader interested in a more lengthy explanation. It is hoped that this strategy will make the findings, as well as the methodology, useful to a much broader audience. Finally, all of the basic empirical results on tax burdens are contained in the appendices so that the interested reader can glean whatever information is desired. Statistical findings on equity for each state and major taxes within a state are presented to allow for comparisons across states or with the average for the nation. Using the information contained herein, anyone interested is in a position to make whatever comparisons are of most interest.

[a]The reader interested in a brief summary of major findings might want to turn first to Chapter 7, pp. 167-170.

Chapter 1

The Analysis of State-Local Tax Equity: Background

The fiscal operations of state and local governments are increasingly coming into the public limelight. Although this notoriety began some time ago, it has been intensified by events such as New York City's financial crisis in the Spring of 1975 and numerous defaults or near defaults by local governments. Taxpayers, legislators, journalists, and state and local public officials have all been made painfully aware of the rising financial pressure (both real and perceived) emerging in this sector of the economy. In mid to late 1978, riding high on the tide of passage of California's Proposition 13, legislators began to advocate tax reform; journalists delved deeper and deeper into the complex, often unfathomable, machinations of state and local financial operations; taxpayers cried for relief of any kind, and public officials, meanwhile, were caught squarely between the jaws of a vise. On the one side were irate citizens demanding more services and, simultaneously, smaller tax bills and on the other were unions, inflation, recession, and a seemingly endless array of unmet demands.

Factors contributing to the situation are often bewildering, tend to be very complex, and have far-reaching effects. One issue at the core of the taxpayers' concern, and more and more that of politicians and policymakers as well, is the question of equity. A great deal (but certainly not all) of the unrest linked to the taxpayers' malaise hinges on issues that pertain to "who pays" and "who benefits" from state and local fiscal operations. Reassessment for the local property tax, reform of the educational finance system, exempting items such as food from the general sales tax, property tax circuit breaker relief, to mention but a few factors, all have their legislative impetus, in part at least, either in attempting to rearrange the tax burden from those with less ability to pay to those with more or in making certain that equals are treated more equally. These are classic statements about horizontal and vertical equity. Education finance provides an outstanding example in which equity has become a prime concern for professional research, public policymaking, and legal precedents such as *Serrano* and its progeny (see Odden, Berne, and Stiefel, 1979).

Despite what amounts to an apparently vast and expanding volume of both concern and anxiety over state-local fiscal operations, there remains a real lack of in-depth, comparative, empirical analysis of the burden imposed by various state-local taxes and the differential claim they make on persons at different income levels (i.e., their equity). This is not meant to imply that no attention has been devoted to the myriad specific facets of state or local tax equity. Merely skimming the annual indices of the *National Tax Journal,* the major professional journal in the field, will attest to this. Its pages contain literally hundreds of studies on various aspects of state and local finances. Rather, what is meant is that little empirical information exists on the burden and equity characteristics of individual states on a tax-by-tax and state-by-state basis (two exceptions are Phares, 1973, and Lile and Soule, 1969).

There is an expansive body of literature dealing with tax equity by governmental sector (e.g., Musgrave, 1952, or Pechman and Okner, 1974), a much smaller body that looks at equity within specific states (e.g., Brownlee, 1960, or Eapen and Eapen, 1970), but very few studies that explicitly examine the distributional impact of state and local taxes within the context of all of the fifty states. Given the attention that is currently being focused on state-local fiscal operations, the marked increase in tax reform, tax cut, and tax limitation type of legislation,[a] and a swelling concern over issues pertaining to equity, there is a definite need for information on the equity of various specific taxes and systems of taxes used by state and local jurisdictions. Armed with such information, more intelligent decisions can be reached about a large number of important public policy questions; to mention but a few:

Who Pays State and Local Taxes? It is imperative to answer this question if we are to devise equitable (or at least less inequitable)

[a] Matched on the other side of the budget by similar actions against spending.

schemes for distributing the cost of state and local operations. For the most part, we know relatively little about this subject. As one of the pioneering studies in the analysis of tax burdens noted, "... the question who pays the taxes must be answered if taxes are to be raised in accordance with the public's ideas of distributional justice ..." (Musgrave et al., 1951: 1).

How Do the Fifty States Compare with Each Other in Terms of the Level of the Tax Burden and the Equity of Their Tax Instruments? High tax burdens and adverse distributional impacts can affect state and local governments in important ways, ranging from their competitive position in a region to the need for intergovernmental assistance (federal to state or state to local) to the need for reform in federal-state-local fiscal arrangements to the deterioration of urban areas.

How Redistributive Are State-Local Fiscal Operations? This question notes a concern over the redistributive impact of the state-local fisc. Although it can only be addressed fully when the complete budget impact is looked at, dealing with the revenue side of the budget is at least a first step toward better understanding how this sector, de facto, performs a redistributive function.

What Progress Has Been Made in Promoting Taxpayer Equity? At present such a question can only be addressed loosely in terms of direction and impression. Without empirical information on who pays, there is simply no way to confront the issue in anything but a qualitative or at very best a crude quantitative manner. Regularization of the type of research done here would allow precise statements about such progress to be made.

How Does Tax Reform Influence Who Pays? Whenever reform to an existing tax system is implemented, there will be gainers and losers either absolutely or relatively. Part of the adjustment process is elicited in response to alterations in the level of tax burden and part will result from the distributional consequences of tax policy. To alter taxes piecemeal, here and there, without realizing the impact is bad enough but to talk of "reform," "cut," or "limitation" without knowing who is affected and by how much seems to defeat the purpose of intelligent public policy formulation. For example, we need only look at the outcome of Proposition 13 in California and see how little of the $7 billion cut in local taxes actually benefited the intended recipients, presumably California homeowners, to have this point driven home.

By having thus far focused a disproportionate share of our empirical efforts on sectoral profiles of burden and equity, we have foregone much of the detail that characterizes the federal system; we have implicitly assumed away, or hidden in statistical aggregates, the one feature of state-local operations that is most dominant – interstate differences. That is, by not examining the variation across states we are "methodologically hiding" valuable information about how they differ in their tax policies and the impact that they have on tax burdens and taxpayer equity in each state.

OBJECTIVES

The purposes of this book are several. First, a methodology is developed that allows for the estimation of measures of actual tax burdens in each of the fifty state-local systems for each tax in use.[b] To accomplish this a synthesis was made of the most recent "conventional wisdom" on the economic incidence of each tax; numerous data sources were scrutinized for their applicability to the empirical analysis of tax equity; estimates were devised of the spatial flow of taxes into and out of states; and statistical series were compiled to reflect crucial phenomena such as the distribution of state individual income tax payments, the distribution of income and families by income class, and the impact of federal tax law on the state-local tax burden.

Second, once estimates are made of who pays the taxes, there remains the tricky question of examining and summarizing the burden and equity of taxes across all states. Complexity of interpretation is now compounded since we are dealing with fifty states. In addition, care must be taken to consider both facets of the equity issue, that is, the *level* of burden and its *pattern.* To state that a tax is a "regressive nightmare," as has often been said or implied of the property tax, is one thing; to say that it is regressive and also exerts a high burden implies something altogether different about its economic impact and, therefore, about tax reform policy. Thus, a second component in studying this problem deals with developing a set of measures that portray each facet of the burden, both its level and pattern.

Finally, findings derived from the quantitative estimates need to be set in the context of issues related to public policy, tax reform, and future research endeavors. With data on tax equity and burden for specific revenue sources, we can use this information to analyze a broad variety of policy concerns ranging from exempting items from the general sales tax to educational finance reform to the competitiveness of states vis-à-vis their tax burdens to the "fairness" of a

[b] The District of Columbia is not included.

state's tax system. Without concrete estimates of who actually pays taxes broken down by state and by type of tax, we can never adequately address the complex issue of taxpayer equity. Without this information, policy and tax reform must proceed in what amounts to at best a partial vacuum and at worst a total void. With such information, however, reform can be much more precisely targeted to achieve a desired effect, and the impact of alternative policies can be simulated within specific systems.

Given the tightness of state and local coffers, it will be increasingly necessary to target the outcomes of tax reform so that they are as cost-effective as possible. The greater the empirical base for targeting reform, the more precise and less wasteful will be the results. It is similar to using a nuclear device to demolish a building instead of a few sticks of strategically placed dynamite. The former is certainly effective but not in terms of cost. We need only turn to the very costly and inefficient changes resulting from California's Proposition 13 and how much more the state's residents *could* have benefited from such a drastic modification in local finance.

CAVEAT RECITATOR: SOME LIMITATIONS

So that the reader will be able to exercise caution in making use of the data and interpreting the results that follow, some warnings have to be made explicit at the outset. As is well known to any student of tax burden or tax equity, a variety of assumptions must be made for the analysis to be completed. It is useful to spell out some of the major assumptions that relate to the methodology adopted here.

Empirical findings in the chapters to follow should not be interpreted as reflecting all possible nuances in state or local tax policy. Perusal, for example, of Commerce Clearing House's *State Tax Reporter* for individual states clearly shows the impossibility of such an undertaking. There are simply too many differing provisions among the fifty states, and within states across their thousands of local governments, to allow us to deal with anything but the major contributors to policy outcomes. The burden estimates are intended to show patterns of incidence and levels of burden with enough precision to allow states to be ranked, classified, compared, and so forth. Directly related to this factor is treatment of all local governments within a state as if they were a single fiscal entity. In effect, an "averaging out" of variation across local jurisdictions within a state is assumed, an obviously necessary assumption given their number, over 78,000 as of 1977. We are, in effect, dealing with fifty states and fifty local sectors, in which the latter stands as representative for local governments within a state.

Some additional caveats need to be kept in mind. First, no attention is given to the expenditure side of the budget or, in other words, the question of "who benefits?" Although there is no doubt that this problem is worthy of attention, it is beyond the intended scope of this book. The reader is warned to keep in mind that high tax burdens in states like California and New York are matched with high expenditure benefits, and low burdens in states like Missouri with low levels of spending. We are addressing only the tax side of the budget and must leave expenditure and net fiscal incidence for future analysis. The importance of the full budget's impact is clearly acknowledged.

Second, no consideration is given to adjusting tax burden measures to compensate for a declining marginal utility of money. Although it is clear that such a phenomenon would affect the interpretation of the burden and how it might be divided up, we are in no position to make the interpersonal utility comparisons necessary to relate a 1-percent burden in the under $3,000 income class to an identical burden in the over $35,000 class.

Third, no attention is given to the excess burden or efficiency aspects of state or local taxes. Attention is focused on estimating the actual impact of various taxes rather than how some hypothetical modification might move us toward a more optimal position, that is, in a Pareto sense. Efficiency features of a tax would, of course, enter into consideration of any reform or revision to an existing tax structure.

Fourth, the incidence of taxation without attempting to delineate the full effect of tax policy is examined. Although the general equilibrium nature of incidence is well recognized and has been given extensive theoretical scrutiny (Break, 1974; Mieszkowski, 1969), at an empirical level ceteris paribus must be invoked. As Break (1974: 124) has so aptly stated, "each and every effect [of a tax on private real incomes] cannot, and indeed should not, be analyzed. Only the important ones are worth the cost and effort of detailed study." An empirical solution must rely on the "best" available theory on shifting and incidence balanced against unavoidable empirical, methodological, and data constraints.

Fifth, because we live in a world of less than perfect information, studying tax burdens is an endeavor in which this lack becomes painfully obvious. Given the vast amount of information required to estimate burden by state, tax, and income class, it is often necessary to use less than perfect statistical series as proxy for incidence effects, income distributions, collections, and so forth. This becomes clearer in Chapters 2 through 4. The reader is warned that the data are not always exactly what theoretical considerations mandate.

Finally, it should be noted that data on burdens are not estimates in an econometric or statistical sense. Rather, they are based on theoretical assumptions concerning shifting and incidence, income measures, spatial tax flows, and the like. They are best viewed as an applied side of tax incidence theory. But they go beyond a mere statement of the difference between statutory and economic incidence by estimating the magnitude of the economic impact at various income levels.

ESTIMATING TAX BURDENS: AN OVERVIEW

The concept of a "tax burden" is far from unequivocal. Depending upon the purpose, many alternative specifications have been used (e.g., Aaron, 1965; Conrad, 1955; Donnahoe, 1947). Usually, however, the notion relates taxes paid, however defined, to a measure of ability to pay that is usually some variant of income.[c] Thus, we can begin the analysis by defining burden as an effective tax rate (*ER*), or actual tax payments as a percentage of income.[d] Exactly what enters into the numerator and denominator of this expression will only be sketched here and then dealt with in detail in Chapters 3 and 4.

Since the concern is with taxpayer equity, burden must be examined at several points along an income distribution. The basic measure, therefore, becomes an effective rate of taxation measured at several points along the income continuum. The income classes actually employed are:[e]

Under		$ 3,000
$ 3,000	–	3,999
4,000	–	4,999
5,000	–	5,999
6,000	–	6,999
7,000	–	7,999
8,000	–	9,999
10,000	–	11,999
12,000	–	14,999

[c] Consumption has been suggested by many as a "better" basis for determining tax liability (Musgrave and Musgrave, 1980: 242-247).

[d] The distinction between a nominal rate, as specified by law, and the effective tax rate is crucial here.

[e] There are other approaches to this measurement. Although we use absolute income levels, others have used population deciles, for example (Pechman and Okner, 1974). The final selection of income classes was conditioned by many factors, not the least of which was data availability. This is discussed in Chapter 3.

15,000	–	19,999
20,000	–	24,999
25,000	–	29,999
30,000	–	34,999
Over		$35,000

For each of these fourteen intervals, effective rates are computed. These figures provide the basic data on the level of the burden as well as the incidence pattern as we move from low to high income. They enable us to address the issue of equity with some degree of precision.

In essence, two basic steps are involved in estimating an effective rate: first, to determine the components that comprise the numerator (actual tax payments); second, to arrive at an appropriate measure of ability to pay, for the denominator. Once this is done tax burden can be defined simply as:

$$ER_{ijk} = \frac{T_{ijk}}{Y_{ij}}$$

where ER = effective rate
T = $(C - E + I - F)$
C = total tax receipts
E = exported taxes
I = imported taxes
F = federal tax offset
Y = income
i = states
j = income classes
k = type of tax

These *ER*s can then be "put together" in whatever manner is most appropriate to the task at hand. The components of the numerator and denominator are discussed fully in Chapters 3 and 4.

The next step is to disaggregate tax collections into categories that are meaningful for policy and detailed enough to allow a separate theoretical treatment for shifting and incidence. Too aggregate a measure of collections, in effect, would disguise some of the variation in burden that characterizes state-local systems. For example, to estimate the impact of property taxation as though it were a "single unified" tax would negate the distinction between personal and real property as well as that between the economic incidence of the real property tax on single-family dwellings as opposed to that on commercial or industrial property. Burden estimates by income level would differ markedly depending on whether the property tax is treated as a $55-billion lump sum or as a group of taxes on various types of personal and real property with often vastly different economic effects.

In order to make the effective rate estimates as "realistic" as possible, collections have been broken down into components whenever it was felt necessary to account for alternative shifting and incidence assumptions or the distinction between the state and local sectors. Accordingly, data on fifty categories of taxation were assembled, and in many instances, alternative incidence assumptions were specified for a particular tax to reflect a range of theoretical opinions (this is discussed in Chapter 3). The final categories are as shown in Table 1-1.

In addition to separate estimates for each of the fifty specific categories in Table 1-1, with seventy-four shifting and incidence assumptions, total effective rates were computed to reflect the following burden for groups of related taxes or levels of government:

Total state selective sales and gross receipts taxes
Total state general and selective sales and gross receipts taxes
Total state license taxes
Total state property taxes
Total state taxes

Table 1-1. Detail on Tax Collection Data

General Tax Category	*Number of Specific Taxes* *Total*	*State*	*Local*	*Number of Incidence Assumptions Employed*[a]
General sales and gross receipts	2	1	1	2
Selective sales and gross receipts	13	8	5	14
Licenses	10	9	1	14
Individual income	2	1	1	2
Corporation net income	1	1	–	3
Death and gift	1	1	–	1
Severance	1	1	–	1
Document and stock transfer	1	1	–	1
Other (n.e.c.)	2	1	1	2
State property	3	3	–	3
Local personal property	6	–	6	8
Local real property	7	–	7	22
Imported	1	(Combined)		1
Total	50	27	22	74

[a] Detail is provided in Chapter 3 and Table 3-1.

Total local nonproperty taxes
Total local personal property taxes
Total local real property taxes
Total local property taxes
Total local taxes
Total state and local taxes

To reflect disagreement over the economic incidence of certain taxes, these totals were computed three ways: (1) benchmark (standard case), (2) most regressive, (3) most progressive (see Chapter 3). When taken all together, this compilation generates ninety-three matrices of effective tax rates showing a specific type of burden in each state across fourteen income classes. These individual matrices of tax rates (in Appendix A) become the empirical basis on which the burden and equity of state-local tax systems can be discussed and analyzed. In effect, they allow a great deal of precision in estimating the incidence of each type of tax and maximum flexibility in developing relevant totals and reflecting alternative theoretical considerations.

When effective rates across income classes are estimated for each specific tax, we have a data base that enables us to determine burdens aggregated in any way desired, for example, across taxes or across governmental sectors. We can then proceed to the in-depth analysis of the burden and equity characteristics of state-local tax systems in Chapter 5 and 6.

PRIMARY ACCOMPLISHMENTS

In fiscal 1976 all state and local governments in the United States raised in excess of $156 billion in revenue from the fifty categories of taxes outlined in Table 1-1. The burden on private income that resulted is what we are concerned with in this book. In other words, how much of a claim did the state-local sector exert on private incomes?

The aggregate claim by major source and by state is indicated in Table 1-2. As can be seen in the table, there is significant variation both across states and by type of tax. By far the highest burden of the state-local system is Alaska at 21.6 percent; the lowest is Alabama at 9.43 percent of income. Looking across the table, we can pick out the high-burden state sector (Alaska at 17.8 percent); the high-burden local sector (New York at 9.42 percent); states that allow more liberal local use of nonproperty taxes (New York at 2.97 percent); Delaware's heavy use of corporate and business license taxes (3.06 percent); high reliance on the individual income tax in states like Alaska (4.36 per-

Table 1-2. State and Local Taxes as a Percentage of Income[a]

	State						Local			
State	Total General Sales	Total Selective Sales	Total Licenses	Individual Income	Corporate Income	Total State	Total Nonproperty	Total Property	Total Local	Total State and Local
Alabama	2.24	2.36	0.51	1.27	0.34	7.03	1.39	1.01	2.40	9.43
Alaska	b	1.87	0.63	4.36	0.92	17.87	0.94	2.80	3.74	21.62
Arizona	3.30	1.46	0.46	1.23	0.35	7.72	0.88	3.99	4.88	12.61
Arkansas	2.45	2.08	0.63	1.50	0.57	7.40	0.20	2.16	2.36	9.77
California	2.59	1.08	- 0.35	2.04	0.88	7.45	0.98	5.93	6.91	14.37
Colorado	1.84	1.07	0.41	1.95	0.42	5.87	1.32	4.25	5.57	11.44
Connecticut	2.58	1.86	0.42	0.24	0.68	6.02	0.05	5.48	5.53	11.55
Delaware	b	1.86	3.06	3.86	0.62	9.80	0.34	2.06	2.41	12.21
Florida	2.59	1.99	0.60	b	0.37	6.06	0.57	3.21	3.78	9.84
Georgia	2.43	1.67	0.27	1.62	0.52	6.59	0.68	3.45	4.13	10.73
Hawaii	5.71	1.84	0.09	3.41	0.65	11.79	0.66	2.83	3.50	15.29
Idaho	1.97	1.40	0.92	2.19	0.70	7.31	0.09	3.50	3.59	10.91
Illinois	2.32	1.52	0.55	1.68	0.43	6.62	0.93	4.41	5.34	11.97
Indiana	2.86	1.16	0.34	1.28	0.27	6.07	0.09	3.72	3.81	9.89
Iowa	2.12	1.29	0.83	2.34	0.46	7.24	0.08	4.81	4.90	12.14
Kansas	2.23	1.26	0.51	1.44	0.69	6.35	0.23	4.60	4.83	11.19
Kentucky	2.43	2.07	0.42	1.74	0.80	8.36	0.93	1.91	2.85	11.21
Louisiana	2.20	1.79	0.59	0.61	0.45	8.67	1.78	1.81	3.59	12.27
Maine	2.81	2.20	0.68	0.97	0.60	9.88	0.02	3.46	3.49	13.38
Mayland	1.50	1.60	0.34	2.82	0.39	7.01	1.72	3.33	5.06	12.07
Massachusetts	0.97	1.92	0.22	3.39	0.90	7.61	0.04	6.98	7.02	14.63
Michigan	1.87	1.21	0.66	1.97	0.58	6.59	0.38	4.95	5.33	11.92
Minnesota	1.85	2.08	0.60	3.70	0.85	9.67	0.16	4.38	4.54	14.21
Mississippi	4.25	2.12	0.58	1.05	0.41	8.74	0.15	2.54	2.70	11.45
Missouri	1.99	1.19	0.55	1.27	0.31	5.41	1.32	3.47	4.80	10.21
Montana	b	1.88	0.63	2.39	0.56	6.80	0.22	6.05	6.27	13.08
Nebraska	1.87	1.54	0.55	1.19	0.32	5.53	0.41	5.59	6.01	11.55
Nevada	2.44	3.12	1.08	b	b	7.17	1.47	3.56	5.04	12.21

Table 1–2 *(continued)*

	State						Local			
State	*Total General Sales*	*Total Selective Sales*	*Total Licenses*	*Individual Income*	*Corporate Income*	*Total State*	*Total Nonproperty*	*Total Property*	*Total Local*	*Total State and Local*
New Hampshire	b	2.34	0.62	0.13	0.50	3.87	0.11	5.90	6.02	9.90
New Jersey	1.76	1.39	0.64	0.21	0.48	4.83	0.67	6.76	7.43	12.27
New Mexico	4.08	1.82	0.64	0.97	0.39	9.65	0.29	1.77	2.07	11.72
New York	1.87	1.47	0.35	3.43	0.98	8.51	2.97	6.45	9.42	17.94
North Carolina	1.70	2.16	0.65	2.21	0.57	7.53	0.52	2.48	3.01	10.54
North Dakota	3.30	1.53	0.91	1.76	0.58	8.62	0.20	4.04	4.24	12.86
Ohio	1.62	1.50	0.66	0.81	0.42	5.24	1.04	3.63	4.67	9.92
Oklahoma	1.21	1.76	0.81	1.34	0.35	6.67	0.81	2.28	3.10	9.77
Oregon	b	1.04	0.80	3.35	0.47	5.86	0.26	5.50	5.77	11.64
Pennsylvania	2.05	1.77	0.87	1.56	0.91	7.56	1.42	2.98	4.40	11.97
Rhode Island	2.10	2.06	0.41	1.76	0.67	7.35	0.04	5.06	5.10	12.46
South Carolina	2.80	2.08	0.37	1.83	0.59	7.83	0.18	2.44	2.63	10.47
South Dakota	2.86	2.17	0.67	b	0.06	5.94	0.59	6.10	6.70	12.64
Tennessee	2.61	1.59	0.82	0.10	0.60	5.98	1.21	2.56	3.78	9.76
Texas	2.08	1.87	0.70	b	b	5.92	0.58	3.69	4.28	10.20
Utah	2.96	1.12	0.36	2.12	0.37	7.19	0.64	3.18	3.83	11.02
Vermont	1.15	3.16	0.90	2.42	0.54	8.44	0.07	6.01	6.08	14.52
Virginia	1.27	1.67	0.40	2.02	0.42	6.00	1.30	2.79	4.09	10.10
Washington	4.41	1.71	0.50	b	b	8.18	0.88	2.57	3.46	11.64
West Virginia	4.34	2.23	0.53	1.51	0.21	8.95	0.45	2.08	2.53	11.49
Wisconsin	2.16	1.41	0.48	3.54	0.70	8.94	0.07	4.44	4.51	13.45
Wyoming	3.30	1.31	1.28	b	b	7.92	0.28	5.53	5.62	13.54
Average	2.23	1.76	0.64	1.66	0.50	7.52	0.66	3.89	4.55	12.07

Source: Derived from data compiled for this study.

a Aggregate tax collections divided by aggregate income for each state. See Chapter 3 for a discussion of the income base used.

b Tax not used in this state.

cent), or Delaware (3.86 percent); or Massachusetts' high property tax burden (6.98 percent). We can see the burden that each of these taxes or sectors imposes but only in the aggregate for all income combined.

The single major accomplishment of this book is to take aggregate data on burden and break them down into the burden imposed on taxpayers at different levels of income. The chapters to follow develop the methodology to permit each of the fifty types of taxes to be examined separately. Thus, we develop estimates of effective tax rates for ninety-three tax categories, fifty states, and fourteen income classes. This represents 65,100 effective tax rates, each showing how the total burdens in Table 1-2 vary by tax, state, and income level. The full results are contained in Appendix A.

A second accomplishment pertains to the issue of "fairness" or equity. By using the basic data on burdens, we can examine the equity of taxes, systems of taxes, or governmental sectors. In Chapters 5 and 6 these phenomena are looked at in detail and states are classified by their degree of progressivity or regressivity.

Another major outcome is providing detail on how tax burdens and equity differ from state to state. As is documented in Chapter 2, to date researchers have concentrated their empirical efforts on entire governmental sectors or on specific states. This method disguises in statistical aggregates vast differences in level of burden and equity across systems, and this variation is of considerable concern for a wide variety of policy issues.

Finally, the data contained in Appendix A allow the reader to tailor an analysis to any purpose at hand. Individual states or sets of states can be compared to others or to the U.S. average and specific taxes can be similarly compared. This affords maximum flexibility for those interested in more elaborate comparisons than those presented here.

Chapter 2

Who Pays and Who Benefits? The Historical Setting of Fiscal Incidence Studies

The question "who pays for government?" is an area of inquiry that has had a long and, it might even be said, venerable tradition in public finance. Since the emergence of public finance as a distinct area of study in economics, a great deal of theoretical and empirical analysis has been devoted to understanding the shifting and incidence of taxation. More recently, this work has been extended to determining the magnitude of the claim associated with specific taxes or governmental sectors. To be useful for policy purposes, this empirical analysis has focused on the incidence of taxation rather than on its legal impact, and the concern has been with "who actually pays" rather than the less interesting question who is liable for payment.

Analysis of shifting and incidence comprises an important segment of public finance literature. By introducing a variety of assumptions about market structure, elasticities, cost conditions, tax instruments, type of tax, and so on, economists are able to isolate theoretically, empirically, or both, the effects of a tax, with varying degrees of success (see Mieszkowski, 1969, or Break, 1974). That there exists controversy over the findings and how they should be interpreted is evident from the recent dialogue between the "new" and "old" views of the property tax (McLure, 1977) or the long-standing debate over the tax on corporate income (Mieszkowski, 1969).

The analytical framework most often employed is partial equilibrium, and in this context any solution of the ultimate incidence of a tax is not forthcoming. A major problem, which should at least be recognized, however, is the general equilibrium nature of tax incidence. Factors that influence shifting are numerous, very complex, and highly interrelated, and the complete ramifications of any levy can only be traced when recognition is given to every adjustment that is elicited in response to the tax. If certain assumptions are made, for example, concerning market structure, and everything else is held under ceteris paribus, the incidence of a tax can be spelled out. However, for a theoretically precise solution, a complete specification of all adjustment processes is entailed.

At an empirical level, a general equilibrium model of incidence is not manageable or even conceptually clear, particularly when the focus is on each tax in each state. The format of a fully specified general equilibrium model for all state-level economies would defy description. Consider for a moment the complexity of large-scale econometric models of the U.S. economy carried to the individual state level and dealing with the complex phenomena operating at this level. Any empirical analysis must make use of existing theory and empirical work on the shifting and incidence of specific taxes balanced against unavoidable empirical constraints. Any study of burdens, including this book, must invoke simplifying assumptions while at the same time attempting to account for as much of the variation in state-local policy as is empirically practicable. That the results may be less than perfect is readily admitted by anyone engaged in such research; that they are useful seems to be self-evident.

Tax burden studies are, in essence, empirical manifestations of assumptions about shifting and incidence; they do not test these assumptions but instead use them to estimate burden. They go one step beyond the qualitative results of incidence theory, however, by determining the size of the impact at its final resting place. To specify that a tax levied against corporate income is fully or partially shifted backward to owners or forward to consumers does nothing more than indicate the direction of movement. A crucial policy consideration is the magnitude of this impact. Therefore, the next logical step is to utilize this information to estimate the dollar amount of these claims. As one of the pioneering tax burden studies emphasized: "There is much qualitative theory on where taxes fall and on their eventual effect on the economy, but very little is known quantitatively in terms of dollar aggregates" (Tarasov, 1942:1). Although this is certainly less true almost forty years later for the analysis of entire governmental sectors, it remains basically true in terms of the comparative status of the fifty states. We still know very little about differences in tax burdens among states.

In order to investigate the impact of state and local taxation, analysis needs to be focused on the distribution of tax payments and income by income category. Burden is then computed by relating taxes paid to income. This ratio – an effective tax rate – reflects the claim on private income that is exerted by various taxes used by the state-local sector. It should be interpreted as an average for a class and does not reflect any attempt to deal with excess burden, the incidence of public sector expenditures, or variations in the marginal utility of money. It is a first cut at how the public sector affects persons at various income levels.

Past research on the distribution of government costs has been concentrated at two nearly polar opposite positions. The great bulk of this empirical work has examined aggregate tax burdens for the federal, state-local, or "all-government" level, the objective being to determine the full impact of government on the economy. At the other extreme are studies that examine taxation in only one particular state system. The vast area in between, which deals with each of the fifty state-local tax systems in a comparative context, is a virtual vacuum with few exceptions (Phares, 1973; Lile and Soule, 1969).

The remainder of this chapter serves two purposes. First, it traces the historical evolution in focus, methodology, and empirical feasibility of fiscal incidence studies. Second, it delineates the polarity that has developed in the literature by indicating the nearly complete lack of attention that has been given to variations in the distributional aspects of tax burdens across states.[a]

FISCAL INCIDENCE: WHO PAYS?

The earliest fiscal incidence studies were done during the late 1930s and early 1940s and only dealt with the revenue side of the budget. They provided the initial impetus for the subsequently much more detailed and refined empirical investigations on the distributive impact of government tax policy. One of the first studies, Newcomer (1937), examined the burden on twenty hypothetical families in various occupations and income positions in New York and Illinois. The focus was very limited, and accordingly, the findings were extremely tentative as generalizations of national patterns. This study, however, coped with numerous theoretical problems relevant to shift-

[a] The model to accomplish this is discussed fully in Chapters 3 and 4. The purpose here is to indicate the relevance of such a study. No attempt will be made to review all the literature, but only to examine the major studies and their general evolution.

ing and incidence, provided estimates based on alternative theoretical stances, and utilized the most recent and refined data sources on income distribution, consumption patterns, taxes, and so on. Nonetheless, the results were vulnerable because of its extremely limited scope.

The first analysis to deal with the actual distribution of national tax burdens was done by the Temporary National Economic Committee (TNEC) for the period 1938-1939 (Tarasov and Colm, 1942). Although the existing data had improved little from that available to Newcomer, the focus was on the actual, rather than a hypothetical, burden. Acdingly, the findings were more generally indicative of the national patterns. In a follow-up study, Tarasov (1942) responded to many of the criticisms leveled against the original TNEC study by introducing refinements in the techniques used to allocate taxes by income class and in the data on income. The result was a more recent and polished version of the TNEC study that was purged of many of its methodological and empirical shortcomings.

The major contribution made by these very early studies lies in their attempt to determine an overall pattern of burden by developing a model that explicitly related shifting and incidence theory to data on income and consumption patterns. Compared to earlier efforts, the TNEC-Tarasov research represented substantial progress in arriving at a representative picture of the national pattern of governmental costs.

Following in the tradition of the Tarasov work came a long series of research concerned with the distribution of aggregate tax burdens. One of the most important studies was by Musgrave and his colleagues (1951) for 1948. This work represented by far the most meticulous investigation that had been undertaken up to that time. More importantly, it provided a theoretical, statistical, and methodological focal point for subsequent research. The rationale for the study was clearly pointed out by the authors, who felt that ". . . the question who pays the taxes must be answered if taxes are to be raised in accordance with the public's ideas of distributional justice . . ." (p. 1).

The authors of the study readily admit to using some "grossly simplifying assumptions" and to relying upon data that are less precise than what they consider desirable. Nonetheless, it has become a classic in the tax burden literature because it was the first attempt at formulating a precise theoretical specification of the problem and then implementing it with careful attention to empirical detail. Effective tax rates are estimated for each major governmental sector, and several alternative assumptions concerning shifting and incidence are shown explicitly to provide a range of theoretically plausible situations.

The research by Musgrave et al. (1951) provided the genesis for a number of follow-up studies that also looked at aggregate burdens. Reverberating through scholarly journals during the 1950s was a lengthy debate on the theoretical and empirical nuances of tax burden analysis. Much of this debate occurred between Musgrave and Tucker with the original Musgrave study as the point of departure for further refinement and discussion.

Tucker (1951) took issue with the findings of this study primarily because of its exclusion of certain elements from the income base in calculating effective rates. He redid Musgrave's analysis for 1948 using a broader income definition that contained an additional $13 billion in nonmonetary income. Tucker feels his refinements on Musgrave's study were "enough to vitiate his principal conclusion" about the high burden on low incomes and the "U-shaped" equity pattern (p. 274). He also incorporated some modifications in shifting and incidence assumptions, but readily admits they do little to alter Musgrave's principal findings. The primary source of discrepancy in results derives directly from the income concept chosen for calculating effective rates. The variation that emerges in the final distribution is most pronounced for the low-end income classes where the $13 billion in nonmonetary income is of greatest relative importance.

The debate between Tucker and Musgrave was brought into focus at a round table discussion, "Who Pays the Taxes?", held at the 1952 National Tax Association conference (Musgrave, 1952; Tucker, 1952a; Pechman, 1952). The outcome was general agreement over the source of differences in tax burden studies but no consensus as to the correct measure of income to be used in computing the burdens.

Still another facet was added to the controversy by Bishop (1961). Using Department of Commerce data on income for 1958, he pointed out that there was a large difference between gross national product (GNP) and personal income – some $83 billion, or almost 20 percent of GNP. He went on to argue: "It can hardly be concluded that no part of the tax burden falls on this sizable amount of 'product' for which there are no corresponding income payments to individuals" (p. 42). To adjust for this he developed estimates using net national product (NNP) as the income base. Findings were, once again, an aggregate for major governmental sector and suggested a proportional overall burden for the classes that contained the majority of the population.

One of the most recent investigations of burdens by governmental sector is by Pechman and Okner (1974) for 1966. This study differs in several ways from its predecessors but probably most significantly in terms of the income base. The authors argue for the use of what they call "adjusted family income" as an income base. The primary difference is the inclusion of $61 billion in indirect business taxes. To accomplish this they developed a microanalytic data base from Internal

Revenue Service and Survey of Economic Opportunity (SEO) data for 1967. This MERGE file, as they call it, contains a sample of records from tens of thousands of individual tax returns and SEO files selected to produce representative results for each level of government. Their income base is then "tailored" to correspond theoretically to incidence assumptions for various taxes. In other words, the income base becomes a function of the tax being examined and is derived from data in the MERGE file. This work is clearly a step forward in empirical and theoretical refinement but obviously is dependent upon a data base that generally is unavailable even at the national level.

FISCAL INCIDENCE: WHO PAYS AND WHO BENEFITS?

One weakness inherent in aggregate tax burden studies, and recognized by their authors, is the focus on the revenue side of the budget in isolation from the effects of government spending. The impact of tax policy can only be fully understood in light of total budgetary impact, including the benefits derived from government expenditures. As Musgrave (1952) pointed out almost thirty years ago, ". . . [a] defect of this . . . approach is that it is based on a concept of *absolute* incidence which is open to considerable theoretical objection. Rather we ought to think in terms of a combined incidence of public expenditures and taxes . . ." (p. 193). Although it may be perfectly legitimate for analysis to focus separately on each component of a budget, an analytically complete picture emerges only when the entire budget, that is, both taxes and expenditures, is given scrutiny. This necessitates an empirical examination of the benefits derived from public programs as they affect persons at different income levels. When tax burdens and expenditure benefits are juxtaposed, we see the net fiscal impact of government operations on the distribution of income.

One of the first research attempts to take into account both the burdens and the benefits of governmental activity was undertaken by Adler (1951). He was interested in determining the redistribution of income that had occurred over the period 1938-1939 to 1946-1947. Thus, his analysis dealt with both the distribution of taxes and expenditures and the net fiscal incidence of the public sector for combined governmental operations. Although the revenue side of his model benefited from an extensive past literature, virtually no statistical or theoretical analysis had been done up to then on the incidence of public spending. Adler was helping to break new ground in the field of fiscal incidence.

Explicitly recognizing the weak conceptual foundation on which to base any study of the distribution of government benefits, Adler put forth a rationale based more on politics than economics. He noted that since "Statesmen and politicians show full awareness of the incidence of benefits of government expenditures ... There is ... strong presumption in favor of the economist's attempt to allocate the benefits of government services to distinct income classes ..." (pp. 366-367). His results are presented for total government – federal, state, and local – combined. The primary weakness of dealing with a composite government category lies in the distortion introduced by not giving account to the differences in redistributive impact by level of government. Although this lack is recognized by Adler, no estimates broken down by governmental sector are developed.

The most significant contribution of his study lies not so much in the precision of the results as in Adler's shift in conceptual emphasis. He seeks to define an aggregate picture of the full fiscal impact of public operations and the extent of redistribution that occurred as a result between 1938-1939 and 1946-1947. This study is a first attempt to deal explicitly with the full government budget and, accordingly, is open to considerable criticism, especially as it pertains to the incidence of certain expenditure categories. However, the genesis is provided for more refined subsequent analysis of net fiscal impact.

Published just after Adler's study was one by Tucker (1953) that also dealt with the incidence of government expenditure benefits. Acknowledging the nearly complete lack of empirical research on the impact of public spending, he attempts to reach "broad conclusions" about the net effect of government on the redistribution of income. Tucker's calculation of burden rests almost entirely on his past research (1951). He goes further, however, by relating this distribution to one estimated for government programs for "all government." Noting that some forms of spending may be viewed as wasteful, actually harmful to certain categories of citizens, or in the extreme "positively injurious to the nation as a whole," he treats every dollar of spending as "representing" a dollar's worth of benefit to someone (p. 528).

Based on expenditure data for the year 1948, Tucker isolates over $30 billion that cannot be identified as accruing to any specific group, of which $19.6 billion is from federal spending and $10.6 from state and local. In face of this situation, he decided to allocate this full amount (55 percent of government spending in 1948) using four alternative assumptions based on proportionality – population, income, consumption, and capital. Needless to say such an approach by itself raises doubts about the results, except as a crude indication of the fiscal impact of government operations.

The next major empirical examination of the complete public budget was undertaken by Gillespie (summarized in Gillespie, 1965), this time using data on each major sector of the U.S. economy for the year 1960. Acutely aware of the precarious empirical and theoretical grounds on which to base such an analysis, Gillespie developed a detailed methodology to approximate expenditure incidence. His study commences with a specification of several possible budget impact situations of the public sector on the private sector, defining incidence in terms of "changes in relative income positions of families due to the tax and expenditure policies of the public sector" (p. 125). Empirically his task has three main facets: (1) measurement of an income base, (2) calculation of tax incidence, and (3) calculation of expenditure incidence. By combining these three dimensions in different ways, Gillespie arrives at ten possible "budget experiments," each of which makes a particular statement about the treatment of income (Y), taxes (T), transfer payments (R), and government expenditures on goods and services (B). Empirical findings are presented for two of these ten budgets; they are:

$$ER = \frac{T}{Y}$$

$$ER = \frac{T}{(Y + B + R - T)}$$

where Y = broad income
$(T + B + R - T)$ = "adjusted broad income"
ER = effective rate

Gillespie explicitly admits that his study adds nothing to the extant tax burden literature. Rather, any contribution lies in estimating the distribution of government expenditure benefits and the combined fiscal impact of tax and spending policy. A similar study was also done by Gillespie (1964) for the Canadian economy as part of the Royal (Carter) Commission on Taxation.

Gillespie's work is meticulous in detailing the allocation of public expenditures by income class. However, painstaking attention to detail does not overcome the many empirical and theoretical pitfalls that plague quantifying the effects of public spending. Brazer noted this in a review of Gillespie's work, suggesting that the number and type of assumptions he was forced to make may render the overall results ". . . worthless, or worse than worthless if anyone should look to them for policy guidelines" (Brazer, 1966).

A more recent analysis of fiscal incidence is that of the Tax Foundation (1967a) done under the aegis of George Bishop. This study concentrates on providing broad estimates of tax burdens, expenditure benefits, and net impact for each level of government. Although the basic methodology does not differ markedly from Gillespie's, there are several notable refinements. First, and perhaps of most consequence for the results, the research benefits from the availability of much more precise and detailed data on consumer expenditure and income patterns as compiled by the Bureau of Labor Statistics (1966). Inclusion of these data allowed for substantial improvement over the allocator series used in earlier research, for the statistical base of this survey was a much larger national sample that provided a more accurate depiction of consumption and income patterns. Second, a tentative attempt was made to determine changes in the pattern of redistribution. Although 1961 was the base year chosen for most detailed scrutiny, fiscal incidence estimates were also computed for 1965. These findings are highly tentative, however, since no correction was made for shifts in the distribution of income between 1961 and 1965. Third, the study employed net national product (NNP) as an income base for effective rates, thus differing from earlier studies by the inclusion of $48 billion in indirect business taxes as an imputed component to individual income. This builds on past work by Bishop (1966) on the use of indirect business taxes in computing effective tax rates.

The most recent aggregate study of fiscal incidence is by Musgrave, Case, and Leonard (1974), which updates Musgrave's earlier work to 1968. They determine the distribution of taxes and expenditures and net fiscal impact by major governmental sector using a wide variety of alternative incidence assumptions.

FISCAL INCIDENCE IN A SPECIFIC STATE-LOCAL SYSTEM

The final major category of fiscal incidence study looks at the public sector within a particular state. The focus here is almost totally opposite to the studies dealing with total public sector activity discussed above. Although a large number of studies on the structure and characteristics of taxes in particular states have been done over the years, many of them either ignore the question of tax burden or treat it casually (see McLure, 1966: 369-370, for a list of some of these studies). Their primary concern has generally been with the overall structure of the tax system; trends in revenue, expenditures, and debt composition; and direct implications for potential legislation; but not with the distribution of the costs of government. More recently this literature has extended to the field of school finance, which has generated dozens of such state studies (refer to Garms, Guthrie, and

Pierce, 1978: Section III). There are, however, several notable exceptions, each of which addresses the issue of the distribution of the cost of public goods. Perhaps the three best known are the studies of Michigan, Minnesota, and Wisconsin. Each offers a detailed analysis of the distribution of the tax burden within a state.

The Michigan work, directed by Harvey Brazer, was one component of a much more comprehensive analysis of the entire fiscal structure of Michigan (Musgrave and Daicoff, 1958). In this study, Musgrave and Daicoff attempt to delineate the incidence of taxes collected in the state, acknowledging the nearly complete lack of precedent for such research and warning that the findings reflect certain assumptions about the shifting of taxes under the application of often "rather insufficient data."

Assumptions about tax incidence in the Michigan study do not differ substantially from research that has already been done. Much of the data from which the allocators were derived came from the Time-Life *Study of Consumer Expenditures* or the University of Michigan, Survey Research Center, *Survey of Consumer Finances* annual data on consumer behavior. In this respect, this work suffers from most of the data weaknesses that plagued its predecessors. The results represent a first attempt at uncovering the distribution of public sector costs within a specific state.

In addition to looking at the pattern of burdens, Musgrave and Daicoff also provide estimates "of a highly tentative sort" concerning the impact of Michigan state and local spending. This is a first attempt at investigating the combined tax and expenditure incidence for a single state, thus allowing some tentative inferences to be drawn about the net fiscal effect of the state of Michigan.

One unique feature of the study is its treatment of Michigan vis-à-vis the balance of the national economy. It is assumed that the state acts as an independent decision-making unit formulating unilateral policies. An "open" economy is the milieu in which Michigan functions, and incidence is handled in this context.[b]

A second major study of tax incidence in a particular state was done for Wisconsin under the direction of Harold Groves (University of Wisconsin, 1959). The major concern was the incidence of taxation in Wisconsin in the context of legislative tax reform. The analysis differs methodologically from the Michigan study because of the assumption that Wisconsin functions in a "closed" economy; that is, Wisconsin is not treated in a national context but rather as it relates to its six surrounding states – Illinois, Indiana, Iowa, Michigan, Minnesota, and

[b] This assumption has implications for the geographical incidence of taxation and is discussed further in Chapter 4.

Ohio. Any so-called openness in its economy is approximated by relating Wisconsin to its neighbor states, the implication being that Wisconsin's fiscal decisions are not unilateral but rather are made in response to decisions in its "fiscal community." In effect, Wisconsin's economy is treated as open with respect to its fiscal community but closed with respect to the nation as a whole. Recognition is given to the exporting of taxes out of state, but aside from the federal offset, tax exporting is handled in a closed economy context. Two alternatives are presented for the treatment of other forms of exporting and tax importing. One assumed that exported and imported taxes offset each other, which in effect assumes away the problem; the other allows for the exporting of taxes (about 21 percent of all taxes) but does not consider burdens flowing into Wisconsin. This represents an improvement, however, over the Michigan study in which the burden on Michigan residents is all that is considered.[c]

Another major individual state study was done on Minnesota by O. H. Brownlee (1960). Emphasis here, as was true in Michigan, is on the complete state budget and the net fiscal impact of all public operations. A caveat is clearly noted about the crude estimate of the benefits of public services, the problems in evaluating government expenditures at other than cost, and the need for a range of incidence assumptions containing plausible estimates with judgments as to the most probable outcomes.

Although Brownlee's study benefits from refinements in earlier work, it also inherits many of the same problems. The most refined information on consumption patterns was still the Time-Life and Survey Research Center data. In addition, conceptual problems involved in allocating benefits from government expenditures, although recognized, remained no less formidable. For example, all government services are evaluated at cost and treated as benefiting either persons or property. They were then allocated to income groups using population, personal services, and income for services benefiting persons, and expenditure series for property-related services. This is, at best, a crude approximation to the actual benefit distributions. Finally, the tax exporting issue is recognized but not handled with precision. Explicit provision is made for the federal tax offset as one type of exporting, but estimates of exporting to residents of other states were difficult to obtain and, thus, only crudely accounted for. The phenomenon of importing is not dealt with at all.

Fiscal incidence was given a thorough analysis for the state of Con-

[c] Methodoligically, a case has been developed for each approach. Chapter 4 discusses the treatment of state-local taxes in the context of the burden on residents of a state from *all* sources of *state-local* taxation.

necticut by Eapen and Eapen (1970) using data for 1967. In many ways this study is enhanced by the refinements introduced in earlier research. Tax burdens and expenditure benefits are examined under three different income concepts using alternative incidence assumptions where appropriate; exporting is accounted for explicitly by type of tax due both to the federal offset and the price/migration effect; and finally net fiscal impact for all Connecticut governmental units is spelled out. This represents a thorough analysis of the impact of one state's fiscal operations.

A similar study for Hawaii was done by Ebel and Kamins (1975) for the year 1970. It generally followed the same procedure as in Connecticut but did not look at the spending side of the budget. More recently, Daicoff and Glass (1978) have looked at who paid the taxes in Kansas for the year 1978. It is clear that the analysis of fiscal incidence within a given state has benefited from, and in large part been made possible by, the evolution of research over the past few decades, from the very early studies by Newcomer, Tarasov, and Colm to the most recent and sophisticated studies by Pechman and Okner and Musgrave and his colleagues.

INTERSTATE COMPARISONS OF TAX BURDENS

If one point emerges from this discussion of the fiscal incidence literature it is that, with a few exceptions, little research has focused on tax burdens in each of the fifty states as distinct fiscal units having unique tax structures, economic conditions, income status, and consumption patterns. None to date has looked at expenditure incidence on a state-by-state basis. What has been done, de facto, is to disguise variation across states, which is characteristic of this governmental sector, in a statistical artifact called the "state-local" sector. Musgrave, Case, and Leonard (1974: 280-281) note this explicitly as it pertains to their work, but it certainly also applies to any study that looks at the subnational governments as a composite sector. The unique features of each state are, in effect, lost through the process of aggregation.

A few studies have attempted to confront this issue. Lile and Soule (1969) examine interstate differences in family tax burdens for 1968. They use, however, a "hypothetical" approach that is limited to families living in the largest city in each state. Tax burdens are computed for combined state and local taxes for a family of four located in each of seven income ranges. Although it is definitely a step in the direction of improving knowledge about interstate variations, its limitations are obvious.

Another study, meanwhile, has attempted to examine the actual distribution of the cost of government by state. Phares (1973) estimated the burden of each major category of state-local taxation for each of nine income classes on a state-by-state basis using data for 1962. Explicitly taken into account was the spatial flow of taxes among the fifty states, both exported and imported. These estimates of effective tax rates were then used to classify states according to equity. Although tentative in methodology, data, and findings, it does represent an attempt to delineate the uniqueness of each state's level and pattern of burden. Another study, albeit only remotely related, was done by Fuchs and Rabin (1979). Their study, however, is qualitative in nature rather than quantitative. It looks at features of the tax system that relate to equity, not quantitative estimates of burden for persons at different income levels.

LACUNA: RATIONALE FOR THE PRESENT STUDY

The purpose of this review of the fiscal incidence literature was twofold. The first was to trace the development in technique, methodology, and data availability and the extremes in the focus of tax burden and benefit studies. Although initially research emphasized the national distribution of tax burdens for various levels of government solely in terms of tax policy, analysis was later extended to include the complete budget. This permitted inference about the total fiscal impact of the public sector. Another group of studies was concerned with fiscal incidence within specific state-local systems.

The second purpose was to point out the gap that has emerged in the literature concerning the nature of interstate variations in tax burdens. It is this distinct void and the initial efforts of Phares (1973) on which this book will build. The next two chapters develop a model for estimating burdens for specific taxes state by state.

Chapter 3

A Model for Estimating Effective Tax Rates

The tasks of this chapter include setting out a methodology for imputing tax payments to income classes and discussing the denominator used in computing effective tax rates. These two major components are necessary for determining the burden imposed on taxpayers at each income level. The imputation of tax payments by income category is presented first, followed by a discussion of the income base used and the primary data sources for the study.

SHIFTING AND INCIDENCE ASSUMPTIONS

A fundamental task confronting any study of equity is to incorporate extant theoretical and empirical knowledge on shifting and incidence into a methodology for allocating lump sum tax collections to various income classes. To say, for example, that the general sales tax is borne by consumers of taxed items is only a first step, a qualitative statement of ultimate resting place or economic incidence. The next step is to obtain a statistical series to serve as a proxy for incidence. "Allocators" must be constructed to reflect the incidence pattern of each tax being examined. Each tax can then be imputed among income classes according to the percentage distribution of the allocator series. This procedure generates a distribution of tax revenue consistent with incidence theory. The accuracy of the final distribution is, of course, a function of the theoretical analysis of shifting and incidence and the accuracy of the allocator in manifesting this theory. This procedure gives us a quantitative measure of tax payments by income category, that is, the numerator of the effective rate.

The propensity of a tax to be shifted from the point of legal or statutory impact to its final resting place on those who bear the economic costs is crucial information in determining burden and equity; whether a tax, such as the corporation income tax, is borne by consumers or by owners of capital makes a distinct difference. Table 3-1 spells out fully the shifting and incidence assumptions adopted in this book and the statistical series used to impute tax receipts to specific income classes. In several instances, alternative assumptions and allocators were employed to reflect theoretical disagreement, as with the "new" versus the "old" view of property tax incidence (Aaron, 1974; Netzer, 1973) or with the corporation income tax (Break, 1974: 138-154). Three cases resulted from this procedure:

Benchmark: This is used as a point of reference or a "standard" case. It allows for partial shifting or is an alternative view felt to provide the most reasonable basis for establishing burden and equity.

Most Regressive: This case allows for greater forward shifting to consumers.

Most Progressive: This case allows for greater backward shifting to owners of capital.

These distinctions are of most consequence for levies on corporate activity and real property. The final selection of a shifting and incidence assumption was made by examining past studies and conventional use. It should be noted, however, that no attempt has been made to resolve the theoretical controversy that surrounds several of these taxes.[a]

General Sales Tax

The general sales tax is assumed to be fully shifted forward to the consumer. This has become a standard assumption about this tax (see Musgrave, Case, and Leonard, 1974: 261, or Pechman and Okner,

[a] Refer to Table 3-1 for detail on incidence assumptions and allocator series used. The literature in this area is extensive. No attempt will be made to present all of the arguments here. Rather, the following is a brief synthesis of this literature with indication of the incidence assumptions used in this book. The interested reader is urged to consult the references for further detail or a general source such as Musgrave and Musgrave (1980).

Table 3-1. Incidence Assumptions and Allocator Series for Individual State and Local Taxes

Tax	*Incidence*[a]	*Allocator*[b]
State Taxes:		
General sales and gross receipts taxes	Consumers of taxed items	Special series on consumption of taxed items
Selective sales and gross receipts:		
Motor fuels	⅓ consumers in general, ⅔ households consuming gasoline	Consumption and gasoline expenditures
Tobacco	Consumers of tobacco products	Tobacco products expenditures
Alcohol	Consumers of alcoholic beverages	Alcoholic beverages expenditures
Insurance (B)[d]	⅗ consumers, ⅖ households consuming insurance	Consumption and insurance expenditures
Insurance	Households consuming insurance	Insurance expenditures
Utilities	Consumers of utility services	Gas, electric, and telephone expenditures
Pari-mutuels	Users of recreational facilities	Recreation expenditures
Amusements	Users of recreational facilities	Recreation expenditures
Other	Consumers in general	Total consumption expenditures
License taxes:		
Motor vehicles (B)[d]	¼ consumers, ¾ drivers	Consumption and vehicle operations expenditures
Motor vehicles	Drivers	Vehicle operations expenditures
Corporations in general (B)[d]	½ consumers, ½ owners of capital	Consumption and dividend income
Corporations in general (R)[e]	Consumers in general	Total consumption expenditures
Corporations in general (P)[f]	Owners of capital	Dividend income
Occupations and businesses (n.e.c.)[g]	Businesses	Business net profit
Motor vehicle operations	Drivers	Vehicle operations expenditures
Hunting and fishing	Hunters and fishers	Recreation expenditures
Alcoholic beverages	Consumers of alcoholic beverages	Alcoholic beverages expenditures
Public utilities	Consumers of utility services	Gas, electric, and telephone expenditures

Table 3–1 (*continued*)

Amusements	Users of recreational facilities	Recreational expenditures
Other licenses	Consumers in general	Total consumption expenditures
Individual income tax	Taxpayers	Special series on state income tax payments
Corporation net income tax:		
Benchmark	½ consumers, ½ owners of capital	Consumption and dividend income
Most regressive	Consumers in general	Total consumption expenditures
Most progressive	Owners of capital	Dividend income
Death and gift tax	All to top income class	Allocated to over $35,000 income class
Severance tax	Consumers in general	Total consumption expenditures
Document and stock transfer taxes	½ owners of housing, ½ owners of businesses	Housing values and dividend income
Other taxes (n.e.c.)[g]	Consumers in general	Total consumption expenditures
Property tax:		
Railroads	¾ consumers, ¼ owners of capital	Consumption and dividend income
Public utilities	½ consumers, ½ owners of capital	Consumption and dividend income
Other (n.e.c.)[g]	Consumers in general	Total consumption expenditures
Local Taxes:		
General sales and gross receipts taxes	Consumers of taxed items	Special series on consumption of taxed items
Selective sales and gross receipts:		
Tobacco	Consumers of tobacco products	Tobacco products expenditures
Alcohol	Consumers of alcoholic beverages	Alcoholic beverages expenditures
Motor fuels	⅓ consumers in general, ⅔ households consuming gasoline	Consumption and gasoline expenditures
Utilities	Consumers of utility services	Gas, electric, and telephone expenditures
Other (n.e.c.)[g]	Consumers in general	Total consumption expenditures

Table 3–1 (*continued*)

License tax on motor vehicles (B)[d]	¼ consumers, ¾ drivers	Consumption and vehicle operations expenditures
License tax on motor vehicles	Drivers	Vehicle operations expenditures
Income taxes	Taxpayers	Household income distribution
Taxes (n.e.c.)[g]	Consumers in general	Total consumption expenditures
Personal property tax:		
Agriculture	⅓ farmers, ⅔ consumers of food	Farm net profit and food expenditures
Commercial and industrial	½ consumers, ¼ incorporated and ¼ unincorporated businesses	Consumption, dividend income, and business and partnership profit
Household property (B)[d]	Households	Housing expenditures
Household property	Households	Household income distribution
Intangibles	Households	Household income distribution
Motor vehicles (B)[d]	Households	Vehicle finance charges
Motor vehicles	Households	Household income distribution
Other (n.e.c.)[g]	Households	Household income distribution
Real property tax:		
Acreage and farms (B)[d]	⅓ farmers, ⅔ consumers of food	Farm net profit and food expenditures
Acreage and farms (R)[e]	Consumers of food	Food expenditures
Acreage and farms	Farmers	Farm net profit
Commercial property (B)[d]	⅔ consumers, ⅙ incorporated and ⅙ unincorporated businesses	Consumption, dividend income, and business and partnership profit
Commercial property (R)[e]	Consumers in general	Total consumption expenditures
Commercial property (P)[f]	½ incorporated, ½ unincorporated	Dividend income and business and partnership profit
Industrial property (B)[d]	⅔ consumers, 2/9 incorporated and 1/9 unincorporated businesses	Consumption, dividend income, and business and partnership profit
Industrial property (R)[e]	Consumers in general	Total consumption expenditures
Industrial property (P)[f]	Owners – ⅔ incorporated and ⅓ unincorporated	Dividend income and business and partnership profit
Vacant lots (B)[d]	Owners of land	Dividend income and rent net income

Table 3–1 *(continued)*

Vacant lots	Households	Household income distribution
Other (n.e.c.)[g] (B)[d]	½ owners of capital, ½ consumers in general	Dividend income and consumption
Other (n.e.c.)[g] (R)[e]	Consumers in general	Total consumption expenditures
Other (n.e.c.)[g] (P)[f]	Owners of capital	Dividend income
Single-family residential (B)[d]	Households	Housing values
Single-family residential (R)[e]	Households	Housing expenditures
Single-family residential (P)[f]	Owners of capital	Dividend income
Single family residential	Households	Real estate tax payments
Multifamily residential (B)[d]	½ tenants, ¼ incorporated and ¼ unincorporated landlords	Rent payments, rent net income, and dividend income
Multifamily residential (R)[e]	Tenants	Rent payments
Multifamily residential (P)[f]	Owners of capital	Dividend income
Multifamily residential	Landlords – ½ incorporated and ½ unincorporated	Dividend income and rent net income
Imported Taxes	c	c

[a] Incidence refers to the theoretical "final resting place" of the tax.

[b] Allocator is the statistical series used to proxy incidence.

[c] Imported taxes are actually a composite of 29 types of taxes exported from one state to other states. Each component was treated separately and then summed to get total imported tax burden; see text for a fuller explanation.

[d] B = the benchmark case.

[e] R = most regressive case.

[f] P = most progressive case.

[g] n.e.c. = not elsewhere classified.

1974: 31) and is employed here for both the state and the local components. To distribute this tax across income classes, it was necessary to construct a data series that measures not total consumption, but consumption of *taxed* items. Each state's policy toward exempting items from the general sales tax base was examined and a statistical series constructed to reflect consumption *net* of the major categories of excluded items. The following list shows the most important types of exemptions and the number of states allowing them:

Food	21
Medicine	36
Admissions	19
Telephone and telegraph	19
Gas and electricity	17
Water	29
Housing	50
Health services	50

It is important to take these into account because they can have a substantial effect on the regressivity of the general sales tax, particularly for food or utilities, which are a major item in low-income budgets.[b]

Selective Sales Taxes

Selective sales taxes are disaggregated into eight types at the state level and five at the local level. Once again, the traditional view of incidence is that they are borne by consumers in proportion to their consumption of the taxed commodity (Musgrave, Case, and Leonard, 1974: 261; Pechman and Okner, 1974: 170). This view of selective sales tax incidence was adhered to in this book with two exceptions.

For the tax on motor fuels, it was assumed that one-third actually rested on business and thus was borne in relation to consumption in general (i.e., it was shifted forward to consumers) while two-thirds became a burden on households that consumed gasoline. Such an assumption has been employed elsewhere (Musgrave, Case, and Leonard, 1974: 261; Boyle, 1974: 574), and it seems a more realistic possibility than the full brunt of the tax falling solely on household users of gasoline. A similar situation applies to the selective sales tax on insurance. Here it was assumed that 60 percent legally impacted on business and was then shifted forward to consumers, while the remain-

[b] The exemption of food or an income tax credit for sales taxes is part of the Advisory Commission's "high quality state-local fiscal system" (1972: 5).

ing 40 percent fell on households in proportion to their expenditures for insurance (Boyle, 1974: 574).

License Taxes

State and local licenses are a mixed bag of revenue sources, nine levied by states and one by local governments. Most of them result in a burden on consumers, on users of commodities, or on various types of activity, as with the selective sales taxes. These taxes are assumed to be borne in proportion to consumption or use of the taxed good or service or involvement in the taxed activity. They are:

Motor vehicle operators (state)
Hunting and fishing (state)
Alcoholic beverages (state)
Public utilities (state)
Amusements (state)
Other, not elsewhere classified (state)

The remainder either are paid partly by business and partly by consumers – motor vehicle licenses (state and local) – fall entirely on business – occupations and business (state) – or are a statutory burden on corporations but then are shifted in part to consumers – licenses on corporations in general (state). Table 3-1 gives the incidence assumption and the statistical allocator that has been used for each type.

Corporation Net Income Tax

The incidence of the corporation net income tax has been the subject of a lengthy theoretical debate in the economics profession (Mieszkowski, 1969). For a long time it was held that it could not be shifted and that the burden rested fully with owners of the firm in the form of a reduced return (Ratchford and Han, 1957). More recent theoretical and empirical analysis altered this stance and has resulted in controversy about who does pay. There are basically three positions in the dispute: (1) little or no shifting, (2) varying and indeterminate amounts of shifting, and (3) most, all, or even more than 100 percent shifting (Cragg, Harberger, and Mieszkowski, 1957); Krzyaniak and Musgrave, 1963). Thus, we confront disagreement covering the extremes of 100 percent shifting to owners of capital and 100 percent (or even more) forward shifting to consumers. Rather than choosing between widely divergent viewpoints, three alternative assumptions were adopted: (1) 100 percent shifting to owners of capital, (2) 100 percent shifting to consumers, and (3) 50 percent shifting to each. The 50-50 case was chosen as the "benchmark" while "all to owners" is the most progressive and "all to consumers" the most regressive possibilities; an allocator was developed for each assumption.

Individual Income Tax

The individual income tax generally is not amenable to shifting. Past studies have assumed that it rests fully with the individual upon whom the statutory liability is imposed (Musgrave, Case, and Leonard, 1974: 261; Pechman and Okner, 1974: 30). The task becomes one of devising a statistical series that will adequately reflect vastly different provisions across the forty-four income tax states in their tax laws. This is crucial because this tax is the greatest potential source of progressivity for a state tax structure and also because relative reliance nationwide on this revenue base has nearly doubled while receipts have gone up sevenfold over the past two decades. Unless the specific provisions that lead to progressivity are incorporated into the allocator series, the equity of this tax and its influence on the total tax structure will be misrepresented.

To manifest the income tax's equity, a statistical series was assembled to account for the following major provisions (see tables in Advisory Commission, 1977a, indicated below):

Deductibility of federal taxes (Table 106)
Individual state tax rates (Table 106)
Tax base, if other than income (Table 106)
Personal and dependent exemptions (Table 107)
Standard deduction, percent and maximum dollar amount (Table 108)
Tax credits for sales tax on food, all state-local taxes, or property tax relief (Tables 106 and 111)

For example, three states tax only interest, dividends, or capital gains rather than a broad-based income, and seventeen allow a credit for taxes paid on food, consumer goods, property, or for all state-local tax payments.

The allocator series for this tax was derived as follows:[c] First, gross income was recorded. Next, personal and dependent exemptions were netted out and the standard deduction was subtracted up to the maximum dollar amount allowed. Finally, payment of federal taxes was netted out where this deduction was allowed. The end result is a figure for taxable income in each state and each income class. Specific tax rates for each state were then applied to taxable income categories to arrive at the total tax bill. Lastly, credits for low income, sales

[c] The provisions used were for a married, joint return.

taxes, local taxes, and the property tax were subtracted, when applicable, to determine the final tax bill. Symbolically, the computations are:

$$TAX = [(TI)(R)] - (C)$$

$$TI = GI - (P + D + S + G)$$
$$D = (F - 2.0)(E)$$
$$S = (GI)(SD) \text{ where } S \leq MAX$$

GI = average gross income ($)
TI = taxable income ($)
TAX = tax payment ($)
R = tax rate (%)
P = personal exemption ($)
D = dependent exemption ($)
S = standard deduction ($)
F = average family size (#)
SD = standard deduction rate (%)
MAX = maximum allowable standard deduction ($)
E = exemption per dependent ($)
G = deduction for federal taxes paid ($)
C = tax credits ($)

In three states *TAX* is based on federal tax liability, and in three states *GI* is based on interest, dividends, or capital gains. *TAX* is computed for each of fourteen income classes in each of the forty-four states using this tax.

This figure (*TAX*), when weighted by number of families in each class for each state, becomes the basis for allocating income tax receipts. Adopting this procedure for constructing an allocator leads to a precise picture of the incidence pattern because it reflects specific provisions of state law.

The local income tax, although used in only ten states, does account for a sizable amount of revenue, just under $3 billion. The states that have enabled local governments to use this revenue source generally restrict the levy to a fixed percentage, usually in the range of 0.5 to 1.0 percent. Only New York City has a rate structure that can be considered graduated; it goes from 0.9 to 4.3 percent (Advisory Commission, 1977a: 225-228). It is assumed that the local income tax rests, as does the state version, on the person with the legal obligation for payment.

State Death and Gift Taxes

The usual stance on the incidence of state death and gift taxes is that they fall entirely on the highest income class. Since the top income class used here is $35,000 and over, this does not seem unreasonable. First, the high level of exemptions permitted suggests that all but a small portion of the yield should be imputed to the top class (Musgrave et al., 1951: 25; Tax Foundation, 1967: 11). Second, an inheritance of even a modest amount would tend to increase a person's income to an amount consistent with the $35,000 level.[d] Either of these reasons would suggest that such an assumption is appropriate.

State Severance Tax

Severance tax revenues are derived from the extraction of natural resources, primarily natural gas and petroleum. Thus, the burden of this tax will most likely be shifted forward in prices to final consumers. Accordingly, it was assumed that its impact fell on consumers in general in proportion to total consumption expenditures. Other approaches that break the severance receipts into components have been employed elsewhere (Boyle 1974: 574).

State Document and Stock Transfer Taxes

This state tax is levied against the recording, registering, and transfer of a variety of legal documents such as deeds and securities. It was assumed that one-half of the tax fell on owners of housing and one-half on businesses. In neither instance was forward shifting allowed for and thus it remained with owners of homes and businesses.

Other Taxes (n.e.c.)

This residual category of both state and local taxes is viewed as being passed on to consumers in general. Although this method perhaps lacks the precision that might be desired, taxes in this category averaged only 0.04 percent of total state tax revenue and 1.18 percent

[d] If this income is not included in the base, this second point is irrelevant. It has been argued that the burden of this tax not be examined because of a lack of data on this income source (Pechman and Okner, 1974: 105-107).

of local tax revenue—hardly a source of great concern or of major consequence.

State Property Taxes

State property tax revenue is divided into three categories: railroads, public utilities, and other (n.e.c.). Detail, however, is not available on collections by property type. To estimate receipts in each category, the percent distribution of assessed valuations for state property was applied to total state property tax collections (this procedure is explained later in this chapter). For railroads, one-fourth was assumed to rest on owners and three-fourths were passed on to consumers in general. With public utilities, the split was assumed to be 50-50 between owners and consumers. Finally, the "other" category was assumed to be shifted fully forward to consumers (see Netzer, 1966: 259).

Local Property Taxes

Property taxes are the fiscal mainstay of local government. Although an average of 42.9 percent of all state-local tax revenue is derived at the local level, these sources alone bring in 35 percent. This exceeds by 5 percent *all* types of state general sales, selective sales, and gross receipts taxes combined and far exceeds any other single tax used by state or local governments; it is more than twice as important as either the state general sales or income tax. The point to be emphasized is that the incidence of these revenues is of major consequence for the equity of an overall tax structure.

Given this fact, it is imperative to reflect incidence as accurately as possible. The first step in doing this is *not* to assign any importance to, per se, "the" in the property tax but rather to concentrate attention upon its component parts. Once this is done, each element can be handled separately vis-à-vis both shifting and incidence and the allocator series used to impute payments among income classes. As mentioned above, the primary problem is that there are no systematic, comparable data available on collections by property type for each state. To overcome this, the local property tax is divided into six categories of personal property and seven of real property based on data on the percentage distribution of local assessed valuations by state; the end result, which is discussed later, is shown in Table 3-5. This categorization allows separate incidence assumptions to be used for each of the thirteen classes of property. Although this procedure suffers from any imprecision inherent in using assessed valuation data to reflect collections, it is far more precise than treating the property tax as though "the" should be taken literally.

For the personal component, all but two types were assumed not to be shifted and thus to rest on owners of the property. These types are household property, intangible property, motor vehicles, and other (n.e.c.). For the remaining two types, part of the tax is shifted forward to consumers and part remains as a burden on owners. Specifically, we have for "agricultural property" one-third falling on farmers and two-thirds on consumers of food and for "commercial-industrial" property one-half shifted to consumers and one-half falling on owners (one-half of which is incorporated and the other half unincorporated). Table 3-1 provides details based on these assumptions (refer to Netzer, 1966: 259, and Eapen and Eapen, 1970, for additional background).

The seven components that comprise real property represent, for most states, the majority of collections. Of these, single-family and multifamily dwellings average nearly one-half of the total for the United States as a whole (see Table 3-5). In selecting incidence assumptions for these seven components, several alternatives were chosen to reflect a range of possible outcomes. The standard case—*benchmark*—represents a middle ground, that is, a more conventional view, falling between the extremes. *Most progressive* is used to reflect the "new view" of property tax incidence in which the capital effects dominate and owners of capital bear the burden (Aaron, 1974 or 1975; Mieszkowski, 1972). Since capital ownership tends to be skewed toward upper-income levels, this would make the burden more progressive. *Most regressive* is used to reflect the possibility that property taxes can be shifted forward to consumers (i.e., the excise effects dominate); see Table 3-1 for the specific details.

Little discussion needs to be given here to the cases of extremes; they simply represent a theoretical stance as to whether the excise or the capital effects prevail. It seems likely, however, that the real impact might well occupy a middle position with partial shifting. To reflect how this would influence burdens, a benchmark case was set up for each component. For the benchmark, part of the tax exerted an excise effect to fall ultimately on consumers; the remainder represented a tax resting on owners of capital, in which ownership was distinguished between incorporated and unincorporated. Needless to say, the percentages used are "guesstimates" that do not pretend absolute precision but rather are approximations of relative orders of magnitude concerning the degree of shifting and the legal status of ownership.

Table 3-1 lists each incidence assumption. It also indicates the relative weighting of the excise and capital effects (i.e., how much falls on consumers and how much on owners) and the relative weighting of incorporated versus unincorporated ownership. The final product is twenty-two sets of assumptions for the seven categories of real property, each reflecting a theoretical position concerning the final resting place of the particular component analyzed.

Imported Taxes

In examining the burden of state-local taxation, one of the phenomena that must be dealt with is the spatial rearrangement of taxes among states. There are four general forces at work to produce this effect; first, the excise effect of a tax as it is passed on in the price of goods, services, or both to residents of other states; second, the shifting of a tax to owners that reside out of state; third, the migration effect of people moving from state to state for tourism, recreation, business, or employment reasons; and finally, the federal offset allowance for certain state-local taxes that can be itemized in determining individual federal liability. In the last case, this component of burden is "shifted" to the federal revenue structure and thus removed from consideration as a claim within the state-local sector. In the first three cases, taxes remain within the state-local system but are "rearranged" geographically. For example, Nevada exports taxes on gambling, Delaware taxes on corporations, and Texas taxes on gas and oil. These taxes ultimately are a claim on resident income in some other state; in other words, they are exported from one state and "imported" into others. On balance, then, we have another category of taxation (albeit implicit) with which to deal. Detail on how the process occurs, as well as its magnitude and how various components are estimated, is discussed in Chapter 4. Suffice it to say here, however, there is one more tax category to be considered, imported taxes.

Imported taxes are actually a composite of a variety of taxes that have been exported from other states into the state in question. As is discussed more fully in the next chapter, there are actually twenty-nine forms of taxation that are exported and therefore ultimately imported (see Table 3-2).

Table 3-2. Detail on Types of Imported Taxes

	Number of Taxes	
Type of Imported Tax	*State*	*Local*
General sales	1	1
Selective sales	7	4
Licenses	5	1
Individual Income	1	1
Corporation net income	1	–
Severance	1	–
State property	2	–
Local personal property	–	1
Local real property	–	3
Total	18	11

The incidence of each of these taxes *as imported* is assumed to be the same as for the specific type of tax as listed in Table 3-1. For example, any component of the selective sales tax on alcohol that is imported is assumed to be borne within that state in proportion to consumption of alcohol, and so on, for all remaining components. Each *element*, therefore, is given separate analytical treatment in terms of incidence. The combined burden of all imported taxes becomes the sum of the individual burdens of the twenty-nine types of imported taxes.

THE "NEW VIEW" OF WHO PAYS THE PROPERTY TAX

The question of who pays the property tax has, of late, received a great deal of professional attention. Controversy surrounding the "new" versus the "old" view is, in effect at least, much like that over the tax on corporate income; is it passed forward to consumers or does it rest on owners of capital? Needless to say, the difference in impact on tax burdens resulting from these alternative theoretical positions is of major consequence. If a tax's economic incidence lies with consumers, it will tend to be regressive; if it falls on owners, it will be more progressive. Since this tax raises over one-third of all state-local tax revenue, the equity of the entire system is heavily influenced by this choice.

The old view of property tax incidence argues that owners of capital are able to shift the burden onto consumers of goods and services produced by the taxed property. Thus, with the exception of single-family, owner-occupied dwellings (for which the owner is also the consumer), forward shifting is possible. The new view rejects the possibility of forward shifting and argues that the tax rests as a burden on capital owners in the form of a reduced rate of return. This comes about since the owners are unable to avoid the tax either by shifting assets to untaxed areas or by increasing prices.

Although the situation can be confusing, it is also rife with consequence for determining tax burden. McLure has noted that a careful reading of the original theoretical work by Mieszkowski (1967 and 1972) reveals that his intent was not to discard the past view, per se, but rather to develop a theoretical analysis that subsumed it into a more general framework (McLure, 1977: 69). The new view focuses on "the" property tax as though it were a uniform national levy whereas the old view considers local situations. In the former instance, the tax cannot be avoided and falls as a burden on owners of capital. In the latter case, intranational differentials in tax rates produce excise effects that allow for forward shifting. The precise nature of the excise effects is complex and a function of the nature of local differentials around an average tax rate for the nation.

For policy purposes both McLure (1977) and Netzer (1973) argue that the past view, entailing some forward shifting (but not as much as assumed before), is the most relevant stance. In other words, changes in the local property tax would have virtually no influence on the national rate and thus the tax will be borne by local consumers and owners of local factors; the excise effects dominate the capital effects. As McLure notes ". . . local policy-makers should assume *not* that . . . a change in the property tax will be borne by capital . . . but that local consumers and owners of locally immobile factors will bear most of the burden of the tax" (1977: 70). In other words, although the revised view is theoretically correct as a more inclusive conceptual framework, its focus is on changes in the incidence of "the" national property tax, not on local differentials. The old view deals with the burden due to the excise effects that result from these local differentials. The new view, therefore, is "largely irrelevant for questions of public policy."

Since we are examining the property tax across local governments within each of the fifty states, the excise tax approach is clearly a more relevant view of incidence for this analysis. We must also exercise caution in interpreting burdens in the context of tax reform. Categorical acceptance of the new view, de facto, arms the state-local fiscal arsenal with one of the most progressive policy instruments possible, a levy on capital ownership. This might well be used as an argument for not adopting circuit breaker legislation, for eliminating the tax advantages due to itemization of property taxes on federal forms, for phasing down school finance reform, and a variety of other types of policy changes (see discussion in Aaron, 1975: 71-91). As Netzer has noted in concluding his article, "The Incidence of the Property Tax Revisited": "I agree with the critics that the property tax need not be obnoxious on equity grounds; I disagree with the implication that benign neglect is the appropriate policy posture" (1973: 535). Differences in burden using these two views are marked as has been demonstrated by Odden and Vincent (1976), Musgrave and Musgrave (1980: 270), or Pechman and Okner (1974: 59). Care must be exercised to not jump on the bandwagon of the new view and thus preclude the possibility of judicious reform of the local property tax or the overall tax structure.

In the empirical analysis reported in Chapters 5 and 6, the "most progressive" alternative reflects the new view position and suggests how it affects tax burdens. The reader is in a position to examine results under either set of assumptions.

ALLOCATING TAX PAYMENTS TO INCOME GROUPS

Determining the shifting and incidence of a tax is only the first step in obtaining a final distribution of tax payments by income class. In effect, all it does is manifest theoretical analysis on the pattern of a tax's economic incidence. The crucial step is to link the theory to a method for empirical implementation. That is, we must make use of a statistical series to serve as a proxy for the economic incidence of each tax being examined; these are the allocators in Table 3-1. Once these variables are selected, we can distribute tax payments in the same proportion as the allocator series. A hypothetical example illustrates the procedure. Suppose we are looking at burden for an alcohol selective sales tax and shifting and incidence theory suggests that its impact ultimately rests on consumers of alcohol. The information as shown in Table 3-3 allows us to take total receipts and impute them to various income intervals. As shown in Table 3-3, 33 percent of all alcohol consumption occurs in the \$10,000-19,999 income class; therefore, this class is allocated that percentage of alcohol tax receipts (\$330).

The basic procedure is simple: (1) determine the value of the allocator for each income interval; (2) weight this figure by number of families to get totals for each class;[e] (3) compute the percentage for each class of the sum for all classes; and (4) assign this percentage of total receipts to each class. The end result is an imputation of collections for a specific tax to each income category. A similar procedure is adopted for each tax under each incidence assumption (seventy-four in all) using the information shown in Table 3-1.

Notice that in many instances part of a tax may be allocated using one series and part using another. For example, real property taxes on industrial property are allocated two-thirds to consumers based on general consumption, two-ninths to incorporated businesses based on dividend income, and one-ninth to unincorporated businesses based on business and partnership profits. The final distribution of tax payments reflects assumptions concerning shifting and incidence.

[e] If the allocator series is specified as an average for a class, say average expenditures on alcohol, it must be weighted by number of families to arrive at total alcohol consumption. If it is in totals, percentages can be computed directly.

Table 3–3. Imputing Tax Receipts by Income Level

Alcohol Tax Receipts = $1,000

Income Class	Average Expenditure on Alcohol	Number of Families	Total Consumption of Alcohol	Percent of Total Consumption	Tax
Under $5,000	$100	10	$ 1,000	5	50
$5,000-$9,999	$200	20	$ 4,000	18	180
$10,000-$19,999	$300	25	$ 7,500	33	330
Over $20,000	$400	25	$10,000	44	440
Total		80	$22,500	100%	$1,000

A QUESTION OF INCOME: CHOICE OF AN APPROPRIATE BASE

Selection of the "best" income concept for computing effective rates is an issue that has reverberated throughout the tax burden literature for decades. There remains some divergence of opinion that is tempered by professional judgment, theoretical disagreements, and the ubiquitous constraints imposed by the adequacy of current reliable data on the distribution of various income components. In some instances, where feasible, authors have attempted to use alternative formulations to test for the sensitivity of their results (such as in Gillespie, 1965, or Eapen and Eapen, 1970).

The crux of the debate focuses on the inclusion or exclusion of imputed and nonmonetary components in the base. In examining tax burdens for 1948, Tucker (1951) made a case that these sources should definitely be included as a part of income because of their greater relative impact on poorer taxpayers. Their inclusion would lessen the burden at the low end to a larger extent than in the mid to upper classes, which would thereby decrease overall regressivity for the system as a whole.

Musgrave (1952), on the other hand, felt that the inclusion of imputed or nonmonetary elements would lead to a conceptual quagmire. Once venturing beyond the security of monetary receipts, he argued that there seems to be no clear logic for the inclusion or exclusion of a wide range of imputed and nonmonetary items, ranging from food grown in a person's backyard to the value of leisure time, which is clearly a diverse range.

A spin-off problem related to the use of "broad income" is the influence these new components would exert on income intervals. Once the income base is redefined to be more inclusive, it is highly probable—especially for low-income groups—that the additions will cause persons to be shifted into another class. If not accounted for by adjusting accordingly, the resulting estimates of burden would be biased. The statistical and data problems inherent in correcting for additional income are formidable.

This debate of twenty-five years ago between Musgrave and Tucker draws into focus the income base controversy. In some respects, it can be viewed as less a dispute than a variance in purpose. Each writer, de facto, chooses to measure a different type of burden. Accordingly, the results, when interpreted in light of purpose, need not necessarily be as contradictory as they seem at first glance. Musgrave considers burden as it relates to a statutory definition for tax purposes, using money income as the base for effective rates. Since the policy manipulations of government influence monetary components much more heavily (nonmonetary components tend to remain more insulated from taxation), his results show the burden most immediately related to policy. Tucker's use of a broader base can be viewed as an attempt to relate burden to a measure of "economic well-being." Thus, his base is not the base as defined for tax purposes but includes additional nonmonetary and imputed elements that contribute to well-being. The logical culmination of Tucker's measure is somewhat ambiguous but would seem to relate to an individual's level of satisfaction or utility. Although it may be clear as a theoretical concept, it certainly lacks empirical tractability.

The core of the income debate revolves around the distinction between income as defined for tax purposes and income that will reflect some notion of overall economic status. Each approach, however, measures a distinct type of burden. The former defines burden in terms more closely linked to tax policy, whereas the latter relates it to the economic position of the taxpayer. A crucial factor lies in the interpretation of the effective rates and overall incidence pattern, not in the choice of one base as being sacrosanct or ultimately correct.

Burdens computed with money income tend to produce a less progressive distribution, especially in the lower classes, than a broader measure. Or with a regressive tax, the regressivity is considerably greater using money instead of broad income. The distinction between the two also has important implications for the type of families under investigation. For example, more inclusive income is clearly more relevant to rural families since a larger portion of their income is likely to be derived from nonmonetary sources. For urban families, burden is more closely linked to cash income since nonmonetary components would be relatively less significant. The logical implication, of course, is that separate analyses should be performed for rural and urban families, something the data will not yet support.[f]

Beyond the Musgrave and Tucker variants, Bishop (1961) and the Tax Foundation (1967a) have added another wrinkle to the debate. In studying the distribution of burdens for 1958, 1961, and 1965, they argued that net national product (NNP), or its income equivalent, is most appropriate for computing effective rates. Using NNP, it was felt, would avoid fluctuations that occur in the definition of national income resulting from any shift in the balance between direct and indirect taxes. Both studies were concerned with inconsistencies that arose out of the use of national income that do not occur when NNP is employed. The rationale hinges on the inclusion of indirect taxes as a form of imputed income. It is argued that these items actually represent private income that has been diverted to governmental use, and therefore, it would be inappropriate to compute burden for a taxpaying unit without assigning this unit all income that is affected by a tax (Bishop, 1966).

More recently, Pechman and Okner (1974) have further refined this approach. Using data compiled from a sample of individuals in the 1967 Survey of Economic Opportunity and the Internal Revenue System tax file, they were able to construct a microanalytic data base they call MERGE. These data enabled them to include indirect business taxes in income and at the same time to account for the influence of alternative incidence assumptions. Their procedure becomes quite complex, for the income base becomes a function of the incidence of the tax under examination (Pechman and Okner, 1974: Appendix A and pp. 37-42), but they are able to apportion indirect business taxes as a component of income in accordance with alternative views of incidence. The end result is that tax burdens are computed with respect to the income base most appropriate to the particular tax being examined. Musgrave (1974), in his most recent analysis for the year 1968, acknowledges the theoretical precision of the Pechman and Okner type of refinements but, in effect, concludes that the added complexity far outweighs any increased accuracy; he chooses not to include indirect business taxes in income (pp. 273-274).

The most recent nuance of the income base controversy follows from Friedman's work on permanent income and considers the appropriateness of this measure as a base for effective rates. Netzer discussed permanent income with respect to the property tax in the *Economics of the Property Tax* (1966), noting that the use of such a

[f] The urban-rural split is only one alternative way of looking at tax burden. Age, life cycle, or family size would also be of interest.

measure would certainly lessen its regressivity and could conceivably cause it to become proportional or even mildly progressive. More recently Netzer has commented further on the permanent income hypothesis as related to property tax burdens and poses the basic question as to whether or not such a measure is the relevant one for formulating policy. Agreed that consumption patterns (especially for housing) may be conditioned by a much longer view of income prospects over far more than a single year and that people may be at low-income levels because of temporary or transitory phenomena, the question still remains as to the implementation of such a theoretically new and empirically "shaky" measure. Many other factors, in fact, can have much more of an influence on housing and other consumption choices, such as racial bias, uncertainty, or institutional barriers. He sums up by asking ". . . whether tax policy should ignore heavy current tax burdens on the grounds that it will all work out in the longer run . . ." (Netzer, 1973: 529). The thinking here can easily be extended to other tax instruments.

There is a growing acceptance that permanent income may be a better approximation to taxpayers' economic well-being, assuming that it can be clearly defined theoretically and then accurately measured (presently a tenuous assumption) and that it may play a role in measuring tax burdens. We seem to have returned once again to the crux of the Musgrave and Tucker debate of years ago – what measure of income is best to use in the denominator of an effective tax rate? Again, there is in part a variance in purpose. It should also be kept firmly in mind, however, that judicious manipulation of an income base can produce, literally, almost any type of equity profile; care must be exercised in interpretation lest regressive taxes miraculously become progressive and tax reform suffers as a consequence.

Proponents of permanent income make the case that a longer time period more accurately portrays family economic circumstances and, therefore, the equity of a tax (Aaron, 1975: 27-32). Others (Netzer, 1973) take the stance that current income pays the taxes and therefore seems the most relevant standard for judging burden. That a difference in the equity of a tax is likely to result has been demonstrated in a limited number of studies using permanent income (Davies, 1960 and 1969; Mayer, 1974); the final choice, however, needs to be tempered somewhat by purpose and very heavily by empirical feasibility.

Given all of the theoretical arguments for the use of permanent income, broad income, imputation of "in kind" and nonmonetary items, net national product, treatment of indirect business taxes, and so on, we are ultimately at the mercy of empirical constraints. That is, how far can we proceed in tailoring an income base to the purpose at hand?

Are we able to obtain accurate data on items to be "added in" and is there a conceptual basis for deciding what to include and what to exclude?

At the aggregate national level (such as all federal or all state and local), data on income are much more plentiful and are available by components so that we can contemplate undertaking such redefinitions. The numerous aggregate tax burden studies undertaken thus far do, in fact, cover the spectrum from use of very narrow measures such as the IRS adjusted gross income to more inclusive measures like money income, "broad" income, personal income, net national product, and even permanent income.[g]

When examining tax burdens in each of the fifty states, such flexibility is not an option. Comparable data on the income distribution in each state are scarce at best. Some data can be obtained from the decennial *Census of Population;* IRS data are readily available but use the narrow adjusted gross income base; beyond these sources the only data published on a regular basis for states consist of *aggregate* personal income from the Bureau of Economic Analysis of the Department of Commerce (U.S. Department of Commerce, 1977). What is needed is accurate data on the state-by-state *distribution* of income; what we have portrays only the *level* of income.

Fortunately, such information has become available recently in a survey by the Bureau of the Census, the Survey of Income and Education (SIE). It covers nearly 200,000 households statistically designed to produce reliable state-by-state data on a variety of items including income (Bureau of the Census, 1977c and 1978a). The measure employed is the Bureau of the Census total money income, which includes receipts from wages and salaries; farm and nonfarm self-employment; Social Security and supplemental Social Security income; dividends, interest, and the like; public assistance and welfare benefits; unemployment compensation; pensions; and annuities, alimony, and other regular contributions (see Bureau of the Census, 1977c: 147-149). These data can be obtained by income class.[h]

Using these SIE data as a starting point, an income measure was developed that included additional components that were not reported in the SIE survey. The objective was to obtain an income distribution series by state that was more inclusive than the money income concept of the Census Bureau. Added to the $1,108 billion in income reported in the SIE survey was an additional $155 billion in other and imputed

[g] It should be noted that other denominators for effective tax rates also have been suggested and used, such as Fisher income, which is based on consumption expenditures (Davies, 1960: 992-993).

[h] It must be noted that even the SIE data are subject to weaknesses, most particularly in some of the poorer southern states.

Table 3-4. Components of the Income Base (millions)

Income Component[a]	Allocator Series	Amount
Survey of Income and Education, "money income"[b]	Distribution available from unpublished SIE data	$1,108,702
Other labor income[c]	Factor income	70,803
Imputed interest[c]	Interest income	42,404
Imputed rent[c]	Housing expenditures	11,049
Food stamps (bonus value)[c]	Derived from data on relative value of "bonus" by income levels	4,568
Capital gains[d]	Value of household assets	26,597
Total income		$1,264,123

[a] *Source:* Adjusted to 1975-1976 level.
[b] *Source:* Bureau of the Census (1978a) and unpublished data.
[c] *Source:* Unpublished state personal income worksheet data from the Bureau of Economic Analysis, Regional Economic Information System.
[d] *Source:* Internal Revenue Service (1978), available only for 1975.

income items as explained in Table 3-4. Each of these five added-on components, however, was only available as a total for a state. To obtain a distribution to be added to the SIE data, each item was imputed to income classes for each state using the indicated statistical series.

The final product is a distribution of income, by state for fourteen income classes, that is as accurate as available statistical information will allow. As implied by Table 3-4, it was not possible to include indirect business taxes as a part of the base as done by Pechman and Okner.

Further refinement of this sort must await a much more detailed data base capable of supporting it. In the aggregate, therefore, income sums to $1.26 trillion, slightly less than personal income for this period in dollar terms ($1.3 trillion) but substantially different in composition and distribution. On a state-by-state basis, this amount is entered as the denominator for effective tax rates.

SOURCES OF DATA

Before proceeding to Chapter 4, which deals with spatial tax movements, and Chapters 5 and 6, which report the empirical findings, it is useful to mention briefly the major sources of data used in this book. There are four, each of which will be dealt with in turn.

Tax Receipts

Before the effective rates can be calculated it is necessary to obtain information on state and local tax receipts broken down into each of the fifty categories discussed in Chapter 1. There is no problem with the state sector since ample detail is available on its collections, with the exception of property tax receipts (Bureau of the Census, 1977b). Such is not the case at the local level, however. It became necessary to assemble information from several sources.

The first problem was to obtain the details of local nonproperty tax collections on a state basis. This information was obtained through a special tabulation performed by the Governments Division, Bureau of the Census. The $12.2 billion in this category was reported in nine component parts as shown in Chapter 1. Each part was given separate theoretical and empirical treatment.

Although local use of nonproperty taxes is still limited, there are several states in which they have taken on a major fiscal status. In certain instances they are major revenue generators, for example, the local income tax in New York City. In two states, Alabama and Louisiana, they raise 50 percent or more of all local tax revenue; in eleven states they raise more than one-quarter. Thus, while these taxes only average 7.8 percent of revenue, the range is considerable and attains a high of almost 17 percent of all state and local tax receipts in New York, which necessitates the effort given to estimating their separate impact.

The remaining $54.7 billion in local collections is derived from real and personal property. To treat this figure as a lump sum would introduce considerable imprecision into estimates of burden; it averages, after all, 35 percent of all state and local tax revenue. Unfortunately, however, no systematic, comparable data are available on collections by type of property (i.e., commercial, industrial, intangibles, multifamily, etc.) for each state. This leaves us in the awkward position of knowing only aggregate amounts for all property combined.

To allow these taxes to be subject to separate theoretical and empirical analysis, component by component, an assumption was necessary; it is that receipts, by type of property, can be approximated by the distribution of assessed valuations (McLure, 1966: 267-268, used this assumption). Following such a procedure enables us to divide the $54.7 billion into six categories of personal property and seven of real property. There seems little doubt that assessed valuation data are not an exact proxy for property tax collections. However, it is argued here that it is certainly much more precise to disaggregate the data in this fashion than to treat all revenue as a lump sum and analyze it accordingly. In effect, this assumption views tax rates across local jurisdictions and classes of property within a state as "averaging out." The need to take such a position is obvious and serves to emphasize the necessity for systematic collection of more detailed data on property tax collections. Table 3-5 shows the percent distribution of local property tax revenue divided into thirteen types based on assessed valuation data. A similar approach was used to break down the $2.1 billion in state collections into the following three categories so that they might be subject to separate analysis: railroads, public utilities, and "other" (n.e.c.).

Income and Family Distribution

The income base has already been explained. The primary data source was SIE unpublished data on income supplemented with the other items listed in Table 3-4. In addition to income, the distribution of family units (related and unrelated individuals) was also obtained from unpublished SIE data. Some adjustments had to be made to this latter series to correct for differences in the definition of income intervals at the high end. A simple Pareto interpolation was used to make these corrections.[i]

Income Components and Tax Itemization

As Table 3-1 reflects, a variety of information is required to allocate taxes to income classes in accordance with shifting and incidence theory. In addition, determination of the federal tax offset, which is explained in Chapter 4, was also necessary. To accomplish both of these tasks, various data were obtained in a special tabulation from the IRS State Tax Model. It contains a random sample of more than 206,000 audited and unaudited individual income tax returns classified by state. Reported in the model are all of the data items that enter into preparation of the IRS *Statistics of Income* volume.[j] A special tabulation of these data by state and income class was done by IRS to conform with the needs of this book. The main refinement was that instead of using IRS adjusted gross income (AGI), which has averaged about 85 percent of personal income over the recent two decades (Pechman, 1977, Appendix B), a broader concept of income was used that included AGI plus several items that are excluded from AGI. The re-

[i] Data on the distribution of families were obtained through a special tabulation from the SIE. The Pareto interpolation procedure was obtained through conversation with the staff responsible for SIE. For detail on the SIE refer to Bureau of the Census (1978a).

[j] See IRS, Statistics Division publications 1023 and 1023-A (July 1977) for full detail on the model.

Table 3.5. Percent Distribution of Local Property Tax Revenue Based on Assessed Valuations (in percent)

State	Personal Property						Real Property						
	Commercial-Industrial	Intangible	Agricultural	Household	Motor Vehicles	Other (n.e.c.)[a]	Acreage and Farms	Industrial	Commercial	Vacant Lots	Single-Family	Multifamily	Other (n.e.c.)[a]
Alabama	0.0	0.0	0.0	0.0	15.2	23.6	4.9	5.7	11.3	1.0	35.5	2.2	0.2
Alaska	0.0	0.0	0.0	0.0	0.0	18.1	4.6	4.8	21.9	11.6	33.4	5.2	0.0
Arizona	9.3	0.0	1.2	0.0	0.0	2.6	5.3	6.2	18.5	7.5	41.1	7.9	0.0
Arkansas	9.6	0.0	4.0	4.4	9.3	2.2	16.9	2.4	10.8	2.0	35.2	2.6	0.0
California	12.5	0.0	0.4	0.0	0.0	0.3	6.0	7.1	11.8	3.6	46.1	10.2	1.4
Colorado	8.4	0.0	2.2	0.0	0.0	0.2	7.8	5.4	19.6	3.2	44.5	5.2	2.9
Connecticut	12.1	0.0	0.1	0.0	0.0	6.8	1.1	6.7	12.9	1.8	50.0	8.0	0.0
Delaware	0.0	0.0	0.0	0.0	0.0	0.0	8.1	8.4	16.5	3.2	57.3	6.3	0.0
Florida	0.0	0.0	0.0	0.0	0.0	14.1	9.8	2.9	13.2	6.9	42.9	9.4	0.4
Georgia	0.0	1.4	0.0	0.0	7.7	14.6	15.9	2.5	13.2	2.8	36.9	4.4	0.0
Hawaii	0.0	0.0	0.0	0.0	0.0	0.0	4.0	6.6	20.4	9.6	39.6	19.5	0.0
Idaho	3.9	0.0	8.4	0.0	0.0	2.2	28.8	3.9	11.1	3.0	37.0	1.1	0.0
Illinois	6.1	0.8	0.6	0.0	1.4	3.9	13.3	10.5	14.4	2.3	36.6	9.6	0.1
Indiana	0.0	0.0	0.0	0.0	0.0	26.4	14.4	5.7	9.8	1.6	39.5	2.3	0.0
Iowa	3.9	0.0	2.4	0.0	0.0	0.2	44.9	3.4	9.3	0.6	33.5	1.3	0.0
Kansas	0.0	0.0	0.0	0.0	0.0	37.6	23.6	1.9	7.4	0.7	26.2	2.3	0.1
Kentucky	8.7	0.0	0.0	0.0	9.7	1.3	21.2	3.4	10.8	1.3	41.0	1.8	0.3
Louisiana	15.0	4.9	0.0	0.0	0.0	17.4	5.2	2.9	12.1	2.1	34.6	5.3	0.0
Maine	10.4	0.0	0.1	0.0	0.0	0.5	5.8	8.4	13.5	2.0	52.1	6.4	0.3
Mayland	0.6	0.0	0.0	0.0	0.0	0.0	4.7	4.7	13.9	4.0	63.2	8.5	0.0
Massachusetts	3.8	0.0	0.0	0.0	0.0	2.0	0.7	7.3	15.6	2.6	56.1	11.6	0.0
Michigan	0.0	0.0	0.0	0.0	0.0	13.5	8.0	9.8	11.8	2.2	48.5	4.9	0.9
Minnesota	0.3	0.0	0.1	0.0	0.0	0.0	19.2	7.6	15.4	1.4	50.4	5.2	0.0
Mississippi	12.0	1.0	0.0	0.0	19.3	0.4	15.2	1.5	9.7	2.5	35.4	2.4	0.0
Missouri	5.6	0.0	2.2	0.0	9.5	5.6	12.3	4.7	12.9	2.8	38.7	5.2	0.0
Montana	11.9	2.3	10.8	0.0	12.5	4.1	17.1	4.2	8.9	1.6	24.6	1.4	0.1
Nebraska	9.3	0.0	9.6	0.0	7.0	3.2	34.4	2.1	8.7	0.9	22.0	2.2	0.0
Nevada	3.5	0.0	1.4	0.0	0.0	10.3	10.6	3.2	22.4	3.7	39.8	4.3	0.3
New Hampshire	0.0	0.0	0.0	0.0	0.0	0.1	5.4	11.9	13.9	1.2	59.1	8.1	0.0
New Jersey	2.0	0.0	0.0	0.0	0.0	0.0	1.9	10.6	13.1	3.9	57.5	10.6	0.0

Table 3.5 (*continued*)

	Personal Property						Real Property						
State	Commercial-Industrial	Intangible	Agricultural	Household	Motor Vehicles	Other (n.e.c.)[a]	Acreage and Farms	Industrial	Commercial	Vacant Lots	Single-Family	Multifamily	Other (n.e.c.)[a]
New Mexico	0.0	0.0	1.4	0.0	0.0	6.2	8.5	4.1	16.2	10.0	46.7	4.0	2.5
New York	0.0	0.0	0.0	0.0	0.0	1.0	2.1	7.2	31.6	2.4	31.4	24.8	0.0
North Carolina	17.0	0.0	0.9	2.5	8.5	1.7	11.6	5.5	9.9	3.4	35.7	2.6	0.0
North Dakota	0.0	0.0	0.0	0.0	0.0	0.0	55.8	0.8	12.2	0.8	26.9	3.2	0.0
Ohio	8.5	0.0	0.5	0.0	0.0	0.0	10.9	7.1	12.9	3.1	51.4	5.2	0.0
Oklahoma	13.4	0.0	3.8	0.0	0.0	7.2	15.1	2.2	12.4	1.9	39.8	3.4	0.3
Oregon	11.2	0.0	1.2	0.0	0.0	1.2	16.0	8.8	12.5	3.4	40.9	4.0	0.3
Pennsylvania	0.0	0.0	0.0	0.0	0.0	0.0	3.8	7.7	18.8	1.8	59.4	7.4	0.7
Rhode Island	0.0	0.0	0.0	0.0	0.0	21.4	1.0	6.8	11.4	3.4	45.7	9.9	0.0
South Carolina	0.3	0.0	0.6	0.0	14.6	2.2	12.9	9.9	10.7	3.7	40.6	4.2	0.0
South Dakota	5.2	0.0	13.2	0.0	0.1	4.0	41.6	0.7	7.6	1.1	22.8	1.7	1.4
Tennessee	0.0	0.0	0.0	0.0	0.0	10.8	11.0	8.2	22.4	2.6	41.0	3.5	0.1
Texas	0.0	0.0	0.0	0.0	0.0	19.0	10.2	8.9	12.7	2.2	27.7	2.9	16.1
Utah	7.7	0.0	1.3	0.0	9.1	1.9	9.0	4.0	11.2	4.2	49.0	2.1	0.0
Vermont	7.3	0.0	0.5	0.0	0.0	0.5	13.7	10.6	10.9	0.1	53.6	2.3	0.0
Virginia	3.0	0.0	0.0	0.0	0.0	13.2	7.4	4.8	13.9	3.3	45.2	8.8	0.0
Washington	12.9	0.0	1.0	0.0	0.0	2.3	13.8	6.1	14.8	4.1	39.2	5.2	0.0
West Virginia	0.0	13.2	1.3	3.3	8.8	20.4	5.6	3.7	7.9	1.4	31.4	1.3	1.1
Wisconsin	11.3	0.0	2.6	0.0	0.0	0.5	10.0	4.5	13.0	2.4	49.3	5.9	0.0
Wyoming	20.5	0.0	8.0	0.0	0.0	3.8	19.3	2.1	10.2	1.0	31.4	1.6	1.5
U.S. Average	5.4	0.5	1.6	0.2	2.7	6.6	13.1	5.6	13.6	3.0	41.4	5.6	0.7

Source: Real property taken from Bureau of the Census, *Taxable Property Values and Assessment Sales-Price Ratios, 1977 Census of Governments*, Vol. 2, Part 2 (Washington, D.C.: U.S. Government Printing Office, 1978), table 4. Personal Property derived from same source for years 1962, 1967, 1972, and 1977.

[a] n.e.c. = not elsewhere classified.

quired data were then tabulated by income class using this broader definition. Although this may not be the perfect data set, it is felt to be, first, the best that is available and, second, accurate enough to portray the *patterns* of incidence even if not the absolute level. These data provide us with information on various components of income (such as salaries and wages or dividends) as well as itemizations for six categories of state and local taxes by fourteen income intervals. They are used as allocators and to compute the federal tax offset discussed in Chapter 4.

Expenditure Patterns

Another source of data for the allocators listed in Table 3-1 is the Bureau of Labor Statistics (BLS) Consumer Expenditure Survey (Bureau of Labor Statistics, 1971 and 1978). This survey, which among other things provides the statistical basis for updating the Consumer Price Index, reports on a vast number of highly detailed spending, income, and financial items (literally hundreds), broken down by income class. Accordingly, it offers an ideal data base from which to construct allocator series for the many consumption-based taxes that ultimately come to rest on consumers of various items (e.g., alcohol, tobacco, or vehicle operations).

Two problems arise, however. First, the income categories reported in the survey did not conform to those used here at the top end of the income spectrum; BLS tops out with the over $25,000 class. In order to get data by expenditure item on the top three classes used here – $25,000-29,999; $30,000-34,999; over $35,000 – a special tabulation was obtained from the computer tapes containing the raw expenditure data from the BLS Interview Survey. Average expenditure items were recomputed for these top three classes.

Second, expenditure data reported in the BLS Interview Survey are only available for four geographical regions, not state by state; the Northeast region includes nine states, the North Central region twelve states, the South sixteen states, and the West thirteen states. In the past, studies undertaken for a specific state have often had to assume that a state's expenditure characteristics conformed to those for the region in which it is located (Eapen and Eapen, 1970) or in some cases for a major metropolitan area in a state; there was usually little choice in the matter. The obvious difficulty lies in the assumption that regional consumption patterns are capable of portraying consumption patterns for each state within that region. That is, the pattern for the Northeast region portrays the pattern in Massachusetts, New York, and Maine, and so forth. Any variation across states would be lost with such a procedure and the resulting imputation of tax payments would suffer accordingly.

Since the distribution of taxes by income group and the variation across states are both critical, it was necessary to develop a methodology for estimating consumption expenditures by income class for *each* of the fifty states. The procedure is as follows and was replicated for all of the consumption items listed as an allocator in Table 3-1. First, the following simple expenditure/income type of relationship was specified:

$$\bar{E}_{abc} = \alpha + \beta\,(\bar{Y})_{ab}$$

where $\bar{E}$ = average expenditure
$\bar{Y}$ = average income
a = region
b = income class
c = expenditure category

This equation was fitted statistically to expenditure and income data using the fourteen income classes as observations. A separate regional equation was estimated for each expenditure allocator. The final product is a set of four regression equations, showing the relationship between income and expenditure for each type of spending; a separate equation was estimated for each of the four regions mentioned above. For example, the equation for average spending on alcohol in the Northeast region is estimated as:

$$\bar{E} = 18.7 + 0.0056\,(\bar{Y}) \qquad (Pr \doteq 0.001;\ R^2 = 0.962)$$

From this relationship, it is easy to estimate consumption items by income class and state simply by plugging into the appropriate regional equation data on state income by income class for every state in a region. This calculation generates fourteen values of average expenditure that, when weighted by number of families, gives total spending by class in a state.[k]

[k] This procedure is simple in concept, relatively easy to do, and yet gives good estimates of spending. In nearly every instance the fit to the data was excellent, with R^2 values exceeding 0.90.

The definition of tax burden presented in Chapter 1 was:

$$ER_{ijk} = \frac{T_{ijk}}{Y_{ij}}$$

where ER = effective tax rate
Y = income
i = states
j = income classes
k = type of tax

and

$$T_{ijk} = (C - E + I - F)$$

where C = total tax receipts
E = exported taxes
I = imported taxes
F = federal tax offset

Thus far, we have developed a model that incorporates all of the information except E, I, and F. These factors are the main components of spatial tax flows among the fifty states and are the topic of the next chapter. Once these elements are estimated, we can compute the 65,100 effective rates for all ninety-three types of taxes, fifty states, and fourteen income classes. The findings are presented in Chapters 5 and 6.

Chapter 4

The Geographical Movement of Taxes and Tax Burdens

The preceding chapters have detailed a methodology for estimating various elements of an effective tax rate, discussed the evolution of the tax burden literature, and described the data problems that any such study confronts. At every step of the analysis attention was given to refinements that would account for the variations that exist across states in critical factors such as the distribution of income, consumption patterns, features of tax instruments used, and so forth. One crucial element remains to be discussed, an element that is absolutely essential to a proper specification of the true burden of taxation resting on the residents of each state.

The explicit focus of this analysis is on determining the burden within a state on its residents and then replicating it for each state. To accomplish this we need to capture all state-local taxes that rest with taxpayers in a state. The difficulty is that geographical boundaries do not serve as a barrier to the flow of tax burdens into and out of a state; we need to consider these tax flows out of (exporting) and into (importing) each state, treating each as a unique fiscal and economic unit. By way of an example, we must account for the fact that someone from New York who goes to Las Vegas to gamble pays gambling taxes to Nevada; these taxes are, in effect, "exported" from Nevada and then "imported" into New York; that is, they ultimately become a burden on someone living in another state. Just as there is a difference between tax impact and tax incidence in a strict interpersonal sense, so also is this distinction important in a spatial setting. A tax's legal impact in one location can be moved spatially and its incidence felt in another.

As long as we deal in aggregate terms by sector, spatial incidence is of little or no importance because it "averages out." However, in the disaggregate focus of this book it is of consequence, for the situation in each state differs. The approach assumed here is to look at tax burdens at their final spatial resting place, not simply where they are legally imposed, at least to the extent that the existing theoretical and empirical base will allow. This chapter outlines the methodology and data used to accomplish this and spells out the magnitude of these imported and exported tax movements.

Thus far we have discussed each component of an effective tax rate with one exception. The numerator of this expression must contain all taxes that exert a claim on taxpayers in a state. Since taxes can be "rearranged" geographically (i.e., exported and imported), this alters the burden of any particular tax and also changes the equity for systems of taxes. This phenomenon must be empirically accounted for prior to calculating effective rates. Before describing the methodology used and the magnitude of the issue, however, it is beneficial to review the somewhat limited literature on spatial tax incidence.

The existing body of literature on geographical incidence is quite limited. McLure, in his pioneering analysis of interregional tax flows, notes that "although there is an extensive literature on the subject of incidence, most of it is in the context of a closed economy, so that all statutory taxpayers and ultimate bearers of the taxes are residents of the taxing region" (McLure, 1964: 187). Adopting the stance that taxes levied in a state impose a burden *only within* that state and that they exhaust the claim on the state's residents is conceptually simplistic and empirically untenable, most particularly when the focus is interstate comparisons. Taxes levied in any state-local system can, and do, have repercussions that extend throughout the entire economy. The problem, therefore, takes on three distinct dimensions. First, exporting must be determined by state and type of tax; second, the importing of taxes into each state must be estimated; finally, the effect of exporting and importing on the level and distribution of burdens must be incorporated into the model presented in Chapter 3 prior to computing effective tax rates.

Only when the methodology explicitly accounts for this flow of taxes among states will the resulting effective rates be representative of the true pattern, since it influences the level of burden as well as equity. States in a position to export heavily, such as with Nevada's gambling taxes or Delaware's corporate franchise tax, impose a lower level of burden on their residents than would be indicated by analysis done on a strictly impact basis. Burden is altered by the flow of taxes, and in effect, part of the cost of providing public goods in a particular state is borne by residents of other states. As will be shown, the federal government also "absorbs" part of the cost of state-local taxes through provisions in the Internal Revenue System code. This alters not only the level but also the equity of the burden. Finally, equity is influenced by the type of taxes most heavily exported, for example, a regressive consumption tax versus a progressive individual income tax. This factor influences the equity of the burden that remains within the system.

HISTORICAL MILIEU OF GEOGRAPHICAL INCIDENCE

The phenomenon of geographical incidence has received two distinct theoretical treatments in the past. It must be recognized, however, that the focus of this research differed from the present analysis. Although tax flows were accounted for, it was in the context of only one state, whereas this book must look at flows for all fifty states. Geographical incidence arises as a consideration whether the unit of analysis is one particular state or all states, but it becomes far more important and complex in the latter instance.

The first method (the "Michigan approach") derives from the research of Musgrave and Daicoff (1958). They assumed that taxes levied in all other states were of no consequence for the state of Michigan. These taxes were, in effect, treated as being beyond the control of the state and as a result only the internal policy of Michigan was considered. The second approach (the "Wisconsin approach") is an outcome of a study on Wisconsin's state and local tax burden done under the aegis of Harold Groves (University of Wisconsin, 1959). He treated taxes levied in Wisconsin in the context of those levied in neighboring states, assuming that the states did not make unilateral decisions but rather were influenced by each other's fiscal circumstances. These two conceptual approaches to policy make nearly opposite assumptions about the nature of the fiscal milieu in which subnational governments operate. Michigan is assumed to have an open economy in which unilateral fiscal decisions are made and Wisconsin a type of closed economy in which decisions are made in interdependent fashion with one's fiscal neighbors.

Musgrave and Daicoff (1958) reflect the exporting of taxes and their influence on the burden for residents of Michigan by accounting for that portion of payments shifted across state borders through price and income changes and instances where the payment of Michigan taxes lowered the federal tax liability. They determined that $374 million, or nearly one-fifth of all Michigan revenue for 1956, was so rearranged. Calculation of effective rates takes exporting into account but the problem of taxes flowing into the state is simply assumed away.

Groves's examination of Wisconsin also recognized exporting. He found that more than 20 percent of this state's taxes were shifted to the federal government or out-of-state consumers in 1956, that is, $156 out of $727 million (1959: 45). However, as with other state studies, importing is dismissed on the assumption that imported and exported taxes offset each other.

Another major study, that of Minnesota by Brownlee (1960), accounts for the exporting of taxes through the federal offset and higher prices. No attempt is made, however, to determine the impact of importing on Minnesota residents. The results, accordingly, understate the burden remaining in the state by an amount that depends on the degree to which exported and imported flows do not offset each other.

More recent studies in other states have also accounted for tax exporting. Eapen and Eapen (1970) in Connecticut, Ebel and Kamin (1975) in Hawaii, and Daicoff (1978) in Kansas each accounted for the lessening of the in-state burden due to the federal offset and the price/migration effect. Thus far, however, imported taxes have received little more than lip service as a factor that should be recognized (see Garrison, Goolsby, and Quindry, 1977, or Phares, 1973).

One empirical model that does make an explicit allowance for the geographical flow of taxes, both into and out of an area, was developed by Hirsch et al. (1969) in a study of the external costs and benefits of providing local education in Clayton, Missouri, a small suburb of St. Louis. In examining cost flows, a spatial incidence model was specified to deal with the spill-in and spill-out of taxes pertaining to the financing of education. Hirsch was not concerned with the rearrangement of costs among all local governments but rather with the tax flows as shown in Table 4-1. The focus is explicitly upon Clayton with other areas included only to make the results more representative of Clayton's situation.

Thus far, all studies with a single state as the unit of analysis do not accurately reflect the burden because that part of the burden represented by taxes imported from elsewhere is not considered. Although in the context of one particular state such a methodology may be acceptable, when all fifty states are considered and the focus is interstate variations, attention needs to be given to both types of flows, exporting and importing.

By far the most comprehensive analysis of interstate tax movements is the pioneering work by McLure (1964, 1966, and 1967). In an exhaustive theoretical and empirical analysis of exporting state by

Table 4–1. An Outline of Hirsch's Spatial Tax Flow Model

	Spatial Incidence for Hirsch Study		
Geographic Area	*Outflow (Export)*	*Inflow (Import)*	*Net Effect*
Remainder of St. Louis County			
City of St. Louis			
Rest of Metropolitan area		(Dollar tax flows)	
Rest of state			
Rest of United States			

Source: Hirsch et al (1969).

state and tax by tax, he develops estimates of the extent to which taxes shifted to out-of-state residents or to the federal revenue structure.[a] His study is the first attempt to set this phenomenon in an interstate context. The importance of exporting becomes evident from a perusal of his findings. McLure (1966) estimates that exported taxes accounted for about 21 percent of all state-local tax receipts, or $8.3 out of $42 billion in 1962. The specific impact of this phenomenon on the geographical distribution of burdens is considerable. One-fifth of the full cost of state-local operations was shifted from the state of legal impact to the state of incidence. The final spatial resting place of these taxes alters the burden in each state and the nature of variations across states.

Total relative exporting ranges from a high of 49 percent in Nevada, owing to the importance of gambling and related activities, to a low of 16 percent in New Hampshire. Thus, even when viewed in the aggregate, the range is considerable. Exporting for specific taxes manifests even more variability. The national average goes from a high of 45 percent for corporate taxes (with a range between 81 percent in Delaware and 33 percent in South Dakota) to a low of 6 percent for miscellaneous taxes (with a range from 65 percent in Nevada to less than 1 percent in states such as Alaska, Iowa, or Kansas). This vast range in the extent of specific exporting is an important contributor to differentials in burdens. Although McLure does provide great detail on the exporting phenomenon, his task is not defined to include importing.

A recent study by Phares (1973) on tax burdens in each of the fifty states made use of McLure's findings to adjust effective tax rates for spatial flows. The findings in this instance were not only that the level of burden was influenced but that the overall pattern of equity was

[a]Bridges (1966) looked at the cost of deductibility of nonbusiness taxes due to IRS provisions for 1962. This is, of course, only part of what McLure accomplished.

also influenced. His results showed that without exporting one state was progressive, sixteen proportional, and thirty-three regressive, whereas with exporting none was progressive, eleven were proportional, and thirty-nine regressive. Generally, exporting made most states more regressive (Phares, 1973: Chapter 6 and Appendix C). Phares also made a crude estimate of tax importing for each state and included it in his estimates of total burden.

SOURCES OF TAX EXPORTING

The task at hand is to determine as precisely as possible the dollar amount of each state and local tax that is exported from each state. Given this information, it can be netted out of tax collections in the numerator of effective tax rates, thus providing a more accurate picture of the equity and burden on residents of a state.

As McLure (1964 and 1966) has discussed in great detail, taxes can be rearranged spatially in three basic ways.[b] First, they can be passed on to the federal revenue structure through provisions in federal law that allow for the deduction of certain state and local taxes in determining federal liability. Second, they can be shifted to out-of-state residents through the interstate movement of taxed commodities or by the migration of people among political jurisdictions. Finally, some taxes may fall as a burden on owners of factors, where the owners do not reside in the state of legal impact. For expository convenience these basic forms of exporting will be called the "federal offset export" for the first category and "price/migration export" for the second two categories lumped together. Each is discussed in turn.

The price/migration effect reflects the spatial shifting of taxes among states due to market conditions that allow them to be passed on to owners of factors of production or consumers of taxed commodities, as reflected in higher prices, or due to the movement of taxpayers. In this instance, however, the owners, consumers, and taxpayers live out of state. The distinction here is little different from the standard type of shifting and incidence theory except that the change in location between point of legal impact and final resting place becomes crucial. In other words, location is critical in determining who really pays a tax. Ideally, we would be able to incorporate all repercussions of a tax as it lowers the real incomes of nonresidents, regardless

[b]The theoretical and empirical detail necessary to accomplish this is substantial. No attempt will be made to present it here. The interested reader should refer to the work by McLure (1966) as a primary reference and Phares (1973) for its use in tax burden analysis.

of the remoteness of the point of impact. This would demand that we have some way of determining the general equilibrium spatial impact of every tax falling on nonresident income.

Attempting to implement such comprehensiveness for the purpose of this book would be an exercise in futility because no empirical base exists to allow us to come even close to approximating this degree of precision, let alone being able to deal with the theoretical difficulties that would surface. Rather, as McLure has noted, attention is much more productively focused on the "... immediate effects taxes have upon real incomes via changes in the prices of factors and products most directly affected by the tax" (1967: 51).

It was decided to adopt McLure's methodology for estimating the price/migration effect on tax-by-tax and state-by-state basis as a reasonable approximation to the relative "orders of magnitude" for this form of exporting. No pretense is made by McLure (1966: 300-302), nor by this author, that his findings are the sine qua non of interstate tax flows. They represent, however, the most detailed and precise information available at this time and do at least enable us to incorporate the exporting phenomenon into estimates of burden. Applying McLure's methodology, adjusted for changes that have occurred between his study year and the year under analysis here,[c] provides a summary of state and local taxes exported nationwide from all states due to the price and migration effect (see Table 4-2). The dollar amount of these exported taxes in each state is "netted" out of collections for each tax to arrive at a figure for nonexported taxes, that is, the amount that remains within the state. This figure is used in computing effective rates.[d]

Taxes that account for the largest volume of exporting include taxes for which a relatively large percentage is exported, such as the severance tax in Texas or Louisiana; taxes with a relatively smaller percentage exported but of a large base, such as the general sales tax in California or New York; or taxes with a high incidence of interstate activity or out-of-state ownership, such as the corporation license tax in Delaware. In total, this form of exporting amounts to well over $13 billion or almost 9 percent of all state and local collections in 1975–1976. Table 4-3 summarizes the relative impact of exporting, showing the average, high-low range, and coefficient of variation.

[c]Changes were made to incorporate more recent data, the adoption of new taxes in a state, and so on, wherever it was felt to be necessary to do so, between 1962 and 1975–1976.

[d]It was not possible to make estimates of the exporting effect by income class. Therefore, exported taxes were netted out of total collections for a tax in a specific state, not out of taxes apportioned by income category. In terms of the formula for burden presented at the end of Chapter 3, we now have C (total tax receipts) and E (exported taxes).

Table 4-2. A Summary of Tax Exporting Nationwide

Tax Category		Amount Exported ($ millions)
General sales		$ 2,038.2
Selective sales:		$ 2,405.0
Motor fuels	$ 633.3	
Tobacco	$ 148.2	
Alcohol	$ 91.0	
Insurance	$ 759.5	
Public utilities	$ 404.7	
Pari-mutuels	$ 312.3	
Amusements	$ 56.0	
Licenses:		$ 1,682.7
Motor vehicles	$1,112.8	
Corporations in general	$ 507.2	
Hunting and fishing	$ 46.2	
Alcohol	$ 7.1	
Public utilities	$ 9.4	
Individual income		$ 303.5
Corporation net income		$ 3,195.5
Severance		$ 1,187.1
State property:		$ 132.7
Railroads	$ 9.2	
Public utilities	$ 123.5	
Local personal property:		
Commercial/industrial		$ 121.5
Local real property:		$ 2,271.0
Commercial	$ 394.7	
Industrial	$1,607.0	
Other	$ 269.3	
Total Exported[a]		$13,336.9

[a]Items do not sum exactly to total due to rounding.

The second component to exporting results from provisions in federal tax law that permit the itemization of selected items in arriving at federal taxable income. The procedure used to estimate the federal offset export is quite a bit less entailed than was McLure's for the price/migration offset and was made possible by data obtained in a special tabulation from the IRS State Tax Model discussed earlier.

For those who are able to itemize deductions, several taxes, as listed below, can be deducted from adjusted gross income to arrive at taxable income on 1040 Schedule A:

Table 4–3. Summary Statistics on Percentage of State-Local Taxes Exported[a]

Tax[c]	Average[b]	Range[b] High	Range[b] Low	Coefficient of Variation[b]
General sales and gross receipts:				
Total	11.9	30.2	6.1	35.7
Federal offset	5.9	15.1	1.4	38.5
Selective sales and gross receipts:	13.9	45.0	8.4	37.4
Tobacco	3.8	15.0	3.0	68.5
Alcohol	3.8	15.0	3.0	68.5
Motor fuels:				
Total	14.6	24.2	9.8	22.3
Federal offset	7.3	15.4	2.7	37.7
All other	22.7	59.4	6.1	39.8
License taxes	21.6	58.4	12.4	32.0
Corporation net income	43.7	51.0	38.0	6.8
Individual income[d]	27.1	125.4	13.3	75.9
Severance	34.7	75.0	25.0	44.4
Other (n.e.c.)	12.4	43.9	0.0	70.5
State property	7.3	15.6	0.0	70.5
Local property:				
Total	10.9	18.2	4.4	32.3
Federal offset	7.5	12.7	2.2	33.2
All local:				
Total	10.8	17.3	4.3	31.2
Federal offset	7.2	13.8	2.2	34.9
All state:				
Total	19.3	38.3	10.4	27.4
Federal offset	7.2	12.9	1.7	42.5
All state and local:				
Total	16.0	34.1	7.8	26.3
Federal offset	7.1	13.1	1.9	34.9

Source: Price/migration factor based on McLure (1966); for federal offset refer to text.

[a]Total percentage exported is comprised of the federal tax offset and the price/migration export.

[b]Computed for states actually using the tax.

[c]State and local taxes combined, where applicable

[d]Exceeds 100 percent in New Jersey, see text for explanation.

State and local income
Real estate
State and local gasoline (until 1979)
General sales (state plus local add-on)
Personal property
Other (e.g., foreign income taxes)

For taxpayers who do itemize, each dollar of deduction becomes, in effect, a "passing on" to the federal government of a part of their state-local tax burden. By allowing these deductions, the federal government is implicitly subsidizing state-local operations but more so for locations that rely more heavily on taxes that can be deducted, particularly sales and income. The amount of the subsidy, however, is not dollar for dollar. Rather, the amount by which the federal liability goes down is a function of the amount deducted, taxable income for the income class in which they are paid, and the marginal tax rate applicable to that income level. Thus, if $1,000 were itemized on a married, joint return for income tax payments on a taxable income of $15,000, the applicable marginal rate would be 25 percent and the federal liability would be reduced by $250. This, in effect, is a shifting of $250 in state-local taxes to the federal revenue structure.[e]

As mentioned earlier, the information necessary to compute the dollar amount of federal offset by state, tax, and income class was obtained from a special tabulation on the IRS State Tax Model for 1975. This model contains a stratified probability sample of over 206,000 federal individual tax returns. It is organized to allow data to be reported for each state then weighted to obtain national totals. Contained in the model are all of the major items listed on individual returns, including itemized deductions. The tabulation provides data on the amount of each tax actually itemized for each of fourteen income classes, by state. Total amounts deducted nationwide are as follows ("other" was not used because no detail was given):

State and local income	$16,701 million
Real estate	15,450 million
State and local gasoline	2,934 million
General sales (state plus local add-on)	7,360 million
Personal property	956 million
Other (n.e.c.)	506 million
Total	$43,907 million

[e]The burden, of course, does not disappear but, assuming an equal yield, is now distributed as a part of the federal burden.

As noted above, however, only some fraction of this $43.9 billion becomes a reduction in the federal liability, where this fraction is a function of the marginal tax rate, the dollar amount deducted, and the level of income.

To obtain estimates of the actual offset, the dollar amount of each itemized deduction in each income class was weighted by the marginal rate applicable to each class. This was done separately for *each* state, *each* income class, and *each* type of tax.[f] Total dollar amounts nationwide are given in the following list. (The death and gift offset was estimated using McLure's methodology).

State and local income	$ 5,525 million
Real estate	4,420 million
State and local gasoline	743 million
General sales (state plus local add-on)	2,038 million
Personal property	263 million
Death and gift	547 million
Total federal offset	$13,481 million

These estimates of the federal offset were used to net out of the effective rate numerator all taxes exported to the federal revenue structure due to IRS provisions. One distinct advantage to this procedure is that these data allow for adjustment in each income class rather than only in the aggregate, as had to be done with the price/migration export. This gives a much more precise picture of the real burden at each income level since the equity effect of the federal offset is taken into account explicitly. Since the value of the offset is a function of the marginal tax rate, the higher the rate, the more the deduction is worth, and the more regressive the influence on the tax in question and the system as a whole.

THE IMPORTING OF TAXES

The other side to the tax flow coin is importing. For the year being examined, more than $26.8 billion in state and local collections were exported from all states nationwide; this is 17.2 percent of all tax revenue for this sector. As outlined above, exporting was accomp-

[f] Totals for property, sales, income, and so on, were allocated to components of these taxes in proportion to receipts. Data on married joint returns were used. We now have data on F (federal tax offset) in the effective rate formula at the end of Chapter 3.

lished in two ways: first, through the price/migration effect; and second, through the federal offset. Taxes shifted to the federal revenue structure are, in effect, "lost" as a claim within the state-local sector. The burden becomes absorbed by the federal system to somehow be "made up" there. In examining state-local equity or burden, then, the federal offset lowers the level in the state-local system (but increases it for the federal structure, assuming constant yield) and alters the equity of each tax instrument it affects. This $13.5 billion offset, a de facto subsidy to subnational governments, is equivalent to 8.6 percent of their total receipts.

The remaining component of exported dollars, $13.3 billion due to the price/migration effect (8.5 percent of all revenue), *does not*, however, "escape" the state-local system. It remains as a burden in the form of taxes that are imported into each state from other states. Nevada's gambling-related taxes (31 percent of its taxes), Texas' severance tax (19 percent of taxes), and Delaware's business-related taxes (26 percent of taxes), to pick some of the blatant cases, become manifest as a cost to residents of the other states. To estimate burden or equity properly, this amount must be allocated back to each state and then treated as though it were just another tax category (albeit implicit), arising out of the openness of subnational fiscal operations. This amount can then be distributed by income class as was done with every other tax.

Two distinct steps are entailed in this process. First, we take the total dollar volume of exporting ($13.3 billion) and determine its composition when exported; that is, how much was a sales tax, an income tax, a property tax, and so forth. It then must be allocated back to each state. Second, once distributed to a state, this amount must be allocated by income class, in accordance with the shifting and incidence assumptions outlined in Chapter 3, in order to arrive at an effective tax rate for imported taxes. When this is done, the picture of the burden in each state-local system is complete.

The procedure for the first step is as follows. Individual types of exported taxes were lumped together according to the statistical series used to proxy their incidence (refer to Table 3-1). That is, the total exporting of $13.3 billion was broken into categories. For example, two forms of exported taxes entailed gasoline expenditures as proxies for incidence and they totaled $633.3 million; eleven entailed consumption (at least in part) and they summed to $6,673 million; and so on. Once these amounts were determined for each exported tax, as specified in Table 4-4, they can be allocated across states. This was accomplished by determining each state's percentage of total national involvement in the allocator series indicated. If, for example, California had 10 percent of total national consumption expenditures, it was given 10 per-

Table 4-4. Imported Taxes: Amounts Allocated by Type of Allocator

Spatial Incidence Allocator Series	*Amount ($ millions)*	*Number of Taxes Involved*
Gasoline expenditures	$ 633.3	2
Tobacco expenditures	148.2	2
Alcohol expenditures	98.1	3
Insurance expenditures	759.5	1
Gas and electric expenditures	414.0	3
Recreation expenditures	414.4	3
Motor vehicle operations expenditures	1,112.8	2
Consumption expenditures	6,672.8	11
Dividend income	2,780.3	8
Income tax allocated to contiguous states[a]	301.0	2
Total imported taxes	$13,334.4	37

[a]Exported individual income tax due to migration was allocated to states contiguous to the states exporting. The District of Columbia imported $2.54 million, which was therefore "netted out" of the state-local system.

cent of the $6,673 billion in consumption-related exported taxes. This distribution was repeated for each of the first nine items listed in Table 4-4, where these categories actually represent thirty-five distinct sources of exporting.

The final category, the individual income tax, reflects the shifting of $301 million due to the migration effect of people living in one state and working in another. The most extreme case results from commutation patterns in the New York metropolition area where residents of Connecticut and New Jersey are liable for taxes levied by jurisdictions in New York state, that is, they import them. To incorporate this phenomenon, the $301 million was allocated to states that are contiguous with those that exported in accordance with relative population shares. Once this is done, all $13.3 billion in exported taxes is fully allocated back to the fifty states in accordance with assumptions concerning spatial incidence.[g]

The second step is relatively straight forward. For each state, the amount imported (e.g., California's 10 percent of consumption-oriented exporting, or $667 million) is now allocated by income class in proportion to the statistical series used to proxy its final incidence (as shown in Table 4-4). These ten individual categories are handled separately and then summed to arrive at an effective tax rate for all types of imported taxes as a composite.

[g] This is the final element in the numerator of the effective tax rate, *I* (imported taxes).

The end result is a complete specification of the claim resting on residents of each state for each income class, taking into account exporting to residents of other states and the federal government as well as importing. Thus, it accounts for the influence on the level of burden as well as the equity effect these flows exert.

THE MAJOR DIMENSIONS OF SPATIAL TAX FLOWS

Thus far we have considered spatial shifting only in aggregate national terms. Since our unit of analysis is the state, it is instructive to examine data on how these flow effect each state. It is in part their differential impact that contributes to differences in the burden and equity of individual taxes. The extent to which any system can export and the amount that it in turn imports helps to determine what the burden will be on its taxpayers and how it will differ from other states. Table 4-3 provides the percentage of major state and local taxes that is exported. Detail is shown for each type of tax and, where relevent, for the contribution of the federal offset. Also reported are the average, the coefficient of variation, and the high-low range for the states actually using a tax.

The greatest propensity for exportability is manifest by the corporation net income tax at an average of 43.7 percent; the high and low is between New York and Rhode Island at 51 percent and Pennsylvania at 38 percent. Next highest comes the severance tax with an average of 34.7 percent and a high of 75 percent in Texas. Following this is the individual income tax, which is exported almost entirely due to the federal offset.[h] Although it averages 27 percent, one state exports *more* than it raises, a curious situation worthy of explanation. New Jersey exports $127.9 million in taxes to the federal revenue structure due to itemization by its residents of state and local income taxes; it only collected $101 million. The reason is New Jersey's contiguous border with New York and the journey-to-work movement of its residents in and out of the area, particularly New York City. People who live in New Jersey and work in New York City (or state) are liable for New York income taxes. As a result, they itemized over $336 million in state and local income taxes on their federal 1040 Schedule A form which reduced their federal liability by $127.9 million, thus more than "offsetting" their own state's income tax levy. A similiar "border" phenomenon was found in Connecticut, which exports 84 per-

[h] There is a small migration effect, mentioned earlier, due to commutation across state borders but it is only $300 million out of $5.5 billion.

cent of its income tax, and New Hampshire, which exports 86 percent. Both of these states border states into which there is a flow of their residents for employment; as a result they have federal offsets of $43 against $51 million in collections and $5.3 against $6.2 million, respectively.

The cumulative impact of exporting averages 16 percent for all state-local taxes, 7.1 percent of which is contributed by the federal offset and the balance by the price/migration effects. The state with the highest exportability is Delaware at 34 percent owing to its taxation of business activity and high reliance on the individual income tax. The low is 7.8 percent in South Dakota. Relatively, the largest federal offset is found in Maryland (13 percent), the smallest in Wyoming (1.9 percent).

Also shown in Table 4-3 is the coefficient of variation for the percent of each tax exported. Variation is clearly present, the greatest being found for the individual income (75.9), state property (70.5), tobacco and alcohol selective sales taxes (68.5), and severance (44.4). Although this variation tends to average out to 26.3 percent overall, it remains a marked contributor to interstate differentials in burden.

An obvious problem with data expressed in percentage terms is that the scale, or absolute level, is hidden. To set spatial flows in an absolute, as opposed to a relative, context, Table 4-5 gives dollar amounts by state. Total state and local collections, exported taxes broken down by type, imported taxes, and the net balance are all shown both in absolute and relative terms. In perusing this table, the vast dollar differences involved become evident. At one extreme lie the fiscal giants, California and New York, with over $20 billion in revenue and $3.8 and $4.2 billion in exporting, respectively. At the other extreme lie Vermont and Wyoming, each with around $350 million in collections and $46 and $49 million in exporting, respectively. The contribution made by the federal offset and the price/migration effect are shown separately. States like Minnesota, Delaware, Wisconsin, Maryland, and Oregon are able to export a larger percentage of their burden to the federal revenue structure because of more extensive use of the individual income tax. Wyoming, South Dakota, and Texas, on the other hand, with no tax on income lose this advantage. In terms of the price/migration effect, the clear advantage is for states such as Delaware that is able to export 23 percent of its burden primarily due to taxation of business activity, Nevada (22 percent) due to gambling, and Texas (18 percent) and Louisiana (18 percent) due to natural resources. At the low end are states like Maryland with a lesser reliance on exportable revenue sources.

On the other side of the export issue is importing. About one-half of the $26.8 billion in exported taxes is simply rearranged among the

Table 4–5. Major Features of Spatial Tax Flows (in millions)

State	Total State and Local Taxes	Exported Taxes[a] Amount	Exported Taxes[a] Percent of Total Taxes	Federal Offset Export Amount	Federal Offset Export Percent of Total Taxes
Alabama	$ 1,668.3	$ 249.0	14.9	$ 113.7	6.8
Alaska	724.3	87.7	12.1	47.6	6.5
Arizona	1,660.4	239.3	14.4	117.4	7.0
Arkansas	957.1	137.9	14.4	60.0	6.2
California	20,749.5	3,841.6	18.5	2,151.3	10.3
Colorado	1,880.6	302.6	16.0	190.6	10.1
Connecticut	2,424.6	443.1	18.2	245.9	10.1
Delaware	447.2	152.6	34.1	51.8	11.5
Florida	4,764.6	755.2	15.8	251.6	5.2
Georgia	2,726.7	377.6	13.8	210.2	7.7
Hawaii	829.1	181.2	21.8	73.7	8.8
Idaho	490.7	72.4	14.7	37.0	7.5
Illinois	8,639.8	1,473.0	17.0	699.8	8.1
Indiana	3,118.2	370.7	11.8	183.2	5.8
Iowa	2,010.9	263.0	13.0	147.4	7.3
Kansas	1,504.5	202.1	13.4	107.5	7.1
Kentucky	1,883.2	335.3	17.8	139.3	7.3
Louisiana	2,342.3	504.9	21.5	79.5	3.3
Maine	718.5	83.3	11.6	34.8	4.8
Mayland	3,374.3	609.7	18.0	448.4	13.2
Massachusetts	5,244.0	885.4	16.8	544.1	10.3
Michigan	6,819.3	1,179.0	17.2	668.5	9.8
Minnesota	3,261.9	614.1	18.8	360.1	11.0
Mississippi	1,144.4	139.7	12.2	60.5	5.2
Missouri	2,724.4	374.1	13.7	200.8	7.3
Montana	533.7	80.3	15.0	32.0	6.0
Nebraska	1,021.2	110.9	10.8	56.9	5.5
Nevada	500.5	129.2	25.8	20.1	4.0
New Hampshire	469.9	75.6	16.1	29.2	6.2
New Jersey	5,816.2	1,120.9	19.2	631.7	10.8
New Mexico	698.6	119.6	17.1	36.3	5.2
New York	20,614.6	4,195.3	20.3	2,373.5	11.5
North Carolina	2,883.6	469.3	16.2	238.4	8.2
North Dakota	428.9	58.8	13.7	26.7	6.2
Ohio	6,262.2	921.5	14.7	439.5	7.0
Oklahoma	1,465.2	259.6	17.7	96.2	6.5
Oregon	1,638.4	273.7	16.7	167.7	10.2
Pennsylvania	8,112.5	1,239.4	15.2	600.3	7.4
Rhode Island	658.7	111.4	16.9	59.4	9.0
South Carolina	1,393.3	202.8	14.5	103.9	7.4
South Dakota	409.2	31.8	7.7	12.1	2.9
Tennessee	2,078.1	284.1	13.6	82.3	3.9
Texas	7,258.7	1,579.3	21.7	297.4	4.0
Utah	727.8	103.9	14.2	62.4	8.5
Vermont	353.2	49.4	14.0	24.8	7.0
Virginia	3,065.5	502.9	16.4	310.3	10.1
Washington	2,629.6	312.9	11.9	145.2	5.5
West Virginia	1,063.5	96.3	9.0	33.1	3.1
Wisconsin	3,643.7	566.3	15.5	368.2	10.1
Wyoming	330.2	46.0	13.9	6.7	2.0
All states	$156,165.8	$26,818.3	17.2	$13,481.4	8.6

[a]Exported taxes equal the sum of federal offset export and price/migration export, except for rounding error.

[b]Excludes $2.6 million in individual income taxes exported to the District of Columbia. Price/migration and importe taxes sum to same amount except for this difference.

[c]Sums to zero except for rounding error and $2.6 million individual income taxes exported to District of Columbi that is, net exporting and importing offset each other in total.

Table 4-5 (continued)

Price/Migration Export		Imported Taxes		Net Export (+) or Import (−) of Taxes	
Amount	Percent of Total Taxes	Amount[b]	Percent of Total Taxes	Amount	Percent of Total Taxes
$ 135.2	8.1	$ 166.9	10.0	$ −31.6	−1.8
40.1	5.5	26.3	3.6	13.8	1.9
121.8	7.3	134.4	8.1	−12.6	−0.7
77.8	8.1	102.3	10.6	−24.4	−2.5
1,690.2	8.1	1,438.5	6.9	251.6	1.2
111.9	5.9	158.5	8.4	−46.6	−2.4
197.1	8.1	280.6	11.5	−83.4	−3.4
100.7	22.5	45.3	10.1	55.4	12.4
503.6	10.5	589.3	12.3	−85.7	−1.8
167.4	6.1	253.4	9.2	−86.0	−3.1
107.4	12.9	53.2	6.4	54.2	6.5
35.3	7.2	41.8	8.5	−6.5	−1.3
773.1	8.9	743.7	8.6	29.3	0.3
187.5	6.0	300.8	9.6	−113.3	−3.6
115.5	5.7	158.4	7.8	−42.8	−2.1
94.5	6.2	136.8	9.0	−42.2	−2.8
196.0	10.4	177.0	9.4	18.9	1.0
425.3	18.1	182.6	7.7	242.7	10.3
48.4	6.7	61.1	8.5	−12.6	−1.7
161.2	4.7	255.3	7.5	−94.0	−2.7
341.3	6.5	390.7	7.4	−49.4	−0.9
510.5	7.4	532.3	7.8	−21.8	−0.3
254.0	7.7	223.9	6.8	30.1	0.9
79.2	6.9	99.8	8.7	−20.6	−1.8
173.3	6.3	279.8	10.2	−106.5	−3.9
48.3	9.0	40.6	7.6	7.6	1.4
53.9	5.2	85.8	8.4	−31.8	−3.1
109.0	21.7	42.7	8.5	66.2	13.2
46.4	9.8	61.8	13.1	−15.4	−3.2
489.2	8.4	734.8	12.6	−245.5	−4.2
83.2	11.9	60.1	8.6	23.1	3.3
1,821.7	8.8	1,338.9	6.4	482.8	2.3
230.8	8.0	298.7	10.3	−67.8	−2.3
32.0	7.4	32.8	7.6	−0.7	−0.3
481.9	7.6	625.2	9.9	−143.2	−2.2
163.4	11.1	146.6	10.0	16.8	1.1
106.0	6.4	140.4	8.5	−34.4	−2.0
639.0	7.8	748.3	9.2	−109.2	−1.3
52.0	7.8	59.4	9.0	−7.4	−1.1
98.9	7.1	136.2	9.7	−37.2	−2.6
19.6	4.8	34.1	8.3	−14.5	−3.5
201.8	9.7	204.4	9.8	−2.6	−0.1
1,281.9	17.6	718.5	9.8	563.4	7.7
41.5	5.7	59.2	8.1	−17.7	−2.4
24.6	6.9	28.9	8.1	−4.3	−1.2
192.5	6.2	292.5	9.5	−99.9	−3.2
167.7	6.3	223.5	8.4	−55.7	−2.1
63.2	5.9	93.4	8.7	−30.2	−2.8
198.1	5.4	268.5	7.3	−70.3	−1.9
39.3	11.9	23.9	7.2	15.3	4.6
$13,336.9	8.5	$13,334.3[b]	8.5	[c]	

fifty states; what is moved out of one state is imported somewhere else. Table 4-5 shows the amount imported by state. The impact here, related to actual collections, is from a peak of 13.1 percent in New Hampshire to a low of 3.6 percent in Alaska. Dollar amounts go from almost $1.5 billion in California to $26 million in Alaska. Comparison of the price/migration export data with imported taxes shows what the net import is for a state as a result of spatial flows.[i] This is shown in the last two columns in Table 4-5. The largest "net exporters" in dollar terms are New York ($482 million) and Texas ($563 million) but, as mentioned, for different reasons. In relative terms Nevada (13.2 percent), Delaware (12.4 percent), and Louisiana (10.3 percent) lead the list. "Net importing" is greatest in New Jersey ($245 million) and Ohio ($143 million) in dollar terms and Missouri (3.9 percent) and Indiana (3.6 percent) in relative terms. As the data show, there is substantial variation on both an absolute and a relative basis.

The nature and impact of these flows can be defined by examining two states that define the extremes. Nevada exports $109 million and imports $43 million. On balance, its public operations are subsidized by $66 million (13 percent of all tax revenue) from residents of other states. Missouri, on the other hand, exports $173 million but imports $280 million, thus helping to subsidize governmental operations elsewhere. Owing to the size of the federal offset, only one state winds up being a *net* loser overall. South Dakota exports $12.1 million due to the federal offset and $19.6 million due to the price/migration effect, but it imports $34.1 million. Even with the federal offset, it is a net overall importer of $2.4 million.

The federal offset as a source of exporting accounts for more than $13.4 billion, the full amount of which ultimately becomes a burden on federal taxpayers but *not* on state-local taxpayers.[j] The net effect is to shift 8.6 percent of all state-local collections onto federal taxpayers in accordance with the equity pattern of federal revenue sources. The magnitude of these offsets, however, is far from identical across the income spectrum. Rather, it is a function of taxable income in an income class and the marginal tax rate applicable to that class. Accordingly, the impact on effective rates varies distinctly as we move from "under $3,000" to "over $35,000." It is of consequence how these effective rates are differentially lowered because this factor alters the progressivity or regressivity of each tax for which the offset is allowed. This, in turn, cumulates to alter the equity of systems of taxes and the total burden.

[i] All states except South Dakota are overall net exporters due to the federal offset. We are looking here at the balance between price/migration export and importing.

[j] They are, of course, the same people but we are only interested in the burden resulting from state and local taxes.

Table 4-6 details combined federal offsets by income class and state, expressed as a percentage of income. The pattern of these "effective rates" is clearly progressive in incidence (i.e., a higher percentage for higher incomes). It ranges on an average, from a few tenths of 1 percent in the lowest class to 2.55 percent at the top. Fluctuation around the mean, however, is extreme; the coefficients of variation go from 151 in the lowest class to 41 at the top. Generally, the degree diminishes when moving up the income spectrum; the bottom seven classes decreases steadily from 151 to 56 while the top 7 all lie in the range 37 to 46.

The net effect of these offsets is to *lessen* the progressivity of the tax structure as a whole and of the specific taxes to which they apply. The extreme case is found in New York where the offset as a percentage of income rises steadily from 0.053 to 6.06, which is far above the average. This has the net effect, for example, of reducing the total state-local burden in the top income class from 23.4 percent without the offset to 17.3 percent with it, a 26 percent decrease. Other states show a similiar phenomenon, although not quite so extreme; for example, compare Delaware or Minnesota. States that benefit the most from these offsets are high-income tax states, such as the states just mentioned. Those that benefit the least are the ones with no individual income tax such as Nevada or Wyoming. All states, however, reap some benefit, owing to itemization of other state-local taxes.

Table 4-6 shows explicitly, as a percentage of income, the influence that federal tax law exerts on burdens by income level. In effect, the total state-local burden would be higher by the amounts shown in the table if the offset were not allowed. The "pro-rich" distribution is evident and the net impact is to increase the regressivity of state-local taxation in each state, but for some states it is much more so than for others (e.g., contrast New York with Wyoming).

The impact of the federal offset as it influences each tax to which it applies is incorporated into the estimates of effective rates on a basis of tax by tax, state by state, and income class by income class, thus adjusting not only the level of burden but also its equity pattern.

Finally, to help set these factors into perspective, we can consider the relationship between each major component of spatial flows and income, as shown in Table 4-7. To provide a benchmark, each element is expressed as a percentage of aggregate income for the state (as defined in Chapter 3). Total exported taxes average nearly 2 percent of income nationwide but go from 4.17 percent in Delaware to 0.98 percent in South Dakota. Imported taxes average slightly over 1 percent but are as high as 1.33 percent in Connecticut and as low as 0.78 percent in Alaska. The difference between these two items is the reduction in burden due to the federal offset (0.90 percent on average).

Table 4.6. Total Federal Tax Offset as a Percentage of Income[a]

	Income Classes					
State	Under $3,000	$3,000-$3,999	$4,000-$4,999	$5,000-$5,999	$6,000-$6,999	$7,000-$7,999
Alabama	0.027	0.000	0.021	0.108	0.124	0.262
Alaska	0.019	0.000	0.299	0.040	0.119	0.078
Arizona	0.015	0.092	0.149	0.101	0.289	0.490
Arkansas	0.000	0.029	0.046	0.048	0.061	0.073
California	0.111	0.117	0.200	0.189	0.319	0.336
Colorado	0.113	0.066	0.116	0.174	0.187	0.288
Connecticut	0.000	0.135	0.322	0.134	0.435	0.121
Delaware	0.000	0.046	0.100	0.020	0.150	0.147
Florida	0.018	0.053	0.181	0.150	0.120	0.151
Georgia	0.016	0.059	0.089	0.128	0.166	0.174
Hawaii	0.041	0.012	0.059	0.038	0.114	0.224
Idaho	0.022	0.034	0.030	0.030	0.088	0.083
Illinois	0.019	0.088	0.076	0.264	0.199	0.146
Indiana	0.005	0.055	0.083	0.071	0.058	0.139
Iowa	0.016	0.013	0.022	0.250	0.079	0.153
Kansas	0.001	0.031	0.104	0.227	0.218	0.253
Kentucky	0.002	0.050	0.050	0.131	0.110	0.180
Louisiana	0.000	0.000	0.041	0.040	0.171	0.160
Maine	0.010	0.082	0.021	0.347	0.083	0.192
Mayland	0.213	0.069	0.032	0.329	0.104	0.114
Massachusetts	0.316	0.163	0.273	0.403	0.352	0.414
Michigan	0.103	0.066	0.120	0.244	0.463	0.301
Minnesota	0.001	0.247	0.355	0.198	0.307	0.096
Mississippi	0.040	0.000	0.005	0.159	0.153	0.107
Missouri	0.007	0.052	0.143	0.106	0.142	0.117
Montana	0.086	0.043	0.052	0.128	0.081	0.088
Nebraska	0.005	0.000	0.026	0.012	0.163	0.172
Nevada	0.014	0.017	0.068	0.166	0.173	0.168
New Hampshire	0.020	0.027	0.142	0.136	0.440	0.237
New Jersey	0.051	0.460	0.541	0.477	0.415	0.586
New Mexico	0.005	0.036	0.006	0.106	0.038	0.243
New York	0.053	0.222	0.251	0.529	0.482	0.444
North Carolina	0.014	0.027	0.147	0.054	0.087	0.211
North Dakota	0.000	0.044	0.051	0.232	0.049	0.169
Ohio	0.021	0.024	0.052	0.109	0.236	0.170
Oklahoma	0.045	0.018	0.093	0.057	0.044	0.213
Oregon	0.194	0.153	0.122	0.101	0.029	0.248
Pennsylvania	0.023	0.098	0.088	0.110	0.215	0.304
Rhode Island	0.011	0.129	0.136	0.023	0.515	0.636
South Carolina	0.000	0.000	0.011	0.191	0.126	0.231
South Dakota	0.100	0.028	0.036	0.086	0.070	0.094
Tennessee	0.009	0.003	0.001	0.072	0.104	0.107
Texas	0.037	0.014	0.046	0.037	0.062	0.104
Utah	0.075	0.114	0.246	0.158	0.109	0.450
Vermont	0.016	0.198	0.062	0.192	0.263	0.352
Virginia	0.037	0.041	0.040	0.109	0.262	0.211
Washington	0.027	0.038	0.109	0.281	0.319	0.235
West Virginia	0.000	0.000	0.043	0.048	0.010	0.113
Wisconsin	0.048	0.139	0.122	0.274	0.193	0.275
Wyoming	0.000	0.008	0.013	0.000	0.096	0.090
Average	0.041	0.069	0.109	0.153	0.184	0.220

[a]*All* state and local taxes "exported" to the federal revenue structure. See chapter 3 for a discussion of the income base used.

[b]All exported death and gift taxes are included in this income class.

Table 4.6 *(continued)*

				Income Classes			
$8,000-$9,999	*$10,000-$11,999*	*$12,000-$14,999*	*$15,000-$19,999*	*$20,000-$24,999*	*$25,000-$29,999*	*$30,000-$34,999*	*Over[b] $35,000*
0.194	0.279	0.467	0.549	0.636	0.708	0.741	2.484
0.070	0.185	0.231	0.436	0.727	0.963	1.391	2.264
0.397	0.623	0.597	0.656	0.988	1.179	1.115	2.006
0.132	0.175	0.369	0.417	0.542	0.646	0.788	3.431
0.583	0.640	0.754	1.025	1.257	1.389	1.654	3.923
0.666	0.770	0.719	0.932	1.149	1.211	1.822	2.581
0.454	0.613	0.653	0.701	0.790	0.894	1.141	2.980
0.167	0.428	0.590	0.612	0.905	1.248	1.782	4.594
0.243	0.260	0.259	0.356	0.375	0.449	0.683	1.818
0.296	0.351	0.429	0.540	0.745	1.071	1.331	2.729
0.472	0.457	0.778	1.127	1.416	1.217	1.905	2.552
0.223	0.359	0.373	0.604	0.883	0.872	1.490	2.865
0.347	0.489	0.503	0.692	0.922	1.029	1.141	2.288
0.310	0.224	0.355	0.433	0.464	1.013	0.669	1.523
0.189	0.309	0.660	0.622	0.845	1.124	1.375	2.364
0.143	0.278	0.410	0.591	0.859	0.731	0.919	2.427
0.266	0.412	0.788	0.724	0.794	0.859	1.135	3.015
0.151	0.239	0.281	0.295	0.335	0.397	0.560	1.266
0.333	0.443	0.470	0.527	0.545	0.786	0.942	2.315
0.463	0.777	1.027	1.234	1.558	1.381	2.246	3.037
0.836	0.585	1.191	1.082	1.406	1.208	1.333	4.180
0.659	0.599	0.776	0.914	1.126	1.303	1.448	2.722
0.455	0.658	0.951	1.310	1.615	1.638	1.960	4.250
0.274	0.359	0.429	0.630	0.565	0.572	0.610	2.330
0.166	0.260	0.434	0.687	0.764	0.817	1.349	2.097
0.288	0.507	0.551	0.528	0.670	0.932	0.874	2.409
0.290	0.303	0.492	0.459	0.504	0.783	0.651	1.867
0.312	0.380	0.521	0.432	0.492	0.468	0.538	0.874
0.230	0.409	0.419	0.424	0.605	0.730	0.660	1.913
0.986	0.631	0.821	0.923	0.994	1.170	1.420	2.994
0.210	0.304	0.426	0.450	0.540	0.808	1.269	1.429
0.620	0.835	1.132	1.336	1.597	1.783	2.022	6.064
0.276	0.464	0.561	0.715	0.888	0.859	1.343	2.823
0.227	0.265	0.355	0.426	0.638	0.882	0.854	2.553
0.222	0.324	0.457	0.443	0.549	0.680	1.000	2.206
0.259	0.227	0.252	0.468	0.561	0.829	0.995	1.815
0.385	0.575	0.748	0.968	1.127	1.259	1.980	3.546
0.336	0.381	0.657	0.630	0.958	1.049	1.003	2.360
0.449	0.772	0.702	0.661	0.805	0.880	1.332	3.781
0.293	0.379	0.584	0.585	0.685	0.831	1.324	3.026
0.310	0.211	0.316	0.321	0.423	0.407	0.531	1.028
0.199	0.186	0.233	0.307	0.366	0.471	0.435	1.381
0.149	0.148	0.244	0.269	0.366	0.454	0.666	1.255
0.554	0.600	0.745	0.910	1.089	1.301	1.008	1.673
0.563	0.531	0.626	0.791	0.870	1.332	1.631	4.005
0.210	0.415	0.548	0.690	0.934	1.008	1.413	2.613
0.547	0.286	0.525	0.557	0.615	0.582	0.983	1.308
0.113	0.103	0.098	0.160	0.279	0.569	0.824	1.746
0.613	0.500	0.893	1.043	1.421	1.603	1.670	3.909
0.245	0.166	0.207	0.263	0.272	0.234	0.269	0.598
0.348	0.414	0.553	0.650	0.810	0.933	1.165	2.550

Table 4–7. Major Components of State-Local Tax Flows as a Percentage of Income[a]

State	*Total Exported Taxes*	*Federal Offset Export*	*Price/Migration Export*	*Imported Taxes*	*Total Taxes Net of Tax Flows*	*Total Taxes*	*Net Reduction (+) in Burden Due to Tax Flows*
Alabama	1.40	0.64	0.76	0.94	8.97	9.43	0.46
Alaska	2.62	1.42	1.19	0.78	19.78	21.62	1.83
Arizona	1.81	0.89	0.92	1.02	11.81	12.61	0.79
Arkansas	1.40	0.61	0.79	1.04	9.41	9.77	0.36
California	2.66	1.49	1.17	0.99	12.70	14.37	1.66
Colorado	1.84	1.16	0.68	0.96	10.56	11.44	0.87
Connecticut	2.11	1.17	0.93	1.33	10.78	11.55	0.77
Delaware	4.17	1.41	2.75	1.23	9.28	12.21	2.93
Florida	1.56	0.52	1.04	1.21	9.50	9.84	0.34
Georgia	1.48	0.82	0.65	0.99	10.24	10.73	0.48
Hawaii	3.34	1.36	1.98	0.98	12.93	15.29	2.36
Idaho	1.61	0.82	0.78	0.93	10.23	10.91	0.67
Illinois	2.04	0.96	1.07	1.03	10.96	11.97	1.01
Indiana	1.17	0.58	0.59	0.95	9.67	9.89	0.22
Iowa	1.58	0.89	0.69	0.95	11.51	12.14	0.63
Kansas	1.50	0.80	0.70	1.01	10.70	11.19	0.48
Kentucky	1.99	0.82	1.16	1.05	10.27	11.21	0.94
Louisiana	2.64	0.41	2.22	0.95	10.58	12.27	1.68
Maine	1.55	0.64	0.90	1.13	12.96	13.38	0.41
Maryland	2.18	1.60	0.57	0.91	10.80	12.07	1.26
Massachusetts	2.47	1.51	0.95	1.09	13.25	14.63	1.38
Michigan	2.06	1.16	0.89	0.93	10.79	11.92	1.13
Minnesota	2.67	1.56	1.10	0.97	12.51	14.21	1.70
Mississippi	1.39	0.60	0.79	0.99	11.05	11.45	0.39
Missouri	1.40	0.75	0.64	1.04	9.86	10.21	0.35

Table 4–7 *(continued)*

Montana	1.97	0.78	1.18	0.99	12.11	13.08	0.97
Nebraska	1.25	0.64	0.61	0.97	11.26	11.55	0.28
Nevada	3.15	0.49	2.66	1.04	10.10	12.21	2.10
New Hampshire	1.59	0.61	0.97	1.30	9.60	9.90	0.29
New Jersey	2.36	1.33	1.03	1.55	11.46	12.27	0.81
New Mexico	2.00	0.61	1.39	1.00	10.72	11.72	0.99
New York	3.65	2.06	1.58	1.16	15.45	17.94	2.48
North Carolina	1.71	0.87	0.84	1.09	9.91	10.54	0.62
North Dakota	1.76	0.80	0.96	0.98	12.08	12.86	0.78
Ohio	1.46	0.69	0.76	0.99	9.45	9.92	0.46
Oklahoma	1.73	0.64	1.09	0.97	9.02	9.77	0.75
Oregon	1.94	1.19	0.75	0.99	10.69	11.64	0.94
Pennsylvania	1.82	0.88	0.94	1.10	11.24	11.97	0.72
Rhode Island	2.10	1.12	0.98	1.12	11.48	12.46	0.98
South Carolina	1.52	0.78	0.74	1.02	9.97	10.47	0.50
South Dakota	0.98	0.37	0.60	1.05	12.71	12.64	−0.07[b]
Tennessee	1.33	0.38	0.94	0.96	9.39	9.76	0.37
Texas	2.22	0.41	1.80	1.01	8.99	10.20	1.21
Utah	1.57	0.94	0.62	0.89	10.34	11.02	0.67
Vermont	2.03	1.02	1.01	1.19	13.68	14.52	0.84
Virginia	1.65	1.02	0.63	0.96	9.40	10.10	0.69
Washington	1.38	0.64	0.74	0.99	11.25	11.64	0.39
West Virginia	1.04	0.35	0.68	1.01	11.46	11.49	0.03
Wisconsin	2.09	1.36	0.73	0.99	12.35	13.45	1.10
Wyoming	1.88	0.27	1.61	0.98	12.64	13.54	0.90
Average	1.94	0.90	1.04	1.04	11.16	12.06	0.90

[a]See chapter 3 for a discussion of the income base used.

[b]Imported taxes as a percentage of income exceeds total exported taxes as a percentage of income.

The overall effect on burden can be gleaned from a perusal of the last three columns. The big "winners" are Delaware (2.93 percent) and New York (2.48 percent). The only absolute loser is South Dakota (−0.07 percent). In many instances the reduction in burden is less than one-half of 1 percent. Again, variance among states is quite distinct with a range between a net reduction of 2.93 percent or a net increase of 0.07 percent.

These data help to summarize the change in burden due to spatial tax flows by major component. We are now in a position to examine the burden of each state and local tax by income level for each of the fifty states. Accounting for the geographical rearrangement of taxation among states and the federal revenue structure is the last adjustment necessary to the numerator of the effective tax rates.

Chapter 5

The Burden of Individual State and Local Taxes

As noted throughout the previous text, past studies of tax burdens share two inherent biases vis-à-vis the treatment of state-local taxes. Either they assume that the level and equity estimated for the entire fifty states are somehow representative of each state or they assume that the pattern in one particular state is reflective of that in others; that is, a regressive general sales tax for the state-local sector or in a particular state means that this applies elsewhere as well. Clearly this assumption is untenable except perhaps as a very crude first approximation. To base policy on such a stance would indeed be naive. If one characteristic is descriptive of the federal system, it is the wide differences in the tax and spending policy that are prevalent. States like New York and California need only to be contrasted with states like Missouri and Ohio for this to become evident. Only when such differences are taken into account will the impact of subnational tax policy be properly understood. Only when each state's particular provisions for exemptions from the general sales tax; property tax circuit breaker allowances; deductions, exemption, and, graduated marginal tax rates for the individual income tax; consumption and income patterns; and so forth, are recognized will tax burdens—both their level and equity—portray the impact of public policy on private income.

The model developed in Chapters 2 through 4 has been designed for this specific purpose. Mindful that no model, no matter how precisely specified, can posibly take into account all of the nuances across fifty states with more than 78,000 local governments, we can nonetheless incorporate the aspects that are of major significance. In this context we are able to treat each system's profile as representative of circumstances in that state and its local sector, with each state treated as a distinct fiscal entity.

The end product of this model, in empirical terms, is an effective tax rate for each individual state and local tax, and totals for categories, using alternative shifting and incidence assumptions, for fifty states and fourteen income classes. This produces 65,100 specific burden measures.

Having generated literally thousands of effective rates, the challenge is to make some sense out of this bevy of numbers. We cannot deal in any meaningful way with ninety-three different effective rate (*ER*) matrices, containing data on each of fifty states and fourteen income categories. There is a pressing need to be able to condense these data in a manner that allows us to note something about the burden pattern within a particular state and how systems and taxes compare with each other. Thus, in addition to the basic data on *ERs*, contained in Appendix A, we need some method of summarization to indicate patterns across both states and income classes.

A logical place to start is with the arithmetic mean of effective rates. This offers a profile of the "average" level of burden at each of fourteen locations along the income distribution. We want in addition, however, to know how much this level differs among states. A second useful summary statistic, therefore, reflects the extent of variation in *ERs* across states for each income class; this is indicated by the coefficient of variation (standard deviation divided by the arithmetic mean). Making use of these two summary measures, we can depict a great deal of information about the prevailing average claim on income and how this changes as we look across states and as we move from low to high-income levels. These two statistics permit us to address directly concerns of horizontal and vertical equity; that is, how "equally" are "equals" treated across states when we compare the same income class and how "unequally" are "unequals" treated as we move up the income spectrum. Consideration along these lines, also permits inferences about variations in tax policy among state-local systems.

Table 5-3 summarizes effective rate data for seventeen major taxes or categories of taxes using the arithmetic mean (see Appendix A for data on other taxes). Table 5-4 provides coefficients of variation for the same data. Both numbers are calculated to include only the states that actually use a tax (e.g., forty-five for the state general sales tax) rather than all states. This is intended to portray features of these taxes as actually used rather than as they might be used.

Obviously, in presenting data in such a condensed format, information is sacrificed. However, there are two distinct advantages not found in other studies on state-local tax burdens. First, the level and pattern reflected in Table 5-3 are based on individual estimates for each state and, in the case of totals, for each tax that enters into the total. Thus, the average is a true average in a statistical sense and not just a composite for a sector. Second, the basic data by tax, state, and income class are available in Appendix A if more specific comparisons are desired.

In interpreting the findings contained in these tables, it must be remembered that we are concerned with two distinct facets of burden. First is the *level* of the effective rate, that is, whether it is 0.5 or 5.0. This shows the intensity of the claim for different types of taxes across the income distribution; the difference, for example, is between local real property taxes, which range from 10.25 to 2.79 percent of income, and the alcohol selective sales tax with *ERs* that decrease from 0.34 to 0.15. Second is the way in which this burden changes, that is, its *pattern* or *equity profile*. The difference here is between a tax like the state general sales tax, which steadily decreases as a percentage of income (from 5.02 to 1.63 percent), and the state individual income tax, which increases when moving upward on the income spectrum (from 0.01 to 1.72 percent). Burden for an entire state-local tax structure is a function of how individual taxes interact. Heavy relative reliance on regressive property taxation (as in New Hampshire) pulls it in one direction while heavy use of an individual income tax (as in Delaware) pulls it in another. The total tax burden represent a balancing of these forces.

We can now turn to a discussion of major individual taxes, their characteristics, and how they interact to generate a burden on each state's residents. This chapter is concerned with a general discussion of each major tax; Chapter 6, meanwhile, discusses the equity of major taxes and systems of taxes and how states compare to each other.

Since the model from Chapters 3 and 4 is applied separately to each of fifty types of taxes under a variety of incidence assumptions, we wind up with ninety-three distinct sets of effective rates. No attempt will be made to interpret each of them. Many will be discussed only in the aggregate, such as local real and personal property taxes (which actually have thirteen separate components); others will not be mentioned because of their trivial financial role, such as the motor vehicle operators license or the document and stock transfer tax. Only major taxes or taxes that have a special status in certain states (e.g., the severance tax in Texas or Louisiana) are dealt with explicitly. State-by-state data on *all* those remaining are contained in Appendix A.

TAXES ON PROPERTY

Taxes on property are by far the largest single revenue source for the state-local system. For the study year they averaged over 35 percent of total revenue and ranged between a high of 60 percent in New Hampshire and a low of 11 percent in Alabama (See Table 5-1 for a summary of all major state and local taxes discussed in this chapter). Although still fiscally dominant, this represents a drop in reliance on this tax instrument that is quite pronounced. In 1962 it averaged 46 percent of revenue with a high of 71 percent in Nebraska and a low of 16 percent in Hawaii. Although dollars collected have not decreased over this period, and instead have risen from $18.9 to $54.7 billion, receipts from other sources have grown much more rapidly. For example, a threefold increase in property tax receipts has been matched with a sevenfold growth in the state individual income tax or a fourfold growth in the state general sales tax. No matter how it is cut, however, property taxation, while on the wane relatively, continues as the major influence in state-local finance.

An important facet of property taxation is the unique status it plays in local finance. As of 1976 it accounted for over 96 percent of all property tax collections and for, on the average, 85 percent of all local revenues, with a range between 42 percent in Alabama and 98 to 99 percent in Massachusetts, Vermont, and New Hampshire. "Localness" is perhaps the most distinguishing attribute of this tax, but even this factor has evolved as the figures show in Tables 5-2. There is a clear movement toward a lessened dependence on local property taxation, which results from expanded use of other instruments by local governments. Nonproperty tax sources now average 15 percent of all local revenue, but in some states they play a dominant role, such as in Alabama (58 percent) or in Louisiana (50 percent). For some local governments, these alternative revenues have become of great consequence, for example, witness the local income tax in New York City or St. Louis, Missouri. This lessened dependence on the property tax is a function mainly of three factors: (1) alterations in local fiscal responsibility for certain functions; (2) greater state and federal involvement in financing local services; and (3) more liberal state legislation enabling local jurisdictions to use nonproperty tax sources not previously available (see Schroeder and Sjoquist, 1975).

Turning first to Table 5-3, we see that the highest burden for a single tax is found with the real property tax; on the average it lies well above

Table 5-1. Summary of Individual State and Local Taxes as a Percentage of Total State and Local Tax Collections

Tax	Average[a]	Range		Coefficient of Variation	Number of States Using Tax
		High	Low		
State Taxes:	57.15	82.67	39.14	17.4	50
Total sales and gross receipts	30.35	57.25	8.68	33.0	50
General sales and gross receipts	17.50	37.88	0.00[c]	51.1	45
Total selective sales and gross receipts:	12.84	25.59	7.52	29.6	50
Motor fuels	5.55	11.89	2.33	29.0	50
Tobacco	2.22	5.85	0.58	42.2	50
Alcohol	1.32	4.96	0.31	62.5	50
Insurance	1.26	2.52	0.71	28.4	50
Public utilities	1.32	5.19	0.00[c]	124.0	40
Pari-mutuels	0.46	3.58	0.00[c]	156.7	30
Amusements	0.07	14.47	0.00[c]	649.6	29
Other (n.e.c.)[b]	0.66	5.01	0.00[c]	155.5	32
Total license taxes:	4.42	25.07	0.62	63.0	50
Motor vehicles	2.59	6.39	0.01	42.6	50
Corporations in general	0.73	15.18	0.00[c]	268.4	49
Occupations and businesses	0.50	5.28	0.15	106.2	50
Motor vehicle operators	0.20	0.45	0.00[c]	49.0	48
Hunting and fishing	0.21	2.63	0.01	111.4	50
Alocoholic beverages	0.10	0.34	0.00[c]	84.8	49
Public utilities	0.05	0.22	0.00[c]	146.2	33
Amusements	0.02	3.98	0.00[c]	635.3	31
Others (n.e.c.)[b]	0.03	0.30	0.00[c]	141.2	43
Individual income	13.73	31.64	0.00[c]	62.6	44
Corporation net income	4.66	7.60	0.00[c]	44.0	46

Table 5-1 (*continued*)

Death and gift	1.00	1.88	0.00[c]	56.6	49
Severance	1.30	23.84	0.00[c]	231.0	31
Document and stock transfer	0.35	2.11	0.00[c]	191.0	30
Other (n.e.c.)[b]	0.03	0.47	0.00[c]	224.9	14
Property	1.36	42.30	0.00[c]	284.7	44
Local Taxes:	42.85	60.82	17.33	28.6	50
Property[d]	35.05	59.67	10.72	35.2	50
Total nonproperty	7.80	16.56	0.22	85.6	50
General sales and gross receipts	2.94	12.38	0.00[c]	144.6	26
Selective sales and gross receipts:	1.50	6.14	0.22	100.2	50
Alcohol	0.06	1.72	0.00[c]	377.0	7
Motor fuels	0.03	1.34	0.00[c]	372.4	7
Public utilities	0.98	4.47	0.00[c]	139.7	39
Tobacco	0.07	0.70	0.00[c]	326.0	7
Other (n.e.c.)[b]	0.35	2.22	0.00[c]	207.6	29
License tax on motor vehicles	0.20	1.91	0.00[c]	187.9	28
Income tax	1.85	10.32	0.00[c]	254.5	10
Other (n.e.c.)[b]	1.31	6.14	0.21	100.2	50

Source: State taxes taken from Bureau of the Census (1977b), Table 7; local property taxes from Bureau of Census, (1977a), Table 17; local nonproperty taxes from a special tabulation by the Governments Division, Bureau of the Census.

[a]This is a weighted average.

[b]n.e.c. = not elsewhere classified.

[c]Tax not in use in certain states.

[d]For a percentage breakdown of the local property tax by type see Table 3.5

Table 5-2. The Role of Property Taxes in Local Finance

Property Taxes as a Percentage of All Local Taxes	*Number of States, 1962*	*Number of States, 1976*
95-99%	17	15
90-94%	14	8
80-89%	9	12
70-79%	8	7
Below 70%	2	8

all others in the claim it exerts on private income. It is by far the major contributor to burden for the entire tax structure[a] in almost every state (refer to Table A-83). Looking over the entire income range, a distinctly regressive incidence pattern is evident. The level of effective rates clearly supports its importance as a revenue source; the pattern demonstrates its regressive influence on the overall tax system. There are, however, marked variations across states that are a function of the relative reliance on the tax; this ranges from nearly 60 percent in New Hampshire to just under 11 percent in Alabama.

Effective rates for local real property taxes, using the benchmark case, drop from 10.25 to 2.79. There is a steady decline from the lowest class up to the $25,000-29,999 class, where they begin to rise slightly. Thus, over the range of income that contains the majority of people, the influence is regressive. When looking at only the middle-income range, however, regressivity is somewhat less pronounced than the overall pattern suggests. Between $6,000 and $24,999 effective rates decline only two points from 4.19 to 2.19; this is a range in which 62 percent of all U.S. families are located (see Table B-1). That regressivity is present is clear, but for most taxpayers it is not as regressive as the full drop from 10.25 to 2.10 would suggest. In fact, there is a mild progressive influence suggested by the top three classes in which the burden rises slightly from 2.10 to 2.79.

In we examine specific states (Table A-83), there is wide variation in the level and pattern of burden manifested. Extreme cases are Alabama and Massachusetts. Over the full range of incomes, the former drops from 1.64 to 0.58 while the latter goes from 23.2 to 4.84. The impact of local real property taxes in these two states is vastly dif-

[a] We are considering here the impact of all real property taxes combined. Tables A-61 to A-82 provide detail on burdens resulting from seven types of real property tax. These estimates were made using the procedure discussed in Chapter 3 as reflected by the data in Table 3-5.

Table 5-3. Average Effective Tax Rates for Major State and Local Taxes[a] (in percent)

	Income Classes					
Tax	*Under $3,000*	*$3,000-$3,999*	*$4,000-$4,999*	*$5,000-$5,999*	*$6,000-$6,999*	*$7,000-$7,999*
State Taxes:						
General sales and gross receipts	5.02	3.49	3.12	2.87	2.75	2.64
Selective sales and gross receipts:						
Motor fuels	2.25	1.40	1.20	1.06	0.99	0.92
Alcohol	0.34	0.25	0.23	0.21	0.21	0.20
Tobacco	1.18	0.67	0.55	0.48	0.43	0.39
Total	4.81	2.99	2.57	2.28	2.12	1.98
Total license taxes	1.16	0.76	0.68	0.62	0.59	0.55
Individual income	0.01	0.12	0.26	0.43	0.57	0.70
Corporation net income:						
Benchmark	0.67	0.42	0.40	0.34	0.32	0.26
Most regressive	0.93	0.58	0.50	0.45	0.42	0.40
Most progressive	0.42	0.26	0.29	0.24	0.21	0.13
Total state property taxes	1.21	0.77	0.69	0.63	0.59	0.52
Total state taxes:						
Benchmark	12.63	8.33	7.50	6.95	6.70	6.41
Most regressive	12.87	8.48	7.60	7.05	6.79	6.53
Most progressive	12.40	8.18	7.41	6.85	6.60	6.28
Local Taxes:						
General sales and gross receipts	1.07	0.72	0.63	0.59	0.56	0.52
Total nonproperty	1.56	1.03	0.91	0.83	0.79	0.75
Total personal property	1.19	0.85	0.78	0.73	0.70	0.68
Total real property:						
Benchmark	10.25	6.11	5.22	4.68	4.19	3.84
Most regressive	8.69	5.53	4.75	4.32	4.01	3.77
Most progressive	5.01	2.98	3.32	2.84	2.30	1.84
Total local taxes:						
Benchmark	12.88	7.90	6.84	6.16	5.60	5.20
Most regressive	11.32	7.33	6.37	5.82	5.42	5.13
Most progressive	7.64	4.77	4.94	4.33	3.71	3.20
Imported Taxes	2.59	1.65	1.48	1.33	1.23	1.14
Total State and Local Taxes:						
Benchmark	28.10	17.88	15.83	14.44	13.53	12.75
Most regressive	26.78	17.46	15.45	14.20	13.45	12.80
Most progressive	22.63	14.60	13.83	12.51	11.54	10.63

Source: Computed from data in Appendix A.
[a]Arithmetic mean across states using tax.
[b]Number of states using this tax.

ferent. Table 5-4 indicates differences across states with coefficients of variation between 52 and 41. With a few exceptions, property tax burdens vary more than any other tax. This is of particular importance given its dominant status in state-local finance.

Two points need to be emphasized in interpreting these results. First, there is some indication that mild progressivity is present at the

Table 5-3 *(continued)*

				Income Classes				
$8,000-$9,999	*$10,000-11,999*	*$12,000-$14,999*	*$15,000-$19,999*	*$20,000-$24,999*	*$25,000-$29,999*	*$30,000-$35,000*	*Over $35,000*	*Number of States[b]*
2.47	2.34	2.20	2.06	1.97	1.91	1.83	1.63	45
0.83	0.75	0.68	0.61	0.57	0.53	0.51	0.45	50
0.19	0.19	0.18	0.17	0.17	0.17	0.16	0.15	50
0.34	0.30	0.27	0.23	0.20	0.18	0.17	0.14	50
1.80	1.64	1.50	1.36	1.26	1.19	1.14	1.01	50
0.52	0.48	0.44	0.41	0.40	0.40	0.42	0.58	50
0.89	1.11	1.32	1.60	1.82	1.92	1.96	1.72	44
0.27	0.24	0.21	0.21	0.21	0.22	0.25	0.71	46
0.36	0.34	0.31	0.28	0.26	0.25	0.24	0.22	46
0.18	0.14	0.11	0.13	0.15	0.18	0.27	1.20	46
0.49	0.45	0.42	0.38	0.35	0.34	0.34	0.43	44
6.17	5.99	5.77	5.68	5.66	5.62	5.58	6.26	50
6.26	6.08	5.87	5.75	5.71	5.65	5.57	5.81	50
6.08	5.90	5.68	5.62	5.61	5.59	5.59	6.71	50
0.49	0.46	0.43	0.40	0.38	0.36	0.35	0.30	26
0.70	0.65	0.60	0.56	0.53	0.50	0.48	0.38	50
0.65	0.61	0.58	0.56	0.55	0.57	0.61	0.87	45
3.43	3.10	2.71	2.39	2.19	2.10	2.13	2.79	50
3.40	3.16	2.88	2.61	2.44	2.35	2.30	2.19	50
2.10	1.70	1.32	1.36	1.49	1.69	2.53	9.57	50
4.71	4.28	3.83	3.45	3.21	3.11	3.15	3.95	50
4.68	4.36	4.00	3.68	3.47	3.36	3.32	3.36	50
3.39	2.90	2.44	2.42	2.51	2.70	3.56	10.74	50
1.08	1.00	0.92	0.86	0.83	0.82	0.86	1.40	50
11.96	11.26	10.52	10.00	9.71	9.55	9.59	11.61	50
12.02	11.44	10.78	10.29	10.01	9.83	9.75	10.57	50
10.55	9.80	9.04	8.90	8.96	9.11	10.01	18.85	50

top end of the income distribution but is being masked by the open-ended "over $35,000" class. Although this may indeed be true, this segment of the income distribution contains relatively few families, less than 5 percent nationwide. Thus, any progressive influence is mitigated by the small proportion of the population that it affects. (Detail by state can be found in Table A-83).

Second, the federal offset for real property tax payments serves to increase regressivity. For the study year, $15.45 billion in payments

Table 5-4. Coefficients of Variation for Effective Tax Rates of Major State and Local Taxes[a]

Tax	Under $3,000	$3,000-$3,999	$4,000-$4,999	$5,000-$5,999	$6,000-$6,999	$7,000-$7,999
	Income Classes					
State Taxes:						
General sales and gross receipts	46	42	41	40	39	39
Selective sales and gross receipts:						
Motor fuels	28	25	24	23	23	22
Alcohol	53	53	54	54	55	56
Tobacco	34	34	34	34	34	34
Total	23	22	23	22	22	22
Total license taxes	41	45	45	44	43	40
Individual income	427	133	106	95	84	80
Corporation net income:						
Benchmark	42	57	54	49	53	40
Most regressive	37	39	38	39	39	39
Most progressive	72	130	102	95	116	88
Total state property taxes	391	389	396	407	405	398
Total state taxes:						
Benchmark	42	40	40	40	39	36
Most regressive	41	39	40	40	39	35
Most progressive	42	42	41	40	39	36
Local Taxes:						
General sales and gross receipts	81	80	80	82	83	82
Total nonproperty	82	83	84	85	86	87
Total personal property	89	83	76	75	77	75
Total real property:						
Benchmark	52	51	50	51	48	47
Most regressive	46	47	44	46	45	45
Most progressive	57	70	88	86	81	73
Total local taxes:						
Benchmark	40	39	38	39	36	35
Most regressive	36	36	34	35	34	34
Most progressive	40	49	57	55	51	49
Imported Taxes	9	10	14	15	13	11
Total State and Local Taxes:						
Benchmark	19	21	21	22	21	19
Most regressive	19	20	20	21	21	19
Most progressive	22	31	28	26	27	24

Source: Computed from data in Appendix A.
[a]Standard deviation divided by the arthmetic mean and then multiplied by 100, for those states using the tax.
[b]Number of states using this tax

were credited against federal taxable income because of itemizations on the 1040 Schedule A form. When these itemizations are weighted by marginal rates, this lowers the total real property tax burden by $4.4 billion, or 8 percent of all local property collections. The beneficiaries of this reduced liability, however, are much more heavily concentrated in the upper-income classes where marginal rates are higher,

Table 5-4 (*continued*)

Income Classes								
$8,000-$9,999	$10,000-11,999	$12,000-$14,999	$15,000-$19,999	$20,000-$24,999	$25,000-$29,999	$30,000-$34,999	Over $35,000	Number of States[b]
38	38	38	37	37	38	37	40	45
22	21	21	21	22	22	22	22	50
56	57	58	59	60	60	60	61	50
35	35	36	38	39	40	41	43	50
23	24	24	25	26	26	26	26	50
44	44	43	40	41	42	48	57	50
71	61	57	53	51	53	55	60	44
49	39	41	44	37	43	44	43	46
39	39	39	39	39	40	40	40	46
94	67	67	64	51	61	69	46	46
404	402	402	392	392	389	376	277	44
36	34	34	32	33	34	35	31	50
35	34	34	31	33	34	35	33	50
36	34	34	32	33	34	34	30	50
83	83	83	84	85	86	86	86	26
88	89	90	91	93	94	94	88	50
74	76	75	76	76	78	80	76	45
48	47	45	44	43	44	46	41	50
44	46	45	45	45	46	47	42	50
103	66	59	46	57	57	76	44	50
35	35	34	33	32	34	37	35	50
33	35	34	34	34	35	37	36	50
64	42	35	33	38	39	56	40	50
16	12	12	13	13	14	19	23	50
20	19	19	19	19	21	22	18	50
19	19	19	19	20	21	22	19	50
28	20	21	21	21	23	28	24	50

larger property tax payments are made, and itemization can be taken full advantage of. Thus, high-income families receive much greater relief than families at the low end; this lowers the level of the burden and makes the pattern more inequitable.

When looking at burdens based on the new view of property tax incidence, a totally different picture emerges. Under the category of "most progressive" in Table 5-3, effective rates exhibit more of a U-shaped configuration, dropping from 5.01 to a low of 1.32 and then rising to 9.57. Initially there is very mild regressivity, which changes to progressivity toward the open-ended top class. Once again, however, the burden over the middle range of income is perhaps more accurately described as nearly proportional, as least as it affects most taxpayers. Progressivity does begin at around $15,000 but becomes pronounced only for incomes above $30,000. With the exception of the state individual and corporate income taxes, this is the only instance where the effective rate in the top class *exceeds* that in the lowest. This U-shaped pattern is consistent with new view aggregate patterns found by Pechman and Okner, (1974: 59), Musgrave *et al.* (1974: 264), or Odden and Vincent (1976: 11-24).

Perusal of Table A-85 shows differences across states in the *ER* pattern with the top income class generally having a substantially greater burden than the lowest. Massachusetts once again defines one extreme with a rate of 22.6 in the *highest* class, almost exactly what it was for the *lowest* class under the benchmark case. Table 5-4 indicates that there is more dispersion across states than with the benchmark case; the coefficients of variation range between 103 and 44 and are higher in every instance.

Taxes on personal property are levied, in one form or another, in all but five states. Table 5-5 indicates the number of states involved for each category and the table in Appendix A that contains estimates of burden.[b] Looking at the total profile, we see that it makes a moderate addition to burden that drops from a high of 1.19 to a low of 0.55 and then increases to 0.87. It is slightly U-shaped overall but essentially proportional over the range $6,000 to $35,000.

Variation in the claim made by this tax is amongst the highest shown in Table 5-4, ranging from 74 to 89. Table A-60 shows the heaviest burden to fall on residents of Montana; the lowest is in New Hampshire, where it virtually rounds to zero. Tables A-52 to A-59 show, with few exceptions, the small overall contribution these taxes make. The blatant exception is Montana, which derives almost 42 percent of its local property tax receipts from personal property. Accordingly, the *ERs* in this state range between 5.62 and 3.12. Table 3-5 indicates the states that raise local revenue from this source and Tables A-52 and A-59 show the burden that is imposed as a result.

The burden of this tax, as with real property, is lessened by the federal offset allowance. For the study year, $956 million was itemized, thus reducing the federal tax liability by $264 million (see Chapter 4). This tends to introduce a regressive influence that is most pronounced

[b] The distribution of property tax receipts had to be estimated with data on assessed valuations; refer to Chapter 3 and Table 3-5 for the procedure employed.

Table 5-5. Detail on Personal Property Taxes

Tax Category	*Number of States*	*Appendix A Table Number*
Agricultural	28	A-52
Commercial/industrial	32	A-53
Household	3	A-54
Intangible(s)	6	A-56
Motor vehicles	14	A-57
Other	42	A-59
Total personal property	45	A-60

in the states that rely heavily on taxation of personal property. The effect is the greatest in states like Alabama, Kansas, or West Virginia where personal property is a large compenent of the base.

State use of property tax, as applied to railroads, public utilities, and "other," is a trivial source of revenue, averaging a mere 1.36 percent of all taxes. Tables A-34 to A-36 show that this results in a negligible addition to overall burden in almost every state. The states that stand out are Arizona and Washington for "public utility" and Alaska, Maine, and Wisconsin for "other."

Alaska deserves further comment given its unique status among property-taxing states; state property taxes bring in 42.3 percent of all collections. No other system even comes close to this position, and in only two other states is it pronounced enough to warrant mention (Maine, 18.3 percent; Washington, 10.3 percent). Alaska's situation derives from the extraction of oil and gas, which began to generate substantial revenue for the state coffers in the study year.[c] As a result, this source became of marked consequence for Alaska's tax system. Total *ERs* fall from a peak of 30.95 at the low end to 7.43 at the top (Table A-37). This tax is the major contributor to the overall burden since it is a fiscal mainstay for the state of Alaska.[d]

THE GENERAL SALES TAX

The second largest source of revenue for state-local operations is the general sales tax. For states, it averaged 17.5 percent of revenue

[c] State property tax receipts jumped from $6.6 to $306.4 million in just one year as the oil began to be extracted and shipped through the pipeline.

[d] Most taxes are collected by the state in Alaska (83 percent). Thus, this is the major revenue source for the state as well as the total state-local system.

(see Table 5-1) with a high of 37.9 percent in Washington, a low of 6.6 percent in Massachusetts, and five states that do not use it at all. This represents a 20 percent expansion in relative use over 1962 when it averaged 14.6; of equal interest, the number of states making no, or virtually no, use of the tax dropped from twelve to five. That the general sales tax is an important and growing source of revenue is indicated by receipts, which expanded from $6.1 to $27.3 billion; growth has occurred both in absolute and relative terms. Although it does not everywhere serve the role suggested by the Advisory Commission on Intergovernmental Relations as a part of a "high quality state-local fiscal system" (1972: 3-6), there is definite movement toward this status. In twenty-two states it actually exceeds the 20-25 percent Commission figure, and in five it exceeds 30 percent.

This source is also becoming an important revenue producer for local jurisdictions. In 1976 it raised almost $4.6 billion. In certain states it has helped to offset an increased dependence on property taxation. For example, it accounts for 42 percent of all local taxes in Louisiana, 28 percent in Alabama, and 21 percent in Oklahoma and Tennessee.

Effective rates for the state component of this tax decrease continually from 5.02 to 1.63. There is little question about its regressive incidence and, therefore, its impact on burden. It is a major revenue source and is distinctly regressive. This picture is softened somewhat when considering only the middle section of the income range, say between $6,000 and $24,999. Regressivity here is less pronounced, on the average, with the *ER*s declining by only 0.78 point.

As was found with the property tax, there is considerable variation across the forty-five states that use the tax; coefficients of variation lie between 46 and 37. The nature of these differences becomes more evident upon examination of Table A-1. Mississippi and West Virginia define one extreme of a high, regressive burden. Low and much less regressive burden is found in Massachusetts, New Jersey, and Vermont.

The local component manifests much the same pattern but at a much lower level. Average effective rates drop continuously from 1.07 to 0.30 for the twenty-six states that permit local jurisdictions to use this tax. As indicated above the major users, relatively, are Louisiana and Alabama. In absolute amounts, New York leads the list with $1.6 billion and California is a distant second at $817 million. In terms of claim on income, Louisiana and Alaska lie at the top with a range between 2.95-1.04 and 2.78-0.46, respectively (see Table A-41). The local burden for these two states is far above the national average and, in fact, is above the burden present for the state component in many states. Variation across states with a local general sales tax is extremely high; coefficients of variation lie in the range of 80-86. This reflects differences in state policies toward local use of this tax at all, and if allowed, how much is permitted (see Advisory Commission, 1977a: 186-189).

Two additional factors need to be accounted for in evaluating these results. First is the impact on both level and equity due to the federal offset for state and local general sales taxes. For 1976, $7.36 billion was itemized on IRS form 1040 Schedule A, which lowered federal tax receipts by $2.04 billion. This represents 6.4 percent of all general sales collections nationwide. As with property taxes, the financial advantage of these deductions concentrates on persons that consume more, have higher marginal tax rates, and are able to itemize; clearly this is "pro-rich." The net effect is to lower their burden by much more than those with low incomes. This exerts a regressive influence on the state-local tax system by making both the state and local general sales tax more regressive.

Second is the influence of exemptions from the base, as discussed in Chapter 3. In 1976, twenty-one states had removed food as a taxable item. Several others allowed additional exemptions such as for medicines or utility services. The policy rationale for this shrinkage in the base is that it softens the regressive sting of sales taxation. It also, of course, lowers the level of the *ER*s from what they would be if exempt items were to be taxed.[e] Past empirical analysis has tended to substantiate the beneficial equity effects of exempting food (Schaefer, 1969; Davies, 1960). State-by-state data (Table A-1) on general sales effective rates do suggest a less regressive pattern in states that exempt food. Contrast, for example, California or New York with Arkansas or Mississippi. In Chapter 6 we deal with the effect of exemptions on equity in more precise terms.

TAXES ON INDIVIDUAL INCOME

The third most significant source of revenue for the state-local fisc is the tax on individual income. In 1976, the state component averaged 13.7 percent of all receipts but ranged between a peak of 31.6 percent in Delaware and six states that did not use the tax. Lowest reliance in the states using it was in the range 1-2 percent in Tennessee, Connecticut, and New Hampshire. Each of these states, however, does not have a broad income base, but rather a base that only applies to interest, dividends, or capital gains. There are at present

[e] Exemption of food from general sales taxation can represent a substantial loss in revenue to state and local governments. The overall equity effects depend on how this loss in revenue is "made up," assuming a constant yield.

eleven states in which this tax brings in excess of 20 percent of all receipts and one in which it exceeds 30 percent.

Interestingly, the fiscal role of the income tax has undergone dramatic change over the past two decades. When looking at data for 1962, we see that it accounted for a shade over 7 percent of revenue, placing it a distant third behind taxes on property at 46 percent and general sales at 15 percent. Or, put another way, more money was raised through the selective sales tax on motor fuels; the taxation of individual income had not yet come into its own.

By 1976 this had changed and state use of the individual income base raised $21.5 billion dollars, more than seven times its 1962 yield. Although thirteen states did not tax individual income at all in 1962, this number had dropped to six as of 1976. It is clear that this source will play an expanding role in state-local finance. It is also of interest to note that it now exceeds the "25 percent" benchmark figure for a high-quality revenue system, as suggested by the Advisory Commission (1974: 5), in four states and is fast approaching this mark in another nine.

That the tax on individual income is becoming a dominant fiscal instrument for the state-local sector and is a major source of revenue in several states (such as Delaware or Oregon) is clear. Its importance for the study of burdens is underlined by its potential to exert a progressive influence on the overall tax system. Perusal of specific features of the tax, as they vary across the forty-four states that use it, illustrates this (refer to Advisory Commission, 1977a: 194-207). Standard deductions range between 10 and 15 percent with maximum allowable deductions on joint returns between $650 and $2,850. Personal exemptions (joint) range from a low of $600 in New Hampshire to a high of $6,500 in Mississippi. A variety of additional exemptions are allowed for dependents, age, or blindness up to $1,500 for each person in Michigan.

Of equal consequence for the distribution of burdens across income levels is the system of marginal rates applied against taxable income. Variation here is even more pronounced. Three states tax only some combination of interest, dividends, or capital gains at a flat percentage (Connecticut, 7 percent; New Hampshire, 4.25 percent; Tennessee, 6 percent). Five others use a much broader base with a flat percentage levy (Illinois, 2.5 percent; Indiana, 2 percent; Michigan, 4.6 percent; Massachusetts, 5 percent; Pennsylvania, 2 percent. Three more tie their liability directly to the federal income tax at a fixed percentage (Nebraska, 15 percent; Rhode Island, 17 percent; or Vermont, 25 percent). This method has the effect of introducing some of the progressivity of the federal system into the states' individual income tax.

The remaining thirty-three states establish liability by using a system of graduated marginal rates applied to ranges of income. The nominally least progressive is Mississippi, which has rates of 3 percent on the first $5,000 and 4 percent above that. The role of the tax in this state, however, is relatively small, bringing in $105 million, or 9.2 percent of total receipts. Nominally the most progressive state is Delaware where the rates begin at 1.6 percent on the first $1,000 and increases steadily to 19.8 percent on all income above $100,000; nominal rate progression in this state is pronounced. Delaware also has the system with the greatest relative reliance on this tax (31.6 percent) and the second largest role for state government (80 percent, second only to Alaska and New Mexico at 82 percent of all state-local tax revenue). The only other state that comes near Delaware in terms of a progressive nominal rate structure is Alaska, which begins at 3 percent on the first $4,000 and tops at 14.5 percent in excess of $300,000. Its progressive rates cover a wider range of income but are not nearly as severe as Delaware's.

A final major feature of the state individual income tax is the provision for various credits or deductions. As of 1976, seventeen states allowed a credit, six for food and consumer-related taxes, twelve for property taxes, and one for all state-local tax payments. The intent of these credits is to ameliorate the regressive sting of various state and local taxes. Finally, sixteen states permit the deduction of federal income tax payments against state taxable income. Needless to say, the latter provision is more valuable the higher a person's income.

The combined effect of all these provisions is what ultimately determines the nature of the individual income tax burden. As discussed in Chapter 3, each major provision was taken into account, state by state, in estimating the burden distribution. The effective tax rates, therefore, reflect their influence on the level of burden and equity.

Because of the built-in features that pertain to exemptions, deductions, tax credits, and graduated marginal rates, it is possible for this tax to be distinctly progressive. If a state chooses to rely on it, it can be a major source of revenue and can exert a strong progressive influence on the overall tax structure. The final result is a function of how each state decides to implement the tax (see Advisory Commission, 1977a: 194-214).

Looking now at the end result of these provisions, we see the average effective rate shown in Table 5-3. The *ER*s increase steadily from 0.01 in the lowest class to a maximum of 1.96 in the $30,000-35,000 class, then falling back to 1.72. On an average, the pattern is unequivocally progressive. Since it is the third largest revenue source, this progression is of importance for the equity of the tax system as a whole.

One problem with the picture reflected by this average is that there is substantial variation around the mean figure. This is shown quite dramatically by the coefficients of variation in Table 5-4, which range from 427 at the low end to the 50s toward the top end.

A major contributor to this extreme variance at the low end are the allowances made for deductions and exemptions that tend to lower drastically or even eliminate any burden whatsoever. Close examination of the data in Table A-26 shows their impact explicitly. Most pronounced is Mississippi where payments are eliminated in the first seven income classes and after that remain below the U.S. average. On the other hand, Minnesota's provisions remove all claim on the lowest six classes, but then it begins at incomes above $8,000 and rises rapidly to attain one of the highest levels of any state in the top class. A convenient way to summarize the effect of these exemption or deduction provisions is to look at the number of instances in which they serve to eliminate burden completely. If we look at all *ER*s for the first six classes (up to $8,000) for the forty-four states using this tax, ninety-four of the two hundred sixty-four instances have a zero tax liability. More interesting is how these zero burdens are distributed, as shown below:

Income Class	*Number of Zero Burdens*
Under $3,000	41
$3,000-3,999	21
4,000-4,999	11
5,000-5,999	10
6,000-6,999	6
7,000-7,999	5
8,000 and over	11

The softening effect of these exemptions, deductions, or credits on the low-income burden is quite distinct in many states with the liability completely removed for the lowest few income classes. Above $8,000 there are only eleven instances of a zero burden; eight of them are in Connecticut and New Hampshire where the tax base is very narrowly defined and the federal offset for taxes paid in contiguous New York and Massachusetts wipes out much of the burden.

Also indicated in Table 5-4 is an increase in variation that begins with incomes above $20,000; the coefficient of variation goes up from 51 to 60. Two other factors come into play at this end of the income distribution. First, sixteen states allow for the deduction of federal taxes against state taxable income. This allowance is more valuable to taxpayers with high incomes because of the nature of the federal and state individual income taxes and their graduated rate structure. The larger the income, the greater the federal tax bill. The more progressive the state rates, the more valuable these deductions are in lowering the state liability. The effect is a larger and larger deduction as income rises and, therefore, a lower and lower state liability.

Needless to say, the impact is more pronounced in states with a greater concentration of income at the high end. As Table B-2 demonstrates, the relative concentration of income by class can be very different across states. In Alaska, for example, almost 39 percent of all income falls in the over $35,000 class; this compares to 15 percent nationwide or less than 10 percent in Alabama, Arkansas, or Mississippi. The fact that Alaska does *not* allow deduction of federal taxes makes its income tax, de facto, more progressive; the fact that Minnesota does allow it makes its tax less progressive. Generally, the sixteen states that permit this deduction are not high-income states, and therefore the lessened progressive impact on the state individual income tax is smaller than it would be in more affluent states like Alaska, California, or New York.

The second factor at operation is somewhat the converse of the factor just discussed. While sixteen states allow for the deduction of federal income taxes, the federal government allows for the deduction of *all* state and local taxes in determining federal liability. Thus, high tax bills in states like Alaska, Delaware, or New York are softened in that the federal revenue structure absorbs part of the cost. In the study year, these itemizations on form 1040 Schedule A totaled $16.7 billion nationwide. This amount, when weighted by the appropriate federal rates (as discussed in Chapter 4), converts into a reduction in federal liability of $5.53 billion. This is slightly less than one-quarter of the yield of all state and local income taxes. As indicated earlier in Table 4-6, the impact of these itemizations is quite progressive, that is, favors high income. In addition, itemization of income taxes is even more pro-rich than the other types. The end result is that the federal offset for individual income taxes lessens the overall progressivity of a state's individual income tax from what it would be in its absence. Not only does it lower the level of burden (shown for all offsets in Table 4-6) but it also tilts equity toward lessened progressivity.[f]

The local income tax is a small but expanding revenue instrument. It averages 1.8 percent nationwide but ranges up to a high of 10.3 percent in Maryland with Ohio close behind at 8.1 percent. In terms of receipts, they are greatest in New York at $1.2 billion because of New York City, followed by $349 million in Maryland because of Baltimore, and $400-500 million in Ohio and Pennsylvania because of more liberal

[f] In a total revenue context this is most likely not true, for the lessening effect on the state-local system is absorbed by the federal revenue structure, which is more progressive. Our concern here, however, is only state-local taxation.

enabling legislation permitting use of this tax by local governments (see Advisory Commission, 1977a: 226-228). Tax rates are generally a flat percentage of income except in a few instances like New York City.

Out of the ten states that allow local taxation of income, the highest burden is in Maryland where it generally exceeds 1.0 percent of income (see Table A-49). Next come New York, Ohio, and Pennsylvania but each of these lies well below Maryland. Overall its average incidence is roughly proportional, in the range 0.44 to 0.46 for much of the income spectrum. Only in a very few states does it influence the total tax burden to any perceptible degree.

SELECTIVE SALES TAXES

Selective sales taxes have always played an important role in generating revenue for support of state and local governments. Collectively in 1976 they raised nearly 12.8 percent of all revenue and ranged from a high of almost 26 percent in Nevada to a low of 7.5 percent in California. In seven states they exceed 20 percent of total receipts. Variation by specific type is quite marked, but with a few notable exceptions, they are individually not of the major consequence of the "big-three" just discussed. Some of the high outliers are over 11 percent for motor fuels in Arkansas and Mississippi and 14.5 percent for gambling-related amusement activities in Nevada. In all, dollars raised exceeded $20 billion for states and another $2.3 billion at the local level, thus nearly equaling the yield from income taxes. This represents a relative contraction, however, from 1962 when they averaged over 17.9 percent, yielded $7.4 billion, and exceeded 25 percent of all receipts in twenty-five states and 30 percent in two.

In considering the magnitude and pattern of burden for these taxes, it should be remembered that their nature can be sumptuary or benefit-oriented, even though this taxonomy may be "loose" at best. Motor fuels taxes could be considered a kind of user charge for transportation-related services, particularly highways, while taxes on alcohol and tobacco products and pari-mutuel activities can be considered to promote the social good by "discouraging the consumption of 'demerit' goods" (Musgrave and Musgrave, 1980: 448). Following this tentative taxonomy, 39 percent of selective sales taxes would be benefit-oriented and 29 percent sumptuary; of the remaining 32 percent, over one-half apply to public utilities and are perhaps best viewed as "just another source of revenue."

Table 5-3 gives the burden of the three major state selective sales taxes and the total for all eight types used by state governments. The motor fuels tax is quite regressive, on the average, dropping steadily from 2.25 to 0.45. Even over the middle range its pattern remains quite regressive although the level is less than 1 percent of income. Table A-2 provides data by state, and as might be anticipated, the burden in Arkansas and Mississippi is well above average. In these two states, and a few others, regressivity is compounded by high yield. If this tax can be accepted as being in accord with benefits received, perhaps its regressive nature is of less consequence because there is some quid pro quo linkage. It seems, however, that any connection to benefits is unclear at best and that its regressive impact may be a concern, especially in light of the rising price of fuel and its necessity for the journey to work of lower-income families. Its regressive burden can be exacerbated by the role it plays in the budget for those with less flexibility to curtail consumption of this taxed commodity, which is not unlike food with the general sales tax.

Turning to the "sumptuary" category, we see that the tax on alcohol is very close to being proportional, ranging from 0.34 to 0.15 overall but generally falling in the range of 0.18 to 0.20 for most taxpayers. The tax on tobacco is clearly regressive and drops steadily from 1.18 to 0.14. Table 5-4 shows that there is nearly twice as much variation across states with the alcohol burden as with tobacco. Perusal of Tables A-3 and A-4 uncovers the nature of these differences. For tobacco, the highest *ER*s are found in New Hampshire, which ranges from 2.23 to 0.32 or almost twice the national average; for alcohol a high burden is seen in Vermont with a range between 0.80 and 0.42. The former tax is regressive, the latter more or less proportional. There are states, however, where the alcohol tax is regressive, for example, Washington, where the *ER*s drop from 0.79 to 0.21.[g] The pari-mutuel tax is shown in Table A-8 and it also is about proportional for the nation as a whole. The highest instance is found in New Hampshire with *ER*s between 0.21 and 0.17.

The remaining selective sales taxes are shown individually in Tables A-5 to A-10. The impact of gambling in Nevada stands out in Table A-9, but it is the only state in which this is true. The influence of the utilities tax is seen in Table A-7. In several states the claim is quite pronounced. Alabama, Hawaii, and North Carolina exhibit *ER*s three times the national average that are markedly regressive over the entire income range; witness North Carolina's *ER*s declining from 1.66 to 0.25. Given the rising cost of energy and the role that utilities play in the low-income budget, the regressivity of this tax as it impacts on poorer families may be of more and more concern as the oil and energy

[g] As shown in Table B-3, the tobacco tax is one of the most regressive of all used by state and local governments.

nexus falls subject to domestic deregulation and further OPEC price increases.

The combined impact from all eight types of state selective sales taxes is shown as "total" in Table 5-3. Regressivity is suggested by the continual decline in *ER*s, from a peak of 4.81 to a low of 1.01. Even over the middle-income range, this pattern is present, although it is not as pronounced as with some of the specific taxes. Table A-11 shows how states compare in terms of the combined burden of selective sales taxes. As suggested by low coefficients of variation in Table 5-4 (range of 22-26), states tend to cluster tightly around the mean. The highest burden is in Vermont, which lies at 1.5 to 2.0 times the national average over the entire income spectrum. Other high-burden states are Alabama, West Virginia, and North Carolina. One of the lowest burdens is in California (*ER*s go from 3.13 to 0.58) because it only raises 7.5 percent of all revenue from these sources. It is interesting to note that although variation for individual taxes can be quite high (e.g., the alcohol tax), total burden manifests very low variation; it tends to average out across revenue sources within a state.

Local selective sales taxes are not shown in Tables 5-3 or 5-4 because of their relative insignificance as revenue sources; on an average they bring in only 1.5 percent of total taxes nationwide with a peak of 4.69 percent in New Jersey. Tables A-42 to A-46 provide state-by-state data for each local selective sales tax. As becomes evident from perusing these data, the only tax worthy of mention is that on public utilities (A-45). This tax is used by local governments in thirty-nine states and in some, such as New Jersey, Florida, or Virginia, it represents a significant and regressive contribution to taxpayer burden. In Virginia, for example, *ER*s range from 1.33 to 0.18.

LICENSE TAXES

State and local governments levy license fees on numerous items or activities. Although in total they are insignificant revenue generators, producing only 4.6 percent nationwide, in two states they are extremely important. Delaware's license tax on corporate activity and occupations and businesses is the extreme example; these two types of licenses comprise over 20 percent of all revenue for this state. No other state even approaches this figure, however. Aside from licenses on motor vehicles, which are used in all fifty states and average 3.0 percent, Nevada's license tax on gambling amusements is next at 4 percent and lies far above all others.

Tables 5-3 gives the profile of total license burdens. The *ER*s decline from a high of 1.16 to a low of 0.40, although there is some reversal toward the top end of the income distribution where the burden rises from 0.40 on incomes of $20,000 to $24,999 to 0.58 over $35,000. The overall pattern, therefore, is U-shaped with a regressive low tail and a mildly progressive upper tail.

Variation in burden for all licenses is fairly high at between 40 and 57 (Table 5-4). Table A-25 shows how this breaks down on an individual state basis. High total burdens are found in Delaware or Nevada for the reasons mentioned and in Wyoming because of relatively high license taxes on motor vehicles and hunting and fishing activity. Low burdens are seen in states like Hawaii or Massachusetts, which are well below average. Tables A-13 to A-24 give details for each individual license tax. With the exception of the tax on motor vehicle licenses, it can be seen that these taxes individually contribute relatively little to overall burden in each system.

Local government use of licenses is predominantly confined to that on motor vehicles, aside from the incredible variety of trivial taxes lumped into "not elsewhere classified." Table A-47 shows the burden of the motor vehicle tax to be of virtually no consequence in almost every state, although greater in Hawaii, Montana, South Dakota, or Virginia than in other states. Even in these cases *ER*s are less than one-half of 1 percent.

STATE CORPORATION NET INCOME TAX

The state tax on corporation net income is, generally speaking, far from a mainstay of state finance. In fact it averages only 4.7 percent of all revenue with a peak of 7.6 percent in Pennsylvania. Four states (Nevada, Texas, Washington, and Wyoming) do not exercise the option to use this tax.

The burden of the tax is shown in Table 5-3 under three alternative incidence assumptions that are intended to reflect a range of theoretical positions about where the economic impact of the tax actually falls (as discussed in Chapter 3). The average burden distribution exhibits a pattern that is best categorized as U-shaped, using the "benchmark" assumptions, and more or less proportional with "most progressive." Under the former category, the *ER*s fall from 0.67 to 0.21 and remain there between $12,000 and $24,999. They then rise again to a high of 0.71 at the top class. Thus, there is a fair degree of regressivity at the low end, near proportionality over the middle range, and slight progressivity at the top. The level of burden, however, is much less than 1 percent in all but two classes. Under the most progressive assumptions, the burden is more nearly proportional over the bulk of taxpayers with progression emerging only in a few upper-income classes; the claim actually exceeds 1 percent on incomes over $35,000. This progressive influence at the high end results from the tax resting with owners of capital as opposed to partly on consumers.

In looking at variance across states, we see that it is relatively high under benchmark but distinctly higher under the most progressive assumptions. Tables A-27 to A-29 contain data by state. In only a handful of instances does the burden exceed 1.0 percent and with few exceptions this is only true for the very bottom or very top income class. Although for "benchmark" (A-27) the low and top end burdens differ somewhat across states, in most instances the middle-income range is quite close to being proportional. Under "most progressive" (A-29), this range of proportionality extends over a larger segment of income with mild progression appearing in the top two or three classes.

OTHER STATE-LOCAL TAXES

Several other taxes are worthy of brief mention because of their unique role in particular states or due to some unusual feature. First in this category would be revenue derived from the extraction of natural resources. This averages 1.30 percent of all state-local revenue nationwide but is heavily concentrated in three states. Of the more than $2 billion in receipts for 1975-1976, $800 million came from Texas alone with another $559 million from Louisiana; the remaining $670 million was raised in the other twenty-nine states that tax extraction of natural resources, with none reaching $100 million.[h] *ER*s for this tax on the average are quite low. However, in a few states they do rise well above the average as shown in Table A-31 (see Alaska, Louisiana, Wyoming). Only in these instances are overall level and equity influenced to any degree.

Second, death and gift taxes account for about 1.0 percent of collections nationwide. Given the assumption that they rest with the highest income taxpayers (see Chapter 3), the full impact is felt above $35,000. Table A-30 shows how much this contributes to the claim on this class, somewhere between zero in Nevada (which does not use the tax) and 1.25 percent in South Dakota. Thus, they exert a mild pro-

[h] The influence of this tax in states like Texas, Louisiana, and Alaska is likely to increase as the energy situation worsens.

[i] There is some mild distortion introduced in estimating the burden of this tax. It was not possible to include in the income base income derived from gifts and inheritances. Thus, burden may be slightly overstated, as has been noted by Pechman and Okner (1974: 105-107).

gressive influence because of the burden on the open-ended top class ($35,000 or above).[i]

Finally, we need to mention the implicit category of taxes that arises out of spatial tax flows. Imported taxes averaged 8.5 percent of revenues in the study year, with a high of 13.1 percent in New Hampshire and a low of 3.6 percent in Alaska.[j] The $13.3 billion in imported taxes represents a substantial component of the burden on residents of each state-local system and is a function of (1) the extent to which taxes are imported into a state and (2) the way in which imported taxes are allocated by income levels. The former phenomenon is shown in Table 4-5, the latter in Table 4-4.

Average burden is indicated in Table 5-3. *ER*s fall steadily from 2.59 to 0.82 but then rise again, to reach 1.40 once income exceeds $30,000. The pattern is mildly regressive and then mildly progressive. Variation across states is the lowest of any tax shown in Table 5-4; for most classes it is around 13 to 14. Table A-90 reflects the tightness of the fifty states as they cluster around the mean value. There is very little difference across systems in the impact of this tax. The largest differences are found in the top income class where the *ER*s vary from 0.71 in Alaska to 2.20 in Delaware.

TAX BURDEN BY GOVERNMENTAL SECTOR

We have up to now considered the claim exerted by each of the more important state and local taxes. Many of them are summarized in Tables 5-3 and 5-4 and data on the rest are in Appendix A. An attempt has been made to portray the nature of the impact involved with each tax, its equity profile, and how these features differ. The discussion was intended to be a summary, not complete analysis. Discussion of each tax in each state and its level and pattern of burden is unnecessary because this information is available in Appendix A, and any state or tax can be compared to any other or the U.S. average by using these data.

The purpose now is to see how these separate taxes interact with each other to produce a burden and equity profile for the entire state sector, all local governments, and the total state-local system. The final result represents a complex interaction of the features of each tax, its relative role in the revenue system, and the influence of spatial tax flows. We will sketch out a general picture as was done with the separate taxes, leaving it up to the reader to tailor an in-depth analysis

[j] Refer to Chapter 4 and Table 4-5 for details on imported taxes by state.

from the data in Appendix A. Chapter 6 summarizes statistically many of the findings in this chapter.

The importance of state government differs considerably across the fifty states. The "fiscal assignment responsibility" for raising revenue[k] goes from a high of 83 percent in Alaska, 82 percent in New Mexico, and 80 percent in Hawaii to a low of 39 percent in New Hampshire and New Jersey. Since the role of the individual states varies widely, so also does the type of tax instruments used and its relative impact on the total system. For example, heavy reliance on a nominally very progressive individual income tax in Delaware, in which the state accounts for 80 percent of all revenue, makes for much more progressivity than in New Jersey, in which the state only raises 39 percent of all revenue and the individual income tax is hardly used at all (1.7 percent of state-local taxes.). It is these types of interactions that generate the final situation for the state sector.

As Table 5-3 indicates, combined state taxes (benchmark case) change from 12.63 percent on incomes less than $3,000 to 6.26 percent over $35,000. At first glance this pattern appears to be regressive. However, closer examination of incomes between, say, $5,000 and over $35,000, shows that it is pretty much proportional, especially when considering that this range contains almost 74 percent of all families nationwide (Table B-1). Thus, on an average, for most taxpayers, the state sector's burden is proportional.

Table 5-4 shows that there is a moderate amount of variance around this mean profile, with coefficients of variation between 31 and 42. In Table A-38, which shows data state by state, the nature of these differences is apparent. Alaska is far above every other state in the nation at three times the national average. *ER*s go from 40.87 to 14.89 but are much less regressive over the middle-range than these numbers might suggest. The dominant fiscal role of the state in Alaska means that the total burden is largely a function of its taxation policy. States with a smaller state role (New Hampshire or New Jersey) manifest much lower *ER*s.

In terms of equity, Wyoming and Nevada are systems with regressive state burdens; the *ER*s fall steadily across the income distribution (e.g., in Wyoming, it is 15.86 to 4.96). Neither of these states has an individual income tax. At the progressive end of the spectrum lie Minnesota or Delaware where the burden profile takes on a U-shape. These tax systems are much closer to being proportional or actually mildly progressive, in large part because of the income tax and its role as a revenue producer. All in all, many states show a pattern that is U-shaped, although the level of burden varies from the high in Alaska or New Mexico to a low in Oregon or Massachusetts.

[k] State taxes as a percentage of total state and local taxes.

The other sector to be considered is local governments in a state. In terms of relative importance, local government goes from playing a very small role in Alaska (17 percent) and New Mexico (18 percent) to a dominant role in New Hampshire and New Jersey (over 60 percent). One factor that distinguishes this sector from the state is that it has a very constrained flexibility in selecting revenue sources. Although states are free to tax a broad variety of items or forms of activity, such is not true at the local level (see Advisory Commission, 1977b). For the most part, local jurisdictions are intimately linked to the property tax. On the average, 85 percent of all local revenue is derived from property taxation. In twenty-three states, it raises 90 percent or more of all revenue. There has been of late, however, an increased willingness by state governments to permit limited local use of sales and income taxes. Currently, there are eight states in which the local sector raises *less* than 70 percent of its taxes from the property tax. The most extreme instances are Alabama (42 percent) and Louisiana (50 percent). In dollar terms, of course, the leaders are New York ($3.4 billion) and California ($1.4 billion).

The single major contributor to the level of burden and equity characteristics of the local sector in every state is the property tax.[1] The profile for this sector, however, is less dominated by this tax in several states than has been the case in the past. The combined effect of all local sources (see Table 5-3) using the benchmark case drops from 12.88 percent at the low end to 3.95 percent at the top. On the average, the pattern is regressive, even over the middle-income range where most families are located. In the top two classes there is a slight increase in *ER*s from 3.11 to 3.95.

Table 5-4 indicates once again a fair amount of dispersion around the mean pattern with coefficients in the range of 33 to 40. If we examine Table A-87 we see the status of each state. The heaviest burden, as expected, is associated with the largest local sectors – New Hampshire, New Jersey, and New York. The lowest is found in Alabama, Delaware, or New Mexico with a relatively small local sector. Thus, the extreme ranges in *ER*s are 26.87 to 7.88 in New York to 5.80 to 1.65 in Delaware, or from about twice the national average to less than one-half. Equity is influenced primarily by the role of the property tax in local finance. Alabama and Louisiana manifest equity profiles that are very mildly regressive. On the other hand, the local tax burden in Massachusetts, which is 99.4 percent from property taxes, is quite regressive; the *ER*s drop steadily from 23.94 to 3.91 at $30,000 to $34,999 and then rise to 5.47 over $35,000.

[1] Details on the contribution to local tax burdens by various types of property taxation are shown in Tables A-52 to A-82. These tables break the burden into thirteen components of real and personal property under different incidence assumptions.

The interaction effects here need to be noted. A large local sector with dominance by the property tax (New Hampshire is 61 percent local taxes and 98 percent property taxes) leads to a high, regressive burden. A small local sector and low reliance on the property tax (Alabama is 25 percent local taxes and 42 percent property taxes) leads to a low, mildly regressive burden. In between are forty-eight situations representing various combinations of the role of local government and reliance on property taxation. The final result is indicated in Table A-87.

Under the most progressive view of the property tax, the situation changes dramatically, as shown in Table 5-3. Burden now averages between 7.64 percent on incomes under $3,000 and 10.74 percent above $35,000. Although there is some U-shape to this pattern, with *ER*s eventually rising substantially in the top two classes to almost 11 percent, burden is roughly proportional in the range of $6,000 to $35,000. States most affected by the new view of property tax incidence are states with heaviest reliance on this tax and with the largest local sector, as epitomized by New Hampshire. The effective rates here range between 11.88 percent on incomes less than $3,000 and 21.52 percent over $35,000 (as opposed to 23.0 to 4.57 under the benchmark case) with wide variation in between (see Table A-89). A similar situation is found elsewhere depending on the state-local and property tax-nonproperty tax balance. Whatever the particular situation, the new view of property tax incidence does alter, often radically, the answer to the question "who pays local taxes?"

Finally, the last burden to be examined is the full claim of all state and local taxes. The picture that emerges is a function of which sources are used, the relative importance of each, and the state-local balance. Each tax's burden enters into the total in the same way that a number enters into an average; the more pronounced the burden, the greater the influence exerted. More importantly, the equity characteristics of each tax, taken in conjunction with its relative usage, help to determine how the total burden is apportioned by income level or, in other words, who pays. Looking at extremes to make the point, the role of the individual income tax in Delaware or Minnesota is dominant and strongly progressive while local property taxes dominate finances in New Hampshire or New Jersey. This influences equity in these two states in distinctly different ways.

Table 5-3 shows that the average *ER* profile (benchmark) varies from 28.10 to a low of 9.55 in the $25,000 to $29,999 income class and then up to 11.61 on incomes exceeding $35,000. Overall, state and local taxes are quite regressive over the entire range up to $29,999. Since this includes 93.5 percent of all family units nationwide (see Table B-1), it seems fair to characterize this sector as regressive, *on the average*. However, the point of this study was to look behind statistical averages or aggregate impressions to the situation prevailing in each system. As Table 5-4 reflects, there is less variation in the overall burden than for any other category except imported taxes (the coefficients fall in the narrow band of 18 to 22). Interestingly, although separate taxes vary markedly in burden across states, most of this balances out when all revenues are combined into an overall tax structure.

The data in Table A-91 show the total claim each state makes on its residents. One state, Alaska, stands well above all others; its cost for providing public goods goes from 53 percent of income at the bottom to 19 percent at the top.[m] The fiscal pressure of very high tax burdens in states such as New York, California, Massachusetts, and Vermont becomes evident; each is well above the average at every income level. Low burdens are found in states like Delaware, Alabama, or South Carolina, which are well below the U.S. average.

In examining the pattern of effective rates across income classes, we can see large differences. Delaware is basically proportional over much of the income range, say $6,000 to $34,999, with a low burden. Minnesota is roughly proportional with a slightly above average burden. New Hampshire, alternatively, is distinctly regressive over the middle-income range. As mentioned, there are the opposite influences of the strongly progressive individual income tax in Delaware and Minnesota and the regressive property tax in New Hampshire producing the final situation.

It is also of interest to note that many states exhibit a U-shaped pattern with regression at the low end and mild progression at the top. In *every* state, the claim on the top class is higher than that on the $30,000 to $34,999 class, and in numerous cases, this progressive influence moves down to several lower income classes as well. Iowa, Minnesota, or New York illustrate the potential influence of a state income tax when it is a major instrument of state-local finance.

When looking at total burden under the most progressive set of incidence assumptions, the profile changes considerably.[n] On an average, *ER*s drop steadily up to the $15,000 to $19,999 class (22.63 to 8.90). At this point the progressive influence emerges, and the *ER*s increase dramatically from 8.90 to 18.85. Equity under this view is mixed with a distinct U-shape to the profile. A similar situation has

[m] In interpreting these data the peculiar income distribution in this state and the role this plays in determining burden should be kept in mind. Table B-2 delineates this quite clearly; almost 40 percent of all income in Alaska is in the top class compared to 15 percent nationwide.

[n] This is primarily a function of the new view of property tax incidence as falling on owners of capital (refer to Chapter 3).

been found by others, such as Musgrave (1974: 264) or Pechman and Okner (1974: 62), for the entire state-local sector's burden.

Turning to data on individual states (Table A-93), the strength of the new view pattern is a function of the role of the property tax and is most evident in the marked jump in burden for the last two classes. The extreme case is New Hampshire where the *ER* jumps by 20 points. In other instances, the increase is much less dramatic. Whatever the case in a particular state, there is little question that the new view of property tax incidence provides a very different answer to the question posed by Aaron (1975) in his book *Who Pays the Property Tax?*

Having discussed in general the features of individual revenue sources in terms of both level and pattern of burden, we are now in a position to scrutinize with more precision the equity of major tax categories for each state. Chapter 6 employs several techniques to summarize the burdens across the fourteen classes into a single measure that allows for direct comparisons across states.

Chapter 6

Taxpayer Equity in the Fifty States

One difficulty inherent in the inferences drawn in the previous chapter is that they are visual and somewhat impressionistic. That is, to make sense out of the tax burden estimates it is necessary to examine visually their magnitude and pattern and then to interpret them. This may be a perfectly acceptable approach when examining aggregate levels of taxation such as done by Pechman and Okner (1974) and Musgrave et al. (1974) or within a single state (Eapen and Eapen, 1970). In these cases an impression can be an accurate description of a tax following a regressive, progressive, proportional, or U-shaped pattern, particularly since the number of taxes dealt with is limited and, therefore, manageable. In addition, comparisons across taxes can also be quite reliable.

However, when we shift attention to the burden pattern across all states, we have, de facto, severely complicated interpretation. We are now in a position to compare any of ninety-three individual sets of taxes in any of fifty states, or groups of states, or the U.S. average, across fourteen income classes. This leads to an incredibly large number of possibilities. Instead of examining the impact of a tax at each of fourteen income classes at an "average" level as was done in Chapter 5 (shown in Table 5-3), we would like to know more about how the individual states compare with each other. A written scenario about the burdens for each tax and each state would be too complex and lengthy. A simplification is in order. Although the data in Tables 5-3 and 5-4 do serve as an accurate summary of the 18,200 burdens they represent (twenty six tax types, fifty states, and fourteen income classes), comprehensive and direct comparisons across states cannot be undertaken easily. To look at each separate *ER* matrix would certainly be confusing.

The task at this point is to select measures that will enable us to summarize the information contained in each (50 × 14) effective rate matrix into a single value for each state, that is, to collapse the data across classes. We can do this for specific taxes or sets of taxes as desired. We must, however, keep track of two phenomena. First, we want to know what the *pattern* of burden looks like as we move from low- to high-income levels, that is, its " 'gressvity." Second, we also want to know how states compare to each other in terms of the *level* of burden. In the first instance we are addressing the equity profile, in the latter the claim that this tax makes on private income. The desired end result is one measure per state for each tax category that will allow direct comparisons and classifications state to state.[a]

To accomplish this we will apply three techniques to the basic data on effective rates derived earlier. First, a simple regression model will look at the responsiveness (elasticity) of the tax burden with respect to income. Second, a Lorenz curve type of analysis will examine inequality in the distribution of payments by income class. Finally, we will use a more complex mathematical technique to construct an overall index of burden that reflects both level and equity.

A REGRESSION MODEL FOR TAX EQUITY PROFILES

Making any general statement about the pattern of effective rates (*ER*) in moving from low to high income (call it an equity profile) for any tax or set of taxes on a state-by-state basis must involve examining and summarizing the change in tax burden as income changes. As has been detailed by Musgrave and Thin (1948) and numerous others in subsequent research, there is no unequivocal way to do this. When we think of " 'gressivity," that is, whether a tax is regressive or progressive, however, the most common association is between burden and some measure of income. We can thus set up the following classification of four general equity patterns:

[a] Not all ninety-three effective rate matrices will be examined. Rather, analysis will be confined to those of most consequence for state-local finance.

1. Regressive: tax burden that declines as income rises
2. Progressive: tax burden that rises as income rises
3. Proportional: tax burden that remains roughly invariant or constant across the income spectrum; the average serving as the best description
4. U-shaped: a mixture of 1, 2, and perhaps 3 with a regressive range for the low incomes and a progressive range for high incomes

All that remains is to define burden and income (this has already been done in earlier chapters) and to decide how to depict the relationship. What we are doing is stating that burden is a function of income and then examining the nature of the relationship.

Past empirical analyses of equity have employed a variety of methods. They range from a simple measure such as the ratio of the sum of weighted (by population) effective rates above to that below the median income level (Ghazanfar, 1978) to much more complex measures of average rate, marginal rate, liability, or effective progression (Musgrave and Thin, 1948). Perusal of recent literature on quantifying equity, however, reveals a leaning toward one general approach.

Since we are interested in the change in *ER*s associated with a change in income, a simple regression model is well suited to classifying the equity profile. It must be remembered that this measure states an average relationship that exists across the entire income spectrum, not between any and every pair of points; that is, it is a summary of a pattern, not a literal description. This simple regression approach has been applied in several variants; they are:

$$B = \alpha + \beta(Y) \qquad (1)$$
$$\log(B) = \alpha + \beta[\log(Y)] \qquad (2)$$
$$\omega \log(B) = \alpha + \beta[\omega \log(Y)] \qquad (3)$$

where B = tax burden or tax base
Y = income
ω = weighting factor
α = constant term
β = slope or elasticity

Variant (1) simply looks at the slope (β) of the relationship between burden and income. Variant (2) follows the same approach but estimates an elasticity (percentage change in burden with respect to the percentage change in income) for the relationship derived from taking the log of each side of the following expression:

$$B = \alpha Y^{\beta}$$

Variant (3) goes one step further and weights each observation (*not* the data itself) in the regression according to the relative concentration of families or income contained in each income class. The intent here is to "adjust" the procedure to account for the fact that some classes have a greater concentration of persons or income than others and should, therefore, be counted more heavily in estimating the elasticity or equity profile measure. Tables B-1 and B-2 show how much this concentration can vary across states.

Phares (1973) used variant (1) in classifying the equity profile of each state for tax burdens in 1962. He fitted a simple unweighted linear regression to data points on effective rates and income for each of nine income classes. Estimates of the statistical significance of the coefficient (β) allowed classification according to the following scheme:

$\beta > 1.0$ progressive
$\beta = 1.0$ proportional
$\beta < 1.0$ regressive

Using this approach, he found no progressive states, eleven that were proportional, and thirty-nine with varying degrees of regressivity (p. 66). The second variant has been used by Davies (1960) in studying the progressiveness of a sales base with respect to various income bases. By changing the base (*B*) and the income measure (*Y*), he was able to analyze how the equity of the general sales tax responded to the composition of the base (e.g., whether food was exempted or not) and the income concept used (e.g., gross, Fisher, or permanent income). Davies's estimates were elasticities and the equity classification was as follows:

$\beta > 1.0$ progressive
$\beta = 1.0$ proportional
$\beta < 1.0$ regressive

Variant (3) is identical to (2) but introduces a weighting factor into the regression so that the observations on income classes are weighted according to the relative concentration of families or income. If one class has twice as many families, it counts in the regression as though it were actually two observations instead of one. Estimates of elasticity (β), therefore, are influenced by the concentration of family units or income. This approach has been widely adopted, for example, to examine the effect of including services in the sales tax base (Davies, 1969), of including housing services (Davies and Black, 1975), of exempting clothing (Schaefer, 1969b; Davies, 1971), and of including or excluding a variety of other items in a sales tax base (Schaefer, 1969a and 1969c).

It was decided to use a form of variant (2) as the basic model for estimating the equity profile for a tax or set of taxes in each state but also to report on the impact that weighting by income and families has on these estimates. The advantage to this approach is that it offers a single, direct measure of the responsiveness of burden to changes in income, that is, the value of the coefficient (β) interpreted as an elasticity. The weighted estimates (variant 3) account for differences in the impact of a tax as it affects a large segment of the population or of income as opposed to affecting a small segment.

Two additional points need to be cleared up before discussing the findings. First, the usual definition of a progressive (regressive) tax in the literature is one in which the ratio of the effective rate to income increases (decreases) as income increases and where the effective tax rate is defined as the ratio of tax payments to income. In most equity studies, however, the author is not working directly with effective rate data but rather is examining the responsiveness of some tax base to a change in income. In these instances tax burden has been defined as a tax base, such as total consumption or total consumption net of food, not as an effective rate per se (e.g., Schaefer, 1969c). In this book, since we have gone to great lengths to estimate effective rates, the final form of the regression was specified as below; call it variant (4):[b]

$$\omega \log (ER) = \alpha + \beta\, [\omega \log (\bar{Y})] \qquad (4)$$

where $ER = T/Y$
T = tax payments
Y = income
$\bar{Y}$ = average income
ω = weighting factor (none, families, income)
α = constant term
β = elasticity

This equation (unweighted) was fitted to the data by income class on the values for effective rates and average income for each class; weighting by number of families or income is reported in the next section. The estimated coefficient (β) serves as an elasticity measure for the percentage change in burden in response to a percentage change in income. Each tax category can be treated individually using this method and states can be classified in equity terms as follows:

$\beta > 0.0$ progressive
$\beta = 0.0$ proportional
$\beta < 0.0$ regressive

[b] Variant (4) is actually mathematically equivalent to variant (3) except that the statistical tests for significance are for $\beta \neq 0.0$ instead of $\beta \neq 1.0$.

Table 6-1. State General Sales and Gross Receipts Tax: Elasticity Estimates, Exemption of Food, and Relative Importance

State	*Elasticity*[a] *(1)*	*Food Exemption* *(2)*	*Tax as Percent of All State and Local Tax Revenue* *(3)*
Alabama	-0.426		23.7
Alaska	*b*		*b*
Arizona	-0.339		26.2
Arkansas	-0.414		25.1
California	-0.233	Yes	18.0
Colorado	-0.362		16.1
Connecticut	-0.113	Yes	22.4
Delaware	*b*		*b*
Florida	-0.320	Yes	26.3
Georgia	-0.397		22.7
Hawaii	-0.231		37.3
Idaho	-0.313		18.1
Illinois	-0.274		19.4
Indiana	-0.239	Yes	28.9
Iowa	-0.234	Yes	17.5
Kansas	-0.309		20.0
Kentucky	-0.320	Yes	21.7
Louisiana	-0.239	Yes	18.0
Maine	-0.183	Yes	21.0
Maryland	-0.335	Yes	12.4
Massachusetts	-0.118	Yes	6.6
Michigan	-0.262	Yes	15.7
Minnesota	-0.247	Yes	13.1
Mississippi	-0.393		37.1
Missouri	-0.336		19.5
Montana	*b*		*b*
Nebraska	-0.291		16.2
Nevada	-0.307		20.0

Second, in examining the basic effective rate data contained in Appendix A, one thing stands out – the "under $3,000" class shows a level, for most instances, that is distinctly higher than the next class. This lowest income class has always proven to be a problem in this type of study and is often treated as a statistical aberration or outlier. It was felt that including it as a data point in the regressions would seriously bias the estimated equity profile in the direction of greater than warranted regressivity.[c] On this basis it was excluded from all regressions and only the thirteen income classes between $3,000 and over $35,000 were used as observations.

[c] The potential for bias is clearly illustrated by examining the "under $3,000" class and the "$3,000 to $3,999" class in, for example, Tables A-1, A-12, A-38, A-87, or A-91.

Table 6-1 *(continued)*

State	Elasticity[a] (1)	Food Exemption (2)	Tax as Percent of All State and Local Tax Revenue (3)
New Hampshire	b		b
New Jersey	-0.103	Yes	14.3
New Mexico	-0.325		34.8
New York	-0.192	Yes	10.4
North Carolina	-0.385		16.2
North Dakota	-0.206	Yes	25.7
Ohio	-0.178	Yes	16.4
Oklahoma	-0.409		12.4
Oregon	b		b
Pennsylvania	-0.106	Yes	17.2
Rhode Island	-0.130	Yes	16.9
South Carolina	-0.384		26.7
South Dakota	-0.283		22.7
Tennessee	-0.402		26.7
Texas	-0.294	Yes	20.4
Utah	-0.334		26.9
Vermont	-0.185	Yes	7.9
Virginia	-0.402		12.6
Washington	-0.291		37.9
West Virginia	-0.354		37.8
Wisconsin	-0.230	Yes	16.0
Wyoming	-0.285		24.4
U.S. total	-0.320		19.5

[a]See text for an explanation of the elasticity measure. All coefficients are significant at the 0.01 level. There are unweighted elasticity estimates.

[b]Tax not used in this state.

State General Sales Tax

Table 6-1 contains estimates of the burden elasticity for the state general sales tax. To help set the tax in perspective, the table also indicates whether or not the state exempts food and its relative importance. The most inequitable pattern is in Alabama (−0.426), and Arkansas (−0.414), with Oklahoma (−0.409), Tennessee (−0.402), and Virginia (−0.402) closed behind. With one exception, the ten most regressive states are all located in the South. This suggests an interaction of low income combined with a concentration of families, and therefore, consumption that is skewed toward the low end of the income distribution. The importance of consumption, and thus any levy on consumption, for low income stands out. In addition, not one of the ten most regressive states exempts food from the tax base. At the opposite end of the spectrum are the least regressive systems, with New Jersey (−0.103), Connecticut (−0.113), and Pennsylvania (−0.106). General sales taxation in these three states is only mildly regressive. Thus, the interstate range in equity is quite pronounced, lying between −0.426 in Alabama and −0.103 in New Jersey. The data in Table 6-2 summarize elasticity values[d] for the forty-five general sales tax states:

Table 6-2. Summary of General Sales Tax Elasticities

Elasticity[a]	*Number of States*	*Number Exempting Food*
0.40 and over	5	0
0.30-0.39	16	3
0.20-0.29	15	9
0.10-0.19	9	9

[a]Elasticity is shown as an absolute value.

Table 6-1, column (2) lists the states that exempt food. The impact on general sales equity can be inferred from these data. All nine states with elasticies below 0.20 exempt food and the lowest in the range of 0.20 to 0.29 also exempt food. At the high end, all states exceeding 0.40 do not exempt food nor do those with values of 0.38 to 0.39. Thus, if we array tax systems according to elasticity values, the highest one-quarter are without an exemption while the lowest one-quarter have such a provision. This is not unequivocal evidence that the exemption of food furthers the cause of taxpayer equity but it is strongly consistent with such a premise. The distribution of food-exempt states is clearly toward less regressive values. This fits with past research both nationwide (Davies, 1959 or 1960) or within a particular state (Schaefer, 1969a). It goes one step further, however, by detailing each state that uses this tax and including the effect of food exemption on its relative status.

The full impact of the sales tax within a state is a function of its equity profile plus its level of burden. The latter depends on how intensely the tax is put to use. Column (3) in Table 6-1 reflects relative dependence. Greatest reliance is indicated in four states—Hawaii, Mississippi, Washington, and West Virginia—at 37 percent of revenue. Although none of these states exempts food, the range in elas-

[d] In the text to follow, we refer to the *absolute* value of the elasticity, to simplify discussion, unless noted otherwise.

ticity is from a low of −0.231 in Hawaii to a high of −0.393 in Mississippi. In the latter case, it acts as a strong regressive influence, which is much less true in Hawaii even though it plays the same relative role. For the five most regressive states, its role is mixed. Three exceed the national average reliance by a substantial amount, whereas the other two fall well below it. In the former instances a strong regressive profile is intensified by heavy reliance on the tax; in the latter, regressivity is mitigated by the smaller role the tax plays as a revenue generator. It is interesting to note that all states with elasticities below 0.20 except two use this revenue source to less than the average degree. Thus, mild regressivity is of less consequence since it yields a below average share of collections.

In summary we can make several statements. First, there is a wide divergence across states in the equity of this tax. Second, the exemption of food does seem to promote greater equity.[e] Finally, the most regressive states tend to use this tax much more intensively than the least regressive.

State Individual Income Tax

The only progressive influence in the arsenal of state-local finance is the tax on individual income. As discussed in Chapter 3, the plethora of provisions relating to deductions, exemptions, credits, marginal tax rates, and so on, provide an opportunity for this source to take a progressive stance. Whether it does or not, and to what degree, is a function of state policy and the income status of its citizenry. When this instrument is also a dominant influence in the revenue system, the influence is further enhanced.

Table 6-3 gives elasticity estimates and relative usage of this tax. As can be seen by skimming columns (1) and (3), there is quite a bit of variance across states. Thirty-eight of them are progressive, five are proportional, and one actually turns out to be regressive. Turning first to the latter two categories we see that New Hampshire has an income tax that is distinctly inequitable with a elasticity of −1.595. New Hampshire represents a peculiar case, however, since its base only includes interest and dividend income and it brings in a mere 1.3 percent of all receipts. In addition, payments are affected by the federal tax offset for New Hampshire residents who work and pay taxes in Massachusetts. As discussed in Chapter 4, 86 percent of the New Hampshire income tax burden is wiped out through itemization on federal form 1040 Schedule A. Table A-26 shows the peculiar pattern that results.

[e] Part of the cost of this equity is the revenue loss resulting from the exemption of food. Thus, equity is furthered but at the cost of yield.

Table 6.3. State Individual Income Tax: Elasticity Estimates and Relative Importance

State	Elasticity[a] (1)	Equity[b] (2)	Tax as Percent of All State and Local Tax Revenue (3)
Alabama	0.627	PP	13.4
Alaska	1.025	PR	20.2
Arizona	0.922	PR	9.8
Arkansas	1.576	PR	15.4
California	2.408	PR[d]	14.3
Colorado	0.859	PR	17.0
Connecticut	1.849	PP	2.1
Delaware	0.844	PR	31.6
Florida	c	c	c
Georgia	1.020	PR	15.2
Hawaii	1.028	PR	22.3
Idaho	0.661	PR[d]	20.1
Illinois	0.506	PR	14.1
Indiana	0.308	PR	13.0
Iowa	1.097	PR	19.3
Kansas	0.690	PR	12.9
Kentucky	1.035	PR	15.5
Louisiana	1.267	PR	5.0
Maine	1.412	PR	7.3
Maryland	0.679	PR	23.4
Massachusetts	0.363	PR[d]	23.2
Michigan	0.869	PR	16.6
Minnesota	0.834	PR[d]	26.0
Mississippi	1.060	PR[d]	9.2
Missouri	1.238	PR	12.4
Montana	0.708	PR	18.3
Nebraska	1.513	PR	10.4
Nevada	c	c	c
New Hampshire	−1.595	R[d]	1.3
New Jersey	1.145	PP	1.7

In the five proportional states there are similar forces at work. Connecticut is heavily influenced by the federal offset, with 84 percent of its payments exported to the federal revenue structure because of itemization; in addition, its base includes only capital gains and dividends. The net effect is that there is a claim present in only three of the fourteen income classes (see Table A-26). Tennessee, likewise, uses a very narrow base—interest and dividends. The remaining three states can be accounted for by looking at their specific provisions. Alabama has a rate structure that tops at 5 percent over $5,000 and allows for the deduction of federal taxes. New Jersey has only two tax

Table 6-3 *(continued)*

State	Elasticity[a] (1)	Equity[b] (2)	Tax as Percent of All State and Local Tax Revenue (3)
New Mexico	1.043	PR	8.3
New York	1.005	PR	19.2
North Carolina	0.744	PR	21.0
North Dakota	1.617	PR	13.7
Ohio	1.300	PR	8.2
Oklahoma	1.555	PR	13.7
Oregon	0.551	PR	28.8
Pennsylvania	−0.055	PP	13.1
Rhode Island	0.736	PR	14.1
South Carolina	1.118	PR	17.5
South Dakota	c	c	c
Tennessee	−0.010	PP	1.1
Texas	c	c	c
Utah	0.884	PR	19.3
Vermont	0.863	PP	16.7
Virginia	0.648	PR	20.0
Washington	c	c	c
West Virginia	0.697	PR	13.2
Wisconsin	0.873	PR	26.3
Wyoming	c	c	c
U.S. Total	1.641	PR	13.7

[a]Unweighted elasticity estimates.

[b]PR = progressive, PP = proportional, R = regressive based on elasticity estimates (see text). Unless noted otherwise, significant at 0.01 level. Degrees of freedom vary from state to state (refer to Table A-26) but significance tests take this into account.

[c]Tax not used in this state.

[d]Significant at 0.05 but not 0.01 level.

brackets – 2 percent on the first $20,000, 2.5 percent over that. It also brings in very little revenue and is heavily influenced by the federal offset for its residents who work in New York. Finally, Pennsylvania has a flat 2 percent levy on all taxable income. Thus, these five states emerge as being proportional, on the average.

Looking at the remaining thirty-eight progressive states, there is a wide divergence in equity. Greatest progression is found in California with an elasticity of 2.408, far above second-place North Dakota at 1.617. Least progressivity is found in Indiana (0.308) and Massachusetts (0.363). The distribution of elasticities for progressive states is as follows:

Elasticity[f]	*Number of States*
Over 2.00	1
1.50 - 2.00	4
1.00 - 1.49	13
0.50 - 0.99	18
Less than 0.50	2

The individual income tax offers an excellent exemplification of the vast difference that can emerge between equity suggested by nominal tax rates and the pattern of effective rates that portrays the actual burden. Delaware, as a case in point, has nominally the most progressive marginal rates, rising from 1.6 percent on less than $1,000 to 19.8 percent over $100,000. When all features of the tax are combined with the distribution of income in the state, however, Delaware ends up being much less progressive than its nominal rate structure might suggest. California, the most progressive state based on effective rates, does not appear to be all that progressive in nominal terms; rates increase from 1 percent for less than $2,000 to 11 percent over $15,500. When all the factors discussed in Chapter 3 for the individual income tax are accounted for, however, the actual equity pattern can, and indeed does, depart radically from the nominal. Table A-26 gives actual rates.

Column (3) in Table 6-3 reflects to what extent each state depends on the income tax; the range is from a high of 31.6 percent in Delaware to less than 2 percent in New Jersey, New Hampshire, and Tennessee. If we combine equity with yield, its complete impact is put into perspective. California, the most progressive state, is just above the U.S. average percentage (14.3 percent versus 13.7 percent). Thus, distinct progressivity is softened somewhat by an average role in raising tax dollars. At the other extreme lie Delaware (31.6 percent), Minnesota (26.0 percent), Oregon (28.8 percent), and Wisconsin (26.3 percent), which use this source much more intensively. Although all are progressive, their elasticities fall in the range +0.551 to +0.873, quite a bit lower than that found in the eighteen states with values exceeding 1.0. Taxpayer equity here is enhanced by the role of the tax but softened by its less progressive impact.

The state individual income tax is the only revenue source with a progressive impact, but it differs widely depending upon specific provisions, the distribution of income, and the strength of the federal offset. States with an above average utilization do benefit from its equity

[f] Elasticity is shown as an absolute value.

effects. States that rely on it to a lesser degree receive some progressive benefit but not as much as if it were a dominant revenue source.

Local Real Property Taxes

Property taxation is the dominant fiscal influence in almost every state. Data in Table 5-3 showed the average equity pattern to be regressive, but Table 5-4 indicated the presence of considerable variation. Elasticity estimates for combined local real property taxes are given in column (2) of Table 6-4. Although all fifty states are regressive, there are substantial differences in degree as the following data show:

Elasticity[g]	*Number of States*
0.50 and over	8
0.40-.49	16
0.30-.39	17
0.20-.29	9

The most regressive state is Connecticut with an elasticity of −0.618, followed closely by Massachusetts, New Jersey, New Hampshire, Vermont, Rhode Island, Pennsylvania, and Wisconsin, all with values exceeding 0.50. The property tax in these eight states is set apart by its clear regressive claim on private income.

At the least regressive end of the spectrum is South Dakota with an elasticity of −0.238, slightly above one-half the U.S. average. Also at the low end are Texas (−0.242), Arkansas (−0.241), and Louisiana (−0.250). The range in extremes, therefore, is between one-half the U.S. average and 40 percent above it.

Contrasting the elasticity of this tax with its role in state-local finance helps to pin down its impact on the tax burden faced by residents of a state. Greatest dependence is in New Hampshire where nearly 60 percent of all revenue comes from the taxation of property; next closest is New Jersey at 55 percent. Both states are also set apart by their very regressive pattern, with elasticities of −0.511 and −0.557, respectively. Other high property tax states are also characterized by an extremely inequitable burden. Witness Connecticut at 47.5 percent of revenue and an elasticity of −0.618; Massachusetts at 47.7 percent and −0.529; or Vermont at 41.4 percent

[g] Elasticity is shown as an absolute value.

Table 6-4. All Local Real Property Taxes: Elasticity Estimates and Relative Importance (benchmark case)

State	Regression Weights			Taxes as Percent of all State and Local Tax Revenue
	Families[a] (1)	None[a] (2)	Income[a] (3)	
Alabama	-0.411	-0.306	-0.197[b]	10.7
Alaska	-0.314	-0.431	-0.150[b]	13.0
Arizona	-0.485	-0.420	-0.236[b]	31.7
Arkansas	-0.367	-0.241	-0.162[b]	22.1
California	-0.500	-0.468	-0.286[c]	41.3
Colorado	-0.457	-0.420	-0.208[b]	37.2
Connecticut	-0.595	-0.618	-0.430	47.4
Delaware	-0.356	-0.352	-0.224	16.9
Florida	-0.346	-0.272	-0.186[c]	32.6
Georgia	-0.376	-0.309	-0.170[b]	32.2
Hawaii	-0.420	-0.432	-0.197[b]	18.6
Idaho	-0.358	-0.288	-0.136[b]	32.1
Illinois	-0.418	-0.391	-0.190[b]	36.9
Indiana	-0.464	-0.429	-0.283	37.6
Iowa	-0.353	-0.310	-0.172[c]	39.6
Kansas	-0.407	-0.361	-0.214[c]	41.2
Kentucky	-0.459	-0.329	-0.242[c]	17.1
Louisiana	-0.309	-0.250	-0.098[b]	14.8
Maine	-0.566	-0.480	-0.370	25.9
Maryland	-0.413	-0.445	-0.262	27.6
Massachusetts	-0.564	-0.529	-0.365	47.7
Michigan	-0.518	-0.485	-0.324	41.5
Minnesota	-0.478	-0.426	-0.293	30.8
Mississippi	-0.398	-0.284	-0.180[b]	22.3
Missouri	-0.480	-0.414	-0.279[c]	34.0
Montana	-0.402	-0.327	-0.170[b]	46.3
Nebraska	-0.355	-0.314	-0.155[b]	48.5
Nevada	-0.392	-0.384	-0.191[b]	29.2

and −0.568. This situation is by no means unequivocal, however. Substantial dependence on property taxes does not always mean a powerful regressive influence in the full revenue system. South Dakota, the least regressive state (−0.238), raises just under 50 percent of all revenue with this instrument. Montana, Nebraska, and Oregon all raise in excess of 46 percent of all collections with this tax and yet their burden elasticities fall in a low to moderate range (0.30-0.36), well below the national average.

In examining the role this tax plays in local finance, we see that it is a distinct source of inequity in several states. Of eight states with elasticities exceeding 0.50, six of them raise 98 percent or more of all

Table 6-4 *(continued)*

State	Regression Weights Families[a] (1)	None[a] (2)	Income[a] (3)	Taxes as Percent of all State and Local Tax Revenue
New Hampshire	-0.567	-0.511	-0.372	59.7
New Jersey	-0.563	-0.557	-0.389	55.1
New Mexico	-0.430	-0.427	-0.276	15.2
New York	-0.434	-0.392	-0.152[b]	36.0
North Carolina	-0.398	-0.358	-0.233[c]	23.6
North Dakota	-0.294	-0.261	-0.105[b]	31.4
Ohio	-0.463	-0.419	-0.256[c]	36.6
Oklahoma	-0.343	-0.329	-0.195[c]	23.4
Oregon	-0.458	-0.367	-0.221[b]	47.3
Pennsylvania	-0.584	-0.550	-0.415	24.9
Rhode Island	-0.567	-0.529	-0.357	40.6
South Carolina	-0.378	-0.304	-0.190[b]	23.4
South Dakota	-0.320	-0.288	-0.173[c]	48.3
Tennessee	-0.354	-0.266	-0.137[b]	26.3
Texas	-0.296	-0.242	-0.060[b]	36.2
Utah	-0.515	-0.478	-0.316	28.9
Vermont	-0.622	-0.568	-0.503	41.4
Virginia	-0.443	-0.433	-0.272	27.7
Washington	-0.464	-0.410	-0.188[b]	22.1
West Virginia	-0.400	-0.307	-0.216[c]	18.1
Wisconsin	-0.553	-0.500	-0.386	33.0
Wyoming	-0.372	-0.336	-0.146[b]	39.4
U.S. total	-0.531	-0.452	-0.272	35.1

[a]Significant at 0.01 level unless noted otherwise.
[b]Coefficient not significant, a proportional burden.
[c]Significant at 0.05 level but not 0.01 level.

local revenue through property taxation. One, New Jersey, raises over 90 percent. In Pennsylvania, which has one of the most regressive property taxes, third only to Connecticut and Vermont, it accounts for only one-quarter of all revenue and 67 percent of local revenue. Here is an instance in which a very regressive local property tax has been mitigated by state-allowed use of local nonproperty revenues.

In states with a very regressive property tax burden and heavy use of the tax (Connecticut, New Jersey, or Massachusetts), the impact on the total system is evident. For states with a regressive claim but lower reliance (e.g., Pennsylvania or Wisconsin), the sting is mitigated by a smaller relative yield. Finally, there are states with mild regressivity and a relatively small role (e.g., Alabama, Louisiana, or West Virginia). Taxpayer equity in these cases benefits from both aspects.

Comparison of property tax and general sales tax equity shows the former to be generally more inequitable. The most regressive general sales tax is in Alabama (−0.426); the most regressive property tax in Connecticut (−0.618). The least regressive sales tax is in New Jersey (−0.103), the least regressive property tax in South Dakota (−0.238). The full range of differences becomes apparent by comparing Table 6-3, column (1) with Table 6-4, column (2). Close scrutiny shows that states with highly regressive property taxes tend to have a much less inequitable sales tax. Connecticut has a property tax elasticity of −0.618 and a sales tax elasticity of −0.113; New Jersey −0.557 and −0.103; Pennsylvania −0.550 and −0.106; the extremes appear to balance out. A few states in between have achieved a balance in equity between these two dominant forces, for example, Texas, North Dakota, and Louisiana.

The tax on property is a clear source of inequity in every state and generally is more so than that on general sales. When a strong regressive influence is combined with heavy fiscal dependence, the situation can result in a powerful source of inequity. The extremes are illustrated by Connecticut and South Dakota, both of which raise just shy of 50 percent of all revenue with this tax. Burden elasticities, however, differ from −0.618 in the former to −0.238 in the latter, a factor of more than 1.5 to 1.0. The impact on the total state-local system can be seen by examining column (2) in Table 6-6; South Dakota's system is quite a bit less regressive than average (−0.207) while Connecticut is the third most severe (−0.336).

Selected Other State and Local Taxes

Because of the sheer number of taxes being considered, it is not feasible to report on each one individually. Many of them are not major generators of revenue and play an important role in only one or a few states. As a reference, Table B-3 gives elasticity values for nine additional categories not discussed above. A few brief comments are in order.

State selective sales taxes generally prove to be regressive, with that on alcohol the least so. The most regressive (and in fact of all taxes) is that on tobacco with elasticities in the range −0.535 to −0.734. Total state license taxes are mixed but wind up proportional in thirteen states and most regressive in Maryland (−0.344). The state levy on corporation net income is found to be proportional in every state because of its impact on capital ownership.

Turning to the local sector, we see that nonproperty sources are quite regressive, with a range between −0.212 in Indiana and −0.522 in Alaska. Local personal property taxes are proportional in twenty-eight states, progressive in six, and regressive in the remaining eleven. In only two states does this source exert much of a regressive influence – Maryland (−0.408) and South Carolina (−0.473).[h] The final column reflects the equity of the entire local sector. In twenty-three states, the profile is 90 percent or more a function of property taxes. In only eight is the elasticity influenced to any appreciable degree by nonproperty revenues. The range is between high property tax states like Connecticut (−0.513), Massachusetts (−0.502), or New Jersey (−0.537) and high nonproperty tax local sectors in Alabama (−0.352) or Louisiana (−0.185).

All State Taxes

The role of state government in fiscal matters varies widely. At one extreme are dominant state governments – such as Alaska, New Mexico, or Delaware – which account for in excess of 80 percent of all yield. At the opposite extreme are strong local government states, like New Hampshire or New Jersey, in which these jurisdictions raise over 60 percent of all receipts. The equity profiles that result from such diverse situations are a function of which taxes are levied in a state; the impact on the overall tax structure depends on the relative role of the state.

Table 6-5, column (2), gives burden elasticity values for all state taxes and indicates the relative role of state government. Generally, the largest contributors to equity are the general sales and the individual income taxes. Exceptions are noted, however, in a few atypical instances where a large percentage of revenue is derived from other sources: corporate activity in Delaware (15.2 percent); gambling in Nevada (14.5 percent); natural resources in Texas (11.0 percent), Louisiana (23.8 percent), New Mexico (12.5 percent), Oklahoma (10.3 percent), and Wyoming (12.4 percent); motor fuels in California and Mississippi (11 percent); and finally, the state property tax in Alaska (42.3 percent), Maine (18.3 percent), and Washington (10.3 percent). In these twelve instances, the state system is influenced by these instruments.

When all sources are combined, we find the most regressive state system to be Wyoming (−0.336) with Florida (−0.331) and Texas (−0.330) very close behind; these are all states with state sectors that are slightly above average in size. Most important for the equity pro-

[h] Minnesota and New Hampshire actually turn out to be extremely regressive but this is due to the peculiar burden pattern, caused by the federal offset, that eliminates all payments in the top several income classes (see Table A-60).

Table 6-5. Total State Taxes: Elasticity Estimates and Relative Importance (benchmark case)

State	Regression Weights			Taxes as Percent of all State and Local Tax Revenue
	Families[a] (1)	None[a] (2)	Income[a] (3)	
Alabama	−0.236	−0.202	−0.163	74.5
Alaska	−0.198	−0.251	−0.124	82.7
Arizona	−0.266	−0.257	−0.203	61.3
Arkansas	−0.208	−0.165	−0.134	75.7
California	+0.010[b]	+0.027[b]	+0.144[c]	51.9
Colorado	−0.094	−0.110	−0.084	51.3
Connecticut	−0.171	−0.184	−0.055[b]	52.1
Delaware	+0.051[b]	+0.058[b]	+0.195[c]	80.2
Florida	−0.346	−0.311	−0.244	61.6
Georgia	−0.133	−0.125	−0.083[c]	61.5
Hawaii	−0.041[c]	−0.047	−0.008[b]	77.1
Idaho	−0.077	−0.068	−0.041[c]	67.0
Illinois	−0.162	−0.157	−0.111	55.4
Indiana	−0.164	−0.157	−0.104	61.4
Iowa	+0.024[b]	+0.041[b]	+0.107[c]	59.6
Kansas	−0.127	−0.110	−0.045[b]	56.8
Kentucky	−0.121	−0.079[b]	−0.019[b]	74.5
Louisiana	−0.214	−0.177	−0.096[b]	70.7
Maine	−0.179	−0.123[c]	−0.058[b]	73.8
Maryland	−0.132	−0.149	−0.106	58.1
Massachusetts	+0.064	+0.065	+0.056	52.0
Michigan	−0.082	−0.071[c]	−0.016[b]	55.3
Minnesota	+0.092[b]	+0.104[c]	+0.159	68.0
Mississippi	−0.249	−0.185	−0.124[c]	76.4
Missouri	−0.121	−0.114	−0.068[c]	53.0
Montana	−0.069[b]	−0.149[b]	+0.026[b]	52.0
Nebraska	−0.095[b]	−0.069[b]	+0.033[b]	47.9
Nevada	−0.300	−0.293	−0.194	58.7

file is the absence of an individual income tax. In addition, they each have an above average reliance on the general sales tax. The other three "no income tax" states—Nevada, South Dakota, Washington—also have a more regressive system than average since they rely more heavily on sales-oriented revenues. Of the states without any general sales tax, two are proportional, one is progressive, and the remaining two, Alaska and New Hampshire, are also heavily influenced by consumption taxes.

At the progressive extreme, there are four state systems: Massachusetts (+0.065), Minnesota (+0.104), New York (+0.139), and Oregon (+0.124). Each relies heavily on the individual income tax

Table 6-5 *(continued)*

State	*Regression Weights*			*Taxes as Percent of all State and Local Tax Revenue*
	Families[a] (1)	*None*[a] (2)	*Income*[a] (3)	
New Hampshire	−0.314	−0.251	−0.103[b]	39.1
New Jersey	−0.174	−0.177	−0.078[b]	39.4
New Mexico	−0.273	−0.255	−0.162	82.3
New York	+0.126[c]	+0.139	+0.205	47.4
North Carolina	−0.119	−0.106	−0.053[b]	71.4
North Dakota	−0.067[b]	−0.067[c]	−0.039[b]	67.0
Ohio	−0.119[c]	−0.102[c]	−0.006[b]	52.9
Oklahoma	−0.151[c]	−0.127[c]	−0.010[b]	68.3
Oregon	+0.129	+0.124	+0.169	50.4
Pennsylvania	−0.073[b]	−0.052[b]	+0.014[b]	63.2
Rhode Island	−0.084[c]	−0.068[c]	+0.006[b]	59.0
South Carolina	−0.130	−0.128	−0.094	74.8
South Dakota	−0.280	−0.230	−0.157[c]	47.0
Tennessee	−0.322	−0.237	−0.116[b]	61.3
Texas	−0.348	−0.330	−0.253	58.1
Utah	−0.124	−0.117	−0.057[c]	65.2
Vermont	−0.015[b]	+0.011[b]	+0.038[b]	58.1
Virginia	−0.153	−0.156	−0.139	59.5
Washington	−0.275	−0.247	−0.112[b]	70.3
West Virginia	−0.244	−0.190	−0.098[b]	77.9
Wisconsin	+0.044[b]	+0.047[b]	+0.089	66.5
Wyoming	−0.347	−0.336	−0.271	58.5
U.S. total	−0.239	−0.172	−0.064[b]	57.2

[a]Significant at 0.01 level unless noted otherwise.
[b]Coefficient not significant, a proportional burden.
[c]Significant at 0.05 level but not 0.01 level.

which, as can be seen in Table 6-3, is progressive in each state, from a low of +0.363 in Massachusetts to a high of +1.005 in New York. One state, Oregon, has no general sales tax, whereas the other three are among the least regressive and exempt food from their base. This further enhances taxpayer equity.

Nine states are proportional overall and each of them has an income tax that is distinctly progressive (e.g., California, 2.408; Nebraska, 1.513). In addition, the general sales tax in these states is either not used at all (Delaware and Montana) or has a low elasticity (Pennsylvania is least regressive at −0.106; the rest are below the average; six of the nine exempt food).

The balancing of all forces – use of the income tax, use of the general sales tax, exemption of food, the elasticity of the two dominant revenue producers – produces the final equity picture for a state tax system. Overall, nine are proportional, four progressive, and another twenty-five lie in a range of relatively mild regressivity (0.19 or less). Use of an individual income tax with its specific provisions offers states an opportunity to introduce progressivity into the system. Only three states have a tax structure that is strongly regressive, and each has elected not to tax income but rather to rely very heavily on consumption-related revenues.

When the equity pattern of all state taxation is combined with a dominant role for the state, the total system is affected accordingly. Oregon and New York are progressive but the state's share of revenue is below the national average. Delaware with a proportional structure influences the overall system by its sheer dominance (80.2 percent of all revenue). This is also true of Alaska with a regressive structure and large state sector (82.7 percent).

Equity in any state depends on how the state balances its income and general sales taxes and implements provisions pertaining to each. The extremes are found in New York with a progressive income tax and a mildly regressive general sales tax and Wyoming with no income tax and a fairly regressive sales tax.

All State and Local Taxes

We are finally in a position to "fit all the pieces together" and to look at equity for the entire state-local tax structure. The picture that emerges is heavily influenced by the balance among the "big three" of state-local finance – property, sales, and income – and the balance between the state and local sectors. Table 6-6, column (2), contains elasticity estimates; they break down as follows:

Elasticity[i]	*Number of States*
0.30 and over	5
0.20 - 0.29	24
0.10 - 0.19	20
Proportional	1

The most regressive state-local tax system is New Jersey (−0.378) with New Hampshire a close second (−0.372) and Connecticut third (−0.336). Each of these three states is affected by a powerful local property tax (elasticities exceed 0.50) with a predominant role in

[i] Elasticity is shown as an absolute value.

Table 6-6. Total State and Local Taxes: Elasticity Estimates (benchmark case)

	Regression Weights		
State	*Families*[a] (1)	*None*[a] (2)	*Income*[a] (3)
Alabama	−0.278	−0.235	−0.185
Alaska	−0.222	−0.280	−0.142
Arizona	−0.332	−0.303	−0.193
Arkansas	−0.257	−0.185	−0.136[c]
California	−0.239	−0.212	−0.058[b]
Colorado	−0.268	−0.256	−0.130[c]
Connecticut	−0.315	−0.336	−0.135[b]
Delaware	−0.058[b]	−0.055[b]	−0.109[b]
Florida	−0.319	−0.268	−0.189
Georgia	−0.217	−0.188	−0.115[c]
Hawaii	−0.150	−0.159	−0.064[b]
Idaho	−0.178	−0.144	−0.063[b]
Illinois	−0.255	−0.240	−0.118[b]
Indiana	−0.232	−0.216	−0.130[c]
Iowa	−0.155[c]	−0.123[c]	−0.014[b]
Kansas	−0.190	−0.165	−0.082[b]
Kentucky	−0.199	−0.134[c]	−0.062[b]
Louisiana	−0.219	−0.181	−0.092[b]
Maine	−0.263	−0.192	−0.107[b]
Maryland	−0.238	−0.254	−0.167
Massachusetts	−0.262	−0.237	−0.126[b]
Michigan	−0.257	−0.237	−0.131[c]
Minnesota	−0.139[c]	−0.108[c]	−0.008[b]
Mississippi	−0.285	−0.207	−0.134[c]
Missouri	−0.252	−0.220	−0.132[c]
Montana	−0.220	−0.173	−0.051[b]
Nebraska	−0.209	−0.173	−0.036[b]
Nevada	−0.315	−0.310	−0.167[c]
New Hampshire	−0.435	−0.372	−0.221[c]
New Jersey	−0.380	−0.378	−0.232
New Mexico	−0.296	−0.277	−0.176
New York	−0.170[c]	−0.147[c]	−0.012[b]
North Carolina	−0.199	−0.169	−0.076[b]
North Dakota	−0.163	−0.151	−0.073[c]
Ohio	−0.246	−0.219	−0.097[b]
Oklahoma	−0.213	−0.189	−0.062[b]
Oregon	−0.179[c]	−0.128[c]	−0.012[b]
Pennsylvania	−0.236	−0.209	−0.111[b]
Rhode Island	−0.249	−0.221	−0.105[b]
South Carolina	−0.208	−0.180	−0.121
South Dakota	−0.274	−0.207	−0.135[c]
Tennessee	−0.318	−0.242	−0.133[b]
Texas	−0.290	−0.260	−0.149[c]
Utah	−0.257	−0.239	−0.135[c]

Table 6-6 *(continued)*

State	Regression Weights: Families[a] (1)	None[a] (2)	Income[a] (3)
Vermont	−0.254	−0.189	−0.126[b]
Virginia	−0.262	−0.260	−0.182
Washington	−0.309	−0.275	−0.121[b]
West Virginia	−0.262	−0.202	−0.111[b]
Wisconsin	−0.170	−0.139	−0.053[b]
Wyoming	−0.308	−0.280	−0.130[b]
U.S. total	−0.352	−0.280	−0.141[c]

[a]Significant at 0.01 level unless noted otherwise.
[b]Coefficient not significant, a proportional burden.
[c]Significant at 0.05 level but not at 0.01 level.

financing local operations. In these states, local property taxation is very regressive, is the major contributor to revenue, and is not softened by a strong individual income tax. In fact, New Hampshire's income tax actually turns out to be regressive. The only mitigating influence is a mildly regressive general sales tax in New Jersey and Connecticut; New Hampshire has none.

At the other extreme is one proportional state, Delaware, in which the state's role is dominant and is financed through a progressive income tax that raises almost 32 percent of all revenue. In addition, Delaware does not tax general sales and does tax business activity to the extent that it accounts for over 25 percent of all yield. The end result is that it is proportional overall, or neutral, in its claim on private income.

Several other systems, although not actually proportional, are only mildly regressive. Oregon, for example, has a strong income tax, that brings in almost 29 percent of all revenue, and no general sales tax; Minnesota and Wisconsin likewise use the income tax heavily and have a moderately regressive general sales tax with food exempted. The most regressive cases are generally states dominated by local property taxation while the less regressive are states in which the income tax is evident.

Whatever the case for specific state-local systems, it becomes obvious that state tax policy is the only pro-equity force at operation. Local governments simply do not have an option to implement more equitable tax policy because of their intimate link to a property base. It remains, for the most part, up to the state to play the role of furthering taxpayer equity; the most powerful weapon it has to do this is a judiciously designed individual income tax that serves as a major source of dollars.

WEIGHTED TAX BURDEN ELASTICITIES: THE IMPACT ON EQUITY

In computing estimates of β in the equation for variant (4), there are three possible alternatives for weighting (ω) that are of interest. The first, and the one the previous discussion is based on, is to introduce no weighting factor at all; that is, each observation counts the same. A second option is to let ω represent the relative concentration of families (taxpaying units). By doing this a class with twice as many families as another would count in the regression as though it were actually two observations instead of one. In other words, estimates of elasticity are adjusted to account for the fact that each class "should" not count the same. This logic also applies to the third possibility, weighting by relative concentration of income. In this instance, observations with a greater amount of income influence the estimate of β more heavily. As an analogy, this can be likened to computing a weighted average rather than a simple average in which families or income serve as weights in estimating β, the average elasticity across the entire income spectrum.

Tables B-1 and B-2 provide data on the percentage distribution of families and income. They show that there are considerable differences among states in how these two variables are concentrated by income category. A good example is Mississippi with a very skewed distribution of families, 48 percent lie below $8,000. For income, Alaska is a good example in that slightly less than 40 percent of all income in the state is in the top (over $35,000) class.

The effect of weighting on three major tax categories is discussed to illustrate how equity profiles are affected when income and family concentration are taken into consideration. This approach has been used in past studies by Schaefer (1969a, b, c), Davies (1969, 1971), and Davies and Black (1975), amongst others, and can be compared with the results found in this book.

Looking first at all local real property taxes, change in the distribution of elasticity values[j] under the three weighting schemes is shown in Table 6-7. Weighting by family concentration leads to the most in-

[j] In the discussion that follows elasticity is also shown in absolute values to simplify matters.

Table 6-7. All Local Real Property Taxes: Summary of Elasticities

	Weight		
Elasticity[a]	Families	None	Income
0.60 and over	1	1	0
0.50-0.59	11	7	1
0.40-0.49	19	16	2
0.30-0.39	17	17	8
0.20-0.29	2	9	13
0.10-0.19	0	0	4
Proportional	0	0	22
Progressive	0	0	0

[a] Elasticity is shown as an absolute value.

equitable situation with more than three-fifths of all states having an elasticity of 0.40 or higher. If we turn next to the "no weight" case, the situation is softened. Only twenty-four states now exceed 0.40, and the number in the range 0.20 to 0.29 has risen from two to nine. Referring to the data in Table 6-4, columns (1) and (2), we see that the elasticities have declined in every state but four (Alaska, Connecticut, Hawaii, and Maryland). In addition, there is some reordering in the extent of inequity. Vermont is most regressive using families (−0.622); Connecticut is with no weight (−0.628); North Dakota is least regressive with families (−0.294); and South Dakota is without a weight (−0.238).

Using income as a weighting factor, elasticity values are lower everywhere, often by a considerable amount. There are now only three states in the range of 0.40 or over and twenty-two that are proportional. Regressivity for the local real property tax is distinctly less pronounced when an adjustment is made to account for the relative concentration of income.

Next we can examine all state revenues. Table 6-8 shows the distribution of elasticities in this instance. With family units as a weight, we have three progressive and ten proportional states and only six that are 0.30 or greater. Most states lie in the range of less than 0.20. The most regressive tax system is in Texas (−0.348); Oregon is most progressive (+.129) (see Table 6-5, columns 1 and 2). Using no weights, the situation is altered. One state shifts from proportional to progressive and three move downward into the range of 0.10 to 0.19. Only three now have elasticities of 0.30 or above. Once again, the values are lower in all but a handful of cases.

Turning to income as a weight, tax systems are progressive in eight and proportional in twenty-one states; all but four have an elasticity of

Table 6-8. Total State Taxes: Summary of Elasticities

	Weight		
Elasticity[a]	*Families*	*None*	*Income*
0.30 and over	6	3	0
0.20-0.29	9	9	4
0.10-0.19	17	20	11
Less than 0.10	5	5	6
Proportional	10	9	21
Progressive	3	4	8

[a]Elasticity is shown as an absolute value.

less than 0.20. State taxes, taken in light of the distribution of income, are much less regressive than with the other weights.

Finally, we can examine the overall state-local tax system; the distribution of elasticities is shown in Table 6-9. Under the family weight case, most states are situated in the range 0.20 or higher with the most inequity in New Hampshire (−0.435). One state is proportional, Delaware. With no weights used, nine states shift down to less than 0.20 and Delaware remains proportional. All but four are now less inequitable than previously (compare columns 1 and 2 in Table 6-6). With income as a weighting factor, the situation changes dramatically. Twenty-eight structures now turn out to be neutral in equity terms with another twenty lying in the low regressivity range of 0.19 or less.

Use of different weights in the equation for estimating burden elasticities has a distinct impact on the empirical results. This has been found true in earlier work (e.g., Schaefer 1969a, b, c; Davies, 1969 and 1971). For almost every state, less inequity is present as we move

Table 6-9. Total State and Local Taxes: Summary of Elasticities

	Weight		
Elasticity[a]	*Families*	*None*	*Income*
0.40 and over	1	0	0
0.30-0.39	8	5	0
0.20-0.29	29	24	2
0.10-0.19	11	20	19
Less than 0.10	0	0	1
Proportional	1	1	28
Progressive	0	0	0

[a] Elasticity is shown as an absolute value.

from family weights to no weight to income as a weight. Thus, when we examine the impact that burdens exert on families, it is distinctly more regressive than it is with respect to income. These findings suggest that families are being subject to a distinctly more inequitable burden than is income.

INEQUALITY IN THE DISTRIBUTION OF TAX PAYMENTS

A second approach to examining the equity of a tax or system of taxes is to focus on how aggregate payments are distributed vis-à-vis the distribution of aggregate taxpaying units (families) or taxpaying ability (income). In Chapters 3 and 4 we developed a methodology for imputing tax payments to fourteen income classes but then used these data to compute effective rates. In this section we return to the original data on aggregate payments to see how unequally they are distributed with respect to the income that is available to "bear" them. More precisely, we look at the percentage distribution of payments (tax burden) with respect to the percentage distribution of income as we move up the income spectrum.

This approach is based upon a Lorenz curve type of analysis that shows, for a given percentage of income, the percentage of families that has received that income. Figure 6-1 (a) shows a typical Lorenz curve that relates cumulated percentage of families and cumulated percentage of total income. The diagonal of the box is a line of equal distribution, in a mathematical *not* a social or an economic sense. It is a locus of points along which y percent of the families receive y percent of the income, that is, an equal percentage distribution. Any deviation from this line, such as the curved line x bounding the shaded area, reflects an unequal distribution of income with respect to family units. It can be seen easily by reading Figure 6-1(a) that 50 percent of all families actually received less than 25 percent of total income (Reynolds and Smolensky, 1977, for example, document how unequally income has been distributed in the United States). If we cumulate all of the inequality in such a distribution we measure, de facto, the area indicated by shading; relating this area to the total triangle under the diagonal provides us with an index of inequality, the Gini ratio. Curve x is called the Lorenz curve, and the shaded area is the relative inequality measured by the Gini ratio.

This approach to measuring inequality in the distribution of taxes with respect to income and family units has been used previously by Phares (1973: 76-79) using data for 1962. More recently Suits (1977a and 1977b) and Guthrie (1979) have shown how a Lorenz-based Gini

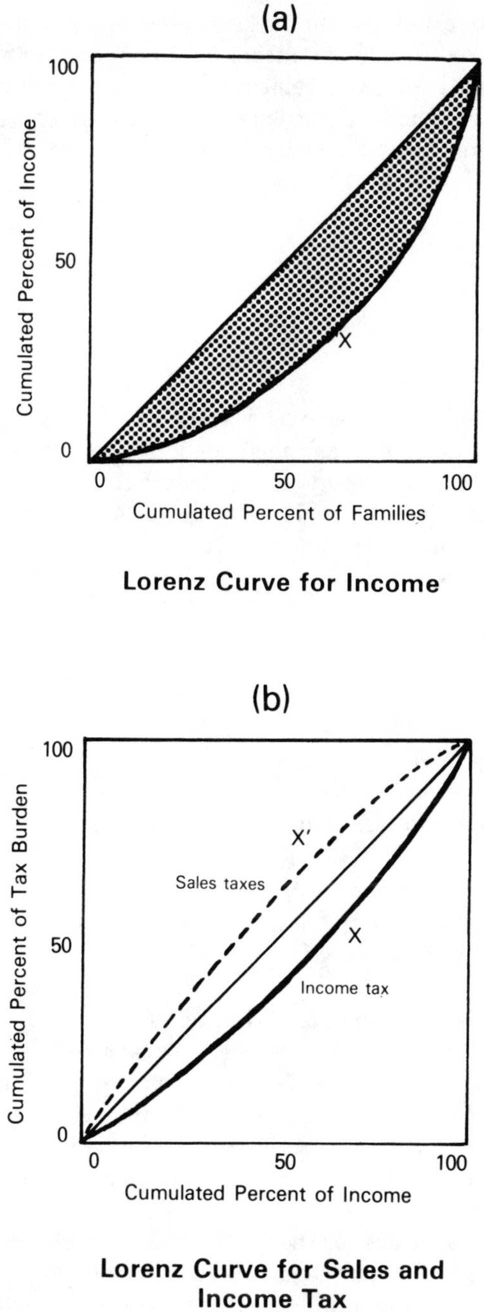

Figure 6.1. Graphic representation of the Suits index of tax progressivity.

ratio can be converted into an index of progressivity for a specific tax or system of taxes. The change from a strict Lorenz curve is indicated by Figure 6-1(b). Instead of relating income to families, Suits's measure begins by relating tax burden (defined as aggregate payments) to aggregate income. Starting with a Gini ratio (L_x), his index (S) for a tax is computed as follows:

$$S = 1.0 - (L_x/K) \qquad (x = \text{tax};\ y = \text{income})$$

$$= 1.0 - (1.0/K) \int_0^{100} T_x(y)dy$$

where $K = 5{,}000$, or the area of the triangle under the diagonal, and L_x is the Gini ratio evaluated as the shaded area relative to K. The value for L_x can be estimated based on a trapezoidal approximation method, using the fourteen points provided by the data on income classes, with the following formula (see Suits, 1977b):

$$L = \int_0^{100} T_x(y)dy$$

$$= \sum_{i=1}^{14} (1/2)\,[T_x(y_i) + T_x(y_{i-1})]\,(y_i - y_{i-1})$$

Taxes can then be classified in equity terms as follows:

Proportional:	$S = 0$	$(L = K)$
Regressive:	$-1.0 \leq S < 0$	$(L > K)$
Progressive:	$+1.0 \geq S > 0$	$(L < K)$

The Suits index (S) is bounded from above by $+1.0$ in the most extreme case where the topmost income class bears all the burden ($L = 0$) and from below by -1.0 in the most extreme case of regressivity ($L = 2K$). The Lorenz curve in these extremes actually lies along the side of the box. A situation where $S = 0$ places on us the diagonal of the box ($L = K$), where y percent of the income pays exactly y percent of the taxes.

Table 6-10 gives values for the Suits index for eight major state-local taxes or systems of taxes; Table B-4 shows support information on nine other categories. The findings are generally consistent with those from the elasticity estimates discussed earlier. It should be kept in mind, however, that these two approaches do measure two different facets of equity. Elasticities indicate how responsive the effective rate (tax burden) is to changes in income; the Suits index shows how inequitable payments are with respect to income. Although they generally point in the same direction, the latter measure does pick up some of the inequality present that the former cannot because it is an average relationship over the entire income spectrum. Thus, the two measures are complements not substitutes.

In pursuing Table 6-10 we see that the general sales tax is regressive in every state. The greatest degree of inequality exists in Alabama (−0.17), Arkansas (−0.18), and Mississippi (−0.18) and the least in Connecticut (−0.04), Massachusetts (−0.04), and New Jersey (−0.03). The amount of inequality in several states is quite small (less than 5 percent) but in several it approaches 20 percent.[k] These findings are consistent with elasticities contained in Table 6-1.

Individual income tax payments are much more unevenly distributed by income class than the general sales tax but in a manner that places the burden more heavily on high incomes. The range in index values is between an extremely regressive, unequal distribution in New Hampshire (−0.62) and a very progressive one for Connecticut (+0.65). These extremes are peculiar cases and help to demonstrate the sensitivity of the Suits index in measuring inequality. As has been noted several times, both New Hampshire and Connecticut have a very narrow income base. As a result, the peculiar pattern of burdens seen in Table A-26 emerges. In Connecticut there is *no* burden whatsoever in all but three income classes, all of which lie at the very top end of the income range. As a result, all payments are concentrated in these classes and the inequality index is a very high +0.65, reflecting a highly progressive impact. In New Hampshire, the level of burden is very low and virtually absent in all top five classes. Accordingly, the Suits index picks up the concentration of payments by lower-income taxpayers and gives a very regressive value of −0.62. Mississippi is the second most progressive state (+0.43) and perusal of Table A-26 shows why; there are no payments at all in the lowest seven classes; all taxes are paid by the top seven. If we check other high-value states (e.g., California, +0.33, or Louisiana, +0.37) we find much the same situation. Elimination of all burden on the lowest income classes through exemptions, deductions, credits, and so on, makes this tax very unequally distributed toward payment by high-income taxpayers. This is consistent with the elasticity measures in Table 6-3, but because of the greater sensitivity of the Suits index to cases of zero

[k] The Suits index can be interpreted as a percentage of inequality with −1.0 totally regressive, +1.0 totally progressive, and 0.0 perfectly equal.

Table 6-10. Suits Index of Tax Progressivity[a] For Major State-Local Taxes by Type of Tax

State	General Sales	Individual Income	Total State (B)[b]	Real Property (B)[b]	Real Property (P)[c]	Imported	Total State And Local (B)[b]	Total State And Local (P)[c]
Alabama	−0.17	0.09	−0.09	−0.13	0.58	−0.07	−0.10	−0.05
Alaska	[d]	0.18	−0.04	−0.06	0.24	−0.07	−0.05	−0.01
Arizona	−0.13	0.06	−0.09	−0.14	0.24	−0.06	−0.10	0.00[e]
Arkansas	−0.18	0.30	−0.08	−0.12	0.20	−0.10	−0.09	−0.03
California	−0.08	0.33	0.04	−0.15	0.29	−0.05	−0.04	0.12
Colorado	−0.13	0.08	−0.04	−0.12	0.37	−0.04	−0.07	0.08
Connecticut	−0.04	0.65	−0.02	−0.19	0.34	0.05	−0.06	0.12
Delaware	[d]	0.13	0.06	−0.10	0.40	0.08	0.02	0.13
Florida	−0.13	[d]	−0.13	−0.11	0.23	−0.01	−0.11	−0.01
Georgia	−0.16	0.24	−0.05	−0.11	0.33	−0.05	−0.07	0.03
Hawaii	−0.07	0.14	0.00[e]	−0.10	0.21	−0.04	−0.03	0.03
Idaho	−0.11	0.09	−0.03	−0.09	0.31	−0.06	−0.04	0.07
Illinois	−0.09	0.05	−0.04	−0.10	0.32	0.00[e]	−0.06	0.07
Indiana	−0.08	0.03	−0.04	−0.14	0.37	−0.01	−0.06	0.07
Iowa	−0.08	0.20	0.02	−0.09	0.17	−0.04	−0.02	0.08
Kansas	−0.11	0.13	−0.03	−0.12	0.22	−0.02	−0.04	0.04
Kentucky	−0.13	0.18	−0.03	−0.15	0.39	−0.01	−0.05	0.03
Louisiana	−0.10	0.37	−0.07	−0.08	0.48	−0.06	−0.07	0.00[e]
Maine	−0.07	0.38	−0.04	−0.20	0.26	−0.02	−0.07	0.02
Maryland	−0.11	0.03	−0.04	−0.11	0.32	−0.03	−0.06	0.05
Massachusetts	−0.04	0.05	0.01	−0.17	0.42	0.03	−0.06	0.20
Michigan	−0.08	0.10	−0.01	−0.15	0.32	−0.02	−0.06	0.10
Minnesota	−0.08	0.23	0.04	−0.15	0.31	−0.02	−0.02	0.13
Mississippi	−0.18	0.43	−0.09	−0.13	0.31	−0.10	−0.10	−0.03
Missouri	−0.13	0.18	−0.04	−0.16	0.37	0.00[e]	−0.08	0.05
Montana	[d]	0.14	0.00[e]	−0.11	0.21	−0.08	−0.04	0.04
Nebraska	−0.10	0.33	0.00[e]	−0.09	0.19	−0.03	−0.04	0.05
Nevada	−0.11	[d]	−0.09	−0.11	0.46	0.02	−0.09	0.05

Table 6-10 *(continued)*

New Hampshire	[d]	−0.62	−0.06	−0.18	0.24	0.00[e]	−0.12	0.11
New Jersey	−0.03	−0.22	−0.03	−0.17	0.17	−0.01	−0.10	0.06
New Mexico	−0.13	0.37	−0.09	−0.16	0.27	−0.07	−0.10	−0.03
New York	−0.07	0.25	0.07	−0.10	0.38	0.03	−0.02	0.16
North Carolina	−0.15	0.12	−0.04	−0.13	0.29	−0.02	−0.05	0.01
North Dakota	−0.08	0.18	−0.02	−0.07	0.12	−0.07	−0.04	0.02
Ohio	−0.06	0.26	−0.01	−0.13	0.34	0.00[e]	−0.05	0.10
Oklahoma	−0.17	0.33	−0.03	−0.12	0.40	−0.05	−0.06	0.03
Oregon	[d]	0.12	0.05	−0.14	0.36	−0.04	−0.03	0.16
Pennsylvania	−0.04	0.03	−0.01	−0.20	0.27	−0.01	−0.06	0.05
Rhode Island	−0.04	0.17	−0.01	−0.18	0.20	−0.02	−0.06	0.05
South Carolina	−0.14	0.17	−0.05	−0.10	0.24	−0.05	−0.06	0.00[e]
South Dakota	−0.11	[d]	−0.08	−0.10	0.10	−0.06	−0.08	−0.01
Tennessee	−0.16	0.02	−0.08	−0.10	0.44	−0.06	−0.09	0.03
Texas	−0.12	[d]	−0.13	−0.06	0.38	−0.02	−0.09	0.02
Utah	−0.11	0.14	−0.03	−0.16	0.29	−0.07	−0.07	0.03
Vermont	−0.06	0.18	0.00[e]	−0.23	0.29	0.02	−0.07	0.11
Virginia	−0.15	0.04	−0.06	−0.13	0.28	−0.04	−0.08	0.01
Washington	−0.10	[d]	−0.06	−0.12	0.39	−0.04	−0.07	0.00[e]
West Virginia	−0.14	0.26	−0.07	−0.13	0.42	−0.04	−0.07	−0.02
Wisconsin	−0.07	0.16	0.02	−0.17	0.27	−0.02	−0.03	0.09
Wyoming	−0.09	[d]	−0.11	−0.08	0.31	0.00[e]	−0.07	0.03
U.S. average	−0.11	0.17	−0.04	0.13	−0.31	−0.03	−0.07	0.05

[a]For a discussion of this index refer to the text or Suits (1977b).
[b]B = benchmark case.
[c]P = most progressive case.
[d]Tax not used in this state.
[e]Rounds to zero.

burden, it reflects the inequality more precisely than a simple elasticity measure.[1]

The real property tax (benchmark case) is also regressive in all fifty states. The most extreme inequality is found in Vermont (−0.23) with Pennsylvania and Maine next (at −0.20). The least inequality is in Texas and Alaska (−0.06) with North Dakota (−0.07) and Louisiana (−0.07) close behind. There is some difference in the ordering of states with this index as compared to the elasticity. Connecticut goes from most regressive using an elasticity to fourth most regressive. Vermont, which was second most regressive initially, now becomes most so. Least regressive using the elasticity was South Dakota; it is now in a group of several states with values of −0.10, far from the least regressive. Again, it must be emphasized that each measure portrays a different facet of the pattern of burdens and thus differences do emerge.

If we look now at all state taxes, the patterns are mixed between six progressive and forty-four regressive states but with several falling very close to zero. The most progressive tax structures are New York (+0.07) and Delaware (+0.06), which comes as little surprise given the results discussed earlier, while the most regressive are Florida (−0.13), Texas (−0.13), and Wyoming (−0.11), once again consistent with findings based on the elasticity measure. Many states manifest very small values on either side of 0.0, suggesting that they are very close to achieving equality in the distribution of tax payments by family units; for example, Massachusetts, Michigan, Ohio, and Pennsylvania all at −0.01, or Iowa and Wisconsin at +0.02.

Imported taxes are also quite equally distributed and fall in the range between +0.08 in Delaware and −0.10 in Mississippi. For most states, however, values are in the narrow range of ±0.05 with five that round to 0.00 (perfect equality).

Finally, we can examine the total state-local tax structure (benchmark). Every state but Delaware (+0.02) turns out to be negative, but the values are all closer to zero than −0.12. Many states are very close to having equality in the distribution of tax payments, falling in the narrow range −0.02 to −0.04, for example, Minnesota, New York, Oregon, and Wisconsin. The most inequality is seen in New Mexico (−0.10), Florida (−0.11), and New Hampshire (−0.12). All in all, however, the extent is not very marked. Figure 6-2 summarizes visually how each state compares.

The final item of information contained in Table 6-10 relates to the new view of the property tax. Although not reported earlier, elasticity

[1] Zero burden observations had to be excluded in the elasticity regressions for statistical reasons.

estimates under the most progressive incidence assumptions classified all states as being proportional. One problem with this measure is that it depicts an average relationship across fourteen income intervals and thus may lose some detail when effective rates are scattered and depict no clear-cut pattern. The elasticity is estimated as not being different from 0.0. An advantage to the Suits measure, in these instances, is that it is much better able to portray how a tax impacts by quantifying the relative extent of inequality in payments.

If we look at Suits values for the new view in Table 6-10, we perhaps get a clearer understanding of how this theoretical stance alters our notion of who is burdened. Index numbers are positive for every state and are distributed as follows:

Suits Index	*Number of States*
0.50 or over	1
0.40 - 0.49	7
0.30 - 0.39	18
0.20 - 0.29	19
0.10 - 0.19	5

Alabama at +0.58 has a distribution of real property tax payments that is distinctly progressive. Less so, but also very high, are Louisiana (0.48), Nevada (0.46), and Tennessee (0.44). The least progressive are South Dakota (0.10) and North Dakota (0.12).

This view of incidence tends to stand the conventional answer to who pays the property tax on its head. Since it is a tax on capital ownership, it is progressive in every state, although it winds up being far more progressive in most states than even the most progressive state income tax. In fact, it changes the property tax from the oft-characterized "regressive nightmare" to the fiscal savior of the low-income taxpayer. Suits's results for a variety of taxes suggest that none can hold a candle to the progressive impact of the property tax qua tax on capital ownership. Consider his findings for other taxes (Suits, 1977b: 750):

Federal individual income tax	+0.19
Federal corporate income tax	+0.32
Federal payroll taxes	−0.13
All federal taxes	−0.09

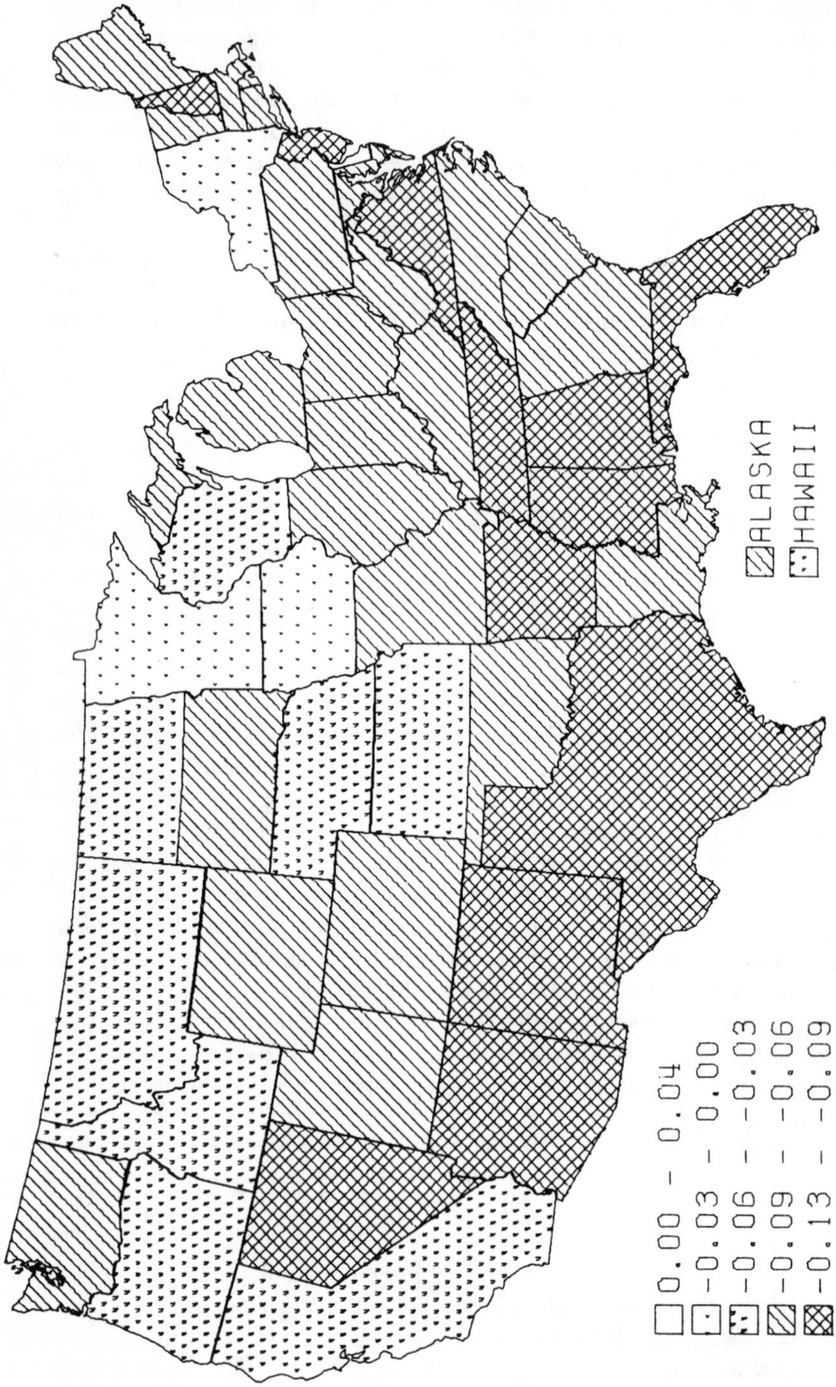

Figure 6.2. Tax progressivity: total staff and local taxes (based on Suits index).

Incorporating the new view into the total tax system gives the following Suits values for combined state-local payments:

Suits Index	*Number of States*
+0.15 - +0.20	3
+0.10 - +0.14	8
+0.01 - +0.09	27
0.00	4
−0.05 - −0.01	8

Massachusetts now has the most progressive tax structure with an index of +0.20 followed by New York and Oregon (+0.16). The most regressive state is Alabama at −0.05. All but twelve now have progressive tax systems and another four are proportional. In fact, of the eight states with a negative Suits value, all are closer to zero than −0.06. For all practical purposes, all state-local tax systems are, if not progressive, then nearly proportional. Although the findings discussed earlier, using the conventional view, did not uncover great regressivity for overall state-local tax systems using either the elasticity or the Suits approach—states were generally found to be mildly regressive—the new view of the property tax burden casts state-local finance in a completely different light.

TOWARD AN OVERALL INDEX OF STATE-LOCAL TAX BURDEN

Measurement of the burden of taxation is an elusive endeavor. As noted earlier, it must start with assumptions concerning shifting and incidence, spatial tax flows, secondary effects, and so forth, and then proceed to an empirical implementation based upon statistical series to allocate receipts by income class. Burden can then be defined as the ratio of tax payments to income. The problem, however, is that interpretation must now cope with as many series of data as there are income classes; this is even further confounded here by having data on each of fifty states.

Contained in the matrices of effective rates in Appendix A is complete information on the burden and equity features of each specific tax or system of taxes. The problem is to summarize or condense it to some manageable format. One solution to this dilemma is to construct an index that synthesizes the information contained in each (50 × 14) effective rate matrix into a single (50 × 1) vector. With a vector of "burden indices," one per state, comparison is greatly simplified. Thus far we have presented two measures that examine the equity aspects of a tax (elasticity and Suits measures). It would be extremely useful, however, if we had a measure that represented the level of burden *and* the equity profile. What we need is to be able to show in one measure the type of information contained in Table 1-1 on absolute level of burden and in Tables 6-6 or 6-10 on the pattern of burden. The major considerations are (1) the information loss inherent in condensing the original (50 × 14) matrix into a (50 × 1) vector and (2) the appropriate technique to perform such a synthesis. The two, needless to say, are closely related.

Before discussing one possible approach to the problem, it is useful to look back briefly on the methodology that has been employed in the past to indicate the burden of public sector activity. Basically, it entails relating taxes paid in an economy to some measure of economic well-being. At the national level, calculation has traditionally compared taxes with gross national product, taking into consideration the level of per capita income. Such analysis provides a crude indication of the aggregate impact of the public sector and is often used to make international or interregional comparisons (Lotz and Morss, 1967; Musgrave, 1969). However, distributional information is totally absent.

A similar method has been applied to states (e.g., refer to Donnahoe, 1947, or Frank, 1959). Once again, discussion revolves around aggregate or per capita taxes relative to taxpaying ability. Tax burden is "some function" that varies directly with tax load and inversely with taxpaying ability, which is some function of income. Although the analysis is slightly more refined than examination of a simple tax-to-income ratio, information on the pattern of burden remains minimal at best.

Examinations of current burden indices points out quite clearly the lack of inclusion of equity considerations in their construction. A major premise of this book is that burden has two distinct components – level and incidence – both of which, ideally, should be considered in its measurement. Empirical implementation of the model developed in Chapters 3 and 4 offers unique data on which to base such an index. Given the effective rate matrices, a technique must be selected to construct an index of burden that will reflect both dimensions.

A mathematical technique designed specifically to accomplish the summarization of large numbers of variables (data reduction) has been given the generic name "factor analysis".[m] The technique was origin-

[m] Factor analysis is capable of far more than data reduction but this is our only concern here (refer to Rummel, 1967: 448-451).

ally designed for the purpose of isolating a general intelligence factor from literally hundreds of variables relating to intelligence. Factor analysis is equally well suited to applications dealing with economic phenomena. It is being suggested here that it be applied as a data reduction tool in order to summarize burdens across the fourteen income classes into single index. This would permit subsequent analysis of the findings to account for both the level of burden and distributional characteristics.

The construction of such an index is given even more credibility in this case since all the data being synthetized relate explicitly to tax burdens. In other applications of factor analysis, interpretation of the index has been made much more complex because the data used did not measure directly the phenomenon to be examined; various proxy variables that indirectly reflected the phenomena have often been employed, as with the use of dozens of measures in attempting to quantify intelligence.

The mechanics of factor analysis can become extremely complex, and many nuances on the basic factor model have been introduced to deal with particular analytical problems. No attempt will be made to present the mathematics here because it would unnecessarily consume a great deal of space and confuse the issue (see Harman, 1960, or Rummel, 1970, for details). Rather, justification for its use in this instance will be given priority.

Application of factor analysis to data reduction relies upon its capacity to synthesize a set of variables into a factor (an index) with minimal loss in information content.[n] The factor is then identified as representing some common dimension of the information in the original input data. In effect, factor analysis is a technique to construct a new variable called a factor in such a way that it accounts for a maximum amount of the total variance that was present in the original variables. In other words, it summarizes or reduces the input data to a common dimension, in this case the burden of a tax (or system of taxes).

Factor analysis was applied to data on total effective rates and factor scores (indices of burden in this case) were computed. The scores are standardized to zero mean and unit variance for ease of comparison and, accordingly, can be interpreted as *Z*-scores or the relative deviation of items in a distribution from the mean of the distribution.[o]

Figure 6-3 depicts visually relative burden for combined state and local taxes (Alaska and Hawaii are shown at the bottom). Remember-

[n] Although several factors may be extracted, the first is the focus of our concern here.

[o] Negative values represent below average burden, positive scores an above average burden.

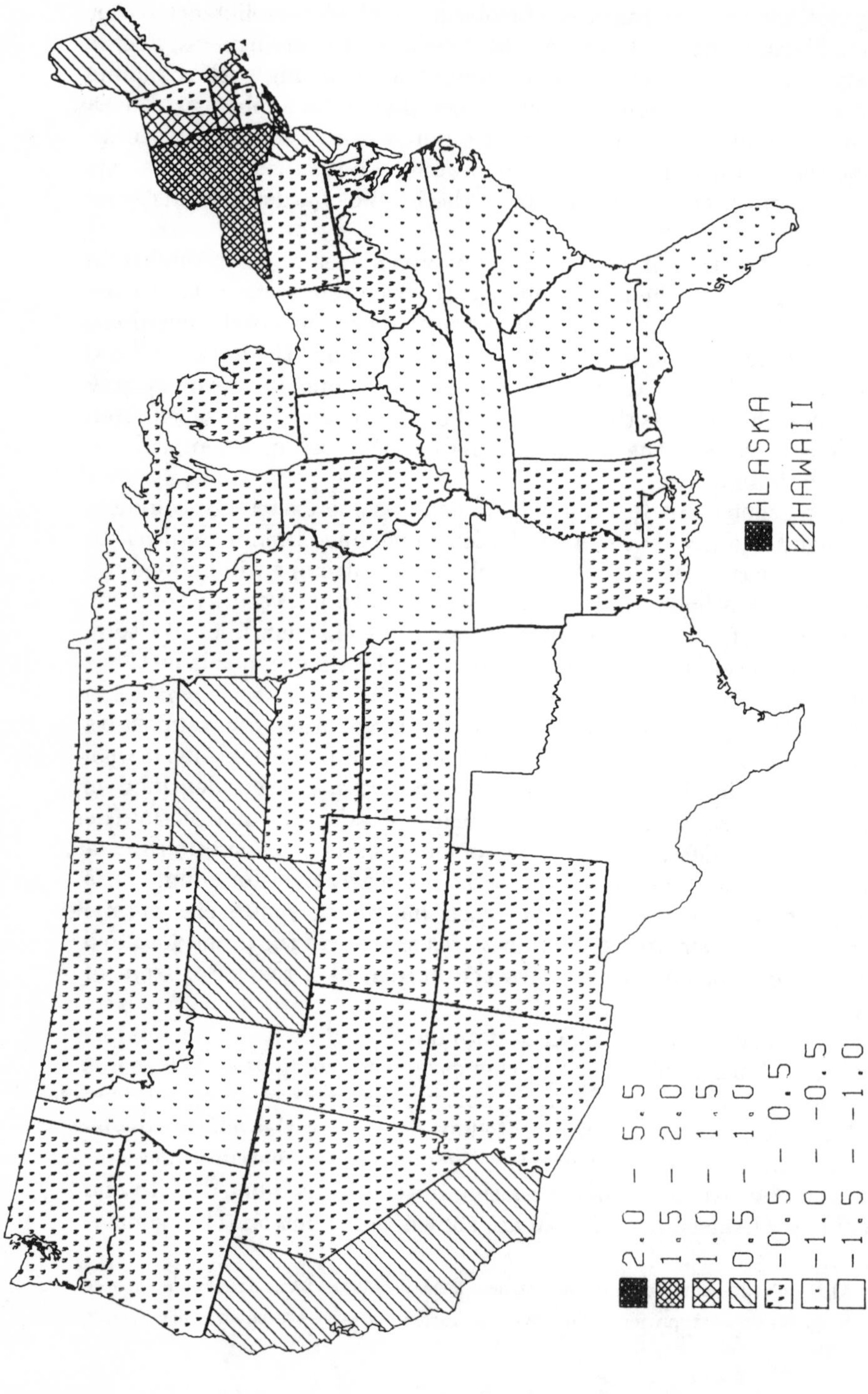

Figure 6.3. Relative tax burden: total state and local taxes.

ing that the score represents a combination of level as well as equity, we can easily pick out high-burden cases. Alaska tops the list with an index of 5.07.[p] The only other state even close to this is New York, a distant second at 1.96. High burdens are also found in Massachusetts, Vermont, California, and Maine. Low burdens are found in Delaware, Texas, and Oklahoma.

The advantage to this measure is that it contains almost all of the information that was in the original input data on total state-local tax burdens. The single factor score on which Figure 6-3 is based accounts for nearly 90 percent of all the variation that was present in the original effective rates for the fourteen income classes. This technique has been applied in the past to data on burdens for 1962 by Phares (1973: 69-76). He computed factors (indices) for several types of burden that accounted for between 78 and 84 percent of all the variation that was contained in the original input data.

Factor analysis indices of burden are presented in Table 6-11 for three major individual taxes, the state and local sectors, and total state-local taxes. These values depict variation around an average value of zero with high positive scores representing high burden and high negative scores low burden.[q]

For general sales taxation, high-burden cases are Hawaii (2.52), Washington (2.01), and West Virginia (2.02). Each of these states tops the list in terms of relative reliance on this tax (37 percent of total revenue) and is more than slightly regressive. This combination leads to a high index for overall burden. Vermont, at the other extreme, only raises 7.9 percent of its revenue with this tax and is slightly regressive; its burden index is a well below average, −0.98. Perusal of the effective rates in Table A-1 and the equity profiles in Table 6-1 helps set this in perspective for individual states.

In terms of the taxation of individual income, the most burdensome states are Massachusetts (2.22), Delaware (1.45), Oregon (2.16), and Wisconsin (1.73). These are all high income tax states with a progressive burden. Low income tax burdens are found in Connecticut (−1.37), New Jersey (−1.33), Tennessee (−1.37), and New Hampshire (−1.21). Each of these states brings in 2 percent or less of all revenue with this source. As Table A-36 shows clearly, the burden in these states is indeed very low and tends to be proportional or, in one case, regressive.

Burden for the local real property tax is highest in Massachusetts (2.32), New Jersey (2.47), and New York (2.10). Each of these states has

[p] This can be interpreted as Alaska being over five standard deviations above the mean.

[q] Actually, they can be interpreted in the same way as a standard deviation.

Table 6-11. Factor Analysis Index[a] of Tax Burden for Selected State-Local Taxes

State	General Sales	Individual Income	Real Property	Total State	Total Local	Total State and Local
Alabama	0.02	−0.25	−1.81	−0.08	−1.42	−1.13
Alaska	[b]	1.49	−0.55	5.67	−0.30	5.07
Arizona	0.91	−0.31	0.14	0.27	0.19	0.40
Arkansas	0.19	−0.17	−1.22	0.00[c]	−1.45	−1.03
California	0.23	−0.41	1.25	−0.34	1.51	0.76
Colorado	−0.27	0.06	0.36	−0.71	0.68	−0.19
Connecticut	0.22	−1.37	0.94	−0.58	0.79	0.18
Delaware	[b]	1.45	−0.83	−0.28	−1.41	−1.19
Florida	0.19	[b]	−0.45	−0.45	−0.58	−0.78
Georgia	0.25	−0.31	−0.49	−0.34	−0.30	−0.57
Hawaii	2.52	1.15	−0.27	1.30	−0.65	0.78
Idaho	−0.17	0.60	−0.16	−0.12	−0.57	−0.58
Illinois	0.04	0.51	0.31	−0.31	0.45	0.01
Indiana	0.58	0.31	−0.27	−0.38	−0.39	−0.69
Iowa	−0.07	0.47	0.92	−0.19	0.32	0.00[c]
Kansas	0.07	0.06	−0.25	−0.41	0.17	−0.31
Kentucky	0.11	0.19	−1.21	0.21	−1.20	−0.65
Louisiana	0.00[c]	−1.00	−1.44	0.12	−0.65	−0.42
Maine	0.39	−0.57	−0.27	1.28	−0.80	0.66
Maryland	−0.58	1.46	0.09	−0.15	0.33	0.05
Massachusetts	−1.10	2.22	2.32	−0.18	1.71	1.11
Michigan	−0.31	0.29	0.71	−0.42	0.54	−0.03
Minnesota	−0.29	0.74	0.78	0.44	0.06	0.46
Mississippi	1.72	−0.68	−1.10	0.64	−1.26	−0.31
Missouri	−0.16	−0.33	−0.43	−0.79	0.11	−0.68
Montana	[b]	1.01	0.16	−0.45	1.14	0.33
Nebraska	−0.23	−0.60	0.54	−0.72	1.04	−0.01

Table 6-11 *(continued)*

Nevada	−0.18	[b]	−0.24	−0.51	0.28	−0.30
New Hampshire	[b]	−1.21	1.77	−1.36	1.00	−0.41
New Jersey	−0.48	−1.33	2.47	−1.05	2.17	0.80
New Mexico	1.76	−0.75	−1.14	0.96	−1.60	−0.23
New York	−0.39	0.85	2.10	−0.13	2.92	1.96
North Carolina	−0.41	0.78	−1.12	−0.03	−1.06	−0.77
North Dakota	1.00	−0.25	0.61	0.40	−0.09	0.28
Ohio	−0.53	−0.76	0.12	−0.83	0.10	−0.74
Oklahoma	−0.78	−0.45	−1.07	−0.43	−0.97	−1.13
Oregon	[b]	2.16	0.89	−0.91	0.70	−0.37
Pennsylvania	−0.19	0.22	−0.18	0.00[c]	−0.06	0.00[c]
Rhode Island	−0.20	0.28	0.45	−0.16	0.34	0.13
South Carolina	0.54	0.11	−0.91	0.17	−1.26	−0.72
South Dakota	0.59	[b]	1.04	−0.33	1.43	0.63
Tennessee	0.35	−1.37	−0.75	−0.46	−0.60	−0.92
Texas	−0.07	[b]	−0.52	−0.64	−0.50	−1.00
Utah	0.73	0.61	−0.42	−0.03	−0.36	−0.31
Vermont	−0.98	0.86	1.26	0.36	0.81	1.01
Virginia	−0.73	0.48	−0.62	−0.55	−0.22	−0.69
Washington	2.01	[b]	−0.83	0.77	−0.75	0.19
West Virginia	2.02	0.34	−1.45	0.98	−1.24	0.03
Wisconsin	−0.04	1.73	0.39	0.43	0.06	0.45
Wyoming	1.16	[b]	0.41	0.39	0.86	0.92
Percent of variance accounted for by factor	97.3	71.0	95.0	91.1	92.8	89.4

[a]Refer to the text for a discussion of this index.
[b]Tax not used in this state.
[c]Rounds to zero.

a noted heavy dependence on property taxation leading to high effective rates (see Table A-83) and, in addition, a regressive equity pattern. The combination generates a high index. Connecticut (0.94) and Vermont (1.26), although not as pronounced, also are well above average. At the low-burden end of the spectrum is Alabama (−1.81), which only raises 10.7 percent of all revenue through its moderately regressive real property taxes, with Arkansas (−1.22) and West Virginia (−1.45) following closely. Low effective rates combined with moderate regressivity account for the situation in these states.

Burden by governmental sector is also shown in Table 6-11. For state taxes, Alaska at 5.67 far exceeds second-place Hawaii (1.30). In these cases, the state government takes in a dominant share of revenue. In New Hampshire (−1.36), New Jersey (−1.05), or Oregon (−0.91), on the other hand, burden and regressivity for the state sector are much less pronounced. The most burdensome local sectors are in New York (2.92), New Jersey (2.17), and Massachusetts (1.71). These are states with a strong local sector that imposes a high and regressive claim (see Table A-87). The end result is an above average index. Although less severe, California (1.51) and New Hampshire (1.00) are in a similar situation. Low burdens, as might be anticipated, are found in states such as New Mexico (−1.60) or Alabama (−1.42) where the claim made by local government operations is much lower and less regressive.

Putting all taxes together, we have the total burden for the state-local tax structure. The dominant state by far is Alaska (5.07). The claim this state exerts on its residents is extremely high (refer to Table A-91) and quite regressive. Others with a high total burden are New York (1.96), Vermont (1.01), and Massachusetts (1.11). Below average burdens are found in Delaware (−1.19), Oklahoma (−1.13), and Texas (−1.00). Figure 6-3 provides a visual impression of how the fifty state-local systems compare in terms of the overall claim on their residents.

It has been suggested here that adopting a factor analysis approach to quantifying burdens using effective rate data as an input gives an accurate representation of both the level of burden as well as the way in which it differentially affects income classes. States with a very high claim (Alaska or New York) clearly stand out as do the low-burden states (Delaware or Alabama). Their position is influenced by the equity effects of the tax as well as the magnitude of the burden since information on all fourteen income classes is used in constructing the index. Thus, it is more than a simple tax-to-income measure, as shown in Table 1-1, in that it contains information on the pattern of effective tax rates. As such, it better manifests the true claim on private income, a claim that can affect persons at different income levels very differently. It gives us a more complete single-valued picture of a state's overall burden, whereas the elasticity and Suits measures indicate only the equity pattern and the basic effective rates leave us with fourteen numbers to interpret.

Chapter 7

Taxpayer Equity and Policy: Conclusions, Implications, and Future Research

The primary objective of this book has been to provide detailed data on differences among the fifty states in the claim they exert on their taxpayers for the support of public activities, with particular attention to the burden imposed on families at various income levels. Substantial effort has gone into the conceptual and empirical methodology necessary to do this, as spelled out in Chapters 1 to 4. A complete set of findings is contained in Appendix A for ninety-three tax categories under a variety of views of tax incidence. These data have been summarized in Chapters 5 and 6. In closing, three areas need to be explored. First, what are the trends over the recent two decades in state-local finance that have a bearing on the issue of taxpayer equity? These trends are summarized along with specific policy moves to promote equity and their influence indicated. Second, what are the implications or uses of the findings of this work for public policy? No attempt is made to make this discussion elaborate or lengthy because it is anticipated that a major application of the findings presented here will be to specific issues within a state or region, or concerning a particular tax. Rather, several broad areas of policy relevance for the results contained herein are noted. Finally, we must discuss where to go from here. To this end, an agenda for future research activities is outlined.

TAX POLICY AND EQUITY: RECENT DEVELOPMENTS IN THE "BIG THREE"

Change in the provisions of state and local tax policy over the recent two decades is best characterized as a continuous process of relatively minor alterations to an existing structure. Commerce Clearing House's, *State Tax Reporter* or the Advisory Commission's, *Significant Features* volumes attest to this. Rates have been increased, deductions and exemptions modified, tax bases redefined, and special provisions developed to cope with concerns that have become politically or socially sensitive. Documentation of all such nuances would serve no purpose and would only leave the reader lost in a mire of seemingly unconnected pieces of information. A more fruitful tactic is to discuss major trends in state-local finance and specific attempts to deal with inequities. Attention is focused, accordingly, on the major revisions that have taken place in policy. Since property, individual income, and general sales and gross receipts taxes comprise the bulk of collections, discussion is limited to these "big three" of state-local finance.

Property Taxation

Property taxation has been a main financial support for government in the United States since its founding. It has evolved from a revenue source to support the federal and then state governments to one that is currently uniquely local. Any discussion of property taxes is a discussion of local finance and all the problems this brings to mind.

Chapters 5 and 6 have documented the strong and regressive influence of this tax in every state. Changes in dependence on it, therefore, are critical determinants of equity within any state-local system; the greater the dependence, generally, the more inequitable the state's entire tax system. One simple approach to delineating the impact of the property tax is to examine relative reliance on this revenue source and the special provisions that have been implemented to deal with its inequities.

Examination of data for 1962 and 1975-1976 uncovers a marked decline in this tax as a proportion of all receipts. Table 7-1 provides a summary distribution of states according to relative *changes* in property taxes as a source of revenue, showing the increase or decrease in dependence. Out of fifty states, all have changed; only one state has increased its importance (a mild 2.6 points in Hawaii) while forty-nine have decreased it. Five states showed a decline of 20 points or more, nineteen fell 10 to 19 points, and twenty-five dropped by 9 points or

Table 7.1. State and Local Taxes as a Percentage of Total Tax Revenue: Changes 1962 to 1975-1976

	Number of States		
Change in Percentage Points[a]	*Property*	*Income*	*General Sales*[b]
Minus 20 and over	5	–	–
Minus 10-19	19	–	–
Minus 0-9	25	1	6
Plus 0-4	1	11	11
Plus 5-9	–	18	14
Plus 10-14	–	12	11
Plus 15-20	–	2	4
New tax	–	7	6
No tax	–	6	4

[a] This is not the percentage change but the number of percentage points that the tax increased or decreased in terms of relative importance.
[b] Alaska is all local.

less. The trend is clearly defined. Property taxation remains the major revenue source for local government, but it is far less important today that it was in 1962. On an average, it has fallen from 46 to 36 percent of all state-local collections. This must, however, be kept in the context of a growth in yield from $19 to $57 billion; it is now a smaller portion but of a much larger pie.

Nationwide, property taxes as a proportion of state-local revenue has declined 10 points over the period 1962 to 1975-1976, that is, 22 percent in relative dependence. To the extent that growth in funds has been maintained by a state tax on individual income, the impact on overall equity has been beneficial. Most of the states that showed the largest fall in the role of the property tax are states that have adopted a state personal income tax (e.g., Illinois, Indiana, Nebraska, and Maine). Many of the remaining states simply altered their existing provisions to increase its role in supporting public operations. The net effect of this shift from property taxation to personal income taxation is lessened regressivity for the overall tax structure. A great deal of the shift from the local property base to the state income or general sales base has occurred in the context of school finance reform. States have picked up a larger share of the cost of local education, obviating the need for adding this burden onto local shoulders (refer to Garms, Guthrie, and Pierce, 1978, or Reischauer and Hartman, 1973).

An important recent development in property tax policy has evolved out of a concern over the financial strain it exerts on low-income households. Prior to 1963, there were virtually no instances of state-financed residential relief for low-income households, that is, a "circuit breaker." At this writing, there are thirty states that have adopted such a plan. Table 7-2 summarizes the main features of these schemes in each state. Several points stand out. First, nearly all of this legislation has been enacted in the 1970s and there have been numerous revisions during this decade on the original laws. Second, the majority of states provide relief to both homeowners (29) and renters (24) but most of them (22) have attached age as a condition of qualification. Third, out of thirty states, twenty-six have an income ceiling; this varies from a low of $3,000 to $5,000 in Arizona to a peak of $20,000 (for renters) in Hawaii. Only four states (Maryland, Michigan, Minnesota, and Vermont) have no ceiling. By far the most liberal states are Minnesota and Michigan with neither an age nor an income criterion for receiving benefit; the cost is, accordingly, much greater than elsewhere. Program cost ranges from miniscule amounts in a few states to about $300 million in Michigan. Nationwide, nearly $1 billion is now being put into property tax relief. This is a quantum leap from two decades ago when virtually none was available. The 1970s was clearly the decade of the circuit breaker.

The net effect of circuit breaker allowances is to lower the property tax burden on those with the least capacity to bear such a burden. It seems unfortunate that limitations in twenty-two of thirty states are couched in terms of age, since age clearly does not have an exclusive claim on poverty. The obvious reason is the cost of financing if such a criterion was eliminated. It is necessary to look only at Michigan or Minnesota to see how costly full-fledged circuit breakers can become. A framework is in place, however, for extending low-income relief to other classes of poor, if and when state government decides to assume the fiscal consequences. The added cost of any new programs will undoubtedly be placed on the income and general sales base in most instances.

As one feature of its quality state-local fiscal system, the Advisory Commission on Intergovernmental Relations has emphasized that the regressive sting of the local property tax should be mitigated by provisions such as the circuit breaker. Although it is now a reality in thirty states, twenty remain that have thus far adopted no such provision. In addition, most states see fit to define poverty in the narrow sense of an elderly homeowner or renter. It seems desirable that the past trend be maintained in the future to include additional states and a broader spectrum of the poor.[a] If this becomes fact, the regressive sting of the local property tax is likely to be softened even further.

[a] Some argue against an expanded use of circuit breakers except as an interim measure, see Aaron (1975: 71-79).

Individual Income Tax

In 1962, thirty-seven states levied a personal income tax; in Pennsylvania it was entirely local. By 1975-1976, this number had risen to forty-four, all of which included a state component. There remain six states that do not as yet tax personal income: Florida, Nevada, South Dakota, Texas, Washington, and Wyoming. During the period 1962 to 1975-1976 reliance on this tax increased in forty-three states and fell in only one. Table 7-1 shows the distribution of these changes. Most (18) lie in the range of an increase of 5-9 points, eleven rose by 4 points, twelve by 10-14 points, and two by 15-20 points. The maximum is almost 19 points in Michigan, which adopted a personal income tax in 1967. The one state showing a decline is Alaska at 3.1 points. Broader use of this tax is evident as indicated by the U.S. average reliance more than doubling from 7.3 to 15.6 percent of revenue. During this period yield expanded over eightfold from $3 to $24 billion. Such a shift implies a less regressive overall impact on residents of states that have either recently adopted the tax or have altered its existing rates, deductions, or exemption provisions toward greater progressivity.

A detailed examination of main features of the income tax gives more insight into the gross shifts indicated above. Table 7-2 summarizes changes in the exemption, standard deduction, and rate provisions since 1962. Eight states have increased the percentage deduction and ten have adopted the federal base. Only one has decreased any of its deduction provisions; California removed its percentage deduction while increasing the maximum allowance. The remaining fifteen states did not change. Maximum deductions (married) were increased in ten states while ten opted for use of the federal base; the rest did not change. The tendency toward increasing the allowance for standard deductions (percentage and maximum amount) helps to increase (albeit mildly) the progressive influence of the personal income tax. Wider use of federal definitions tends to work in the same direction.

Another important feature of this tax is the personal exemption allowance. Between 1962 and 1975-1976, seven states increased their personal exemption (married joint) and fifteen the dependency exemption (see Table 7-2). One the other side, five states decreased the personal exemption and one the allowance for dependents. Three states adopted the federal base for both. Thus, there is a clear tendency toward raising the exemption allowance. The net effect of larger exemptions is also to increase progressivity.

A final and important aspect of the personal income tax is its rate structure. Most states, but not all, have an explicit system of marginal rates applied to ranges of income. Nominal rates vary from flat propor-

Table 7-2. Promoting Taxpayer Equity: Changes in Major Provisions[a] of the "Big-Three" State-Local Taxes

	General Sales Tax Food Exemption		Property Tax Circuit Breaker Provisions				State Individual Income Tax					
								Change in Exemptions[e]		Change in Standard Deduction[e]		
State	1962	1975-1976	Year Enacted (number of revisions)	Beneficiaries[b]	Income Ceiling	Cost[c] ($'000)	Credits[d]	Personal	Dependent	Percentage	Maximum	Change in Rates[f]
Alabama								0	0	+	+	0
Alaska	—— all local ——							F	F	F	F	+
Arizona			1973 (1)	H R A	$3,750-5,500	$ 7,762	P	0	0	0	0	+M
Arkansas			1973 (1)	H A	8,000	676	P	0	0	0	0	+M
California	X	X	1967 (3)	H R A	20,000	95,000	P	+	–	Out	+	+S
Colorado			1971 (5)	H R A	7,300-8,300	11,003	P S	0	0	0	0	+VM
Connecticut	X	X	1973 (1)	H R A	6,000	24,754				New tax (1969)		
Delaware	g	g						0	0	0	0	+S
Florida	X	X					g	g	g	g	g	g
Georgia								0	+	F	F	0
Hawaii			1977	R	20,000	4,200	S	+	+	0	0	+M
Idaho			1974 (2)	H A	7,500	4,000	S	+	+	F	F	+M
Illinois			1972 (3)	H R A	10,000	100,000				New tax (1969)		
Indiana		X	1973 (1)	H R A	5,000	844	P			New tax (1963)		
Iowa		X	1973 (1)	H R A	9,000	9,600		0	0	+	+	+VS
Kansas			1970 (3)	H R A	8,150	8,824		0	0	F	F	+VM
Kentucky		X						0	+	0	+	0
Louisiana		X						0	0	F	F	0
Maine	X	X	1971 (3)	H R A	5,000-6,000	4,347				New tax (1969)		
Maryland	X	X	1975 (1)	H	None	20,808		0	0	0	0	+S
Massachusetts		X					S	0	+	0	0	+VM
Michigan		X	1973 (1)	H R	None	275,582	P			New tax (1967)		
Minnesota		X	1967 (5)	H R	None	134,200	P	0	0	0	0	+VS
Mississippi								–	+	+	+	–S
Missouri			1973 (2)	H R A	7,500	7,008	P	0	0	F	F	+M
Montana	g	g						+	+	0	0	+VS
Nebraska							S			New tax (1967)		
Nevada			1973 (2)	H R A	11,000	1,350	g	g	g	g	g	g
New Hampshire	g	g						0	0	0	0	0
New Jersey		X								New tax (1976)		
New Mexico			1977	H R A	16,000	1,500	A	–	+	F	F	+VS
New York		X	1978	H R	12,000	n.a.[h]		+	+	+	+	+VS
North Carolina								0	+	0	0	0

Table 7-2 (continued)

North Dakota		X	1969 (3)	H	R	A	8,000	1,198				+	+	F	F	−S
Ohio	X	X	1971 (3)	H		A	10,000	44,614				New tax (1971, all local in 1962)				
Oklahoma			1974	H		A	6,000	357	P			−	+	+	+	0
Oregon	g	g	1971 (2)	H	R		15,999	74,140	P			+	+	+	+	−VM
Pennsylvania	X	X	1971 (1)	H	R	A	7,500	58,918				New tax (1971, all local in 1962)				
Rhode Island	X	X	1977	H	R	A	5,000	n.a.[h]				New tax (1971)				
South Carolina												0	0	0	0	0
South Dakota			1976 (1)	H		A	4,625-7,375	1,487	g			g	g	g	g	g
Tennessee												0	0	0	0	0
Texas	X	X							g			g	g	g	g	g
Utah			1977	H	R	A	7,000	950				F	F	F	F	+S
Vermont		X	1969 (2)	H	R		None	7,670	P	S		F	F	F	F	+VS
Virginia												−	+	+	+	+M
Washington									g			g	g	g	g	g
West Virginia			1972	H	R	A	5,000	18				0	0	0	0	+VS
Wisconsin		X	1964 (3)	H	R		9,300	48,139	P			−	+	+	+	+M
Wyoming									g			g	g	g	g	g
Total	9	21	30	29	24	22	26	$949,561	12	6	1					

Source: Advisory Commission (1961, 1964, 1977a).
[a]Provisions are as close to years indicated as data allow.
[b]H = homeowners, R = renters, A = aged.
[c]For the most recent year available (1976 to 1979).
[d]P = property taxes, S = sales taxes, A = all state-local taxes.
[e]Between 1962 and 1975-1976 (married joint); + = increase, − = decrease, 0 = no change, F = uses federal base.
[f]Between 1962 and 1975-1976; these are qualitative judgments; + = increase, 0 = no change, − = decrease, V = very, M = mild, S = significant.
[g]No tax in effect.
[h]n.a. = not available.

tionality in Indiana, Illinois, Massachusetts, or Pennsylvania to marked rate progressivity in Alaska or Delaware.[b] Three states tax only a narrow base of interest, dividends, or capital gains, while three others set their bill at a percentage of the federal liability. This is, de facto, a scaled-down system of federal marginal rates.

During the period 1962 to 1975-1976, twenty-two states revised their system of marginal rates nominally in the direction of increased progression (two opted for less progressive rates). This resulted from either an increase in the rates on higher-income classes or greater subdivision of income into more classes with an adjustment of rates to produce a nominal increase in progression. The last column in Table 7-2 attempts to judge, *qualitatively*, the nature of the changes. Major revisions are found, for example, in Iowa, Montana, and New York.

No matter the perspective from which this tax is viewed, it becomes obvious that the individual income tax is assuming a more and more dominant status in state-local finance. It has grown from 7 to almost 16 percent of all collections and nine additional states have adopted it between 1962 and 1975-1976. Of states with such a tax already in effect in 1962, the trend has been in the direction of altering rates, exemptions, and deductions toward producing a greater share of revenue for the system and at the same time increasing its progressive influence.

The Advisory Commission on Intergovernmental Relations in defining a high-quality state-local fiscal system notes that "the personal income tax should stand out as the single most important revenue instrument in the State capable of producing close to 25 percent of total State-local tax revenue" (1972:5).

Although this is not yet a reality everywhere, there are four states that meet such a standard – Delaware, Minnesota, Oregon, and Wisconsin – and three others that come very close – Hawaii, Maryland, and Massachusetts. If we include the local income tax as well, Maryland and New York must be added to this list. Continued movement toward greater reliance on the personal income tax will help to "tone up the equity features of the system and insure an overall State-local system [revenue] elasticity of between 1 and 1.2" (Advisory Commission, 1972:5). Both seem desirable goals for which policy should strive.

General Sales and Gross Receipts Taxes

The third major tax for the state-local sector is that levied on general sales and gross receipts. For 1962 there were forty-one states that had

[b] Nominal rate progressivity is not the same as progressivity in effective rates.

such a tax; in four states the levy was entirely local. By 1975-1976, this had expanded to forty-six, and only Alaska remained entirely local. At present, Delaware, Montana, New Hampshire, and Oregon have not yet adopted a general sales tax either at the state or local level.

Examination of changes since 1962 helps to define the expanded reliance on this tax. Table 7-1 shows these changes. Five states had a small relative decrease of 0.3 to 2.7 points, while one (Michigan) fell 8.6 points. The remaining forty increased their usage. Eleven went up from 0-4 points, fourteen between 5-9, eleven between 10-14, and four by over 15 points. The maximum increase was 18 points in Idaho and Nebraska, both of which adopted the tax during this period. Six new states turned to this revenue source over this period. Between 1962 and 1975-1976, the nationwide average rose from 14.6 to 20.4 percent of total collections, while yield rose from $6 to $32 billion.

The general sales tax has increasingly become one of the most important sources of tax dollars for the state-local sector and has been subject to numerous rate increases since 1962. During the period 1962 to 1975-1976, rates rose in all but three states. In several, the increases were 3 percentage points or more, attaining a maximum rate of 7 percent in Connecticut. Currently, the model rate is 4 percent (in eighteen states) up from 3 percent (in seventeen states) in 1962. This constant revision of rates accounts for much of the increase in yield over the past two decades. In Virginia, for example, this source went from 0.1 percent of taxes in 1962 (a small local levy in Bristol) to 17 percent in 1975-1976, most of which is due to adoption of the tax by the state in 1966. In addition, six new states enacted a sales tax during this period. This accounts for the two largest increases of 18 points in Idaho and Nebraska. The trend clearly has been in favor of more intensive and extensive use of the sales base.

Change at the local level has been almost as widespread. As of 1962, local sales taxation was permitted in twelve states; the number currently stands at twenty-six. One state, Mississippi, stopped the local component but the rest have, generally speaking, allowed increased local use. The trend here is also clearly defined. Within the legal limitations established by respective state governments, local jurisdictions have expanded their reliance on the local general sales tax. Although the modal rate has remained at 1 percent, the number of states permitting a local levy has more than doubled. As a result, the number of local governments (of all types) relying on this tax has risen from just less than 1,900 in 1962 to nearly 5,000 as of 1976.

As has been documented empirically in Chapter 5, the general sales tax tends to be regressive in incidence. To soften some of its regressivity, many states have enacted corrective legislation. These provisions are indicated in Table 7-2. In 1962 only nine states exempted food. As of 1976, twenty-one had removed food from the base. Based on existing research, exemption of food does serve to soften the regressivity of the general sales tax. Exemption of other items such as clothing or medicine, however, does not have the same beneficial impact of the food exemption (see Schaefer, 1969b).

In addition to exemption provisions, six states have adopted a personal income tax rebate to soften the impact of the general sales tax – all since 1962. While the form and amount allowed varies, Colorado, Hawaii, Idaho, Indiana, Massachusetts, Nebraska, and Vermont all give rebates tied to the state personal income tax. One state, New Mexico, gives a credit for all state and local tax payments. Thus, in addition to the states with a specific food exemption, several have chosen to enact a personal income tax credit to offset the inequity of the general sales tax (see Billings, 1972, or Boyle, 1974).

All in all, there is a definite trend toward more widespread use of a general sales tax, expanded local use of this tax, and an increased reliance on the tax. Simultaneously, there is clear movement in the design of policy to lessen some of its regressivity. Currently, twenty-six states either exempt food or allow a personal income tax rebate. Expanded use of this source has been tempered by policy designed to deal with its impact on low-income taxpayers.

Summary

The "big-three" of state-local finance – property, income, and general sales taxation – accounted for 72.4 percent of all revenue in 1975-1976, up from 67.8 percent in 1962. Over this period there have been two clear patterns emerging in their use:

Decreased reliance on local property taxation compensated for by an expanded use of the income and general sales base

Widespread enactment of policies to offset the regressive burden of the property and general sales taxes and to increase the progressivity of the personal income tax

Both of these trends clearly operate to further the cause of taxpayer equity, although the impact can differ quite dramatically state by state.

DATA ON STATE-LOCAL TAX BURDENS: USES AND IMPLICATIONS

After a brief recapitulation of general findings, this section discusses some of the areas of policy to which the results in this book might be applied. No attempt will be made to wring out all nuances of these data but, rather, to suggest where they would be useful in helping formulate, implement, and refine policy decision making.

Recapitulation

One of the glaring deficiences in the literature on state-local tax burdens is that it focuses on entire sectors or single states. Lost in this process is the variation across the states in the claim they exert on residents for the support of public operations. As a result, we have little knowledge about how this sector affects people at different income levels within a state. The findings of Chapters 5 and 6 have helped to fill this vacuum by quantifying the burden imposed by each state and local tax at fourteen points along the income spectrum for each state. Several items need to be noted by way of a brief summary.

First, to compute burden accurately attention must be given to disaggregating collection data into a detailed format that allows separate theoretical and empirical treatment of each tax and identification of each governmental sector. This allows the final results to manifest the differentials that actually exist in burden. Chapter 3 has outlined a methodology to accomplish this.

Second, computing an effective rate that portrays *actual* burden entials far more than a simple tax-to-income ratio. The denominator must contain a measure of income that is more inclusive than the narrow measures that are often employed. Chapter 4 discussed the development of such an income base from data sources recently made available. The numerator of an effective rate must contain all taxes that come to rest as a burden on taxpayers in a state. To measure this accurately, it is necessary to account for the geographical flow of taxes into and out of the fifty states and between the state-local and federal sectors. Through this process billions of dollars are rearranged from point of legal impact to ultimate "spatial resting place."

Third, for the study year, this spatial rearrangement of taxes involved almost $27 billion, or 17.2 percent of all state-local collections. These flows were of three main types:

1. Exported taxes – taxes exported from a state due to the price/migration effect.
2. Federal offset – taxes exported to the federal revenue structure due to IRS provisions.
3. Imported taxes – taxes in category 1 as they are imported back into other states

This process of exporting and importing benefited residents of every state to the extent that part of the cost was passed on to the federal government to be then apportioned according to the features of the federal revenue system. In total, this phemonenom amounted to a $13.5 billion decrease in the burden attributable to *state-local* taxation. The states that gained the most here are states that make heavy use of the income and general sales base. The movement of taxes due to the price/migration effect, on the other hand, benefited certain states at the expense of others. States like Nevada, Delaware, Texas, or Louisiana are in a position to export a larger part of their burden out of state because of the special circumstances they confront (see Table 4-5, last column). Thus, there are clear winners and losers "relatively," owing to the geographical movement of taxes. Only one state winds up a loser in absolute terms, however, which is South Dakota by $2.4 million. Interstate tax flows were found to be an extremely important determinant of the actual burden imposed on residents of a state.

Fourth, as mentioned above, one component to exporting is the federal offset. This resulted from the deduction of $43.9 billion in state and local tax payments on federal form 1040 Schedule A in the study year. When weighted by appropriate marginal rates, these deductions lowered the federal liability by $13.5 billion. This is, de facto, a subsidy to the state-local sector by the federal government through IRS provisions, and it was treated as a reduction in burden for each tax that was deducted. The impact of these deductions, however, is far from equally distributed. As Table 4-6 documents for all federal offsets, they are distinctly progressive in incidence, that is, "pro-rich." The outcome of the federal offset, therefore, was to make the state-local system *more regressive* than it would have been in its absence. How much more depends on the income distribution in a state and to what extent it employs deductible taxes. IRS itemization provisions serve to provide larger rewards to residents of states that use income and sales taxation more heavily.

Fifth, as Chapter 5 documents in considerable detail, there are marked differences across the states and across taxes in the burden they impose. Owing to variations in income distribution, spending patterns, taxes used and their importance, and spatial tax flows, effective tax rates differ, often radically, among states. Probably the best example is the state individual income tax (see Tables 5-3 and A-26). Marked policy differences in deductions, exemptions, credits, and marginal rate structures result in vastly different patterns of burden. These, in turn, influence the overall burden for the entire tax structure, depending upon their relative strength. If one thing characterizes the burden of state-local taxation it is that it differs substantially across states.

Sixth, just as the level of burden varies so does its equity pattern. Chapter 6 documents by how much states differ on a continuum of regressivity or progressivity. The only progressive influence in the entire system derives from the state individual income tax. Here we have a range between distinct progressivity in California and marked regressivity in New Hampshire. Property and general sales taxation are regressive in every state but much more so in some than in others. It is the balancing of the big-three revenue producers that determines what the final burden will look like in any particular state. A very progressive income tax raising a large share of collections will have a much different impact from a small (or no) income tax and a very regressive property tax; it is the difference, for example, between Delaware and Connecticut.

The most regressive and strongest influence almost everywhere is the local property tax. It remains the major revenue producer for most systems and is consistently more regressive than any other major tax. It is, in addition, a prime source of receipts for local governments. Although states do have some flexibility in altering their revenue sources (i.e., new or expanded use of sales or income taxes), this is most often not true at the local level. Some states have enacted more liberal enabling legislation permitting expanded local use of the general sales or income base, but for most local governments property taxes are the "only game in town." Any growth in the local sector that is not financed through federal or state aid falls on one of the most inequitable taxes. Any furtherance of taxpayer equity, therefore, must come through actions initiated and financed by the state. These would include the exemption of food from the general sales base, circuit breaker provisions for the property tax, liberalization of exemption or deductions and more progressive rates on the income tax, and a reassignment of financial responsibility onto a progressive state income tax from the local property tax. A great deal of the latter has already occurred in the context of school finance reform. Whatever the specific action, the state's role in promoting taxpayer equity is pivotal.

One of the raging points of contention in state-local finance concerns property tax incidence and whether it falls on capital ownership or on products produced with taxed property; the new versus the old view, as it has come to be called. Setting aside for a moment which stance is correct, as it were, the implication of adopting one or the other can be spelled out. This was done is Chapter 6 using the Suits index of progressivity. Comparison of findings from each view reveals a vast difference in the equity of property taxation (see Table 6-10). Under the old position, clear regressivity prevails in every state, generally more so than with most other taxes in use. Adherence to the new theory shifts the property tax to marked progressivity; in fact, more progressivity is present in most states than with the state individual income tax. Furthermore, this revenue source is actually found to be more progressive, for most states, than the federal individual or corporate income tax. We have a confusing situation in which property taxation can be condemned for its inequity, on the one hand, or praised for its equity, on the other. This produces a certain schizophrenia in perceiving the reality of state-local finance. It certainly stands the conventional wisdon about state-local taxation on its head. Undoubtedly, debate over the incidence of this tax will continue for some time, but it has been suggested here that the old view is probably more appropriate to the policy analysis of tax burdens for subnational political jurisdictions.

Finally, it has been noted that quantification of the equity and burden of a tax or system of taxes can be an elusive endeavor. As discussed in Chapter 6, there is no unequivocal method to be employed. Three measures have been suggested and used here:

1. Burden elasticity – based on a regression model
2. Inequality in tax payments – based on a Lorenz curve method developed by Suits
3. Factor analysis – to produce an overall index of burden

Each of these measures has its advantages and each looks at a different facet of burden. The first two address the equity issue directly but *not* the *level* of burden. The factor analysis method, shown visually in Figure 6-3, looks at the *overall* burden of a tax or tax system taking into account how it varies in impact across the income spectrum. Using the basic data on effective rates (Appendix A), an index can be computed that reflects most of the information contained in these data for all fourteen income classes. Lower scores indicate the interaction of low burden and a less regressive (more progressive with the income tax) impact, higher scores the opposite. It is felt that use of factor analysis offers considerable promise in condensing information on the distribution of tax burdens into a single value for each state. This greatly facilitates comparative analysis and offers an opportunity to develop measures that take into account information on distributional consequences.

Tax Burden and Intergovernmental Aid

Measurement of burden can have implications for the allocation of federal dollars among states. Most aid formulas use some factor to allow for above or below average effort. The amount of aid (say per capita) is adjusted upward or downward according to relative effort. It is being suggested here that such a measure may not accurately reflect actual effort for a state because in ignores two important phenomena. First, there are the distributional consequences of taxation relative to income. For example, total tax collections per $1,000 of personal income in a state tells nothing of how this burden differentially affects various income levels. A more accurate measure would indicate both the level of burden and how it is distributed. As the data discussed earlier clearly show, there can be a vast difference between an average tax-to-income ratio (as in Table 1-1) and how this affects different income categories (as summarized in Table 5-3). Second, it is important to account for the spatial rearrangement of taxes as it pertains to quantifying effort. The flow of taxes in and out of states will influence an effort index upward or downward depending upon the exporting and importing balance. Just such an index was developed in Chapter 6 by applying factor analysis to data on effective tax rates.

A simple formula to allocate aid according to population, per capita personal income, and tax effort might look as follows (see Break, 1967: 128-129; Lile and Soule, 1969: 438):

$$F_i = \frac{(P_i \cdot Y)}{Y_i} (E_i)$$

where F_i = state i's share of total aid
E_i = tax effort of ith state
P_i = population of ith state
Y_i = per capita personal income for i^{th} state
Y = per capita personal income for United States
P = population of United States

Traditionally, tax effort (E_i) has been defined as:

$$\frac{T_i}{(Y_i \cdot P_i)} \Big/ \frac{T}{(Y \cdot P)}$$

This measure relates taxes paid as a percentage of personal income in the ith state to that for the total United States. It is suggested here that effort be redefined to reflect both spatial tax flows and equity considerations. Table 6-11 contains data that do just that. Use of such data to construct an index would adjust the distribution of aid to be more reflective of variations in tax effort and tax flows among states. This would lead to a more equitable allocation of intergovernmental funds (see Lile and Soule, 1969).

Tax Burden and the Local Sector

One important policy implication of this research relates to the fiscal integrity of the local sector. The extreme dependence of local government on property taxation as a prime source of revenue is a strong source of inequity. The impact is extreme from two points of view: first, the level of burden is by far the highest; second, its impact is regressive. Combined, the effects place the local sector in an increasingly less tenable position.

Local reliance on property taxation in a particular state depends upon the nature of fiscal assignment. A state with a high local responsibility for raising revenue will exhibit a level of property tax burden considerably above states that raise revenue at the state level. High local assignment forces local units to utilize this source more intensively. Empirical examination of the local sector's burden serves to emphasize its regressiveness. Although in many instances the *state's* burden is proportional or even progressive, the local component is regressive everywhere (see Table B-3).

This regressive burden has substantial import for the capacity of this sector to maintain or expand its public services, particularly in the face of double-digit inflation. In a system where the state has assumed greater responsibility for raising revenue, the tax instruments are considerably more responsive to expanding needs. Consider, for example, the windfall in revenue from the inflation-related growth in yield for the state income and general sales taxes and the surpluses that have accrued as a result. At the local level, however, the base is more narrowly defined and elastic ("responsive") forms of taxatin are generally not available. Most estimates of property tax elasticity place it well below 1.0 (Advisory Commission, 1977a: 254; Netzer, 1966:189). In face of the existing situation, the capacity of this sector to keep pace with demands exerted upon it out of local sources looks more and more dismal. Despite a rather remarkable track record, increasing financial pressure raises serious doubt about the maintenance of past trends out of "own" resources. This tension is already manifest in the extreme dependence of the entire state-local sector on "outside" funds to finance programs. Federal grants as a percentage of state-local receipts from *own* sources has risen steadily from 16.8 percent in 1960 to over 35 percent in 1977. If we look at specific *local* governments, the situation can be even more extreme. Direct federal aid as a percentage of own source general revenue has reached 76 percent in Buffalo, 60 percent in Cleveland, 56 percent in St. Louis, and averages about 48 percent for fifteen large cities.

Fiscal problems of local governments are increasing in intensity. A person need only read local newspapers, Senate hearings, or academic journals to get some feel for their plight. The severity of the situation has been brought home in recent years by the New York City fiscal crisis of Spring of 1975; the passage of California's Proposition 13 in June 1978; numerous defaults or near defaults by local governments in between and since; and the growing threat of cuts in and more stringent limitations on local revenue raising potential, most particularly property taxation (Advisory Commission, 1977b).

It seems as though the state-local sector, but especially the local, has become a second-rate partner in the American federal system. The burden of the local tax structure has been rising steadily, in large part in response to the process of urbanization and demands for public action to cope with resulting problems. At the same time, the distributional impact of local tax instruments raises concerns over questions of equity. To a considerable extent local governments have borne a disproportionate share of the costs associated with urban America and these costs have been placed on a tax system that is inferior when viewed relative to either the state or federal revenue structures. The resulting burden, imposed almost entirely on the local property base, has lead to widespread taxpayer resistance to any local tax increase, resounding defeat for most local referendum issues that "cost anything," and a flurry of activity to cut and limit local and state activity. It seems likely that things will become more intense as economic factors make the burden on private income even more pronounced.

Many of the financial problems that contribute to the plight of local governments relate to the burden and inequity of their revenue sources. A partial listing would include:

The inequity of local property taxes and the taxpayer and legislative impetus for cuts and limitations, in the manner of Proposition 13 and its progeny

Taxpayer resistence to passage of almost any referendum that even remotely suggests an added tax burden

Pressure for functional reassignment of the cost of local services upward to the state or federal revenue base

Implementation of reform measures to deal with the regressive sting of local property taxation, such as the circuit breaker

Expansion of intergovernmental aid for the support of local programs

What to do with the billions of dollars in "surplus" state funds to ease the pressure on taxpayers or on local jurisdictions

Equity and Revenue Potential

Equity is a separate policy issue from the elasticity of a tax, that is, its expansion in yield relative to growth in economic circumstances (usually related to personal income). These two facets of a tax are, however, linked. Past research has tended to demonstrate that regressive taxes have the least elasticity. As personal income grows, their yield tends to increase less than proportionately. The property and individual income taxes provide good examples and define the extremes.

The property tax has been documented as being one of the most regressive or inequitable. Elasticity estimates have found that it tends to expand in yield much less than in proportion to growth in income. Odden and Vincent (1976: 23) found an elasticity of 0.5 in Missouri and 0.4 in South Dakota. McLoone found elasticities for the forty-eight contiguous states in the following ranges (cited in Netzer, 1966: 189):

Elasticity	*Number of States*
0.85 and above	8
0.75 - 0.84	15
0.65 - 0.74	13
Less than 0.65	12

Thus, a 1-percent expansion of personal income is likely to elicit much less than a 1-percent growth in yield. The problem as Odden and Vincent state it (1976: 23) is that:

> Since the demand for governmental services tends at least to keep pace with increases in personal income, annual debates over tax rate increases become nearly unavoidable if government expenditures are financed by regressive tax sources.

One the other hand, the elasticity of the individual income tax is consistently estimated as exceeding 1.0 and even approaching 2.0 in some states (Advisory Commission, 1977a: 254); the more progressive the tax, generally, the higher its elasticity. It seems then that reducing the regressivity of the state-local tax system by deemphasizing local property taxation has a twofold advantage; first, it promotes taxpayer equity; second, it makes the state-local revenue system more responsive in terms of yield.

School Finance Reform

The decade of the 1970s clearly was the heyday of school finance reform. Its impact has been felt in twenty to twenty-five states and has probably affected local education for well over 50 percent of the nation's pupils. The primary approach has been to "level up" low-spending school districts while maintaining levels elsewhere; this has been accomplished in a variety of ways. Substantial impetus for this movement was provided by a variety of court cases that dealt with the unconstitutionality of property taxation for the support of local education. This, it was argued, led to often vast differences in resources available to fund schools and thus represented a denial of equal protection under the 14th Amendment to the U.S. Constitution. *Serrano* v. *Priest* in California and *Robinson* v. *Cahill* in New Jersey represent two successful attempts to have the system of local finance for education declared unconstitutional. In 1973, however, the U.S. Supreme Court in a 5-to-4 decision overturned a *Serrano*-type school finance suit from Texas. The *Rodriguez* v. *San Antonio* decision stated, in essence, that the school finance problem was *not* a *federal* issue but one to be dealt with state by state.

One this premise, nearly one-half of the states have poured in billions of dollars in additional funds for local schools. In eighteen states that have recently adopted aid programs, their commitment to supporting education has risen from 39 to 51 percent of total revenues. In California, for example, compliance with *Serrano* led to a $4.6 billion appropriation over a four-year period.

Much of the reform in school finance has had a direct impact on the absolute or relative growth in the burden of the local property tax. Education being the single largest item in the local sector's budget, any additional external support served to take some pressure off of the property base. Thus, greater state involvement in financing schools has definitely had a beneficial impact on taxpayer equity. The impact has been more extensive in states with a strong, progressive individual income tax to generate needed additional tax dollars.

Whether or not this trend will be continued in the 1980s, which may prove to be the decade of "fiscal retrenchment," remains to be seen. One thing is clear, however. The equity of local education finance is likely to be challenged even further, whether it is in a milieu of expanding budgets or environment of "cuts and limitations." Data on burden and equity for local property taxation and state revenue sources for each state will be a useful input to further research, analysis, and policy designed to deal with school finance equity. One purpose to which the data in this book might be put is to examine the impact of shifting from local taxation to state revenue sources.

AN AGENDA FOR FUTURE RESEARCH

Problems encountered in bringing to fruition a study on the burden of taxation in each state, by income category, for all major state and local taxes have been discussed throughout Chapters 1-4. A restatement can now be made in terms of directions for future research on subnational fiscal incidence.

One of the main diffulties to be confronted directly is the paucity of timely, comparable data detailing various facets of economic and fiscal phenomena within each state, particularly as they pertain to distribution by income level. Without an adequate base of information, studies of this type tend to be unique and not repeatable, which is undesirable from the point of view of documenting the progress that has been made in advancing taxpayer equity. It is argued here that this type of analysis should be undertaken on a regular basis to arm policymakers at all governmental levels with data on tax burdens in each state-local system. In order to accomplish this, the following types of data would have to be made available on a comparable, periodic basis (e.g., every 5-10 years):

Detail on state and local tax collections, most especially the latter, which tends to be reported in much less detail than state data

Data on property tax collection by class of property, which are not now available on a *comparable* basis for *all* states

Data on consumption and expenditure patterns by state, which are not now available except by region (see Chapter 3)

Data on income distribution patterns by income source for each state, which are not generally available (SIE was a "one-shot" survey)

Data on tax itemizations, which are available through the IRS State Tax Model, although not readily

If these kinds of information could be collected regularly and in a coordinated fashion, it would greatly simplify replication of the study done here for 1975-1976 and earlier for 1962 by Phares (1973).

A second area that needs attention pertains to spatial tax flows. More resources need to be put into refining and updating the methodology initiated by McLure for estimating interstate tax movements. This would entail further refinement in the theory underlying spatial incidence as well as the development of a data base to permit its empirical implementation. Despite widespread acknowledgment of the importance of this phenomenon, there has been relatively little effort given to refining and updating McLure's earlier work. It seems appropriate that spatial incidence be given greater conceptual and empirical attention in future research endeavors.

A final critical area for future research relates to the expenditure side of the budget for state and local governments. As noted at the outset, nothing can be said at present about the impact of spending operations on taxpayers at various income levels. We thus look at taxes (costs) in isolation from the benefits that result from public programs. A complete analysis would look at *both* sides of the budget and net fiscal incidence to get a picture of the full redistributive impact of public operations. As Thurow has noted in a review essay on the

Pechman and Okner (1974) book: "I would agrue that the economic analysis of the incidence of public expenditures stands as the number one gap in the analysis of public finance. It is the place where analysis and research funds should be concentrated" (1975: 186). Although we do have some information on the full budget impact for entire governmental sectors or single states in isolation, to date there is no study that looks at every state and the economic incidence of spending operations. It is the logical sequel to this book.

Appendix A

Individual State Data on Effective Tax Rates by Type of Tax

The data contained in Tables A-1 through A-93 are the basic measures of tax burden that were estimated using the empirical model in Chapters 3 and 4. Effective tax rates are shown for each of fourteen income classes—under $3,000 to over $35,000—for each of the fifty states, for each individual state and local tax, and for appropriate totals by category (e.g., all licenses) or governmental sector (state, local, or total). In addition, several taxes are treated differently in terms of shifting and incidence. These estimates are also shown separately (e.g., Tables A-75 to A-78 shown four separate theoretical treatments of the local real property tax on single-family residential property). The three primary theoretical approaches are distinguished as follows (see Chapter 3 for detail):

Benchmark—more generally accepted consensus assumptions about incidence
Most regressive—most regressive incidence assumptions
Most progressive—most progressive incidence assumptions

The bottom line of each table provides the average effective tax rate across the states that actually use the type of tax (e.g., 45 for the state general sales tax shown in Table A-1). States that do not use a tax are indicated by a row of asterisks (*) across *all* fourteen income classes.

Given the detail of information provided, the reader is able to compare any state to any other as well as to the average for all states and also to tailor further analysis to the purpose at hand.

TABLE A-1
EFFECTIVE TAX RATES: STATE GENERAL SALES AND GROSS RECEIPTS TAXES
INCIDENCE: CONSUMERS OF TAXED ITEMS
ALLOCATOR: SPECIAL SERIES ON CONSUMPTION OF TAXED ITEMS

STATE	UNDER $3,000	$3,000 -3,999	$4,000 -4,999	$5,000 -5,999	$6,000 -6,999	$7,000 -7,999	$8,000 -9,999	$10,000 -11,999	$12,000 -14,999	$15,000 -19,999	$20,000 -24,999	$25,000 -29,999	$30,000 -34,999	OVER $35,000
ALABAMA	5.76	3.65	3.18	2.82	2.57	2.49	2.33	2.10	1.91	1.76	1.66	1.56	1.56	1.04
ALASKA	*	*	*	*	*	*	*	*	*	*	*	*	*	*
ARIZONA	7.71	5.13	4.10	4.14	3.68	3.39	3.34	3.08	2.90	2.71	2.47	2.30	2.33	2.10
ARKANSAS	6.20	3.92	3.44	3.08	2.96	2.71	2.53	2.27	2.09	1.89	1.78	1.67	1.64	1.25
CALIFORNIA	4.21	3.40	3.01	2.87	2.73	2.62	2.46	2.36	2.27	2.14	2.05	2.01	1.97	1.82
COLORADO	4.24	2.98	2.52	2.31	2.29	2.04	1.87	1.79	1.68	1.54	1.44	1.42	1.23	1.16
CONNECTICUT	2.80	2.70	2.55	2.63	2.47	2.79	2.43	2.43	2.34	2.27	2.29	2.27	2.21	1.97
DELAWARE	*	*	*	*	*	*	*	*	*	*	*	*	*	*
FLORIDA	5.31	3.61	3.13	2.88	2.82	2.68	2.48	2.31	2.21	2.03	1.95	1.86	1.71	1.49
GEORGIA	6.47	3.80	3.50	3.18	2.99	2.86	2.54	2.32	2.18	2.02	1.86	1.73	1.64	1.39
HAWAII	8.39	6.28	6.47	6.05	5.68	5.50	5.18	4.90	4.70	4.38	4.24	4.30	4.02	3.85
IDAHO	4.23	2.87	2.48	2.48	2.31	2.14	2.08	1.90	1.82	1.67	1.57	1.52	1.43	1.29
ILLINOIS	4.14	3.15	2.85	2.67	2.48	2.43	2.29	2.13	2.08	1.94	1.83	1.80	1.74	1.53
INDIANA	5.35	3.90	3.40	3.36	3.23	3.09	2.81	2.79	2.65	2.49	2.44	2.20	2.29	2.09
IOWA	3.79	2.78	2.73	2.27	2.33	2.25	2.10	2.08	1.92	1.86	1.79	1.71	1.65	1.55
KANSAS	4.92	3.34	3.06	2.56	2.61	2.44	2.45	2.17	2.08	1.89	1.75	1.79	1.71	1.46
KENTUCKY	5.06	3.44	3.11	2.75	2.61	2.52	2.42	2.26	2.03	1.94	1.88	1.83	1.73	1.38
LOUISIANA	4.29	2.89	2.57	2.58	2.42	2.35	2.30	2.09	1.96	1.89	1.87	1.82	1.71	1.51
MAINE	4.30	3.39	3.17	2.77	2.91	2.69	2.69	2.56	2.47	2.37	2.38	2.24	2.20	2.04
MARYLAND	3.32	2.31	2.07	1.76	1.77	1.67	1.61	1.46	1.34	1.26	1.17	1.18	1.06	0.97
MASSACHUSETTS	1.09	1.11	0.99	0.95	0.95	0.94	0.93	0.94	0.86	0.86	0.84	0.86	0.87	0.73
MICHIGAN	3.46	2.63	2.29	2.06	1.97	2.01	1.82	1.79	1.68	1.57	1.51	1.46	1.43	1.26
MINNESOTA	3.41	2.62	2.15	2.13	2.03	2.10	1.82	1.78	1.69	1.58	1.53	1.49	1.50	1.30
MISSISSIPPI	10.90	7.04	5.80	5.22	4.71	4.72	4.28	3.96	3.57	3.23	3.09	3.01	2.91	2.29
MISSOURI	4.61	2.82	2.81	2.45	2.32	2.21	2.07	1.95	1.77	1.63	1.58	1.52	1.37	1.24
MONTANA	*	*	*	*	*	*	*	*	*	*	*	*	*	*
NEBRASKA	4.15	2.92	2.37	2.23	2.13	2.05	1.91	1.83	1.70	1.61	1.56	1.48	1.47	1.30
NEVADA	3.85	2.92	2.57	2.33	2.34	2.20	2.04	1.88	1.75	1.67	1.57	1.51	1.49	1.29
NEW HAMPSHIRE	*	*	*	*	*	*	*	*	*	*	*	*	*	*
NEW JERSEY	1.95	1.79	1.74	1.71	1.70	1.71	1.61	1.64	1.59	1.56	1.53	1.53	1.47	1.34
NEW MEXICO	8.96	6.28	5.83	5.13	5.05	4.56	4.36	4.02	3.66	3.48	3.35	3.16	2.89	2.89
NEW YORK	2.94	2.24	2.01	1.89	1.89	1.84	1.72	1.71	1.60	1.55	1.53	1.51	1.49	1.26
NORTH CAROLINA	4.35	2.76	2.44	2.06	2.04	1.85	1.77	1.60	1.51	1.36	1.27	1.25	1.16	0.98
NORTH DAKOTA	6.20	4.39	4.05	3.68	3.54	3.48	3.28	3.24	3.14	2.98	2.83	2.75	2.78	2.52
OHIO	2.40	1.93	1.83	1.69	1.64	1.70	1.60	1.52	1.46	1.45	1.42	1.38	1.33	1.17
OKLAHOMA	3.58	2.07	1.81	1.69	1.59	1.43	1.31	1.22	1.11	0.98	0.93	0.86	0.83	0.74
OREGON	*	*	*	*	*	*	*	*	*	*	*	*	*	*
PENNSYLVANIA	2.66	2.22	2.13	1.98	2.05	1.99	2.00	1.97	1.86	1.86	1.77	1.77	1.79	1.65
RHODE ISLAND	2.84	2.14	2.30	2.15	1.92	1.95	1.98	1.88	1.89	1.84	1.81	1.78	1.70	1.55
SOUTH CAROLINA	6.95	4.49	3.82	3.51	3.23	3.17	2.88	2.72	2.45	2.28	2.15	2.05	1.89	1.61
SOUTH DAKOTA	6.00	4.04	3.72	3.41	3.28	3.05	2.83	2.79	2.59	2.49	2.34	2.30	2.17	1.94
TENNESSEE	6.50	4.25	3.70	3.42	3.10	2.99	2.68	2.53	2.33	2.11	1.99	1.84	1.85	1.39
TEXAS	4.34	3.03	2.64	2.54	2.38	2.26	2.18	2.06	1.91	1.79	1.72	1.62	1.55	1.35
UTAH	6.99	4.73	3.96	3.50	3.78	3.30	3.06	2.90	2.69	2.47	2.33	2.22	2.19	2.01
VERMONT	1.67	1.30	1.30	1.18	1.14	1.13	1.05	1.07	1.02	1.01	0.99	0.89	0.88	0.80
VIRGINIA	3.58	2.06	1.91	1.76	1.56	1.47	1.42	1.29	1.17	1.07	0.99	0.95	0.88	0.75
WASHINGTON	9.69	6.70	5.71	5.28	4.86	4.94	4.52	4.41	4.10	3.82	3.68	3.59	3.21	3.03
WEST VIRGINIA	11.53	7.47	6.13	5.45	5.24	5.00	4.38	4.32	3.89	3.66	3.44	3.22	3.01	2.89
WISCONSIN	4.03	2.80	2.55	2.44	2.41	2.37	2.08	2.05	1.95	1.87	1.78	1.75	1.74	1.56
WYOMING	6.66	4.94	4.68	4.26	3.99	3.83	3.52	3.39	3.20	2.93	2.81	2.82	2.80	2.39
AVERAGE	5.02	3.49	3.12	2.87	2.75	2.64	2.47	2.34	2.19	2.06	1.97	1.91	1.83	1.63

* EFFECTIVE TAX RATE EQUALS ZERO BEFORE ROUNDING. AN ENTIRE ROW OF * MEANS THAT THIS TAX IS NOT USED IN THIS STATE.

TABLE A-2

EFFECTIVE TAX RATES: STATE SELECTIVE SALES AND GROSS RECEIPTS TAXES-MOTOR FUELS
INCIDENCE: 1/3 CONSUMERS IN GENERAL, 2/3 HOUSEHOLDS CONSUMING GASOLINE
ALLOCATOR: CONSUMPTION AND GASOLINE EXPENDITURES

STATE	UNDER $3,000	$3,000 -3,999	$4,000 -4,999	$5,000 -5,999	$6,000 -6,999	$7,000 -7,999	$8,000 -9,999	$10,000 -11,999	$12,000 -14,999	$15,000 -19,999	$20,000 -24,999	$25,000 -29,999	$30,000 -34,999	OVER $35,000
ALABAMA	2.84	1.66	1.41	1.21	1.08	1.01	0.93	0.82	0.72	0.63	0.58	0.54	0.54	0.39
ALASKA	2.22	1.42	1.29	1.23	1.14	0.98	0.95	0.87	0.79	0.68	0.63	0.59	0.54	0.49
ARIZONA	2.64	1.60	1.24	1.20	1.02	0.93	0.87	0.77	0.70	0.62	0.54	0.49	0.50	0.45
ARKANSAS	3.38	2.01	1.72	1.51	1.43	1.27	1.17	1.02	0.90	0.81	0.75	0.69	0.67	0.54
CALIFORNIA	1.63	1.07	0.87	0.78	0.70	0.64	0.55	0.49	0.44	0.38	0.34	0.32	0.31	0.29
COLORADO	1.91	1.22	0.99	0.88	0.85	0.74	0.64	0.58	0.52	0.47	0.42	0.41	0.35	0.33
CONNECTICUT	1.33	1.01	0.88	0.85	0.77	0.84	0.66	0.63	0.57	0.54	0.51	0.50	0.47	0.43
DELAWARE	2.45	1.43	1.36	1.11	1.04	0.97	0.88	0.72	0.69	0.62	0.57	0.51	0.47	0.41
FLORIDA	2.27	1.35	1.11	0.97	0.92	0.85	0.75	0.66	0.60	0.51	0.47	0.44	0.38	0.33
GEORGIA	2.89	1.59	1.44	1.26	1.16	1.09	0.95	0.84	0.76	0.69	0.62	0.55	0.53	0.47
HAWAII	1.32	0.87	0.85	0.77	0.69	0.65	0.58	0.53	0.47	0.43	0.39	0.39	0.36	0.34
IDAHO	2.59	1.55	1.30	1.24	1.12	1.01	0.94	0.82	0.76	0.66	0.59	0.56	0.52	0.46
ILLINOIS	1.30	0.90	0.79	0.70	0.64	0.62	0.56	0.50	0.47	0.42	0.38	0.36	0.36	0.32
INDIANA	2.15	1.37	1.14	1.08	1.01	0.93	0.80	0.78	0.70	0.64	0.60	0.51	0.55	0.48
IOWA	1.97	1.26	1.19	0.95	0.93	0.87	0.79	0.76	0.66	0.62	0.58	0.54	0.52	0.48
KANSAS	1.92	1.22	1.08	0.88	0.89	0.81	0.80	0.68	0.63	0.57	0.51	0.53	0.48	0.44
KENTUCKY	3.12	1.86	1.59	1.36	1.25	1.17	1.07	0.95	0.81	0.75	0.70	0.66	0.62	0.51
LOUISIANA	2.74	1.55	1.28	1.22	1.08	0.99	0.93	0.80	0.71	0.65	0.60	0.57	0.50	0.45
MAINE	2.16	1.46	1.30	1.07	1.10	1.01	0.95	0.88	0.81	0.76	0.74	0.68	0.68	0.62
MARYLAND	2.30	1.38	1.19	0.98	0.92	0.85	0.78	0.68	0.58	0.50	0.44	0.44	0.38	0.35
MASSACHUSETTS	1.16	0.94	0.78	0.70	0.67	0.63	0.58	0.56	0.47	0.46	0.42	0.44	0.44	0.36
MICHIGAN	1.97	1.30	1.05	0.92	0.85	0.85	0.72	0.68	0.60	0.54	0.50	0.48	0.46	0.42
MINNESOTA	2.22	1.49	1.16	1.09	1.01	1.02	0.84	0.79	0.71	0.64	0.59	0.57	0.57	0.50
MISSISSIPPI	3.87	2.36	1.89	1.65	1.47	1.45	1.27	1.14	1.01	0.89	0.83	0.81	0.77	0.61
MISSOURI	2.03	1.16	1.12	0.95	0.89	0.83	0.76	0.69	0.61	0.55	0.52	0.51	0.45	0.43
MONTANA	2.94	1.88	1.61	1.40	1.34	1.23	1.07	0.96	0.88	0.81	0.74	0.70	0.67	0.61
NEBRASKA	2.50	1.63	1.29	1.19	1.10	1.06	0.97	0.90	0.82	0.75	0.71	0.67	0.67	0.60
NEVADA	1.72	1.15	0.98	0.85	0.84	0.75	0.65	0.58	0.52	0.48	0.43	0.41	0.39	0.34
NEW HAMPSHIRE	1.83	1.27	1.01	1.02	0.94	0.84	0.84	0.76	0.72	0.69	0.64	0.61	0.60	0.52
NEW JERSEY	1.25	0.88	0.80	0.72	0.68	0.65	0.58	0.57	0.52	0.49	0.47	0.45	0.43	0.40
NEW MEXICO	2.97	1.89	1.69	1.44	1.37	1.20	1.11	0.99	0.87	0.79	0.74	0.68	0.60	0.60
NEW YORK	0.98	0.63	0.54	0.48	0.46	0.44	0.39	0.36	0.32	0.29	0.28	0.27	0.28	0.23
NORTH CAROLINA	3.21	1.88	1.61	1.32	1.28	1.14	1.04	0.90	0.83	0.73	0.66	0.65	0.59	0.53
NORTH DAKOTA	2.10	1.29	1.13	1.00	0.93	0.88	0.80	0.76	0.71	0.65	0.60	0.57	0.56	0.51
OHIO	1.55	1.02	0.89	0.78	0.71	0.71	0.64	0.57	0.52	0.49	0.46	0.43	0.41	0.36
OKLAHOMA	2.67	1.45	1.24	1.13	1.05	0.91	0.81	0.73	0.66	0.57	0.52	0.47	0.45	0.42
OREGON	1.90	1.15	0.96	0.89	0.79	0.75	0.67	0.59	0.51	0.45	0.41	0.40	0.36	0.34
PENNSYLVANIA	1.62	1.05	0.94	0.83	0.82	0.76	0.72	0.68	0.61	0.58	0.53	0.51	0.52	0.48
RHODE ISLAND	1.72	1.06	1.06	0.95	0.80	0.76	0.77	0.68	0.65	0.62	0.59	0.58	0.54	0.50
SOUTH CAROLINA	2.97	1.80	1.49	1.32	1.22	1.14	1.02	0.93	0.83	0.74	0.69	0.64	0.58	0.51
SOUTH DAKOTA	2.69	1.69	1.51	1.35	1.28	1.18	1.05	1.03	0.94	0.88	0.82	0.79	0.75	0.68
TENNESSEE	2.56	1.57	1.33	1.21	1.07	1.02	0.87	0.81	0.72	0.64	0.58	0.52	0.53	0.40
TEXAS	1.90	1.15	0.95	0.87	0.78	0.72	0.66	0.59	0.52	0.47	0.42	0.39	0.35	0.31
UTAH	2.52	1.55	1.24	1.09	1.12	0.94	0.84	0.77	0.68	0.60	0.55	0.51	0.50	0.46
VERMONT	2.02	1.30	1.22	1.06	0.98	0.95	0.84	0.83	0.76	0.73	0.70	0.63	0.62	0.56
VIRGINIA	3.00	1.60	1.44	1.29	1.09	1.01	0.97	0.84	0.74	0.66	0.59	0.56	0.51	0.44
WASHINGTON	2.46	1.51	1.22	1.10	0.95	0.95	0.81	0.77	0.67	0.60	0.55	0.51	0.46	0.42
WEST VIRGINIA	2.87	1.72	1.36	1.17	1.12	1.03	0.88	0.84	0.74	0.67	0.60	0.54	0.50	0.47
WISCONSIN	1.63	0.98	0.85	0.78	0.74	0.71	0.59	0.56	0.51	0.47	0.43	0.41	0.42	0.37
WYOMING	2.54	1.70	1.55	1.37	1.25	1.16	1.02	0.96	0.88	0.77	0.72	0.70	0.68	0.57
AVERAGE	2.25	1.40	1.20	1.06	0.99	0.92	0.83	0.75	0.68	0.61	0.56	0.53	0.51	0.45

* EFFECTIVE TAX RATE EQUALS ZERO BEFORE ROUNDING. AN ENTIRE ROW OF * MEANS THAT THIS TAX IS NOT USED IN THIS STATE.

TABLE A-3
EFFECTIVE TAX RATES: STATE SELECTIVE SALES AND GROSS RECEIPTS TAXES-TOBACCO
INCIDENCE: CONSUMERS OF TOBACCO PRODUCTS
ALLOCATOR: TOBACCO PRODUCTS EXPENDITURES

STATE	UNDER $3,000	$3,000 -3,999	$4,000 -4,999	$5,000 -5,999	$6,000 -6,999	$7,000 -7,999	$8,000 -9,999	$10,000 -11,999	$12,000 -14,999	$15,000 -19,999	$20,000 -24,999	$25,000 -29,999	$30,000 -34,999	OVER $35,000
ALABAMA	1.29	0.69	0.56	0.47	0.40	0.38	0.33	0.28	0.24	0.20	0.17	0.15	0.14	0.10
ALASKA	0.77	0.44	0.39	0.35	0.31	0.26	0.24	0.21	0.18	0.15	0.13	0.12	0.11	0.09
ARIZONA	1.31	0.72	0.54	0.51	0.43	0.38	0.35	0.30	0.26	0.22	0.18	0.16	0.15	0.12
ARKANSAS	1.94	1.05	0.86	0.73	0.67	0.58	0.51	0.43	0.37	0.31	0.26	0.23	0.21	0.16
CALIFORNIA	0.87	0.52	0.41	0.36	0.31	0.28	0.24	0.21	0.18	0.15	0.13	0.12	0.11	0.08
COLORADO	0.96	0.55	0.43	0.38	0.35	0.30	0.26	0.23	0.20	0.17	0.14	0.13	0.11	0.09
CONNECTICUT	1.25	0.82	0.68	0.63	0.56	0.57	0.46	0.42	0.37	0.32	0.29	0.27	0.25	0.21
DELAWARE	1.72	0.91	0.84	0.66	0.60	0.54	0.47	0.40	0.36	0.30	0.26	0.22	0.20	0.16
FLORIDA	1.66	0.91	0.72	0.61	0.56	0.50	0.43	0.37	0.32	0.26	0.23	0.20	0.18	0.14
GEORGIA	1.38	0.70	0.60	0.52	0.46	0.42	0.36	0.30	0.27	0.22	0.19	0.17	0.15	0.12
HAWAII	0.67	0.40	0.37	0.32	0.28	0.26	0.23	0.20	0.17	0.15	0.13	0.12	0.11	0.08
IDAHO	0.81	0.44	0.35	0.33	0.29	0.25	0.23	0.19	0.17	0.14	0.12	0.10	0.10	0.08
ILLINOIS	0.94	0.59	0.50	0.44	0.39	0.36	0.32	0.29	0.26	0.23	0.21	0.19	0.18	0.15
INDIANA	0.68	0.40	0.32	0.29	0.26	0.24	0.21	0.19	0.17	0.15	0.13	0.12	0.11	0.10
IOWA	1.05	0.61	0.55	0.43	0.41	0.38	0.33	0.31	0.27	0.24	0.21	0.19	0.18	0.16
KANSAS	0.93	0.53	0.46	0.37	0.36	0.32	0.30	0.26	0.23	0.20	0.18	0.17	0.16	0.13
KENTUCKY	0.59	0.32	0.27	0.22	0.19	0.18	0.16	0.14	0.11	0.10	0.08	0.07	0.07	0.05
LOUISIANA	1.41	0.72	0.58	0.53	0.46	0.42	0.37	0.31	0.27	0.22	0.19	0.17	0.15	0.12
MAINE	1.64	0.96	0.81	0.65	0.63	0.56	0.51	0.45	0.40	0.35	0.31	0.28	0.27	0.23
MARYLAND	1.13	0.62	0.51	0.41	0.37	0.33	0.30	0.26	0.22	0.18	0.16	0.14	0.13	0.10
MASSACHUSETTS	1.39	0.95	0.76	0.64	0.60	0.55	0.50	0.45	0.39	0.34	0.31	0.29	0.27	0.22
MICHIGAN	1.00	0.60	0.48	0.41	0.37	0.36	0.31	0.28	0.25	0.21	0.19	0.18	0.17	0.14
MINNESOTA	1.42	0.87	0.66	0.60	0.54	0.53	0.44	0.40	0.36	0.31	0.28	0.26	0.24	0.20
MISSISSIPPI	1.34	0.74	0.57	0.49	0.42	0.40	0.34	0.30	0.25	0.21	0.18	0.16	0.15	0.11
MISSOURI	0.88	0.46	0.43	0.36	0.32	0.29	0.26	0.24	0.20	0.18	0.16	0.15	0.14	0.12
MONTANA	1.21	0.70	0.58	0.49	0.45	0.40	0.34	0.30	0.26	0.22	0.19	0.17	0.15	0.12
NEBRASKA	1.01	0.60	0.46	0.41	0.37	0.35	0.31	0.28	0.25	0.22	0.20	0.18	0.17	0.15
NEVADA	1.12	0.68	0.55	0.47	0.44	0.39	0.34	0.29	0.25	0.21	0.18	0.16	0.15	0.11
NEW HAMPSHIRE	2.23	1.34	1.02	0.97	0.88	0.75	0.72	0.63	0.57	0.50	0.44	0.41	0.39	0.32
NEW JERSEY	1.33	0.82	0.70	0.62	0.56	0.53	0.47	0.43	0.38	0.33	0.30	0.28	0.26	0.22
NEW MEXICO	1.00	0.58	0.50	0.41	0.38	0.33	0.29	0.25	0.21	0.18	0.16	0.14	0.12	0.10
NEW YORK	1.22	0.69	0.55	0.48	0.45	0.41	0.36	0.33	0.29	0.25	0.23	0.21	0.20	0.16
NORTH CAROLINA	0.38	0.20	0.17	0.13	0.12	0.11	0.10	0.08	0.07	0.06	0.05	0.05	0.04	0.03
NORTH DAKOTA	1.04	0.58	0.49	0.42	0.38	0.35	0.31	0.29	0.26	0.23	0.20	0.18	0.18	0.15
OHIO	1.17	0.70	0.59	0.51	0.46	0.44	0.39	0.34	0.31	0.27	0.25	0.23	0.21	0.18
OKLAHOMA	1.75	0.87	0.71	0.63	0.56	0.49	0.42	0.36	0.31	0.26	0.22	0.19	0.18	0.14
OREGON	1.04	0.58	0.47	0.41	0.35	0.33	0.29	0.25	0.21	0.18	0.15	0.14	0.12	0.10
PENNSYLVANIA	1.45	0.81	0.68	0.57	0.55	0.50	0.45	0.40	0.35	0.31	0.28	0.26	0.25	0.21
RHODE ISLAND	1.81	0.97	0.92	0.77	0.66	0.62	0.57	0.50	0.46	0.40	0.36	0.33	0.31	0.26
SOUTH CAROLINA	0.79	0.44	0.35	0.31	0.27	0.25	0.21	0.19	0.16	0.14	0.12	0.10	0.09	0.07
SOUTH DAKOTA	1.01	0.57	0.49	0.43	0.39	0.35	0.31	0.29	0.26	0.23	0.20	0.19	0.18	0.15
TENNESSEE	1.37	0.77	0.62	0.55	0.47	0.43	0.37	0.32	0.28	0.23	0.20	0.17	0.16	0.12
TEXAS	1.91	1.05	0.83	0.74	0.64	0.57	0.51	0.44	0.37	0.31	0.27	0.23	0.21	0.16
UTAH	0.56	0.31	0.24	0.20	0.20	0.17	0.15	0.13	0.11	0.10	0.08	0.07	0.06	0.05
VERMONT	1.48	0.83	0.73	0.61	0.56	0.51	0.45	0.41	0.36	0.32	0.29	0.26	0.24	0.21
VIRGINIA	0.33	0.16	0.14	0.12	0.10	0.09	0.08	0.07	0.06	0.05	0.04	0.04	0.03	0.03
WASHINGTON	1.29	0.72	0.56	0.48	0.42	0.40	0.34	0.30	0.26	0.22	0.19	0.17	0.15	0.12
WEST VIRGINIA	1.43	0.78	0.60	0.50	0.45	0.41	0.34	0.31	0.25	0.21	0.18	0.16	0.14	0.12
WISCONSIN	1.24	0.69	0.57	0.51	0.47	0.45	0.37	0.34	0.31	0.27	0.24	0.22	0.21	0.18
WYOMING	0.80	0.48	0.42	0.36	0.32	0.29	0.25	0.22	0.19	0.16	0.14	0.12	0.12	0.09
AVERAGE	1.18	0.67	0.55	0.48	0.43	0.39	0.34	0.30	0.26	0.23	0.20	0.18	0.17	0.14

* EFFECTIVE TAX RATE EQUALS ZERO BEFORE ROUNDING. AN ENTIRE ROW OF * MEANS THAT THIS TAX IS NOT USED IN THIS STATE.

TABLE A-4

EFFECTIVE TAX RATES: STATE SELECTIVE SALES AND GROSS RECEIPTS TAXES-ALCOHOL
INCIDENCE: CONSUMERS OF ALCOHOLIC BEVERAGES
ALLOCATOR: ALCOHOLIC BEVERAGES EXPENDITURES

STATE	UNDER $3,000	$3,000 -3,999	$4,000 -4,999	$5,000 -5,999	$6,000 -6,999	$7,000 -7,999	$8,000 -9,999	$10,000 -11,999	$12,000 -14,999	$15,000 -19,999	$20,000 -24,999	$25,000 -29,999	$30,000 -34,999	OVER $35,000
ALABAMA	0.59	0.47	0.44	0.41	0.39	0.40	0.39	0.38	0.37	0.36	0.36	0.35	0.36	0.32
ALASKA	0.58	0.39	0.37	0.36	0.34	0.30	0.29	0.28	0.26	0.23	0.23	0.22	0.21	0.20
ARIZONA	0.36	0.23	0.18	0.18	0.16	0.15	0.15	0.14	0.13	0.12	0.11	0.10	0.10	0.09
ARKANSAS	0.26	0.21	0.20	0.19	0.19	0.19	0.18	0.17	0.17	0.17	0.16	0.16	0.16	0.15
CALIFORNIA	0.22	0.15	0.13	0.12	0.11	0.10	0.10	0.09	0.08	0.08	0.07	0.07	0.07	0.06
COLORADO	0.27	0.18	0.15	0.14	0.14	0.12	0.11	0.11	0.10	0.09	0.09	0.08	0.08	0.07
CONNECTICUT	0.16	0.14	0.13	0.13	0.13	0.13	0.12	0.12	0.11	0.11	0.11	0.11	0.11	0.10
DELAWARE	0.17	0.14	0.14	0.13	0.13	0.13	0.13	0.12	0.12	0.12	0.12	0.11	0.11	0.11
FLORIDA	0.52	0.42	0.39	0.37	0.37	0.37	0.36	0.34	0.34	0.33	0.32	0.32	0.31	0.30
GEORGIA	0.44	0.33	0.33	0.32	0.32	0.32	0.30	0.29	0.29	0.28	0.28	0.27	0.27	0.26
HAWAII	0.52	0.36	0.36	0.33	0.31	0.30	0.28	0.26	0.25	0.23	0.22	0.22	0.21	0.20
IDAHO	0.40	0.26	0.22	0.21	0.20	0.18	0.17	0.16	0.15	0.14	0.13	0.12	0.12	0.11
ILLINOIS	0.20	0.15	0.14	0.13	0.12	0.12	0.11	0.11	0.10	0.10	0.09	0.09	0.09	0.09
INDIANA	0.18	0.13	0.11	0.11	0.10	0.10	0.09	0.09	0.08	0.08	0.08	0.07	0.07	0.07
IOWA	0.18	0.12	0.12	0.10	0.10	0.10	0.09	0.09	0.08	0.08	0.08	0.08	0.07	0.07
KANSAS	0.27	0.18	0.17	0.15	0.15	0.14	0.14	0.13	0.12	0.12	0.11	0.11	0.11	0.10
KENTUCKY	0.13	0.11	0.10	0.09	0.09	0.09	0.09	0.09	0.09	0.08	0.09	0.08	0.08	0.08
LOUISIANA	0.34	0.26	0.24	0.25	0.25	0.24	0.24	0.23	0.22	0.22	0.22	0.22	0.21	0.20
MAINE	0.69	0.54	0.50	0.44	0.46	0.44	0.44	0.42	0.41	0.39	0.39	0.38	0.38	0.36
MARYLAND	0.15	0.12	0.11	0.10	0.10	0.10	0.10	0.10	0.10	0.10	0.09	0.09	0.09	0.09
MASSACHUSETTS	0.30	0.28	0.25	0.23	0.23	0.23	0.22	0.22	0.21	0.20	0.20	0.20	0.20	0.19
MICHIGAN	0.29	0.21	0.18	0.16	0.16	0.16	0.15	0.14	0.13	0.13	0.12	0.12	0.12	0.11
MINNESOTA	0.46	0.34	0.28	0.27	0.25	0.26	0.23	0.22	0.21	0.20	0.19	0.19	0.19	0.17
MISSISSIPPI	0.38	0.32	0.28	0.27	0.26	0.27	0.26	0.26	0.24	0.24	0.24	0.24	0.23	0.21
MISSOURI	0.19	0.12	0.12	0.11	0.10	0.10	0.09	0.09	0.08	0.08	0.08	0.07	0.07	0.07
MONTANA	0.52	0.35	0.31	0.28	0.27	0.25	0.22	0.21	0.20	0.19	0.18	0.17	0.16	0.15
NEBRASKA	0.25	0.18	0.14	0.14	0.13	0.13	0.12	0.12	0.11	0.11	0.10	0.10	0.10	0.09
NEVADA	0.51	0.36	0.31	0.28	0.28	0.26	0.24	0.22	0.21	0.19	0.18	0.17	0.17	0.15
NEW HAMPSHIRE	0.13	0.10	0.09	0.09	0.09	0.08	0.08	0.08	0.08	0.08	0.08	0.08	0.08	0.07
NEW JERSEY	0.17	0.14	0.13	0.13	0.12	0.13	0.12	0.12	0.12	0.11	0.11	0.11	0.11	0.10
NEW MEXICO	0.28	0.19	0.17	0.15	0.15	0.13	0.13	0.12	0.11	0.10	0.10	0.09	0.08	0.08
NEW YORK	0.22	0.17	0.15	0.14	0.14	0.14	0.13	0.13	0.13	0.12	0.12	0.12	0.12	0.11
NORTH CAROLINA	0.46	0.37	0.35	0.31	0.33	0.31	0.31	0.30	0.30	0.29	0.29	0.29	0.28	0.27
NORTH DAKOTA	0.39	0.26	0.24	0.21	0.20	0.20	0.19	0.18	0.18	0.17	0.16	0.16	0.16	0.15
OHIO	0.23	0.16	0.15	0.13	0.13	0.13	0.12	0.11	0.11	0.11	0.10	0.10	0.10	0.09
OKLAHOMA	0.35	0.26	0.24	0.24	0.24	0.23	0.22	0.22	0.21	0.20	0.20	0.20	0.20	0.19
OREGON	0.10	0.06	0.05	0.05	0.05	0.04	0.04	0.04	0.03	0.03	0.03	0.03	0.03	0.03
PENNSYLVANIA	0.25	0.19	0.18	0.16	0.17	0.16	0.16	0.16	0.15	0.15	0.14	0.14	0.14	0.14
RHODE ISLAND	0.23	0.16	0.17	0.16	0.15	0.15	0.15	0.14	0.14	0.14	0.14	0.13	0.13	0.13
SOUTH CAROLINA	0.72	0.60	0.55	0.54	0.52	0.53	0.52	0.52	0.50	0.49	0.49	0.49	0.47	0.45
SOUTH DAKOTA	0.44	0.30	0.28	0.25	0.25	0.23	0.22	0.22	0.21	0.20	0.19	0.18	0.18	0.17
TENNESSEE	0.27	0.22	0.21	0.21	0.20	0.20	0.19	0.19	0.18	0.18	0.18	0.17	0.17	0.16
TEXAS	0.27	0.22	0.20	0.20	0.20	0.19	0.19	0.19	0.18	0.17	0.17	0.17	0.17	0.16
UTAH	0.18	0.12	0.10	0.09	0.09	0.08	0.08	0.07	0.07	0.06	0.06	0.05	0.05	0.05
VERMONT	0.80	0.60	0.59	0.54	0.53	0.52	0.49	0.49	0.47	0.47	0.46	0.44	0.43	0.42
VIRGINIA	0.28	0.21	0.20	0.20	0.19	0.18	0.19	0.18	0.18	0.17	0.17	0.17	0.16	0.16
WASHINGTON	0.79	0.51	0.43	0.39	0.36	0.36	0.33	0.31	0.29	0.26	0.25	0.24	0.23	0.21
WEST VIRGINIA	0.33	0.27	0.24	0.22	0.23	0.22	0.21	0.21	0.20	0.20	0.19	0.19	0.19	0.19
WISCONSIN	0.31	0.20	0.18	0.17	0.17	0.17	0.15	0.14	0.14	0.13	0.13	0.12	0.12	0.11
WYOMING	0.11	0.08	0.08	0.07	0.06	0.06	0.06	0.05	0.05	0.05	0.04	0.04	0.04	0.04
AVERAGE	0.34	0.25	0.23	0.21	0.21	0.20	0.19	0.19	0.18	0.17	0.17	0.17	0.16	0.15

* EFFECTIVE TAX RATE EQUALS ZERO BEFORE ROUNDING. AN ENTIRE ROW OF * MEANS THAT THIS TAX IS NOT USED IN THIS STATE.

TABLE A-5

EFFECTIVE TAX RATES: STATE SELECTIVE SALES AND GROSS RECEIPTS TAXES-INSURANCE (BENCHMARK)
INCIDENCE: 3/5 CONSUMERS, 2/5 HOUSEHOLDS CONSUMING INSURANCE
ALLOCATOR: CONSUMPTION AND INSURANCE EXPENDITURES

STATE	UNDER $3,000	$3,000 -3,999	$4,000 -4,999	$5,000 -5,999	$6,000 -6,999	$7,000 -7,999	$8,000 -9,999	$10,000 -11,999	$12,000 -14,999	$15,000 -19,999	$20,000 -24,999	$25,000 -29,999	$30,000 -34,999	OVER $35,000
ALABAMA	0.25	0.18	0.16	0.15	0.14	0.14	0.13	0.12	0.12	0.11	0.11	0.11	0.11	0.09
ALASKA	0.29	0.21	0.20	0.20	0.19	0.17	0.17	0.16	0.15	0.14	0.14	0.14	0.13	0.12
ARIZONA	0.18	0.13	0.11	0.11	0.10	0.09	0.09	0.09	0.09	0.08	0.08	0.07	0.08	0.07
ARKANSAS	0.22	0.15	0.14	0.13	0.13	0.12	0.12	0.11	0.10	0.10	0.10	0.09	0.09	0.09
CALIFORNIA	0.22	0.17	0.15	0.14	0.13	0.13	0.12	0.12	0.11	0.11	0.10	0.10	0.10	0.09
COLORADO	0.16	0.12	0.10	0.09	0.09	0.09	0.08	0.08	0.08	0.07	0.07	0.07	0.07	0.06
CONNECTICUT	0.15	0.12	0.11	0.11	0.11	0.11	0.10	0.10	0.09	0.09	0.09	0.09	0.08	0.08
DELAWARE	0.17	0.12	0.12	0.10	0.10	0.10	0.09	0.08	0.09	0.08	0.08	0.08	0.07	0.07
FLORIDA	0.17	0.12	0.11	0.10	0.10	0.09	0.09	0.08	0.08	0.08	0.07	0.07	0.07	0.06
GEORGIA	0.19	0.12	0.12	0.11	0.11	0.11	0.10	0.09	0.09	0.09	0.08	0.08	0.08	0.07
HAWAII	0.26	0.20	0.20	0.19	0.18	0.18	0.17	0.16	0.16	0.15	0.15	0.15	0.14	0.14
IDAHO	0.25	0.17	0.15	0.15	0.15	0.14	0.14	0.13	0.12	0.12	0.11	0.11	0.11	0.10
ILLINOIS	0.11	0.08	0.08	0.07	0.07	0.07	0.06	0.06	0.05	0.06	0.05	0.05	0.05	0.05
INDIANA	0.15	0.11	0.09	0.09	0.09	0.08	0.08	0.07	0.07	0.07	0.06	0.06	0.06	0.06
IOWA	0.20	0.15	0.14	0.12	0.12	0.11	0.11	0.11	0.10	0.10	0.09	0.09	0.09	0.09
KANSAS	0.22	0.15	0.14	0.12	0.12	0.12	0.12	0.11	0.10	0.10	0.09	0.09	0.09	0.09
KENTUCKY	0.33	0.24	0.22	0.19	0.19	0.18	0.18	0.17	0.16	0.16	0.15	0.15	0.15	0.13
LOUISIANA	0.26	0.18	0.16	0.16	0.15	0.14	0.14	0.13	0.12	0.12	0.12	0.12	0.11	0.10
MAINE	0.16	0.12	0.11	0.10	0.10	0.09	0.09	0.09	0.09	0.08	0.08	0.08	0.08	0.07
MARYLAND	0.19	0.13	0.12	0.10	0.10	0.10	0.10	0.09	0.09	0.08	0.08	0.08	0.08	0.07
MASSACHUSETTS	0.27	0.24	0.21	0.19	0.19	0.18	0.18	0.17	0.16	0.16	0.16	0.16	0.15	0.14
MICHIGAN	0.11	0.08	0.07	0.06	0.06	0.06	0.06	0.06	0.05	0.05	0.05	0.05	0.05	0.04
MINNESOTA	0.23	0.17	0.14	0.14	0.13	0.13	0.12	0.12	0.11	0.11	0.10	0.10	0.10	0.09
MISSISSIPPI	0.30	0.22	0.19	0.18	0.16	0.17	0.16	0.15	0.14	0.14	0.13	0.13	0.13	0.12
MISSOURI	0.20	0.13	0.13	0.12	0.11	0.11	0.10	0.10	0.09	0.09	0.09	0.08	0.08	0.08
MONTANA	0.29	0.22	0.20	0.18	0.18	0.17	0.16	0.16	0.15	0.14	0.14	0.14	0.13	0.13
NEBRASKA	0.20	0.15	0.12	0.12	0.11	0.11	0.10	0.10	0.10	0.09	0.09	0.09	0.09	0.08
NEVADA	0.20	0.15	0.14	0.13	0.13	0.12	0.12	0.11	0.11	0.10	0.10	0.09	0.09	0.08
NEW HAMPSHIRE	0.17	0.13	0.11	0.11	0.11	0.10	0.10	0.09	0.09	0.09	0.09	0.09	0.09	0.08
NEW JERSEY	0.12	0.09	0.09	0.08	0.08	0.08	0.08	0.07	0.07	0.07	0.07	0.07	0.06	0.06
NEW MEXICO	0.24	0.18	0.17	0.15	0.15	0.14	0.14	0.13	0.12	0.12	0.12	0.11	0.11	0.11
NEW YORK	0.20	0.15	0.13	0.12	0.12	0.12	0.11	0.11	0.10	0.10	0.10	0.10	0.10	0.09
NORTH CAROLINA	0.23	0.16	0.15	0.13	0.13	0.12	0.12	0.11	0.11	0.11	0.10	0.10	0.10	0.09
NORTH DAKOTA	0.25	0.17	0.15	0.14	0.13	0.13	0.12	0.12	0.12	0.11	0.11	0.10	0.10	0.10
OHIO	0.16	0.12	0.11	0.10	0.09	0.09	0.09	0.08	0.08	0.08	0.08	0.07	0.07	0.07
OKLAHOMA	0.33	0.21	0.19	0.19	0.18	0.17	0.16	0.15	0.14	0.14	0.13	0.13	0.13	0.12
OREGON	0.18	0.13	0.11	0.11	0.10	0.10	0.10	0.09	0.09	0.08	0.08	0.08	0.07	0.07
PENNSYLVANIA	0.16	0.11	0.11	0.10	0.10	0.09	0.09	0.09	0.08	0.08	0.08	0.08	0.08	0.07
RHODE ISLAND	0.16	0.11	0.11	0.10	0.09	0.09	0.09	0.09	0.09	0.08	0.08	0.08	0.08	0.07
SOUTH CAROLINA	0.19	0.13	0.12	0.11	0.11	0.11	0.10	0.10	0.10	0.09	0.09	0.09	0.08	0.08
SOUTH DAKOTA	0.27	0.19	0.18	0.16	0.16	0.15	0.14	0.14	0.13	0.13	0.13	0.12	0.12	0.11
TENNESSEE	0.21	0.16	0.14	0.13	0.13	0.12	0.12	0.11	0.11	0.10	0.10	0.10	0.10	0.09
TEXAS	0.21	0.15	0.14	0.13	0.12	0.12	0.12	0.11	0.10	0.10	0.10	0.09	0.09	0.08
UTAH	0.18	0.13	0.11	0.10	0.11	0.10	0.09	0.09	0.09	0.08	0.08	0.08	0.08	0.07
VERMONT	0.22	0.16	0.15	0.14	0.13	0.13	0.12	0.12	0.12	0.12	0.11	0.11	0.11	0.10
VIRGINIA	0.24	0.15	0.14	0.13	0.12	0.12	0.12	0.11	0.10	0.10	0.10	0.09	0.09	0.09
WASHINGTON	0.15	0.11	0.09	0.09	0.08	0.08	0.08	0.07	0.07	0.07	0.07	0.06	0.06	0.06
WEST VIRGINIA	0.23	0.17	0.14	0.13	0.13	0.12	0.11	0.11	0.10	0.10	0.10	0.09	0.09	0.09
WISCONSIN	0.14	0.09	0.08	0.08	0.08	0.08	0.07	0.07	0.06	0.06	0.06	0.06	0.06	0.05
WYOMING	0.16	0.13	0.12	0.11	0.11	0.10	0.10	0.09	0.09	0.09	0.08	0.08	0.08	0.08
AVERAGE	0.21	0.15	0.14	0.13	0.12	0.12	0.11	0.11	0.10	0.10	0.10	0.09	0.09	0.09

* EFFECTIVE TAX RATE EQUALS ZERO BEFORE ROUNDING. AN ENTIRE ROW OF * MEANS THAT THIS TAX IS NOT USED IN THIS STATE.

TABLE A-6
EFFECTIVE TAX RATES: STATE SELECTIVE SALES AND GROSS RECEIPTS TAXES-INSURANCE
INCIDENCE: HOUSEHOLDS CONSUMING INSURANCE
ALLOCATOR: INSURANCE EXPENDITURES

STATE	UNDER $3,000	$3,000 -3,999	$4,000 -4,999	$5,000 -5,999	$6,000 -6,999	$7,000 -7,999	$8,000 -9,999	$10,000 -11,999	$12,000 -14,999	$15,000 -19,999	$20,000 -24,999	$25,000 -29,999	$30,000 -34,999	OVER $35,000
ALABAMA	0.08	0.11	0.11	0.11	0.11	0.12	0.12	0.12	0.12	0.12	0.13	0.13	0.13	0.12
ALASKA	0.02	0.08	0.10	0.11	0.12	0.11	0.12	0.13	0.14	0.13	0.14	0.14	0.14	0.14
ARIZONA	*	0.05	0.05	0.06	0.07	0.07	0.08	0.08	0.09	0.09	0.09	0.09	0.09	0.10
ARKANSAS	0.07	0.10	0.10	0.10	0.11	0.11	0.11	0.11	0.11	0.11	0.11	0.11	0.11	0.11
CALIFORNIA	0.00	0.06	0.07	0.08	0.09	0.09	0.10	0.10	0.11	0.11	0.12	0.12	0.12	0.12
COLORADO	*	0.04	0.05	0.06	0.06	0.06	0.07	0.07	0.08	0.08	0.08	0.08	0.08	0.08
CONNECTICUT	0.02	0.06	0.06	0.07	0.08	0.09	0.08	0.09	0.09	0.09	0.09	0.10	0.10	0.09
DELAWARE	0.05	0.06	0.08	0.07	0.08	0.08	0.08	0.08	0.08	0.08	0.09	0.08	0.08	0.08
FLORIDA	0.05	0.07	0.07	0.07	0.08	0.08	0.08	0.08	0.08	0.08	0.08	0.08	0.08	0.08
GEORGIA	0.06	0.07	0.08	0.08	0.09	0.09	0.09	0.09	0.09	0.09	0.09	0.09	0.09	0.09
HAWAII	0.01	0.07	0.10	0.11	0.12	0.13	0.13	0.14	0.15	0.15	0.16	0.16	0.16	0.17
IDAHO	0.00	0.07	0.08	0.10	0.10	0.10	0.12	0.12	0.12	0.13	0.13	0.13	0.14	0.14
ILLINOIS	0.03	0.05	0.05	0.05	0.05	0.05	0.05	0.05	0.06	0.06	0.06	0.06	0.06	0.06
INDIANA	0.04	0.06	0.06	0.06	0.06	0.07	0.07	0.07	0.07	0.07	0.07	0.07	0.07	0.07
IOWA	0.06	0.08	0.09	0.08	0.09	0.09	0.09	0.10	0.10	0.10	0.10	0.10	0.10	0.11
KANSAS	0.06	0.08	0.09	0.09	0.10	0.10	0.10	0.10	0.10	0.10	0.10	0.11	0.11	0.11
KENTUCKY	0.11	0.14	0.15	0.15	0.15	0.16	0.17	0.17	0.17	0.17	0.18	0.18	0.17	0.17
LOUISIANA	0.09	0.10	0.11	0.12	0.12	0.12	0.13	0.13	0.13	0.13	0.13	0.13	0.13	0.13
MAINE	0.03	0.06	0.07	0.07	0.08	0.08	0.09	0.09	0.09	0.09	0.10	0.09	0.10	0.10
MARYLAND	0.05	0.07	0.07	0.07	0.08	0.08	0.08	0.08	0.08	0.08	0.08	0.09	0.09	0.09
MASSACHUSETTS	0.04	0.12	0.12	0.13	0.14	0.14	0.15	0.16	0.16	0.17	0.17	0.18	0.18	0.17
MICHIGAN	0.03	0.04	0.04	0.04	0.05	0.05	0.05	0.05	0.05	0.05	0.05	0.05	0.05	0.05
MINNESOTA	0.06	0.09	0.09	0.10	0.10	0.11	0.10	0.11	0.11	0.11	0.11	0.11	0.12	0.11
MISSISSIPPI	0.10	0.14	0.14	0.14	0.14	0.15	0.15	0.15	0.15	0.15	0.16	0.16	0.16	0.15
MISSOURI	0.06	0.07	0.09	0.08	0.09	0.09	0.09	0.09	0.09	0.09	0.10	0.10	0.10	0.09
MONTANA	0.00	0.09	0.11	0.12	0.13	0.13	0.14	0.15	0.15	0.16	0.16	0.17	0.17	0.17
NEBRASKA	0.06	0.08	0.08	0.08	0.09	0.09	0.09	0.10	0.10	0.10	0.10	0.10	0.10	0.10
NEVADA	0.00	0.06	0.07	0.08	0.09	0.09	0.09	0.10	0.10	0.11	0.11	0.11	0.11	0.11
NEW HAMPSHIRE	0.03	0.06	0.06	0.08	0.08	0.08	0.09	0.09	0.09	0.10	0.10	0.10	0.10	0.10
NEW JERSEY	0.02	0.05	0.05	0.06	0.06	0.06	0.06	0.07	0.07	0.07	0.07	0.07	0.07	0.07
NEW MEXICO	0.00	0.07	0.09	0.10	0.11	0.11	0.12	0.12	0.12	0.13	0.14	0.14	0.14	0.14
NEW YORK	0.04	0.07	0.08	0.08	0.09	0.09	0.09	0.10	0.10	0.10	0.11	0.11	0.11	0.11
NORTH CAROLINA	0.08	0.10	0.10	0.10	0.11	0.10	0.11	0.11	0.11	0.11	0.11	0.12	0.12	0.11
NORTH DAKOTA	0.07	0.10	0.10	0.10	0.10	0.11	0.11	0.11	0.12	0.12	0.12	0.12	0.12	0.12
OHIO	0.04	0.06	0.07	0.07	0.07	0.08	0.08	0.08	0.08	0.08	0.08	0.08	0.08	0.08
OKLAHOMA	0.10	0.13	0.13	0.14	0.15	0.14	0.14	0.15	0.15	0.15	0.15	0.15	0.15	0.15
OREGON	0.00	0.05	0.06	0.07	0.07	0.08	0.08	0.09	0.09	0.09	0.09	0.10	0.09	0.10
PENNSYLVANIA	0.03	0.06	0.06	0.07	0.07	0.08	0.08	0.08	0.08	0.09	0.09	0.09	0.09	0.09
RHODE ISLAND	0.03	0.05	0.07	0.07	0.07	0.07	0.08	0.08	0.09	0.09	0.09	0.09	0.09	0.09
SOUTH CAROLINA	0.06	0.08	0.08	0.09	0.09	0.09	0.09	0.10	0.10	0.10	0.10	0.10	0.10	0.10
SOUTH DAKOTA	0.08	0.11	0.12	0.12	0.13	0.13	0.13	0.14	0.14	0.14	0.14	0.14	0.14	0.14
TENNESSEE	0.07	0.09	0.10	0.10	0.10	0.11	0.11	0.11	0.11	0.11	0.11	0.11	0.12	0.11
TEXAS	0.07	0.09	0.09	0.10	0.10	0.10	0.10	0.10	0.10	0.11	0.11	0.11	0.11	0.10
UTAH	*	0.05	0.05	0.06	0.07	0.07	0.08	0.08	0.09	0.09	0.09	0.09	0.09	0.10
VERMONT	0.04	0.08	0.10	0.10	0.11	0.11	0.11	0.12	0.12	0.13	0.13	0.13	0.13	0.13
VIRGINIA	0.07	0.08	0.09	0.09	0.09	0.10	0.10	0.10	0.10	0.10	0.11	0.11	0.10	0.10
WASHINGTON	0.00	0.04	0.05	0.05	0.06	0.06	0.06	0.07	0.07	0.07	0.08	0.08	0.07	0.08
WEST VIRGINIA	0.08	0.10	0.10	0.10	0.10	0.11	0.10	0.11	0.11	0.11	0.11	0.11	0.11	0.11
WISCONSIN	0.04	0.05	0.05	0.06	0.06	0.06	0.06	0.06	0.06	0.07	0.07	0.07	0.07	0.07
WYOMING	0.00	0.05	0.06	0.07	0.07	0.08	0.08	0.09	0.09	0.09	0.09	0.10	0.10	0.10
AVERAGE	0.04	0.08	0.08	0.09	0.09	0.10	0.10	0.10	0.10	0.11	0.11	0.11	0.11	0.11

* EFFECTIVE TAX RATE EQUALS ZERO BEFORE ROUNDING. AN ENTIRE ROW OF * MEANS THAT THIS TAX IS NOT USED IN THIS STATE.

TABLE A-7

EFFECTIVE TAX RATES: STATE SELECTIVE SALES AND GROSS RECEIPTS TAXES-UTILITIES
INCIDENCE: CONSUMERS OF UTILITY SERVICES
ALLOCATOR: GAS, ELECTRIC, AND TELEPHONE EXPENDITURES

STATE	UNDER $3,000	$3,000 -3,999	$4,000 -4,999	$5,000 -5,999	$6,000 -6,999	$7,000 -7,999	$8,000 -9,999	$10,000 -11,999	$12,000 -14,999	$15,000 -19,999	$20,000 -24,999	$25,000 -29,999	$30,000 -34,999	OVER $35,000
ALABAMA	1.60	0.90	0.76	0.65	0.57	0.55	0.49	0.43	0.38	0.33	0.30	0.28	0.27	0.21
ALASKA	0.10	0.06	0.05	0.05	0.04	0.04	0.04	0.03	0.03	0.03	0.02	0.02	0.02	0.02
ARIZONA	0.25	0.15	0.11	0.11	0.09	0.08	0.08	0.07	0.06	0.06	0.05	0.04	0.04	0.04
ARKANSAS	*	*	*	*	*	*	*	*	*	*	*	*	*	*
CALIFORNIA	0.03	0.02	0.02	0.01	0.01	0.01	0.01	0.01	0.01	0.01	0.01	0.01	0.01	0.01
COLORADO	0.01	0.01	0.01	0.00	0.00	0.00	0.00	0.00	0.00	0.00	0.00	0.00	0.00	0.00
CONNECTICUT	1.32	0.89	0.74	0.69	0.62	0.63	0.52	0.48	0.43	0.38	0.35	0.33	0.31	0.27
DELAWARE	0.79	0.44	0.42	0.33	0.31	0.29	0.26	0.22	0.21	0.19	0.17	0.15	0.14	0.12
FLORIDA	0.41	0.24	0.19	0.17	0.16	0.14	0.13	0.11	0.10	0.09	0.08	0.07	0.07	0.06
GEORGIA	*	*	*	*	*	*	*	*	*	*	*	*	*	*
HAWAII	1.51	0.95	0.92	0.82	0.73	0.69	0.62	0.55	0.51	0.45	0.41	0.39	0.37	0.32
IDAHO	0.08	0.05	0.04	0.04	0.03	0.03	0.03	0.02	0.02	0.02	0.02	0.02	0.01	0.01
ILLINOIS	1.30	0.82	0.69	0.62	0.54	0.51	0.46	0.41	0.38	0.33	0.30	0.28	0.27	0.23
INDIANA	*	*	*	*	*	*	*	*	*	*	*	*	*	*
IOWA	*	*	*	*	*	*	*	*	*	*	*	*	*	*
KANSAS	0.01	0.00	0.00	0.00	0.00	0.00	0.00	0.00	0.00	0.00	0.00	0.00	0.00	0.00
KENTUCKY	*	*	*	*	*	*	*	*	*	*	*	*	*	*
LOUISIANA	0.26	0.14	0.12	0.11	0.10	0.09	0.08	0.07	0.06	0.06	0.05	0.05	0.04	0.04
MAINE	0.57	0.34	0.29	0.24	0.23	0.21	0.19	0.17	0.15	0.13	0.12	0.11	0.11	0.09
MARYLAND	0.52	0.30	0.25	0.21	0.19	0.18	0.16	0.15	0.13	0.11	0.10	0.09	0.09	0.08
MASSACHUSETTS	*	*	*	*	*	*	*	*	*	*	*	*	*	*
MICHIGAN	*	*	*	*	*	*	*	*	*	*	*	*	*	*
MINNESOTA	0.85	0.53	0.40	0.37	0.33	0.33	0.27	0.25	0.22	0.20	0.18	0.16	0.16	0.13
MISSISSIPPI	[illegible]	0.01	0.01	0.01	0.01	0.01	0.01	0.01	0.00	0.00	0.00	0.00	0.00	0.00
MISSOURI	0.00	0.00	0.00	0.00	0.00	0.00	0.00	0.00	0.00	0.00	0.00	0.00	0.00	0.00
MONTANA	0.26	0.16	0.13	0.12	0.11	0.10	0.09	0.08	0.07	0.06	0.06	0.05	0.05	0.04
NEBRASKA	*	*	*	*	*	*	*	*	*	*	*	*	*	*
NEVADA	0.07	0.05	0.04	0.03	0.03	0.03	0.03	0.02	0.02	0.02	0.02	0.02	0.01	0.01
NEW HAMPSHIRE	0.17	0.11	0.08	0.08	0.07	0.06	0.06	0.05	0.05	0.04	0.04	0.04	0.03	0.03
NEW JERSEY	0.29	0.19	0.16	0.14	0.13	0.13	0.11	0.10	0.09	0.08	0.08	0.07	0.07	0.06
NEW MEXICO	0.17	0.10	0.09	0.08	0.07	0.06	0.06	0.05	0.04	0.04	0.04	0.03	0.03	0.03
NEW YORK	1.15	0.67	0.54	0.47	0.44	0.41	0.36	0.34	0.30	0.27	0.25	0.23	0.22	0.18
NORTH CAROLINA	1.66	0.94	0.80	0.64	0.62	0.55	0.51	0.45	0.41	0.35	0.32	0.30	0.28	0.24
NORTH DAKOTA	0.22	0.12	0.10	0.09	0.08	0.08	0.07	0.06	0.06	0.05	0.04	0.04	0.04	0.03
OHIO	0.99	0.60	0.51	0.43	0.40	0.38	0.34	0.30	0.27	0.24	0.22	0.20	0.19	0.16
OKLAHOMA	0.07	0.04	0.03	0.03	0.03	0.02	0.02	0.02	0.02	0.01	0.01	0.01	0.01	0.01
OREGON	0.02	0.01	0.01	0.01	0.01	0.01	0.01	0.01	0.01	0.01	0.01	0.00	0.00	0.00
PENNSYLVANIA	1.19	0.69	0.58	0.50	0.47	0.44	0.40	0.36	0.32	0.29	0.26	0.25	0.24	0.20
RHODE ISLAND	1.50	0.82	0.79	0.67	0.57	0.55	0.50	0.45	0.42	0.37	0.34	0.32	0.30	0.26
SOUTH CAROLINA	0.37	0.21	0.17	0.16	0.14	0.13	0.12	0.11	0.10	0.08	0.08	0.07	0.07	0.06
SOUTH DAKOTA	0.02	0.01	0.01	0.01	0.01	0.01	0.01	0.01	0.01	0.01	0.00	0.00	0.00	0.00
TENNESSEE	0.13	0.08	0.06	0.06	0.05	0.05	0.04	0.04	0.03	0.03	0.03	0.02	0.02	0.02
TEXAS	0.43	0.25	0.21	0.19	0.17	0.15	0.14	0.12	0.11	0.10	0.09	0.08	0.07	0.06
UTAH	0.03	0.02	0.01	0.01	0.01	0.01	0.01	0.01	0.01	0.01	0.01	0.01	0.01	0.00
VERMONT	1.10	0.63	0.56	0.47	0.43	0.40	0.36	0.33	0.29	0.27	0.24	0.22	0.20	0.18
VIRGINIA	1.08	0.56	0.49	0.44	0.38	0.35	0.32	0.29	0.25	0.22	0.20	0.18	0.17	0.15
WASHINGTON	0.96	0.56	0.45	0.40	0.36	0.34	0.31	0.28	0.25	0.22	0.20	0.18	0.17	0.15
WEST VIRGINIA	*	*	*	*	*	*	*	*	*	*	*	*	*	*
WISCONSIN	0.93	0.52	0.44	0.39	0.36	0.34	0.29	0.26	0.24	0.21	0.19	0.18	0.17	0.14
WYOMING	*	*	*	*	*	*	*	*	*	*	*	*	*	*
AVERAGE	0.56	0.33	0.28	0.25	0.22	0.21	0.19	0.17	0.15	0.13	0.12	0.11	0.11	0.09

* EFFECTIVE TAX RATE EQUALS ZERO BEFORE ROUNDING. AN ENTIRE ROW OF * MEANS THAT THIS TAX IS NOT USED IN THIS STATE.

TABLE A-8
EFFECTIVE TAX RATES: STATE SELECTIVE SALES AND GROSS RECEIPTS TAXES-PARIMUTUELS
INCIDENCE: USERS OF RECREATIONAL FACILITIES
ALLOCATOR: RECREATION EXPENDITURES

STATE	UNDER $3,000	$3,000 -3,999	$4,000 -4,999	$5,000 -5,999	$6,000 -6,999	$7,000 -7,999	$8,000 -9,999	$10,000 -11,999	$12,000 -14,999	$15,000 -19,999	$20,000 -24,999	$25,000 -29,999	$30,000 -34,999	OVER $35,000
ALABAMA	*	*	*	*	*	*	*	*	*	*	*	*	*	*
ALASKA	*	*	*	*	*	*	*	*	*	*	*	*	*	*
ARIZONA	0.10	0.07	0.06	0.06	0.06	0.05	0.05	0.05	0.05	0.05	0.05	0.04	0.04	0.04
ARKANSAS	0.10	0.08	0.07	0.07	0.07	0.06	0.06	0.06	0.06	0.05	0.05	0.05	0.05	0.05
CALIFORNIA	0.07	0.05	0.05	0.04	0.04	0.04	0.04	0.04	0.03	0.03	0.03	0.03	0.03	0.03
COLORADO	0.08	0.06	0.05	0.05	0.05	0.04	0.04	0.04	0.04	0.04	0.04	0.04	0.03	0.03
CONNECTICUT	0.04	0.04	0.04	0.04	0.04	0.04	0.04	0.04	0.04	0.04	0.04	0.04	0.04	0.04
DELAWARE	0.19	0.14	0.14	0.12	0.12	0.12	0.12	0.11	0.11	0.11	0.10	0.10	0.10	0.09
FLORIDA	0.15	0.12	0.10	0.10	0.10	0.09	0.09	0.09	0.08	0.08	0.08	0.08	0.07	0.07
GEORGIA	*	*	*	*	*	*	*	*	*	*	*	*	*	*
HAWAII	*	*	*	*	*	*	*	*	*	*	*	*	*	*
IDAHO	0.01	0.01	0.01	0.01	0.01	0.01	0.01	0.01	0.01	0.01	0.01	0.01	0.01	0.01
ILLINOIS	0.07	0.06	0.06	0.06	0.05	0.05	0.05	0.05	0.05	0.05	0.05	0.05	0.05	0.05
INDIANA	*	*	*	*	*	*	*	*	*	*	*	*	*	*
IOWA	*	*	*	*	*	*	*	*	*	*	*	*	*	*
KANSAS	*	*	*	*	*	*	*	*	*	*	*	*	*	*
KENTUCKY	0.06	0.04	0.04	0.04	0.04	0.03	0.03	0.03	0.03	0.03	0.03	0.03	0.03	0.03
LOUISIANA	0.10	0.07	0.06	0.06	0.06	0.06	0.06	0.05	0.05	0.05	0.05	0.05	0.05	0.04
MAINE	0.03	0.03	0.03	0.02	0.02	0.02	0.02	0.02	0.02	0.02	0.02	0.02	0.02	0.02
MARYLAND	0.07	0.05	0.05	0.04	0.04	0.04	0.04	0.04	0.04	0.04	0.04	0.04	0.03	0.03
MASSACHUSETTS	0.05	0.05	0.05	0.05	0.05	0.05	0.05	0.05	0.05	0.05	0.05	0.05	0.05	0.05
MICHIGAN	0.07	0.06	0.06	0.05	0.05	0.05	0.05	0.05	0.05	0.05	0.05	0.05	0.05	0.04
MINNESOTA	*	*	*	*	*	*	*	*	*	*	*	*	*	*
MISSISSIPPI	*	*	*	*	*	*	*	*	*	*	*	*	*	*
MISSOURI	*	*	*	*	*	*	*	*	*	*	*	*	*	*
MONTANA	*	*	*	*	*	*	*	*	*	*	*	*	*	*
NEBRASKA	0.05	0.04	0.03	0.03	0.03	0.03	0.03	0.03	0.03	0.03	0.03	0.03	0.03	0.03
NEVADA	0.01	0.01	0.01	0.01	0.01	0.00	0.00	0.00	0.00	0.00	0.00	0.00	0.00	0.00
NEW HAMPSHIRE	0.21	0.19	0.17	0.18	0.18	0.17	0.18	0.18	0.18	0.18	0.18	0.18	0.18	0.17
NEW JERSEY	0.04	0.04	0.04	0.04	0.04	0.04	0.04	0.04	0.04	0.04	0.04	0.04	0.04	0.04
NEW MEXICO	0.06	0.05	0.04	0.04	0.04	0.04	0.04	0.03	0.03	0.03	0.03	0.03	0.03	0.03
NEW YORK	0.10	0.09	0.08	0.08	0.08	0.08	0.08	0.08	0.08	0.08	0.08	0.08	0.08	0.07
NORTH CAROLINA	*	*	*	*	*	*	*	*	*	*	*	*	*	*
NORTH DAKOTA	*	*	*	*	*	*	*	*	*	*	*	*	*	*
OHIO	0.03	0.02	0.02	0.02	0.02	0.02	0.02	0.02	0.02	0.02	0.02	0.02	0.02	0.02
OKLAHOMA	*	*	*	*	*	*	*	*	*	*	*	*	*	*
OREGON	0.06	0.04	0.04	0.04	0.04	0.04	0.03	0.03	0.03	0.03	0.03	0.03	0.03	0.03
PENNSYLVANIA	0.05	0.04	0.04	0.04	0.04	0.04	0.04	0.04	0.04	0.04	0.04	0.04	0.04	0.04
RHODE ISLAND	0.05	0.04	0.05	0.04	0.04	0.04	0.04	0.04	0.04	0.04	0.04	0.04	0.04	0.04
SOUTH CAROLINA	*	*	*	*	*	*	*	*	*	*	*	*	*	*
SOUTH DAKOTA	0.04	0.03	0.03	0.03	0.03	0.03	0.03	0.03	0.03	0.03	0.03	0.03	0.02	0.02
TENNESSEE	*	*	*	*	*	*	*	*	*	*	*	*	*	*
TEXAS	*	*	*	*	*	*	*	*	*	*	*	*	*	*
UTAH	*	*	*	*	*	*	*	*	*	*	*	*	*	*
VERMONT	0.06	0.05	0.05	0.05	0.05	0.05	0.05	0.05	0.05	0.05	0.05	0.05	0.05	0.04
VIRGINIA	*	*	*	*	*	*	*	*	*	*	*	*	*	*
WASHINGTON	0.05	0.03	0.03	0.03	0.03	0.03	0.03	0.02	0.02	0.02	0.02	0.02	0.02	0.02
WEST VIRGINIA	0.13	0.10	0.09	0.08	0.08	0.08	0.07	0.07	0.07	0.07	0.06	0.06	0.06	0.06
WISCONSIN	*	*	*	*	*	*	*	*	*	*	*	*	*	*
WYOMING	0.00	0.00	0.00	0.00	0.00	0.00	0.00	0.00	0.00	0.00	0.00	0.00	0.00	0.00
AVERAGE	0.07	0.06	0.05	0.05	0.05	0.05	0.05	0.05	0.05	0.04	0.04	0.04	0.04	0.04

* EFFECTIVE TAX RATE EQUALS ZERO BEFORE ROUNDING. AN ENTIRE ROW OF * MEANS THAT THIS TAX IS NOT USED IN THIS STATE.

TABLE A-9

EFFECTIVE TAX RATES: STATE SELECTIVE SALES AND GROSS RECEIPTS TAXES-AMUSEMENTS
INCIDENCE: USERS OF RECREATIONAL FACILITIES
ALLOCATOR: RECREATION EXPENDITURES

STATE	UNDER $3,000	$3,000 -3,999	$4,000 -4,999	$5,000 -5,999	$6,000 -6,999	$7,000 -7,999	$8,000 -9,999	$10,000 -11,999	$12,000 -14,999	$15,000 -19,999	$20,000 -24,999	$25,000 -29,999	$30,000 -34,999	OVER $35,000
ALABAMA	0.00	0.00	0.00	0.00	0.00	0.00	0.00	0.00	0.00	0.00	0.00	0.00	0.00	0.00
ALASKA	*	*	*	*	*	*	*	*	*	*	*	*	*	*
ARIZONA	*	*	*	*	*	*	*	*	*	*	*	*	*	*
ARKANSAS	*	*	*	*	*	*	*	*	*	*	*	*	*	*
CALIFORNIA	0.00	0.00	0.00	0.00	0.00	0.00	0.00	0.00	0.00	0.00	0.00	0.00	0.00	0.00
COLORADO	0.00	0.00	0.00	0.00	0.00	0.00	0.00	0.00	0.00	0.00	0.00	0.00	0.00	0.00
CONNECTICUT	0.04	0.05	0.04	0.05	0.04	0.05	0.04	0.04	0.04	0.04	0.04	0.04	0.04	0.04
DELAWARE	0.00	0.00	0.00	0.00	0.00	0.00	0.00	0.00	0.00	0.00	0.00	0.00	0.00	0.00
FLORIDA	0.01	0.01	0.01	0.01	0.01	0.01	0.00	0.00	0.00	0.00	0.00	0.00	0.00	0.00
GEORGIA	*	*	*	*	*	*	*	*	*	*	*	*	*	*
HAWAII	*	*	*	*	*	*	*	*	*	*	*	*	*	*
IDAHO	*	*	*	*	*	*	*	*	*	*	*	*	*	*
ILLINOIS	0.02	0.02	0.01	0.01	0.01	0.01	0.01	0.01	0.01	0.01	0.01	0.01	0.01	0.01
INDIANA	0.00	0.00	0.00	0.00	0.00	0.00	0.00	0.00	0.00	0.00	0.00	0.00	0.00	0.00
IOWA	*	*	*	*	*	*	*	*	*	*	*	*	*	*
KANSAS	0.00	0.00	0.00	0.00	0.00	0.00	0.00	0.00	0.00	0.00	0.00	0.00	0.00	0.00
KENTUCKY	0.00	0.00	0.00	0.00	0.00	0.00	0.00	0.00	0.00	0.00	0.00	0.00	0.00	0.00
LOUISIANA	0.00	0.00	0.00	0.00	0.00	0.00	0.00	0.00	0.00	0.00	0.00	0.00	0.00	0.00
MAINE	*	*	*	*	*	*	*	*	*	*	*	*	*	*
MARYLAND	0.00	0.00	0.00	0.00	0.00	0.00	0.00	0.00	0.00	0.00	0.00	0.00	0.00	0.00
MASSACHUSETTS	0.02	0.02	0.02	0.02	0.02	0.02	0.02	0.02	0.02	0.02	0.02	0.02	0.02	0.02
MICHIGAN	0.00	0.00	0.00	0.00	0.00	0.00	0.00	0.00	0.00	0.00	0.00	0.00	0.00	0.00
MINNESOTA	0.00	0.00	0.00	0.00	0.00	0.00	0.00	0.00	0.00	0.00	0.00	0.00	0.00	0.00
MISSISSIPPI	0.02	0.01	0.01	0.01	0.01	0.01	0.01	0.01	0.01	0.01	0.01	0.01	0.01	0.01
MISSOURI	*	*	*	*	*	*	*	*	*	*	*	*	*	*
MONTANA	*	*	*	*	*	*	*	*	*	*	*	*	*	*
NEBRASKA	0.01	0.01	0.01	0.01	0.01	0.01	0.01	0.01	0.01	0.01	0.01	0.01	0.01	0.01
NEVADA	0.82	0.65	0.58	0.54	0.55	0.53	0.50	0.47	0.45	0.43	0.41	0.41	0.41	0.37
NEW HAMPSHIRE	*	*	*	*	*	*	*	*	*	*	*	*	*	*
NEW JERSEY	0.00	0.00	0.00	0.00	0.00	0.00	0.00	0.00	0.00	0.00	0.00	0.00	0.00	0.00
NEW MEXICO	0.00	0.00	0.00	0.00	0.00	0.00	0.00	0.00	0.00	0.00	0.00	0.00	0.00	0.00
NEW YORK	0.00	0.00	0.00	0.00	0.00	0.00	0.00	0.00	0.00	0.00	0.00	0.00	0.00	0.00
NORTH CAROLINA	*	*	*	*	*	*	*	*	*	*	*	*	*	*
NORTH DAKOTA	*	*	*	*	*	*	*	*	*	*	*	*	*	*
OHIO	*	*	*	*	*	*	*	*	*	*	*	*	*	*
OKLAHOMA	*	*	*	*	*	*	*	*	*	*	*	*	*	*
OREGON	*	*	*	*	*	*	*	*	*	*	*	*	*	*
PENNSYLVANIA	0.00	0.00	0.00	0.00	0.00	0.00	0.00	0.00	0.00	0.00	0.00	0.00	0.00	0.00
RHODE ISLAND	0.00	0.00	0.00	0.00	0.00	0.00	0.00	0.00	0.00	0.00	0.00	0.00	0.00	0.00
SOUTH CAROLINA	0.05	0.04	0.03	0.03	0.03	0.03	0.03	0.03	0.03	0.03	0.03	0.03	0.03	0.02
SOUTH DAKOTA	*	*	*	*	*	*	*	*	*	*	*	*	*	*
TENNESSEE	0.00	0.00	0.00	0.00	0.00	0.00	0.00	0.00	0.00	0.00	0.00	0.00	0.00	0.00
TEXAS	0.00	0.00	0.00	0.00	0.00	0.00	0.00	0.00	0.00	0.00	0.00	0.00	0.00	0.00
UTAH	*	*	*	*	*	*	*	*	*	*	*	*	*	*
VERMONT	*	*	*	*	*	*	*	*	*	*	*	*	*	*
VIRGINIA	0.00	0.00	0.00	0.00	0.00	0.00	0.00	0.00	0.00	0.00	0.00	0.00	0.00	0.00
WASHINGTON	0.00	0.00	0.00	0.00	0.00	0.00	0.00	0.00	0.00	0.00	0.00	0.00	0.00	0.00
WEST VIRGINIA	*	*	*	*	*	*	*	*	*	*	*	*	*	*
WISCONSIN	0.00	0.00	0.00	0.00	0.00	0.00	0.00	0.00	0.00	0.00	0.00	0.00	0.00	0.00
WYOMING	*	*	*	*	*	*	*	*	*	*	*	*	*	*
AVERAGE	0.03	0.03	0.03	0.02	0.02	0.02	0.02	0.02	0.02	0.02	0.02	0.02	0.02	0.02

* EFFECTIVE TAX RATE EQUALS ZERO BEFORE ROUNDING. AN ENTIRE ROW OF * MEANS THAT THIS TAX IS NOT USED IN THIS STATE.

TABLE A-10
EFFECTIVE TAX RATES: STATE SELECTIVE SALES AND GROSS RECEIPTS TAXES-OTHER N.E.C.
INCIDENCE: CONSUMERS IN GENERAL
ALLOCATOR: TOTAL CONSUMPTION EXPENDITURES

STATE	UNDER $3,000	$3,000 -3,999	$4,000 -4,999	$5,000 -5,999	$6,000 -6,999	$7,000 -7,999	$8,000 -9,999	$10,000 -11,999	$12,000 -14,999	$15,000 -19,999	$20,000 -24,999	$25,000 -29,999	$30,000 -34,999	OVER $35,000
ALABAMA	0.33	0.20	0.17	0.15	0.14	0.13	0.12	0.11	0.10	0.09	0.09	0.08	0.08	0.07
ALASKA	1.93	1.22	1.12	1.05	0.98	0.84	0.81	0.75	0.69	0.60	0.57	0.54	0.52	0.46
ARIZONA	*	*	*	*	*	*	*	*	*	*	*	*	*	*
ARKANSAS	*	*	*	*	*	*	*	*	*	*	*	*	*	*
CALIFORNIA	0.09	0.06	0.05	0.05	0.04	0.04	0.03	0.03	0.03	0.03	0.02	0.02	0.02	0.02
COLORADO	0.00	0.00	0.00	0.00	0.00	0.00	0.00	0.00	0.00	0.00	0.00	0.00	0.00	0.00
CONNECTICUT	*	*	*	*	*	*	*	*	*	*	*	*	*	*
DELAWARE	0.05	0.03	0.03	0.02	0.02	0.02	0.02	0.02	0.02	0.02	0.02	0.01	0.01	0.01
FLORIDA	0.19	0.12	0.10	0.09	0.08	0.08	0.07	0.06	0.06	0.05	0.05	0.05	0.05	0.04
GEORGIA	*	*	*	*	*	*	*	*	*	*	*	*	*	*
HAWAII	*	*	*	*	*	*	*	*	*	*	*	*	*	*
IDAHO	*	*	*	*	*	*	*	*	*	*	*	*	*	*
ILLINOIS	0.07	0.05	0.04	0.04	0.03	0.03	0.03	0.03	0.03	0.02	0.02	0.02	0.02	0.02
INDIANA	*	*	*	*	*	*	*	*	*	*	*	*	*	*
IOWA	0.00	0.00	0.00	0.00	0.00	0.00	0.00	0.00	0.00	0.00	0.00	0.00	0.00	0.00
KANSAS	*	*	*	*	*	*	*	*	*	*	*	*	*	*
KENTUCKY	1.29	0.80	0.70	0.61	0.56	0.54	0.51	0.47	0.43	0.39	0.38	0.36	0.34	0.30
LOUISIANA	0.16	0.09	0.08	0.08	0.07	0.07	0.06	0.06	0.05	0.05	0.05	0.04	0.04	0.04
MAINE	*	*	*	*	*	*	*	*	*	*	*	*	*	*
MARYLAND	1.05	0.65	0.56	0.48	0.46	0.42	0.41	0.37	0.34	0.31	0.29	0.28	0.26	0.24
MASSACHUSETTS	0.98	0.74	0.61	0.54	0.52	0.48	0.46	0.43	0.39	0.36	0.34	0.33	0.32	0.28
MICHIGAN	*	*	*	*	*	*	*	*	*	*	*	*	*	*
MINNESOTA	0.83	0.55	0.43	0.40	0.37	0.37	0.31	0.30	0.27	0.25	0.23	0.22	0.22	0.19
MISSISSIPPI	0.05	0.03	0.02	0.02	0.02	0.02	0.02	0.02	0.01	0.01	0.01	0.01	0.01	0.01
MISSOURI	*	*	*	*	*	*	*	*	*	*	*	*	*	*
MONTANA	0.24	0.15	0.13	0.11	0.11	0.10	0.09	0.08	0.07	0.07	0.06	0.06	0.05	0.05
NEBRASKA	0.04	0.02	0.02	0.02	0.02	0.01	0.01	0.01	0.01	0.01	0.01	0.01	0.01	0.01
NEVADA	0.02	0.01	0.01	0.01	0.01	0.01	0.01	0.01	0.01	0.00	0.00	0.00	0.00	0.00
NEW HAMPSHIRE	0.87	0.57	0.45	0.44	0.41	0.36	0.36	0.33	0.31	0.29	0.27	0.26	0.25	0.22
NEW JERSEY	0.10	0.07	0.06	0.06	0.05	0.05	0.05	0.04	0.04	0.04	0.04	0.03	0.03	0.03
NEW MEXICO	0.61	0.39	0.34	0.29	0.28	0.25	0.23	0.21	0.18	0.17	0.16	0.15	0.13	0.12
NEW YORK	*	*	*	*	*	*	*	*	*	*	*	*	*	*
NORTH CAROLINA	0.22	0.13	0.12	0.10	0.10	0.09	0.08	0.08	0.07	0.06	0.06	0.06	0.06	0.05
NORTH DAKOTA	0.22	0.13	0.11	0.10	0.09	0.09	0.08	0.08	0.07	0.06	0.06	0.06	0.06	0.05
OHIO	*	*	*	*	*	*	*	*	*	*	*	*	*	*
OKLAHOMA	0.62	0.35	0.30	0.28	0.26	0.24	0.22	0.20	0.18	0.17	0.16	0.15	0.14	0.13
OREGON	*	*	*	*	*	*	*	*	*	*	*	*	*	*
PENNSYLVANIA	0.00	0.00	0.00	0.00	0.00	0.00	0.00	0.00	0.00	0.00	0.00	0.00	0.00	0.00
RHODE ISLAND	*	*	*	*	*	*	*	*	*	*	*	*	*	*
SOUTH CAROLINA	0.18	0.11	0.10	0.09	0.08	0.08	0.07	0.07	0.06	0.06	0.05	0.05	0.05	0.04
SOUTH DAKOTA	0.87	0.53	0.47	0.42	0.40	0.36	0.33	0.32	0.29	0.27	0.25	0.24	0.23	0.21
TENNESSEE	0.05	0.03	0.03	0.03	0.02	0.02	0.02	0.02	0.02	0.02	0.02	0.01	0.01	0.01
TEXAS	1.23	0.77	0.65	0.60	0.55	0.51	0.49	0.45	0.41	0.37	0.35	0.33	0.32	0.28
UTAH	*	*	*	*	*	*	*	*	*	*	*	*	*	*
VERMONT	2.04	1.25	1.15	0.99	0.93	0.88	0.80	0.76	0.69	0.65	0.61	0.57	0.55	0.50
VIRGINIA	0.57	0.32	0.29	0.27	0.24	0.22	0.21	0.19	0.18	0.16	0.15	0.14	0.14	0.12
WASHINGTON	*	*	*	*	*	*	*	*	*	*	*	*	*	*
WEST VIRGINIA	1.64	1.02	0.83	0.73	0.69	0.65	0.57	0.55	0.49	0.46	0.42	0.40	0.38	0.36
WISCONSIN	0.00	0.00	0.00	0.00	0.00	0.00	0.00	0.00	0.00	0.00	0.00	0.00	0.00	0.00
WYOMING	*	*	*	*	*	*	*	*	*	*	*	*	*	*
AVERAGE	0.52	0.33	0.28	0.25	0.23	0.22	0.20	0.19	0.17	0.16	0.15	0.14	0.13	0.12

* EFFECTIVE TAX RATE EQUALS ZERO BEFORE ROUNDING. AN ENTIRE ROW OF * MEANS THAT THIS TAX IS NOT USED IN THIS STATE.

TABLE A-11
EFFECTIVE TAX RATES: TOTAL STATE SELECTIVE SALES AND GROSS RECEIPTS TAXES
INCIDENCE: SUM OF EFFECTIVE TAX RATES FOR INDIVIDUAL TAXES
ALLOCATOR: BASED ON INDIVIDUAL TAXES

STATE	UNDER $3,000	$3,000 -3,999	$4,000 -4,999	$5,000 -5,999	$6,000 -6,999	$7,000 -7,999	$8,000 -9,999	$10,000 -11,999	$12,000 -14,999	$15,000 -19,999	$20,000 -24,999	$25,000 -29,999	$30,000 -34,999	OVER $35,000
ALABAMA	6.90	4.09	3.49	3.04	2.72	2.61	2.40	2.14	1.93	1.73	1.61	1.51	1.49	1.18
ALASKA	5.89	3.74	3.42	3.23	3.00	2.59	2.50	2.30	2.10	1.84	1.71	1.63	1.53	1.38
ARIZONA	4.84	2.91	2.24	2.17	1.86	1.69	1.59	1.42	1.28	1.14	1.01	0.92	0.92	0.81
ARKANSAS	5.90	3.51	3.00	2.62	2.49	2.23	2.04	1.78	1.61	1.43	1.32	1.23	1.18	0.98
CALIFORNIA	3.13	2.04	1.68	1.50	1.35	1.24	1.10	0.99	0.89	0.78	0.71	0.67	0.64	0.58
COLORADO	3.39	2.13	1.74	1.54	1.48	1.30	1.14	1.05	0.94	0.84	0.76	0.73	0.65	0.59
CONNECTICUT	4.29	3.07	2.61	2.50	2.27	2.38	1.94	1.82	1.66	1.51	1.44	1.38	1.31	1.18
DELAWARE	5.53	3.20	3.05	2.48	2.32	2.17	1.97	1.67	1.61	1.43	1.31	1.19	1.12	0.99
FLORIDA	5.38	3.27	2.72	2.41	2.30	2.13	1.92	1.72	1.59	1.40	1.31	1.23	1.13	1.00
GEORGIA	4.90	2.74	2.49	2.21	2.05	1.93	1.70	1.52	1.41	1.28	1.17	1.08	1.03	0.91
HAWAII	4.27	2.78	2.72	2.44	2.20	2.07	1.88	1.70	1.56	1.41	1.30	1.27	1.18	1.08
IDAHO	4.14	2.49	2.07	1.98	1.78	1.61	1.51	1.32	1.22	1.08	0.97	0.92	0.86	0.77
ILLINOIS	4.01	2.67	2.30	2.07	1.86	1.77	1.61	1.45	1.35	1.22	1.12	1.07	1.03	0.92
INDIANA	3.16	2.00	1.66	1.57	1.46	1.35	1.17	1.13	1.03	0.93	0.87	0.76	0.80	0.71
IOWA	3.40	2.15	2.01	1.60	1.57	1.46	1.32	1.26	1.12	1.03	0.96	0.91	0.87	0.80
KANSAS	3.35	2.10	1.86	1.52	1.52	1.40	1.37	1.18	1.10	0.98	0.90	0.90	0.84	0.76
KENTUCKY	5.53	3.37	2.92	2.51	2.32	2.19	2.04	1.85	1.64	1.52	1.43	1.36	1.29	1.10
LOUISIANA	5.28	3.01	2.52	2.41	2.17	2.02	1.89	1.65	1.48	1.36	1.28	1.22	1.11	0.99
MAINE	5.25	3.45	3.04	2.52	2.56	2.32	2.20	2.03	1.87	1.74	1.68	1.56	1.54	1.40
MARYLAND	5.40	3.27	2.79	2.34	2.20	2.02	1.90	1.69	1.49	1.33	1.20	1.17	1.06	0.97
MASSACHUSETTS	4.17	3.22	2.68	2.37	2.28	2.14	2.01	1.90	1.69	1.60	1.49	1.48	1.45	1.26
MICHIGAN	3.45	2.26	1.83	1.61	1.49	1.48	1.29	1.20	1.09	0.98	0.91	0.87	0.84	0.76
MINNESOTA	6.00	3.94	3.07	2.87	2.64	2.64	2.21	2.07	1.89	1.70	1.57	1.51	1.47	1.29
MISSISSIPPI	5.97	3.68	2.97	2.63	2.35	2.32	2.07	1.88	1.67	1.50	1.41	1.37	1.30	1.07
MISSOURI	3.31	1.87	1.80	1.52	1.43	1.33	1.22	1.12	0.99	0.89	0.84	0.81	0.73	0.68
MONTANA	5.46	3.46	2.96	2.58	2.45	2.24	1.96	1.78	1.63	1.49	1.36	1.28	1.23	1.10
NEBRASKA	4.04	2.62	2.07	1.90	1.77	1.70	1.55	1.44	1.32	1.21	1.14	1.09	1.07	0.96
NEVADA	4.46	3.06	2.62	2.31	2.29	2.10	1.88	1.71	1.57	1.45	1.32	1.27	1.23	1.08
NEW HAMPSHIRE	5.60	3.71	2.92	2.89	2.69	2.36	2.34	2.12	1.99	1.86	1.73	1.65	1.61	1.40
NEW JERSEY	3.29	2.23	1.98	1.79	1.67	1.60	1.45	1.38	1.26	1.17	1.10	1.05	1.00	0.91
NEW MEXICO	5.33	3.38	3.01	2.56	2.45	2.15	1.99	1.78	1.57	1.43	1.34	1.23	1.11	1.07
NEW YORK	3.87	2.39	1.99	1.78	1.70	1.59	1.43	1.35	1.22	1.12	1.05	1.01	0.99	0.85
NORTH CAROLINA	6.16	3.69	3.20	2.63	2.58	2.31	2.17	1.93	1.79	1.61	1.47	1.44	1.34	1.21
NORTH DAKOTA	4.21	2.56	2.23	1.95	1.81	1.72	1.56	1.49	1.39	1.26	1.17	1.11	1.09	1.00
OHIO	4.13	2.62	2.27	1.97	1.81	1.79	1.60	1.43	1.31	1.21	1.12	1.06	1.01	0.87
OKLAHOMA	5.80	3.18	2.72	2.50	2.32	2.06	1.85	1.69	1.52	1.35	1.25	1.16	1.11	1.00
OREGON	3.31	1.97	1.65	1.51	1.33	1.26	1.13	1.01	0.88	0.77	0.71	0.67	0.61	0.56
PENNSYLVANIA	4.72	2.90	2.53	2.20	2.14	1.98	1.86	1.72	1.55	1.45	1.32	1.28	1.26	1.14
RHODE ISLAND	5.47	3.16	3.10	2.69	2.32	2.21	2.12	1.91	1.79	1.66	1.55	1.48	1.39	1.26
SOUTH CAROLINA	5.27	3.33	2.80	2.57	2.37	2.27	2.08	1.94	1.77	1.63	1.54	1.47	1.37	1.24
SOUTH DAKOTA	5.32	3.32	2.97	2.66	2.51	2.30	2.09	2.02	1.86	1.74	1.62	1.55	1.48	1.35
TENNESSEE	4.61	2.83	2.40	2.18	1.94	1.84	1.60	1.48	1.34	1.19	1.09	1.00	1.00	0.80
TEXAS	5.95	3.59	2.98	2.73	2.46	2.27	2.11	1.90	1.69	1.52	1.39	1.30	1.21	1.06
UTAH	3.47	2.13	1.71	1.49	1.54	1.30	1.17	1.07	0.96	0.85	0.77	0.72	0.70	0.64
VERMONT	7.71	4.81	4.46	3.86	3.60	3.44	3.12	3.00	2.74	2.60	2.46	2.27	2.19	2.02
VIRGINIA	5.50	3.00	2.71	2.45	2.12	1.97	1.89	1.69	1.51	1.36	1.25	1.18	1.11	0.98
WASHINGTON	5.70	3.44	2.77	2.49	2.19	2.16	1.89	1.75	1.55	1.39	1.27	1.19	1.08	0.98
WEST VIRGINIA	6.65	4.06	3.25	2.83	2.69	2.52	2.17	2.10	1.85	1.71	1.56	1.45	1.37	1.28
WISCONSIN	4.24	2.48	2.13	1.94	1.83	1.74	1.46	1.37	1.25	1.14	1.04	0.99	0.98	0.85
WYOMING	3.61	2.39	2.17	1.91	1.74	1.62	1.42	1.33	1.21	1.05	0.98	0.96	0.92	0.77
AVERAGE	4.81	2.99	2.57	2.28	2.12	1.98	1.80	1.64	1.49	1.36	1.26	1.19	1.14	1.01

* EFFECTIVE TAX RATE EQUALS ZERO BEFORE ROUNDING. AN ENTIRE ROW OF * MEANS THAT THIS TAX IS NOT USED IN THIS STATE.

TABLE A-12
EFFECTIVE TAX RATES: TOTAL STATE SALES AND GROSS RECEIPTS TAXES
INCIDENCE: SUM OF EFFECTIVE TAX RATES FOR INDIVIDUAL TAXES
ALLOCATOR: BASED ON INDIVIDUAL TAXES

STATE	UNDER $3,000	$3,000 -3,999	$4,000 -4,999	$5,000 -5,999	$6,000 -6,999	$7,000 -7,999	$8,000 -9,999	$10,000 -11,999	$12,000 -14,999	$15,000 -19,999	$20,000 -24,999	$25,000 -29,999	$30,000 -34,999	OVER $35,000
ALABAMA	12.66	7.74	6.68	5.86	5.29	5.11	4.72	4.24	3.85	3.49	3.27	3.07	3.04	2.22
ALASKA	5.89	3.74	3.42	3.23	3.00	2.59	2.50	2.30	2.10	1.84	1.71	1.63	1.53	1.38
ARIZONA	12.55	8.03	6.34	6.31	5.54	5.08	4.93	4.49	4.18	3.85	3.47	3.22	3.25	2.91
ARKANSAS	12.10	7.43	6.44	5.70	5.46	4.93	4.57	4.05	3.69	3.33	3.10	2.91	2.82	2.24
CALIFORNIA	7.34	5.44	4.68	4.37	4.07	3.86	3.56	3.35	3.16	2.92	2.77	2.68	2.62	2.40
COLORADO	7.62	5.12	4.26	3.85	3.77	3.34	3.01	2.84	2.63	2.39	2.20	2.14	1.88	1.75
CONNECTICUT	7.08	5.78	5.16	5.13	4.74	5.17	4.37	4.25	4.00	3.79	3.73	3.65	3.52	3.15
DELAWARE	5.53	3.20	3.05	2.48	2.32	2.17	1.97	1.67	1.61	1.43	1.31	1.19	1.12	0.99
FLORIDA	10.69	6.88	5.85	5.29	5.12	4.81	4.40	4.03	3.80	3.43	3.25	3.09	2.84	2.49
GEORGIA	11.38	6.54	5.98	5.40	5.05	4.80	4.25	3.84	3.58	3.30	3.03	2.81	2.67	2.31
HAWAII	12.66	9.07	9.19	8.49	7.89	7.57	7.06	6.59	6.26	5.79	5.54	5.57	5.20	4.93
IDAHO	8.38	5.35	4.55	4.46	4.09	3.75	3.58	3.22	3.04	2.75	2.54	2.43	2.29	2.06
ILLINOIS	8.15	5.82	5.16	4.75	4.34	4.21	3.90	3.59	3.43	3.16	2.95	2.86	2.77	2.45
INDIANA	8.50	5.90	5.06	4.93	4.69	4.44	3.98	3.92	3.67	3.41	3.31	2.96	3.09	2.80
IOWA	7.18	4.93	4.74	3.87	3.89	3.71	3.41	3.35	3.03	2.89	2.75	2.62	2.52	2.35
KANSAS	8.27	5.44	4.92	4.08	4.13	3.84	3.82	3.35	3.18	2.88	2.65	2.69	2.56	2.23
KENTUCKY	10.58	6.81	6.03	5.26	4.93	4.70	4.46	4.11	3.67	3.45	3.31	3.19	3.02	2.48
LOUISIANA	9.57	5.90	5.09	4.99	4.59	4.37	4.19	3.75	3.45	3.26	3.15	3.04	2.82	2.49
MAINE	9.55	6.84	6.21	5.30	5.47	5.01	4.89	4.59	4.34	4.11	4.06	3.79	3.73	3.44
MARYLAND	8.72	5.58	4.86	4.10	3.96	3.70	3.50	3.15	2.83	2.59	2.37	2.35	2.12	1.94
MASSACHUSETTS	5.26	4.33	3.67	3.32	3.23	3.07	2.94	2.84	2.55	2.46	2.33	2.35	2.32	1.99
MICHIGAN	6.91	4.90	4.12	3.67	3.46	3.49	3.10	2.99	2.76	2.55	2.42	2.34	2.27	2.02
MINNESOTA	9.41	6.56	5.22	5.00	4.67	4.74	4.03	3.85	3.58	3.28	3.10	3.00	2.97	2.59
MISSISSIPPI	16.88	10.73	8.77	7.84	7.06	7.03	6.35	5.83	5.24	4.73	4.50	4.38	4.21	3.36
MISSOURI	7.92	4.69	4.61	3.97	3.74	3.54	3.29	3.07	2.75	2.53	2.42	2.33	2.11	1.93
MONTANA	5.46	3.46	2.96	2.58	2.45	2.24	1.96	1.78	1.63	1.49	1.36	1.28	1.23	1.10
NEBRASKA	8.20	5.54	4.44	4.13	3.89	3.75	3.47	3.27	3.02	2.83	2.70	2.56	2.53	2.26
NEVADA	8.31	5.98	5.19	4.64	4.62	4.30	3.92	3.59	3.32	3.12	2.89	2.78	2.72	2.37
NEW HAMPSHIRE	5.60	3.71	2.92	2.89	2.69	2.36	2.34	2.12	1.99	1.86	1.73	1.65	1.61	1.40
NEW JERSEY	5.24	4.02	3.72	3.50	3.37	3.32	3.06	3.02	2.85	2.73	2.63	2.58	2.47	2.25
NEW MEXICO	14.29	9.67	8.84	7.69	7.49	6.71	6.36	5.80	5.23	4.90	4.69	4.39	4.00	3.97
NEW YORK	6.81	4.63	4.00	3.67	3.59	3.43	3.15	3.05	2.82	2.67	2.58	2.53	2.48	2.11
NORTH CAROLINA	10.52	6.45	5.64	4.69	4.62	4.17	3.93	3.52	3.30	2.97	2.73	2.68	2.50	2.19
NORTH DAKOTA	10.41	6.94	6.27	5.63	5.36	5.20	4.84	4.73	4.53	4.24	4.00	3.86	3.88	3.52
OHIO	6.53	4.55	4.10	3.66	3.45	3.49	3.20	2.95	2.77	2.66	2.54	2.44	2.33	2.04
OKLAHOMA	9.37	5.25	4.53	4.18	3.91	3.49	3.16	2.90	2.62	2.33	2.18	2.02	1.94	1.74
OREGON	3.31	1.97	1.65	1.51	1.33	1.26	1.13	1.01	0.88	0.77	0.71	0.67	0.61	0.56
PENNSYLVANIA	7.38	5.12	4.66	4.18	4.19	3.97	3.86	3.69	3.42	3.30	3.09	3.05	3.06	2.78
RHODE ISLAND	8.31	5.31	5.40	4.85	4.24	4.16	4.10	3.79	3.68	3.50	3.36	3.27	3.10	2.81
SOUTH CAROLINA	12.22	7.82	6.62	6.08	5.60	5.44	4.96	4.66	4.23	3.91	3.69	3.53	3.26	2.84
SOUTH DAKOTA	11.32	7.36	6.69	6.06	5.80	5.35	4.92	4.81	4.45	4.23	3.97	3.85	3.65	3.29
TENNESSEE	11.11	7.08	6.09	5.61	5.03	4.83	4.28	4.01	3.68	3.30	3.09	2.84	2.85	2.19
TEXAS	10.29	6.62	5.62	5.27	4.85	4.53	4.29	3.96	3.60	3.31	3.11	2.92	2.76	2.41
UTAH	10.46	6.86	5.67	4.99	5.32	4.60	4.23	3.97	3.65	3.32	3.10	2.94	2.89	2.65
VERMONT	9.38	6.11	5.76	5.05	4.74	4.57	4.17	4.07	3.76	3.62	3.45	3.16	3.07	2.82
VIRGINIA	9.09	5.06	4.63	4.21	3.67	3.44	3.31	2.97	2.68	2.43	2.24	2.13	1.99	1.74
WASHINGTON	15.38	10.14	8.49	7.76	7.05	7.10	6.40	6.16	5.65	5.21	4.96	4.78	4.29	4.01
WEST VIRGINIA	18.18	11.53	9.37	8.28	7.93	7.52	6.55	6.42	5.74	5.37	5.00	4.67	4.38	4.17
WISCONSIN	8.27	5.28	4.69	4.38	4.23	4.12	3.54	3.42	3.20	3.01	2.82	2.73	2.72	2.42
WYOMING	10.27	7.34	6.86	6.17	5.73	5.45	4.93	4.72	4.41	3.98	3.79	3.78	3.72	3.15
AVERAGE	9.33	6.13	5.38	4.87	4.59	4.36	4.02	3.75	3.47	3.21	3.03	2.91	2.79	2.47

* EFFECTIVE TAX RATE EQUALS ZERO BEFORE ROUNDING. AN ENTIRE ROW OF * MEANS THAT THIS TAX IS NOT USED IN THIS STATE.

TABLE A-13
EFFECTIVE TAX RATES: STATE LICENSE TAXES-MOTOR VEHICLES (BENCHMARK)
INCIDENCE: 1/4 CONSUMERS, 3/4 DRIVERS
ALLOCATOR: CONSUMPTION AND VEHICLE OPERATIONS EXPENDITURES

STATE	UNDER $3,000	$3,000 -3,999	$4,000 -4,999	$5,000 -5,999	$6,000 -6,999	$7,000 -7,999	$8,000 -9,999	$10,000 -11,999	$12,000 -14,999	$15,000 -19,999	$20,000 -24,999	$25,000 -29,999	$30,000 -34,999	OVER $35,000
ALABAMA	0.46	0.27	0.23	0.20	0.18	0.18	0.16	0.15	0.13	0.12	0.11	0.11	0.10	0.09
ALASKA	0.83	0.53	0.50	0.47	0.44	0.38	0.37	0.34	0.32	0.28	0.27	0.26	0.25	0.22
ARIZONA	0.83	0.51	0.40	0.39	0.34	0.31	0.30	0.27	0.25	0.23	0.21	0.19	0.19	0.17
ARKANSAS	0.97	0.59	0.51	0.45	0.43	0.39	0.36	0.32	0.29	0.27	0.25	0.23	0.22	0.19
CALIFORNIA	0.59	0.39	0.32	0.29	0.27	0.25	0.23	0.21	0.19	0.17	0.16	0.15	0.15	0.13
COLORADO	0.59	0.38	0.31	0.28	0.27	0.24	0.22	0.21	0.19	0.17	0.16	0.15	0.14	0.13
CONNECTICUT	0.42	0.33	0.29	0.29	0.27	0.29	0.25	0.24	0.23	0.22	0.21	0.21	0.20	0.19
DELAWARE	1.16	0.69	0.67	0.54	0.52	0.49	0.45	0.40	0.39	0.35	0.33	0.30	0.29	0.26
FLORIDA	0.95	0.58	0.48	0.43	0.41	0.38	0.35	0.31	0.29	0.26	0.24	0.23	0.21	0.19
GEORGIA	0.37	0.21	0.19	0.17	0.16	0.15	0.13	0.12	0.11	0.10	0.10	0.09	0.09	0.08
HAWAII	0.00	0.00	0.00	0.00	0.00	0.00	0.00	0.00	0.00	0.00	0.00	0.00	0.00	0.00
IDAHO	1.34	0.82	0.68	0.66	0.60	0.54	0.52	0.46	0.43	0.39	0.36	0.34	0.32	0.29
ILLINOIS	0.84	0.59	0.52	0.48	0.44	0.42	0.39	0.37	0.35	0.32	0.31	0.30	0.29	0.27
INDIANA	0.58	0.38	0.32	0.30	0.28	0.26	0.24	0.23	0.21	0.19	0.18	0.17	0.17	0.16
IOWA	1.32	0.86	0.81	0.66	0.65	0.62	0.56	0.55	0.50	0.47	0.44	0.43	0.41	0.39
KANSAS	0.72	0.47	0.42	0.35	0.35	0.33	0.32	0.28	0.27	0.25	0.23	0.23	0.22	0.20
KENTUCKY	0.60	0.36	0.32	0.27	0.25	0.24	0.22	0.20	0.18	0.17	0.16	0.15	0.14	0.13
LOUISIANA	0.39	0.22	0.19	0.18	0.16	0.15	0.14	0.13	0.12	0.11	0.10	0.10	0.09	0.08
MAINE	0.65	0.46	0.41	0.35	0.36	0.33	0.32	0.30	0.29	0.27	0.27	0.25	0.25	0.24
MARYLAND	0.79	0.48	0.41	0.35	0.33	0.30	0.29	0.26	0.24	0.22	0.20	0.19	0.18	0.16
MASSACHUSETTS	0.20	0.17	0.14	0.13	0.13	0.12	0.12	0.11	0.10	0.10	0.10	0.10	0.09	0.09
MICHIGAN	0.56	0.38	0.31	0.28	0.26	0.26	0.23	0.22	0.21	0.19	0.18	0.17	0.17	0.15
MINNESOTA	0.89	0.60	0.48	0.46	0.42	0.43	0.37	0.35	0.33	0.30	0.29	0.28	0.27	0.24
MISSISSIPPI	0.44	0.27	0.22	0.20	0.18	0.17	0.16	0.14	0.13	0.12	0.11	0.11	0.10	0.09
MISSOURI	0.81	0.47	0.46	0.39	0.37	0.35	0.32	0.30	0.28	0.26	0.25	0.24	0.22	0.20
MONTANA	0.59	0.38	0.33	0.29	0.28	0.25	0.23	0.21	0.19	0.18	0.17	0.16	0.15	0.14
NEBRASKA	0.83	0.55	0.44	0.41	0.39	0.37	0.34	0.33	0.30	0.28	0.27	0.26	0.25	0.23
NEVADA	0.85	0.58	0.49	0.43	0.43	0.40	0.36	0.33	0.30	0.27	0.25	0.24	0.23	0.20
NEW HAMPSHIRE	0.64	0.46	0.37	0.38	0.36	0.32	0.33	0.31	0.30	0.28	0.27	0.27	0.26	0.24
NEW JERSEY	0.56	0.42	0.39	0.36	0.35	0.34	0.32	0.31	0.30	0.28	0.27	0.27	0.26	0.25
NEW MEXICO	1.02	0.66	0.59	0.51	0.49	0.44	0.41	0.37	0.33	0.30	0.29	0.27	0.25	0.24
NEW YORK	0.42	0.29	0.25	0.23	0.22	0.21	0.20	0.20	0.18	0.18	0.17	0.17	0.16	0.15
NORTH CAROLINA	0.85	0.51	0.44	0.36	0.35	0.32	0.30	0.27	0.26	0.23	0.21	0.21	0.19	0.17
NORTH DAKOTA	1.43	0.90	0.79	0.70	0.65	0.63	0.58	0.56	0.53	0.49	0.46	0.44	0.44	0.41
OHIO	0.76	0.51	0.45	0.40	0.37	0.37	0.34	0.31	0.29	0.28	0.26	0.25	0.25	0.22
OKLAHOMA	1.48	0.82	0.70	0.65	0.60	0.54	0.49	0.45	0.41	0.37	0.35	0.32	0.31	0.28
OREGON	1.20	0.74	0.63	0.58	0.52	0.50	0.46	0.42	0.38	0.34	0.32	0.30	0.28	0.26
PENNSYLVANIA	0.60	0.40	0.36	0.33	0.33	0.31	0.30	0.29	0.27	0.26	0.25	0.24	0.24	0.23
RHODE ISLAND	0.55	0.35	0.36	0.32	0.29	0.28	0.28	0.26	0.25	0.24	0.23	0.23	0.22	0.21
SOUTH CAROLINA	0.45	0.28	0.23	0.21	0.19	0.19	0.17	0.16	0.14	0.13	0.12	0.12	0.11	0.10
SOUTH DAKOTA	0.80	0.51	0.46	0.42	0.40	0.36	0.34	0.33	0.30	0.29	0.27	0.26	0.25	0.23
TENNESSEE	0.62	0.39	0.33	0.30	0.27	0.26	0.23	0.21	0.20	0.18	0.17	0.16	0.15	0.13
TEXAS	0.73	0.45	0.38	0.35	0.32	0.29	0.28	0.25	0.23	0.21	0.19	0.18	0.17	0.15
UTAH	0.57	0.36	0.29	0.26	0.26	0.23	0.21	0.20	0.18	0.16	0.15	0.14	0.14	0.12
VERMONT	1.12	0.75	0.71	0.63	0.60	0.58	0.54	0.53	0.50	0.48	0.46	0.44	0.43	0.41
VIRGINIA	0.74	0.40	0.36	0.33	0.29	0.27	0.26	0.23	0.21	0.19	0.18	0.17	0.16	0.14
WASHINGTON	0.66	0.41	0.34	0.30	0.27	0.27	0.25	0.23	0.21	0.19	0.18	0.17	0.16	0.14
WEST VIRGINIA	1.06	0.65	0.52	0.46	0.43	0.41	0.35	0.34	0.30	0.28	0.25	0.24	0.23	0.21
WISCONSIN	0.69	0.42	0.37	0.34	0.33	0.32	0.27	0.26	0.25	0.23	0.22	0.21	0.21	0.19
WYOMING	1.82	1.24	1.14	1.01	0.93	0.87	0.79	0.74	0.68	0.61	0.57	0.56	0.55	0.47
AVERAGE	0.77	0.49	0.43	0.38	0.36	0.34	0.31	0.29	0.27	0.25	0.24	0.22	0.22	0.20

* EFFECTIVE TAX RATE EQUALS ZERO BEFORE ROUNDING. AN ENTIRE ROW OF * MEANS THAT THIS TAX IS NOT USED IN THIS STATE.

TABLE A-14
EFFECTIVE TAX RATES: STATE LICENSE TAXES-MOTOR VEHICLES
INCIDENCE: DRIVERS
ALLOCATOR: VEHICLE OPERATIONS EXPENDITURES

STATE	UNDER $3,000	$3,000 -3,999	$4,000 -4,999	$5,000 -5,999	$6,000 -6,999	$7,000 -7,999	$8,000 -9,999	$10,000 -11,999	$12,000 -14,999	$15,000 -19,999	$20,000 -24,999	$25,000 -29,999	$30,000 -34,999	OVER $35,000
ALABAMA	0.47	0.28	0.24	0.21	0.18	0.18	0.16	0.15	0.13	0.12	0.11	0.11	0.10	0.09
ALASKA	0.80	0.52	0.48	0.46	0.43	0.37	0.37	0.34	0.32	0.28	0.27	0.26	0.25	0.23
ARIZONA	0.81	0.50	0.39	0.38	0.34	0.31	0.30	0.27	0.25	0.23	0.21	0.20	0.19	0.17
ARKANSAS	0.99	0.60	0.51	0.45	0.43	0.39	0.36	0.32	0.29	0.26	0.25	0.23	0.22	0.19
CALIFORNIA	0.57	0.38	0.32	0.29	0.26	0.25	0.23	0.21	0.19	0.18	0.16	0.16	0.15	0.14
COLORADO	0.58	0.37	0.31	0.28	0.27	0.24	0.22	0.21	0.19	0.17	0.16	0.15	0.14	0.13
CONNECTICUT	0.37	0.31	0.28	0.28	0.26	0.28	0.24	0.24	0.23	0.22	0.21	0.21	0.21	0.20
DELAWARE	1.18	0.70	0.68	0.55	0.52	0.49	0.45	0.40	0.39	0.35	0.33	0.30	0.29	0.26
FLORIDA	0.97	0.59	0.49	0.43	0.41	0.38	0.35	0.31	0.29	0.26	0.24	0.22	0.21	0.19
GEORGIA	0.38	0.21	0.19	0.17	0.16	0.15	0.13	0.12	0.11	0.10	0.09	0.09	0.09	0.08
HAWAII	0.00	0.00	0.00	0.00	0.00	0.00	0.00	0.00	0.00	0.00	0.00	0.00	0.00	0.00
IDAHO	1.31	0.81	0.67	0.65	0.59	0.54	0.51	0.46	0.43	0.39	0.36	0.34	0.33	0.30
ILLINOIS	0.81	0.57	0.51	0.47	0.43	0.42	0.39	0.36	0.35	0.33	0.31	0.30	0.29	0.27
INDIANA	0.55	0.37	0.31	0.30	0.28	0.26	0.23	0.23	0.21	0.19	0.19	0.17	0.17	0.16
IOWA	1.26	0.83	0.79	0.64	0.64	0.61	0.56	0.55	0.50	0.47	0.45	0.43	0.42	0.39
KANSAS	0.69	0.45	0.41	0.34	0.34	0.32	0.32	0.28	0.27	0.25	0.23	0.23	0.22	0.20
KENTUCKY	0.61	0.37	0.32	0.27	0.25	0.24	0.22	0.20	0.18	0.17	0.16	0.15	0.14	0.12
LOUISIANA	0.39	0.22	0.19	0.18	0.16	0.15	0.14	0.13	0.12	0.11	0.10	0.09	0.09	0.08
MAINE	0.59	0.43	0.39	0.34	0.35	0.33	0.32	0.30	0.29	0.28	0.27	0.26	0.26	0.25
MARYLAND	0.80	0.49	0.42	0.35	0.33	0.31	0.29	0.27	0.24	0.22	0.20	0.19	0.18	0.16
MASSACHUSETTS	0.18	0.16	0.13	0.12	0.12	0.12	0.11	0.11	0.10	0.10	0.10	0.10	0.10	0.09
MICHIGAN	0.54	0.37	0.31	0.27	0.26	0.25	0.23	0.22	0.21	0.19	0.18	0.18	0.17	0.16
MINNESOTA	0.85	0.59	0.47	0.45	0.42	0.42	0.36	0.35	0.33	0.30	0.29	0.28	0.28	0.25
MISSISSIPPI	0.44	0.27	0.22	0.20	0.18	0.17	0.16	0.14	0.13	0.12	0.11	0.10	0.10	0.08
MISSOURI	0.78	0.46	0.45	0.39	0.36	0.34	0.32	0.30	0.28	0.26	0.25	0.24	0.23	0.21
MONTANA	0.57	0.37	0.32	0.29	0.27	0.25	0.22	0.21	0.20	0.18	0.17	0.16	0.15	0.14
NEBRASKA	0.80	0.54	0.43	0.40	0.38	0.37	0.34	0.32	0.30	0.28	0.27	0.26	0.26	0.24
NEVADA	0.83	0.57	0.48	0.43	0.42	0.39	0.36	0.32	0.30	0.27	0.25	0.24	0.23	0.20
NEW HAMPSHIRE	0.57	0.43	0.35	0.36	0.35	0.31	0.32	0.30	0.30	0.29	0.28	0.27	0.27	0.25
NEW JERSEY	0.50	0.39	0.36	0.34	0.33	0.33	0.31	0.31	0.29	0.28	0.28	0.27	0.26	0.25
NEW MEXICO	0.99	0.65	0.58	0.50	0.48	0.43	0.40	0.37	0.33	0.31	0.29	0.27	0.25	0.24
NEW YORK	0.38	0.27	0.23	0.22	0.21	0.21	0.19	0.19	0.18	0.18	0.17	0.17	0.17	0.15
NORTH CAROLINA	0.86	0.51	0.44	0.36	0.36	0.32	0.30	0.27	0.26	0.23	0.21	0.20	0.19	0.17
NORTH DAKOTA	1.37	0.87	0.77	0.69	0.64	0.62	0.57	0.56	0.53	0.49	0.46	0.45	0.44	0.41
OHIO	0.73	0.49	0.44	0.39	0.37	0.37	0.34	0.31	0.29	0.28	0.27	0.26	0.25	0.23
OKLAHOMA	1.50	0.83	0.71	0.65	0.61	0.55	0.50	0.45	0.41	0.37	0.34	0.32	0.31	0.28
OREGON	1.17	0.73	0.62	0.57	0.51	0.49	0.45	0.42	0.38	0.34	0.32	0.31	0.29	0.26
PENNSYLVANIA	0.53	0.38	0.35	0.31	0.31	0.30	0.30	0.28	0.27	0.26	0.25	0.25	0.25	0.23
RHODE ISLAND	0.49	0.33	0.34	0.31	0.28	0.28	0.27	0.26	0.25	0.24	0.24	0.23	0.23	0.22
SOUTH CAROLINA	0.46	0.28	0.23	0.21	0.19	0.19	0.17	0.16	0.14	0.13	0.12	0.12	0.11	0.10
SOUTH DAKOTA	0.77	0.50	0.45	0.41	0.39	0.36	0.34	0.33	0.31	0.29	0.27	0.26	0.25	0.24
TENNESSEE	0.63	0.39	0.33	0.31	0.27	0.26	0.23	0.21	0.20	0.18	0.17	0.15	0.15	0.13
TEXAS	0.75	0.46	0.38	0.35	0.32	0.30	0.28	0.25	0.23	0.21	0.19	0.18	0.17	0.15
UTAH	0.56	0.35	0.29	0.25	0.26	0.23	0.21	0.20	0.18	0.16	0.15	0.14	0.14	0.13
VERMONT	1.01	0.70	0.68	0.61	0.58	0.57	0.54	0.53	0.50	0.49	0.47	0.45	0.44	0.42
VIRGINIA	0.75	0.41	0.37	0.33	0.29	0.27	0.26	0.23	0.21	0.19	0.18	0.17	0.16	0.14
WASHINGTON	0.64	0.40	0.33	0.30	0.27	0.27	0.24	0.23	0.21	0.19	0.18	0.17	0.16	0.15
WEST VIRGINIA	1.08	0.66	0.53	0.46	0.43	0.41	0.35	0.34	0.30	0.27	0.25	0.24	0.22	0.21
WISCONSIN	0.66	0.41	0.36	0.34	0.32	0.31	0.27	0.26	0.25	0.23	0.22	0.21	0.21	0.19
WYOMING	1.78	1.21	1.12	0.99	0.92	0.87	0.78	0.74	0.68	0.61	0.58	0.57	0.55	0.48
AVERAGE	0.75	0.48	0.42	0.38	0.36	0.34	0.31	0.29	0.27	0.25	0.24	0.23	0.22	0.20

* EFFECTIVE TAX RATE EQUALS ZERO BEFORE ROUNDING. AN ENTIRE ROW OF * MEANS THAT THIS TAX IS NOT USED IN THIS STATE.

TABLE A-15
EFFECTIVE TAX RATES: STATE LICENSE TAXES-CORPORATIONS IN GENERAL (BENCHMARK)
INCIDENCE: 1/2 CONSUMERS, 1/2 OWNERS OF CAPITAL
ALLOCATOR: CONSUMPTION AND DIVIDEND INCOME

STATE	UNDER $3,000	$3,000 -3,999	$4,000 -4,999	$5,000 -5,999	$6,000 -6,999	$7,000 -7,999	$8,000 -9,999	$10,000 -11,999	$12,000 -14,999	$15,000 -19,999	$20,000 -24,999	$25,000 -29,999	$30,000 -34,999	OVER $35,000
ALABAMA	0.19	0.11	0.10	0.08	0.08	0.08	0.06	0.07	0.06	0.05	0.08	0.05	0.07	0.43
ALASKA	0.02	0.03	0.02	0.01	0.01	0.01	0.01	0.01	0.01	0.01	0.01	0.01	0.01	0.01
ARIZONA	0.01	0.01	0.01	0.01	0.01	0.00	0.00	0.01	0.00	0.00	0.00	0.00	0.00	0.01
ARKANSAS	0.03	0.02	0.02	0.02	0.01	0.01	0.01	0.01	0.01	0.01	0.01	0.01	0.01	0.04
CALIFORNIA	0.00	0.00	0.00	0.00	0.00	0.00	0.00	0.00	0.00	0.00	0.00	0.00	0.00	0.00
COLORADO	0.02	0.01	0.02	0.01	0.01	0.01	0.01	0.00	0.00	0.00	0.00	0.00	0.01	0.02
CONNECTICUT	0.00	0.00	0.01	0.00	0.00	0.00	0.00	0.00	0.00	0.00	0.00	0.00	0.00	0.01
DELAWARE	0.43	0.22	0.20	0.15	0.13	0.22	0.12	0.13	0.15	0.13	0.13	0.13	0.11	0.41
FLORIDA	0.01	0.01	0.01	0.01	0.01	0.00	0.00	0.00	0.00	0.00	0.00	0.00	0.01	0.01
GEORGIA	0.04	0.02	0.01	0.02	0.02	0.01	0.01	0.01	0.01	0.01	0.01	0.01	0.02	0.04
HAWAII	0.01	0.01	0.00	0.01	0.01	0.00	0.00	0.00	0.00	0.00	0.00	0.00	0.00	0.01
IDAHO	0.03	0.02	0.01	0.01	0.01	0.01	0.01	0.01	0.01	0.01	0.01	0.01	0.02	0.03
ILLINOIS	0.04	0.03	0.02	0.03	0.02	0.02	0.02	0.02	0.01	0.01	0.01	0.01	0.01	0.04
INDIANA	0.01	0.01	0.00	0.00	0.00	0.00	0.00	0.00	0.00	0.00	0.00	0.00	0.00	0.01
IOWA	0.03	0.02	0.02	0.03	0.02	0.01	0.02	0.02	0.01	0.01	0.01	0.01	0.03	0.04
KANSAS	0.04	0.02	0.02	0.02	0.03	0.02	0.02	0.02	0.01	0.01	0.02	0.02	0.01	0.04
KENTUCKY	0.05	0.03	0.03	0.04	0.02	0.02	0.02	0.02	0.02	0.02	0.02	0.03	0.02	0.11
LOUISIANA	0.25	0.13	0.14	0.10	0.10	0.10	0.09	0.09	0.07	0.08	0.07	0.08	0.11	0.34
MAINE	0.01	0.01	0.01	0.01	0.00	0.00	0.01	0.00	0.00	0.00	0.00	0.01	0.00	0.01
MARYLAND	0.01	0.01	0.01	0.01	0.00	0.00	0.00	0.00	0.00	0.00	0.00	0.00	0.00	0.01
MASSACHUSETTS	0.01	0.01	0.01	0.01	0.01	0.00	0.01	0.00	0.00	0.00	0.00	0.01	0.00	0.02
MICHIGAN	0.38	0.27	0.24	0.18	0.17	0.21	0.16	0.12	0.11	0.11	0.11	0.16	0.11	0.35
MINNESOTA	0.01	0.00	0.01	0.00	0.00	0.00	0.00	0.00	0.00	0.00	0.00	0.00	0.00	0.01
MISSISSIPPI	0.19	0.11	0.11	0.08	0.14	0.08	0.09	0.09	0.07	0.07	0.11	0.08	0.09	0.33
MISSOURI	0.08	0.04	0.04	0.05	0.03	0.04	0.03	0.03	0.03	0.02	0.03	0.03	0.03	0.11
MONTANA	0.01	0.01	0.00	0.00	0.00	0.00	0.00	0.00	0.00	0.00	0.00	0.00	0.00	0.01
NEBRASKA	0.03	0.02	0.01	0.01	0.02	0.01	0.01	0.01	0.01	0.01	0.01	0.01	0.01	0.03
NEVADA	0.03	0.02	0.01	0.01	0.01	0.01	0.01	0.01	0.01	0.01	0.01	0.01	0.01	0.03
NEW HAMPSHIRE	0.06	0.03	0.06	0.05	0.02	0.02	0.02	0.03	0.02	0.02	0.02	0.01	0.02	0.07
NEW JERSEY	0.16	0.11	0.15	0.14	0.11	0.09	0.18	0.09	0.07	0.06	0.07	0.06	0.07	0.15
NEW MEXICO	0.03	0.02	0.01	0.01	0.01	0.01	0.01	0.01	0.01	0.01	0.01	0.01	0.01	0.02
NEW YORK	0.01	0.00	0.00	0.00	0.00	0.00	0.00	0.00	0.00	0.00	0.00	0.00	0.00	0.01
NORTH CAROLINA	0.16	0.07	0.12	0.06	0.06	0.05	0.05	0.05	0.04	0.04	0.05	0.05	0.04	0.17
NORTH DAKOTA	0.01	0.01	0.01	0.00	0.01	0.00	0.00	0.00	0.00	0.00	0.00	0.00	0.00	0.01
OHIO	0.22	0.16	0.13	0.14	0.08	0.09	0.09	0.08	0.07	0.07	0.07	0.08	0.11	0.24
OKLAHOMA	0.09	0.04	0.03	0.03	0.04	0.04	0.03	0.02	0.03	0.03	0.03	0.03	0.02	0.10
OREGON	0.02	0.01	0.01	0.01	0.01	0.00	0.00	0.01	0.00	0.00	0.01	0.00	0.01	0.02
PENNSYLVANIA	0.45	0.29	0.20	0.24	0.28	0.13	0.20	0.13	0.12	0.13	0.11	0.12	0.15	0.39
RHODE ISLAND	0.02	0.02	0.01	0.01	0.02	0.01	0.01	0.01	0.01	0.01	0.01	0.01	0.01	0.02
SOUTH CAROLINA	0.03	0.01	0.01	0.01	0.02	0.02	0.01	0.02	0.01	0.01	0.01	0.01	0.01	0.05
SOUTH DAKOTA	0.01	0.00	0.00	0.00	0.00	0.01	0.00	0.00	0.00	0.00	0.00	0.00	0.00	0.01
TENNESSEE	0.18	0.08	0.08	0.06	0.07	0.06	0.07	0.07	0.05	0.06	0.05	0.06	0.06	0.29
TEXAS	0.43	0.18	0.22	0.17	0.13	0.13	0.12	0.12	0.12	0.11	0.10	0.14	0.15	0.42
UTAH	*	*	*	*	*	*	*	*	*	*	*	*	*	*
VERMONT	0.01	0.00	0.00	0.01	0.00	0.00	0.00	0.00	0.00	0.00	0.00	0.00	0.01	0.01
VIRGINIA	0.02	0.01	0.01	0.01	0.02	0.01	0.01	0.01	0.01	0.01	0.01	0.01	0.01	0.02
WASHINGTON	0.02	0.01	0.01	0.01	0.01	0.01	0.01	0.00	0.01	0.01	0.00	0.00	0.01	0.02
WEST VIRGINIA	0.02	0.03	0.02	0.01	0.01	0.01	0.01	0.01	0.01	0.01	0.01	0.01	0.03	0.04
WISCONSIN	0.01	0.00	0.00	0.00	0.00	0.00	0.00	0.00	0.00	0.00	0.00	0.00	0.00	0.01
WYOMING	0.02	0.01	0.01	0.01	0.01	0.01	0.01	0.00	0.00	0.00	0.00	0.00	0.00	0.02
AVERAGE	0.08	0.05	0.04	0.04	0.04	0.03	0.03	0.03	0.03	0.02	0.03	0.03	0.03	0.09

* EFFECTIVE TAX RATE EQUALS ZERO BEFORE ROUNDING. AN ENTIRE ROW OF * MEANS THAT THIS TAX IS NOT USED IN THIS STATE.

TABLE A-16

EFFECTIVE TAX RATES: STATE LICENSE TAXES-CORPORATIONS IN GENERAL (MOST REGRESSIVE)
INCIDENCE: CONSUMERS IN GENERAL
ALLOCATOR: TOTAL CONSUMPTION EXPENDITURES

STATE	UNDER $3,000	$3,000 -3,999	$4,000 -4,999	$5,000 -5,999	$6,000 -6,999	$7,000 -7,999	$8,000 -9,999	$10,000 -11,999	$12,000 -14,999	$15,000 -19,999	$20,000 -24,999	$25,000 -29,999	$30,000 -34,999	OVER $35,000
ALABAMA	0.32	0.19	0.16	0.15	0.13	0.13	0.12	0.11	0.10	0.09	0.08	0.08	0.08	0.07
ALASKA	0.04	0.02	0.02	0.02	0.02	0.02	0.02	0.01	0.01	0.01	0.01	0.01	0.01	0.01
ARIZONA	0.02	0.01	0.01	0.01	0.01	0.01	0.01	0.01	0.01	0.01	0.00	0.00	0.00	0.00
ARKANSAS	0.04	0.03	0.02	0.02	0.02	0.02	0.02	0.01	0.01	0.01	0.01	0.01	0.01	0.01
CALIFORNIA	0.00	0.00	0.00	0.00	0.00	0.00	0.00	0.00	0.00	0.00	0.00	0.00	0.00	0.00
COLORADO	0.02	0.02	0.01	0.01	0.01	0.01	0.01	0.01	0.01	0.01	0.01	0.01	0.01	0.00
CONNECTICUT	0.01	0.01	0.00	0.00	0.00	0.00	0.00	0.00	0.00	0.00	0.00	0.00	0.00	0.00
DELAWARE	0.56	0.34	0.33	0.27	0.26	0.24	0.23	0.20	0.20	0.18	0.17	0.16	0.15	0.14
FLORIDA	0.02	0.01	0.01	0.01	0.01	0.01	0.01	0.01	0.01	0.00	0.00	0.00	0.00	0.00
GEORGIA	0.04	0.03	0.02	0.02	0.02	0.02	0.02	0.02	0.01	0.01	0.01	0.01	0.01	0.01
HAWAII	0.01	0.01	0.01	0.01	0.01	0.01	0.01	0.00	0.00	0.00	0.00	0.00	0.00	0.00
IDAHO	0.04	0.02	0.02	0.02	0.02	0.02	0.02	0.01	0.01	0.01	0.01	0.01	0.01	0.01
ILLINOIS	0.06	0.04	0.03	0.03	0.03	0.03	0.02	0.02	0.02	0.02	0.02	0.02	0.02	0.01
INDIANA	0.01	0.01	0.01	0.01	0.01	0.01	0.00	0.00	0.00	0.00	0.00	0.00	0.00	0.00
IOWA	0.05	0.03	0.03	0.03	0.02	0.02	0.02	0.02	0.02	0.02	0.02	0.01	0.01	0.01
KANSAS	0.06	0.04	0.03	0.03	0.03	0.02	0.02	0.02	0.02	0.02	0.02	0.02	0.02	0.01
KENTUCKY	0.08	0.05	0.05	0.04	0.04	0.03	0.03	0.03	0.03	0.03	0.02	0.02	0.02	0.02
LOUISIANA	0.38	0.22	0.19	0.18	0.17	0.16	0.15	0.13	0.12	0.11	0.11	0.10	0.10	0.09
MAINE	0.02	0.01	0.01	0.01	0.01	0.01	0.01	0.01	0.01	0.00	0.00	0.00	0.00	0.00
MARYLAND	0.02	0.01	0.01	0.01	0.01	0.01	0.01	0.01	0.01	0.00	0.00	0.00	0.00	0.00
MASSACHUSETTS	0.02	0.01	0.01	0.01	0.01	0.01	0.01	0.01	0.01	0.01	0.01	0.01	0.01	0.00
MICHIGAN	0.53	0.34	0.28	0.24	0.23	0.22	0.20	0.19	0.17	0.15	0.14	0.14	0.13	0.12
MINNESOTA	0.01	0.00	0.00	0.00	0.00	0.00	0.00	0.00	0.00	0.00	0.00	0.00	0.00	0.00
MISSISSIPPI	0.33	0.21	0.17	0.16	0.14	0.14	0.13	0.12	0.11	0.10	0.09	0.09	0.08	0.07
MISSOURI	0.13	0.07	0.07	0.06	0.06	0.05	0.05	0.04	0.04	0.04	0.03	0.03	0.03	0.03
MONTANA	0.01	0.01	0.01	0.01	0.01	0.01	0.00	0.00	0.00	0.00	0.00	0.00	0.00	0.00
NEBRASKA	0.04	0.03	0.02	0.02	0.02	0.02	0.02	0.01	0.01	0.01	0.01	0.01	0.01	0.01
NEVADA	0.04	0.03	0.02	0.02	0.02	0.02	0.02	0.01	0.01	0.01	0.01	0.01	0.01	0.01
NEW HAMPSHIRE	0.07	0.05	0.04	0.04	0.03	0.03	0.03	0.03	0.03	0.02	0.02	0.02	0.02	0.02
NEW JERSEY	0.24	0.16	0.15	0.13	0.13	0.12	0.11	0.11	0.10	0.09	0.09	0.08	0.08	0.07
NEW MEXICO	0.04	0.03	0.02	0.02	0.02	0.02	0.02	0.01	0.01	0.01	0.01	0.01	0.01	0.01
NEW YORK	0.01	0.00	0.00	0.00	0.00	0.00	0.00	0.00	0.00	0.00	0.00	0.00	0.00	0.00
NORTH CAROLINA	0.20	0.12	0.11	0.09	0.09	0.08	0.08	0.07	0.07	0.06	0.06	0.05	0.05	0.05
NORTH DAKOTA	0.01	0.01	0.01	0.01	0.01	0.01	0.01	0.00	0.00	0.00	0.00	0.00	0.00	0.00
OHIO	0.31	0.20	0.17	0.15	0.14	0.14	0.12	0.11	0.11	0.10	0.09	0.09	0.08	0.07
OKLAHOMA	0.14	0.08	0.07	0.06	0.06	0.05	0.05	0.05	0.04	0.04	0.04	0.03	0.03	0.03
OREGON	0.02	0.01	0.01	0.01	0.01	0.01	0.01	0.01	0.01	0.01	0.01	0.01	0.01	0.00
PENNSYLVANIA	0.53	0.33	0.29	0.25	0.24	0.23	0.22	0.20	0.18	0.17	0.16	0.15	0.15	0.14
RHODE ISLAND	0.03	0.02	0.02	0.01	0.01	0.01	0.01	0.01	0.01	0.01	0.01	0.01	0.01	0.01
SOUTH CAROLINA	0.05	0.03	0.02	0.02	0.02	0.02	0.02	0.02	0.02	0.01	0.01	0.01	0.01	0.01
SOUTH DAKOTA	0.01	0.01	0.01	0.00	0.00	0.00	0.00	0.00	0.00	0.00	0.00	0.00	0.00	0.00
TENNESSEE	0.26	0.16	0.14	0.13	0.12	0.11	0.10	0.09	0.09	0.08	0.07	0.07	0.07	0.06
TEXAS	0.52	0.33	0.28	0.26	0.23	0.22	0.21	0.19	0.17	0.16	0.15	0.14	0.14	0.12
UTAH	*	*	*	*	*	*	*	*	*	*	*	*	*	*
VERMONT	0.01	0.01	0.01	0.01	0.01	0.01	0.01	0.01	0.00	0.00	0.00	0.00	0.00	0.00
VIRGINIA	0.03	0.02	0.02	0.02	0.01	0.01	0.01	0.01	0.01	0.01	0.01	0.01	0.01	0.01
WASHINGTON	0.03	0.02	0.01	0.01	0.01	0.01	0.01	0.01	0.01	0.01	0.01	0.01	0.01	0.01
WEST VIRGINIA	0.05	0.03	0.02	0.02	0.02	0.02	0.02	0.02	0.01	0.01	0.01	0.01	0.01	0.01
WISCONSIN	0.01	0.01	0.01	0.00	0.00	0.00	0.00	0.00	0.00	0.00	0.00	0.00	0.00	0.00
WYOMING	0.02	0.01	0.01	0.01	0.01	0.01	0.01	0.01	0.01	0.01	0.01	0.01	0.01	0.00
AVERAGE	0.11	0.07	0.06	0.05	0.05	0.05	0.04	0.04	0.04	0.03	0.03	0.03	0.03	0.03

* EFFECTIVE TAX RATE EQUALS ZERO BEFORE ROUNDING. AN ENTIRE ROW OF * MEANS THAT THIS TAX IS NOT USED IN THIS STATE.

TABLE A-17

EFFECTIVE TAX RATES: STATE LICENSE TAXES-CORPORATIONS IN GENERAL (MOST PROGRESSIVE)
INCIDENCE: OWNERS OF CAPITAL
ALLOCATOR: DIVIDEND INCOME

STATE	UNDER $3,000	$3,000 -3,999	$4,000 -4,999	$5,000 -5,999	$6,000 -6,999	$7,000 -7,999	$8,000 -9,999	$10,000 -11,999	$12,000 -14,999	$15,000 -19,999	$20,000 -24,999	$25,000 -29,999	$30,000 -34,999	OVER $35,000
ALABAMA	0.07	0.02	0.04	0.01	0.04	0.02	0.00	0.03	0.02	0.01	0.07	0.03	0.06	0.79
ALASKA	0.01	0.04	0.02	0.00	0.00	0.00	0.00	0.00	0.00	0.01	0.01	0.01	0.01	0.02
ARIZONA	0.01	0.01	0.01	0.01	0.01	0.00	0.00	0.00	0.00	0.00	0.00	0.00	0.01	0.02
ARKANSAS	0.02	0.01	0.01	0.03	0.00	*	0.01	0.01	0.01	0.00	0.01	0.01	0.01	0.08
CALIFORNIA	0.00	0.00	0.00	0.00	0.00	0.00	0.00	0.00	0.00	0.00	0.00	0.00	0.00	0.00
COLORADO	0.02	0.00	0.02	0.00	0.00	0.01	0.00	0.00	0.00	0.00	0.00	0.00	0.01	0.03
CONNECTICUT	0.00	0.00	0.01	0.00	0.00	0.00	0.00	0.00	0.00	0.00	0.00	0.00	0.00	0.01
DELAWARE	0.31	0.11	0.07	0.03	0.01	0.20	0.01	0.05	0.11	0.07	0.09	0.09	0.06	0.68
FLORIDA	0.01	0.00	0.00	0.00	0.00	0.00	0.00	0.00	0.00	0.00	0.00	0.00	0.01	0.02
GEORGIA	0.03	0.01	0.01	0.01	0.01	0.00	0.00	0.00	0.00	0.01	0.01	0.01	0.03	0.07
HAWAII	0.02	0.00	0.00	0.00	0.01	0.00	0.00	0.00	0.00	0.00	0.00	0.00	0.00	0.01
IDAHO	0.02	0.01	0.00	0.00	0.00	0.01	0.00	0.00	0.00	0.00	0.01	0.01	0.03	0.05
ILLINOIS	0.03	0.02	0.01	0.02	0.01	0.01	0.01	0.01	0.01	0.01	0.01	0.01	0.01	0.07
INDIANA	0.00	0.00	0.00	0.00	0.00	0.00	0.00	0.00	0.00	0.00	0.00	0.00	0.00	0.02
IOWA	0.00	0.01	0.02	0.03	0.01	0.00	0.02	0.02	0.00	0.01	0.01	0.01	0.04	0.06
KANSAS	0.02	0.01	0.01	0.01	0.03	0.01	0.01	0.01	0.00	0.01	0.01	0.01	0.01	0.07
KENTUCKY	0.01	0.00	0.01	0.05	0.00	0.00	0.01	0.00	0.00	0.01	0.01	0.03	0.01	0.21
LOUISIANA	0.11	0.04	0.09	0.02	0.03	0.05	0.03	0.04	0.03	0.05	0.03	0.05	0.12	0.60
MAINE	0.01	0.00	0.00	0.01	0.00	0.00	0.01	0.00	0.00	0.00	0.00	0.01	0.00	0.02
MARYLAND	0.00	0.02	0.00	0.00	0.00	0.00	0.00	0.00	0.00	0.00	0.00	0.00	0.00	0.01
MASSACHUSETTS	0.01	0.00	0.01	0.01	0.01	0.00	0.00	0.00	0.00	0.00	0.00	0.01	0.00	0.03
MICHIGAN	0.24	0.20	0.19	0.11	0.11	0.19	0.12	0.06	0.05	0.06	0.08	0.18	0.08	0.59
MINNESOTA	0.00	0.00	0.01	0.00	0.00	0.00	0.00	0.00	0.00	0.00	0.00	0.00	0.00	0.01
MISSISSIPPI	0.05	0.00	0.05	0.00	0.15	0.02	0.06	0.06	0.04	0.04	0.13	0.07	0.09	0.60
MISSOURI	0.02	0.01	0.01	0.03	0.01	0.02	0.02	0.02	0.02	0.01	0.02	0.02	0.02	0.19
MONTANA	0.01	0.01	0.00	0.00	0.00	0.00	0.00	0.01	0.00	0.00	0.00	0.00	0.00	0.02
NEBRASKA	0.02	0.01	0.00	0.00	0.01	0.00	0.01	0.00	0.00	0.00	0.01	0.01	0.01	0.05
NEVADA	0.01	0.01	0.00	0.00	0.00	0.00	0.00	0.01	0.00	0.01	0.00	0.00	0.00	0.05
NEW HAMPSHIRE	0.04	0.01	0.08	0.07	0.01	0.00	0.01	0.02	0.01	0.01	0.01	0.01	0.02	0.11
NEW JERSEY	0.08	0.06	0.16	0.15	0.09	0.07	0.25	0.07	0.04	0.04	0.05	0.04	0.05	0.22
NEW MEXICO	0.01	0.02	0.00	0.00	0.00	0.01	0.00	0.01	0.01	0.01	0.01	0.02	0.02	0.03
NEW YORK	0.00	0.00	0.00	0.00	0.00	0.00	0.00	0.00	0.00	0.00	0.00	0.00	0.00	0.01
NORTH CAROLINA	0.12	0.02	0.13	0.03	0.03	0.02	0.03	0.02	0.02	0.03	0.04	0.04	0.04	0.30
NORTH DAKOTA	0.01	0.00	0.01	0.00	0.01	0.00	0.00	0.00	0.00	0.00	0.00	0.00	0.00	0.01
OHIO	0.14	0.11	0.09	0.13	0.01	0.05	0.06	0.05	0.03	0.04	0.05	0.06	0.13	0.41
OKLAHOMA	0.05	0.00	0.00	0.00	0.02	0.02	0.01	0.00	0.01	0.02	0.02	0.03	0.01	0.18
OREGON	0.02	0.00	0.00	0.00	0.00	*	0.00	0.00	0.00	0.00	0.00	0.00	0.01	0.03
PENNSYLVANIA	0.36	0.25	0.12	0.23	0.31	0.03	0.19	0.06	0.06	0.09	0.07	0.09	0.14	0.64
RHODE ISLAND	0.01	0.02	0.01	0.01	0.03	0.00	0.00	0.01	0.01	0.00	0.00	0.00	0.01	0.03
SOUTH CAROLINA	0.01	*	0.01	0.00	0.03	0.02	0.01	0.02	0.01	0.01	0.00	0.00	0.01	0.09
SOUTH DAKOTA	0.00	0.00	0.00	0.00	0.00	0.01	0.00	0.00	0.00	0.00	0.00	0.00	0.00	0.01
TENNESSEE	0.10	0.00	0.01	0.00	0.03	0.00	0.03	0.05	0.01	0.05	0.04	0.05	0.05	0.51
TEXAS	0.34	0.04	0.17	0.08	0.03	0.04	0.03	0.04	0.07	0.06	0.05	0.14	0.17	0.71
UTAH	*	*	*	*	*	*	*	*	*	*	*	*	*	*
VERMONT	0.00	0.00	0.00	0.00	0.00	0.00	0.00	0.00	0.00	0.00	0.00	0.00	0.01	0.02
VIRGINIA	0.01	0.01	0.00	0.01	0.02	0.00	0.01	0.01	0.00	0.00	0.00	0.01	0.01	0.03
WASHINGTON	0.00	0.00	0.01	0.01	0.00	0.01	0.00	0.00	0.00	0.00	0.00	0.00	0.01	0.03
WEST VIRGINIA	0.00	0.03	0.01	0.00	0.00	0.01	0.00	0.00	0.00	0.01	0.01	0.01	0.04	0.08
WISCONSIN	0.00	0.00	0.00	0.00	0.00	0.00	0.01	0.00	0.00	0.00	0.00	0.00	0.00	0.01
WYOMING	0.01	0.01	0.00	0.00	0.00	0.01	0.01	0.00	0.00	0.00	0.00	0.00	0.00	0.03
AVERAGE	0.05	0.02	0.03	0.02	0.02	0.02	0.02	0.02	0.01	0.01	0.02	0.02	0.03	0.16

* EFFECTIVE TAX RATE EQUALS ZERO BEFORE ROUNDING. AN ENTIRE ROW OF * MEANS THAT THIS TAX IS NOT USED IN THIS STATE.

TABLE A-18
EFFECTIVE TAX RATES: STATE LICENSE TAXES-OCCUPATIONS AND BUSINESSES N.E.C.
INCIDENCE: BUSINESSES
ALLOCATOR: BUSINESS NET PROFIT

STATE	UNDER $3,000	$3,000 -3,999	$4,000 -4,999	$5,000 -5,999	$6,000 -6,999	$7,000 -7,999	$8,000 -9,999	$10,000 -11,999	$12,000 -14,999	$15,000 -19,999	$20,000 -24,999	$25,000 -29,999	$30,000 -34,999	OVER $35,000
ALABAMA	0.09	0.06	0.06	0.12	0.05	0.14	0.04	0.03	0.03	0.04	0.06	0.06	0.11	0.32
ALASKA	0.30	0.04	0.23	0.10	0.36	0.26	0.05	0.08	0.08	0.08	0.13	0.08	0.09	0.19
ARIZONA	0.08	0.09	0.02	0.06	0.04	0.05	0.04	0.04	0.02	0.03	0.04	0.03	0.08	0.09
ARKANSAS	0.08	0.07	0.11	0.06	0.05	0.07	0.03	0.03	0.04	0.04	0.03	0.06	0.05	0.16
CALIFORNIA	0.07	0.04	0.04	0.04	0.04	0.04	0.04	0.04	0.03	0.03	0.04	0.04	0.06	0.12
COLORADO	0.08	0.03	0.06	0.04	0.03	0.06	0.04	0.05	0.04	0.04	0.05	0.04	0.08	0.13
CONNECTICUT	0.06	0.04	0.06	0.04	0.05	0.06	0.07	0.06	0.03	0.04	0.03	0.05	0.04	0.11
DELAWARE	0.85	1.04	0.91	0.88	0.62	0.35	0.76	0.65	0.43	0.28	0.26	0.45	0.86	1.49
FLORIDA	0.12	0.08	0.07	0.09	0.07	0.08	0.06	0.06	0.04	0.06	0.07	0.06	0.13	0.24
GEORGIA	0.05	0.04	0.03	0.03	0.02	0.04	0.03	0.04	0.02	0.02	0.02	0.03	0.06	0.10
HAWAII	0.12	0.06	0.04	0.04	0.07	0.05	0.07	0.04	0.05	0.06	0.03	0.03	0.06	0.14
IDAHO	0.30	0.20	0.19	0.13	0.19	0.15	0.15	0.12	0.14	0.12	0.22	0.21	0.22	0.53
ILLINOIS	0.04	0.02	0.03	0.05	0.03	0.03	0.03	0.03	0.02	0.03	0.02	0.02	0.04	0.10
INDIANA	0.05	0.03	0.02	0.02	0.02	0.03	0.02	0.01	0.02	0.02	0.02	0.03	0.03	0.07
IOWA	0.05	0.03	0.04	0.02	0.02	0.06	0.04	0.03	0.02	0.03	0.03	0.05	0.07	0.11
KANSAS	0.10	0.06	0.04	0.07	0.06	0.05	0.03	0.06	0.04	0.05	0.04	0.07	0.06	0.19
KENTUCKY	0.06	0.07	0.05	0.08	0.02	0.07	0.05	0.02	0.04	0.03	0.03	0.07	0.06	0.23
LOUISIANA	0.13	0.11	0.12	0.11	0.12	0.16	0.11	0.10	0.10	0.08	0.08	0.09	0.11	0.40
MAINE	0.14	0.12	0.15	0.11	0.09	0.11	0.14	0.09	0.09	0.08	0.10	0.18	0.12	0.36
MARYLAND	0.07	0.05	0.04	0.04	0.05	0.04	0.03	0.04	0.03	0.02	0.02	0.02	0.04	0.09
MASSACHUSETTS	0.07	0.03	0.05	0.06	0.06	0.06	0.05	0.03	0.03	0.02	0.02	0.02	0.03	0.11
MICHIGAN	0.04	0.03	0.03	0.03	0.04	0.04	0.03	0.02	0.02	0.02	0.02	0.02	0.03	0.09
MINNESOTA	0.16	0.12	0.08	0.13	0.09	0.09	0.08	0.08	0.06	0.06	0.08	0.07	0.10	0.18
MISSISSIPPI	0.11	0.11	0.10	0.13	0.08	0.09	0.10	0.03	0.08	0.07	0.05	0.07	0.14	0.36
MISSOURI	0.06	0.04	0.05	0.05	0.03	0.03	0.04	0.03	0.02	0.04	0.03	0.03	0.04	0.11
MONTANA	0.10	0.04	0.07	0.09	0.10	0.06	0.07	0.08	0.05	0.06	0.05	0.10	0.11	0.18
NEBRASKA	0.13	0.09	0.07	0.04	0.06	0.08	0.09	0.06	0.03	0.06	0.05	0.10	0.10	0.16
NEVADA	0.14	0.06	0.07	0.06	0.06	0.09	0.07	0.05	0.06	0.05	0.06	0.05	0.09	0.20
NEW HAMPSHIRE	0.14	0.09	0.11	0.10	0.11	0.11	0.08	0.08	0.08	0.04	0.07	0.06	0.08	0.22
NEW JERSEY	0.04	0.03	0.03	0.03	0.04	0.04	0.04	0.03	0.03	0.02	0.02	0.02	0.02	0.06
NEW MEXICO	0.09	0.09	0.08	0.05	0.05	0.03	0.05	0.06	0.05	0.05	0.05	0.05	0.12	0.14
NEW YORK	0.04	0.03	0.04	0.04	0.03	0.03	0.03	0.02	0.02	0.02	0.02	0.02	0.03	0.08
NORTH CAROLINA	0.18	0.12	0.19	0.13	0.11	0.11	0.11	0.11	0.07	0.07	0.11	0.05	0.11	0.33
NORTH DAKOTA	0.23	0.22	0.07	0.15	0.22	0.07	0.11	0.10	0.12	0.11	0.11	0.14	0.22	0.30
OHIO	0.04	0.02	0.02	0.03	0.02	0.03	0.02	0.02	0.02	0.02	0.01	0.02	0.03	0.07
OKLAHOMA	0.09	0.03	0.04	0.04	0.03	0.06	0.02	0.03	0.03	0.03	0.02	0.03	0.04	0.08
OREGON	0.13	0.15	0.07	0.07	0.13	0.14	0.09	0.09	0.07	0.09	0.11	0.20	0.13	0.30
PENNSYLVANIA	0.12	0.08	0.07	0.11	0.13	0.10	0.10	0.09	0.05	0.05	0.07	0.10	0.09	0.27
RHODE ISLAND	0.03	0.02	0.03	0.03	0.03	0.05	0.03	0.03	0.02	0.02	0.02	0.02	0.04	0.09
SOUTH CAROLINA	0.06	0.10	0.10	0.07	0.08	0.10	0.06	0.06	0.04	0.05	0.05	0.12	0.08	0.26
SOUTH DAKOTA	0.14	0.07	0.07	0.09	0.14	0.07	0.09	0.05	0.11	0.09	0.12	0.14	0.22	0.34
TENNESSEE	0.28	0.12	0.20	0.17	0.14	0.12	0.17	0.09	0.09	0.12	0.13	0.21	0.34	0.83
TEXAS	0.04	0.03	0.04	0.02	0.03	0.02	0.02	0.02	0.01	0.02	0.02	0.03	0.03	0.09
UTAH	0.04	0.04	0.04	0.03	0.05	0.03	0.03	0.02	0.03	0.03	0.03	0.04	0.04	0.09
VERMONT	0.10	0.05	0.13	0.02	0.05	0.06	0.05	0.07	0.04	0.03	0.04	0.05	0.07	0.25
VIRGINIA	0.12	0.07	0.06	0.07	0.06	0.05	0.04	0.05	0.03	0.04	0.05	0.05	0.04	0.15
WASHINGTON	0.09	0.07	0.05	0.09	0.07	0.10	0.07	0.05	0.07	0.05	0.08	0.07	0.13	0.25
WEST VIRGINIA	0.01	0.01	0.02	0.02	0.03	0.01	0.01	0.02	0.02	0.01	0.01	0.03	0.03	0.09
WISCONSIN	0.07	0.08	0.04	0.05	0.04	0.05	0.07	0.05	0.04	0.03	0.04	0.06	0.06	0.13
WYOMING	0.03	0.00	0.01	0.01	0.01	0.01	0.01	0.02	0.01	0.02	0.01	0.01	0.03	0.05
AVERAGE	0.11	0.09	0.09	0.08	0.08	0.08	0.07	0.06	0.05	0.05	0.06	0.07	0.10	0.22

* EFFECTIVE TAX RATE EQUALS ZERO BEFORE ROUNDING. AN ENTIRE ROW OF * MEANS THAT THIS TAX IS NOT USED IN THIS STATE.

TABLE A-19
EFFECTIVE TAX RATES: STATE LICENSE TAXES-MOTOR VEHICLE OPERATORS
INCIDENCE: DRIVERS
ALLOCATOR: VEHICLE OPERATIONS EXPENDITURES

STATE	UNDER $3,000	$3,000 -3,999	$4,000 -4,999	$5,000 -5,999	$6,000 -6,999	$7,000 -7,999	$8,000 -9,999	$10,000 -11,999	$12,000 -14,999	$15,000 -19,999	$20,000 -24,999	$25,000 -29,999	$30,000 -34,999	OVER $35,000
ALABAMA	0.08	0.05	0.04	0.04	0.03	0.03	0.03	0.03	0.02	0.02	0.02	0.02	0.02	0.01
ALASKA	0.04	0.03	0.03	0.03	0.02	0.02	0.02	0.02	0.02	0.02	0.01	0.01	0.01	0.01
ARIZONA	0.08	0.05	0.04	0.04	0.03	0.03	0.03	0.03	0.02	0.02	0.02	0.02	0.02	0.02
ARKANSAS	0.13	0.08	0.07	0.06	0.06	0.05	0.05	0.04	0.04	0.04	0.03	0.03	0.03	0.03
CALIFORNIA	0.03	0.02	0.02	0.02	0.01	0.01	0.01	0.01	0.01	0.01	0.01	0.01	0.01	0.01
COLORADO	0.04	0.02	0.02	0.02	0.02	0.02	0.01	0.01	0.01	0.01	0.01	0.01	0.01	0.01
CONNECTICUT	0.09	0.07	0.07	0.07	0.06	0.07	0.06	0.06	0.05	0.05	0.05	0.05	0.05	0.05
DELAWARE	0.11	0.06	0.06	0.05	0.05	0.04	0.04	0.04	0.04	0.03	0.03	0.03	0.03	0.02
FLORIDA	0.14	0.08	0.07	0.06	0.06	0.05	0.05	0.04	0.04	0.04	0.03	0.03	0.03	0.03
GEORGIA	0.06	0.04	0.03	0.03	0.03	0.03	0.02	0.02	0.02	0.02	0.02	0.02	0.01	0.01
HAWAII	*	*	*	*	*	*	*	*	*	*	*	*	*	*
IDAHO	0.11	0.07	0.06	0.05	0.05	0.04	0.04	0.04	0.04	0.03	0.03	0.03	0.03	0.02
ILLINOIS	0.07	0.05	0.04	0.04	0.04	0.03	0.03	0.03	0.03	0.03	0.03	0.03	0.02	0.02
INDIANA	*	*	*	*	*	*	*	*	*	*	*	*	*	*
IOWA	0.10	0.07	0.06	0.05	0.05	0.05	0.05	0.04	0.04	0.04	0.04	0.03	0.03	0.03
KANSAS	0.07	0.05	0.04	0.04	0.04	0.03	0.03	0.03	0.03	0.03	0.02	0.02	0.02	0.02
KENTUCKY	0.05	0.03	0.02	0.02	0.02	0.02	0.02	0.02	0.01	0.01	0.01	0.01	0.01	0.01
LOUISIANA	0.08	0.04	0.04	0.03	0.03	0.03	0.03	0.02	0.02	0.02	0.02	0.02	0.02	0.01
MAINE	0.08	0.06	0.05	0.04	0.05	0.04	0.04	0.04	0.04	0.04	0.04	0.03	0.03	0.03
MARYLAND	0.07	0.04	0.03	0.03	0.03	0.02	0.02	0.02	0.02	0.02	0.02	0.02	0.01	0.01
MASSACHUSETTS	0.05	0.04	0.03	0.03	0.03	0.03	0.03	0.03	0.03	0.03	0.02	0.02	0.02	0.02
MICHIGAN	0.05	0.03	0.03	0.02	0.02	0.02	0.02	0.02	0.02	0.02	0.02	0.01	0.01	0.01
MINNESOTA	0.07	0.05	0.04	0.04	0.04	0.04	0.03	0.03	0.03	0.03	0.02	0.02	0.02	0.02
MISSISSIPPI	0.12	0.08	0.06	0.06	0.05	0.05	0.04	0.04	0.04	0.03	0.03	0.03	0.03	0.02
MISSOURI	0.05	0.03	0.03	0.03	0.02	0.02	0.02	0.02	0.02	0.02	0.02	0.02	0.01	0.01
MONTANA	0.09	0.06	0.05	0.05	0.04	0.04	0.04	0.03	0.03	0.03	0.03	0.03	0.02	0.02
NEBRASKA	0.05	0.03	0.03	0.02	0.02	0.02	0.02	0.02	0.02	0.02	0.02	0.02	0.02	0.01
NEVADA	0.05	0.03	0.03	0.03	0.03	0.02	0.02	0.02	0.02	0.02	0.01	0.01	0.01	0.01
NEW HAMPSHIRE	0.08	0.06	0.05	0.05	0.05	0.04	0.04	0.04	0.04	0.04	0.04	0.04	0.04	0.03
NEW JERSEY	0.07	0.05	0.05	0.05	0.05	0.05	0.04	0.04	0.04	0.04	0.04	0.04	0.04	0.04
NEW MEXICO	0.07	0.04	0.04	0.03	0.03	0.03	0.03	0.03	0.02	0.02	0.02	0.02	0.02	0.02
NEW YORK	0.03	0.02	0.02	0.02	0.02	0.02	0.02	0.02	0.01	0.01	0.01	0.01	0.01	0.01
NORTH CAROLINA	0.08	0.05	0.04	0.04	0.03	0.03	0.03	0.03	0.02	0.02	0.02	0.02	0.02	0.02
NORTH DAKOTA	0.06	0.04	0.04	0.03	0.03	0.03	0.03	0.03	0.02	0.02	0.02	0.02	0.02	0.02
OHIO	0.04	0.03	0.03	0.02	0.02	0.02	0.02	0.02	0.02	0.02	0.02	0.02	0.02	0.01
OKLAHOMA	0.15	0.08	0.07	0.07	0.06	0.05	0.05	0.05	0.04	0.04	0.03	0.03	0.03	0.03
OREGON	0.11	0.07	0.06	0.06	0.05	0.05	0.04	0.04	0.04	0.03	0.03	0.03	0.03	0.03
PENNSYLVANIA	0.08	0.06	0.05	0.05	0.05	0.05	0.04	0.04	0.04	0.04	0.04	0.04	0.04	0.04
RHODE ISLAND	0.10	0.06	0.07	0.06	0.05	0.05	0.05	0.05	0.05	0.05	0.05	0.05	0.04	0.04
SOUTH CAROLINA	0.02	0.01	0.01	0.01	0.01	0.01	0.01	0.01	0.01	0.01	0.01	0.01	0.01	0.00
SOUTH DAKOTA	0.07	0.04	0.04	0.04	0.03	0.03	0.03	0.03	0.03	0.03	0.02	0.02	0.02	0.02
TENNESSEE	0.09	0.05	0.05	0.04	0.04	0.04	0.03	0.03	0.03	0.02	0.02	0.02	0.02	0.02
TEXAS	0.09	0.05	0.05	0.04	0.04	0.03	0.03	0.03	0.03	0.02	0.02	0.02	0.02	0.02
UTAH	0.08	0.05	0.04	0.03	0.04	0.03	0.03	0.03	0.02	0.02	0.02	0.02	0.02	0.02
VERMONT	0.08	0.06	0.05	0.05	0.05	0.05	0.04	0.04	0.04	0.04	0.04	0.04	0.04	0.03
VIRGINIA	0.13	0.07	0.06	0.06	0.05	0.05	0.04	0.04	0.04	0.03	0.03	0.03	0.03	0.02
WASHINGTON	0.13	0.08	0.07	0.06	0.06	0.05	0.05	0.05	0.04	0.04	0.04	0.03	0.03	0.03
WEST VIRGINIA	0.07	0.04	0.03	0.03	0.03	0.03	0.02	0.02	0.02	0.02	0.02	0.02	0.01	0.01
WISCONSIN	0.08	0.05	0.04	0.04	0.04	0.04	0.03	0.03	0.03	0.03	0.03	0.03	0.03	0.02
WYOMING	0.03	0.02	0.02	0.02	0.02	0.02	0.01	0.01	0.01	0.01	0.01	0.01	0.01	0.01
AVERAGE	0.08	0.05	0.04	0.04	0.04	0.03	0.03	0.03	0.03	0.03	0.02	0.02	0.02	0.02

* EFFECTIVE TAX RATE EQUALS ZERO BEFORE ROUNDING. AN ENTIRE ROW OF * MEANS THAT THIS TAX IS NOT USED IN THIS STATE.

TABLE A-20

EFFECTIVE TAX RATES: STATE LICENSE TAXES-HUNTING AND FISHING
INCIDENCE: HUNTERS AND FISHERS
ALLOCATOR: RECREATION EXPENDITURES

STATE	UNDER $3,000	$3,000 -3,999	$4,000 -4,999	$5,000 -5,999	$6,000 -6,999	$7,000 -7,999	$8,000 -9,999	$10,000 -11,999	$12,000 -14,999	$15,000 -19,999	$20,000 -24,999	$25,000 -29,999	$30,000 -34,999	OVER $35,000
ALABAMA	0.05	0.04	0.03	0.03	0.03	0.03	0.03	0.03	0.03	0.03	0.02	0.02	0.02	0.02
ALASKA	0.09	0.07	0.07	0.07	0.06	0.06	0.06	0.06	0.05	0.05	0.05	0.05	0.05	0.05
ARIZONA	0.07	0.05	0.04	0.04	0.04	0.03	0.03	0.03	0.03	0.03	0.03	0.03	0.03	0.03
ARKANSAS	0.06	0.05	0.04	0.04	0.04	0.04	0.04	0.03	0.03	0.03	0.03	0.03	0.03	0.03
CALIFORNIA	0.04	0.03	0.02	0.02	0.02	0.02	0.02	0.02	0.02	0.02	0.02	0.02	0.02	0.02
COLORADO	0.08	0.06	0.05	0.05	0.05	0.05	0.04	0.04	0.04	0.04	0.04	0.04	0.04	0.03
CONNECTICUT	0.01	0.01	0.01	0.01	0.01	0.01	0.01	0.01	0.01	0.01	0.01	0.01	0.01	0.00
DELAWARE	0.01	0.01	0.01	0.01	0.01	0.01	0.01	0.01	0.01	0.01	0.01	0.01	0.01	0.01
FLORIDA	0.02	0.01	0.01	0.01	0.01	0.01	0.01	0.01	0.01	0.01	0.01	0.01	0.01	0.01
GEORGIA	0.04	0.03	0.03	0.03	0.03	0.03	0.02	0.02	0.02	0.02	0.02	0.02	0.02	0.02
HAWAII	0.00	0.00	0.00	0.00	0.00	0.00	0.00	0.00	0.00	0.00	0.00	0.00	0.00	0.00
IDAHO	0.13	0.09	0.08	0.08	0.08	0.07	0.07	0.07	0.06	0.06	0.06	0.06	0.06	0.05
ILLINOIS	0.01	0.01	0.01	0.01	0.01	0.01	0.01	0.01	0.01	0.01	0.01	0.01	0.01	0.01
INDIANA	0.02	0.02	0.02	0.02	0.01	0.01	0.01	0.01	0.01	0.01	0.01	0.01	0.01	0.01
IOWA	0.04	0.03	0.03	0.03	0.03	0.03	0.03	0.03	0.03	0.03	0.03	0.03	0.03	0.03
KANSAS	0.04	0.03	0.03	0.03	0.03	0.03	0.03	0.03	0.03	0.03	0.03	0.03	0.03	0.02
KENTUCKY	0.05	0.04	0.04	0.03	0.03	0.03	0.03	0.03	0.03	0.03	0.03	0.03	0.03	0.03
LOUISIANA	0.03	0.02	0.02	0.02	0.02	0.02	0.02	0.02	0.02	0.02	0.02	0.02	0.02	0.02
MAINE	0.05	0.05	0.05	0.04	0.05	0.05	0.05	0.05	0.04	0.04	0.04	0.04	0.04	0.04
MARYLAND	0.02	0.01	0.01	0.01	0.01	0.01	0.01	0.01	0.01	0.01	0.01	0.01	0.01	0.01
MASSACHUSETTS	0.01	0.01	0.01	0.01	0.01	0.01	0.01	0.01	0.01	0.01	0.01	0.01	0.01	0.01
MICHIGAN	0.04	0.03	0.03	0.03	0.03	0.03	0.03	0.03	0.03	0.03	0.03	0.03	0.03	0.02
MINNESOTA	0.06	0.05	0.05	0.05	0.05	0.05	0.04	0.04	0.04	0.04	0.04	0.04	0.04	0.04
MISSISSIPPI	0.07	0.05	0.04	0.04	0.04	0.04	0.04	0.04	0.03	0.03	0.03	0.03	0.03	0.03
MISSOURI	0.06	0.05	0.05	0.04	0.04	0.04	0.04	0.04	0.04	0.04	0.04	0.04	0.04	0.03
MONTANA	0.19	0.14	0.13	0.12	0.12	0.11	0.10	0.10	0.10	0.09	0.09	0.09	0.09	0.09
NEBRASKA	0.05	0.04	0.04	0.04	0.04	0.04	0.04	0.03	0.03	0.03	0.03	0.03	0.03	0.03
NEVADA	0.08	0.07	0.06	0.06	0.06	0.05	0.05	0.05	0.05	0.04	0.04	0.04	0.04	0.04
NEW HAMPSHIRE	0.03	0.02	0.02	0.02	0.02	0.02	0.02	0.02	0.02	0.02	0.02	0.02	0.02	0.02
NEW JERSEY	0.01	0.01	0.01	0.01	0.01	0.01	0.01	0.01	0.01	0.01	0.01	0.01	0.01	0.01
NEW MEXICO	0.11	0.08	0.07	0.07	0.07	0.06	0.06	0.06	0.05	0.05	0.05	0.05	0.05	0.05
NEW YORK	0.01	0.01	0.01	0.01	0.01	0.01	0.01	0.01	0.01	0.01	0.01	0.01	0.01	0.01
NORTH CAROLINA	0.04	0.03	0.03	0.03	0.03	0.02	0.02	0.02	0.02	0.02	0.02	0.02	0.02	0.02
NORTH DAKOTA	0.06	0.05	0.05	0.04	0.04	0.04	0.04	0.04	0.04	0.04	0.04	0.04	0.04	0.04
OHIO	0.02	0.01	0.01	0.01	0.01	0.01	0.01	0.01	0.01	0.01	0.01	0.01	0.01	0.01
OKLAHOMA	0.07	0.04	0.04	0.04	0.04	0.04	0.03	0.03	0.03	0.03	0.03	0.03	0.03	0.03
OREGON	0.07	0.05	0.05	0.04	0.04	0.04	0.04	0.04	0.03	0.03	0.03	0.03	0.03	0.03
PENNSYLVANIA	0.04	0.03	0.03	0.03	0.03	0.03	0.03	0.03	0.03	0.03	0.03	0.03	0.03	0.03
RHODE ISLAND	0.00	0.00	0.00	0.00	0.00	0.00	0.00	0.00	0.00	0.00	0.00	0.00	0.00	0.00
SOUTH CAROLINA	0.04	0.03	0.03	0.03	0.03	0.03	0.03	0.03	0.03	0.02	0.02	0.02	0.02	0.02
SOUTH DAKOTA	0.07	0.06	0.05	0.05	0.05	0.05	0.05	0.05	0.05	0.05	0.05	0.05	0.04	0.04
TENNESSEE	0.05	0.04	0.04	0.04	0.03	0.03	0.03	0.03	0.03	0.03	0.03	0.03	0.03	0.03
TEXAS	0.03	0.02	0.02	0.02	0.02	0.02	0.02	0.02	0.02	0.01	0.01	0.01	0.01	0.01
UTAH	0.08	0.06	0.05	0.05	0.05	0.04	0.04	0.04	0.04	0.04	0.04	0.04	0.03	0.03
VERMONT	0.07	0.06	0.06	0.06	0.06	0.06	0.06	0.06	0.05	0.06	0.06	0.05	0.05	0.05
VIRGINIA	0.04	0.03	0.03	0.03	0.02	0.02	0.02	0.02	0.02	0.02	0.02	0.02	0.02	0.02
WASHINGTON	0.10	0.07	0.06	0.06	0.06	0.06	0.05	0.05	0.05	0.05	0.05	0.04	0.04	0.04
WEST VIRGINIA	0.07	0.05	0.05	0.04	0.04	0.04	0.04	0.04	0.04	0.04	0.03	0.03	0.03	0.03
WISCONSIN	0.09	0.07	0.06	0.06	0.06	0.06	0.06	0.06	0.06	0.06	0.05	0.05	0.05	0.05
WYOMING	0.31	0.25	0.24	0.22	0.21	0.21	0.19	0.19	0.18	0.17	0.17	0.17	0.17	0.15
AVERAGE	0.06	0.04	0.04	0.04	0.04	0.04	0.04	0.03	0.03	0.03	0.03	0.03	0.03	0.03

* EFFECTIVE TAX RATE EQUALS ZERO BEFORE ROUNDING. AN ENTIRE ROW OF * MEANS THAT THIS TAX IS NOT USED IN THIS STATE.

TABLE A-21
EFFECTIVE TAX RATES: STATE LICENSE TAXES-ALCOHOLIC BEVERAGES
INCIDENCE: CONSUMERS OF ALCOHOLIC BEVERAGES
ALLOCATOR: ALCOHOLIC BEVERAGES EXPENDITURES

STATE	UNDER $3,000	$3,000 -3,999	$4,000 -4,999	$5,000 -5,999	$6,000 -6,999	$7,000 -7,999	$8,000 -9,999	$10,000 -11,999	$12,000 -14,999	$15,000 -19,999	$20,000 -24,999	$25,000 -29,999	$30,000 -34,999	OVER $35,000
ALABAMA	0.03	0.02	0.02	0.02	0.02	0.02	0.02	0.02	0.02	0.02	0.02	0.02	0.02	0.01
ALASKA	0.07	0.05	0.04	0.04	0.04	0.03	0.03	0.03	0.03	0.03	0.03	0.03	0.02	0.02
ARIZONA	0.03	0.02	0.02	0.02	0.01	0.01	0.01	0.01	0.01	0.01	0.01	0.01	0.01	0.01
ARKANSAS	0.01	0.01	0.01	0.01	0.01	0.01	0.01	0.01	0.01	0.01	0.01	0.01	0.01	0.01
CALIFORNIA	0.03	0.02	0.02	0.02	0.02	0.02	0.02	0.01	0.01	0.01	0.01	0.01	0.01	0.01
COLORADO	0.02	0.02	0.01	0.01	0.01	0.01	0.01	0.01	0.01	0.01	0.01	0.01	0.01	0.01
CONNECTICUT	0.03	0.03	0.03	0.03	0.03	0.03	0.02	0.02	0.02	0.02	0.02	0.02	0.02	0.02
DELAWARE	0.02	0.01	0.01	0.01	0.01	0.01	0.01	0.01	0.01	0.01	0.01	0.01	0.01	0.01
FLORIDA	0.03	0.03	0.03	0.02	0.02	0.02	0.02	0.02	0.02	0.02	0.02	0.02	0.02	0.02
GEORGIA	0.00	0.00	0.00	0.00	0.00	0.00	0.00	0.00	0.00	0.00	0.00	0.00	0.00	0.00
HAWAII	*	*	*	*	*	*	*	*	*	*	*	*	*	*
IDAHO	0.03	0.02	0.02	0.02	0.02	0.02	0.02	0.01	0.01	0.01	0.01	0.01	0.01	0.01
ILLINOIS	0.00	0.00	0.00	0.00	0.00	0.00	0.00	0.00	0.00	0.00	0.00	0.00	0.00	0.00
INDIANA	0.04	0.03	0.03	0.03	0.02	0.02	0.02	0.02	0.02	0.02	0.02	0.02	0.02	0.02
IOWA	0.05	0.04	0.04	0.03	0.03	0.03	0.03	0.03	0.03	0.02	0.02	0.02	0.02	0.02
KANSAS	0.01	0.01	0.01	0.01	0.01	0.01	0.01	0.01	0.01	0.01	0.01	0.01	0.01	0.01
KENTUCKY	0.01	0.01	0.01	0.01	0.01	0.01	0.01	0.01	0.01	0.01	0.01	0.01	0.01	0.01
LOUISIANA	0.01	0.01	0.01	0.01	0.01	0.01	0.01	0.01	0.01	0.01	0.01	0.01	0.01	0.01
MAINE	0.04	0.03	0.03	0.02	0.02	0.02	0.02	0.02	0.02	0.02	0.02	0.02	0.02	0.02
MARYLAND	0.00	0.00	0.00	0.00	0.00	0.00	0.00	0.00	0.00	0.00	0.00	0.00	0.00	0.00
MASSACHUSETTS	0.00	0.00	0.00	0.00	0.00	0.00	0.00	0.00	0.00	0.00	0.00	0.00	0.00	0.00
MICHIGAN	0.04	0.03	0.02	0.02	0.02	0.02	0.02	0.02	0.02	0.02	0.01	0.01	0.01	0.01
MINNESOTA	0.00	0.00	0.00	0.00	0.00	0.00	0.00	0.00	0.00	0.00	0.00	0.00	0.00	0.00
MISSISSIPPI	0.03	0.02	0.02	0.02	0.02	0.02	0.02	0.02	0.02	0.02	0.02	0.02	0.02	0.01
MISSOURI	0.02	0.01	0.01	0.01	0.01	0.01	0.01	0.01	0.01	0.01	0.01	0.01	0.01	0.01
MONTANA	0.11	0.07	0.07	0.06	0.06	0.05	0.05	0.04	0.04	0.04	0.04	0.04	0.03	0.03
NEBRASKA	0.00	0.00	0.00	0.00	0.00	0.00	0.00	0.00	0.00	0.00	0.00	0.00	0.00	0.00
NEVADA	0.00	0.00	0.00	0.00	0.00	0.00	0.00	0.00	0.00	0.00	0.00	0.00	0.00	0.00
NEW HAMPSHIRE	0.02	0.01	0.01	0.01	0.01	0.01	0.01	0.01	0.01	0.01	0.01	0.01	0.01	0.01
NEW JERSEY	0.01	0.01	0.01	0.01	0.00	0.00	0.00	0.00	0.00	0.00	0.00	0.00	0.00	0.00
NEW MEXICO	0.01	0.01	0.01	0.01	0.01	0.01	0.01	0.01	0.00	0.00	0.00	0.00	0.00	0.00
NEW YORK	0.05	0.04	0.03	0.03	0.03	0.03	0.03	0.03	0.03	0.03	0.03	0.03	0.03	0.02
NORTH CAROLINA	0.00	0.00	0.00	0.00	0.00	0.00	0.00	0.00	0.00	0.00	0.00	0.00	0.00	0.00
NORTH DAKOTA	0.01	0.01	0.01	0.01	0.01	0.01	0.01	0.01	0.01	0.01	0.01	0.01	0.01	0.00
OHIO	0.03	0.02	0.02	0.02	0.02	0.02	0.02	0.02	0.02	0.02	0.02	0.01	0.01	0.01
OKLAHOMA	0.01	0.01	0.01	0.01	0.01	0.01	0.01	0.01	0.01	0.01	0.01	0.01	0.01	0.01
OREGON	0.02	0.01	0.01	0.01	0.01	0.01	0.01	0.01	0.01	0.01	0.01	0.01	0.01	0.01
PENNSYLVANIA	0.02	0.02	0.01	0.01	0.01	0.01	0.01	0.01	0.01	0.01	0.01	0.01	0.01	0.01
RHODE ISLAND	0.00	0.00	0.00	0.00	0.00	0.00	0.00	0.00	0.00	0.00	0.00	0.00	0.00	0.00
SOUTH CAROLINA	0.02	0.02	0.02	0.02	0.02	0.02	0.02	0.02	0.02	0.02	0.02	0.02	0.02	0.01
SOUTH DAKOTA	0.01	0.00	0.00	0.00	0.00	0.00	0.00	0.00	0.00	0.00	0.00	0.00	0.00	0.00
TENNESSEE	0.01	0.00	0.00	0.00	0.00	0.00	0.00	0.00	0.00	0.00	0.00	0.00	0.00	0.00
TEXAS	0.02	0.01	0.01	0.01	0.01	0.01	0.01	0.01	0.01	0.01	0.01	0.01	0.01	0.01
UTAH	0.00	0.00	0.00	0.00	0.00	0.00	0.00	0.00	0.00	0.00	0.00	0.00	0.00	0.00
VERMONT	0.03	0.02	0.02	0.02	0.02	0.02	0.02	0.02	0.02	0.02	0.02	0.01	0.01	0.01
VIRGINIA	0.01	0.01	0.01	0.01	0.01	0.01	0.01	0.01	0.00	0.00	0.00	0.00	0.00	0.00
WASHINGTON	0.03	0.02	0.02	0.02	0.02	0.02	0.01	0.01	0.01	0.01	0.01	0.01	0.01	0.01
WEST VIRGINIA	0.02	0.02	0.01	0.01	0.01	0.01	0.01	0.01	0.01	0.01	0.01	0.01	0.01	0.01
WISCONSIN	0.00	0.00	0.00	0.00	0.00	0.00	0.00	0.00	0.00	0.00	0.00	0.00	0.00	0.00
WYOMING	0.00	0.00	0.00	0.00	0.00	0.00	0.00	0.00	0.00	0.00	0.00	0.00	0.00	0.00
AVERAGE	0.02	0.02	0.01	0.01	0.01	0.01	0.01	0.01	0.01	0.01	0.01	0.01	0.01	0.01

* EFFECTIVE TAX RATE EQUALS ZERO BEFORE ROUNDING. AN ENTIRE ROW OF * MEANS THAT THIS TAX IS NOT USED IN THIS STATE.

TABLE A-22

EFFECTIVE TAX RATES: STATE LICENSE TAXES-PUBLIC UTILITIES

INCIDENCE: CONSUMERS OF UTILITY SERVICES

ALLOCATOR: GAS, ELECTRIC, AND TELEPHONE EXPENDITURES

STATE	UNDER $3,000	$3,000 -3,999	$4,000 -4,999	$5,000 -5,999	$6,000 -6,999	$7,000 -7,999	$8,000 -9,999	$10,000 -11,999	$12,000 -14,999	$15,000 -19,999	$20,000 -24,999	$25,000 -29,999	$30,000 -34,999	OVER $35,000
ALABAMA	0.01	0.01	0.00	0.00	0.00	0.00	0.00	0.00	0.00	0.00	0.00	0.00	0.00	0.00
ALASKA	*	*	*	*	*	*	*	*	*	*	*	*	*	*
ARIZONA	*	*	*	*	*	*	*	*	*	*	*	*	*	*
ARKANSAS	0.06	0.03	0.03	0.02	0.02	0.02	0.02	0.02	0.01	0.01	0.01	0.01	0.01	0.01
CALIFORNIA	0.02	0.01	0.01	0.01	0.01	0.01	0.01	0.01	0.01	0.01	0.00	0.00	0.00	0.00
COLORADO	0.00	0.00	0.00	0.00	0.00	0.00	0.00	0.00	0.00	0.00	0.00	0.00	0.00	0.00
CONNECTICUT	*	*	*	*	*	*	*	*	*	*	*	*	*	*
DELAWARE	0.09	0.05	0.05	0.04	0.04	0.03	0.03	0.03	0.03	0.02	0.02	0.02	0.02	0.01
FLORIDA	0.03	0.02	0.02	0.01	0.01	0.01	0.01	0.01	0.01	0.01	0.01	0.01	0.01	0.00
GEORGIA	*	*	*	*	*	*	*	*	*	*	*	*	*	*
HAWAII	0.04	0.03	0.03	0.02	0.02	0.02	0.02	0.02	0.01	0.01	0.01	0.01	0.01	0.01
IDAHO	0.01	0.01	0.01	0.01	0.01	0.00	0.00	0.00	0.00	0.00	0.00	0.00	0.00	0.00
ILLINOIS	*	*	*	*	*	*	*	*	*	*	*	*	*	*
INDIANA	0.00	0.00	0.00	0.00	0.00	0.00	0.00	0.00	0.00	0.00	0.00	0.00	0.00	0.00
IOWA	0.00	0.00	0.00	0.00	0.00	0.00	0.00	0.00	0.00	0.00	0.00	0.00	0.00	0.00
KANSAS	0.01	0.00	0.00	0.00	0.00	0.00	0.00	0.00	0.00	0.00	0.00	0.00	0.00	0.00
KENTUCKY	0.02	0.01	0.01	0.01	0.01	0.01	0.01	0.01	0.01	0.00	0.00	0.00	0.00	0.00
LOUISIANA	0.01	0.00	0.00	0.00	0.00	0.00	0.00	0.00	0.00	0.00	0.00	0.00	0.00	0.00
MAINE	*	*	*	*	*	*	*	*	*	*	*	*	*	*
MARYLAND	*	*	*	*	*	*	*	*	*	*	*	*	*	*
MASSACHUSETTS	*	*	*	*	*	*	*	*	*	*	*	*	*	*
MICHIGAN	0.00	0.00	0.00	0.00	0.00	0.00	0.00	0.00	0.00	0.00	0.00	0.00	0.00	0.00
MINNESOTA	0.00	0.00	0.00	0.00	0.00	0.00	0.00	0.00	0.00	0.00	0.00	0.00	0.00	0.00
MISSISSIPPI	*	*	*	*	*	*	*	*	*	*	*	*	*	*
MISSOURI	0.03	0.01	0.01	0.01	0.01	0.01	0.01	0.01	0.01	0.01	0.01	0.00	0.00	0.00
MONTANA	*	*	*	*	*	*	*	*	*	*	*	*	*	*
NEBRASKA	*	*	*	*	*	*	*	*	*	*	*	*	*	*
NEVADA	*	*	*	*	*	*	*	*	*	*	*	*	*	*
NEW HAMPSHIRE	0.03	0.02	0.01	0.01	0.01	0.01	0.01	0.01	0.01	0.01	0.01	0.01	0.01	0.00
NEW JERSEY	0.00	0.00	0.00	0.00	0.00	0.00	0.00	0.00	0.00	0.00	0.00	0.00	0.00	0.00
NEW MEXICO	0.01	0.00	0.00	0.00	0.00	0.00	0.00	0.00	0.00	0.00	0.00	0.00	0.00	0.00
NEW YORK	0.08	0.04	0.04	0.03	0.03	0.03	0.02	0.02	0.02	0.02	0.02	0.02	0.01	0.01
NORTH CAROLINA	0.00	0.00	0.00	0.00	0.00	0.00	0.00	0.00	0.00	0.00	0.00	0.00	0.00	0.00
NORTH DAKOTA	0.03	0.02	0.02	0.01	0.01	0.01	0.01	0.01	0.01	0.01	0.01	0.01	0.01	0.01
OHIO	0.03	0.02	0.02	0.01	0.01	0.01	0.01	0.01	0.01	0.01	0.01	0.01	0.01	0.01
OKLAHOMA	0.00	0.00	0.00	0.00	0.00	0.00	0.00	0.00	0.00	0.00	0.00	0.00	0.00	0.00
OREGON	0.07	0.04	0.03	0.03	0.03	0.03	0.02	0.02	0.02	0.02	0.01	0.01	0.01	0.01
PENNSYLVANIA	0.08	0.05	0.04	0.03	0.03	0.03	0.03	0.02	0.02	0.02	0.02	0.02	0.02	0.01
RHODE ISLAND	*	*	*	*	*	*	*	*	*	*	*	*	*	*
SOUTH CAROLINA	*	*	*	*	*	*	*	*	*	*	*	*	*	*
SOUTH DAKOTA	*	*	*	*	*	*	*	*	*	*	*	*	*	*
TENNESSEE	0.01	0.01	0.01	0.01	0.01	0.00	0.00	0.00	0.00	0.00	0.00	0.00	0.00	0.00
TEXAS	0.00	0.00	0.00	0.00	0.00	0.00	0.00	0.00	0.00	0.00	0.00	0.00	0.00	0.00
UTAH	0.01	0.00	0.00	0.00	0.00	0.00	0.00	0.00	0.00	0.00	0.00	0.00	0.00	0.00
VERMONT	*	*	*	*	*	*	*	*	*	*	*	*	*	*
VIRGINIA	*	*	*	*	*	*	*	*	*	*	*	*	*	*
WASHINGTON	0.07	0.04	0.03	0.03	0.03	0.02	0.02	0.02	0.02	0.02	0.01	0.01	0.01	0.01
WEST VIRGINIA	0.05	0.03	0.02	0.02	0.02	0.02	0.01	0.01	0.01	0.01	0.01	0.01	0.01	0.01
WISCONSIN	0.00	0.00	0.00	0.00	0.00	0.00	0.00	0.00	0.00	0.00	0.00	0.00	0.00	0.00
WYOMING	0.04	0.02	0.02	0.02	0.02	0.02	0.01	0.01	0.01	0.01	0.01	0.01	0.01	0.01
AVERAGE	0.03	0.02	0.01	0.01	0.01	0.01	0.01	0.01	0.01	0.01	0.01	0.01	0.00	0.00

* EFFECTIVE TAX RATE EQUALS ZERO BEFORE ROUNDING. AN ENTIRE ROW OF * MEANS THAT THIS TAX IS NOT USED IN THIS STATE.

TABLE A-23
EFFECTIVE TAX RATES: STATE LICENSE TAXES-AMUSEMENTS
INCIDENCE: USERS OF RECREATIONAL FACILITIES
ALLOCATOR: RECREATION EXPENDITURES

STATE	UNDER $3,000	$3,000 -3,999	$4,000 -4,999	$5,000 -5,999	$6,000 -6,999	$7,000 -7,999	$8,000 -9,999	$10,000 -11,999	$12,000 -14,999	$15,000 -19,999	$20,000 -24,999	$25,000 -29,999	$30,000 -34,999	OVER $35,000
ALABAMA	*	*	*	*	*	*	*	*	*	*	*	*	*	*
ALASKA	0.01	0.00	0.00	0.00	0.00	0.00	0.00	0.00	0.00	0.00	0.00	0.00	0.00	0.00
ARIZONA	*	*	*	*	*	*	*	*	*	*	*	*	*	*
ARKANSAS	0.00	0.00	0.00	0.00	0.00	0.00	0.00	0.00	0.00	0.00	0.00	0.00	0.00	0.00
CALIFORNIA	0.00	0.00	0.00	0.00	0.00	0.00	0.00	0.00	0.00	0.00	0.00	0.00	0.00	0.00
COLORADO	0.00	0.00	0.00	0.00	0.00	0.00	0.00	0.00	0.00	0.00	0.00	0.00	0.00	0.00
CONNECTICUT	0.00	0.00	0.00	0.00	0.00	0.00	0.00	0.00	0.00	0.00	0.00	0.00	0.00	0.00
DELAWARE	0.00	0.00	0.00	0.00	0.00	0.00	0.00	0.00	0.00	0.00	0.00	0.00	0.00	0.00
FLORIDA	0.00	0.00	0.00	0.00	0.00	0.00	0.00	0.00	0.00	0.00	0.00	0.00	0.00	0.00
GEORGIA	*	*	*	*	*	*	*	*	*	*	*	*	*	*
HAWAII	*	*	*	*	*	*	*	*	*	*	*	*	*	*
IDAHO	*	*	*	*	*	*	*	*	*	*	*	*	*	*
ILLINOIS	0.00	0.00	0.00	0.00	0.00	0.00	0.00	0.00	0.00	0.00	0.00	0.00	0.00	0.00
INDIANA	0.00	0.00	0.00	0.00	0.00	0.00	0.00	0.00	0.00	0.00	0.00	0.00	0.00	0.00
IOWA	*	*	*	*	*	*	*	*	*	*	*	*	*	*
KANSAS	0.00	0.00	0.00	0.00	0.00	0.00	0.00	0.00	0.00	0.00	0.00	0.00	0.00	0.00
KENTUCKY	0.00	0.00	0.00	0.00	0.00	0.00	0.00	0.00	0.00	0.00	0.00	0.00	0.00	0.00
LOUISIANA	0.00	0.00	0.00	0.00	0.00	0.00	0.00	0.00	0.00	0.00	0.00	0.00	0.00	0.00
MAINE	0.00	0.00	0.00	0.00	0.00	0.00	0.00	0.00	0.00	0.00	0.00	0.00	0.00	0.00
MARYLAND	0.00	0.00	0.00	0.00	0.00	0.00	0.00	0.00	0.00	0.00	0.00	0.00	0.00	0.00
MASSACHUSETTS	0.00	0.00	0.00	0.00	0.00	0.00	0.00	0.00	0.00	0.00	0.00	0.00	0.00	0.00
MICHIGAN	0.00	0.00	0.00	0.00	0.00	0.00	0.00	0.00	0.00	0.00	0.00	0.00	0.00	0.00
MINNESOTA	0.00	0.00	0.00	0.00	0.00	0.00	0.00	0.00	0.00	0.00	0.00	0.00	0.00	0.00
MISSISSIPPI	*	*	*	*	*	*	*	*	*	*	*	*	*	*
MISSOURI	*	*	*	*	*	*	*	*	*	*	*	*	*	*
MONTANA	*	*	*	*	*	*	*	*	*	*	*	*	*	*
NEBRASKA	0.00	0.00	0.00	0.00	0.00	0.00	0.00	0.00	0.00	0.00	0.00	0.00	0.00	0.00
NEVADA	0.90	0.71	0.64	0.59	0.61	0.58	0.55	0.52	0.50	0.48	0.46	0.45	0.45	0.41
NEW HAMPSHIRE	0.00	0.00	0.00	0.00	0.00	0.00	0.00	0.00	0.00	0.00	0.00	0.00	0.00	0.00
NEW JERSEY	*	*	*	*	*	*	*	*	*	*	*	*	*	*
NEW MEXICO	0.00	0.00	0.00	0.00	0.00	0.00	0.00	0.00	0.00	0.00	0.00	0.00	0.00	0.00
NEW YORK	0.00	0.00	0.00	0.00	0.00	0.00	0.00	0.00	0.00	0.00	0.00	0.00	0.00	0.00
NORTH CAROLINA	0.01	0.01	0.01	0.01	0.01	0.01	0.01	0.01	0.01	0.01	0.01	0.01	0.01	0.01
NORTH DAKOTA	0.00	0.00	0.00	0.00	0.00	0.00	0.00	0.00	0.00	0.00	0.00	0.00	0.00	0.00
OHIO	*	*	*	*	*	*	*	*	*	*	*	*	*	*
OKLAHOMA	0.01	0.01	0.01	0.01	0.01	0.01	0.01	0.00	0.00	0.00	0.00	0.00	0.00	0.00
OREGON	0.01	0.00	0.00	0.00	0.00	0.00	0.00	0.00	0.00	0.00	0.00	0.00	0.00	0.00
PENNSYLVANIA	0.00	0.00	0.00	0.00	0.00	0.00	0.00	0.00	0.00	0.00	0.00	0.00	0.00	0.00
RHODE ISLAND	0.00	0.00	0.00	0.00	0.00	0.00	0.00	0.00	0.00	0.00	0.00	0.00	0.00	0.00
SOUTH CAROLINA	0.02	0.01	0.01	0.01	0.01	0.01	0.01	0.01	0.01	0.01	0.01	0.01	0.01	0.01
SOUTH DAKOTA	*	*	*	*	*	*	*	*	*	*	*	*	*	*
TENNESSEE	*	*	*	*	*	*	*	*	*	*	*	*	*	*
TEXAS	*	*	*	*	*	*	*	*	*	*	*	*	*	*
UTAH	*	*	*	*	*	*	*	*	*	*	*	*	*	*
VERMONT	0.00	0.00	0.00	0.00	0.00	0.00	0.00	0.00	0.00	0.00	0.00	0.00	0.00	0.00
VIRGINIA	0.00	0.00	0.00	0.00	0.00	0.00	0.00	0.00	0.00	0.00	0.00	0.00	0.00	0.00
WASHINGTON	*	*	*	*	*	*	*	*	*	*	*	*	*	*
WEST VIRGINIA	*	*	*	*	*	*	*	*	*	*	*	*	*	*
WISCONSIN	*	*	*	*	*	*	*	*	*	*	*	*	*	*
WYOMING	*	*	*	*	*	*	*	*	*	*	*	*	*	*
AVERAGE	0.03	0.03	0.02	0.02	0.02	0.02	0.02	0.02	0.02	0.02	0.02	0.02	0.02	0.01

* EFFECTIVE TAX RATE EQUALS ZERO BEFORE ROUNDING. AN ENTIRE ROW OF * MEANS THAT THIS TAX IS NOT USED IN THIS STATE.

TABLE A-24
EFFECTIVE TAX RATES: STATE LICENSE TAXES-OTHER N.E.C.
INCIDENCE: CONSUMERS IN GENERAL
ALLOCATOR: TOTAL CONSUMPTION EXPENDITURES

STATE	UNDER $3,000	$3,000 -3,999	$4,000 -4,999	$5,000 -5,999	$6,000 -6,999	$7,000 -7,999	$8,000 -9,999	$10,000 -11,999	$12,000 -14,999	$15,000 -19,999	$20,000 -24,999	$25,000 -29,999	$30,000 -34,999	OVER $35,000
ALABAMA	*	*	*	*	*	*	*	*	*	*	*	*	*	*
ALASKA	*	*	*	*	*	*	*	*	*	*	*	*	*	*
ARIZONA	0.01	0.00	0.00	0.00	0.00	0.00	0.00	0.00	0.00	0.00	0.00	0.00	0.00	0.00
ARKANSAS	0.01	0.00	0.00	0.00	0.00	0.00	0.00	0.00	0.00	0.00	0.00	0.00	0.00	0.00
CALIFORNIA	0.00	0.00	0.00	0.00	0.00	0.00	0.00	0.00	0.00	0.00	0.00	0.00	0.00	0.00
COLORADO	0.00	0.00	0.00	0.00	0.00	0.00	0.00	0.00	0.00	0.00	0.00	0.00	0.00	0.00
CONNECTICUT	0.00	0.00	0.00	0.00	0.00	0.00	0.00	0.00	0.00	0.00	0.00	0.00	0.00	0.00
DELAWARE	0.02	0.01	0.01	0.01	0.01	0.01	0.01	0.01	0.01	0.01	0.01	0.00	0.00	0.00
FLORIDA	0.03	0.02	0.02	0.02	0.01	0.01	0.01	0.01	0.01	0.01	0.01	0.01	0.01	0.01
GEORGIA	0.00	0.00	0.00	0.00	0.00	0.00	0.00	0.00	0.00	0.00	0.00	0.00	0.00	0.00
HAWAII	*	*	*	*	*	*	*	*	*	*	*	*	*	*
IDAHO	*	*	*	*	*	*	*	*	*	*	*	*	*	*
ILLINOIS	0.00	0.00	0.00	0.00	0.00	0.00	0.00	0.00	0.00	0.00	0.00	0.00	0.00	0.00
INDIANA	0.01	0.01	0.01	0.01	0.01	0.01	0.00	0.00	0.00	0.00	0.00	0.00	0.00	0.00
IOWA	0.01	0.01	0.01	0.01	0.01	0.01	0.00	0.00	0.00	0.00	0.00	0.00	0.00	0.00
KANSAS	0.01	0.00	0.00	0.00	0.00	0.00	0.00	0.00	0.00	0.00	0.00	0.00	0.00	0.00
KENTUCKY	0.01	0.01	0.00	0.00	0.00	0.00	0.00	0.00	0.00	0.00	0.00	0.00	0.00	0.00
LOUISIANA	0.01	0.00	0.00	0.00	0.00	0.00	0.00	0.00	0.00	0.00	0.00	0.00	0.00	0.00
MAINE	0.03	0.02	0.02	0.01	0.01	0.01	0.01	0.01	0.01	0.01	0.01	0.01	0.01	0.01
MARYLAND	0.01	0.00	0.00	0.00	0.00	0.00	0.00	0.00	0.00	0.00	0.00	0.00	0.00	0.00
MASSACHUSETTS	0.01	0.00	0.00	0.00	0.00	0.00	0.00	0.00	0.00	0.00	0.00	0.00	0.00	0.00
MICHIGAN	0.01	0.00	0.00	0.00	0.00	0.00	0.00	0.00	0.00	0.00	0.00	0.00	0.00	0.00
MINNESOTA	0.04	0.02	0.02	0.02	0.02	0.02	0.01	0.01	0.01	0.01	0.01	0.01	0.01	0.01
MISSISSIPPI	*	*	*	*	*	*	*	*	*	*	*	*	*	*
MISSOURI	0.01	0.01	0.01	0.01	0.01	0.00	0.00	0.00	0.00	0.00	0.00	0.00	0.00	0.00
MONTANA	0.00	0.00	0.00	0.00	0.00	0.00	0.00	0.00	0.00	0.00	0.00	0.00	0.00	0.00
NEBRASKA	0.01	0.00	0.00	0.00	0.00	0.00	0.00	0.00	0.00	0.00	0.00	0.00	0.00	0.00
NEVADA	0.07	0.05	0.04	0.03	0.03	0.03	0.03	0.03	0.02	0.02	0.02	0.02	0.02	0.01
NEW HAMPSHIRE	0.04	0.03	0.02	0.02	0.02	0.02	0.02	0.02	0.01	0.01	0.01	0.01	0.01	0.01
NEW JERSEY	0.01	0.00	0.00	0.00	0.00	0.00	0.00	0.00	0.00	0.00	0.00	0.00	0.00	0.00
NEW MEXICO	*	*	*	*	*	*	*	*	*	*	*	*	*	*
NEW YORK	0.00	0.00	0.00	0.00	0.00	0.00	0.00	0.00	0.00	0.00	0.00	0.00	0.00	0.00
NORTH CAROLINA	0.01	0.00	0.00	0.00	0.00	0.00	0.00	0.00	0.00	0.00	0.00	0.00	0.00	0.00
NORTH DAKOTA	*	*	*	*	*	*	*	*	*	*	*	*	*	*
OHIO	0.01	0.00	0.00	0.00	0.00	0.00	0.00	0.00	0.00	0.00	0.00	0.00	0.00	0.00
OKLAHOMA	0.10	0.05	0.05	0.04	0.04	0.04	0.03	0.03	0.03	0.03	0.02	0.02	0.02	0.02
OREGON	0.03	0.02	0.01	0.01	0.01	0.01	0.01	0.01	0.01	0.01	0.01	0.01	0.01	0.01
PENNSYLVANIA	0.01	0.01	0.00	0.00	0.00	0.00	0.00	0.00	0.00	0.00	0.00	0.00	0.00	0.00
RHODE ISLAND	0.01	0.00	0.00	0.00	0.00	0.00	0.00	0.00	0.00	0.00	0.00	0.00	0.00	0.00
SOUTH CAROLINA	0.03	0.02	0.02	0.02	0.02	0.01	0.01	0.01	0.01	0.01	0.01	0.01	0.01	0.01
SOUTH DAKOTA	0.03	0.02	0.01	0.01	0.01	0.01	0.01	0.01	0.01	0.01	0.01	0.01	0.01	0.01
TENNESSEE	0.01	0.00	0.00	0.00	0.00	0.00	0.00	0.00	0.00	0.00	0.00	0.00	0.00	0.00
TEXAS	0.01	0.00	0.00	0.00	0.00	0.00	0.00	0.00	0.00	0.00	0.00	0.00	0.00	0.00
UTAH	0.01	0.01	0.01	0.00	0.00	0.00	0.00	0.00	0.00	0.00	0.00	0.00	0.00	0.00
VERMONT	0.03	0.02	0.02	0.02	0.02	0.01	0.01	0.01	0.01	0.01	0.01	0.01	0.01	0.01
VIRGINIA	0.01	0.00	0.00	0.00	0.00	0.00	0.00	0.00	0.00	0.00	0.00	0.00	0.00	0.00
WASHINGTON	0.00	0.00	0.00	0.00	0.00	0.00	0.00	0.00	0.00	0.00	0.00	0.00	0.00	0.00
WEST VIRGINIA	0.00	0.00	0.00	0.00	0.00	0.00	0.00	0.00	0.00	0.00	0.00	0.00	0.00	0.00
WISCONSIN	0.04	0.02	0.02	0.02	0.02	0.02	0.01	0.01	0.01	0.01	0.01	0.01	0.01	0.01
WYOMING	0.01	0.01	0.01	0.01	0.01	0.01	0.01	0.00	0.00	0.00	0.00	0.00	0.00	0.00
AVERAGE	0.02	0.01	0.01	0.01	0.01	0.01	0.01	0.01	0.01	0.00	0.00	0.00	0.00	0.00

* EFFECTIVE TAX RATE EQUALS ZERO BEFORE ROUNDING. AN ENTIRE ROW OF * MEANS THAT THIS TAX IS NOT USED IN THIS STATE.

TABLE A-25
EFFECTIVE TAX RATES: TOTAL STATE LICENSE TAXES (BENCHMARK)
INCIDENCE: SUM OF EFFECTIVE TAX RATES FOR INDIVIDUAL TAXES
ALLOCATOR: BASED ON INDIVIDUAL TAXES

STATE	UNDER $3,000	$3,000 -3,999	$4,000 -4,999	$5,000 -5,999	$6,000 -6,999	$7,000 -7,999	$8,000 -9,999	$10,000 -11,999	$12,000 -14,999	$15,000 -19,999	$20,000 -24,999	$25,000 -29,999	$30,000 -34,999	OVER $35,000
ALABAMA	0.90	0.55	0.50	0.49	0.39	0.48	0.34	0.32	0.29	0.28	0.31	0.28	0.34	0.88
ALASKA	1.35	0.75	0.89	0.72	0.93	0.77	0.54	0.54	0.51	0.46	0.50	0.44	0.44	0.51
ARIZONA	1.11	0.72	0.53	0.55	0.47	0.44	0.43	0.39	0.35	0.33	0.31	0.29	0.33	0.33
ARKANSAS	1.35	0.85	0.78	0.67	0.63	0.58	0.52	0.46	0.44	0.40	0.37	0.38	0.36	0.47
CALIFORNIA	0.79	0.52	0.44	0.41	0.38	0.36	0.33	0.31	0.28	0.26	0.25	0.24	0.25	0.30
COLORADO	0.84	0.52	0.48	0.41	0.39	0.38	0.34	0.33	0.30	0.27	0.27	0.26	0.28	0.33
CONNECTICUT	0.62	0.49	0.46	0.44	0.43	0.46	0.41	0.39	0.35	0.34	0.33	0.34	0.32	0.38
DELAWARE	2.69	2.10	1.93	1.70	1.39	1.17	1.43	1.27	1.06	0.84	0.79	0.95	1.33	2.23
FLORIDA	1.34	0.84	0.70	0.65	0.61	0.58	0.52	0.48	0.43	0.40	0.39	0.36	0.42	0.50
GEORGIA	0.57	0.34	0.30	0.28	0.25	0.25	0.23	0.21	0.18	0.18	0.17	0.17	0.20	0.25
HAWAII	0.18	0.09	0.08	0.07	0.10	0.08	0.09	0.07	0.07	0.08	0.05	0.05	0.07	0.16
IDAHO	1.95	1.22	1.04	0.96	0.94	0.84	0.81	0.71	0.69	0.62	0.70	0.65	0.66	0.94
ILLINOIS	1.01	0.71	0.63	0.61	0.53	0.51	0.49	0.45	0.42	0.40	0.38	0.37	0.38	0.44
INDIANA	0.71	0.47	0.39	0.37	0.35	0.34	0.30	0.28	0.27	0.25	0.24	0.24	0.24	0.27
IOWA	1.61	1.06	1.02	0.82	0.81	0.80	0.72	0.71	0.63	0.60	0.57	0.57	0.60	0.61
KANSAS	1.02	0.65	0.57	0.52	0.52	0.47	0.44	0.43	0.39	0.37	0.35	0.37	0.35	0.49
KENTUCKY	0.84	0.56	0.48	0.47	0.36	0.39	0.36	0.31	0.30	0.28	0.27	0.30	0.27	0.52
LOUISIANA	0.89	0.55	0.52	0.47	0.44	0.48	0.41	0.37	0.34	0.31	0.30	0.31	0.35	0.86
MAINE	1.00	0.74	0.71	0.60	0.59	0.57	0.59	0.52	0.50	0.47	0.48	0.54	0.48	0.71
MARYLAND	0.96	0.61	0.52	0.44	0.43	0.39	0.36	0.34	0.30	0.28	0.26	0.24	0.25	0.28
MASSACHUSETTS	0.35	0.26	0.25	0.24	0.24	0.23	0.21	0.19	0.18	0.17	0.16	0.16	0.17	0.25
MICHIGAN	1.12	0.78	0.67	0.56	0.54	0.58	0.49	0.43	0.40	0.37	0.37	0.40	0.37	0.65
MINNESOTA	1.23	0.86	0.68	0.70	0.62	0.62	0.54	0.53	0.48	0.44	0.44	0.43	0.45	0.50
MISSISSIPPI	0.96	0.63	0.55	0.52	0.50	0.45	0.45	0.36	0.37	0.34	0.35	0.33	0.40	0.85
MISSOURI	1.12	0.66	0.65	0.58	0.52	0.50	0.47	0.44	0.40	0.39	0.37	0.36	0.35	0.49
MONTANA	1.09	0.71	0.65	0.60	0.60	0.52	0.49	0.47	0.42	0.40	0.38	0.41	0.41	0.47
NEBRASKA	1.11	0.74	0.59	0.53	0.52	0.53	0.50	0.45	0.40	0.40	0.38	0.42	0.42	0.47
NEVADA	2.12	1.51	1.35	1.22	1.22	1.19	1.08	1.00	0.96	0.89	0.85	0.82	0.85	0.90
NEW HAMPSHIRE	1.03	0.72	0.66	0.65	0.61	0.55	0.54	0.51	0.49	0.43	0.45	0.43	0.45	0.60
NEW JERSEY	0.85	0.63	0.64	0.59	0.55	0.54	0.60	0.49	0.45	0.42	0.41	0.40	0.40	0.51
NEW MEXICO	1.33	0.90	0.80	0.68	0.66	0.58	0.57	0.53	0.48	0.44	0.42	0.41	0.46	0.47
NEW YORK	0.64	0.44	0.39	0.36	0.35	0.33	0.31	0.30	0.28	0.27	0.26	0.26	0.26	0.30
NORTH CAROLINA	1.34	0.80	0.83	0.62	0.60	0.54	0.53	0.49	0.43	0.39	0.42	0.36	0.40	0.72
NORTH DAKOTA	1.85	1.24	0.98	0.96	0.98	0.79	0.78	0.75	0.74	0.68	0.65	0.65	0.73	0.78
OHIO	1.15	0.78	0.68	0.64	0.54	0.56	0.52	0.47	0.44	0.42	0.40	0.40	0.43	0.58
OKLAHOMA	1.99	1.08	0.95	0.88	0.82	0.78	0.67	0.63	0.58	0.53	0.49	0.48	0.46	0.55
OREGON	1.66	1.09	0.87	0.81	0.79	0.77	0.67	0.63	0.56	0.54	0.52	0.60	0.51	0.66
PENNSYLVANIA	1.39	0.93	0.78	0.80	0.86	0.66	0.72	0.62	0.55	0.55	0.53	0.56	0.58	0.98
RHODE ISLAND	0.71	0.46	0.48	0.43	0.40	0.40	0.38	0.36	0.34	0.32	0.31	0.30	0.32	0.36
SOUTH CAROLINA	0.68	0.49	0.43	0.38	0.37	0.39	0.32	0.31	0.27	0.26	0.24	0.31	0.27	0.46
SOUTH DAKOTA	1.12	0.71	0.65	0.62	0.64	0.54	0.52	0.47	0.50	0.46	0.47	0.48	0.55	0.66
TENNESSEE	1.24	0.70	0.70	0.63	0.57	0.52	0.54	0.45	0.40	0.42	0.41	0.48	0.61	1.30
TEXAS	1.34	0.76	0.71	0.61	0.55	0.51	0.48	0.45	0.42	0.39	0.36	0.40	0.40	0.70
UTAH	0.79	0.51	0.43	0.37	0.40	0.35	0.33	0.29	0.28	0.26	0.24	0.25	0.23	0.27
VERMONT	1.44	0.96	1.00	0.80	0.80	0.79	0.73	0.74	0.67	0.64	0.63	0.61	0.62	0.78
VIRGINIA	1.07	0.60	0.53	0.51	0.45	0.41	0.38	0.36	0.31	0.30	0.29	0.28	0.26	0.36
WASHINGTON	1.09	0.70	0.58	0.56	0.50	0.53	0.47	0.41	0.41	0.36	0.36	0.35	0.39	0.51
WEST VIRGINIA	1.31	0.83	0.68	0.59	0.57	0.53	0.46	0.45	0.40	0.37	0.35	0.35	0.35	0.40
WISCONSIN	0.98	0.65	0.54	0.52	0.49	0.49	0.45	0.42	0.39	0.36	0.35	0.37	0.36	0.41
WYOMING	2.27	1.56	1.44	1.29	1.20	1.13	1.04	0.99	0.91	0.83	0.78	0.77	0.77	0.72
AVERAGE	1.16	0.76	0.68	0.62	0.59	0.55	0.52	0.48	0.44	0.41	0.40	0.40	0.42	0.58

[illegible] TAX RATE EQUALS ZERO BEFORE ROUNDING. AN ENTIRE ROW OF * MEANS THAT THIS TAX IS NOT USED IN THIS STATE.

TABLE A-26
EFFECTIVE TAX RATES: STATE INDIVIDUAL INCOME TAX
INCIDENCE: TAXPAYERS
ALLOCATOR: SPECIAL SERIES ON STATE INCOME TAX PAYMENTS

STATE	UNDER $3,000	$3,000 -3,999	$4,000 -4,999	$5,000 -5,999	$6,000 -6,999	$7,000 -7,999	$8,000 -9,999	$10,000 -11,999	$12,000 -14,999	$15,000 -19,999	$20,000 -24,999	$25,000 -29,999	$30,000 -34,999	OVER $35,000
ALABAMA	*	*	0.09	0.32	0.40	0.49	0.85	1.14	1.21	1.28	1.34	1.36	1.40	0.39
ALASKA	*	0.18	0.62	0.96	1.04	1.12	1.51	1.76	2.10	2.10	3.09	3.48	3.95	4.52
ARIZONA	*	0.04	0.19	0.27	0.38	0.48	0.76	0.91	1.16	1.25	1.23	1.06	1.09	0.64
ARKANSAS	*	*	0.02	0.12	0.16	0.52	0.55	0.95	1.01	1.40	2.01	2.13	2.44	1.28
CALIFORNIA	*	*	*	*	*	*	0.02	0.29	0.57	1.33	2.22	2.63	2.61	2.07
COLORADO	*	*	0.14	0.34	0.51	0.49	0.74	1.30	1.63	2.00	1.96	1.96	1.55	1.01
CONNECTICUT	*	*	*	*	*	*	*	*	*	*	0.04	0.06	*	0.18
DELAWARE	*	0.32	0.66	0.71	0.97	1.28	1.74	1.99	2.68	2.71	2.79	2.67	2.66	3.64
FLORIDA	*	*	*	*	*	*	*	*	*	*	*	*	*	*
GEORGIA	*	*	*	*	0.21	0.31	0.53	0.63	1.02	1.72	1.87	1.87	1.85	1.38
HAWAII	*	*	0.15	0.67	0.91	1.40	1.51	2.09	2.23	2.53	2.71	3.38	3.02	3.26
IDAHO	*	*	0.21	0.59	0.91	1.10	1.36	1.79	2.03	2.02	2.10	2.23	1.91	1.44
ILLINOIS	*	0.25	0.55	0.81	1.00	1.15	1.23	1.33	1.45	1.47	1.49	1.48	1.50	1.35
INDIANA	*	0.35	0.63	0.82	0.94	0.99	0.99	1.12	1.15	1.19	1.23	1.03	1.19	1.07
IOWA	*	*	0.17	0.37	0.52	0.78	1.24	1.36	1.63	2.11	2.12	2.33	2.67	2.73
KANSAS	*	0.31	0.41	0.41	0.46	0.46	0.93	1.01	1.08	1.29	1.25	1.86	1.81	1.11
KENTUCKY	*	0.06	0.34	0.45	0.40	0.66	0.67	1.32	1.50	1.87	2.01	2.06	1.89	1.19
LOUISIANA	*	*	*	*	*	*	0.10	0.19	0.26	0.34	0.91	1.00	1.00	0.72
MAINE	*	*	0.10	0.12	0.15	0.17	0.38	0.40	0.44	0.85	1.27	1.38	1.77	1.66
MARYLAND	*	0.25	0.42	1.13	1.61	1.89	2.03	2.18	2.22	2.38	2.41	2.58	2.23	2.08
MASSACHUSETTS	*	*	0.99	1.52	1.88	2.10	2.46	2.88	2.80	3.10	3.16	3.43	3.46	2.25
MICHIGAN	*	*	0.10	0.47	0.75	1.10	1.11	1.40	1.56	1.66	1.76	1.82	1.84	1.75
MINNESOTA	*	*	*	*	*	*	0.69	1.66	2.33	3.17	3.82	4.18	4.64	3.20
MISSISSIPPI	*	*	*	*	*	*	*	0.27	0.52	1.17	1.47	1.71	1.76	1.48
MISSOURI	*	0.03	0.10	0.24	0.36	0.42	0.54	0.81	0.92	1.28	1.42	1.48	1.29	1.09
MONTANA	*	0.40	0.52	0.82	0.95	1.22	1.21	1.44	1.84	2.29	2.59	2.41	2.78	1.92
NEBRASKA	*	*	*	*	0.03	0.27	0.43	0.56	0.66	0.83	1.11	1.08	1.47	2.09
NEVADA	*	*	*	*	*	*	*	*	*	*	*	*	*	*
NEW HAMPSHIRE	0.11	0.16	0.41	0.18	0.12	0.11	0.10	0.05	0.09	0.00	*	*	0.02	*
NEW JERSEY	*	*	*	*	*	0.01	0.06	0.10	0.11	0.11	0.12	0.03	*	*
NEW MEXICO	*	*	*	0.16	0.23	0.23	0.29	0.37	0.44	0.55	0.82	0.94	0.89	1.70
NEW YORK	*	*	*	0.48	0.77	0.83	1.07	1.39	1.64	2.02	3.08	3.84	4.48	3.38
NORTH CAROLINA	*	0.27	0.41	0.69	0.79	0.86	1.44	1.76	1.82	2.27	2.27	2.40	2.14	1.53
NORTH DAKOTA	*	0.04	0.06	*	0.20	0.19	0.36	0.70	1.27	1.85	2.01	1.89	2.15	1.13
OHIO	*	0.07	0.09	0.10	0.10	0.25	0.25	0.27	0.58	0.60	0.86	1.06	0.99	1.06
OKLAHOMA	*	0.04	0.07	0.17	0.18	0.18	0.18	0.44	0.70	1.06	1.75	1.69	1.66	1.70
OREGON	*	0.55	1.06	1.64	1.63	1.71	2.13	1.94	2.42	3.19	3.36	3.29	2.78	2.85
PENNSYLVANIA	*	*	*	*	1.20	1.52	1.53	1.54	1.46	1.47	1.36	1.35	1.37	1.23
RHODE ISLAND	0.03	0.18	0.48	0.69	0.84	0.81	0.93	1.10	1.11	1.33	1.51	1.61	1.59	2.11
SOUTH CAROLINA	*	0.10	0.17	0.23	0.47	0.51	0.79	1.16	1.49	1.98	2.12	2.13	1.87	1.12
SOUTH DAKOTA	*	*	*	*	*	*	*	*	*	*	*	*	*	*
TENNESSEE	0.17	0.13	0.08	0.05	0.11	0.08	0.07	0.08	0.03	0.06	0.05	0.06	0.10	0.13
TEXAS	*	*	*	*	*	*	*	*	*	*	*	*	*	*
UTAH	*	0.19	0.35	0.66	0.79	1.04	1.07	1.38	1.68	1.95	2.03	2.04	2.21	2.23
VERMONT	*	*	0.24	0.75	0.78	0.87	1.66	1.75	2.02	2.30	2.48	2.48	2.81	2.68
VIRGINIA	*	0.30	0.42	0.50	0.67	0.77	1.44	1.48	1.54	1.88	1.91	1.86	1.78	1.15
WASHINGTON	*	*	*	*	*	*	*	*	*	*	*	*	*	*
WEST VIRGINIA	*	0.40	0.52	0.59	0.66	0.79	0.74	0.83	1.10	1.32	1.45	1.55	1.70	3.03
WISCONSIN	*	0.47	0.61	0.75	1.18	1.45	1.44	1.79	2.53	3.23	3.62	3.63	3.88	3.09
WYOMING	*	*	*	*	*	*	*	*	*	*	*	*	*	*
AVERAGE	0.01	0.12	0.26	0.43	0.57	0.70	0.89	1.11	1.32	1.60	1.82	1.92	1.96	1.72

* EFFECTIVE TAX RATE EQUALS ZERO BEFORE ROUNDING. AN ENTIRE ROW OF * MEANS THAT THIS TAX IS NOT USED IN THIS STATE.

TABLE A-27
EFFECTIVE TAX RATES: STATE CORPORATION NET INCOME TAX (BENCHMARK)
INCIDENCE: 1/2 CONSUMERS, 1/2 OWNERS OF CAPITAL
ALLOCATOR: CONSUMPTION AND DIVIDEND INCOME

STATE	UNDER $3,000	$3,000 -3,999	$4,000 -4,999	$5,000 -5,999	$6,000 -6,999	$7,000 -7,999	$8,000 -9,999	$10,000 -11,999	$12,000 -14,999	$15,000 -19,999	$20,000 -24,999	$25,000 -29,999	$30,000 -34,999	OVER $35,000
ALABAMA	0.37	0.20	0.19	0.15	0.16	0.15	0.11	0.13	0.11	0.10	0.14	0.11	0.13	0.82
ALASKA	1.01	1.53	1.01	0.50	0.43	0.44	0.45	0.39	0.35	0.50	0.37	0.35	0.35	0.64
ARIZONA	0.46	0.36	0.31	0.24	0.26	0.14	0.16	0.17	0.14	0.16	0.13	0.14	0.16	0.36
ARKANSAS	0.73	0.39	0.39	0.55	0.26	0.20	0.32	0.29	0.28	0.18	0.22	0.20	0.18	0.99
CALIFORNIA	1.32	0.76	0.65	0.69	0.52	0.46	0.48	0.44	0.44	0.35	0.33	0.38	0.39	0.92
COLORADO	0.67	0.27	0.57	0.23	0.18	0.37	0.19	0.15	0.15	0.13	0.15	0.14	0.23	0.55
CONNECTICUT	0.58	0.63	0.68	0.58	0.40	0.26	0.24	0.24	0.29	0.29	0.21	0.21	0.19	0.69
DELAWARE	0.80	0.41	0.37	0.28	0.25	0.41	0.22	0.23	0.29	0.23	0.24	0.23	0.20	0.76
FLORIDA	0.51	0.25	0.27	0.24	0.22	0.20	0.17	0.20	0.16	0.16	0.14	0.18	0.22	0.41
GEORGIA	0.68	0.36	0.28	0.32	0.29	0.19	0.19	0.15	0.18	0.18	0.17	0.19	0.35	0.75
HAWAII	1.23	0.45	0.42	0.46	0.65	0.36	0.36	0.27	0.24	0.31	0.20	0.19	0.25	0.59
IDAHO	1.05	0.52	0.40	0.34	0.31	0.39	0.27	0.28	0.22	0.23	0.39	0.31	0.59	0.93
ILLINOIS	0.49	0.35	0.27	0.31	0.23	0.21	0.21	0.22	0.16	0.15	0.15	0.16	0.16	0.50
INDIANA	0.34	0.22	0.17	0.13	0.12	0.14	0.11	0.12	0.10	0.11	0.12	0.15	0.12	0.39
IOWA	0.45	0.36	0.37	0.39	0.25	0.18	0.29	0.30	0.16	0.18	0.18	0.18	0.45	0.56
KANSAS	0.86	0.49	0.44	0.40	0.60	0.39	0.32	0.36	0.25	0.25	0.31	0.32	0.24	0.87
KENTUCKY	0.73	0.44	0.44	0.71	0.32	0.28	0.33	0.24	0.25	0.29	0.25	0.41	0.28	1.80
LOUISIANA	0.51	0.27	0.29	0.21	0.20	0.22	0.18	0.18	0.15	0.17	0.14	0.16	0.23	0.71
MAINE	0.67	0.41	0.35	0.50	0.26	0.25	0.45	0.21	0.23	0.31	0.20	0.39	0.27	0.77
MARYLAND	0.45	0.62	0.30	0.25	0.18	0.18	0.17	0.21	0.15	0.17	0.19	0.14	0.17	0.39
MASSACHUSETTS	1.06	0.58	0.72	0.61	0.60	0.38	0.42	0.39	0.39	0.32	0.32	0.43	0.31	1.22
MICHIGAN	0.81	0.57	0.50	0.37	0.36	0.43	0.34	0.26	0.23	0.22	0.24	0.33	0.23	0.75
MINNESOTA	0.99	0.55	1.12	0.41	0.42	0.34	0.50	0.35	0.33	0.27	0.31	0.36	0.31	1.19
MISSISSIPPI	0.40	0.22	0.23	0.16	0.29	0.16	0.19	0.18	0.15	0.15	0.23	0.16	0.18	0.69
MISSOURI	0.31	0.18	0.16	0.19	0.14	0.15	0.14	0.13	0.12	0.10	0.12	0.11	0.11	0.46
MONTANA	0.71	0.67	0.33	0.34	0.33	0.35	0.25	0.36	0.19	0.18	0.20	0.19	0.24	0.68
NEBRASKA	0.46	0.23	0.15	0.16	0.22	0.14	0.19	0.12	0.12	0.10	0.13	0.12	0.18	0.46
NEVADA	*	*	*	*	*	*	*	*	*	*	*	*	*	*
NEW HAMPSHIRE	0.67	0.34	0.66	0.61	0.24	0.19	0.24	0.29	0.21	0.20	0.19	0.16	0.22	0.75
NEW JERSEY	0.44	0.30	0.41	0.38	0.29	0.26	0.49	0.24	0.18	0.17	0.18	0.17	0.18	0.41
NEW MEXICO	0.43	0.35	0.20	0.17	0.17	0.22	0.15	0.17	0.19	0.16	0.16	0.20	0.22	0.34
NEW YORK	1.03	0.69	0.65	0.60	0.43	0.43	0.39	0.35	0.34	0.33	0.32	0.32	0.40	1.02
NORTH CAROLINA	0.73	0.33	0.54	0.27	0.27	0.22	0.23	0.21	0.20	0.19	0.22	0.22	0.20	0.78
NORTH DAKOTA	0.74	0.35	0.41	0.28	0.49	0.22	0.22	0.19	0.23	0.17	0.23	0.24	0.27	0.51
OHIO	0.55	0.38	0.31	0.34	0.19	0.23	0.23	0.20	0.16	0.17	0.18	0.18	0.26	0.59
OKLAHOMA	0.47	0.20	0.17	0.16	0.19	0.20	0.14	0.12	0.13	0.13	0.15	0.16	0.12	0.53
OREGON	0.84	0.28	0.30	0.20	0.19	0.17	0.17	0.21	0.15	0.17	0.19	0.16	0.35	0.60
PENNSYLVANIA	1.38	0.89	0.63	0.74	0.85	0.40	0.62	0.40	0.38	0.41	0.35	0.37	0.45	1.20
RHODE ISLAND	0.74	0.65	0.47	0.38	0.66	0.24	0.28	0.32	0.26	0.23	0.20	0.19	0.31	0.65
SOUTH CAROLINA	0.57	0.31	0.32	0.28	0.50	0.40	0.30	0.38	0.28	0.22	0.18	0.19	0.25	1.05
SOUTH DAKOTA	0.07	0.05	0.04	0.03	0.04	0.06	0.04	0.03	0.02	0.02	0.03	0.03	0.03	0.09
TENNESSEE	0.70	0.33	0.31	0.26	0.29	0.23	0.26	0.29	0.19	0.26	0.22	0.24	0.23	1.13
TEXAS	*	*	*	*	*	*	*	*	*	*	*	*	*	*
UTAH	0.87	0.23	0.33	0.27	0.18	0.21	0.19	0.16	0.13	0.14	0.15	0.13	0.16	0.47
VERMONT	0.53	0.29	0.27	0.35	0.27	0.30	0.30	0.25	0.25	0.20	0.28	0.19	0.55	0.83
VIRGINIA	0.52	0.36	0.23	0.32	0.37	0.19	0.22	0.24	0.15	0.18	0.16	0.19	0.17	0.48
WASHINGTON	*	*	*	*	*	*	*	*	*	*	*	*	*	*
WEST VIRGINIA	0.21	0.26	0.15	0.10	0.10	0.12	0.08	0.07	0.07	0.08	0.09	0.11	0.23	0.37
WISCONSIN	0.86	0.47	0.60	0.34	0.29	0.42	0.60	0.32	0.25	0.28	0.32	0.26	0.39	0.93
WYOMING	*	*	*	*	*	*	*	*	*	*	*	*	*	*
AVERAGE	0.67	0.42	0.40	0.34	0.32	0.26	0.27	0.24	0.21	0.21	0.21	0.22	0.25	0.71

[illegible] TAX RATE EQUALS ZERO BEFORE ROUNDING. AN ENTIRE ROW OF * MEANS THAT THIS TAX IS NOT USED IN THIS STATE.

TABLE A-28
EFFECTIVE TAX RATES: STATE CORPORATION NET INCOME TAX (MOST REGRESSIVE)
INCIDENCE: CONSUMERS IN GENERAL
ALLOCATOR: TOTAL CONSUMPTION EXPENDITURES

STATE	UNDER $3,000	$3,000 -3,999	$4,000 -4,999	$5,000 -5,999	$6,000 -6,999	$7,000 -7,999	$8,000 -9,999	$10,000 -11,999	$12,000 -14,999	$15,000 -19,999	$20,000 -24,999	$25,000 -29,999	$30,000 -34,999	OVER $35,000
ALABAMA	0.60	0.37	0.32	0.28	0.25	0.25	0.23	0.20	0.19	0.17	0.16	0.15	0.15	0.13
ALASKA	1.70	1.07	0.99	0.92	0.86	0.74	0.71	0.66	0.60	0.53	0.50	0.48	0.45	0.41
ARIZONA	0.70	0.42	0.33	0.32	0.28	0.25	0.24	0.22	0.20	0.18	0.16	0.15	0.15	0.13
ARKANSAS	0.96	0.60	0.52	0.46	0.44	0.40	0.37	0.33	0.31	0.28	0.27	0.25	0.24	0.21
CALIFORNIA	1.75	1.14	0.94	0.85	0.77	0.71	0.64	0.58	0.53	0.48	0.44	0.41	0.40	0.35
COLORADO	0.81	0.51	0.42	0.38	0.36	0.32	0.29	0.27	0.25	0.22	0.20	0.19	0.18	0.16
CONNECTICUT	0.91	0.66	0.56	0.54	0.50	0.51	0.43	0.41	0.38	0.35	0.33	0.32	0.31	0.28
DELAWARE	1.03	0.63	0.61	0.50	0.48	0.45	0.42	0.38	0.37	0.34	0.32	0.29	0.28	0.26
FLORIDA	0.66	0.41	0.34	0.31	0.29	0.27	0.25	0.23	0.21	0.19	0.18	0.17	0.16	0.14
GEORGIA	0.85	0.49	0.45	0.40	0.38	0.36	0.32	0.29	0.28	0.25	0.24	0.22	0.22	0.19
HAWAII	0.98	0.64	0.63	0.56	0.51	0.48	0.44	0.40	0.38	0.34	0.32	0.31	0.29	0.26
IDAHO	1.32	0.79	0.65	0.63	0.56	0.51	0.48	0.43	0.39	0.35	0.32	0.30	0.29	0.26
ILLINOIS	0.67	0.45	0.39	0.36	0.32	0.31	0.28	0.26	0.25	0.22	0.21	0.20	0.19	0.18
INDIANA	0.51	0.32	0.26	0.25	0.23	0.21	0.19	0.18	0.16	0.15	0.14	0.13	0.13	0.12
IOWA	0.83	0.52	0.49	0.39	0.38	0.36	0.32	0.31	0.28	0.26	0.24	0.23	0.22	0.20
KANSAS	1.24	0.77	0.68	0.56	0.55	0.51	0.49	0.43	0.41	0.37	0.34	0.33	0.32	0.28
KENTUCKY	1.33	0.83	0.72	0.62	0.58	0.55	0.52	0.48	0.44	0.41	0.39	0.37	0.35	0.31
LOUISIANA	0.79	0.46	0.39	0.38	0.35	0.33	0.31	0.28	0.25	0.23	0.22	0.21	0.20	0.18
MAINE	0.98	0.63	0.55	0.46	0.46	0.41	0.40	0.36	0.34	0.31	0.29	0.27	0.27	0.24
MARYLAND	0.75	0.47	0.40	0.34	0.33	0.31	0.29	0.27	0.25	0.22	0.21	0.20	0.19	0.17
MASSACHUSETTS	1.34	1.01	0.84	0.74	0.71	0.66	0.62	0.58	0.53	0.49	0.46	0.45	0.44	0.39
MICHIGAN	1.11	0.72	0.59	0.51	0.48	0.47	0.42	0.39	0.36	0.33	0.30	0.29	0.28	0.25
MINNESOTA	1.48	0.97	0.77	0.72	0.66	0.66	0.56	0.53	0.49	0.44	0.41	0.39	0.38	0.34
MISSISSIPPI	0.69	0.43	0.35	0.32	0.29	0.28	0.26	0.24	0.22	0.20	0.19	0.18	0.17	0.15
MISSOURI	0.54	0.31	0.29	0.25	0.23	0.22	0.20	0.18	0.16	0.15	0.14	0.14	0.13	0.11
MONTANA	0.99	0.63	0.54	0.47	0.45	0.41	0.36	0.33	0.31	0.28	0.26	0.24	0.23	0.21
NEBRASKA	0.58	0.37	0.29	0.27	0.25	0.24	0.22	0.20	0.19	0.17	0.16	0.15	0.15	0.13
NEVADA	*	*	*	*	*	*	*	*	*	*	*	*	*	*
NEW HAMPSHIRE	0.84	0.55	0.43	0.43	0.40	0.35	0.35	0.32	0.30	0.28	0.26	0.25	0.24	0.21
NEW JERSEY	0.66	0.45	0.40	0.37	0.34	0.33	0.31	0.29	0.27	0.25	0.23	0.23	0.22	0.20
NEW MEXICO	0.68	0.43	0.38	0.33	0.31	0.28	0.26	0.23	0.20	0.19	0.17	0.16	0.15	0.14
NEW YORK	1.49	0.93	0.77	0.69	0.67	0.62	0.57	0.54	0.50	0.46	0.44	0.42	0.40	0.36
NORTH CAROLINA	0.92	0.56	0.49	0.41	0.40	0.36	0.35	0.32	0.30	0.27	0.25	0.24	0.23	0.21
NORTH DAKOTA	0.90	0.54	0.47	0.41	0.38	0.36	0.33	0.31	0.29	0.27	0.25	0.24	0.23	0.21
OHIO	0.75	0.48	0.42	0.37	0.34	0.34	0.30	0.28	0.26	0.24	0.22	0.21	0.20	0.18
OKLAHOMA	0.70	0.40	0.34	0.32	0.30	0.27	0.25	0.23	0.21	0.19	0.18	0.17	0.16	0.15
OREGON	0.87	0.52	0.44	0.40	0.36	0.34	0.31	0.28	0.25	0.23	0.21	0.20	0.18	0.16
PENNSYLVANIA	1.64	1.01	0.89	0.77	0.75	0.71	0.66	0.62	0.57	0.53	0.49	0.48	0.47	0.42
RHODE ISLAND	0.95	0.56	0.55	0.48	0.42	0.40	0.38	0.36	0.34	0.31	0.29	0.28	0.27	0.24
SOUTH CAROLINA	0.98	0.62	0.52	0.48	0.44	0.43	0.39	0.37	0.34	0.31	0.29	0.28	0.27	0.24
SOUTH DAKOTA	0.11	0.07	0.06	0.05	0.05	0.04	0.04	0.04	0.04	0.03	0.03	0.03	0.03	0.03
TENNESSEE	1.02	0.65	0.55	0.51	0.46	0.44	0.40	0.37	0.34	0.31	0.30	0.28	0.27	0.23
TEXAS	*	*	*	*	*	*	*	*	*	*	*	*	*	*
UTAH	0.74	0.45	0.37	0.32	0.33	0.29	0.26	0.24	0.22	0.19	0.18	0.17	0.16	0.14
VERMONT	0.90	0.55	0.51	0.44	0.41	0.39	0.35	0.34	0.31	0.29	0.27	0.25	0.24	0.22
VIRGINIA	0.83	0.46	0.42	0.38	0.34	0.32	0.30	0.28	0.25	0.23	0.22	0.21	0.20	0.18
WASHINGTON	*	*	*	*	*	*	*	*	*	*	*	*	*	*
WEST VIRGINIA	0.40	0.25	0.20	0.18	0.17	0.16	0.14	0.13	0.12	0.11	0.10	0.10	0.09	0.09
WISCONSIN	1.29	0.77	0.66	0.61	0.57	0.55	0.47	0.44	0.42	0.38	0.35	0.34	0.33	0.29
WYOMING	*	*	*	*	*	*	*	*	*	*	*	*	*	*
AVERAGE	0.93	0.58	0.50	0.45	0.42	0.40	0.36	0.34	0.31	0.28	0.26	0.25	0.24	0.22

* EFFECTIVE TAX RATE EQUALS ZERO BEFORE ROUNDING. AN ENTIRE ROW OF * MEANS THAT THIS TAX IS NOT USED IN THIS STATE.

TABLE A-29
EFFECTIVE TAX RATES: STATE CORPORATION NET INCOME TAX (MOST PROGRESSIVE)
INCIDENCE: OWNERS OF CAPITAL
ALLOCATOR: DIVIDEND INCOME

STATE	UNDER $3,000	$3,000 -3,999	$4,000 -4,999	$5,000 -5,999	$6,000 -6,999	$7,000 -7,999	$8,000 -9,999	$10,000 -11,999	$12,000 -14,999	$15,000 -19,999	$20,000 -24,999	$25,000 -29,999	$30,000 -34,999	OVER $35,000
ALABAMA	0.14	0.04	0.07	0.01	0.07	0.05	0.00	0.06	0.03	0.02	0.13	0.06	0.11	1.51
ALASKA	0.32	1.99	1.04	0.08	0.01	0.13	0.18	0.11	0.09	0.47	0.23	0.23	0.24	0.88
ARIZONA	0.22	0.30	0.29	0.17	0.23	0.04	0.09	0.12	0.08	0.13	0.11	0.13	0.17	0.59
ARKANSAS	0.50	0.18	0.26	0.63	0.08	*	0.26	0.24	0.24	0.08	0.16	0.15	0.12	1.76
CALIFORNIA	0.88	0.37	0.35	0.54	0.27	0.21	0.33	0.29	0.34	0.23	0.23	0.35	0.39	1.48
COLORADO	0.53	0.02	0.72	0.09	0.01	0.42	0.08	0.03	0.05	0.04	0.09	0.08	0.29	0.94
CONNECTICUT	0.26	0.60	0.79	0.62	0.30	0.01	0.04	0.06	0.20	0.24	0.08	0.10	0.07	1.10
DELAWARE	0.58	0.20	0.13	0.05	0.01	0.38	0.02	0.09	0.20	0.13	0.16	0.17	0.12	1.26
FLORIDA	0.36	0.09	0.20	0.17	0.15	0.12	0.10	0.17	0.10	0.13	0.10	0.20	0.28	0.67
GEORGIA	0.50	0.24	0.11	0.24	0.21	0.01	0.07	0.01	0.08	0.10	0.11	0.15	0.47	1.31
HAWAII	1.48	0.25	0.22	0.36	0.80	0.24	0.28	0.14	0.10	0.27	0.08	0.07	0.21	0.91
IDAHO	0.77	0.26	0.14	0.06	0.05	0.27	0.07	0.14	0.04	0.11	0.46	0.32	0.89	1.61
ILLINOIS	0.31	0.25	0.15	0.27	0.15	0.11	0.13	0.18	0.07	0.08	0.10	0.11	0.13	0.82
INDIANA	0.17	0.11	0.07	0.00	0.01	0.06	0.03	0.07	0.04	0.07	0.10	0.17	0.10	0.67
IOWA	0.07	0.20	0.25	0.40	0.12	0.00	0.26	0.29	0.05	0.10	0.11	0.13	0.67	0.91
KANSAS	0.48	0.21	0.20	0.24	0.65	0.27	0.14	0.29	0.09	0.14	0.29	0.31	0.17	1.46
KENTUCKY	0.14	0.06	0.16	0.79	0.06	0.01	0.14	0.01	0.07	0.17	0.12	0.46	0.21	3.28
LOUISIANA	0.23	0.08	0.19	0.05	0.06	0.10	0.06	0.09	0.05	0.10	0.06	0.10	0.26	1.25
MAINE	0.35	0.19	0.15	0.55	0.06	0.09	0.50	0.06	0.13	0.31	0.11	0.51	0.27	1.31
MARYLAND	0.15	0.77	0.20	0.16	0.03	0.05	0.04	0.15	0.06	0.12	0.18	0.09	0.15	0.61
MASSACHUSETTS	0.78	0.15	0.61	0.48	0.50	0.11	0.21	0.19	0.26	0.14	0.18	0.41	0.18	2.05
MICHIGAN	0.51	0.43	0.40	0.22	0.24	0.39	0.25	0.12	0.10	0.12	0.18	0.37	0.17	1.24
MINNESOTA	0.49	0.12	1.47	0.11	0.19	0.03	0.44	0.18	0.17	0.10	0.20	0.34	0.24	2.05
MISSISSIPPI	0.11	0.00	0.11	0.00	0.30	0.03	0.12	0.12	0.09	0.09	0.26	0.14	0.19	1.23
MISSOURI	0.08	0.05	0.03	0.13	0.05	0.08	0.08	0.08	0.07	0.05	0.10	0.08	0.10	0.80
MONTANA	0.42	0.70	0.12	0.20	0.22	0.29	0.14	0.39	0.08	0.09	0.15	0.13	0.25	1.16
NEBRASKA	0.35	0.08	0.01	0.06	0.19	0.04	0.17	0.03	0.06	0.03	0.11	0.08	0.20	0.78
NEVADA	*	*	*	*	*	*	*	*	*	*	*	*	*	*
NEW HAMPSHIRE	0.50	0.14	0.88	0.80	0.07	0.03	0.13	0.27	0.13	0.11	0.13	0.08	0.21	1.30
NEW JERSEY	0.22	0.15	0.43	0.40	0.24	0.18	0.67	0.20	0.10	0.10	0.12	0.11	0.15	0.61
NEW MEXICO	0.18	0.26	0.01	0.01	0.03	0.17	0.05	0.12	0.17	0.13	0.15	0.24	0.30	0.54
NEW YORK	0.56	0.46	0.52	0.51	0.20	0.24	0.22	0.17	0.19	0.21	0.21	0.23	0.39	1.68
NORTH CAROLINA	0.54	0.10	0.58	0.13	0.14	0.07	0.12	0.11	0.09	0.12	0.20	0.20	0.17	1.35
NORTH DAKOTA	0.58	0.16	0.35	0.15	0.59	0.07	0.11	0.07	0.18	0.08	0.21	0.25	0.31	0.80
OHIO	0.34	0.28	0.21	0.31	0.03	0.11	0.15	0.12	0.07	0.10	0.13	0.16	0.31	0.99
OKLAHOMA	0.23	0.01	0.00	0.00	0.08	0.12	0.04	0.00	0.06	0.08	0.12	0.15	0.07	0.91
OREGON	0.82	0.03	0.15	0.00	0.03	*	0.03	0.15	0.05	0.12	0.16	0.12	0.52	1.04
PENNSYLVANIA	1.11	0.77	0.37	0.72	0.95	0.10	0.58	0.19	0.19	0.28	0.21	0.27	0.44	1.98
RHODE ISLAND	0.52	0.74	0.38	0.28	0.90	0.09	0.18	0.29	0.19	0.16	0.10	0.11	0.36	1.06
SOUTH CAROLINA	0.17	*	0.11	0.08	0.57	0.37	0.21	0.39	0.22	0.12	0.07	0.10	0.24	1.85
SOUTH DAKOTA	0.04	0.03	0.02	0.01	0.03	0.08	0.04	0.02	0.01	0.01	0.03	0.03	0.04	0.15
TENNESSEE	0.39	0.01	0.06	0.00	0.12	0.01	0.12	0.20	0.04	0.20	0.14	0.20	0.20	2.03
TEXAS	*	*	*	*	*	*	*	*	*	*	*	*	*	*
UTAH	1.00	0.01	0.30	0.23	0.04	0.14	0.13	0.08	0.04	0.08	0.12	0.10	0.16	0.80
VERMONT	0.16	0.02	0.03	0.27	0.13	0.20	0.25	0.16	0.20	0.11	0.29	0.12	0.85	1.44
VIRGINIA	0.21	0.27	0.03	0.26	0.41	0.07	0.13	0.20	0.05	0.12	0.10	0.17	0.15	0.78
WASHINGTON	*	*	*	*	*	*	*	*	*	*	*	*	*	*
WEST VIRGINIA	0.01	0.28	0.09	0.03	0.03	0.09	0.03	0.00	0.03	0.04	0.08	0.12	0.36	0.65
WISCONSIN	0.42	0.16	0.55	0.07	0.01	0.29	0.73	0.20	0.09	0.19	0.29	0.18	0.46	1.57
WYOMING	*	*	*	*	*	*	*	*	*	*	*	*	*	*
AVERAGE	0.42	0.26	0.29	0.24	0.21	0.13	0.18	0.14	0.11	0.13	0.15	0.18	0.27	1.20

[illegible] TAX RATE EQUALS ZERO BEFORE ROUNDING. AN ENTIRE ROW OF * MEANS THAT THIS TAX IS NOT USED IN THIS STATE.

TABLE A-30
EFFECTIVE TAX RATES: STATE DEATH AND GIFT TAX
INCIDENCE: PERSONS IN THE HIGHEST INCOME CLASS ONLY
ALLOCATOR: ALLOCATED ENTIRELY TO THE "OVER $35,000" INCOME CLASS

STATE	UNDER $3,000	$3,000 -3,999	$4,000 -4,999	$5,000 -5,999	$6,000 -6,999	$7,000 -7,999	$8,000 -9,999	$10,000 -11,999	$12,000 -14,999	$15,000 -19,999	$20,000 -24,999	$25,000 -29,999	$30,000 -34,999	OVER $35,000
ALABAMA	*	*	*	*	*	*	*	*	*	*	*	*	*	0.10
ALASKA	*	*	*	*	*	*	*	*	*	*	*	*	*	0.01
ARIZONA	*	*	*	*	*	*	*	*	*	*	*	*	*	0.05
ARKANSAS	*	*	*	*	*	*	*	*	*	*	*	*	*	0.05
CALIFORNIA	*	*	*	*	*	*	*	*	*	*	*	*	*	0.78
COLORADO	*	*	*	*	*	*	*	*	*	*	*	*	*	0.55
CONNECTICUT	*	*	*	*	*	*	*	*	*	*	*	*	*	0.62
DELAWARE	*	*	*	*	*	*	*	*	*	*	*	*	*	0.66
FLORIDA	*	*	*	*	*	*	*	*	*	*	*	*	*	0.08
GEORGIA	*	*	*	*	*	*	*	*	*	*	*	*	*	0.06
HAWAII	*	*	*	*	*	*	*	*	*	*	*	*	*	0.18
IDAHO	*	*	*	*	*	*	*	*	*	*	*	*	*	0.58
ILLINOIS	*	*	*	*	*	*	*	*	*	*	*	*	*	0.33
INDIANA	*	*	*	*	*	*	*	*	*	*	*	*	*	0.40
IOWA	*	*	*	*	*	*	*	*	*	*	*	*	*	1.07
KANSAS	*	*	*	*	*	*	*	*	*	*	*	*	*	0.41
KENTUCKY	*	*	*	*	*	*	*	*	*	*	*	*	*	0.81
LOUISIANA	*	*	*	*	*	*	*	*	*	*	*	*	*	0.33
MAINE	*	*	*	*	*	*	*	*	*	*	*	*	*	1.13
MARYLAND	*	*	*	*	*	*	*	*	*	*	*	*	*	0.18
MASSACHUSETTS	*	*	*	*	*	*	*	*	*	*	*	*	*	0.77
MICHIGAN	*	*	*	*	*	*	*	*	*	*	*	*	*	0.27
MINNESOTA	*	*	*	*	*	*	*	*	*	*	*	*	*	1.07
MISSISSIPPI	*	*	*	*	*	*	*	*	*	*	*	*	*	0.32
MISSOURI	*	*	*	*	*	*	*	*	*	*	*	*	*	0.32
MONTANA	*	*	*	*	*	*	*	*	*	*	*	*	*	0.97
NEBRASKA	*	*	*	*	*	*	*	*	*	*	*	*	*	0.08
NEVADA	*	*	*	*	*	*	*	*	*	*	*	*	*	*
NEW HAMPSHIRE	*	*	*	*	*	*	*	*	*	*	*	*	*	0.87
NEW JERSEY	*	*	*	*	*	*	*	*	*	*	*	*	*	0.64
NEW MEXICO	*	*	*	*	*	*	*	*	*	*	*	*	*	0.14
NEW YORK	*	*	*	*	*	*	*	*	*	*	*	*	*	0.30
NORTH CAROLINA	*	*	*	*	*	*	*	*	*	*	*	*	*	0.65
NORTH DAKOTA	*	*	*	*	*	*	*	*	*	*	*	*	*	0.42
OHIO	*	*	*	*	*	*	*	*	*	*	*	*	*	0.24
OKLAHOMA	*	*	*	*	*	*	*	*	*	*	*	*	*	0.75
OREGON	*	*	*	*	*	*	*	*	*	*	*	*	*	1.14
PENNSYLVANIA	*	*	*	*	*	*	*	*	*	*	*	*	*	1.05
RHODE ISLAND	*	*	*	*	*	*	*	*	*	*	*	*	*	0.48
SOUTH CAROLINA	*	*	*	*	*	*	*	*	*	*	*	*	*	0.27
SOUTH DAKOTA	*	*	*	*	*	*	*	*	*	*	*	*	*	1.25
TENNESSEE	*	*	*	*	*	*	*	*	*	*	*	*	*	1.03
TEXAS	*	*	*	*	*	*	*	*	*	*	*	*	*	0.23
UTAH	*	*	*	*	*	*	*	*	*	*	*	*	*	0.29
VERMONT	*	*	*	*	*	*	*	*	*	*	*	*	*	0.90
VIRGINIA	*	*	*	*	*	*	*	*	*	*	*	*	*	0.21
WASHINGTON	*	*	*	*	*	*	*	*	*	*	*	*	*	0.99
WEST VIRGINIA	*	*	*	*	*	*	*	*	*	*	*	*	*	0.68
WISCONSIN	*	*	*	*	*	*	*	*	*	*	*	*	*	1.01
WYOMING	*	*	*	*	*	*	*	*	*	*	*	*	*	0.21
AVERAGE	*	*	*	*	*	*	*	*	*	*	*	*	*	0.53

* EFFECTIVE TAX RATE EQUALS ZERO BEFORE ROUNDING. AN ENTIRE ROW OF * MEANS THAT THIS TAX IS NOT USED IN THIS STATE.

TABLE A-31
EFFECTIVE TAX RATES: STATE SEVERANCE TAX
INCIDENCE: CONSUMERS IN GENERAL
ALLOCATOR: TOTAL CONSUMPTION EXPENDITURES

STATE	UNDER $3,000	$3,000 -3,999	$4,000 -4,999	$5,000 -5,999	$6,000 -6,999	$7,000 -7,999	$8,000 -9,999	$10,000 -11,999	$12,000 -14,999	$15,000 -19,999	$20,000 -24,999	$25,000 -29,999	$30,000 -34,999	OVER $35,000
ALABAMA	0.15	0.09	0.08	0.07	0.06	0.06	0.06	0.05	0.05	0.04	0.04	0.04	0.04	0.03
ALASKA	1.41	0.89	0.82	0.77	0.72	0.62	0.60	0.55	0.50	0.44	0.42	0.40	0.38	0.34
ARIZONA	*	*	*	*	*	*	*	*	*	*	*	*	*	*
ARKANSAS	0.19	0.12	0.10	0.09	0.09	0.08	0.08	0.07	0.06	0.06	0.05	0.05	0.05	0.04
CALIFORNIA	0.00	0.00	0.00	0.00	0.00	0.00	0.00	0.00	0.00	0.00	0.00	0.00	0.00	0.00
COLORADO	0.07	0.04	0.04	0.03	0.03	0.03	0.02	0.02	0.02	0.02	0.02	0.02	0.01	0.01
CONNECTICUT	*	*	*	*	*	*	*	*	*	*	*	*	*	*
DELAWARE	*	*	*	*	*	*	*	*	*	*	*	*	*	*
FLORIDA	0.22	0.14	0.12	0.10	0.10	0.09	0.08	0.08	0.07	0.06	0.06	0.06	0.05	0.05
GEORGIA	*	*	*	*	*	*	*	*	*	*	*	*	*	*
HAWAII	*	*	*	*	*	*	*	*	*	*	*	*	*	*
IDAHO	0.02	0.01	0.01	0.01	0.01	0.01	0.01	0.01	0.01	0.01	0.01	0.01	0.00	0.00
ILLINOIS	*	*	*	*	*	*	*	*	*	*	*	*	*	*
INDIANA	0.00	0.00	0.00	0.00	0.00	0.00	0.00	0.00	0.00	0.00	0.00	0.00	0.00	0.00
IOWA	*	*	*	*	*	*	*	*	*	*	*	*	*	*
KANSAS	0.01	0.01	0.01	0.01	0.01	0.01	0.01	0.00	0.00	0.00	0.00	0.00	0.00	0.00
KENTUCKY	0.78	0.48	0.42	0.37	0.34	0.32	0.31	0.28	0.26	0.24	0.23	0.21	0.21	0.18
LOUISIANA	4.41	2.58	2.19	2.11	1.94	1.83	1.73	1.54	1.41	1.30	1.25	1.19	1.13	0.99
MAINE	*	*	*	*	*	*	*	*	*	*	*	*	*	*
MARYLAND	*	*	*	*	*	*	*	*	*	*	*	*	*	*
MASSACHUSETTS	*	*	*	*	*	*	*	*	*	*	*	*	*	*
MICHIGAN	0.03	0.02	0.02	0.01	0.01	0.01	0.01	0.01	0.01	0.01	0.01	0.01	0.01	0.01
MINNESOTA	0.20	0.13	0.10	0.09	0.09	0.09	0.07	0.07	0.06	0.06	0.05	0.05	0.05	0.04
MISSISSIPPI	0.51	0.32	0.26	0.24	0.21	0.21	0.19	0.18	0.16	0.15	0.14	0.13	0.13	0.11
MISSOURI	*	*	*	*	*	*	*	*	*	*	*	*	*	*
MONTANA	1.23	0.78	0.66	0.58	0.55	0.50	0.44	0.41	0.38	0.34	0.32	0.30	0.28	0.26
NEBRASKA	0.03	0.02	0.01	0.01	0.01	0.01	0.01	0.01	0.01	0.01	0.01	0.01	0.01	0.01
NEVADA	0.01	0.01	0.01	0.01	0.01	0.01	0.00	0.00	0.00	0.00	0.00	0.00	0.00	0.00
NEW HAMPSHIRE	0.00	0.00	0.00	0.00	0.00	0.00	0.00	0.00	0.00	0.00	0.00	0.00	0.00	0.00
NEW JERSEY	*	*	*	*	*	*	*	*	*	*	*	*	*	*
NEW MEXICO	2.33	1.48	1.31	1.12	1.07	0.96	0.88	0.79	0.70	0.64	0.60	0.56	0.52	0.48
NEW YORK	*	*	*	*	*	*	*	*	*	*	*	*	*	*
NORTH CAROLINA	*	*	*	*	*	*	*	*	*	*	*	*	*	*
NORTH DAKOTA	0.59	0.36	0.31	0.27	0.25	0.24	0.22	0.21	0.19	0.17	0.16	0.15	0.15	0.14
OHIO	0.01	0.01	0.01	0.01	0.01	0.01	0.01	0.01	0.00	0.00	0.00	0.00	0.00	0.00
OKLAHOMA	1.66	0.93	0.81	0.75	0.70	0.64	0.58	0.54	0.49	0.45	0.42	0.40	0.39	0.35
OREGON	0.06	0.04	0.03	0.03	0.03	0.02	0.02	0.02	0.02	0.02	0.02	0.01	0.01	0.01
PENNSYLVANIA	*	*	*	*	*	*	*	*	*	*	*	*	*	*
RHODE ISLAND	*	*	*	*	*	*	*	*	*	*	*	*	*	*
SOUTH CAROLINA	*	*	*	*	*	*	*	*	*	*	*	*	*	*
SOUTH DAKOTA	0.02	0.01	0.01	0.01	0.01	0.01	0.01	0.01	0.01	0.01	0.01	0.01	0.01	0.00
TENNESSEE	0.02	0.01	0.01	0.01	0.01	0.01	0.01	0.01	0.01	0.01	0.01	0.00	0.00	0.00
TEXAS	0.85	0.53	0.45	0.41	0.38	0.35	0.33	0.31	0.28	0.26	0.24	0.23	0.22	0.19
UTAH	0.46	0.28	0.23	0.20	0.21	0.18	0.16	0.15	0.14	0.12	0.11	0.10	0.10	0.09
VERMONT	*	*	*	*	*	*	*	*	*	*	*	*	*	*
VIRGINIA	0.01	0.00	0.00	0.00	0.00	0.00	0.00	0.00	0.00	0.00	0.00	0.00	0.00	0.00
WASHINGTON	0.44	0.27	0.22	0.19	0.17	0.17	0.15	0.14	0.13	0.11	0.11	0.10	0.09	0.08
WEST VIRGINIA	*	*	*	*	*	*	*	*	*	*	*	*	*	*
WISCONSIN	0.00	0.00	0.00	0.00	0.00	0.00	0.00	0.00	0.00	0.00	0.00	0.00	0.00	0.00
WYOMING	2.52	1.68	1.53	1.34	1.23	1.15	1.03	0.96	0.88	0.78	0.72	0.70	0.68	0.58
AVERAGE	0.59	0.36	0.32	0.29	0.27	0.25	0.23	0.21	0.19	0.17	0.16	0.15	0.15	0.13

[illegible] BEFORE ROUNDING. AN ENTIRE ROW OF * MEANS THAT THIS TAX IS NOT USED IN THIS STATE.

TABLE A-32
EFFECTIVE TAX RATES: STATE DOCUMENT AND STOCK TRANSFER TAXES
INCIDENCE: 1/2 OWNERS OF HOUSING, 1/2 OWNERS OF BUSINESSES
ALLOCATOR: HOUSING VALUES AND DIVIDEND INCOME

STATE	UNDER $3,000	$3,000 -3,999	$4,000 -4,999	$5,000 -5,999	$6,000 -6,999	$7,000 -7,999	$8,000 -9,999	$10,000 -11,999	$12,000 -14,999	$15,000 -19,999	$20,000 -24,999	$25,000 -29,999	$30,000 -34,999	OVER $35,000
ALABAMA	0.05	0.03	0.03	0.02	0.02	0.02	0.02	0.02	0.01	0.01	0.02	0.01	0.02	0.11
ALASKA	*	*	*	*	*	*	*	*	*	*	*	*	*	*
ARIZONA	*	*	*	*	*	*	*	*	*	*	*	*	*	*
ARKANSAS	0.04	0.02	0.02	0.03	0.01	0.01	0.02	0.01	0.01	0.01	0.01	0.01	0.01	0.05
CALIFORNIA	*	*	*	*	*	*	*	*	*	*	*	*	*	*
COLORADO	*	*	*	*	*	*	*	*	*	*	*	*	*	*
CONNECTICUT	*	*	*	*	*	*	*	*	*	*	*	*	*	*
DELAWARE	0.48	0.25	0.22	0.17	0.15	0.25	0.13	0.14	0.18	0.14	0.15	0.14	0.12	0.46
FLORIDA	0.48	0.24	0.26	0.23	0.21	0.19	0.17	0.19	0.15	0.15	0.14	0.18	0.21	0.39
GEORGIA	0.04	0.02	0.01	0.02	0.02	0.01	0.01	0.01	0.01	0.01	0.01	0.01	0.02	0.04
HAWAII	0.06	0.02	0.02	0.02	0.03	0.02	0.02	0.01	0.01	0.01	0.01	0.01	0.01	0.02
IDAHO	*	*	*	*	*	*	*	*	*	*	*	*	*	*
ILLINOIS	0.02	0.01	0.01	0.01	0.01	0.01	0.01	0.01	0.00	0.00	0.00	0.00	0.00	0.01
INDIANA	*	*	*	*	*	*	*	*	*	*	*	*	*	*
IOWA	0.03	0.02	0.02	0.02	0.01	0.01	0.01	0.01	0.01	0.01	0.01	0.01	0.02	0.02
KANSAS	*	*	*	*	*	*	*	*	*	*	*	*	*	*
KENTUCKY	0.02	0.01	0.01	0.02	0.01	0.01	0.01	0.01	0.01	0.01	0.01	0.01	0.01	0.05
LOUISIANA	*	*	*	*	*	*	*	*	*	*	*	*	*	*
MAINE	0.03	0.02	0.02	0.02	0.01	0.01	0.02	0.01	0.01	0.01	0.01	0.01	0.01	0.03
MARYLAND	0.12	0.17	0.08	0.07	0.05	0.05	0.04	0.06	0.04	0.05	0.05	0.04	0.05	0.11
MASSACHUSETTS	0.06	0.03	0.03	0.03	0.03	0.02	0.02	0.02	0.02	0.01	0.01	0.02	0.01	0.05
MICHIGAN	*	*	*	*	*	*	*	*	*	*	*	*	*	*
MINNESOTA	0.10	0.06	0.10	0.04	0.04	0.03	0.04	0.03	0.03	0.02	0.03	0.03	0.02	0.10
MISSISSIPPI	*	*	*	*	*	*	*	*	*	*	*	*	*	*
MISSOURI	0.01	0.00	0.00	0.00	0.00	0.00	0.00	0.00	0.00	0.00	0.00	0.00	0.00	0.01
MONTANA	*	*	*	*	*	*	*	*	*	*	*	*	*	*
NEBRASKA	0.04	0.02	0.01	0.01	0.02	0.01	0.01	0.01	0.01	0.01	0.01	0.01	0.01	0.03
NEVADA	0.05	0.03	0.02	0.02	0.02	0.02	0.01	0.02	0.01	0.01	0.01	0.01	0.01	0.05
NEW HAMPSHIRE	0.07	0.03	0.06	0.05	0.02	0.02	0.02	0.02	0.02	0.01	0.01	0.01	0.02	0.06
NEW JERSEY	0.04	0.02	0.03	0.03	0.02	0.02	0.03	0.02	0.01	0.01	0.01	0.01	0.01	0.02
NEW MEXICO	*	*	*	*	*	*	*	*	*	*	*	*	*	*
NEW YORK	0.69	0.42	0.37	0.34	0.24	0.24	0.21	0.18	0.17	0.16	0.15	0.14	0.17	0.47
NORTH CAROLINA	*	*	*	*	*	*	*	*	*	*	*	*	*	*
NORTH DAKOTA	*	*	*	*	*	*	*	*	*	*	*	*	*	*
OHIO	*	*	*	*	*	*	*	*	*	*	*	*	*	*
OKLAHOMA	0.03	0.01	0.01	0.01	0.01	0.01	0.01	0.01	0.01	0.01	0.01	0.01	0.01	0.04
OREGON	0.01	0.00	0.00	0.00	0.00	0.00	0.00	0.00	0.00	0.00	0.00	0.00	0.00	0.00
PENNSYLVANIA	0.26	0.16	0.11	0.12	0.13	0.07	0.10	0.06	0.05	0.06	0.05	0.05	0.06	0.17
RHODE ISLAND	0.03	0.02	0.02	0.01	0.02	0.01	0.01	0.01	0.01	0.01	0.01	0.00	0.01	0.02
SOUTH CAROLINA	0.07	0.04	0.04	0.04	0.06	0.05	0.04	0.05	0.04	0.03	0.02	0.02	0.03	0.13
SOUTH DAKOTA	*	*	*	*	*	*	*	*	*	*	*	*	*	*
TENNESSEE	0.12	0.05	0.05	0.04	0.05	0.04	0.04	0.05	0.03	0.04	0.04	0.04	0.04	0.19
TEXAS	*	*	*	*	*	*	*	*	*	*	*	*	*	*
UTAH	*	*	*	*	*	*	*	*	*	*	*	*	*	*
VERMONT	0.17	0.09	0.08	0.09	0.07	0.07	0.07	0.06	0.06	0.04	0.06	0.04	0.12	0.18
VIRGINIA	0.13	0.09	0.06	0.08	0.10	0.05	0.06	0.06	0.04	0.05	0.04	0.05	0.04	0.12
WASHINGTON	0.03	0.02	0.02	0.02	0.01	0.01	0.01	0.01	0.01	0.01	0.01	0.01	0.01	0.03
WEST VIRGINIA	0.03	0.04	0.02	0.02	0.02	0.02	0.01	0.01	0.01	0.01	0.01	0.02	0.04	0.06
WISCONSIN	0.02	0.01	0.01	0.01	0.00	0.01	0.01	0.00	0.00	0.00	0.00	0.00	0.01	0.01
WYOMING	*	*	*	*	*	*	*	*	*	*	*	*	*	*
AVERAGE	0.11	0.06	0.06	0.05	0.05	0.04	0.04	0.04	0.03	0.03	0.03	0.03	0.04	0.10

* EFFECTIVE TAX RATE EQUALS ZERO BEFORE ROUNDING. AN ENTIRE ROW OF * MEANS THAT THIS TAX IS NOT USED IN THIS STATE.

TABLE A-33
EFFECTIVE TAX RATES: OTHER STATE TAXES N.E.C.
INCIDENCE: CONSUMERS IN GENERAL
ALLOCATOR: TOTAL CONSUMPTION EXPENDITURES

STATE	UNDER $3,000	$3,000 -3,999	$4,000 -4,999	$5,000 -5,999	$6,000 -6,999	$7,000 -7,999	$8,000 -9,999	$10,000 -11,999	$12,000 -14,999	$15,000 -19,999	$20,000 -24,999	$25,000 -29,999	$30,000 -34,999	OVER $35,000
ALABAMA	*	*	*	*	*	*	*	*	*	*	*	*	*	*
ALASKA	0.26	0.17	0.15	0.14	0.13	0.11	0.11	0.10	0.09	0.08	0.08	0.07	0.07	0.06
ARIZONA	*	*	*	*	*	*	*	*	*	*	*	*	*	*
ARKANSAS	0.03	0.02	0.02	0.02	0.01	0.01	0.01	0.01	0.01	0.01	0.01	0.01	0.01	0.01
CALIFORNIA	*	*	*	*	*	*	*	*	*	*	*	*	*	*
COLORADO	0.08	0.05	0.04	0.04	0.03	0.03	0.03	0.03	0.02	0.02	0.02	0.02	0.02	0.01
CONNECTICUT	*	*	*	*	*	*	*	*	*	*	*	*	*	*
DELAWARE	*	*	*	*	*	*	*	*	*	*	*	*	*	*
FLORIDA	*	*	*	*	*	*	*	*	*	*	*	*	*	*
GEORGIA	0.01	0.01	0.01	0.01	0.00	0.00	0.00	0.00	0.00	0.00	0.00	0.00	0.00	0.00
HAWAII	*	*	*	*	*	*	*	*	*	*	*	*	*	*
IDAHO	*	*	*	*	*	*	*	*	*	*	*	*	*	*
ILLINOIS	*	*	*	*	*	*	*	*	*	*	*	*	*	*
INDIANA	*	*	*	*	*	*	*	*	*	*	*	*	*	*
IOWA	*	*	*	*	*	*	*	*	*	*	*	*	*	*
KANSAS	*	*	*	*	*	*	*	*	*	*	*	*	*	*
KENTUCKY	*	*	*	*	*	*	*	*	*	*	*	*	*	*
LOUISIANA	*	*	*	*	*	*	*	*	*	*	*	*	*	*
MAINE	*	*	*	*	*	*	*	*	*	*	*	*	*	*
MARYLAND	0.04	0.02	0.02	0.02	0.02	0.01	0.01	0.01	0.01	0.01	0.01	0.01	0.01	0.01
MASSACHUSETTS	*	*	*	*	*	*	*	*	*	*	*	*	*	*
MICHIGAN	*	*	*	*	*	*	*	*	*	*	*	*	*	*
MINNESOTA	0.20	0.13	0.11	0.10	0.09	0.09	0.08	0.07	0.07	0.06	0.06	0.05	0.05	0.05
MISSISSIPPI	*	*	*	*	*	*	*	*	*	*	*	*	*	*
MISSOURI	0.00	0.00	0.00	0.00	0.00	0.00	0.00	0.00	0.00	0.00	0.00	0.00	0.00	0.00
MONTANA	0.04	0.02	0.02	0.02	0.02	0.02	0.01	0.01	0.01	0.01	0.01	0.01	0.01	0.01
NEBRASKA	*	*	*	*	*	*	*	*	*	*	*	*	*	*
NEVADA	*	*	*	*	*	*	*	*	*	*	*	*	*	*
NEW HAMPSHIRE	*	*	*	*	*	*	*	*	*	*	*	*	*	*
NEW JERSEY	*	*	*	*	*	*	*	*	*	*	*	*	*	*
NEW MEXICO	*	*	*	*	*	*	*	*	*	*	*	*	*	*
NEW YORK	*	*	*	*	*	*	*	*	*	*	*	*	*	*
NORTH CAROLINA	*	*	*	*	*	*	*	*	*	*	*	*	*	*
NORTH DAKOTA	*	*	*	*	*	*	*	*	*	*	*	*	*	*
OHIO	*	*	*	*	*	*	*	*	*	*	*	*	*	*
OKLAHOMA	0.02	0.01	0.01	0.01	0.01	0.01	0.01	0.01	0.01	0.01	0.01	0.01	0.01	0.01
OREGON	*	*	*	*	*	*	*	*	*	*	*	*	*	*
PENNSYLVANIA	*	*	*	*	*	*	*	*	*	*	*	*	*	*
RHODE ISLAND	0.08	0.05	0.05	0.04	0.04	0.03	0.03	0.03	0.03	0.03	0.03	0.02	0.02	0.02
SOUTH CAROLINA	*	*	*	*	*	*	*	*	*	*	*	*	*	*
SOUTH DAKOTA	*	*	*	*	*	*	*	*	*	*	*	*	*	*
TENNESSEE	0.06	0.04	0.04	0.03	0.03	0.03	0.03	0.02	0.02	0.02	0.02	0.02	0.02	0.01
TEXAS	*	*	*	*	*	*	*	*	*	*	*	*	*	*
UTAH	*	*	*	*	*	*	*	*	*	*	*	*	*	*
VERMONT	0.16	0.10	0.09	0.08	0.07	0.07	0.06	0.06	0.05	0.05	0.05	0.05	0.04	0.04
VIRGINIA	0.02	0.01	0.01	0.01	0.01	0.01	0.01	0.01	0.01	0.01	0.00	0.00	0.00	0.00
WASHINGTON	*	*	*	*	*	*	*	*	*	*	*	*	*	*
WEST VIRGINIA	*	*	*	*	*	*	*	*	*	*	*	*	*	*
WISCONSIN	0.03	0.02	0.01	0.01	0.01	0.01	0.01	0.01	0.01	0.01	0.01	0.01	0.01	0.01
WYOMING	*	*	*	*	*	*	*	*	*	*	*	*	*	*
AVERAGE	0.07	0.05	0.04	0.04	0.03	0.03	0.03	0.03	0.02	0.02	0.02	0.02	0.02	0.02

* EFFECTIVE TAX RATE EQUALS ZERO BEFORE ROUNDING. AN ENTIRE ROW OF * MEANS THAT THIS TAX IS NOT USED IN THIS STATE.

TABLE A-34
EFFECTIVE TAX RATES: STATE PROPERTY TAX-RAILROADS
INCIDENCE: 3/4 CONSUMERS, 1/4 OWNERS OF CAPITAL
ALLOCATOR: CONSUMPTION AND DIVIDEND INCOME

STATE	UNDER $3,000	$3,000 -3,999	$4,000 -4,999	$5,000 -5,999	$6,000 -6,999	$7,000 -7,999	$8,000 -9,999	$10,000 -11,999	$12,000 -14,999	$15,000 -19,999	$20,000 -24,999	$25,000 -29,999	$30,000 -34,999	OVER $35,000
ALABAMA	0.06	0.03	0.03	0.02	0.02	0.02	0.02	0.02	0.02	0.02	0.02	0.01	0.02	0.05
ALASKA	*	*	*	*	*	*	*	*	*	*	*	*	*	*
ARIZONA	0.09	0.06	0.05	0.04	0.04	0.03	0.03	0.03	0.03	0.03	0.02	0.02	0.02	0.04
ARKANSAS	0.01	0.00	0.00	0.00	0.00	0.00	0.00	0.00	0.00	0.00	0.00	0.00	0.00	0.00
CALIFORNIA	0.04	0.02	0.02	0.02	0.01	0.01	0.01	0.01	0.01	0.01	0.01	0.01	0.01	0.01
COLORADO	0.00	0.00	0.00	0.00	0.00	0.00	0.00	0.00	0.00	0.00	0.00	0.00	0.00	0.00
CONNECTICUT	*	*	*	*	*	*	*	*	*	*	*	*	*	*
DELAWARE	*	*	*	*	*	*	*	*	*	*	*	*	*	*
FLORIDA	0.26	0.15	0.14	0.12	0.11	0.10	0.09	0.09	0.08	0.08	0.07	0.08	0.08	0.12
GEORGIA	0.01	0.00	0.00	0.00	0.00	0.00	0.00	0.00	0.00	0.00	0.00	0.00	0.00	0.00
HAWAII	*	*	*	*	*	*	*	*	*	*	*	*	*	*
IDAHO	0.00	0.00	0.00	0.00	0.00	0.00	0.00	0.00	0.00	0.00	0.00	0.00	0.00	0.00
ILLINOIS	0.00	0.00	0.00	0.00	0.00	0.00	0.00	0.00	0.00	0.00	0.00	0.00	0.00	0.00
INDIANA	0.05	0.03	0.02	0.02	0.02	0.02	0.02	0.02	0.02	0.01	0.01	0.02	0.01	0.03
IOWA	0.00	0.00	0.00	0.00	0.00	0.00	0.00	0.00	0.00	0.00	0.00	0.00	0.00	0.00
KANSAS	0.03	0.02	0.02	0.01	0.02	0.01	0.01	0.01	0.01	0.01	0.01	0.01	0.01	0.02
KENTUCKY	0.34	0.21	0.19	0.22	0.15	0.14	0.14	0.12	0.11	0.12	0.11	0.13	0.10	0.35
LOUISIANA	0.00	0.00	0.00	0.00	0.00	0.00	0.00	0.00	0.00	0.00	0.00	0.00	0.00	0.00
MAINE	*	*	*	*	*	*	*	*	*	*	*	*	*	*
MARYLAND	0.01	0.01	0.00	0.00	0.00	0.00	0.00	0.00	0.00	0.00	0.00	0.00	0.00	0.00
MASSACHUSETTS	*	*	*	*	*	*	*	*	*	*	*	*	*	*
MICHIGAN	*	*	*	*	*	*	*	*	*	*	*	*	*	*
MINNESOTA	*	*	*	*	*	*	*	*	*	*	*	*	*	*
MISSISSIPPI	0.01	0.00	0.00	0.00	0.00	0.00	0.00	0.00	0.00	0.00	0.00	0.00	0.00	0.00
MISSOURI	0.01	0.00	0.00	0.00	0.00	0.00	0.00	0.00	0.00	0.00	0.00	0.00	0.00	0.00
MONTANA	0.04	0.03	0.02	0.02	0.02	0.02	0.01	0.02	0.01	0.01	0.01	0.01	0.01	0.02
NEBRASKA	0.00	0.00	0.00	0.00	0.00	0.00	0.00	0.00	0.00	0.00	0.00	0.00	0.00	0.00
NEVADA	0.11	0.07	0.06	0.05	0.05	0.04	0.04	0.04	0.03	0.03	0.03	0.03	0.02	0.06
NEW HAMPSHIRE	*	*	*	*	*	*	*	*	*	*	*	*	*	*
NEW JERSEY	*	*	*	*	*	*	*	*	*	*	*	*	*	*
NEW MEXICO	0.03	0.02	0.01	0.01	0.01	0.01	0.01	0.01	0.01	0.01	0.01	0.01	0.01	0.01
NEW YORK	*	*	*	*	*	*	*	*	*	*	*	*	*	*
NORTH CAROLINA	0.02	0.01	0.01	0.01	0.01	0.01	0.01	0.01	0.01	0.01	0.01	0.01	0.01	0.01
NORTH DAKOTA	0.04	0.02	0.02	0.02	0.02	0.01	0.01	0.01	0.01	0.01	0.01	0.01	0.01	0.02
OHIO	0.02	0.01	0.01	0.01	0.01	0.01	0.01	0.01	0.01	0.00	0.00	0.00	0.01	0.01
OKLAHOMA	*	*	*	*	*	*	*	*	*	*	*	*	*	*
OREGON	0.00	0.00	0.00	0.00	0.00	0.00	0.00	0.00	0.00	0.00	0.00	0.00	0.00	0.00
PENNSYLVANIA	*	*	*	*	*	*	*	*	*	*	*	*	*	*
RHODE ISLAND	*	*	*	*	*	*	*	*	*	*	*	*	*	*
SOUTH CAROLINA	0.00	0.00	0.00	0.00	0.00	0.00	0.00	0.00	0.00	0.00	0.00	0.00	0.00	0.00
SOUTH DAKOTA	*	*	*	*	*	*	*	*	*	*	*	*	*	*
TENNESSEE	*	*	*	*	*	*	*	*	*	*	*	*	*	*
TEXAS	0.02	0.01	0.01	0.01	0.01	0.01	0.01	0.01	0.01	0.01	0.01	0.01	0.01	0.01
UTAH	0.00	0.00	0.00	0.00	0.00	0.00	0.00	0.00	0.00	0.00	0.00	0.00	0.00	0.00
VERMONT	*	*	*	*	*	*	*	*	*	*	*	*	*	*
VIRGINIA	0.02	0.01	0.01	0.01	0.01	0.01	0.01	0.01	0.01	0.01	0.01	0.01	0.01	0.01
WASHINGTON	0.24	0.14	0.13	0.12	0.11	0.10	0.09	0.08	0.08	0.07	0.06	0.06	0.07	0.13
WEST VIRGINIA	0.00	0.00	0.00	0.00	0.00	0.00	0.00	0.00	0.00	0.00	0.00	0.00	0.00	0.00
WISCONSIN	*	*	*	*	*	*	*	*	*	*	*	*	*	*
WYOMING	0.04	0.03	0.02	0.02	0.02	0.02	0.02	0.01	0.01	0.01	0.01	0.01	0.01	0.02
AVERAGE	0.05	0.03	0.03	0.02	0.02	0.02	0.02	0.02	0.01	0.01	0.01	0.01	0.01	0.03

* EFFECTIVE TAX RATE EQUALS ZERO BEFORE ROUNDING. AN ENTIRE ROW OF * MEANS THAT THIS TAX IS NOT USED IN THIS STATE.

TABLE A-35
EFFECTIVE TAX RATES: STATE PROPERTY TAX-PUBLIC UTILITIES
INCIDENCE: 1/2 CONSUMERS, 1/2 OWNERS OF CAPITAL
ALLOCATOR: CONSUMPTION AND DIVIDEND INCOME

STATE	UNDER $3,000	$3,000 -3,999	$4,000 -4,999	$5,000 -5,999	$6,000 -6,999	$7,000 -7,999	$8,000 -9,999	$10,000 -11,999	$12,000 -14,999	$15,000 -19,999	$20,000 -24,999	$25,000 -29,999	$30,000 -34,999	OVER $35,000
ALABAMA	0.24	0.13	0.13	0.10	0.10	0.10	0.08	0.09	0.07	0.06	0.09	0.07	0.09	0.54
ALASKA	*	*	*	*	*	*	*	*	*	*	*	*	*	*
ARIZONA	1.18	0.92	0.78	0.62	0.65	0.37	0.42	0.44	0.36	0.40	0.34	0.35	0.40	0.91
ARKANSAS	0.03	0.02	0.02	0.02	0.01	0.01	0.01	0.01	0.01	0.01	0.01	0.01	0.01	0.04
CALIFORNIA	0.55	0.32	0.27	0.29	0.22	0.19	0.20	0.18	0.18	0.15	0.14	0.16	0.17	0.39
COLORADO	0.02	0.01	0.02	0.01	0.01	0.01	0.01	0.01	0.01	0.00	0.01	0.00	0.01	0.02
CONNECTICUT	*	*	*	*	*	*	*	*	*	*	*	*	*	*
DELAWARE	*	*	*	*	*	*	*	*	*	*	*	*	*	*
FLORIDA	0.03	0.01	0.02	0.01	0.01	0.01	0.01	0.01	0.01	0.01	0.01	0.01	0.01	0.02
GEORGIA	0.05	0.03	0.02	0.02	0.02	0.01	0.01	0.01	0.01	0.01	0.01	0.01	0.03	0.06
HAWAII	*	*	*	*	*	*	*	*	*	*	*	*	*	*
IDAHO	0.01	0.01	0.00	0.00	0.00	0.00	0.00	0.00	0.00	0.00	0.00	0.00	0.01	0.01
ILLINOIS	*	*	*	*	*	*	*	*	*	*	*	*	*	*
INDIANA	0.11	0.07	0.05	0.04	0.04	0.04	0.03	0.04	0.03	0.03	0.04	0.05	0.04	0.12
IOWA	0.00	0.00	0.00	0.00	0.00	0.00	0.00	0.00	0.00	0.00	0.00	0.00	0.00	0.00
KANSAS	0.17	0.10	0.09	0.08	0.12	0.08	0.06	0.07	0.05	0.05	0.06	0.06	0.05	0.17
KENTUCKY	0.04	0.02	0.02	0.04	0.02	0.02	0.02	0.01	0.01	0.02	0.01	0.02	0.02	0.10
LOUISIANA	0.00	0.00	0.00	0.00	0.00	0.00	0.00	0.00	0.00	0.00	0.00	0.00	0.00	0.00
MAINE	*	*	*	*	*	*	*	*	*	*	*	*	*	*
MARYLAND	0.24	0.33	0.16	0.13	0.10	0.09	0.09	0.11	0.08	0.09	0.10	0.08	0.09	0.21
MASSACHUSETTS	0.00	0.00	0.00	0.00	0.00	0.00	0.00	0.00	0.00	0.00	0.00	0.00	0.00	0.00
MICHIGAN	*	*	*	*	*	*	*	*	*	*	*	*	*	*
MINNESOTA	0.02	0.01	0.02	0.01	0.01	0.01	0.01	0.01	0.01	0.00	0.01	0.01	0.01	0.02
MISSISSIPPI	0.04	0.02	0.02	0.02	0.03	0.02	0.02	0.02	0.02	0.02	0.02	0.02	0.02	0.07
MISSOURI	0.02	0.01	0.01	0.01	0.01	0.01	0.01	0.01	0.01	0.01	0.01	0.01	0.01	0.03
MONTANA	0.23	0.21	0.11	0.11	0.11	0.11	0.08	0.12	0.06	0.06	0.07	0.06	0.08	0.22
NEBRASKA	*	*	*	*	*	*	*	*	*	*	*	*	*	*
NEVADA	0.68	0.43	0.34	0.29	0.26	0.26	0.24	0.32	0.20	0.24	0.17	0.20	0.14	0.81
NEW HAMPSHIRE	*	*	*	*	*	*	*	*	*	*	*	*	*	*
NEW JERSEY	*	*	*	*	*	*	*	*	*	*	*	*	*	*
NEW MEXICO	0.20	0.16	0.09	0.08	0.08	0.11	0.07	0.08	0.09	0.08	0.08	0.09	0.11	0.16
NEW YORK	0.04	0.03	0.03	0.03	0.02	0.02	0.02	0.01	0.01	0.01	0.01	0.01	0.02	0.04
NORTH CAROLINA	0.23	0.11	0.17	0.09	0.09	0.07	0.07	0.07	0.06	0.06	0.07	0.07	0.06	0.25
NORTH DAKOTA	0.09	0.04	0.05	0.04	0.06	0.03	0.03	0.02	0.03	0.02	0.03	0.03	0.03	0.06
OHIO	0.11	0.08	0.07	0.07	0.04	0.05	0.05	0.04	0.03	0.03	0.04	0.04	0.05	0.12
OKLAHOMA	*	*	*	*	*	*	*	*	*	*	*	*	*	*
OREGON	0.00	0.00	0.00	0.00	0.00	0.00	0.00	0.00	0.00	0.00	0.00	0.00	0.00	0.00
PENNSYLVANIA	*	*	*	*	*	*	*	*	*	*	*	*	*	*
RHODE ISLAND	*	*	*	*	*	*	*	*	*	*	*	*	*	*
SOUTH CAROLINA	0.01	0.01	0.01	0.01	0.01	0.01	0.01	0.01	0.01	0.00	0.00	0.00	0.01	0.02
SOUTH DAKOTA	*	*	*	*	*	*	*	*	*	*	*	*	*	*
TENNESSEE	*	*	*	*	*	*	*	*	*	*	*	*	*	*
TEXAS	0.08	0.03	0.04	0.03	0.02	0.02	0.02	0.02	0.02	0.02	0.02	0.03	0.03	0.08
UTAH	0.00	0.00	0.00	0.00	0.00	0.00	0.00	0.00	0.00	0.00	0.00	0.00	0.00	0.00
VERMONT	*	*	*	*	*	*	*	*	*	*	*	*	*	*
VIRGINIA	0.11	0.08	0.05	0.07	0.08	0.04	0.05	0.05	0.03	0.04	0.03	0.04	0.04	0.10
WASHINGTON	1.98	1.10	1.29	1.10	0.99	1.01	0.85	0.59	0.76	0.68	0.61	0.57	0.87	2.27
WEST VIRGINIA	0.00	0.01	0.00	0.00	0.00	0.00	0.00	0.00	0.00	0.00	0.00	0.00	0.01	0.01
WISCONSIN	*	*	*	*	*	*	*	*	*	*	*	*	*	*
WYOMING	0.12	0.09	0.06	0.05	0.04	0.05	0.06	0.03	0.03	0.03	0.03	0.03	0.03	0.13
AVERAGE	0.20	0.13	0.12	0.10	0.09	0.08	0.08	0.07	0.07	0.06	0.06	0.06	0.07	0.21

* EFFECTIVE TAX RATE EQUALS ZERO BEFORE ROUNDING. AN ENTIRE ROW OF * MEANS THAT THIS TAX IS NOT USED IN THIS STATE.

TABLE A-36
EFFECTIVE TAX RATES: STATE PROPERTY TAX N.E.C.
INCIDENCE: CONSUMERS IN GENERAL
ALLOCATOR: TOTAL CONSUMPTION EXPENDITURES

STATE	UNDER $3,000	$3,000 -3,999	$4,000 -4,999	$5,000 -5,999	$6,000 -6,999	$7,000 -7,999	$8,000 -9,999	$10,000 -11,999	$12,000 -14,999	$15,000 -19,999	$20,000 -24,999	$25,000 -29,999	$30,000 -34,999	OVER $35,000
ALABAMA	*	*	*	*	*	*	*	*	*	*	*	*	*	*
ALASKA	30.95	19.56	17.98	16.87	15.65	13.54	13.04	12.00	11.01	9.67	9.09	8.69	8.28	7.43
ARIZONA	0.90	0.54	0.42	0.41	0.36	0.32	0.31	0.28	0.25	0.23	0.21	0.19	0.19	0.16
ARKANSAS	*	*	*	*	*	*	*	*	*	*	*	*	*	*
CALIFORNIA	*	*	*	*	*	*	*	*	*	*	*	*	*	*
COLORADO	*	*	*	*	*	*	*	*	*	*	*	*	*	*
CONNECTICUT	*	*	*	*	*	*	*	*	*	*	*	*	*	*
DELAWARE	*	*	*	*	*	*	*	*	*	*	*	*	*	*
FLORIDA	*	*	*	*	*	*	*	*	*	*	*	*	*	*
GEORGIA	*	*	*	*	*	*	*	*	*	*	*	*	*	*
HAWAII	*	*	*	*	*	*	*	*	*	*	*	*	*	*
IDAHO	*	*	*	*	*	*	*	*	*	*	*	*	*	*
ILLINOIS	0.01	0.01	0.01	0.01	0.01	0.01	0.01	0.00	0.00	0.00	0.00	0.00	0.00	0.00
INDIANA	*	*	*	*	*	*	*	*	*	*	*	*	*	*
IOWA	*	*	*	*	*	*	*	*	*	*	*	*	*	*
KANSAS	*	*	*	*	*	*	*	*	*	*	*	*	*	*
KENTUCKY	0.09	0.06	0.05	0.04	0.04	0.04	0.04	0.03	0.03	0.03	0.03	0.03	0.02	0.02
LOUISIANA	0.00	0.00	0.00	0.00	0.00	0.00	0.00	0.00	0.00	0.00	0.00	0.00	0.00	0.00
MAINE	6.85	4.39	3.82	3.19	3.19	2.89	2.75	2.52	2.33	2.13	2.04	1.90	1.86	1.69
MARYLAND	0.24	0.15	0.13	0.11	0.10	0.10	0.09	0.08	0.08	0.07	0.07	0.06	0.06	0.06
MASSACHUSETTS	*	*	*	*	*	*	*	*	*	*	*	*	*	*
MICHIGAN	0.68	0.44	0.36	0.32	0.29	0.29	0.26	0.24	0.22	0.20	0.19	0.18	0.17	0.15
MINNESOTA	0.00	0.00	0.00	0.00	0.00	0.00	0.00	0.00	0.00	0.00	0.00	0.00	0.00	0.00
MISSISSIPPI	*	*	*	*	*	*	*	*	*	*	*	*	*	*
MISSOURI	*	*	*	*	*	*	*	*	*	*	*	*	*	*
MONTANA	0.92	0.58	0.50	0.43	0.41	0.38	0.33	0.31	0.28	0.26	0.24	0.22	0.21	0.19
NEBRASKA	0.00	0.00	0.00	0.00	0.00	0.00	0.00	0.00	0.00	0.00	0.00	0.00	0.00	0.00
NEVADA	0.20	0.14	0.12	0.10	0.10	0.09	0.08	0.07	0.07	0.06	0.05	0.05	0.05	0.04
NEW HAMPSHIRE	0.33	0.22	0.17	0.17	0.16	0.14	0.14	0.13	0.12	0.11	0.10	0.10	0.10	0.08
NEW JERSEY	0.39	0.27	0.24	0.22	0.21	0.20	0.18	0.17	0.16	0.15	0.14	0.14	0.13	0.12
NEW MEXICO	0.34	0.22	0.19	0.16	0.16	0.14	0.13	0.12	0.10	0.09	0.09	0.08	0.08	0.07
NEW YORK	*	*	*	*	*	*	*	*	*	*	*	*	*	*
NORTH CAROLINA	*	*	*	*	*	*	*	*	*	*	*	*	*	*
NORTH DAKOTA	*	*	*	*	*	*	*	*	*	*	*	*	*	*
OHIO	0.26	0.17	0.14	0.13	0.12	0.12	0.10	0.10	0.09	0.08	0.08	0.07	0.07	0.06
OKLAHOMA	*	*	*	*	*	*	*	*	*	*	*	*	*	*
OREGON	*	*	*	*	*	*	*	*	*	*	*	*	*	*
PENNSYLVANIA	0.26	0.16	0.14	0.12	0.12	0.11	0.10	0.10	0.09	0.08	0.08	0.07	0.07	0.07
RHODE ISLAND	0.29	0.17	0.17	0.14	0.13	0.12	0.12	0.11	0.10	0.09	0.09	0.09	0.08	0.07
SOUTH CAROLINA	0.06	0.04	0.03	0.03	0.03	0.02	0.02	0.02	0.02	0.02	0.02	0.02	0.02	0.01
SOUTH DAKOTA	*	*	*	*	*	*	*	*	*	*	*	*	*	*
TENNESSEE	*	*	*	*	*	*	*	*	*	*	*	*	*	*
TEXAS	0.02	0.01	0.01	0.01	0.01	0.01	0.01	0.01	0.01	0.00	0.00	0.00	0.00	0.00
UTAH	0.01	0.00	0.00	0.00	0.00	0.00	0.00	0.00	0.00	0.00	0.00	0.00	0.00	0.00
VERMONT	0.06	0.04	0.03	0.03	0.03	0.02	0.02	0.02	0.02	0.02	0.02	0.02	0.02	0.01
VIRGINIA	*	*	*	*	*	*	*	*	*	*	*	*	*	*
WASHINGTON	*	*	*	*	*	*	*	*	*	*	*	*	*	*
WEST VIRGINIA	*	*	*	*	*	*	*	*	*	*	*	*	*	*
WISCONSIN	1.48	0.88	0.76	0.70	0.66	0.63	0.54	0.51	0.48	0.44	0.41	0.39	0.38	0.33
WYOMING	0.64	0.43	0.39	0.34	0.31	0.29	0.26	0.24	0.22	0.20	0.18	0.18	0.17	0.15
AVERAGE	1.87	1.18	1.07	0.98	0.92	0.81	0.77	0.71	0.65	0.58	0.55	0.52	0.50	0.45

* EFFECTIVE TAX RATE EQUALS ZERO BEFORE ROUNDING. AN ENTIRE ROW OF * MEANS THAT THIS TAX IS NOT USED IN THIS STATE.

TABLE A-37
EFFECTIVE TAX RATES: TOTAL STATE PROPERTY TAXES
INCIDENCE: SUM OF EFFECTIVE TAX RATES FOR INDIVIDUAL TAXES
ALLOCATOR: BASED ON INDIVIDUAL TAXES

STATE	UNDER $3,000	$3,000 -3,999	$4,000 -4,999	$5,000 -5,999	$6,000 -6,999	$7,000 -7,999	$8,000 -9,999	$10,000 -11,999	$12,000 -14,999	$15,000 -19,999	$20,000 -24,999	$25,000 -29,999	$30,000 -34,999	OVER $35,000
ALABAMA	0.30	0.17	0.16	0.12	0.13	0.12	0.09	0.11	0.09	0.08	0.11	0.08	0.10	0.59
ALASKA	30.95	19.56	17.98	16.87	15.65	13.54	13.04	12.00	11.01	9.67	9.09	8.69	8.28	7.43
ARIZONA	2.17	1.53	1.25	1.07	1.05	0.72	0.76	0.75	0.64	0.65	0.57	0.57	0.61	1.11
ARKANSAS	0.04	0.02	0.02	0.03	0.01	0.01	0.02	0.01	0.01	0.01	0.01	0.01	0.01	0.04
CALIFORNIA	0.59	0.34	0.29	0.31	0.23	0.21	0.22	0.20	0.20	0.16	0.15	0.17	0.17	0.40
COLORADO	0.03	0.01	0.02	0.01	0.01	0.01	0.01	0.01	0.01	0.01	0.01	0.01	0.01	0.02
CONNECTICUT	*	*	*	*	*	*	*	*	*	*	*	*	*	*
DELAWARE	*	*	*	*	*	*	*	*	*	*	*	*	*	*
FLORIDA	0.29	0.16	0.15	0.13	0.13	0.12	0.10	0.11	0.09	0.09	0.08	0.09	0.10	0.14
GEORGIA	0.06	0.03	0.02	0.03	0.02	0.02	0.02	0.01	0.02	0.01	0.01	0.02	0.03	0.06
HAWAII	*	*	*	*	*	*	*	*	*	*	*	*	*	*
IDAHO	0.02	0.01	0.01	0.01	0.00	0.01	0.00	0.00	0.00	0.00	0.01	0.00	0.01	0.01
ILLINOIS	0.02	0.01	0.01	0.01	0.01	0.01	0.01	0.01	0.01	0.01	0.01	0.01	0.00	0.01
INDIANA	0.16	0.10	0.08	0.06	0.06	0.06	0.05	0.06	0.05	0.05	0.05	0.06	0.05	0.15
IOWA	0.00	0.00	0.00	0.00	0.00	0.00	0.00	0.00	0.00	0.00	0.00	0.00	0.00	0.00
KANSAS	0.20	0.11	0.10	0.09	0.14	0.09	0.07	0.08	0.06	0.06	0.07	0.07	0.06	0.19
KENTUCKY	0.48	0.29	0.27	0.30	0.21	0.19	0.20	0.17	0.16	0.16	0.15	0.18	0.14	0.47
LOUISIANA	0.00	0.00	0.00	0.00	0.00	0.00	0.00	0.00	0.00	0.00	0.00	0.00	0.00	0.00
MAINE	6.85	4.39	3.82	3.19	3.19	2.89	2.75	2.52	2.33	2.13	2.04	1.90	1.86	1.69
MARYLAND	0.49	0.49	0.29	0.25	0.20	0.19	0.18	0.20	0.16	0.17	0.17	0.14	0.15	0.27
MASSACHUSETTS	0.00	0.00	0.00	0.00	0.00	0.00	0.00	0.00	0.00	0.00	0.00	0.00	0.00	0.00
MICHIGAN	0.68	0.44	0.36	0.32	0.29	0.29	0.26	0.24	0.22	0.20	0.19	0.18	0.17	0.15
MINNESOTA	0.02	0.01	0.02	0.01	0.01	0.01	0.01	0.01	0.01	0.00	0.01	0.01	0.01	0.02
MISSISSIPPI	0.05	0.03	0.03	0.02	0.03	0.02	0.02	0.02	0.02	0.02	0.03	0.02	0.02	0.08
MISSOURI	0.03	0.02	0.02	0.02	0.01	0.01	0.01	0.01	0.01	0.01	0.01	0.01	0.01	0.04
MONTANA	1.18	0.82	0.62	0.56	0.54	0.50	0.42	0.44	0.35	0.32	0.31	0.29	0.30	0.43
NEBRASKA	0.00	0.00	0.00	0.00	0.00	0.00	0.00	0.00	0.00	0.00	0.00	0.00	0.00	0.00
NEVADA	0.99	0.64	0.51	0.44	0.41	0.39	0.36	0.43	0.30	0.34	0.25	0.28	0.22	0.92
NEW HAMPSHIRE	0.33	0.22	0.17	0.17	0.16	0.14	0.14	0.13	0.12	0.11	0.10	0.10	0.10	0.08
NEW JERSEY	0.39	0.27	0.24	0.22	0.21	0.20	0.18	0.17	0.16	0.15	0.14	0.14	0.13	0.12
NEW MEXICO	0.57	0.40	0.30	0.26	0.25	0.26	0.21	0.21	0.20	0.18	0.17	0.19	0.19	0.24
NEW YORK	0.04	0.03	0.03	0.03	0.02	0.02	0.02	0.01	0.01	0.01	0.01	0.01	0.02	0.04
NORTH CAROLINA	0.25	0.12	0.19	0.09	0.10	0.08	0.08	0.07	0.07	0.07	0.08	0.08	0.07	0.26
NORTH DAKOTA	0.13	0.06	0.07	0.05	0.08	0.04	0.04	0.04	0.04	0.03	0.04	0.04	0.05	0.08
OHIO	0.39	0.26	0.22	0.21	0.16	0.17	0.16	0.14	0.13	0.12	0.12	0.12	0.13	0.19
OKLAHOMA	*	*	*	*	*	*	*	*	*	*	*	*	*	*
OREGON	0.00	0.00	0.00	0.00	0.00	0.00	0.00	0.00	0.00	0.00	0.00	0.00	0.00	0.00
PENNSYLVANIA	0.26	0.16	0.14	0.12	0.12	0.11	0.10	0.10	0.09	0.08	0.08	0.07	0.07	0.07
RHODE ISLAND	0.29	0.17	0.17	0.14	0.13	0.12	0.12	0.11	0.10	0.09	0.09	0.09	0.08	0.07
SOUTH CAROLINA	0.07	0.04	0.04	0.03	0.04	0.03	0.03	0.03	0.03	0.02	0.02	0.02	0.02	0.04
SOUTH DAKOTA	*	*	*	*	*	*	*	*	*	*	*	*	*	*
TENNESSEE	*	*	*	*	*	*	*	*	*	*	*	*	*	*
TEXAS	0.12	0.06	0.06	0.05	0.04	0.04	0.04	0.03	0.04	0.03	0.03	0.04	0.04	0.09
UTAH	0.01	0.01	0.00	0.00	0.00	0.00	0.00	0.00	0.00	0.00	0.00	0.00	0.00	0.00
VERMONT	0.06	0.04	0.03	0.03	0.03	0.02	0.02	0.02	0.02	0.02	0.02	0.02	0.02	0.01
VIRGINIA	0.13	0.09	0.06	0.08	0.09	0.05	0.06	0.06	0.04	0.05	0.04	0.05	0.04	0.11
WASHINGTON	2.22	1.24	1.42	1.22	1.09	1.11	0.94	0.67	0.84	0.75	0.67	0.63	0.94	2.40
WEST VIRGINIA	0.01	0.01	0.00	0.00	0.00	0.00	0.00	0.00	0.00	0.00	0.00	0.00	0.01	0.01
WISCONSIN	1.48	0.88	0.76	0.70	0.66	0.63	0.54	0.51	0.48	0.44	0.41	0.39	0.38	0.33
WYOMING	0.80	0.54	0.47	0.41	0.37	0.36	0.33	0.29	0.27	0.24	0.22	0.22	0.22	0.30
AVERAGE	1.21	0.77	0.69	0.63	0.59	0.52	0.49	0.45	0.42	0.38	0.35	0.34	0.34	0.42

* EFFECTIVE TAX RATE EQUALS ZERO BEFORE ROUNDING. AN ENTIRE ROW OF * MEANS THAT THIS TAX IS NOT USED IN THIS STATE.

TABLE A-38
EFFECTIVE TAX RATES: TOTAL STATE TAXES (BENCHMARK)
INCIDENCE: SUM OF EFFECTIVE TAX RATES FOR INDIVIDUAL TAXES
ALLOCATOR: BASED ON INDIVIDUAL TAXES

STATE	UNDER $3,000	$3,000 -3,999	$4,000 -4,999	$5,000 -5,999	$6,000 -6,999	$7,000 -7,999	$8,000 -9,999	$10,000 -11,999	$12,000 -14,999	$15,000 -19,999	$20,000 -24,999	$25,000 -29,999	$30,000 -34,999	OVER $35,000
ALABAMA	14.43	8.78	7.72	7.02	6.46	6.42	6.19	6.01	5.61	5.28	5.23	4.95	5.07	5.15
ALASKA	40.87	26.83	24.89	23.18	21.91	19.19	18.74	17.64	16.66	15.10	15.24	15.07	14.99	14.89
ARIZONA	16.29	10.69	8.62	8.45	7.70	6.87	7.04	6.71	6.47	6.23	5.73	5.27	5.44	5.40
ARKANSAS	14.49	8.85	7.79	7.19	6.63	6.35	6.08	5.86	5.52	5.40	5.78	5.69	5.87	5.17
CALIFORNIA	10.05	7.05	6.07	5.79	5.20	4.89	4.61	4.58	4.64	5.01	5.72	6.10	6.05	6.86
COLORADO	9.30	6.01	5.55	4.92	4.93	4.65	4.33	4.68	4.76	4.83	4.62	4.53	3.98	4.23
CONNECTICUT	8.28	6.90	6.30	6.14	5.56	5.89	5.01	4.88	4.63	4.42	4.30	4.26	4.03	5.03
DELAWARE	9.51	6.29	6.23	5.32	5.07	5.28	5.49	5.30	5.82	5.36	5.28	5.19	5.43	8.73
FLORIDA	13.53	8.49	7.35	6.64	6.38	5.98	5.44	5.08	4.71	4.30	4.07	3.96	3.84	4.07
GEORGIA	12.72	7.30	6.61	6.05	5.84	5.57	5.22	4.86	4.99	5.41	5.27	5.06	5.11	4.85
HAWAII	14.13	9.63	9.86	9.71	9.58	9.43	9.04	9.03	8.81	8.71	8.51	9.19	8.56	9.15
IDAHO	11.41	7.12	6.21	6.37	6.26	6.09	6.04	6.02	5.98	5.63	5.75	5.64	5.47	5.97
ILLINOIS	9.68	7.15	6.63	6.50	6.12	6.10	5.83	5.60	5.48	5.20	4.98	4.88	4.82	5.07
INDIANA	9.72	7.03	6.33	6.31	6.17	5.98	5.43	5.50	5.25	5.01	4.95	4.45	4.68	5.09
IOWA	9.27	6.37	6.31	5.48	5.49	5.47	5.68	5.73	5.47	5.79	5.63	5.71	6.25	7.34
KANSAS	10.35	7.01	6.45	5.51	5.86	5.26	5.59	5.24	4.96	4.86	4.63	5.31	5.02	5.30
KENTUCKY	13.44	8.65	8.00	7.58	6.57	6.56	6.34	6.45	6.15	6.29	6.21	6.37	5.81	7.50
LOUISIANA	15.39	9.29	8.08	7.78	7.18	6.89	6.61	6.03	5.60	5.38	5.74	5.69	5.53	6.12
MAINE	18.10	12.41	11.20	9.74	9.67	8.90	9.08	8.26	7.85	7.88	8.06	8.02	8.12	9.43
MARYLAND	10.78	7.74	6.49	6.26	6.44	6.41	6.31	6.15	5.72	5.65	5.47	5.51	4.99	5.26
MASSACHUSETTS	6.73	5.21	5.67	5.71	5.99	5.80	6.05	6.31	5.94	6.06	5.99	6.38	6.27	6.53
MICHIGAN	9.56	6.71	5.76	5.39	5.41	5.90	5.31	5.33	5.18	5.01	4.98	5.07	4.88	5.60
MINNESOTA	12.15	8.30	7.34	6.35	5.93	5.92	5.96	6.57	6.87	7.31	7.81	8.11	8.51	8.76
MISSISSIPPI	18.79	11.93	9.84	8.79	8.10	7.87	7.20	6.84	6.47	6.55	6.70	6.73	6.70	6.89
MISSOURI	9.39	5.59	5.54	5.00	4.78	4.64	4.46	4.47	4.21	4.31	4.34	4.29	3.88	4.32
MONTANA	9.70	6.86	5.76	5.50	5.44	5.35	4.79	4.92	4.82	5.03	5.17	4.89	5.26	5.84
NEBRASKA	9.84	6.55	5.20	4.85	4.70	4.71	4.62	4.42	4.21	4.17	4.34	4.20	4.62	5.39
NEVADA	11.48	8.16	7.09	6.32	6.27	5.90	5.38	5.05	4.59	4.37	4.00	3.89	3.80	4.23
NEW HAMPSHIRE	7.82	5.19	4.87	4.55	3.84	3.36	3.38	3.12	2.92	2.62	2.49	2.36	2.43	3.78
NEW JERSEY	6.97	5.24	5.04	4.72	4.44	4.33	4.42	4.03	3.75	3.60	3.49	3.33	3.19	3.95
NEW MEXICO	18.95	12.79	11.46	10.07	9.87	8.97	8.46	7.87	7.24	6.88	6.86	6.68	6.27	7.34
NEW YORK	9.21	6.21	5.43	5.48	5.40	5.27	5.14	5.30	5.27	5.46	6.41	7.10	7.80	7.61
NORTH CAROLINA	12.84	7.96	7.60	6.36	6.38	5.87	6.21	6.06	5.81	5.90	5.72	5.74	5.31	6.13
NORTH DAKOTA	13.72	9.00	8.10	7.19	7.35	6.68	6.45	6.61	7.01	7.16	7.10	6.84	7.22	6.57
OHIO	8.63	6.04	5.40	4.95	4.44	4.70	4.36	4.03	4.09	3.97	4.10	4.21	4.15	4.71
OKLAHOMA	13.55	7.54	6.56	6.16	5.83	5.30	4.76	4.64	4.53	4.50	5.01	4.77	4.58	5.66
OREGON	5.88	3.93	3.91	4.19	3.98	3.94	4.13	3.82	4.04	4.69	4.79	4.74	4.26	5.82
PENNSYLVANIA	10.66	7.26	6.32	5.97	7.35	6.73	6.94	6.42	5.95	5.87	5.45	5.45	5.59	7.47
RHODE ISLAND	10.18	6.84	7.05	6.55	6.32	5.78	5.84	5.72	5.53	5.51	5.51	5.49	5.43	6.54
SOUTH CAROLINA	13.62	8.79	7.61	7.04	7.04	6.82	6.44	6.59	6.32	6.42	6.29	6.20	5.71	5.92
SOUTH DAKOTA	12.53	8.13	7.39	6.72	6.49	5.96	5.49	5.32	4.98	4.71	4.47	4.36	4.24	5.29
TENNESSEE	13.42	8.35	7.28	6.63	6.10	5.72	5.23	4.90	4.36	4.10	3.83	3.69	3.85	5.98
TEXAS	12.60	7.97	6.84	6.34	5.82	5.44	5.14	4.74	4.34	3.98	3.74	3.59	3.42	3.62
UTAH	12.60	8.08	7.02	6.50	6.90	6.38	5.99	5.95	5.88	5.79	5.63	5.46	5.60	6.00
VERMONT	11.74	7.57	7.47	7.15	6.76	6.69	7.01	6.95	6.83	6.87	6.96	6.54	7.22	8.25
VIRGINIA	10.96	6.53	5.92	5.71	5.36	4.92	5.47	5.19	4.77	4.89	4.69	4.55	4.29	4.18
WASHINGTON	19.17	12.36	10.73	9.76	8.84	8.93	7.98	7.39	7.03	6.44	6.11	5.87	5.73	8.01
WEST VIRGINIA	19.73	13.08	10.75	9.58	9.27	8.98	7.84	7.78	7.33	7.16	6.91	6.70	6.69	8.73
WISCONSIN	11.63	7.77	7.23	6.71	6.87	7.14	6.59	6.47	6.86	7.33	7.53	7.39	7.74	8.21
WYOMING	15.86	11.11	10.30	9.20	8.53	8.09	7.33	6.95	6.47	5.84	5.51	5.46	5.38	4.96
AVERAGE	12.63	8.33	7.50	6.95	6.70	6.41	6.17	5.99	5.77	5.68	5.66	5.62	5.58	6.26

* EFFECTIVE TAX RATE EQUALS ZERO BEFORE ROUNDING. AN ENTIRE ROW OF * MEANS THAT THIS TAX IS NOT USED IN THIS STATE.

TABLE A-39
EFFECTIVE TAX RATES: TOTAL STATE TAXES (MOST REGRESSIVE)
INCIDENCE: SUM OF EFFECTIVE TAX RATES FOR INDIVIDUAL TAXES
ALLOCATOR: BASED ON INDIVIDUAL TAXES

STATE	UNDER $3,000	$3,000 -3,999	$4,000 -4,999	$5,000 -5,999	$6,000 -6,999	$7,000 -7,999	$8,000 -9,999	$10,000 -11,999	$12,000 -14,999	$15,000 -19,999	$20,000 -24,999	$25,000 -29,999	$30,000 -34,999	OVER $35,000
ALABAMA	14.66	8.94	7.84	7.16	6.55	6.52	6.30	6.08	5.68	5.36	5.25	5.00	5.09	4.45
ALASKA	41.56	26.37	24.86	23.61	22.34	19.50	19.01	17.91	16.91	15.13	15.38	15.20	15.09	14.66
ARIZONA	16.53	10.75	8.64	8.53	7.73	6.98	7.12	6.76	6.53	6.25	5.75	5.28	5.43	5.17
ARKANSAS	14.72	9.05	7.91	7.11	6.81	6.55	6.13	5.91	5.55	5.50	5.83	5.75	5.93	4.39
CALIFORNIA	10.48	7.44	6.36	5.94	5.45	5.14	4.76	4.73	4.73	5.14	5.83	6.13	6.06	6.30
COLORADO	9.45	6.25	5.40	5.06	5.10	4.60	4.44	4.80	4.86	4.92	4.67	4.58	3.92	3.85
CONNECTICUT	8.61	6.92	6.19	6.10	5.66	6.14	5.21	5.05	4.72	4.47	4.43	4.37	4.15	4.62
DELAWARE	9.74	6.50	6.47	5.55	5.31	5.31	5.69	5.45	5.90	5.46	5.36	5.25	5.52	8.23
FLORIDA	13.68	8.65	7.42	6.71	6.45	6.06	5.52	5.11	4.76	4.33	4.10	3.94	3.78	3.81
GEORGIA	12.89	7.42	6.78	6.13	5.93	5.75	5.35	5.00	5.09	5.49	5.33	5.10	4.99	4.29
HAWAII	13.88	9.82	10.06	9.81	9.44	9.55	9.12	9.16	8.95	8.75	8.63	9.31	8.60	8.82
IDAHO	11.69	7.39	6.47	6.65	6.52	6.21	6.25	6.16	6.16	5.75	5.68	5.63	5.17	5.29
ILLINOIS	9.86	7.25	6.75	6.55	6.21	6.19	5.91	5.64	5.57	5.27	5.04	4.92	4.85	4.75
INDIANA	9.88	7.13	6.43	6.43	6.28	6.05	5.51	5.56	5.31	5.05	4.97	4.42	4.70	4.81
IOWA	9.65	6.53	6.43	5.47	5.62	5.65	5.71	5.74	5.58	5.87	5.69	5.76	6.03	6.99
KANSAS	10.73	7.29	6.69	5.67	5.81	5.38	5.76	5.31	5.12	4.97	4.66	5.32	5.09	4.71
KENTUCKY	14.03	9.03	8.28	7.49	6.82	6.83	6.54	6.69	6.33	6.40	6.35	6.33	5.88	6.01
LOUISIANA	15.67	9.48	8.19	7.95	7.32	7.00	6.74	6.12	5.70	5.44	5.82	5.75	5.50	5.58
MAINE	18.42	12.63	11.40	9.69	9.87	9.06	9.03	8.41	7.95	7.88	8.16	7.90	8.12	8.90
MARYLAND	11.08	7.58	6.59	6.35	6.59	6.54	6.43	6.21	5.81	5.70	5.48	5.57	5.01	5.04
MASSACHUSETTS	7.01	5.63	5.78	5.84	6.09	6.08	6.26	6.51	6.08	6.23	6.13	6.40	6.40	5.70
MICHIGAN	9.86	6.85	5.85	5.54	5.54	5.94	5.40	5.47	5.31	5.11	5.05	5.03	4.94	5.10
MINNESOTA	12.65	8.72	6.99	6.66	6.17	6.23	6.02	6.75	7.03	7.48	7.91	8.14	8.58	7.91
MISSISSIPPI	19.08	12.14	9.96	8.94	8.10	8.00	7.27	6.91	6.53	6.61	6.67	6.76	6.70	6.35
MISSOURI	9.62	5.71	5.68	5.06	4.88	4.70	4.52	4.52	4.26	4.36	4.36	4.32	3.89	3.97
MONTANA	9.99	6.82	5.97	5.63	5.55	5.41	4.90	4.89	4.94	5.13	5.23	4.94	5.25	5.36
NEBRASKA	9.96	6.69	5.34	4.95	4.73	4.81	4.64	4.50	4.28	4.24	4.37	4.24	4.59	5.07
NEVADA	11.48	8.16	7.09	6.32	6.27	5.90	5.38	5.05	4.59	4.37	4.00	3.89	3.80	4.23
NEW HAMPSHIRE	7.99	5.39	4.65	4.36	4.00	3.53	3.48	3.14	3.01	2.70	2.56	2.44	2.44	3.23
NEW JERSEY	7.19	5.39	5.03	4.70	4.49	4.41	4.24	4.08	3.84	3.67	3.55	3.39	3.22	3.74
NEW MEXICO	19.20	12.87	11.64	10.23	10.01	9.02	8.57	7.92	7.26	6.91	6.88	6.64	6.20	7.14
NEW YORK	9.67	6.44	5.55	5.57	5.64	5.46	5.31	5.49	5.42	5.59	6.52	7.20	7.81	6.95
NORTH CAROLINA	13.03	8.20	7.56	6.50	6.51	6.01	6.33	6.16	5.92	5.97	5.75	5.76	5.34	5.57
NORTH DAKOTA	13.87	9.19	8.16	7.32	7.25	6.82	6.56	6.73	7.07	7.25	7.12	6.84	7.18	6.27
OHIO	8.83	6.14	5.51	4.98	4.60	4.82	4.43	4.11	4.18	4.04	4.14	4.23	4.10	4.30
OKLAHOMA	13.79	7.73	6.73	6.32	5.94	5.38	4.86	4.75	4.60	4.56	5.04	4.78	4.62	5.28
OREGON	5.91	4.18	4.05	4.39	4.14	4.11	4.27	3.88	4.13	4.74	4.81	4.78	4.09	5.39
PENNSYLVANIA	10.93	7.38	6.58	6.00	7.25	7.03	6.98	6.63	6.14	5.99	5.59	5.56	5.61	6.70
RHODE ISLAND	10.39	6.75	7.13	6.64	6.08	5.94	5.95	5.75	5.61	5.59	5.60	5.58	5.39	6.13
SOUTH CAROLINA	14.03	9.10	7.81	7.24	6.98	6.85	6.52	6.58	6.38	6.51	6.40	6.30	5.72	5.11
SOUTH DAKOTA	12.57	8.15	7.41	6.74	6.50	5.94	5.50	5.33	4.99	4.73	4.48	4.36	4.23	5.22
TENNESSEE	13.73	8.67	7.53	6.88	6.27	5.94	5.36	4.99	4.52	4.16	3.90	3.73	3.89	5.09
TEXAS	12.60	7.97	6.84	6.34	5.82	5.44	5.14	4.74	4.34	3.98	3.74	3.59	3.42	3.62
UTAH	12.47	8.31	7.05	6.55	7.04	6.45	6.06	6.03	5.97	5.84	5.66	5.50	5.60	5.67
VERMONT	12.11	7.84	7.71	7.24	6.90	6.79	7.07	7.04	6.88	6.96	6.96	6.60	6.91	7.64
VIRGINIA	11.27	6.62	6.12	5.77	5.33	5.05	5.56	5.23	4.87	4.95	4.75	4.57	4.32	3.88
WASHINGTON	19.17	12.36	10.73	9.76	8.84	8.93	7.98	7.39	7.03	6.44	6.11	5.87	5.73	8.01
WEST VIRGINIA	19.93	13.07	10.80	9.65	9.34	9.02	7.90	7.85	7.38	7.19	6.92	6.69	6.56	8.45
WISCONSIN	12.07	8.07	7.29	6.97	7.15	7.27	6.46	6.59	7.02	7.43	7.56	7.47	7.68	7.57
WYOMING	15.86	11.11	10.30	9.20	8.53	8.09	7.33	6.95	6.47	5.84	5.51	5.46	5.38	4.96
AVERAGE	12.87	8.48	7.60	7.05	6.79	6.53	6.26	6.08	5.87	5.75	5.71	5.65	5.57	5.81

* EFFECTIVE TAX RATE EQUALS ZERO BEFORE ROUNDING. AN ENTIRE ROW OF * MEANS THAT THIS TAX IS NOT USED IN THIS STATE.

TABLE A-40
EFFECTIVE TAX RATES: TOTAL STATE TAXES (MOST PROGRESSIVE)
INCIDENCE: SUM OF EFFECTIVE TAX RATES FOR INDIVIDUAL TAXES
ALLOCATOR: BASED ON INDIVIDUAL TAXES

STATE	UNDER $3,000	$3,000 -3,999	$4,000 -4,999	$5,000 -5,999	$6,000 -6,999	$7,000 -7,999	$8,000 -9,999	$10,000 -11,999	$12,000 -14,999	$15,000 -19,999	$20,000 -24,999	$25,000 -29,999	$30,000 -34,999	OVER $35,000
ALABAMA	14.19	8.61	7.59	6.89	6.37	6.32	6.08	5.94	5.53	5.21	5.22	4.91	5.05	5.84
ALASKA	40.18	27.29	24.92	22.76	21.49	18.89	18.48	17.37	16.41	15.06	15.11	14.95	14.88	15.13
ARIZONA	16.05	10.63	8.59	8.38	7.68	6.76	6.96	6.65	6.41	6.21	5.70	5.26	5.45	5.63
ARKANSAS	14.26	8.64	7.66	7.28	6.45	6.15	6.02	5.81	5.49	5.29	5.73	5.64	5.81	5.94
CALIFORNIA	9.61	6.67	5.77	5.63	4.95	4.64	4.45	4.43	4.54	4.89	5.61	6.07	6.05	7.43
COLORADO	9.16	5.76	5.70	4.78	4.75	4.70	4.23	4.56	4.66	4.75	4.56	4.48	4.04	4.62
CONNECTICUT	7.96	6.87	6.42	6.18	5.46	5.64	4.82	4.71	4.54	4.36	4.18	4.16	3.90	5.43
DELAWARE	9.28	6.07	5.99	5.10	4.84	5.24	5.29	5.16	5.74	5.26	5.20	5.13	5.35	9.23
FLORIDA	13.38	8.34	7.28	6.57	6.31	5.91	5.36	5.05	4.65	4.26	4.03	3.97	3.90	4.33
GEORGIA	12.55	7.17	6.44	5.97	5.76	5.40	5.09	4.72	4.89	5.33	5.20	5.02	5.24	5.41
HAWAII	14.38	9.43	9.65	9.61	9.72	9.31	8.96	8.90	8.67	8.68	8.39	9.07	8.52	9.47
IDAHO	11.14	6.85	5.96	6.08	6.01	5.97	5.83	5.87	5.81	5.51	5.82	5.65	5.77	6.64
ILLINOIS	9.50	7.05	6.51	6.46	6.03	6.00	5.75	5.56	5.39	5.12	4.92	4.83	4.78	5.39
INDIANA	9.55	6.93	6.23	6.19	6.06	5.90	5.35	5.45	5.18	4.97	4.93	4.47	4.67	5.37
IOWA	8.89	6.21	6.19	5.48	5.36	5.30	5.65	5.72	5.35	5.71	5.56	5.66	6.48	7.70
KANSAS	9.97	6.73	6.21	5.35	5.91	5.14	5.41	5.16	4.80	4.75	4.61	5.30	4.94	5.88
KENTUCKY	12.84	8.27	7.72	7.66	6.31	6.29	6.15	6.21	5.96	6.17	6.08	6.42	5.74	8.99
LOUISIANA	15.10	9.10	7.98	7.62	7.03	6.78	6.49	5.94	5.50	5.31	5.66	5.64	5.56	6.65
MAINE	17.78	12.19	11.01	9.78	9.47	8.74	9.13	8.10	7.75	7.88	7.97	8.14	8.12	9.96
MARYLAND	10.48	7.89	6.39	6.17	6.29	6.28	6.18	6.09	5.63	5.59	5.45	5.45	4.97	5.48
MASSACHUSETTS	6.45	4.78	5.55	5.59	5.89	5.53	5.85	6.12	5.81	5.88	5.85	6.36	6.14	7.36
MICHIGAN	9.26	6.56	5.66	5.25	5.29	5.86	5.23	5.20	5.05	4.91	4.92	5.11	4.83	6.09
MINNESOTA	11.66	7.87	7.69	6.05	5.70	5.60	5.90	6.40	6.71	7.14	7.70	8.08	8.44	9.62
MISSISSIPPI	18.50	11.71	9.72	8.63	8.11	7.74	7.13	6.78	6.41	6.50	6.74	6.71	6.71	7.43
MISSOURI	9.16	5.46	5.41	4.94	4.69	4.57	4.40	4.41	4.17	4.26	4.32	4.27	3.86	4.66
MONTANA	9.42	6.89	5.56	5.37	5.33	5.29	4.68	4.95	4.71	4.94	5.12	4.83	5.26	6.31
NEBRASKA	9.72	6.40	5.07	4.74	4.67	4.61	4.59	4.33	4.15	4.10	4.32	4.17	4.65	5.72
NEVADA	11.48	8.16	7.09	6.32	6.27	5.90	5.38	5.05	4.59	4.37	4.00	3.89	3.80	4.23
NEW HAMPSHIRE	7.65	4.98	5.09	4.74	3.67	3.20	3.27	3.10	2.84	2.54	2.43	2.27	2.41	4.32
NEW JERSEY	6.75	5.09	5.05	4.74	4.39	4.26	4.61	3.99	3.67	3.52	3.44	3.27	3.15	4.16
NEW MEXICO	18.70	12.71	11.27	9.91	9.73	8.91	8.36	7.81	7.22	6.85	6.85	6.72	6.35	7.54
NEW YORK	8.75	5.97	5.30	5.38	5.17	5.08	4.96	5.11	5.12	5.33	6.29	7.01	7.79	8.27
NORTH CAROLINA	12.65	7.73	7.65	6.23	6.25	5.72	6.10	5.96	5.71	5.82	5.69	5.72	5.28	6.70
NORTH DAKOTA	13.56	8.81	8.04	7.06	7.46	6.53	6.34	6.49	6.95	7.06	7.08	6.85	7.27	6.87
OHIO	8.43	5.93	5.30	4.92	4.29	4.59	4.28	3.96	4.00	3.90	4.05	4.18	4.20	5.12
OKLAHOMA	13.32	7.34	6.39	6.00	5.72	5.23	4.65	4.53	4.46	4.45	4.98	4.77	4.53	6.04
OREGON	5.86	3.69	3.76	3.99	3.82	3.77	3.99	3.75	3.94	4.64	4.77	4.70	4.43	6.26
PENNSYLVANIA	10.40	7.14	6.06	5.94	7.45	6.42	6.89	6.20	5.76	5.74	5.31	5.35	5.58	8.25
RHODE ISLAND	9.97	6.94	6.97	6.45	6.56	5.62	5.74	5.68	5.46	5.44	5.41	5.40	5.48	6.94
SOUTH CAROLINA	13.21	8.48	7.40	6.84	7.10	6.80	6.35	6.60	6.26	6.32	6.18	6.11	5.70	6.72
SOUTH DAKOTA	12.50	8.11	7.37	6.70	6.48	5.98	5.49	5.31	4.96	4.70	4.47	4.36	4.24	5.35
TENNESSEE	13.10	8.04	7.03	6.37	5.93	5.51	5.09	4.82	4.21	4.05	3.75	3.65	3.81	6.88
TEXAS	12.60	7.97	6.84	6.34	5.82	5.44	5.14	4.74	4.34	3.98	3.74	3.59	3.42	3.62
UTAH	12.73	7.86	6.98	6.46	6.75	6.31	5.93	5.87	5.79	5.73	5.60	5.43	5.60	6.33
VERMONT	11.37	7.31	7.23	7.06	6.62	6.60	6.96	6.86	6.77	6.79	6.97	6.47	7.52	8.86
VIRGINIA	10.65	6.43	5.73	5.65	5.39	4.79	5.38	5.15	4.67	4.84	4.63	4.53	4.27	4.48
WASHINGTON	19.17	12.36	10.73	9.76	8.84	8.93	7.98	7.39	7.03	6.44	6.11	5.87	5.73	8.01
WEST VIRGINIA	19.54	13.10	10.69	9.51	9.21	8.95	7.79	7.72	7.29	7.12	6.90	6.72	6.82	9.01
WISCONSIN	11.20	7.47	7.17	6.44	6.59	7.01	6.72	6.35	6.69	7.24	7.50	7.32	7.81	8.85
WYOMING	15.86	11.11	10.30	9.20	8.53	8.09	7.33	6.95	6.47	5.84	5.51	5.46	5.38	4.96
AVERAGE	12.40	8.18	7.41	6.85	6.60	6.28	6.08	5.90	5.68	5.62	5.61	5.59	5.59	6.71

* EFFECTIVE TAX RATE EQUALS ZERO BEFORE ROUNDING. AN ENTIRE ROW OF * MEANS THAT THIS TAX IS NOT USED IN THIS STATE.

TABLE A-41
EFFECTIVE TAX RATES: LOCAL GENERAL SALES AND GROSS RECEIPTS TAXES
INCIDENCE: CONSUMERS OF TAXED ITEMS
ALLOCATOR: SPECIAL SERIES ON CONSUMPTION OF TAXED ITEMS

STATE	UNDER $3,000	$3,000 -3,999	$4,000 -4,999	$5,000 -5,999	$6,000 -6,999	$7,000 -7,999	$8,000 -9,999	$10,000 -11,999	$12,000 -14,999	$15,000 -19,999	$20,000 -24,999	$25,000 -29,999	$30,000 -34,999	OVER $35,000
ALABAMA	1.73	1.10	0.96	0.85	0.77	0.75	0.70	0.63	0.58	0.53	0.50	0.47	0.47	0.31
ALASKA	2.78	1.76	1.62	1.51	1.40	1.18	1.16	1.07	0.96	0.79	0.74	0.66	0.61	0.46
ARIZONA	1.53	1.01	0.81	0.82	0.73	0.67	0.66	0.61	0.57	0.54	0.49	0.46	0.46	0.42
ARKANSAS	0.02	0.01	0.01	0.01	0.01	0.01	0.01	0.01	0.01	0.00	0.00	0.00	0.00	0.00
CALIFORNIA	0.92	0.74	0.66	0.63	0.60	0.57	0.54	0.52	0.49	0.47	0.45	0.44	0.43	0.40
COLORADO	2.38	1.67	1.41	1.29	1.28	1.15	1.05	1.00	0.94	0.87	0.81	0.79	0.69	0.65
CONNECTICUT	*	*	*	*	*	*	*	*	*	*	*	*	*	*
DELAWARE	*	*	*	*	*	*	*	*	*	*	*	*	*	*
FLORIDA	*	*	*	*	*	*	*	*	*	*	*	*	*	*
GEORGIA	0.53	0.31	0.29	0.26	0.25	0.24	0.21	0.19	0.18	0.17	0.15	0.14	0.14	0.11
HAWAII	*	*	*	*	*	*	*	*	*	*	*	*	*	*
IDAHO	*	*	*	*	*	*	*	*	*	*	*	*	*	*
ILLINOIS	0.87	0.66	0.60	0.56	0.52	0.51	0.48	0.45	0.44	0.41	0.38	0.38	0.36	0.32
INDIANA	*	*	*	*	*	*	*	*	*	*	*	*	*	*
IOWA	*	*	*	*	*	*	*	*	*	*	*	*	*	*
KANSAS	0.07	0.05	0.04	0.04	0.04	0.04	0.04	0.03	0.03	0.03	0.03	0.03	0.03	0.02
KENTUCKY	*	*	*	*	*	*	*	*	*	*	*	*	*	*
LOUISIANA	2.95	1.99	1.77	1.78	1.67	1.62	1.59	1.44	1.35	1.30	1.29	1.25	1.18	1.04
MAINE	*	*	*	*	*	*	*	*	*	*	*	*	*	*
MARYLAND	*	*	*	*	*	*	*	*	*	*	*	*	*	*
MASSACHUSETTS	*	*	*	*	*	*	*	*	*	*	*	*	*	*
MICHIGAN	*	*	*	*	*	*	*	*	*	*	*	*	*	*
MINNESOTA	0.02	0.02	0.01	0.01	0.01	0.01	0.01	0.01	0.01	0.01	0.01	0.01	0.01	0.01
MISSISSIPPI	*	*	*	*	*	*	*	*	*	*	*	*	*	*
MISSOURI	1.00	0.61	0.61	0.53	0.50	0.48	0.45	0.42	0.38	0.35	0.34	0.33	0.30	0.27
MONTANA	*	*	*	*	*	*	*	*	*	*	*	*	*	*
NEBRASKA	0.50	0.35	0.28	0.27	0.25	0.25	0.23	0.22	0.20	0.19	0.19	0.18	0.18	0.16
NEVADA	0.42	0.32	0.28	0.25	0.25	0.24	0.22	0.20	0.19	0.18	0.17	0.16	0.16	0.14
NEW HAMPSHIRE	*	*	*	*	*	*	*	*	*	*	*	*	*	*
NEW JERSEY	*	*	*	*	*	*	*	*	*	*	*	*	*	*
NEW MEXICO	0.10	0.07	0.07	0.06	0.06	0.05	0.05	0.05	0.04	0.04	0.04	0.04	0.03	0.03
NEW YORK	2.13	1.63	1.45	1.37	1.37	1.34	1.25	1.24	1.16	1.12	1.11	1.10	1.08	0.91
NORTH CAROLINA	1.18	0.75	0.66	0.56	0.55	0.50	0.48	0.43	0.41	0.37	0.34	0.34	0.31	0.27
NORTH DAKOTA	*	*	*	*	*	*	*	*	*	*	*	*	*	*
OHIO	0.14	0.11	0.11	0.10	0.10	0.10	0.09	0.09	0.09	0.08	0.08	0.08	0.08	0.07
OKLAHOMA	1.96	1.13	0.99	0.92	0.87	0.78	0.71	0.67	0.60	0.54	0.51	0.47	0.45	0.40
OREGON	*	*	*	*	*	*	*	*	*	*	*	*	*	*
PENNSYLVANIA	*	*	*	*	*	*	*	*	*	*	*	*	*	*
RHODE ISLAND	*	*	*	*	*	*	*	*	*	*	*	*	*	*
SOUTH CAROLINA	*	*	*	*	*	*	*	*	*	*	*	*	*	*
SOUTH DAKOTA	0.58	0.39	0.36	0.33	0.31	0.29	0.27	0.27	0.25	0.24	0.22	0.22	0.21	0.19
TENNESSEE	2.00	1.31	1.14	1.05	0.95	0.92	0.83	0.78	0.72	0.65	0.61	0.57	0.57	0.43
TEXAS	0.77	0.54	0.47	0.45	0.43	0.40	0.39	0.37	0.34	0.32	0.31	0.29	0.28	0.24
UTAH	1.13	0.76	0.64	0.57	0.61	0.53	0.49	0.47	0.43	0.40	0.38	0.36	0.35	0.32
VERMONT	*	*	*	*	*	*	*	*	*	*	*	*	*	*
VIRGINIA	1.22	0.70	0.65	0.60	0.53	0.50	0.49	0.44	0.40	0.37	0.34	0.32	0.30	0.26
WASHINGTON	0.67	0.46	0.39	0.36	0.33	0.34	0.31	0.30	0.28	0.26	0.25	0.25	0.22	0.21
WEST VIRGINIA	*	*	*	*	*	*	*	*	*	*	*	*	*	*
WISCONSIN	*	*	*	*	*	*	*	*	*	*	*	*	*	*
WYOMING	0.31	0.23	0.21	0.20	0.18	0.18	0.16	0.16	0.15	0.13	0.13	0.13	0.13	0.11
AVERAGE	1.07	0.72	0.63	0.59	0.56	0.52	0.49	0.46	0.43	0.40	0.38	0.36	0.35	0.30

* EFFECTIVE TAX RATE EQUALS ZERO BEFORE ROUNDING. AN ENTIRE ROW OF * MEANS THAT THIS TAX IS NOT USED IN THIS STATE.

TABLE A-42

EFFECTIVE TAX RATES: LOCAL SELECTIVE SALES AND GROSS RECEIPTS TAXES-TOBACCO
INCIDENCE: CONSUMERS OF TOBACCO PRODUCTS
ALLOCATOR: TOBACCO PRODUCTS EXPENDITURES

STATE	UNDER $3,000	$3,000 -3,999	$4,000 -4,999	$5,000 -5,999	$6,000 -6,999	$7,000 -7,999	$8,000 -9,999	$10,000 -11,999	$12,000 -14,999	$15,000 -19,999	$20,000 -24,999	$25,000 -29,999	$30,000 -34,999	OVER $35,000
ALABAMA	0.22	0.12	0.09	0.08	0.07	0.06	0.06	0.05	0.04	0.03	0.03	0.03	0.02	0.02
ALASKA	*	*	*	*	*	*	*	*	*	*	*	*	*	*
ARIZONA	*	*	*	*	*	*	*	*	*	*	*	*	*	*
ARKANSAS	*	*	*	*	*	*	*	*	*	*	*	*	*	*
CALIFORNIA	*	*	*	*	*	*	*	*	*	*	*	*	*	*
COLORADO	*	*	*	*	*	*	*	*	*	*	*	*	*	*
CONNECTICUT	*	*	*	*	*	*	*	*	*	*	*	*	*	*
DELAWARE	*	*	*	*	*	*	*	*	*	*	*	*	*	*
FLORIDA	*	*	*	*	*	*	*	*	*	*	*	*	*	*
GEORGIA	*	*	*	*	*	*	*	*	*	*	*	*	*	*
HAWAII	*	*	*	*	*	*	*	*	*	*	*	*	*	*
IDAHO	*	*	*	*	*	*	*	*	*	*	*	*	*	*
ILLINOIS	0.09	0.05	0.05	0.04	0.04	0.03	0.03	0.03	0.02	0.02	0.02	0.02	0.02	0.01
INDIANA	*	*	*	*	*	*	*	*	*	*	*	*	*	*
IOWA	*	*	*	*	*	*	*	*	*	*	*	*	*	*
KANSAS	*	*	*	*	*	*	*	*	*	*	*	*	*	*
KENTUCKY	*	*	*	*	*	*	*	*	*	*	*	*	*	*
LOUISIANA	*	*	*	*	*	*	*	*	*	*	*	*	*	*
MAINE	*	*	*	*	*	*	*	*	*	*	*	*	*	*
MARYLAND	*	*	*	*	*	*	*	*	*	*	*	*	*	*
MASSACHUSETTS	*	*	*	*	*	*	*	*	*	*	*	*	*	*
MICHIGAN	*	*	*	*	*	*	*	*	*	*	*	*	*	*
MINNESOTA	*	*	*	*	*	*	*	*	*	*	*	*	*	*
MISSISSIPPI	*	*	*	*	*	*	*	*	*	*	*	*	*	*
MISSOURI	0.29	0.15	0.14	0.12	0.10	0.10	0.09	0.08	0.07	0.06	0.05	0.05	0.04	0.04
MONTANA	*	*	*	*	*	*	*	*	*	*	*	*	*	*
NEBRASKA	*	*	*	*	*	*	*	*	*	*	*	*	*	*
NEVADA	*	*	*	*	*	*	*	*	*	*	*	*	*	*
NEW HAMPSHIRE	*	*	*	*	*	*	*	*	*	*	*	*	*	*
NEW JERSEY	0.00	0.00	0.00	0.00	0.00	0.00	0.00	0.00	0.00	0.00	0.00	0.00	0.00	0.00
NEW MEXICO	*	*	*	*	*	*	*	*	*	*	*	*	*	*
NEW YORK	0.18	0.10	0.08	0.07	0.07	0.06	0.05	0.05	0.04	0.04	0.03	0.03	0.03	0.02
NORTH CAROLINA	*	*	*	*	*	*	*	*	*	*	*	*	*	*
NORTH DAKOTA	*	*	*	*	*	*	*	*	*	*	*	*	*	*
OHIO	*	*	*	*	*	*	*	*	*	*	*	*	*	*
OKLAHOMA	*	*	*	*	*	*	*	*	*	*	*	*	*	*
OREGON	*	*	*	*	*	*	*	*	*	*	*	*	*	*
PENNSYLVANIA	*	*	*	*	*	*	*	*	*	*	*	*	*	*
RHODE ISLAND	*	*	*	*	*	*	*	*	*	*	*	*	*	*
SOUTH CAROLINA	*	*	*	*	*	*	*	*	*	*	*	*	*	*
SOUTH DAKOTA	*	*	*	*	*	*	*	*	*	*	*	*	*	*
TENNESSEE	0.02	0.01	0.01	0.01	0.01	0.01	0.01	0.00	0.00	0.00	0.00	0.00	0.00	0.00
TEXAS	*	*	*	*	*	*	*	*	*	*	*	*	*	*
UTAH	*	*	*	*	*	*	*	*	*	*	*	*	*	*
VERMONT	*	*	*	*	*	*	*	*	*	*	*	*	*	*
VIRGINIA	0.24	0.12	0.10	0.09	0.07	0.07	0.06	0.05	0.04	0.04	0.03	0.03	0.02	0.02
WASHINGTON	*	*	*	*	*	*	*	*	*	*	*	*	*	*
WEST VIRGINIA	*	*	*	*	*	*	*	*	*	*	*	*	*	*
WISCONSIN	*	*	*	*	*	*	*	*	*	*	*	*	*	*
WYOMING	*	*	*	*	*	*	*	*	*	*	*	*	*	*
AVERAGE	0.15	0.08	0.07	0.06	0.05	0.05	0.04	0.04	0.03	0.03	0.02	0.02	0.02	0.02

* EFFECTIVE TAX RATE EQUALS ZERO BEFORE ROUNDING. AN ENTIRE ROW OF * MEANS THAT THIS TAX IS NOT USED IN THIS STATE.

TABLE A-43
EFFECTIVE TAX RATES: LOCAL SELECTIVE SALES AND GROSS RECEIPTS TAXES-ALCOHOL
INCIDENCE: CONSUMERS OF ALCOHOLIC BEVERAGES
ALLOCATOR: ALCOHOLIC BEVERAGES EXPENDITURES

STATE	UNDER $3,000	$3,000 -3,999	$4,000 -4,999	$5,000 -5,999	$6,000 -6,999	$7,000 -7,999	$8,000 -9,999	$10,000 -11,999	$12,000 -14,999	$15,000 -19,999	$20,000 -24,999	$25,000 -29,999	$30,000 -34,999	OVER $35,000
ALABAMA	0.12	0.10	0.09	0.09	0.08	0.09	0.08	0.08	0.08	0.08	0.08	0.07	0.08	0.07
ALASKA	*	*	*	*	*	*	*	*	*	*	*	*	*	*
ARIZONA	*	*	*	*	*	*	*	*	*	*	*	*	*	*
ARKANSAS	0.01	0.01	0.01	0.01	0.01	0.01	0.01	0.01	0.01	0.01	0.01	0.01	0.01	0.01
CALIFORNIA	*	*	*	*	*	*	*	*	*	*	*	*	*	*
COLORADO	*	*	*	*	*	*	*	*	*	*	*	*	*	*
CONNECTICUT	*	*	*	*	*	*	*	*	*	*	*	*	*	*
DELAWARE	*	*	*	*	*	*	*	*	*	*	*	*	*	*
FLORIDA	*	*	*	*	*	*	*	*	*	*	*	*	*	*
GEORGIA	0.28	0.21	0.21	0.20	0.20	0.20	0.19	0.18	0.18	0.18	0.17	0.17	0.17	0.16
HAWAII	*	*	*	*	*	*	*	*	*	*	*	*	*	*
IDAHO	*	*	*	*	*	*	*	*	*	*	*	*	*	*
ILLINOIS	*	*	*	*	*	*	*	*	*	*	*	*	*	*
INDIANA	*	*	*	*	*	*	*	*	*	*	*	*	*	*
IOWA	*	*	*	*	*	*	*	*	*	*	*	*	*	*
KANSAS	*	*	*	*	*	*	*	*	*	*	*	*	*	*
KENTUCKY	*	*	*	*	*	*	*	*	*	*	*	*	*	*
LOUISIANA	0.03	0.02	0.02	0.02	0.02	0.02	0.02	0.02	0.02	0.02	0.02	0.02	0.02	0.02
MAINE	*	*	*	*	*	*	*	*	*	*	*	*	*	*
MARYLAND	0.00	0.00	0.00	0.00	0.00	0.00	0.00	0.00	0.00	0.00	0.00	0.00	0.00	0.00
MASSACHUSETTS	*	*	*	*	*	*	*	*	*	*	*	*	*	*
MICHIGAN	*	*	*	*	*	*	*	*	*	*	*	*	*	*
MINNESOTA	*	*	*	*	*	*	*	*	*	*	*	*	*	*
MISSISSIPPI	*	*	*	*	*	*	*	*	*	*	*	*	*	*
MISSOURI	*	*	*	*	*	*	*	*	*	*	*	*	*	*
MONTANA	*	*	*	*	*	*	*	*	*	*	*	*	*	*
NEBRASKA	*	*	*	*	*	*	*	*	*	*	*	*	*	*
NEVADA	*	*	*	*	*	*	*	*	*	*	*	*	*	*
NEW HAMPSHIRE	*	*	*	*	*	*	*	*	*	*	*	*	*	*
NEW JERSEY	*	*	*	*	*	*	*	*	*	*	*	*	*	*
NEW MEXICO	*	*	*	*	*	*	*	*	*	*	*	*	*	*
NEW YORK	*	*	*	*	*	*	*	*	*	*	*	*	*	*
NORTH CAROLINA	*	*	*	*	*	*	*	*	*	*	*	*	*	*
NORTH DAKOTA	*	*	*	*	*	*	*	*	*	*	*	*	*	*
OHIO	*	*	*	*	*	*	*	*	*	*	*	*	*	*
OKLAHOMA	*	*	*	*	*	*	*	*	*	*	*	*	*	*
OREGON	*	*	*	*	*	*	*	*	*	*	*	*	*	*
PENNSYLVANIA	*	*	*	*	*	*	*	*	*	*	*	*	*	*
RHODE ISLAND	*	*	*	*	*	*	*	*	*	*	*	*	*	*
SOUTH CAROLINA	*	*	*	*	*	*	*	*	*	*	*	*	*	*
SOUTH DAKOTA	*	*	*	*	*	*	*	*	*	*	*	*	*	*
TENNESSEE	0.22	0.18	0.17	0.17	0.16	0.16	0.15	0.15	0.15	0.14	0.14	0.14	0.14	0.13
TEXAS	*	*	*	*	*	*	*	*	*	*	*	*	*	*
UTAH	*	*	*	*	*	*	*	*	*	*	*	*	*	*
VERMONT	*	*	*	*	*	*	*	*	*	*	*	*	*	*
VIRGINIA	*	*	*	*	*	*	*	*	*	*	*	*	*	*
WASHINGTON	*	*	*	*	*	*	*	*	*	*	*	*	*	*
WEST VIRGINIA	0.04	0.03	0.03	0.02	0.02	0.02	0.02	0.02	0.02	0.02	0.02	0.02	0.02	0.02
WISCONSIN	*	*	*	*	*	*	*	*	*	*	*	*	*	*
WYOMING	*	*	*	*	*	*	*	*	*	*	*	*	*	*
AVERAGE	0.10	0.08	0.07	0.07	0.07	0.07	0.07	0.07	0.06	0.06	0.06	0.06	0.06	0.06

* EFFECTIVE TAX RATE EQUALS ZERO BEFORE ROUNDING. AN ENTIRE ROW OF * MEANS THAT THIS TAX IS NOT USED IN THIS STATE.

TABLE A-44
EFFECTIVE TAX RATES: LOCAL SELECTIVE SALES AND GROSS RECEIPTS TAXES-MOTOR FUELS
INCIDENCE: 1/3 CONSUMERS IN GENERAL, 2/3 HOUSEHOLDS CONSUMING GASOLINE
ALLOCATOR: CONSUMPTION AND GASOLINE EXPENDITURES

STATE	UNDER $3,000	$3,000 -3,999	$4,000 -4,999	$5,000 -5,999	$6,000 -6,999	$7,000 -7,999	$8,000 -9,999	$10,000 -11,999	$12,000 -14,999	$15,000 -19,999	$20,000 -24,999	$25,000 -29,999	$30,000 -34,999	OVER $35,000
ALABAMA	0.37	0.22	0.18	0.16	0.14	0.13	0.12	0.11	0.09	0.08	0.08	0.07	0.07	0.05
ALASKA	*	*	*	*	*	*	*	*	*	*	*	*	*	*
ARIZONA	*	*	*	*	*	*	*	*	*	*	*	*	*	*
ARKANSAS	0.00	0.00	0.00	0.00	0.00	0.00	0.00	0.00	0.00	0.00	0.00	0.00	0.00	0.00
CALIFORNIA	*	*	*	*	*	*	*	*	*	*	*	*	*	*
COLORADO	*	*	*	*	*	*	*	*	*	*	*	*	*	*
CONNECTICUT	*	*	*	*	*	*	*	*	*	*	*	*	*	*
DELAWARE	*	*	*	*	*	*	*	*	*	*	*	*	*	*
FLORIDA	*	*	*	*	*	*	*	*	*	*	*	*	*	*
GEORGIA	*	*	*	*	*	*	*	*	*	*	*	*	*	*
HAWAII	0.45	0.30	0.29	0.26	0.24	0.22	0.20	0.18	0.16	0.15	0.13	0.13	0.12	0.12
IDAHO	*	*	*	*	*	*	*	*	*	*	*	*	*	*
ILLINOIS	0.00	0.00	0.00	0.00	0.00	0.00	0.00	0.00	0.00	0.00	0.00	0.00	0.00	0.00
INDIANA	*	*	*	*	*	*	*	*	*	*	*	*	*	*
IOWA	*	*	*	*	*	*	*	*	*	*	*	*	*	*
KANSAS	*	*	*	*	*	*	*	*	*	*	*	*	*	*
KENTUCKY	*	*	*	*	*	*	*	*	*	*	*	*	*	*
LOUISIANA	*	*	*	*	*	*	*	*	*	*	*	*	*	*
MAINE	*	*	*	*	*	*	*	*	*	*	*	*	*	*
MARYLAND	*	*	*	*	*	*	*	*	*	*	*	*	*	*
MASSACHUSETTS	*	*	*	*	*	*	*	*	*	*	*	*	*	*
MICHIGAN	*	*	*	*	*	*	*	*	*	*	*	*	*	*
MINNESOTA	*	*	*	*	*	*	*	*	*	*	*	*	*	*
MISSISSIPPI	0.09	0.05	0.04	0.04	0.03	0.03	0.03	0.03	0.02	0.02	0.02	0.02	0.02	0.01
MISSOURI	*	*	*	*	*	*	*	*	*	*	*	*	*	*
MONTANA	*	*	*	*	*	*	*	*	*	*	*	*	*	*
NEBRASKA	*	*	*	*	*	*	*	*	*	*	*	*	*	*
NEVADA	0.42	0.28	0.24	0.21	0.20	0.18	0.16	0.14	0.13	0.12	0.10	0.10	0.10	0.08
NEW HAMPSHIRE	*	*	*	*	*	*	*	*	*	*	*	*	*	*
NEW JERSEY	*	*	*	*	*	*	*	*	*	*	*	*	*	*
NEW MEXICO	*	*	*	*	*	*	*	*	*	*	*	*	*	*
NEW YORK	0.01	0.01	0.01	0.01	0.01	0.01	0.00	0.00	0.00	0.00	0.00	0.00	0.00	0.00
NORTH CAROLINA	*	*	*	*	*	*	*	*	*	*	*	*	*	*
NORTH DAKOTA	*	*	*	*	*	*	*	*	*	*	*	*	*	*
OHIO	*	*	*	*	*	*	*	*	*	*	*	*	*	*
OKLAHOMA	*	*	*	*	*	*	*	*	*	*	*	*	*	*
OREGON	*	*	*	*	*	*	*	*	*	*	*	*	*	*
PENNSYLVANIA	*	*	*	*	*	*	*	*	*	*	*	*	*	*
RHODE ISLAND	*	*	*	*	*	*	*	*	*	*	*	*	*	*
SOUTH CAROLINA	*	*	*	*	*	*	*	*	*	*	*	*	*	*
SOUTH DAKOTA	*	*	*	*	*	*	*	*	*	*	*	*	*	*
TENNESSEE	*	*	*	*	*	*	*	*	*	*	*	*	*	*
TEXAS	*	*	*	*	*	*	*	*	*	*	*	*	*	*
UTAH	*	*	*	*	*	*	*	*	*	*	*	*	*	*
VERMONT	*	*	*	*	*	*	*	*	*	*	*	*	*	*
VIRGINIA	*	*	*	*	*	*	*	*	*	*	*	*	*	*
WASHINGTON	*	*	*	*	*	*	*	*	*	*	*	*	*	*
WEST VIRGINIA	*	*	*	*	*	*	*	*	*	*	*	*	*	*
WISCONSIN	*	*	*	*	*	*	*	*	*	*	*	*	*	*
WYOMING	*	*	*	*	*	*	*	*	*	*	*	*	*	*
AVERAGE	0.19	0.12	0.11	0.10	0.09	0.08	0.07	0.07	0.06	0.05	0.05	0.05	0.04	0.04

* EFFECTIVE TAX RATE EQUALS ZERO BEFORE ROUNDING. AN ENTIRE ROW OF * MEANS THAT THIS TAX IS NOT USED IN THIS STATE.

TABLE A-45
EFFECTIVE TAX RATES: LOCAL SELECTIVE SALES AND GROSS RECEIPTS TAXES-UTILITIES
INCIDENCE: CONSUMERS OF UTILITY SERVICES
ALLOCATOR: GAS, ELECTRIC, AND TELEPHONE EXPENDITURES

STATE	UNDER $3,000	$3,000 -3,999	$4,000 -4,999	$5,000 -5,999	$6,000 -6,999	$7,000 -7,999	$8,000 -9,999	$10,000 -11,999	$12,000 -14,999	$15,000 -19,999	$20,000 -24,999	$25,000 -29,999	$30,000 -34,999	OVER $35,000
ALABAMA	0.14	0.08	0.07	0.06	0.05	0.05	0.04	0.04	0.03	0.03	0.03	0.02	0.02	0.02
ALASKA	0.04	0.03	0.02	0.02	0.02	0.02	0.02	0.01	0.01	0.01	0.01	0.01	0.01	0.01
ARIZONA	0.33	0.19	0.15	0.14	0.12	0.11	0.10	0.09	0.08	0.07	0.06	0.06	0.06	0.05
ARKANSAS	0.34	0.19	0.16	0.14	0.13	0.12	0.11	0.09	0.08	0.07	0.07	0.06	0.06	0.05
CALIFORNIA	0.51	0.32	0.26	0.23	0.21	0.19	0.17	0.15	0.14	0.12	0.11	0.10	0.10	0.08
COLORADO	0.31	0.19	0.15	0.14	0.13	0.11	0.10	0.09	0.08	0.07	0.07	0.06	0.06	0.05
CONNECTICUT	*	*	*	*	*	*	*	*	*	*	*	*	*	*
DELAWARE	0.01	0.01	0.01	0.00	0.00	0.00	0.00	0.00	0.00	0.00	0.00	0.00	0.00	0.00
FLORIDA	1.49	0.86	0.70	0.61	0.57	0.52	0.46	0.41	0.37	0.32	0.29	0.26	0.24	0.21
GEORGIA	0.30	0.16	0.14	0.13	0.11	0.11	0.09	0.08	0.07	0.07	0.06	0.05	0.05	0.04
HAWAII	0.30	0.19	0.18	0.16	0.14	0.13	0.12	0.11	0.10	0.09	0.08	0.08	0.07	0.06
IDAHO	0.08	0.04	0.04	0.03	0.03	0.03	0.03	0.02	0.02	0.02	0.02	0.01	0.01	0.01
ILLINOIS	0.66	0.42	0.35	0.32	0.28	0.26	0.23	0.21	0.19	0.17	0.15	0.14	0.14	0.12
INDIANA	*	*	*	*	*	*	*	*	*	*	*	*	*	*
IOWA	0.03	0.02	0.02	0.01	0.01	0.01	0.01	0.01	0.01	0.01	0.01	0.01	0.01	0.01
KANSAS	0.34	0.20	0.17	0.14	0.13	0.12	0.11	0.10	0.09	0.08	0.07	0.07	0.06	0.05
KENTUCKY	0.72	0.41	0.35	0.29	0.27	0.25	0.23	0.20	0.18	0.16	0.14	0.13	0.13	0.10
LOUISIANA	0.21	0.11	0.09	0.09	0.08	0.07	0.07	0.06	0.05	0.05	0.04	0.04	0.04	0.03
MAINE	*	*	*	*	*	*	*	*	*	*	*	*	*	*
MARYLAND	0.58	0.34	0.28	0.23	0.22	0.20	0.18	0.16	0.14	0.13	0.11	0.11	0.10	0.08
MASSACHUSETTS	*	*	*	*	*	*	*	*	*	*	*	*	*	*
MICHIGAN	0.16	0.10	0.08	0.07	0.06	0.06	0.05	0.05	0.04	0.04	0.03	0.03	0.03	0.02
MINNESOTA	0.20	0.12	0.10	0.09	0.08	0.08	0.06	0.06	0.05	0.05	0.04	0.04	0.04	0.03
MISSISSIPPI	0.17	0.10	0.08	0.07	0.06	0.06	0.05	0.05	0.04	0.04	0.03	0.03	0.03	0.02
MISSOURI	1.30	0.69	0.65	0.54	0.49	0.45	0.40	0.36	0.31	0.28	0.25	0.24	0.22	0.19
MONTANA	*	*	*	*	*	*	*	*	*	*	*	*	*	*
NEBRASKA	0.14	0.08	0.06	0.06	0.05	0.05	0.04	0.04	0.04	0.03	0.03	0.03	0.02	0.02
NEVADA	0.38	0.24	0.20	0.17	0.17	0.15	0.14	0.12	0.11	0.09	0.08	0.08	0.08	0.06
NEW HAMPSHIRE	*	*	*	*	*	*	*	*	*	*	*	*	*	*
NEW JERSEY	1.72	1.09	0.95	0.84	0.77	0.74	0.66	0.60	0.54	0.49	0.44	0.42	0.39	0.34
NEW MEXICO	0.23	0.14	0.12	0.10	0.10	0.09	0.08	0.07	0.06	0.05	0.05	0.04	0.04	0.04
NEW YORK	0.34	0.20	0.16	0.14	0.13	0.12	0.11	0.10	0.09	0.08	0.07	0.07	0.07	0.05
NORTH CAROLINA	*	*	*	*	*	*	*	*	*	*	*	*	*	*
NORTH DAKOTA	0.08	0.04	0.04	0.03	0.03	0.03	0.02	0.02	0.02	0.02	0.02	0.02	0.01	0.01
OHIO	0.00	0.00	0.00	0.00	0.00	0.00	0.00	0.00	0.00	0.00	0.00	0.00	0.00	0.00
OKLAHOMA	0.36	0.19	0.16	0.14	0.13	0.12	0.10	0.09	0.08	0.07	0.06	0.06	0.06	0.05
OREGON	0.32	0.19	0.16	0.14	0.12	0.12	0.10	0.09	0.08	0.07	0.07	0.06	0.06	0.05
PENNSYLVANIA	*	*	*	*	*	*	*	*	*	*	*	*	*	*
RHODE ISLAND	*	*	*	*	*	*	*	*	*	*	*	*	*	*
SOUTH CAROLINA	0.01	0.01	0.01	0.01	0.00	0.00	0.00	0.00	0.00	0.00	0.00	0.00	0.00	0.00
SOUTH DAKOTA	0.01	0.01	0.01	0.00	0.00	0.00	0.00	0.00	0.00	0.00	0.00	0.00	0.00	0.00
TENNESSEE	0.10	0.06	0.05	0.04	0.04	0.04	0.03	0.03	0.02	0.02	0.02	0.02	0.02	0.01
TEXAS	0.35	0.21	0.17	0.15	0.14	0.12	0.11	0.10	0.09	0.08	0.07	0.06	0.06	0.05
UTAH	0.23	0.13	0.11	0.09	0.09	0.08	0.07	0.07	0.06	0.05	0.05	0.04	0.04	0.03
VERMONT	*	*	*	*	*	*	*	*	*	*	*	*	*	*
VIRGINIA	1.33	0.69	0.61	0.54	0.47	0.43	0.40	0.35	0.31	0.27	0.25	0.23	0.21	0.18
WASHINGTON	0.69	0.40	0.32	0.29	0.25	0.24	0.22	0.20	0.18	0.15	0.14	0.13	0.12	0.10
WEST VIRGINIA	0.17	0.10	0.08	0.07	0.06	0.06	0.05	0.05	0.04	0.04	0.03	0.03	0.03	0.02
WISCONSIN	*	*	*	*	*	*	*	*	*	*	*	*	*	*
WYOMING	0.12	0.08	0.07	0.06	0.06	0.05	0.05	0.04	0.04	0.03	0.03	0.03	0.03	0.02
AVERAGE	0.38	0.22	0.19	0.16	0.15	0.14	0.12	0.11	0.10	0.09	0.08	0.07	0.07	0.06

* EFFECTIVE TAX RATE EQUALS ZERO BEFORE ROUNDING. AN ENTIRE ROW OF * MEANS THAT THIS TAX IS NOT USED IN THIS STATE.

TABLE A-46

EFFECTIVE TAX RATES: LOCAL SELECTIVE SALES AND GROSS RECEIPTS TAXES-OTHER N.E.C.
INCIDENCE: CONSUMERS IN GENERAL
ALLOCATOR: TOTAL CONSUMPTION EXPENDITURES

STATE	UNDER $3,000	$3,000 -3,999	$4,000 -4,999	$5,000 -5,999	$6,000 -6,999	$7,000 -7,999	$8,000 -9,999	$10,000 -11,999	$12,000 -14,999	$15,000 -19,999	$20,000 -24,999	$25,000 -29,999	$30,000 -34,999	OVER $35,000
ALABAMA	0.03	0.02	0.02	0.01	0.01	0.01	0.01	0.01	0.01	0.01	0.01	0.01	0.01	0.01
ALASKA	*	*	*	*	*	*	*	*	*	*	*	*	*	*
ARIZONA	0.11	0.07	0.05	0.05	0.04	0.04	0.04	0.03	0.03	0.03	0.02	0.02	0.02	0.02
ARKANSAS	0.03	0.02	0.01	0.01	0.01	0.01	0.01	0.01	0.01	0.01	0.01	0.01	0.01	0.01
CALIFORNIA	0.14	0.09	0.08	0.07	0.06	0.06	0.05	0.05	0.04	0.04	0.04	0.03	0.03	0.03
COLORADO	0.08	0.05	0.04	0.03	0.03	0.03	0.03	0.03	0.02	0.02	0.02	0.02	0.02	0.01
CONNECTICUT	*	*	*	*	*	*	*	*	*	*	*	*	*	*
DELAWARE	*	*	*	*	*	*	*	*	*	*	*	*	*	*
FLORIDA	0.08	0.05	0.04	0.04	0.03	0.03	0.03	0.03	0.03	0.02	0.02	0.02	0.02	0.02
GEORGIA	0.14	0.08	0.07	0.07	0.06	0.06	0.05	0.05	0.05	0.04	0.04	0.04	0.04	0.03
HAWAII	*	*	*	*	*	*	*	*	*	*	*	*	*	*
IDAHO	*	*	*	*	*	*	*	*	*	*	*	*	*	*
ILLINOIS	0.05	0.04	0.03	0.03	0.03	0.02	0.02	0.02	0.02	0.02	0.02	0.02	0.02	0.01
INDIANA	0.01	0.01	0.01	0.00	0.00	0.00	0.00	0.00	0.00	0.00	0.00	0.00	0.00	0.00
IOWA	*	*	*	*	*	*	*	*	*	*	*	*	*	*
KANSAS	*	*	*	*	*	*	*	*	*	*	*	*	*	*
KENTUCKY	0.13	0.08	0.07	0.06	0.06	0.05	0.05	0.05	0.04	0.04	0.04	0.04	0.03	0.03
LOUISIANA	0.07	0.04	0.04	0.03	0.03	0.03	0.03	0.03	0.02	0.02	0.02	0.02	0.02	0.02
MAINE	*	*	*	*	*	*	*	*	*	*	*	*	*	*
MARYLAND	0.23	0.15	0.13	0.11	0.10	0.09	0.09	0.08	0.08	0.07	0.06	0.06	0.06	0.05
MASSACHUSETTS	*	*	*	*	*	*	*	*	*	*	*	*	*	*
MICHIGAN	*	*	*	*	*	*	*	*	*	*	*	*	*	*
MINNESOTA	0.04	0.03	0.02	0.02	0.02	0.02	0.02	0.02	0.01	0.01	0.01	0.01	0.01	0.01
MISSISSIPPI	*	*	*	*	*	*	*	*	*	*	*	*	*	*
MISSOURI	0.03	0.02	0.02	0.01	0.01	0.01	0.01	0.01	0.01	0.01	0.01	0.01	0.01	0.01
MONTANA	*	*	*	*	*	*	*	*	*	*	*	*	*	*
NEBRASKA	*	*	*	*	*	*	*	*	*	*	*	*	*	*
NEVADA	0.87	0.58	0.49	0.43	0.42	0.38	0.34	0.31	0.28	0.25	0.23	0.22	0.21	0.18
NEW HAMPSHIRE	*	*	*	*	*	*	*	*	*	*	*	*	*	*
NEW JERSEY	0.07	0.05	0.04	0.04	0.04	0.04	0.03	0.03	0.03	0.03	0.02	0.02	0.02	0.02
NEW MEXICO	0.06	0.04	0.04	0.03	0.03	0.03	0.02	0.02	0.02	0.02	0.02	0.02	0.01	0.01
NEW YORK	0.76	0.47	0.39	0.35	0.34	0.32	0.29	0.28	0.25	0.23	0.22	0.21	0.21	0.18
NORTH CAROLINA	*	*	*	*	*	*	*	*	*	*	*	*	*	*
NORTH DAKOTA	*	*	*	*	*	*	*	*	*	*	*	*	*	*
OHIO	0.02	0.02	0.01	0.01	0.01	0.01	0.01	0.01	0.01	0.01	0.01	0.01	0.01	0.01
OKLAHOMA	0.02	0.01	0.01	0.01	0.01	0.01	0.01	0.01	0.01	0.01	0.01	0.00	0.00	0.00
OREGON	0.07	0.04	0.04	0.03	0.03	0.03	0.02	0.02	0.02	0.02	0.02	0.02	0.01	0.01
PENNSYLVANIA	0.04	0.03	0.02	0.02	0.02	0.02	0.02	0.02	0.01	0.01	0.01	0.01	0.01	0.01
RHODE ISLAND	*	*	*	*	*	*	*	*	*	*	*	*	*	*
SOUTH CAROLINA	*	*	*	*	*	*	*	*	*	*	*	*	*	*
SOUTH DAKOTA	0.01	0.01	0.00	0.00	0.00	0.00	0.00	0.00	0.00	0.00	0.00	0.00	0.00	0.00
TENNESSEE	0.04	0.03	0.02	0.02	0.02	0.02	0.02	0.02	0.01	0.01	0.01	0.01	0.01	0.01
TEXAS	0.07	0.05	0.04	0.04	0.03	0.03	0.03	0.03	0.02	0.02	0.02	0.02	0.02	0.02
UTAH	0.04	0.02	0.02	0.02	0.02	0.01	0.01	0.01	0.01	0.01	0.01	0.01	0.01	0.01
VERMONT	*	*	*	*	*	*	*	*	*	*	*	*	*	*
VIRGINIA	0.15	0.08	0.07	0.07	0.06	0.06	0.05	0.05	0.04	0.04	0.04	0.04	0.03	0.03
WASHINGTON	0.66	0.40	0.33	0.29	0.26	0.26	0.23	0.21	0.19	0.17	0.16	0.15	0.14	0.13
WEST VIRGINIA	*	*	*	*	*	*	*	*	*	*	*	*	*	*
WISCONSIN	0.02	0.01	0.01	0.01	0.01	0.01	0.01	0.01	0.01	0.00	0.00	0.00	0.00	0.00
WYOMING	*	*	*	*	*	*	*	*	*	*	*	*	*	*
AVERAGE	0.14	0.09	0.07	0.07	0.06	0.06	0.05	0.05	0.04	0.04	0.04	0.04	0.03	0.03

* EFFECTIVE TAX RATE EQUALS ZERO BEFORE ROUNDING. AN ENTIRE ROW OF * MEANS THAT THIS TAX IS NOT USED IN THIS STATE.

TABLE A-47
EFFECTIVE TAX RATES: LOCAL LICENSE TAX ON MOTOR VEHICLES (BENCHMARK)
INCIDENCE: 1/4 CONSUMERS, 3/4 DRIVERS
ALLOCATOR: CONSUMPTION AND VEHICLE OPERATIONS EXPENDITURES

STATE	UNDER $3,000	$3,000 -3,999	$4,000 -4,999	$5,000 -5,999	$6,000 -6,999	$7,000 -7,999	$8,000 -9,999	$10,000 -11,999	$12,000 -14,999	$15,000 -19,999	$20,000 -24,999	$25,000 -29,999	$30,000 -34,999	OVER $35,000
ALABAMA	0.14	0.08	0.07	0.06	0.06	0.05	0.05	0.05	0.04	0.04	0.03	0.03	0.03	0.03
ALASKA	*	*	*	*	*	*	*	*	*	*	*	*	*	*
ARIZONA	0.04	0.03	0.02	0.02	0.02	0.02	0.01	0.01	0.01	0.01	0.01	0.01	0.01	0.01
ARKANSAS	0.00	0.00	0.00	0.00	0.00	0.00	0.00	0.00	0.00	0.00	0.00	0.00	0.00	0.00
CALIFORNIA	*	*	*	*	*	*	*	*	*	*	*	*	*	*
COLORADO	0.11	0.07	0.06	0.05	0.05	0.05	0.04	0.04	0.04	0.03	0.03	0.03	0.03	0.02
CONNECTICUT	*	*	*	*	*	*	*	*	*	*	*	*	*	*
DELAWARE	*	*	*	*	*	*	*	*	*	*	*	*	*	*
FLORIDA	0.06	0.04	0.03	0.03	0.03	0.02	0.02	0.02	0.02	0.02	0.02	0.01	0.01	0.01
GEORGIA	0.01	0.01	0.01	0.01	0.01	0.01	0.01	0.00	0.00	0.00	0.00	0.00	0.00	0.00
HAWAII	0.55	0.36	0.36	0.33	0.30	0.28	0.26	0.24	0.23	0.21	0.20	0.19	0.18	0.17
IDAHO	0.02	0.01	0.01	0.01	0.01	0.01	0.01	0.01	0.01	0.01	0.01	0.01	0.01	0.01
ILLINOIS	0.15	0.10	0.09	0.09	0.08	0.07	0.07	0.06	0.06	0.06	0.05	0.05	0.05	0.05
INDIANA	0.00	0.00	0.00	0.00	0.00	0.00	0.00	0.00	0.00	0.00	0.00	0.00	0.00	0.00
IOWA	0.04	0.03	0.03	0.02	0.02	0.02	0.02	0.02	0.02	0.02	0.02	0.01	0.01	0.01
KANSAS	0.01	0.01	0.01	0.01	0.01	0.01	0.01	0.01	0.01	0.00	0.00	0.00	0.00	0.00
KENTUCKY	0.08	0.05	0.04	0.04	0.03	0.03	0.03	0.03	0.02	0.02	0.02	0.02	0.02	0.02
LOUISIANA	0.01	0.01	0.01	0.01	0.01	0.00	0.00	0.00	0.00	0.00	0.00	0.00	0.00	0.00
MAINE	*	*	*	*	*	*	*	*	*	*	*	*	*	*
MARYLAND	*	*	*	*	*	*	*	*	*	*	*	*	*	*
MASSACHUSETTS	*	*	*	*	*	*	*	*	*	*	*	*	*	*
MICHIGAN	0.00	0.00	0.00	0.00	0.00	0.00	0.00	0.00	0.00	0.00	0.00	0.00	0.00	0.00
MINNESOTA	0.01	0.01	0.01	0.01	0.01	0.01	0.01	0.01	0.01	0.00	0.00	0.00	0.00	0.00
MISSISSIPPI	0.05	0.03	0.03	0.02	0.02	0.02	0.02	0.02	0.02	0.01	0.01	0.01	0.01	0.01
MISSOURI	0.07	0.04	0.04	0.03	0.03	0.03	0.03	0.03	0.02	0.02	0.02	0.02	0.02	0.02
MONTANA	0.39	0.25	0.22	0.19	0.18	0.17	0.15	0.14	0.13	0.12	0.11	0.10	0.10	0.09
NEBRASKA	0.08	0.05	0.04	0.04	0.04	0.04	0.03	0.03	0.03	0.03	0.03	0.02	0.02	0.02
NEVADA	*	*	*	*	*	*	*	*	*	*	*	*	*	*
NEW HAMPSHIRE	*	*	*	*	*	*	*	*	*	*	*	*	*	*
NEW JERSEY	*	*	*	*	*	*	*	*	*	*	*	*	*	*
NEW MEXICO	*	*	*	*	*	*	*	*	*	*	*	*	*	*
NEW YORK	0.06	0.04	0.03	0.03	0.03	0.03	0.03	0.03	0.02	0.02	0.02	0.02	0.02	0.02
NORTH CAROLINA	0.01	0.00	0.00	0.00	0.00	0.00	0.00	0.00	0.00	0.00	0.00	0.00	0.00	0.00
NORTH DAKOTA	*	*	*	*	*	*	*	*	*	*	*	*	*	*
OHIO	0.08	0.05	0.04	0.04	0.04	0.04	0.03	0.03	0.03	0.03	0.03	0.03	0.02	0.02
OKLAHOMA	*	*	*	*	*	*	*	*	*	*	*	*	*	*
OREGON	*	*	*	*	*	*	*	*	*	*	*	*	*	*
PENNSYLVANIA	*	*	*	*	*	*	*	*	*	*	*	*	*	*
RHODE ISLAND	*	*	*	*	*	*	*	*	*	*	*	*	*	*
SOUTH CAROLINA	*	*	*	*	*	*	*	*	*	*	*	*	*	*
SOUTH DAKOTA	0.49	0.31	0.28	0.25	0.24	0.22	0.20	0.20	0.18	0.17	0.16	0.16	0.15	0.14
TENNESSEE	0.12	0.07	0.06	0.06	0.05	0.05	0.04	0.04	0.04	0.03	0.03	0.03	0.03	0.02
TEXAS	0.13	0.08	0.07	0.06	0.05	0.05	0.05	0.04	0.04	0.04	0.03	0.03	0.03	0.03
UTAH	*	*	*	*	*	*	*	*	*	*	*	*	*	*
VERMONT	*	*	*	*	*	*	*	*	*	*	*	*	*	*
VIRGINIA	0.33	0.18	0.16	0.15	0.13	0.12	0.11	0.10	0.09	0.09	0.08	0.08	0.07	0.06
WASHINGTON	0.03	0.02	0.01	0.01	0.01	0.01	0.01	0.01	0.01	0.01	0.01	0.01	0.01	0.01
WEST VIRGINIA	*	*	*	*	*	*	*	*	*	*	*	*	*	*
WISCONSIN	*	*	*	*	*	*	*	*	*	*	*	*	*	*
WYOMING	*	*	*	*	*	*	*	*	*	*	*	*	*	*
AVERAGE	0.11	0.07	0.06	0.06	0.05	0.05	0.04	0.04	0.04	0.04	0.03	0.03	0.03	0.03

* EFFECTIVE TAX RATE EQUALS ZERO BEFORE ROUNDING. AN ENTIRE ROW OF * MEANS THAT THIS TAX IS NOT USED IN THIS STATE.

TABLE A-48
EFFECTIVE TAX RATES: LOCAL LICENSE TAX ON MOTOR VEHICLES
INCIDENCE: DRIVERS
ALLOCATOR: VEHICLE OPERATIONS EXPENDITURES

STATE	UNDER $3,000	$3,000 -3,999	$4,000 -4,999	$5,000 -5,999	$6,000 -6,999	$7,000 -7,999	$8,000 -9,999	$10,000 -11,999	$12,000 -14,999	$15,000 -19,999	$20,000 -24,999	$25,000 -29,999	$30,000 -34,999	OVER $35,000
ALABAMA	0.14	0.08	0.07	0.06	0.06	0.06	0.05	0.05	0.04	0.04	0.03	0.03	0.03	0.03
ALASKA	*	*	*	*	*	*	*	*	*	*	*	*	*	*
ARIZONA	0.04	0.02	0.02	0.02	0.02	0.02	0.01	0.01	0.01	0.01	0.01	0.01	0.01	0.01
ARKANSAS	0.00	0.00	0.00	0.00	0.00	0.00	0.00	0.00	0.00	0.00	0.00	0.00	0.00	0.00
CALIFORNIA	*	*	*	*	*	*	*	*	*	*	*	*	*	*
COLORADO	0.11	0.07	0.06	0.05	0.05	0.04	0.04	0.04	0.04	0.03	0.03	0.03	0.03	0.02
CONNECTICUT	*	*	*	*	*	*	*	*	*	*	*	*	*	*
DELAWARE	*	*	*	*	*	*	*	*	*	*	*	*	*	*
FLORIDA	0.06	0.04	0.03	0.03	0.03	0.02	0.02	0.02	0.02	0.02	0.02	0.01	0.01	0.01
GEORGIA	0.02	0.01	0.01	0.01	0.01	0.01	0.01	0.00	0.00	0.00	0.00	0.00	0.00	0.00
HAWAII	0.53	0.36	0.35	0.32	0.29	0.28	0.26	0.24	0.23	0.21	0.20	0.19	0.18	0.17
IDAHO	0.02	0.01	0.01	0.01	0.01	0.01	0.01	0.01	0.01	0.01	0.01	0.01	0.01	0.01
ILLINOIS	0.14	0.10	0.09	0.08	0.08	0.07	0.07	0.06	0.06	0.06	0.05	0.05	0.05	0.05
INDIANA	0.00	0.00	0.00	0.00	0.00	0.00	0.00	0.00	0.00	0.00	0.00	0.00	0.00	0.00
IOWA	0.04	0.03	0.03	0.02	0.02	0.02	0.02	0.02	0.02	0.02	0.02	0.01	0.01	0.01
KANSAS	0.01	0.01	0.01	0.01	0.01	0.01	0.01	0.01	0.01	0.00	0.00	0.00	0.00	0.00
KENTUCKY	0.08	0.05	0.04	0.04	0.03	0.03	0.03	0.03	0.02	0.02	0.02	0.02	0.02	0.02
LOUISIANA	0.01	0.01	0.01	0.01	0.01	0.00	0.00	0.00	0.00	0.00	0.00	0.00	0.00	0.00
MAINE	*	*	*	*	*	*	*	*	*	*	*	*	*	*
MARYLAND	*	*	*	*	*	*	*	*	*	*	*	*	*	*
MASSACHUSETTS	*	*	*	*	*	*	*	*	*	*	*	*	*	*
MICHIGAN	0.00	0.00	0.00	0.00	0.00	0.00	0.00	0.00	0.00	0.00	0.00	0.00	0.00	0.00
MINNESOTA	0.01	0.01	0.01	0.01	0.01	0.01	0.01	0.01	0.01	0.00	0.00	0.00	0.00	0.00
MISSISSIPPI	0.05	0.03	0.03	0.02	0.02	0.02	0.02	0.02	0.02	0.01	0.01	0.01	0.01	0.01
MISSOURI	0.07	0.04	0.04	0.03	0.03	0.03	0.03	0.03	0.02	0.02	0.02	0.02	0.02	0.02
MONTANA	0.38	0.25	0.21	0.19	0.18	0.17	0.15	0.14	0.13	0.12	0.11	0.10	0.10	0.09
NEBRASKA	0.08	0.05	0.04	0.04	0.04	0.03	0.03	0.03	0.03	0.03	0.03	0.02	0.02	0.02
NEVADA	*	*	*	*	*	*	*	*	*	*	*	*	*	*
NEW HAMPSHIRE	*	*	*	*	*	*	*	*	*	*	*	*	*	*
NEW JERSEY	*	*	*	*	*	*	*	*	*	*	*	*	*	*
NEW MEXICO	*	*	*	*	*	*	*	*	*	*	*	*	*	*
NEW YORK	0.05	0.04	0.03	0.03	0.03	0.03	0.03	0.03	0.02	0.02	0.02	0.02	0.02	0.02
NORTH CAROLINA	0.01	0.00	0.00	0.00	0.00	0.00	0.00	0.00	0.00	0.00	0.00	0.00	0.00	0.00
NORTH DAKOTA	*	*	*	*	*	*	*	*	*	*	*	*	*	*
OHIO	0.07	0.05	0.04	0.04	0.04	0.04	0.03	0.03	0.03	0.03	0.03	0.03	0.02	0.02
OKLAHOMA	*	*	*	*	*	*	*	*	*	*	*	*	*	*
OREGON	*	*	*	*	*	*	*	*	*	*	*	*	*	*
PENNSYLVANIA	*	*	*	*	*	*	*	*	*	*	*	*	*	*
RHODE ISLAND	*	*	*	*	*	*	*	*	*	*	*	*	*	*
SOUTH CAROLINA	*	*	*	*	*	*	*	*	*	*	*	*	*	*
SOUTH DAKOTA	0.47	0.30	0.27	0.25	0.24	0.22	0.20	0.20	0.18	0.17	0.17	0.16	0.15	0.14
TENNESSEE	0.12	0.07	0.06	0.06	0.05	0.05	0.04	0.04	0.04	0.03	0.03	0.03	0.03	0.02
TEXAS	0.13	0.08	0.07	0.06	0.06	0.05	0.05	0.04	0.04	0.04	0.03	0.03	0.03	0.03
UTAH	*	*	*	*	*	*	*	*	*	*	*	*	*	*
VERMONT	*	*	*	*	*	*	*	*	*	*	*	*	*	*
VIRGINIA	0.34	0.18	0.16	0.15	0.13	0.12	0.12	0.10	0.09	0.09	0.08	0.07	0.07	0.06
WASHINGTON	0.03	0.02	0.01	0.01	0.01	0.01	0.01	0.01	0.01	0.01	0.01	0.01	0.01	0.01
WEST VIRGINIA	*	*	*	*	*	*	*	*	*	*	*	*	*	*
WISCONSIN	*	*	*	*	*	*	*	*	*	*	*	*	*	*
WYOMING	*	*	*	*	*	*	*	*	*	*	*	*	*	*
AVERAGE	0.11	0.07	0.06	0.06	0.05	0.05	0.04	0.04	0.04	0.04	0.03	0.03	0.03	0.03

* EFFECTIVE TAX RATE EQUALS ZERO BEFORE ROUNDING. AN ENTIRE ROW OF * MEANS THAT THIS TAX IS NOT USED IN THIS STATE.

TABLE A-49
EFFECTIVE TAX RATES: LOCAL INCOME TAXES
INCIDENCE: TAXPAYERS
ALLOCATOR: HOUSEHOLD INCOME DISTRIBUTION

STATE	UNDER $3,000	$3,000 -3,999	$4,000 -4,999	$5,000 -5,999	$6,000 -6,999	$7,000 -7,999	$8,000 -9,999	$10,000 -11,999	$12,000 -14,999	$15,000 -19,999	$20,000 -24,999	$25,000 -29,999	$30,000 -34,999	OVER $35,000
ALABAMA	0.08	0.10	0.10	0.10	0.09	0.10	0.10	0.10	0.09	0.09	0.09	0.08	0.08	*
ALASKA	*	*	*	*	*	*	*	*	*	*	*	*	*	*
ARIZONA	*	*	*	*	*	*	*	*	*	*	*	*	*	*
ARKANSAS	*	*	*	*	*	*	*	*	*	*	*	*	*	*
CALIFORNIA	*	*	*	*	*	*	*	*	*	*	*	*	*	*
COLORADO	*	*	*	*	*	*	*	*	*	*	*	*	*	*
CONNECTICUT	*	*	*	*	*	*	*	*	*	*	*	*	*	*
DELAWARE	0.15	0.18	0.20	0.19	0.20	0.20	0.21	0.20	0.20	0.20	0.19	0.17	0.14	0.01
FLORIDA	*	*	*	*	*	*	*	*	*	*	*	*	*	*
GEORGIA	*	*	*	*	*	*	*	*	*	*	*	*	*	*
HAWAII	*	*	*	*	*	*	*	*	*	*	*	*	*	*
IDAHO	*	*	*	*	*	*	*	*	*	*	*	*	*	*
ILLINOIS	*	*	*	*	*	*	*	*	*	*	*	*	*	*
INDIANA	0.05	0.06	0.06	0.07	0.07	0.07	0.06	0.07	0.07	0.06	0.06	0.05	0.06	0.04
IOWA	*	*	*	*	*	*	*	*	*	*	*	*	*	*
KANSAS	*	*	*	*	*	*	*	*	*	*	*	*	*	*
KENTUCKY	0.42	0.50	0.52	0.51	0.52	0.53	0.54	0.53	0.48	0.49	0.49	0.47	0.41	0.10
LOUISIANA	*	*	*	*	*	*	*	*	*	*	*	*	*	*
MAINE	*	*	*	*	*	*	*	*	*	*	*	*	*	*
MARYLAND	0.88	1.09	1.12	1.07	1.13	1.14	1.16	1.13	1.08	1.06	1.00	1.05	0.87	0.69
MASSACHUSETTS	*	*	*	*	*	*	*	*	*	*	*	*	*	*
MICHIGAN	0.19	0.25	0.25	0.25	0.25	0.27	0.25	0.25	0.25	0.24	0.23	0.22	0.21	0.12
MINNESOTA	*	*	*	*	*	*	*	*	*	*	*	*	*	*
MISSISSIPPI	*	*	*	*	*	*	*	*	*	*	*	*	*	*
MISSOURI	0.21	0.23	0.26	0.26	0.27	0.27	0.27	0.27	0.26	0.24	0.24	0.24	0.19	0.09
MONTANA	*	*	*	*	*	*	*	*	*	*	*	*	*	*
NEBRASKA	*	*	*	*	*	*	*	*	*	*	*	*	*	*
NEVADA	*	*	*	*	*	*	*	*	*	*	*	*	*	*
NEW HAMPSHIRE	*	*	*	*	*	*	*	*	*	*	*	*	*	*
NEW JERSEY	*	*	*	*	*	*	*	*	*	*	*	*	*	*
NEW MEXICO	*	*	*	*	*	*	*	*	*	*	*	*	*	*
NEW YORK	0.72	0.86	0.85	0.86	0.91	0.92	0.89	0.92	0.88	0.87	0.85	0.82	0.78	0.10
NORTH CAROLINA	*	*	*	*	*	*	*	*	*	*	*	*	*	*
NORTH DAKOTA	*	*	*	*	*	*	*	*	*	*	*	*	*	*
OHIO	0.53	0.67	0.70	0.70	0.71	0.77	0.75	0.73	0.73	0.74	0.73	0.71	0.63	0.29
OKLAHOMA	*	*	*	*	*	*	*	*	*	*	*	*	*	*
OREGON	*	*	*	*	*	*	*	*	*	*	*	*	*	*
PENNSYLVANIA	0.48	0.56	0.58	0.58	0.61	0.61	0.62	0.62	0.58	0.60	0.56	0.55	0.56	0.39
RHODE ISLAND	*	*	*	*	*	*	*	*	*	*	*	*	*	*
SOUTH CAROLINA	*	*	*	*	*	*	*	*	*	*	*	*	*	*
SOUTH DAKOTA	*	*	*	*	*	*	*	*	*	*	*	*	*	*
TENNESSEE	*	*	*	*	*	*	*	*	*	*	*	*	*	*
TEXAS	*	*	*	*	*	*	*	*	*	*	*	*	*	*
UTAH	*	*	*	*	*	*	*	*	*	*	*	*	*	*
VERMONT	*	*	*	*	*	*	*	*	*	*	*	*	*	*
VIRGINIA	*	*	*	*	*	*	*	*	*	*	*	*	*	*
WASHINGTON	*	*	*	*	*	*	*	*	*	*	*	*	*	*
WEST VIRGINIA	*	*	*	*	*	*	*	*	*	*	*	*	*	*
WISCONSIN	*	*	*	*	*	*	*	*	*	*	*	*	*	*
WYOMING	*	*	*	*	*	*	*	*	*	*	*	*	*	*
AVERAGE	0.37	0.45	0.46	0.46	0.47	0.49	0.48	0.48	0.46	0.46	0.44	0.44	0.39	0.18

* EFFECTIVE TAX RATE EQUALS ZERO BEFORE ROUNDING. AN ENTIRE ROW OF * MEANS THAT THIS TAX IS NOT USED IN THIS STATE.

TABLE A-50
EFFECTIVE TAX RATES: OTHER LOCAL TAXES N.E.C.
INCIDENCE: CONSUMERS IN GENERAL
ALLOCATOR: TOTAL CONSUMPTION EXPENDITURES

STATE	UNDER $3,000	$3,000 -3,999	$4,000 -4,999	$5,000 -5,999	$6,000 -6,999	$7,000 -7,999	$8,000 -9,999	$10,000 -11,999	$12,000 -14,999	$15,000 -19,999	$20,000 -24,999	$25,000 -29,999	$30,000 -34,999	OVER $35,000
ALABAMA	0.79	0.48	0.41	0.37	0.33	0.32	0.30	0.27	0.25	0.23	0.21	0.20	0.20	0.17
ALASKA	0.21	0.13	0.12	0.12	0.11	0.09	0.09	0.08	0.08	0.07	0.06	0.06	0.06	0.05
ARIZONA	0.32	0.19	0.15	0.14	0.13	0.11	0.11	0.10	0.09	0.08	0.07	0.07	0.07	0.06
ARKANSAS	0.21	0.13	0.11	0.10	0.09	0.09	0.08	0.07	0.07	0.06	0.06	0.05	0.05	0.05
CALIFORNIA	0.78	0.51	0.42	0.38	0.34	0.32	0.29	0.26	0.24	0.21	0.20	0.19	0.18	0.16
COLORADO	0.45	0.28	0.23	0.21	0.20	0.17	0.16	0.15	0.13	0.12	0.11	0.10	0.10	0.09
CONNECTICUT	0.13	0.09	0.08	0.08	0.07	0.07	0.06	0.06	0.05	0.05	0.05	0.05	0.04	0.04
DELAWARE	0.32	0.19	0.19	0.16	0.15	0.14	0.13	0.12	0.11	0.10	0.10	0.09	0.09	0.08
FLORIDA	0.31	0.20	0.16	0.15	0.14	0.13	0.12	0.11	0.10	0.09	0.09	0.08	0.08	0.07
GEORGIA	0.47	0.27	0.24	0.22	0.21	0.20	0.18	0.16	0.15	0.14	0.13	0.12	0.12	0.11
HAWAII	0.23	0.15	0.15	0.13	0.12	0.12	0.11	0.10	0.09	0.08	0.08	0.07	0.07	0.06
IDAHO	0.19	0.12	0.10	0.09	0.08	0.07	0.07	0.06	0.06	0.05	0.05	0.04	0.04	0.04
ILLINOIS	0.37	0.25	0.21	0.20	0.17	0.17	0.15	0.14	0.13	0.12	0.11	0.11	0.11	0.10
INDIANA	0.07	0.04	0.04	0.03	0.03	0.03	0.03	0.02	0.02	0.02	0.02	0.02	0.02	0.02
IOWA	0.17	0.11	0.10	0.08	0.08	0.07	0.07	0.06	0.06	0.05	0.05	0.05	0.04	0.04
KANSAS	0.28	0.17	0.16	0.13	0.13	0.12	0.11	0.10	0.09	0.08	0.08	0.08	0.07	0.06
KENTUCKY	0.18	0.11	0.10	0.08	0.08	0.07	0.07	0.06	0.06	0.05	0.05	0.05	0.05	0.04
LOUISIANA	0.45	0.26	0.22	0.22	0.20	0.19	0.18	0.16	0.14	0.13	0.13	0.12	0.12	0.10
MAINE	0.08	0.05	0.05	0.04	0.04	0.04	0.03	0.03	0.03	0.03	0.02	0.02	0.02	0.02
MARYLAND	0.86	0.54	0.46	0.39	0.38	0.35	0.34	0.31	0.28	0.26	0.24	0.23	0.22	0.20
MASSACHUSETTS	0.11	0.09	0.07	0.06	0.06	0.06	0.05	0.05	0.04	0.04	0.04	0.04	0.04	0.03
MICHIGAN	0.20	0.13	0.10	0.09	0.08	0.08	0.07	0.07	0.06	0.06	0.05	0.05	0.05	0.04
MINNESOTA	0.22	0.14	0.11	0.10	0.10	0.10	0.08	0.08	0.07	0.06	0.06	0.06	0.06	0.05
MISSISSIPPI	0.14	0.09	0.07	0.06	0.06	0.06	0.05	0.05	0.04	0.04	0.04	0.04	0.03	0.03
MISSOURI	0.44	0.24	0.24	0.20	0.19	0.17	0.16	0.15	0.13	0.12	0.11	0.11	0.10	0.09
MONTANA	0.15	0.09	0.08	0.07	0.07	0.06	0.05	0.05	0.05	0.04	0.04	0.04	0.03	0.03
NEBRASKA	0.37	0.23	0.18	0.17	0.16	0.15	0.14	0.13	0.12	0.11	0.10	0.10	0.09	0.08
NEVADA	2.11	1.41	1.19	1.04	1.02	0.94	0.84	0.76	0.69	0.62	0.56	0.54	0.52	0.44
NEW HAMPSHIRE	0.33	0.22	0.17	0.17	0.16	0.14	0.14	0.13	0.12	0.11	0.10	0.10	0.10	0.08
NEW JERSEY	0.26	0.18	0.16	0.14	0.14	0.13	0.12	0.11	0.11	0.10	0.09	0.09	0.09	0.08
NEW MEXICO	0.51	0.32	0.29	0.24	0.23	0.21	0.19	0.17	0.15	0.14	0.13	0.12	0.11	0.10
NEW YORK	0.46	0.28	0.24	0.21	0.20	0.19	0.17	0.17	0.15	0.14	0.13	0.13	0.12	0.11
NORTH CAROLINA	0.19	0.12	0.10	0.08	0.08	0.08	0.07	0.07	0.06	0.06	0.05	0.05	0.05	0.04
NORTH DAKOTA	0.55	0.33	0.29	0.25	0.23	0.22	0.20	0.19	0.18	0.16	0.15	0.14	0.14	0.13
OHIO	0.29	0.19	0.16	0.14	0.13	0.13	0.12	0.11	0.10	0.09	0.09	0.08	0.08	0.07
OKLAHOMA	0.17	0.10	0.08	0.08	0.07	0.06	0.06	0.05	0.05	0.05	0.04	0.04	0.04	0.04
OREGON	0.51	0.31	0.26	0.24	0.21	0.20	0.18	0.16	0.15	0.13	0.12	0.12	0.11	0.10
PENNSYLVANIA	2.14	1.32	1.15	1.00	0.98	0.92	0.86	0.80	0.74	0.69	0.64	0.62	0.61	0.55
RHODE ISLAND	0.14	0.08	0.08	0.07	0.06	0.06	0.05	0.05	0.05	0.04	0.04	0.04	0.04	0.03
SOUTH CAROLINA	0.52	0.33	0.28	0.26	0.23	0.23	0.21	0.20	0.18	0.17	0.16	0.15	0.14	0.13
SOUTH DAKOTA	0.22	0.14	0.12	0.11	0.10	0.09	0.08	0.08	0.07	0.07	0.06	0.06	0.06	0.05
TENNESSEE	0.40	0.26	0.22	0.20	0.18	0.18	0.16	0.15	0.14	0.12	0.12	0.11	0.11	0.09
TEXAS	0.10	0.06	0.05	0.05	0.04	0.04	0.04	0.04	0.03	0.03	0.03	0.03	0.03	0.02
UTAH	0.31	0.19	0.16	0.13	0.14	0.12	0.11	0.10	0.09	0.08	0.08	0.07	0.07	0.06
VERMONT	[illegible]	0.13	0.12	0.10	0.09	0.09	0.08	0.08	0.07	0.07	0.06	0.06	0.06	0.05
VIRGINIA	1.14	0.63	0.58	0.53	0.47	0.44	0.42	0.38	0.35	0.32	0.30	0.28	0.27	0.25
WASHINGTON	0.68	0.41	0.34	0.30	0.27	0.26	0.24	0.22	0.20	0.18	0.17	0.16	0.14	0.13
WEST VIRGINIA	1.20	0.75	0.61	0.53	0.50	0.48	0.42	0.40	0.36	0.33	0.31	0.29	0.28	0.26
WISCONSIN	0.21	0.12	0.11	0.10	0.09	0.09	0.08	0.07	0.07	0.06	0.06	0.05	0.05	0.05
WYOMING	0.28	0.19	0.17	0.15	0.14	0.13	0.12	0.11	0.10	0.09	0.08	0.08	0.08	0.06
AVERAGE	0.43	0.27	0.23	0.20	0.19	0.18	0.16	0.15	0.14	0.13	0.12	0.11	0.11	0.10

* EFFECTIVE TAX RATE EQUALS ZERO BEFORE ROUNDING. AN ENTIRE ROW OF * MEANS THAT THIS TAX IS NOT USED IN THIS STATE.

TABLE A-51
EFFECTIVE TAX RATES: TOTAL LOCAL NON-PROPERTY TAXES (BENCHMARK)
INCIDENCE: SUM OF EFFECTIVE TAX RATES FOR INDIVIDUAL TAXES
ALLOCATOR: BASED ON INDIVIDUAL TAXES

STATE	UNDER $3,000	$3,000 -3,999	$4,000 -4,999	$5,000 -5,999	$6,000 -6,999	$7,000 -7,999	$8,000 -9,999	$10,000 -11,999	$12,000 -14,999	$15,000 -19,999	$20,000 -24,999	$25,000 -29,999	$30,000 -34,999	OVER $35,000
ALABAMA	3.63	2.29	1.99	1.77	1.61	1.57	1.46	1.33	1.22	1.11	1.05	0.99	0.98	0.67
ALASKA	3.04	1.92	1.76	1.65	1.53	1.29	1.26	1.17	1.05	0.86	0.81	0.73	0.68	0.52
ARIZONA	2.33	1.49	1.18	1.18	1.04	0.95	0.93	0.85	0.79	0.73	0.66	0.61	0.62	0.55
ARKANSAS	0.60	0.36	0.31	0.27	0.26	0.23	0.21	0.19	0.17	0.15	0.14	0.13	0.13	0.11
CALIFORNIA	2.36	1.67	1.42	1.31	1.21	1.14	1.05	0.98	0.91	0.84	0.79	0.76	0.74	0.67
COLORADO	3.32	2.26	1.89	1.72	1.69	1.51	1.37	1.31	1.22	1.11	1.03	1.01	0.88	0.82
CONNECTICUT	0.13	0.09	0.08	0.08	0.07	0.07	0.06	0.06	0.05	0.05	0.05	0.05	0.04	0.04
DELAWARE	0.48	0.38	0.40	0.35	0.35	0.35	0.34	0.31	0.32	0.30	0.29	0.26	0.23	0.09
FLORIDA	1.94	1.14	0.93	0.82	0.77	0.71	0.63	0.56	0.51	0.45	0.41	0.38	0.35	0.30
GEORGIA	1.73	1.04	0.96	0.88	0.84	0.80	0.72	0.67	0.63	0.60	0.56	0.53	0.51	0.46
HAWAII	1.53	1.00	0.98	0.88	0.80	0.76	0.69	0.63	0.58	0.52	0.49	0.48	0.44	0.41
IDAHO	0.29	0.17	0.14	0.14	0.12	0.11	0.10	0.09	0.08	0.08	0.07	0.06	0.06	0.05
ILLINOIS	2.18	1.52	1.33	1.23	1.11	1.07	0.99	0.91	0.87	0.79	0.74	0.72	0.69	0.61
INDIANA	0.13	0.11	0.10	0.10	0.10	0.10	0.09	0.09	0.09	0.09	0.09	0.07	0.08	0.06
IOWA	0.25	0.16	0.14	0.12	0.11	0.11	0.10	0.09	0.08	0.08	0.07	0.07	0.06	0.06
KANSAS	0.71	0.43	0.38	0.31	0.30	0.28	0.27	0.23	0.22	0.19	0.18	0.17	0.16	0.14
KENTUCKY	1.52	1.16	1.08	0.98	0.95	0.94	0.92	0.87	0.78	0.76	0.74	0.71	0.64	0.30
LOUISIANA	3.73	2.44	2.15	2.15	2.00	1.93	1.88	1.70	1.59	1.53	1.50	1.45	1.37	1.21
MAINE	0.08	0.05	0.05	0.04	0.04	0.04	0.03	0.03	0.03	0.03	0.02	0.02	0.02	0.02
MARYLAND	2.56	2.11	1.99	1.80	1.83	1.78	1.77	1.68	1.58	1.51	1.41	1.45	1.24	1.03
MASSACHUSETTS	0.11	0.09	0.07	0.06	0.06	0.06	0.05	0.05	0.04	0.04	0.04	0.04	0.04	0.03
MICHIGAN	0.55	0.47	0.43	0.40	0.39	0.41	0.37	0.37	0.35	0.33	0.31	0.30	0.29	0.19
MINNESOTA	0.50	0.32	0.25	0.23	0.21	0.21	0.18	0.17	0.15	0.14	0.13	0.12	0.12	0.10
MISSISSIPPI	0.45	0.27	0.22	0.19	0.17	0.17	0.15	0.14	0.12	0.11	0.10	0.10	0.09	0.08
MISSOURI	3.34	1.98	1.95	1.69	1.59	1.51	1.40	1.32	1.18	1.09	1.03	0.99	0.87	0.70
MONTANA	0.54	0.35	0.30	0.26	0.25	0.23	0.20	0.19	0.17	0.16	0.15	0.14	0.13	0.12
NEBRASKA	1.08	0.72	0.57	0.53	0.50	0.48	0.44	0.42	0.38	0.36	0.34	0.32	0.32	0.28
NEVADA	4.19	2.83	2.40	2.10	2.07	1.90	1.70	1.53	1.40	1.27	1.15	1.10	1.06	0.91
NEW HAMPSHIRE	0.33	0.22	0.17	0.17	0.16	0.14	0.14	0.13	0.12	0.11	0.10	0.10	0.10	0.08
NEW JERSEY	2.06	1.32	1.15	1.03	0.94	0.91	0.81	0.75	0.68	0.61	0.56	0.53	0.50	0.44
NEW MEXICO	0.90	0.57	0.51	0.44	0.42	0.37	0.34	0.31	0.27	0.25	0.23	0.22	0.20	0.19
NEW YORK	4.67	3.59	3.22	3.05	3.06	2.98	2.80	2.78	2.61	2.51	2.45	2.39	2.31	1.41
NORTH CAROLINA	1.38	0.87	0.77	0.65	0.64	0.58	0.55	0.50	0.47	0.43	0.40	0.39	0.36	0.31
NORTH DAKOTA	0.63	0.38	0.33	0.29	0.26	0.25	0.23	0.22	0.20	0.18	0.17	0.16	0.16	0.14
OHIO	1.06	1.04	1.03	0.99	0.99	1.05	1.01	0.97	0.95	0.95	0.93	0.91	0.82	0.46
OKLAHOMA	2.51	1.43	1.24	1.15	1.08	0.97	0.88	0.82	0.74	0.66	0.62	0.58	0.55	0.49
OREGON	0.90	0.54	0.45	0.41	0.36	0.34	0.31	0.28	0.25	0.22	0.20	0.19	0.18	0.16
PENNSYLVANIA	2.65	1.91	1.76	1.60	1.60	1.54	1.50	1.44	1.34	1.30	1.21	1.19	1.18	0.95
RHODE ISLAND	0.14	0.08	0.08	0.07	0.06	0.06	0.05	0.05	0.05	0.04	0.04	0.04	0.04	0.03
SOUTH CAROLINA	0.53	0.33	0.28	0.26	0.24	0.23	0.21	0.20	0.18	0.17	0.16	0.15	0.14	0.13
SOUTH DAKOTA	1.30	0.84	0.77	0.69	0.66	0.61	0.57	0.55	0.51	0.49	0.46	0.44	0.42	0.38
TENNESSEE	2.90	1.91	1.67	1.55	1.41	1.36	1.23	1.17	1.08	0.99	0.94	0.88	0.88	0.70
TEXAS	1.42	0.93	0.79	0.75	0.69	0.65	0.62	0.57	0.53	0.48	0.46	0.43	0.41	0.36
UTAH	1.70	1.11	0.92	0.81	0.86	0.75	0.69	0.65	0.60	0.54	0.51	0.48	0.47	0.43
VERMONT	0.21	0.13	0.12	0.10	0.09	0.09	0.08	0.08	0.07	0.07	0.06	0.06	0.06	0.05
VIRGINIA	4.41	2.41	2.18	1.97	1.73	1.61	1.53	1.38	1.24	1.12	1.03	0.97	0.91	0.80
WASHINGTON	2.72	1.70	1.39	1.26	1.13	1.12	1.01	0.94	0.86	0.78	0.73	0.69	0.63	0.58
WEST VIRGINIA	1.41	0.88	0.71	0.62	0.59	0.56	0.49	0.47	0.42	0.39	0.36	0.34	0.33	0.31
WISCONSIN	0.22	0.13	0.12	0.11	0.10	0.10	0.08	0.08	0.07	0.07	0.06	0.06	0.06	0.05
WYOMING	0.71	0.49	0.46	0.41	0.38	0.36	0.32	0.31	0.28	0.25	0.24	0.24	0.23	0.20
AVERAGE	1.56	1.03	0.91	0.83	0.79	0.75	0.70	0.65	0.60	0.56	0.53	0.50	0.48	0.38

* EFFECTIVE TAX RATE EQUALS ZERO BEFORE ROUNDING. AN ENTIRE ROW OF * MEANS THAT THIS TAX IS NOT USED IN THIS STATE.

TABLE A-52
EFFECTIVE TAX RATES: LOCAL PERSONAL PROPERTY TAX-AGRICULTURAL
INCIDENCE: 1/3 FARMERS, 2/3 CONSUMERS OF FOOD
ALLOCATOR: FARM NET PROFIT AND FOOD EXPENDITURES

STATE	UNDER $3,000	$3,000 -3,999	$4,000 -4,999	$5,000 -5,999	$6,000 -6,999	$7,000 -7,999	$8,000 -9,999	$10,000 -11,999	$12,000 -14,999	$15,000 -19,999	$20,000 -24,999	$25,000 -29,999	$30,000 -34,999	OVER $35,000
ALABAMA	*	*	*	*	*	*	*	*	*	*	*	*	*	*
ALASKA	*	*	*	*	*	*	*	*	*	*	*	*	*	*
ARIZONA	0.11	0.07	0.05	0.05	0.07	0.04	0.04	0.03	0.03	0.05	0.02	0.06	0.02	0.07
ARKANSAS	0.23	0.12	0.10	0.11	0.11	0.07	0.06	0.08	0.06	0.06	0.06	0.08	0.10	0.16
CALIFORNIA	0.08	0.05	0.04	0.03	0.04	0.03	0.02	0.02	0.02	0.02	0.02	0.02	0.02	0.04
COLORADO	0.26	0.13	0.14	0.10	0.22	0.13	0.11	0.08	0.07	0.07	0.07	0.08	0.04	0.12
CONNECTICUT	0.01	0.00	0.00	0.00	0.00	0.00	0.01	0.00	0.00	0.00	0.00	0.00	0.00	0.00
DELAWARE	*	*	*	*	*	*	*	*	*	*	*	*	*	*
FLORIDA	*	*	*	*	*	*	*	*	*	*	*	*	*	*
GEORGIA	*	*	*	*	*	*	*	*	*	*	*	*	*	*
HAWAII	*	*	*	*	*	*	*	*	*	*	*	*	*	*
IDAHO	0.70	0.38	0.37	0.30	0.33	0.30	0.29	0.24	0.23	0.25	0.27	0.25	0.32	0.44
ILLINOIS	0.06	0.04	0.03	0.03	0.03	0.03	0.03	0.02	0.02	0.02	0.02	0.02	0.03	0.04
INDIANA	*	*	*	*	*	*	*	*	*	*	*	*	*	*
IOWA	0.26	0.17	0.15	0.14	0.13	0.13	0.10	0.10	0.11	0.09	0.09	0.11	0.10	0.14
KANSAS	*	*	*	*	*	*	*	*	*	*	*	*	*	*
KENTUCKY	*	*	*	*	*	*	*	*	*	*	*	*	*	*
LOUISIANA	*	*	*	*	*	*	*	*	*	*	*	*	*	*
MAINE	0.02	0.01	0.02	0.01	0.01	0.01	0.01	0.00	0.00	0.00	0.01	0.00	0.00	0.01
MARYLAND	*	*	*	*	*	*	*	*	*	*	*	*	*	*
MASSACHUSETTS	0.00	0.00	0.00	0.00	0.00	0.00	0.00	0.00	0.00	0.00	0.00	0.00	0.00	0.00
MICHIGAN	*	*	*	*	*	*	*	*	*	*	*	*	*	*
MINNESOTA	0.01	0.01	0.00	0.00	0.01	0.01	0.00	*	*	*	*	*	0.00	*
MISSISSIPPI	*	*	*	*	*	*	*	*	*	*	*	*	*	*
MISSOURI	0.22	0.16	0.13	0.07	0.09	0.07	0.10	0.07	0.07	0.07	0.06	0.05	0.11	0.05
MONTANA	1.37	0.98	0.93	0.64	0.79	0.59	0.57	0.48	0.52	0.53	0.46	0.73	0.77	0.93
NEBRASKA	1.26	0.85	0.72	0.77	0.59	0.71	0.44	0.54	0.48	0.41	0.50	0.44	0.53	0.61
NEVADA	0.11	0.07	0.06	0.05	0.05	0.05	0.04	0.06	0.04	0.03	0.08	0.05	0.04	0.05
NEW HAMPSHIRE	*	*	*	*	*	*	*	*	*	*	*	*	*	*
NEW JERSEY	*	*	*	*	*	*	*	*	*	*	*	*	*	*
NEW MEXICO	0.07	0.07	0.03	0.03	0.03	0.02	0.03	0.02	0.04	0.02	0.02	0.02	0.01	0.02
NEW YORK	*	*	*	*	*	*	*	*	*	*	*	*	*	*
NORTH CAROLINA	0.09	0.03	0.03	0.02	0.04	0.02	0.03	0.02	0.02	0.02	0.03	0.02	0.01	0.02
NORTH DAKOTA	*	*	*	*	*	*	*	*	*	*	*	*	*	*
OHIO	0.04	0.02	0.03	0.03	0.03	0.02	0.02	0.02	0.02	0.02	0.01	0.02	0.02	0.02
OKLAHOMA	0.29	0.12	0.13	0.15	0.09	0.08	0.08	0.06	0.07	0.08	0.06	0.11	0.03	0.08
OREGON	0.16	0.09	0.07	0.07	0.09	0.06	0.09	0.05	0.06	0.04	0.05	0.07	0.07	0.10
PENNSYLVANIA	*	*	*	*	*	*	*	*	*	*	*	*	*	*
RHODE ISLAND	*	*	*	*	*	*	*	*	*	*	*	*	*	*
SOUTH CAROLINA	0.04	0.04	0.02	0.02	0.02	0.01	0.02	0.01	0.01	0.01	0.02	0.01	0.01	0.02
SOUTH DAKOTA	1.81	1.06	0.98	0.93	0.89	0.90	0.73	0.72	0.74	0.74	0.64	0.75	1.06	0.80
TENNESSEE	*	*	*	*	*	*	*	*	*	*	*	*	*	*
TEXAS	*	*	*	*	*	*	*	*	*	*	*	*	*	*
UTAH	0.09	0.06	0.09	0.11	0.05	0.04	0.04	0.06	0.03	0.03	0.02	0.05	0.02	0.04
VERMONT	0.11	0.12	0.03	0.06	0.03	0.03	0.03	0.04	0.03	0.03	0.03	0.01	0.01	0.02
VIRGINIA	*	*	*	*	*	*	*	*	*	*	*	*	*	*
WASHINGTON	0.07	0.04	0.03	0.03	0.03	0.03	0.02	0.02	0.02	0.02	0.01	0.02	0.01	0.05
WEST VIRGINIA	0.15	0.04	0.03	0.03	0.03	0.19	0.02	0.02	0.02	0.02	0.01	0.01	0.03	0.02
WISCONSIN	0.28	0.27	0.20	0.17	0.20	0.13	0.13	0.13	0.13	0.13	0.08	0.09	0.07	0.09
WYOMING	0.82	0.74	0.49	0.82	0.41	0.51	0.35	0.37	0.38	0.32	0.39	0.30	0.54	0.56
AVERAGE	0.31	0.21	0.18	0.17	0.16	0.15	0.12	0.12	0.12	0.11	0.11	0.12	0.14	0.16

* EFFECTIVE TAX RATE EQUALS ZERO BEFORE ROUNDING. AN ENTIRE ROW OF * MEANS THAT THIS TAX IS NOT USED IN THIS STATE.

TABLE A-53

EFFECTIVE TAX RATES: LOCAL PERSONAL PROPERTY TAX-COMMERCIAL AND INDUSTRIAL
INCIDENCE: 1/2 CONSUMERS, 1/4 INCORPORATED BUSINESSES, 1/4 UNINCORPORATED BUSINESSES
ALLOCATOR: CONSUMPTION, DIVIDEND INCOME, BUSINESS AND PARTNERSHIP PROFIT

STATE	UNDER $3,000	$3,000 -3,999	$4,000 -4,999	$5,000 -5,999	$6,000 -6,999	$7,000 -7,999	$8,000 -9,999	$10,000 -11,999	$12,000 -14,999	$15,000 -19,999	$20,000 -24,999	$25,000 -29,999	$30,000 -34,999	OVER $35,000
ALABAMA	*	*	*	*	*	*	*	*	*	*	*	*	*	*
ALASKA	*	*	*	*	*	*	*	*	*	*	*	*	*	*
ARIZONA	0.90	0.64	0.45	0.46	0.40	0.29	0.30	0.28	0.24	0.24	0.23	0.21	0.33	0.58
ARKANSAS	0.43	0.29	0.26	0.27	0.18	0.16	0.17	0.15	0.15	0.12	0.11	0.14	0.17	0.52
CALIFORNIA	1.68	0.98	0.86	0.87	0.71	0.65	0.64	0.58	0.54	0.46	0.44	0.48	0.56	1.13
COLORADO	0.90	0.42	0.64	0.35	0.30	0.43	0.27	0.24	0.23	0.19	0.22	0.19	0.29	0.70
CONNECTICUT	1.09	0.94	1.00	0.85	0.66	0.59	0.59	0.53	0.47	0.51	0.39	0.41	0.40	1.08
DELAWARE	*	*	*	*	*	*	*	*	*	*	*	*	*	*
FLORIDA	*	*	*	*	*	*	*	*	*	*	*	*	*	*
GEORGIA	*	*	*	*	*	*	*	*	*	*	*	*	*	*
HAWAII	*	*	*	*	*	*	*	*	*	*	*	*	*	*
IDAHO	0.36	0.21	0.16	0.13	0.12	0.14	0.11	0.11	0.09	0.08	0.13	0.10	0.17	0.28
ILLINOIS	0.51	0.34	0.29	0.33	0.25	0.24	0.24	0.23	0.18	0.18	0.17	0.18	0.19	0.50
INDIANA	*	*	*	*	*	*	*	*	*	*	*	*	*	*
IOWA	0.34	0.23	0.23	0.25	0.16	0.15	0.17	0.17	0.11	0.12	0.11	0.13	0.23	0.34
KANSAS	*	*	*	*	*	*	*	*	*	*	*	*	*	*
KENTUCKY	0.28	0.19	0.17	0.22	0.11	0.13	0.13	0.10	0.10	0.10	0.10	0.13	0.10	0.50
LOUISIANA	0.50	0.29	0.28	0.24	0.23	0.24	0.21	0.20	0.17	0.17	0.16	0.19	0.24	0.63
MAINE	0.67	0.43	0.40	0.45	0.29	0.29	0.38	0.23	0.23	0.25	0.22	0.33	0.26	0.66
MARYLAND	0.05	0.05	0.03	0.02	0.02	0.02	0.01	0.02	0.01	0.01	0.01	0.01	0.01	0.03
MASSACHUSETTS	0.50	0.30	0.34	0.30	0.30	0.24	0.21	0.18	0.17	0.14	0.13	0.15	0.14	0.48
MICHIGAN	*	*	*	*	*	*	*	*	*	*	*	*	*	*
MINNESOTA	0.03	0.02	0.02	0.01	0.01	0.01	0.00	*	*	*	*	*	*	0.01
MISSISSIPPI	0.53	0.33	0.30	0.27	0.34	0.23	0.26	0.20	0.20	0.18	0.22	0.18	0.24	0.74
MISSOURI	0.37	0.23	0.21	0.21	0.17	0.17	0.16	0.14	0.13	0.12	0.13	0.12	0.14	0.43
MONTANA	1.61	1.17	0.79	0.77	0.79	0.71	0.68	0.72	0.45	0.47	0.48	0.50	0.64	1.29
NEBRASKA	1.28	0.65	0.47	0.57	0.52	0.43	0.49	0.37	0.34	0.30	0.34	0.42	0.49	1.05
NEVADA	0.23	0.14	0.12	0.10	0.10	0.10	0.08	0.09	0.07	0.07	0.06	0.06	0.07	0.21
NEW HAMPSHIRE	*	*	*	*	*	*	*	*	*	*	*	*	*	*
NEW JERSEY	0.24	0.17	0.19	0.16	0.15	0.14	0.20	0.12	0.11	0.09	0.09	0.09	0.08	0.21
NEW MEXICO	*	*	*	*	*	*	*	*	*	*	*	*	*	*
NEW YORK	*	*	*	*	*	*	*	*	*	*	*	*	*	*
NORTH CAROLINA	0.93	0.52	0.66	0.43	0.38	0.37	0.36	0.32	0.27	0.25	0.32	0.26	0.26	0.91
NORTH DAKOTA	*	*	*	*	*	*	*	*	*	*	*	*	*	*
OHIO	0.62	0.42	0.36	0.37	0.28	0.33	0.27	0.24	0.21	0.21	0.20	0.22	0.28	0.47
OKLAHOMA	0.72	0.32	0.31	0.27	0.27	0.34	0.22	0.20	0.21	0.18	0.17	0.18	0.21	0.56
OREGON	1.61	0.80	0.66	0.53	0.54	0.51	0.48	0.47	0.38	0.42	0.42	0.48	0.67	1.29
PENNSYLVANIA	*	*	*	*	*	*	*	*	*	*	*	*	*	*
RHODE ISLAND	*	*	*	*	*	*	*	*	*	*	*	*	*	*
SOUTH CAROLINA	0.01	0.01	0.01	0.01	0.01	0.01	0.01	0.01	0.01	0.00	0.00	0.01	0.01	0.02
SOUTH DAKOTA	0.63	0.38	0.33	0.28	0.33	0.37	0.29	0.23	0.23	0.21	0.27	0.25	0.31	0.65
TENNESSEE	*	*	*	*	*	*	*	*	*	*	*	*	*	*
TEXAS	*	*	*	*	*	*	*	*	*	*	*	*	*	*
UTAH	0.76	0.30	0.33	0.28	0.25	0.23	0.23	0.18	0.16	0.15	0.16	0.16	0.19	0.44
VERMONT	0.79	0.44	0.52	0.44	0.39	0.41	0.37	0.36	0.34	0.30	0.32	0.26	0.54	1.06
VIRGINIA	0.19	0.12	0.09	0.10	0.11	0.08	0.07	0.07	0.05	0.06	0.05	0.05	0.05	0.14
WASHINGTON	0.66	0.39	0.38	0.35	0.31	0.32	0.28	0.22	0.22	0.20	0.19	0.19	0.25	0.65
WEST VIRGINIA	*	*	*	*	*	*	*	*	*	*	*	*	*	*
WISCONSIN	1.07	0.63	0.72	0.46	0.46	0.50	0.61	0.42	0.34	0.34	0.37	0.39	0.49	1.01
WYOMING	2.61	1.48	1.21	1.02	0.94	0.98	1.19	0.81	0.74	0.75	0.63	0.71	0.79	2.27
AVERAGE	0.72	0.43	0.40	0.36	0.31	0.31	0.30	0.26	0.22	0.22	0.21	0.22	0.28	0.65

* EFFECTIVE TAX RATE EQUALS ZERO BEFORE ROUNDING. AN ENTIRE ROW OF * MEANS THAT THIS TAX IS NOT USED IN THIS STATE.

TABLE A-54
EFFECTIVE TAX RATES: LOCAL PERSONAL PROPERTY TAX-HOUSEHOLD PROPERTY (BENCHMARK)
INCIDENCE: HOUSEHOLDS
ALLOCATOR: HOUSING EXPENDITURES

STATE	UNDER $3,000	$3,000 -3,999	$4,000 -4,999	$5,000 -5,999	$6,000 -6,999	$7,000 -7,999	$8,000 -9,999	$10,000 -11,999	$12,000 -14,999	$15,000 -19,999	$20,000 -24,999	$25,000 -29,999	$30,000 -34,999	OVER $35,000
ALABAMA	*	*	*	*	*	*	*	*	*	*	*	*	*	*
ALASKA	*	*	*	*	*	*	*	*	*	*	*	*	*	*
ARIZONA	*	*	*	*	*	*	*	*	*	*	*	*	*	*
ARKANSAS	0.21	0.14	0.13	0.12	0.12	0.11	0.10	0.09	0.09	0.08	0.08	0.08	0.07	0.06
CALIFORNIA	*	*	*	*	*	*	*	*	*	*	*	*	*	*
COLORADO	*	*	*	*	*	*	*	*	*	*	*	*	*	*
CONNECTICUT	*	*	*	*	*	*	*	*	*	*	*	*	*	*
DELAWARE	*	*	*	*	*	*	*	*	*	*	*	*	*	*
FLORIDA	*	*	*	*	*	*	*	*	*	*	*	*	*	*
GEORGIA	*	*	*	*	*	*	*	*	*	*	*	*	*	*
HAWAII	*	*	*	*	*	*	*	*	*	*	*	*	*	*
IDAHO	*	*	*	*	*	*	*	*	*	*	*	*	*	*
ILLINOIS	*	*	*	*	*	*	*	*	*	*	*	*	*	*
INDIANA	*	*	*	*	*	*	*	*	*	*	*	*	*	*
IOWA	*	*	*	*	*	*	*	*	*	*	*	*	*	*
KANSAS	*	*	*	*	*	*	*	*	*	*	*	*	*	*
KENTUCKY	*	*	*	*	*	*	*	*	*	*	*	*	*	*
LOUISIANA	*	*	*	*	*	*	*	*	*	*	*	*	*	*
MAINE	*	*	*	*	*	*	*	*	*	*	*	*	*	*
MARYLAND	*	*	*	*	*	*	*	*	*	*	*	*	*	*
MASSACHUSETTS	*	*	*	*	*	*	*	*	*	*	*	*	*	*
MICHIGAN	*	*	*	*	*	*	*	*	*	*	*	*	*	*
MINNESOTA	*	*	*	*	*	*	*	*	*	*	*	*	*	*
MISSISSIPPI	*	*	*	*	*	*	*	*	*	*	*	*	*	*
MISSOURI	*	*	*	*	*	*	*	*	*	*	*	*	*	*
MONTANA	*	*	*	*	*	*	*	*	*	*	*	*	*	*
NEBRASKA	*	*	*	*	*	*	*	*	*	*	*	*	*	*
NEVADA	*	*	*	*	*	*	*	*	*	*	*	*	*	*
NEW HAMPSHIRE	*	*	*	*	*	*	*	*	*	*	*	*	*	*
NEW JERSEY	*	*	*	*	*	*	*	*	*	*	*	*	*	*
NEW MEXICO	*	*	*	*	*	*	*	*	*	*	*	*	*	*
NEW YORK	*	*	*	*	*	*	*	*	*	*	*	*	*	*
NORTH CAROLINA	0.15	0.10	0.09	0.08	0.08	0.07	0.07	0.07	0.06	0.06	0.06	0.06	0.05	0.05
NORTH DAKOTA	*	*	*	*	*	*	*	*	*	*	*	*	*	*
OHIO	*	*	*	*	*	*	*	*	*	*	*	*	*	*
OKLAHOMA	*	*	*	*	*	*	*	*	*	*	*	*	*	*
OREGON	*	*	*	*	*	*	*	*	*	*	*	*	*	*
PENNSYLVANIA	*	*	*	*	*	*	*	*	*	*	*	*	*	*
RHODE ISLAND	*	*	*	*	*	*	*	*	*	*	*	*	*	*
SOUTH CAROLINA	*	*	*	*	*	*	*	*	*	*	*	*	*	*
SOUTH DAKOTA	*	*	*	*	*	*	*	*	*	*	*	*	*	*
TENNESSEE	*	*	*	*	*	*	*	*	*	*	*	*	*	*
TEXAS	*	*	*	*	*	*	*	*	*	*	*	*	*	*
UTAH	*	*	*	*	*	*	*	*	*	*	*	*	*	*
VERMONT	*	*	*	*	*	*	*	*	*	*	*	*	*	*
VIRGINIA	*	*	*	*	*	*	*	*	*	*	*	*	*	*
WASHINGTON	*	*	*	*	*	*	*	*	*	*	*	*	*	*
WEST VIRGINIA	0.17	0.12	0.10	0.09	0.09	0.08	0.07	0.07	0.07	0.06	0.06	0.06	0.05	0.05
WISCONSIN	*	*	*	*	*	*	*	*	*	*	*	*	*	*
WYOMING	*	*	*	*	*	*	*	*	*	*	*	*	*	*
AVERAGE	0.18	0.12	0.11	0.09	0.09	0.09	0.08	0.08	0.07	0.07	0.07	0.06	0.06	0.06

* EFFECTIVE TAX RATE EQUALS ZERO BEFORE ROUNDING. AN ENTIRE ROW OF * MEANS THAT THIS TAX IS NOT USED IN THIS STATE.

TABLE A-55
EFFECTIVE TAX RATES: LOCAL PERSONAL PROPERTY TAX-HOUSEHOLD PROPERTY
INCIDENCE: HOUSEHOLDS
ALLOCATOR: HOUSEHOLD INCOME DISTRIBUTION

STATE	UNDER $3,000	$3,000 -3,999	$4,000 -4,999	$5,000 -5,999	$6,000 -6,999	$7,000 -7,999	$8,000 -9,999	$10,000 -11,999	$12,000 -14,999	$15,000 -19,999	$20,000 -24,999	$25,000 -29,999	$30,000 -34,999	OVER $35,000
ALABAMA	*	*	*	*	*	*	*	*	*	*	*	*	*	*
ALASKA	*	*	*	*	*	*	*	*	*	*	*	*	*	*
ARIZONA	*	*	*	*	*	*	*	*	*	*	*	*	*	*
ARKANSAS	0.07	0.09	0.09	0.09	0.10	0.09	0.10	0.09	0.09	0.09	0.10	0.10	0.10	0.09
CALIFORNIA	*	*	*	*	*	*	*	*	*	*	*	*	*	*
COLORADO	*	*	*	*	*	*	*	*	*	*	*	*	*	*
CONNECTICUT	*	*	*	*	*	*	*	*	*	*	*	*	*	*
DELAWARE	*	*	*	*	*	*	*	*	*	*	*	*	*	*
FLORIDA	*	*	*	*	*	*	*	*	*	*	*	*	*	*
GEORGIA	*	*	*	*	*	*	*	*	*	*	*	*	*	*
HAWAII	*	*	*	*	*	*	*	*	*	*	*	*	*	*
IDAHO	*	*	*	*	*	*	*	*	*	*	*	*	*	*
ILLINOIS	*	*	*	*	*	*	*	*	*	*	*	*	*	*
INDIANA	*	*	*	*	*	*	*	*	*	*	*	*	*	*
IOWA	*	*	*	*	*	*	*	*	*	*	*	*	*	*
KANSAS	*	*	*	*	*	*	*	*	*	*	*	*	*	*
KENTUCKY	*	*	*	*	*	*	*	*	*	*	*	*	*	*
LOUISIANA	*	*	*	*	*	*	*	*	*	*	*	*	*	*
MAINE	*	*	*	*	*	*	*	*	*	*	*	*	*	*
MARYLAND	*	*	*	*	*	*	*	*	*	*	*	*	*	*
MASSACHUSETTS	*	*	*	*	*	*	*	*	*	*	*	*	*	*
MICHIGAN	*	*	*	*	*	*	*	*	*	*	*	*	*	*
MINNESOTA	*	*	*	*	*	*	*	*	*	*	*	*	*	*
MISSISSIPPI	*	*	*	*	*	*	*	*	*	*	*	*	*	*
MISSOURI	*	*	*	*	*	*	*	*	*	*	*	*	*	*
MONTANA	*	*	*	*	*	*	*	*	*	*	*	*	*	*
NEBRASKA	*	*	*	*	*	*	*	*	*	*	*	*	*	*
NEVADA	*	*	*	*	*	*	*	*	*	*	*	*	*	*
NEW HAMPSHIRE	*	*	*	*	*	*	*	*	*	*	*	*	*	*
NEW JERSEY	*	*	*	*	*	*	*	*	*	*	*	*	*	*
NEW MEXICO	*	*	*	*	*	*	*	*	*	*	*	*	*	*
NEW YORK	*	*	*	*	*	*	*	*	*	*	*	*	*	*
NORTH CAROLINA	0.05	0.06	0.06	0.06	0.06	0.06	0.06	0.06	0.06	0.06	0.06	0.07	0.06	0.06
NORTH DAKOTA	*	*	*	*	*	*	*	*	*	*	*	*	*	*
OHIO	*	*	*	*	*	*	*	*	*	*	*	*	*	*
OKLAHOMA	*	*	*	*	*	*	*	*	*	*	*	*	*	*
OREGON	*	*	*	*	*	*	*	*	*	*	*	*	*	*
PENNSYLVANIA	*	*	*	*	*	*	*	*	*	*	*	*	*	*
RHODE ISLAND	*	*	*	*	*	*	*	*	*	*	*	*	*	*
SOUTH CAROLINA	*	*	*	*	*	*	*	*	*	*	*	*	*	*
SOUTH DAKOTA	*	*	*	*	*	*	*	*	*	*	*	*	*	*
TENNESSEE	*	*	*	*	*	*	*	*	*	*	*	*	*	*
TEXAS	*	*	*	*	*	*	*	*	*	*	*	*	*	*
UTAH	*	*	*	*	*	*	*	*	*	*	*	*	*	*
VERMONT	*	*	*	*	*	*	*	*	*	*	*	*	*	*
VIRGINIA	*	*	*	*	*	*	*	*	*	*	*	*	*	*
WASHINGTON	*	*	*	*	*	*	*	*	*	*	*	*	*	*
WEST VIRGINIA	0.06	0.07	0.07	0.07	0.07	0.07	0.07	0.07	0.07	0.07	0.07	0.07	0.07	0.07
WISCONSIN	*	*	*	*	*	*	*	*	*	*	*	*	*	*
WYOMING	*	*	*	*	*	*	*	*	*	*	*	*	*	*
AVERAGE	0.06	0.07	0.07	0.07	0.08	0.08	0.08	0.08	0.08	0.08	0.08	0.08	0.08	0.07

* EFFECTIVE TAX RATE EQUALS ZERO BEFORE ROUNDING. AN ENTIRE ROW OF * MEANS THAT THIS TAX IS NOT USED IN THIS STATE.

TABLE A-56
EFFECTIVE TAX RATES: LOCAL PERSONAL PROPERTY TAX-INTANGIBLES
INCIDENCE: HOUSEHOLDS
ALLOCATOR: HOUSEHOLD INCOME DISTRIBUTION

STATE	UNDER $3,000	$3,000 -3,999	$4,000 -4,999	$5,000 -5,999	$6,000 -6,999	$7,000 -7,999	$8,000 -9,999	$10,000 -11,999	$12,000 -14,999	$15,000 -19,999	$20,000 -24,999	$25,000 -29,999	$30,000 -34,999	OVER $35,000
ALABAMA	*	*	*	*	*	*	*	*	*	*	*	*	*	*
ALASKA	*	*	*	*	*	*	*	*	*	*	*	*	*	*
ARIZONA	*	*	*	*	*	*	*	*	*	*	*	*	*	*
ARKANSAS	*	*	*	*	*	*	*	*	*	*	*	*	*	*
CALIFORNIA	*	*	*	*	*	*	*	*	*	*	*	*	*	*
COLORADO	*	*	*	*	*	*	*	*	*	*	*	*	*	*
CONNECTICUT	*	*	*	*	*	*	*	*	*	*	*	*	*	*
DELAWARE	*	*	*	*	*	*	*	*	*	*	*	*	*	*
FLORIDA	*	*	*	*	*	*	*	*	*	*	*	*	*	*
GEORGIA	0.04	0.04	0.05	0.05	0.05	0.05	0.05	0.05	0.05	0.05	0.05	0.05	0.05	0.05
HAWAII	*	*	*	*	*	*	*	*	*	*	*	*	*	*
IDAHO	*	*	*	*	*	*	*	*	*	*	*	*	*	*
ILLINOIS	0.02	0.03	0.03	0.03	0.03	0.03	0.03	0.03	0.04	0.04	0.04	0.04	0.04	0.04
INDIANA	*	*	*	*	*	*	*	*	*	*	*	*	*	*
IOWA	*	*	*	*	*	*	*	*	*	*	*	*	*	*
KANSAS	*	*	*	*	*	*	*	*	*	*	*	*	*	*
KENTUCKY	*	*	*	*	*	*	*	*	*	*	*	*	*	*
LOUISIANA	0.07	0.08	0.08	0.09	0.09	0.09	0.09	0.09	0.09	0.09	0.09	0.09	0.09	0.09
MAINE	*	*	*	*	*	*	*	*	*	*	*	*	*	*
MARYLAND	*	*	*	*	*	*	*	*	*	*	*	*	*	*
MASSACHUSETTS	*	*	*	*	*	*	*	*	*	*	*	*	*	*
MICHIGAN	*	*	*	*	*	*	*	*	*	*	*	*	*	*
MINNESOTA	*	*	*	*	*	*	*	*	*	*	*	*	*	*
MISSISSIPPI	0.02	0.03	0.02	0.02	0.02	0.03	0.03	0.03	0.03	0.03	0.03	0.03	0.03	0.02
MISSOURI	*	*	*	*	*	*	*	*	*	*	*	*	*	*
MONTANA	0.09	0.12	0.13	0.13	0.13	0.13	0.13	0.13	0.14	0.14	0.14	0.14	0.14	0.14
NEBRASKA	*	*	*	*	*	*	*	*	*	*	*	*	*	*
NEVADA	*	*	*	*	*	*	*	*	*	*	*	*	*	*
NEW HAMPSHIRE	*	*	*	*	*	*	*	*	*	*	*	*	*	*
NEW JERSEY	*	*	*	*	*	*	*	*	*	*	*	*	*	*
NEW MEXICO	*	*	*	*	*	*	*	*	*	*	*	*	*	*
NEW YORK	*	*	*	*	*	*	*	*	*	*	*	*	*	*
NORTH CAROLINA	*	*	*	*	*	*	*	*	*	*	*	*	*	*
NORTH DAKOTA	*	*	*	*	*	*	*	*	*	*	*	*	*	*
OHIO	*	*	*	*	*	*	*	*	*	*	*	*	*	*
OKLAHOMA	*	*	*	*	*	*	*	*	*	*	*	*	*	*
OREGON	*	*	*	*	*	*	*	*	*	*	*	*	*	*
PENNSYLVANIA	*	*	*	*	*	*	*	*	*	*	*	*	*	*
RHODE ISLAND	*	*	*	*	*	*	*	*	*	*	*	*	*	*
SOUTH CAROLINA	*	*	*	*	*	*	*	*	*	*	*	*	*	*
SOUTH DAKOTA	*	*	*	*	*	*	*	*	*	*	*	*	*	*
TENNESSEE	*	*	*	*	*	*	*	*	*	*	*	*	*	*
TEXAS	*	*	*	*	*	*	*	*	*	*	*	*	*	*
UTAH	*	*	*	*	*	*	*	*	*	*	*	*	*	*
VERMONT	*	*	*	*	*	*	*	*	*	*	*	*	*	*
VIRGINIA	*	*	*	*	*	*	*	*	*	*	*	*	*	*
WASHINGTON	*	*	*	*	*	*	*	*	*	*	*	*	*	*
WEST VIRGINIA	0.22	0.27	0.26	0.26	0.27	0.28	0.26	0.28	0.27	0.28	0.28	0.27	0.26	0.28
WISCONSIN	*	*	*	*	*	*	*	*	*	*	*	*	*	*
WYOMING	*	*	*	*	*	*	*	*	*	*	*	*	*	*
AVERAGE	0.08	0.09	0.09	0.10	0.10	0.10	0.10	0.10	0.10	0.10	0.10	0.10	0.10	0.10

* EFFECTIVE TAX RATE EQUALS ZERO BEFORE ROUNDING. AN ENTIRE ROW OF * MEANS THAT THIS TAX IS NOT USED IN THIS STATE.

TABLE A-57
EFFECTIVE TAX RATES: LOCAL PERSONAL PROPERTY TAX-MOTOR VEHICLES (BENCHMARK)
INCIDENCE: HOUSEHOLDS
ALLOCATOR: VEHICLE FINANCE CHARGES

STATE	UNDER $3,000	$3,000 -3,999	$4,000 -4,999	$5,000 -5,999	$6,000 -6,999	$7,000 -7,999	$8,000 -9,999	$10,000 -11,999	$12,000 -14,999	$15,000 -19,999	$20,000 -24,999	$25,000 -29,999	$30,000 -34,999	OVER $35,000
ALABAMA	0.59	0.34	0.28	0.24	0.21	0.20	0.18	0.16	0.14	0.12	0.11	0.10	0.09	0.07
ALASKA	*	*	*	*	*	*	*	*	*	*	*	*	*	*
ARIZONA	*	*	*	*	*	*	*	*	*	*	*	*	*	*
ARKANSAS	0.72	0.41	0.35	0.30	0.28	0.25	0.23	0.19	0.17	0.15	0.14	0.12	0.12	0.09
CALIFORNIA	*	*	*	*	*	*	*	*	*	*	*	*	*	*
COLORADO	*	*	*	*	*	*	*	*	*	*	*	*	*	*
CONNECTICUT	*	*	*	*	*	*	*	*	*	*	*	*	*	*
DELAWARE	*	*	*	*	*	*	*	*	*	*	*	*	*	*
FLORIDA	*	*	*	*	*	*	*	*	*	*	*	*	*	*
GEORGIA	1.02	0.55	0.49	0.43	0.39	0.36	0.31	0.28	0.25	0.22	0.19	0.17	0.16	0.13
HAWAII	*	*	*	*	*	*	*	*	*	*	*	*	*	*
IDAHO	*	*	*	*	*	*	*	*	*	*	*	*	*	*
ILLINOIS	0.12	0.09	0.08	0.08	0.07	0.07	0.07	0.07	0.07	0.06	0.06	0.06	0.06	0.05
INDIANA	*	*	*	*	*	*	*	*	*	*	*	*	*	*
IOWA	*	*	*	*	*	*	*	*	*	*	*	*	*	*
KANSAS	*	*	*	*	*	*	*	*	*	*	*	*	*	*
KENTUCKY	0.68	0.39	0.33	0.28	0.25	0.24	0.21	0.19	0.16	0.14	0.13	0.12	0.11	0.07
LOUISIANA	*	*	*	*	*	*	*	*	*	*	*	*	*	*
MAINE	*	*	*	*	*	*	*	*	*	*	*	*	*	*
MARYLAND	*	*	*	*	*	*	*	*	*	*	*	*	*	*
MASSACHUSETTS	*	*	*	*	*	*	*	*	*	*	*	*	*	*
MICHIGAN	*	*	*	*	*	*	*	*	*	*	*	*	*	*
MINNESOTA	*	*	*	*	*	*	*	*	*	*	*	*	*	*
MISSISSIPPI	1.77	1.04	0.82	0.72	0.63	0.61	0.54	0.48	0.41	0.35	0.32	0.30	0.28	0.20
MISSOURI	0.73	0.46	0.47	0.41	0.39	0.38	0.36	0.34	0.32	0.30	0.29	0.28	0.26	0.25
MONTANA	2.37	1.52	1.30	1.14	1.08	0.99	0.87	0.80	0.74	0.67	0.62	0.58	0.56	0.50
NEBRASKA	0.82	0.60	0.50	0.47	0.45	0.44	0.42	0.41	0.39	0.37	0.36	0.35	0.35	0.32
NEVADA	*	*	*	*	*	*	*	*	*	*	*	*	*	*
NEW HAMPSHIRE	*	*	*	*	*	*	*	*	*	*	*	*	*	*
NEW JERSEY	*	*	*	*	*	*	*	*	*	*	*	*	*	*
NEW MEXICO	*	*	*	*	*	*	*	*	*	*	*	*	*	*
NEW YORK	*	*	*	*	*	*	*	*	*	*	*	*	*	*
NORTH CAROLINA	0.82	0.47	0.39	0.32	0.31	0.27	0.25	0.22	0.20	0.17	0.16	0.15	0.13	0.10
NORTH DAKOTA	*	*	*	*	*	*	*	*	*	*	*	*	*	*
OHIO	*	*	*	*	*	*	*	*	*	*	*	*	*	*
OKLAHOMA	*	*	*	*	*	*	*	*	*	*	*	*	*	*
OREGON	*	*	*	*	*	*	*	*	*	*	*	*	*	*
PENNSYLVANIA	*	*	*	*	*	*	*	*	*	*	*	*	*	*
RHODE ISLAND	*	*	*	*	*	*	*	*	*	*	*	*	*	*
SOUTH CAROLINA	1.29	0.76	0.62	0.55	0.50	0.47	0.41	0.37	0.33	0.29	0.25	0.24	0.21	0.17
SOUTH DAKOTA	0.01	0.01	0.01	0.01	0.01	0.01	0.01	0.01	0.00	0.00	0.00	0.00	0.00	0.00
TENNESSEE	*	*	*	*	*	*	*	*	*	*	*	*	*	*
TEXAS	*	*	*	*	*	*	*	*	*	*	*	*	*	*
UTAH	1.00	0.61	0.49	0.43	0.44	0.38	0.34	0.31	0.28	0.25	0.23	0.21	0.20	0.18
VERMONT	*	*	*	*	*	*	*	*	*	*	*	*	*	*
VIRGINIA	*	*	*	*	*	*	*	*	*	*	*	*	*	*
WASHINGTON	*	*	*	*	*	*	*	*	*	*	*	*	*	*
WEST VIRGINIA	0.73	0.42	0.33	0.28	0.26	0.25	0.21	0.20	0.17	0.15	0.13	0.12	0.11	0.10
WISCONSIN	*	*	*	*	*	*	*	*	*	*	*	*	*	*
WYOMING	*	*	*	*	*	*	*	*	*	*	*	*	*	*
AVERAGE	0.91	0.55	0.46	0.40	0.38	0.35	0.32	0.29	0.26	0.23	0.21	0.20	0.19	0.16

* EFFECTIVE TAX RATE EQUALS ZERO BEFORE ROUNDING. AN ENTIRE ROW OF * MEANS THAT THIS TAX IS NOT USED IN THIS STATE.

TABLE A-58
EFFECTIVE TAX RATES: LOCAL PERSONAL PROPERTY TAX-MOTOR VEHICLES
INCIDENCE: HOUSEHOLDS
ALLOCATOR: HOUSEHOLD INCOME DISTRIBUTION

STATE	UNDER $3,000	$3,000 -3,999	$4,000 -4,999	$5,000 -5,999	$6,000 -6,999	$7,000 -7,999	$8,000 -9,999	$10,000 -11,999	$12,000 -14,999	$15,000 -19,999	$20,000 -24,999	$25,000 -29,999	$30,000 -34,999	OVER $35,000
ALABAMA	0.12	0.14	0.15	0.14	0.14	0.15	0.15	0.15	0.15	0.15	0.15	0.15	0.15	0.13
ALASKA	*	*	*	*	*	*	*	*	*	*	*	*	*	*
ARIZONA	*	*	*	*	*	*	*	*	*	*	*	*	*	*
ARKANSAS	0.15	0.18	0.19	0.19	0.20	0.20	0.20	0.20	0.20	0.20	0.20	0.20	0.20	0.19
CALIFORNIA	*	*	*	*	*	*	*	*	*	*	*	*	*	*
COLORADO	*	*	*	*	*	*	*	*	*	*	*	*	*	*
CONNECTICUT	*	*	*	*	*	*	*	*	*	*	*	*	*	*
DELAWARE	*	*	*	*	*	*	*	*	*	*	*	*	*	*
FLORIDA	*	*	*	*	*	*	*	*	*	*	*	*	*	*
GEORGIA	0.20	0.22	0.24	0.25	0.26	0.26	0.26	0.26	0.26	0.27	0.26	0.26	0.26	0.25
HAWAII	*	*	*	*	*	*	*	*	*	*	*	*	*	*
IDAHO	*	*	*	*	*	*	*	*	*	*	*	*	*	*
ILLINOIS	0.04	0.05	0.06	0.06	0.06	0.06	0.06	0.06	0.06	0.06	0.06	0.07	0.07	0.06
INDIANA	*	*	*	*	*	*	*	*	*	*	*	*	*	*
IOWA	*	*	*	*	*	*	*	*	*	*	*	*	*	*
KANSAS	*	*	*	*	*	*	*	*	*	*	*	*	*	*
KENTUCKY	0.14	0.17	0.17	0.17	0.17	0.18	0.18	0.19	0.18	0.18	0.19	0.19	0.19	0.15
LOUISIANA	*	*	*	*	*	*	*	*	*	*	*	*	*	*
MAINE	*	*	*	*	*	*	*	*	*	*	*	*	*	*
MARYLAND	*	*	*	*	*	*	*	*	*	*	*	*	*	*
MASSACHUSETTS	*	*	*	*	*	*	*	*	*	*	*	*	*	*
MICHIGAN	*	*	*	*	*	*	*	*	*	*	*	*	*	*
MINNESOTA	*	*	*	*	*	*	*	*	*	*	*	*	*	*
MISSISSIPPI	0.38	0.47	0.45	0.46	0.45	0.49	0.48	0.49	0.48	0.47	0.48	0.49	0.49	0.44
MISSOURI	0.25	0.28	0.32	0.31	0.32	0.32	0.33	0.33	0.32	0.32	0.33	0.33	0.32	0.32
MONTANA	0.51	0.67	0.69	0.69	0.74	0.74	0.72	0.74	0.75	0.76	0.77	0.78	0.78	0.78
NEBRASKA	0.28	0.36	0.33	0.35	0.36	0.37	0.38	0.38	0.39	0.39	0.40	0.40	0.41	0.40
NEVADA	*	*	*	*	*	*	*	*	*	*	*	*	*	*
NEW HAMPSHIRE	*	*	*	*	*	*	*	*	*	*	*	*	*	*
NEW JERSEY	*	*	*	*	*	*	*	*	*	*	*	*	*	*
NEW MEXICO	*	*	*	*	*	*	*	*	*	*	*	*	*	*
NEW YORK	*	*	*	*	*	*	*	*	*	*	*	*	*	*
NORTH CAROLINA	0.16	0.19	0.20	0.19	0.21	0.20	0.21	0.21	0.21	0.21	0.21	0.22	0.21	0.20
NORTH DAKOTA	*	*	*	*	*	*	*	*	*	*	*	*	*	*
OHIO	*	*	*	*	*	*	*	*	*	*	*	*	*	*
OKLAHOMA	*	*	*	*	*	*	*	*	*	*	*	*	*	*
OREGON	*	*	*	*	*	*	*	*	*	*	*	*	*	*
PENNSYLVANIA	*	*	*	*	*	*	*	*	*	*	*	*	*	*
RHODE ISLAND	*	*	*	*	*	*	*	*	*	*	*	*	*	*
SOUTH CAROLINA	0.25	0.31	0.31	0.32	0.33	0.34	0.34	0.35	0.35	0.35	0.35	0.36	0.34	0.33
SOUTH DAKOTA	0.00	0.00	0.00	0.00	0.00	0.00	0.00	0.00	0.00	0.01	0.01	0.01	0.01	0.00
TENNESSEE	*	*	*	*	*	*	*	*	*	*	*	*	*	*
TEXAS	*	*	*	*	*	*	*	*	*	*	*	*	*	*
UTAH	0.20	0.25	0.24	0.24	0.29	0.27	0.27	0.28	0.28	0.28	0.28	0.28	0.28	0.29
VERMONT	*	*	*	*	*	*	*	*	*	*	*	*	*	*
VIRGINIA	*	*	*	*	*	*	*	*	*	*	*	*	*	*
WASHINGTON	*	*	*	*	*	*	*	*	*	*	*	*	*	*
WEST VIRGINIA	0.15	0.18	0.17	0.17	0.18	0.18	0.18	0.19	0.18	0.19	0.19	0.18	0.17	0.19
WISCONSIN	*	*	*	*	*	*	*	*	*	*	*	*	*	*
WYOMING	*	*	*	*	*	*	*	*	*	*	*	*	*	*
AVERAGE	0.20	0.25	0.25	0.25	0.26	0.27	0.27	0.27	0.27	0.27	0.28	0.28	0.28	0.27

* EFFECTIVE TAX RATE EQUALS ZERO BEFORE ROUNDING. AN ENTIRE ROW OF * MEANS THAT THIS TAX IS NOT USED IN THIS STATE.

TABLE A-59
EFFECTIVE TAX RATES: LOCAL PERSONAL PROPERTY TAX-OTHER N.E.C.
INCIDENCE: HOUSEHOLDS
ALLOCATOR: HOUSEHOLD INCOME DISTRIBUTION

STATE	UNDER $3,000	$3,000 -3,999	$4,000 -4,999	$5,000 -5,999	$6,000 -6,999	$7,000 -7,999	$8,000 -9,999	$10,000 -11,999	$12,000 -14,999	$15,000 -19,999	$20,000 -24,999	$25,000 -29,999	$30,000 -34,999	OVER $35,000
ALABAMA	0.19	0.22	0.23	0.22	0.22	0.23	0.24	0.23	0.23	0.23	0.23	0.24	0.23	0.21
ALASKA	0.32	0.41	0.45	0.49	0.50	0.47	0.50	0.50	0.50	0.49	0.49	0.50	0.49	0.48
ARIZONA	0.08	0.09	0.09	0.10	0.09	0.09	0.10	0.10	0.10	0.10	0.10	0.10	0.10	0.10
ARKANSAS	0.04	0.04	0.05	0.05	0.05	0.05	0.05	0.05	0.05	0.05	0.05	0.05	0.05	0.04
CALIFORNIA	0.01	0.02	0.02	0.02	0.02	0.02	0.02	0.02	0.02	0.02	0.02	0.02	0.02	0.02
COLORADO	0.01	0.01	0.01	0.01	0.01	0.01	0.01	0.01	0.01	0.01	0.01	0.01	0.01	0.01
CONNECTICUT	0.22	0.31	0.32	0.34	0.33	0.39	0.35	0.36	0.36	0.36	0.37	0.38	0.37	0.36
DELAWARE	*	*	*	*	*	*	*	*	*	*	*	*	*	*
FLORIDA	0.34	0.41	0.41	0.42	0.42	0.45	0.45	0.45	0.46	0.46	0.47	0.46	0.44	0.39
GEORGIA	0.38	0.42	0.46	0.47	0.49	0.50	0.49	0.49	0.50	0.50	0.50	0.49	0.49	0.48
HAWAII	*	*	*	*	*	*	*	*	*	*	*	*	*	*
IDAHO	0.06	0.07	0.07	0.08	0.08	0.08	0.08	0.08	0.08	0.08	0.08	0.08	0.08	0.08
ILLINOIS	0.11	0.15	0.15	0.16	0.16	0.17	0.17	0.17	0.17	0.18	0.18	0.18	0.18	0.18
INDIANA	0.69	0.85	0.85	0.92	0.94	0.94	0.91	0.97	0.96	0.96	0.98	0.92	0.98	0.95
IOWA	0.01	0.01	0.01	0.01	0.01	0.01	0.01	0.01	0.01	0.01	0.01	0.01	0.01	0.01
KANSAS	1.23	1.51	1.58	1.45	1.61	1.61	1.75	1.68	1.72	1.69	1.67	1.74	1.73	1.63
KENTUCKY	0.02	0.02	0.02	0.02	0.02	0.02	0.03	0.03	0.03	0.02	0.03	0.03	0.03	0.02
LOUISIANA	0.24	0.27	0.28	0.30	0.30	0.31	0.32	0.32	0.31	0.32	0.33	0.33	0.32	0.31
MAINE	0.01	0.02	0.02	0.02	0.02	0.02	0.02	0.02	0.02	0.02	0.02	0.02	0.02	0.02
MARYLAND	*	*	*	*	*	*	*	*	*	*	*	*	*	*
MASSACHUSETTS	0.08	0.13	0.12	0.12	0.13	0.13	0.13	0.13	0.12	0.13	0.13	0.13	0.14	0.11
MICHIGAN	0.47	0.61	0.60	0.59	0.62	0.66	0.64	0.67	0.67	0.66	0.68	0.69	0.69	0.67
MINNESOTA	0.00	0.00	0.00	0.00	0.00	0.00	0.00	*	*	*	*	*	0.00	*
MISSISSIPPI	0.01	0.01	0.01	0.01	0.01	0.01	0.01	0.01	0.01	0.01	0.01	0.01	0.01	0.01
MISSOURI	0.15	0.16	0.19	0.18	0.19	0.19	0.19	0.19	0.19	0.19	0.19	0.19	0.19	0.19
MONTANA	0.17	0.22	0.23	0.23	0.24	0.24	0.24	0.24	0.25	0.25	0.25	0.26	0.26	0.26
NEBRASKA	0.13	0.16	0.15	0.16	0.17	0.17	0.17	0.18	0.18	0.18	0.18	0.19	0.19	0.18
NEVADA	0.24	0.32	0.32	0.33	0.36	0.36	0.34	0.35	0.35	0.35	0.34	0.35	0.36	0.34
NEW HAMPSHIRE	0.01	0.00	0.01	0.01	0.01	0.00	0.00	*	*	*	*	*	*	*
NEW JERSEY	*	*	*	*	*	*	*	*	*	*	*	*	*	*
NEW MEXICO	0.07	0.10	0.10	0.10	0.11	0.11	0.11	0.11	0.11	0.10	0.11	0.11	0.10	0.11
NEW YORK	*	*	*	*	*	*	*	*	*	*	*	*	*	*
NORTH CAROLINA	0.03	0.04	0.04	0.04	0.04	0.04	0.04	0.04	0.04	0.04	0.04	0.04	0.04	0.04
NORTH DAKOTA	*	*	*	*	*	*	*	*	*	*	*	*	*	*
OHIO	*	*	*	*	*	*	*	*	*	*	*	*	*	*
OKLAHOMA	0.13	0.15	0.15	0.16	0.16	0.16	0.16	0.16	0.16	0.15	0.15	0.15	0.15	0.15
OREGON	0.05	0.06	0.06	0.07	0.07	0.07	0.07	0.07	0.07	0.07	0.07	0.07	0.07	0.07
PENNSYLVANIA	*	*	*	*	*	*	*	*	*	*	*	*	*	*
RHODE ISLAND	0.76	0.86	1.00	0.99	0.94	0.93	1.03	1.03	1.04	1.06	1.09	1.08	1.08	1.04
SOUTH CAROLINA	0.04	0.05	0.05	0.05	0.05	0.05	0.05	0.05	0.05	0.05	0.05	0.05	0.05	0.05
SOUTH DAKOTA	0.17	0.21	0.22	0.22	0.23	0.23	0.23	0.25	0.25	0.25	0.26	0.25	0.25	0.25
TENNESSEE	0.20	0.25	0.26	0.27	0.27	0.28	0.27	0.28	0.28	0.28	0.29	0.28	0.29	0.27
TEXAS	0.52	0.64	0.64	0.67	0.68	0.68	0.70	0.71	0.70	0.70	0.72	0.71	0.70	0.68
UTAH	0.04	0.05	0.05	0.05	0.06	0.06	0.06	0.06	0.06	0.06	0.06	0.06	0.06	0.06
VERMONT	0.02	0.03	0.03	0.03	0.03	0.03	0.03	0.03	0.03	0.03	0.03	0.03	0.03	0.03
VIRGINIA	0.28	0.31	0.34	0.34	0.34	0.34	0.36	0.35	0.35	0.35	0.34	0.34	0.34	0.32
WASHINGTON	0.04	0.05	0.05	0.05	0.05	0.06	0.05	0.06	0.06	0.06	0.06	0.06	0.05	0.05
WEST VIRGINIA	0.34	0.41	0.40	0.40	0.41	0.43	0.41	0.43	0.42	0.43	0.43	0.42	0.40	0.43
WISCONSIN	0.02	0.02	0.02	0.02	0.02	0.02	0.02	0.02	0.02	0.02	0.02	0.02	0.03	0.02
WYOMING	0.13	0.17	0.19	0.19	0.19	0.19	0.19	0.20	0.20	0.20	0.21	0.21	0.22	0.20
AVERAGE	0.19	0.23	0.24	0.25	0.25	0.26	0.26	0.26	0.27	0.27	0.27	0.27	0.27	0.26

* EFFECTIVE TAX RATE EQUALS ZERO BEFORE ROUNDING. AN ENTIRE ROW OF * MEANS THAT THIS TAX IS NOT USED IN THIS STATE.

TABLE A-60

EFFECTIVE TAX RATES: TOTAL LOCAL PERSONAL PROPERTY TAXES (BENCHMARK)
INCIDENCE: SUM OF EFFECTIVE TAX RATES FOR INDIVIDUAL TAXES
ALLOCATOR: BASED ON INDIVIDUAL TAXES

STATE	UNDER $3,000	$3,000 -3,999	$4,000 -4,999	$5,000 -5,999	$6,000 -6,999	$7,000 -7,999	$8,000 -9,999	$10,000 -11,999	$12,000 -14,999	$15,000 -19,999	$20,000 -24,999	$25,000 -29,999	$30,000 -34,999	OVER $35,000
ALABAMA	0.78	0.56	0.51	0.46	0.43	0.43	0.42	0.39	0.37	0.35	0.34	0.33	0.33	0.27
ALASKA	0.32	0.41	0.45	0.49	0.50	0.47	0.50	0.50	0.50	0.49	0.49	0.50	0.49	0.48
ARIZONA	1.09	0.80	0.59	0.61	0.57	0.42	0.44	0.41	0.37	0.39	0.35	0.36	0.45	0.75
ARKANSAS	1.62	1.01	0.88	0.85	0.74	0.64	0.61	0.56	0.52	0.46	0.44	0.46	0.51	0.88
CALIFORNIA	1.77	1.05	0.91	0.93	0.76	0.70	0.68	0.62	0.58	0.50	0.48	0.53	0.59	1.20
COLORADO	1.16	0.55	0.79	0.45	0.53	0.56	0.39	0.33	0.31	0.27	0.30	0.29	0.34	0.83
CONNECTICUT	1.32	1.26	1.31	1.19	0.99	0.98	0.95	0.89	0.84	0.88	0.77	0.79	0.77	1.45
DELAWARE	*	*	*	*	*	*	*	*	*	*	*	*	*	*
FLORIDA	0.34	0.41	0.41	0.42	0.42	0.45	0.45	0.45	0.46	0.46	0.47	0.46	0.44	0.39
GEORGIA	1.44	1.01	0.99	0.95	0.93	0.92	0.85	0.81	0.80	0.77	0.74	0.72	0.70	0.66
HAWAII	*	*	*	*	*	*	*	*	*	*	*	*	*	*
IDAHO	1.11	0.66	0.60	0.51	0.53	0.51	0.47	0.43	0.39	0.41	0.48	0.44	0.57	0.80
ILLINOIS	0.83	0.65	0.60	0.63	0.54	0.54	0.54	0.53	0.48	0.48	0.47	0.48	0.50	0.81
INDIANA	0.69	0.85	0.85	0.92	0.94	0.94	0.91	0.97	0.96	0.96	0.98	0.92	0.98	0.95
IOWA	0.60	0.41	0.39	0.40	0.30	0.30	0.28	0.28	0.23	0.22	0.21	0.25	0.34	0.48
KANSAS	1.23	1.51	1.58	1.45	1.61	1.61	1.75	1.68	1.72	1.69	1.67	1.74	1.73	1.63
KENTUCKY	0.98	0.60	0.52	0.52	0.39	0.39	0.36	0.31	0.29	0.26	0.26	0.28	0.24	0.58
LOUISIANA	0.81	0.64	0.64	0.63	0.62	0.64	0.62	0.61	0.58	0.58	0.58	0.61	0.66	1.03
MAINE	0.70	0.46	0.43	0.47	0.32	0.31	0.41	0.25	0.26	0.27	0.24	0.35	0.28	0.69
MARYLAND	0.05	0.05	0.03	0.02	0.02	0.02	0.01	0.02	0.01	0.01	0.01	0.01	0.01	0.03
MASSACHUSETTS	0.59	0.43	0.46	0.43	0.44	0.37	0.34	0.31	0.29	0.27	0.26	0.29	0.27	0.60
MICHIGAN	0.47	0.61	0.60	0.59	0.62	0.66	0.64	0.67	0.67	0.66	0.68	0.69	0.69	0.67
MINNESOTA	0.04	0.03	0.02	0.02	0.01	0.02	0.01	*	*	*	*	*	0.00	0.01
MISSISSIPPI	2.33	1.40	1.16	1.02	1.01	0.88	0.83	0.72	0.65	0.57	0.58	0.51	0.56	0.97
MISSOURI	1.47	1.02	0.99	0.88	0.84	0.80	0.81	0.75	0.71	0.68	0.67	0.65	0.70	0.91
MONTANA	5.62	4.01	3.37	2.90	3.04	2.67	2.48	2.37	2.10	2.06	1.96	2.21	2.38	3.12
NEBRASKA	3.49	2.27	1.84	1.98	1.73	1.76	1.53	1.49	1.39	1.27	1.39	1.40	1.56	2.17
NEVADA	0.57	0.53	0.50	0.48	0.51	0.51	0.46	0.49	0.46	0.45	0.48	0.46	0.46	0.60
NEW HAMPSHIRE	0.01	0.00	0.01	0.01	0.01	0.00	0.00	*	*	*	*	*	*	*
NEW JERSEY	0.24	0.17	0.19	0.16	0.15	0.14	0.20	0.12	0.11	0.09	0.09	0.09	0.08	0.21
NEW MEXICO	0.14	0.17	0.13	0.13	0.14	0.13	0.14	0.12	0.14	0.12	0.13	0.13	0.11	0.14
NEW YORK	*	*	*	*	*	*	*	*	*	*	*	*	*	*
NORTH CAROLINA	2.02	1.16	1.22	0.89	0.85	0.78	0.75	0.67	0.60	0.54	0.60	0.53	0.50	1.12
NORTH DAKOTA	*	*	*	*	*	*	*	*	*	*	*	*	*	*
OHIO	0.66	0.45	0.39	0.40	0.30	0.35	0.29	0.26	0.23	0.22	0.21	0.24	0.30	0.49
OKLAHOMA	1.14	0.59	0.59	0.58	0.52	0.57	0.46	0.42	0.44	0.42	0.38	0.43	0.40	0.79
OREGON	1.82	0.95	0.80	0.66	0.70	0.63	0.64	0.59	0.51	0.54	0.54	0.62	0.82	1.46
PENNSYLVANIA	*	*	*	*	*	*	*	*	*	*	*	*	*	*
RHODE ISLAND	0.76	0.86	1.00	0.99	0.94	0.93	1.03	1.03	1.04	1.06	1.09	1.08	1.08	1.04
SOUTH CAROLINA	1.38	0.85	0.69	0.63	0.58	0.55	0.50	0.45	0.40	0.36	0.33	0.31	0.28	0.26
SOUTH DAKOTA	2.61	1.65	1.54	1.44	1.47	1.51	1.26	1.20	1.22	1.21	1.17	1.26	1.63	1.70
TENNESSEE	0.20	0.25	0.26	0.27	0.27	0.28	0.27	0.28	0.28	0.28	0.29	0.28	0.29	0.27
TEXAS	0.52	0.64	0.64	0.67	0.68	0.68	0.70	0.71	0.70	0.70	0.72	0.71	0.70	0.68
UTAH	1.89	1.02	0.96	0.87	0.30	0.70	0.66	0.61	0.54	0.50	0.47	0.48	0.47	0.73
VERMONT	0.92	0.59	0.58	0.53	0.45	0.46	0.43	0.42	0.40	0.36	0.39	0.31	0.59	1.11
VIRGINIA	0.47	0.43	0.42	0.45	0.45	0.42	0.43	0.42	0.40	0.40	0.39	0.40	0.39	0.46
WASHINGTON	0.78	0.49	0.46	0.43	0.39	0.41	0.36	0.30	0.29	0.28	0.26	0.27	0.32	0.76
WEST VIRGINIA	1.61	1.26	1.12	1.05	1.06	1.22	0.97	1.00	0.94	0.94	0.92	0.89	0.85	0.88
WISCONSIN	1.36	0.92	0.94	0.65	0.69	0.65	0.77	0.57	0.49	0.49	0.47	0.51	0.59	1.12
WYOMING	3.55	2.39	1.88	2.03	1.54	1.68	1.73	1.38	1.33	1.27	1.22	1.23	1.54	3.03
AVERAGE	1.19	0.85	0.78	0.73	0.70	0.68	0.65	0.61	0.58	0.56	0.55	0.57	0.61	0.87

* EFFECTIVE TAX RATE EQUALS ZERO BEFORE ROUNDING. AN ENTIRE ROW OF * MEANS THAT THIS TAX IS NOT USED IN THIS STATE.

TABLE A-61
EFFECTIVE TAX RATES: LOCAL REAL PROPERTY TAX-ACREAGE AND FARMS (BENCHMARK)
INCIDENCE: 1/3 FARMERS, 2/3 CONSUMERS OF FOOD
ALLOCATOR: FARM NET PROFIT AND FOOD EXPENDITURES

STATE	UNDER $3,000	$3,000 -3,999	$4,000 -4,999	$5,000 -5,999	$6,000 -6,999	$7,000 -7,999	$8,000 -9,999	$10,000 -11,999	$12,000 -14,999	$15,000 -19,999	$20,000 -24,999	$25,000 -29,999	$30,000 -34,999	OVER $35,000
ALABAMA	0.17	0.15	0.06	0.05	0.04	0.06	0.04	0.04	0.03	0.04	0.02	0.06	0.07	0.04
ALASKA	0.26	0.17	0.14	0.15	0.14	0.12	0.12	0.10	0.10	0.08	0.07	0.07	0.07	0.16
ARIZONA	0.49	0.28	0.22	0.22	0.30	0.16	0.16	0.14	0.13	0.21	0.10	0.25	0.09	0.31
ARKANSAS	0.95	0.50	0.41	0.47	0.47	0.30	0.27	0.32	0.24	0.22	0.25	0.30	0.40	0.60
CALIFORNIA	1.00	0.58	0.45	0.42	0.46	0.37	0.30	0.25	0.25	0.23	0.22	0.29	0.18	0.50
COLORADO	0.90	0.45	0.48	0.33	0.77	0.45	0.36	0.26	0.25	0.24	0.24	0.28	0.14	0.39
CONNECTICUT	0.13	0.08	0.07	0.07	0.06	0.06	0.14	0.04	0.08	0.09	0.03	0.03	0.03	0.02
DELAWARE	0.42	0.24	0.24	0.42	0.18	0.16	0.18	0.12	0.12	0.12	0.15	0.12	0.35	0.09
FLORIDA	1.04	0.50	0.37	0.47	0.46	0.27	0.25	0.32	0.27	0.16	0.21	0.26	0.48	0.24
GEORGIA	1.50	1.03	0.69	0.81	0.77	0.51	0.50	0.67	0.51	0.34	0.38	0.24	0.19	0.71
HAWAII	0.56	0.13	0.14	0.12	0.13	0.25	0.09	0.09	0.09	0.12	0.07	0.07	0.07	0.13
IDAHO	2.37	1.31	1.27	1.02	1.13	1.00	0.96	0.80	0.74	0.79	0.87	0.80	0.99	1.38
ILLINOIS	1.23	0.74	0.73	0.64	0.54	0.60	0.61	0.47	0.51	0.44	0.45	0.42	0.53	0.71
INDIANA	1.35	1.06	0.57	0.82	0.77	0.65	0.57	0.54	0.47	0.41	0.40	0.44	0.55	0.55
IOWA	4.79	3.03	2.71	2.63	2.43	2.48	1.83	1.83	2.01	1.71	1.60	2.10	1.92	2.46
KANSAS	2.54	1.51	1.28	1.20	0.96	1.17	1.20	0.98	0.94	0.75	0.72	0.93	0.84	1.34
KENTUCKY	1.60	0.79	0.92	0.47	0.57	0.37	0.44	0.42	0.23	0.26	0.19	0.20	0.53	0.36
LOUISIANA	0.23	0.13	0.14	0.19	0.09	0.13	0.08	0.07	0.07	0.05	0.10	0.04	0.04	0.14
MAINE	0.66	0.28	0.48	0.17	0.24	0.16	0.26	0.13	0.12	0.10	0.16	0.08	0.11	0.36
MARYLAND	0.44	0.26	0.42	0.64	0.17	0.16	0.15	0.13	0.24	0.17	0.15	0.07	0.05	0.08
MASSACHUSETTS	0.19	0.19	0.06	0.10	0.05	0.04	0.04	0.04	0.03	0.05	0.08	0.03	0.03	0.02
MICHIGAN	0.89	1.10	0.44	0.44	0.51	0.34	0.44	0.33	0.42	0.37	0.22	0.25	0.34	0.39
MINNESOTA	2.31	1.37	0.97	0.86	1.08	1.11	0.81	0.83	0.75	0.68	0.64	0.59	1.02	0.69
MISSISSIPPI	1.03	0.53	0.69	0.46	0.36	0.62	0.49	0.39	0.25	0.19	0.16	0.16	0.17	0.73
MISSOURI	1.20	0.86	0.72	0.41	0.48	0.36	0.52	0.40	0.39	0.38	0.32	0.26	0.56	0.21
MONTANA	2.16	1.54	1.47	0.98	1.24	0.93	0.87	0.71	0.79	0.80	0.69	1.06	1.18	1.36
NEBRASKA	4.50	3.05	2.56	2.75	2.09	2.49	1.51	1.92	1.65	1.41	1.74	1.49	1.80	2.00
NEVADA	0.77	0.50	0.42	0.36	0.36	0.34	0.30	0.40	0.25	0.21	0.57	0.33	0.29	0.31
NEW HAMPSHIRE	2.67	0.42	0.32	0.32	0.28	0.25	0.25	0.41	0.23	0.34	0.21	0.15	0.14	0.25
NEW JERSEY	0.94	0.16	0.14	0.14	0.21	0.11	0.10	0.52	0.08	0.08	0.07	0.06	0.13	0.06
NEW MEXICO	0.40	0.41	0.17	0.14	0.19	0.12	0.19	0.10	0.20	0.10	0.12	0.08	0.06	0.12
NEW YORK	0.32	0.19	0.16	0.14	0.25	0.29	0.15	0.15	0.31	0.08	0.07	0.14	0.06	0.07
NORTH CAROLINA	1.12	0.42	0.41	0.28	0.45	0.26	0.32	0.23	0.22	0.21	0.32	0.19	0.11	0.16
NORTH DAKOTA	4.69	3.04	2.77	2.47	2.38	2.77	2.13	2.07	1.91	1.67	1.83	1.89	2.07	2.70
OHIO	0.82	0.49	0.70	0.55	0.55	0.43	0.35	0.37	0.35	0.30	0.26	0.35	0.43	0.48
OKLAHOMA	1.13	0.49	0.52	0.58	0.35	0.30	0.32	0.24	0.28	0.31	0.23	0.43	0.12	0.28
OREGON	2.02	1.11	0.94	0.93	1.13	0.75	1.14	0.62	0.75	0.50	0.54	0.91	0.84	1.15
PENNSYLVANIA	0.35	0.24	0.19	0.11	0.15	0.10	0.17	0.23	0.14	0.09	0.06	0.07	0.05	0.04
RHODE ISLAND	0.11	0.06	0.06	0.05	0.04	0.04	0.04	0.03	0.03	0.03	0.03	0.02	0.02	0.13
SOUTH CAROLINA	0.78	0.78	0.35	0.45	0.49	0.27	0.51	0.27	0.26	0.18	0.35	0.15	0.10	0.31
SOUTH DAKOTA	5.63	3.32	3.08	2.90	2.79	2.79	2.25	2.20	2.27	2.26	1.94	2.32	3.22	2.35
TENNESSEE	1.04	0.47	0.43	0.38	0.59	0.25	0.42	0.30	0.26	0.17	0.14	0.12	0.11	0.28
TEXAS	1.16	0.70	0.62	0.41	0.45	0.42	0.43	0.29	0.31	0.29	0.22	0.34	0.39	0.36
UTAH	0.63	0.39	0.58	0.78	0.31	0.23	0.29	0.40	0.22	0.21	0.16	0.35	0.13	0.26
VERMONT	2.89	3.13	0.91	1.58	0.72	0.65	0.72	0.93	0.65	0.63	0.84	0.33	0.30	0.25
VIRGINIA	0.59	0.31	1.04	0.24	0.20	0.44	0.24	0.39	0.17	0.12	0.20	0.10	0.07	0.09
WASHINGTON	0.90	0.57	0.38	0.32	0.45	0.46	0.25	0.25	0.22	0.24	0.17	0.21	0.17	0.62
WEST VIRGINIA	0.63	0.17	0.14	0.12	0.11	0.79	0.09	0.08	0.07	0.07	0.05	0.04	0.10	0.06
WISCONSIN	1.06	1.02	0.74	0.62	0.76	0.48	0.47	0.47	0.46	0.43	0.25	0.30	0.20	0.26
WYOMING	1.96	1.78	1.18	1.97	0.97	1.23	0.86	0.88	0.91	0.77	0.93	0.72	1.28	1.31
AVERAGE	1.35	0.84	0.70	0.66	0.61	0.58	0.50	0.48	0.44	0.39	0.40	0.41	0.46	0.56

* EFFECTIVE TAX RATE EQUALS ZERO BEFORE ROUNDING. AN ENTIRE ROW OF * MEANS THAT THIS TAX IS NOT USED IN THIS STATE.

TABLE A-62

EFFECTIVE TAX RATES: LOCAL REAL PROPERTY TAX-ACREAGE AND FARMS (MOST REGRESSIVE)
INCIDENCE: CONSUMERS OF FOOD
ALLOCATOR: FOOD EXPENDITURES

STATE	UNDER $3,000	$3,000 -3,999	$4,000 -4,999	$5,000 -5,999	$6,000 -6,999	$7,000 -7,999	$8,000 -9,999	$10,000 -11,999	$12,000 -14,999	$15,000 -19,999	$20,000 -24,999	$25,000 -29,999	$30,000 -34,999	OVER $35,000
ALABAMA	0.18	0.10	0.09	0.08	0.07	0.06	0.06	0.05	0.04	0.04	0.03	0.03	0.03	0.01
ALASKA	0.39	0.25	0.22	0.22	0.20	0.18	0.17	0.16	0.15	0.13	0.12	0.11	0.11	0.08
ARIZONA	0.69	0.42	0.33	0.32	0.29	0.25	0.25	0.22	0.20	0.18	0.16	0.15	0.15	0.12
ARKANSAS	1.24	0.72	0.61	0.53	0.50	0.45	0.40	0.35	0.30	0.27	0.24	0.21	0.20	0.11
CALIFORNIA	1.09	0.73	0.60	0.55	0.49	0.46	0.41	0.38	0.34	0.30	0.28	0.26	0.25	0.19
COLORADO	1.05	0.67	0.55	0.50	0.48	0.43	0.37	0.35	0.33	0.29	0.26	0.25	0.22	0.19
CONNECTICUT	0.17	0.12	0.10	0.10	0.09	0.09	0.07	0.07	0.06	0.05	0.05	0.05	0.04	0.03
DELAWARE	0.63	0.36	0.34	0.27	0.25	0.24	0.21	0.18	0.17	0.15	0.13	0.12	0.10	0.07
FLORIDA	1.15	0.68	0.54	0.48	0.45	0.41	0.36	0.32	0.29	0.25	0.22	0.20	0.17	0.08
GEORGIA	2.00	1.08	0.96	0.85	0.78	0.74	0.63	0.56	0.50	0.45	0.39	0.35	0.32	0.20
HAWAII	0.29	0.20	0.20	0.18	0.16	0.15	0.14	0.13	0.12	0.11	0.10	0.09	0.08	0.07
IDAHO	3.08	1.89	1.57	1.52	1.38	1.25	1.18	1.04	0.96	0.85	0.78	0.73	0.66	0.56
ILLINOIS	1.61	1.10	0.96	0.86	0.77	0.75	0.68	0.62	0.59	0.53	0.48	0.46	0.43	0.34
INDIANA	1.64	1.04	0.86	0.81	0.75	0.70	0.61	0.59	0.53	0.48	0.45	0.38	0.40	0.32
IOWA	6.19	3.93	3.69	2.92	2.90	2.71	2.46	2.36	2.07	1.92	1.74	1.66	1.52	1.38
KANSAS	3.22	2.02	1.77	1.46	1.44	1.34	1.31	1.14	1.06	0.92	0.81	0.82	0.78	0.58
KENTUCKY	1.39	0.81	0.70	0.57	0.54	0.49	0.46	0.41	0.34	0.31	0.28	0.26	0.23	0.12
LOUISIANA	0.34	0.19	0.16	0.15	0.13	0.12	0.11	0.10	0.09	0.08	0.07	0.07	0.06	0.04
MAINE	0.62	0.38	0.33	0.26	0.27	0.24	0.22	0.20	0.18	0.16	0.15	0.13	0.12	0.08
MARYLAND	0.65	0.39	0.33	0.26	0.26	0.23	0.21	0.19	0.16	0.14	0.12	0.12	0.10	0.08
MASSACHUSETTS	0.15	0.11	0.09	0.08	0.07	0.07	0.06	0.06	0.05	0.05	0.04	0.04	0.04	0.03
MICHIGAN	1.22	0.80	0.65	0.56	0.51	0.52	0.45	0.43	0.39	0.34	0.32	0.29	0.28	0.22
MINNESOTA	2.50	1.62	1.27	1.22	1.12	1.14	0.94	0.89	0.80	0.72	0.66	0.64	0.59	0.46
MISSISSIPPI	1.32	0.79	0.63	0.56	0.49	0.48	0.42	0.38	0.33	0.28	0.26	0.25	0.22	0.13
MISSOURI	1.32	0.75	0.71	0.61	0.56	0.53	0.49	0.45	0.39	0.35	0.33	0.31	0.26	0.22
MONTANA	3.02	1.96	1.69	1.48	1.42	1.31	1.13	1.04	0.97	0.88	0.81	0.73	0.74	0.61
NEBRASKA	5.75	3.71	2.93	2.70	2.49	2.36	2.16	2.03	1.83	1.69	1.58	1.46	1.42	1.17
NEVADA	1.10	0.75	0.64	0.55	0.55	0.51	0.45	0.40	0.36	0.33	0.30	0.29	0.27	0.19
NEW HAMPSHIRE	0.99	0.63	0.49	0.48	0.43	0.38	0.37	0.33	0.30	0.28	0.25	0.23	0.23	0.16
NEW JERSEY	0.38	0.24	0.21	0.19	0.18	0.17	0.15	0.15	0.13	0.12	0.11	0.10	0.09	0.07
NEW MEXICO	0.44	0.28	0.26	0.22	0.21	0.18	0.17	0.16	0.13	0.12	0.11	0.10	0.08	0.08
NEW YORK	0.47	0.28	0.23	0.20	0.19	0.18	0.16	0.15	0.14	0.12	0.11	0.11	0.10	0.07
NORTH CAROLINA	1.06	0.61	0.51	0.42	0.41	0.36	0.33	0.29	0.26	0.22	0.20	0.18	0.16	0.09
NORTH DAKOTA	6.74	4.09	3.58	3.15	2.92	2.77	2.50	2.38	2.21	2.01	1.85	1.73	1.71	1.48
OHIO	1.13	0.73	0.64	0.56	0.51	0.51	0.46	0.42	0.38	0.36	0.33	0.31	0.29	0.23
OKLAHOMA	1.37	0.73	0.61	0.56	0.52	0.45	0.40	0.37	0.32	0.27	0.25	0.22	0.19	0.15
OREGON	2.70	1.67	1.42	1.32	1.19	1.12	1.01	0.91	0.81	0.72	0.66	0.63	0.54	0.45
PENNSYLVANIA	0.37	0.22	0.19	0.16	0.16	0.14	0.13	0.12	0.11	0.10	0.09	0.08	0.08	0.06
RHODE ISLAND	0.16	0.09	0.09	0.08	0.06	0.06	0.06	0.05	0.05	0.04	0.04	0.04	0.03	0.02
SOUTH CAROLINA	1.08	0.64	0.53	0.47	0.43	0.41	0.36	0.33	0.29	0.26	0.23	0.22	0.17	0.13
SOUTH DAKOTA	6.95	4.34	3.88	3.45	3.26	2.98	2.69	2.59	2.37	2.19	2.03	1.92	1.80	1.50
TENNESSEE	0.97	0.58	0.49	0.44	0.39	0.37	0.32	0.29	0.26	0.23	0.20	0.18	0.17	0.11
TEXAS	1.37	0.81	0.67	0.61	0.55	0.50	0.46	0.41	0.36	0.31	0.28	0.25	0.22	0.15
UTAH	0.92	0.58	0.46	0.41	0.43	0.36	0.33	0.30	0.28	0.24	0.22	0.20	0.20	0.17
VERMONT	2.51	1.47	1.36	1.15	1.06	0.99	0.88	0.83	0.74	0.67	0.62	0.54	0.49	0.36
VIRGINIA	0.86	0.46	0.40	0.36	0.31	0.29	0.27	0.23	0.21	0.18	0.15	0.14	0.12	0.08
WASHINGTON	1.13	0.71	0.57	0.50	0.46	0.45	0.39	0.38	0.33	0.29	0.26	0.25	0.20	0.15
WEST VIRGINIA	0.44	0.26	0.20	0.18	0.16	0.15	0.13	0.12	0.11	0.09	0.08	0.07	0.07	0.05
WISCONSIN	1.36	0.81	0.70	0.63	0.61	0.59	0.48	0.46	0.42	0.38	0.34	0.32	0.31	0.24
WYOMING	2.80	1.91	1.76	1.56	1.42	1.35	1.21	1.14	1.05	0.94	0.88	0.86	0.82	0.68
AVERAGE	1.60	0.99	0.86	0.75	0.71	0.66	0.59	0.55	0.50	0.45	0.41	0.38	0.36	0.28

* EFFECTIVE TAX RATE EQUALS ZERO BEFORE ROUNDING. AN ENTIRE ROW OF * MEANS THAT THIS TAX IS NOT USED IN THIS STATE.

TABLE A-63

EFFECTIVE TAX RATES: LOCAL REAL PROPERTY TAX-ACREAGE AND FARMS (MOST PROGRESSIVE)
INCIDENCE: FARMERS
ALLOCATOR: FARM NET PROFIT

STATE	UNDER $3,000	$3,000 -3,999	$4,000 -4,999	$5,000 -5,999	$6,000 -6,999	$7,000 -7,999	$8,000 -9,999	$10,000 -11,999	$12,000 -14,999	$15,000 -19,999	$20,000 -24,999	$25,000 -29,999	$30,000 -34,999	OVER $35,000
ALABAMA	0.16	0.24	0.00	0.01	*	0.06	*	0.02	*	0.03	0.01	0.11	0.14	0.11
ALASKA	*	*	*	*	*	*	*	*	*	*	*	*	*	0.31
ARIZONA	0.09	*	*	*	0.32	*	*	*	*	0.26	*	0.45	*	0.70
ARKANSAS	0.37	0.04	*	0.36	0.40	*	*	0.25	0.12	0.13	0.25	0.48	0.80	1.61
CALIFORNIA	0.82	0.28	0.13	0.17	0.40	0.18	0.08	*	0.07	0.09	0.11	0.35	0.05	1.13
COLORADO	0.61	*	0.32	*	1.35	0.51	0.35	0.08	0.08	0.13	0.19	0.35	*	0.80
CONNECTICUT	0.03	*	*	*	*	*	0.26	*	0.13	0.16	*	*	0.02	0.01
DELAWARE	*	*	0.05	0.72	0.04	*	0.10	*	0.00	0.05	0.18	0.13	0.85	0.14
FLORIDA	0.82	0.15	0.01	0.45	0.47	*	0.01	0.32	0.23	*	0.19	0.40	1.13	0.56
GEORGIA	0.48	0.94	0.13	0.73	0.76	0.05	0.23	0.91	0.53	0.13	0.35	0.02	*	1.74
HAWAII	1.10	*	0.02	*	0.05	0.45	*	*	0.02	0.14	0.02	0.02	0.03	0.24
IDAHO	0.92	0.13	0.65	*	0.62	0.49	0.51	0.30	0.29	0.66	1.06	0.94	1.67	3.06
ILLINOIS	0.44	0.03	0.28	0.20	0.08	0.29	0.47	0.19	0.34	0.26	0.38	0.34	0.72	1.46
INDIANA	0.76	1.11	*	0.82	0.82	0.57	0.49	0.45	0.33	0.27	0.31	0.56	0.85	1.01
IOWA	1.94	1.21	0.73	2.05	1.47	2.02	0.55	0.77	1.87	1.30	1.32	3.00	2.72	4.65
KANSAS	1.16	0.49	0.28	0.66	*	0.83	0.97	0.65	0.70	0.41	0.53	1.16	0.98	2.89
KENTUCKY	2.01	0.75	1.37	0.26	0.64	0.12	0.40	0.44	0.01	0.16	0.01	0.08	1.14	0.84
LOUISIANA	0.01	*	0.10	0.28	*	0.14	*	*	0.04	*	0.17	*	*	0.33
MAINE	0.76	0.07	0.78	*	0.18	*	0.33	*	*	*	0.18	*	0.08	0.92
MARYLAND	*	0.00	0.59	1.42	*	*	0.01	0.03	0.39	0.22	0.20	*	*	0.09
MASSACHUSETTS	0.26	0.36	*	0.15	0.00	*	*	*	*	0.06	0.16	*	0.00	0.00
MICHIGAN	0.23	1.72	*	0.20	0.49	*	0.42	0.14	0.48	0.41	0.04	0.16	0.47	0.74
MINNESOTA	1.91	0.87	0.36	0.13	0.99	1.04	0.55	0.71	0.63	0.59	0.60	0.50	1.90	1.15
MISSISSIPPI	0.45	*	0.81	0.26	0.10	0.91	0.63	0.41	0.09	0.01	*	*	0.05	1.94
MISSOURI	0.96	1.08	0.74	*	0.32	*	0.60	0.29	0.38	0.43	0.31	0.17	1.18	0.19
MONTANA	0.41	0.69	1.00	*	0.87	0.14	0.34	0.05	0.42	0.63	0.44	1.74	2.06	2.90
NEBRASKA	1.96	1.71	1.81	2.86	1.29	2.76	0.20	1.70	1.30	0.85	2.06	1.54	2.59	3.70
NEVADA	0.10	*	*	*	*	*	*	0.38	0.02	*	1.13	0.40	0.33	0.54
NEW HAMPSHIRE	6.08	*	*	*	*	*	*	0.58	0.08	0.45	0.12	*	*	0.44
NEW JERSEY	2.07	*	*	0.01	0.26	*	*	1.27	*	0.01	*	*	0.21	0.05
NEW MEXICO	0.33	0.67	0.01	*	0.14	*	0.24	*	0.34	0.06	0.13	0.04	0.01	0.20
NEW YORK	*	*	*	0.01	0.38	0.52	0.12	0.14	0.65	*	*	0.20	*	0.06
NORTH CAROLINA	1.24	0.03	0.20	*	0.55	0.05	0.29	0.12	0.13	0.20	0.57	0.21	0.01	0.29
NORTH DAKOTA	0.55	0.93	1.13	1.09	1.28	2.77	1.37	1.44	1.29	0.98	1.79	2.22	2.82	5.16
OHIO	0.19	0.01	0.83	0.52	0.62	0.25	0.11	0.28	0.29	0.18	0.11	0.41	0.71	1.01
OKLAHOMA	0.66	*	0.33	0.60	*	*	0.15	*	0.19	0.41	0.20	0.88	*	0.54
OREGON	0.65	*	*	0.15	1.03	*	1.42	0.03	0.63	0.04	0.29	1.48	1.43	2.58
PENNSYLVANIA	0.30	0.28	0.18	*	0.14	*	0.24	0.46	0.21	0.07	*	0.04	*	0.01
RHODE ISLAND	*	*	*	*	*	*	*	*	*	*	*	*	*	0.36
SOUTH CAROLINA	0.18	1.06	*	0.41	0.61	*	0.81	0.14	0.18	0.01	0.59	0.01	*	0.69
SOUTH DAKOTA	2.95	1.23	1.46	1.79	1.83	2.42	1.36	1.42	2.07	2.40	1.76	3.13	6.11	4.06
TENNESSEE	1.19	0.24	0.31	0.27	1.00	0.02	0.62	0.33	0.25	0.05	0.01	*	*	0.61
TEXAS	0.74	0.46	0.51	0.02	0.24	0.26	0.37	0.05	0.21	0.23	0.09	0.51	0.73	0.79
UTAH	0.04	0.00	0.81	1.53	0.08	*	0.22	0.60	0.11	0.15	0.03	0.65	*	0.45
VERMONT	3.67	6.51	*	2.45	0.02	*	0.39	1.15	0.47	0.56	1.30	*	*	0.03
VIRGINIA	0.03	0.02	2.32	0.00	*	0.75	0.20	0.72	0.10	*	0.30	0.01	*	0.09
WASHINGTON	0.43	0.30	*	*	0.43	0.47	*	*	*	0.14	*	0.14	0.09	1.57
WEST VIRGINIA	1.01	*	*	0.00	*	2.08	*	0.00	*	0.01	*	*	0.18	0.08
WISCONSIN	0.45	1.45	0.84	0.59	1.08	0.27	0.46	0.48	0.54	0.55	0.09	0.26	*	0.32
WYOMING	0.25	1.52	*	2.80	0.05	0.99	0.14	0.34	0.63	0.41	1.03	0.44	2.20	2.59
AVERAGE	0.83	0.53	0.38	0.48	0.43	0.43	0.32	0.35	0.34	0.29	0.37	0.47	0.68	1.11

* EFFECTIVE TAX RATE EQUALS ZERO BEFORE ROUNDING. AN ENTIRE ROW OF * MEANS THAT THIS TAX IS NOT USED IN THIS STATE.

TABLE A-64

EFFECTIVE TAX RATES: LOCAL REAL PROPERTY TAX-COMMERCIAL PROPERTY (BENCHMARK)
INCIDENCE: 2/3 CONSUMERS, 1/6 INCORPORATED BUSINESSES, 1/6 UNINCORPORATED BUSINESSES
ALLOCATOR: CONSUMPTION, DIVIDEND INCOME, BUSINESS AND PARTNERSHIP PROFIT

STATE	UNDER $3,000	$3,000 -3,999	$4,000 -4,999	$5,000 -5,999	$6,000 -6,999	$7,000 -7,999	$8,000 -9,999	$10,000 -11,999	$12,000 -14,999	$15,000 -19,999	$20,000 -24,999	$25,000 -29,999	$30,000 -34,999	OVER $35,000
ALABAMA	0.26	0.15	0.14	0.12	0.11	0.11	0.09	0.08	0.07	0.07	0.08	0.06	0.09	0.23
ALASKA	1.58	1.38	1.05	0.80	0.86	0.76	0.66	0.59	0.52	0.53	0.48	0.42	0.41	0.53
ARIZONA	2.03	1.35	1.00	0.99	0.87	0.68	0.69	0.62	0.55	0.54	0.49	0.44	0.60	0.87
ARKANSAS	0.54	0.35	0.31	0.30	0.23	0.21	0.21	0.19	0.17	0.14	0.14	0.14	0.17	0.39
CALIFORNIA	1.80	1.10	0.94	0.90	0.76	0.70	0.66	0.60	0.54	0.46	0.43	0.44	0.47	0.76
COLORADO	2.32	1.23	1.46	0.97	0.87	1.03	0.72	0.66	0.63	0.53	0.54	0.48	0.59	1.17
CONNECTICUT	1.36	1.08	1.03	0.94	0.78	0.75	0.68	0.60	0.54	0.54	0.44	0.43	0.40	0.79
DELAWARE	0.81	0.54	0.47	0.44	0.33	0.36	0.31	0.27	0.27	0.24	0.21	0.21	0.20	0.44
FLORIDA	0.95	0.57	0.48	0.45	0.42	0.39	0.34	0.33	0.29	0.27	0.26	0.26	0.29	0.42
GEORGIA	1.09	0.63	0.58	0.57	0.49	0.43	0.39	0.35	0.34	0.31	0.28	0.29	0.39	0.66
HAWAII	1.42	0.74	0.69	0.65	0.74	0.56	0.53	0.44	0.40	0.40	0.32	0.29	0.30	0.57
IDAHO	1.08	0.64	0.50	0.44	0.41	0.42	0.35	0.32	0.27	0.24	0.31	0.27	0.36	0.55
ILLINOIS	1.38	0.91	0.78	0.80	0.64	0.63	0.59	0.55	0.46	0.43	0.39	0.39	0.40	0.80
INDIANA	0.89	0.56	0.44	0.39	0.37	0.38	0.32	0.31	0.27	0.26	0.26	0.27	0.25	0.55
IOWA	0.97	0.64	0.63	0.59	0.46	0.43	0.44	0.44	0.33	0.32	0.29	0.32	0.47	0.61
KANSAS	0.81	0.49	0.42	0.37	0.42	0.34	0.31	0.31	0.25	0.23	0.22	0.24	0.20	0.46
KENTUCKY	0.42	0.28	0.24	0.26	0.18	0.18	0.18	0.14	0.13	0.13	0.12	0.15	0.12	0.42
LOUISIANA	0.49	0.28	0.26	0.23	0.22	0.22	0.19	0.18	0.16	0.15	0.14	0.15	0.17	0.36
MAINE	1.00	0.64	0.58	0.56	0.45	0.42	0.49	0.34	0.34	0.34	0.30	0.39	0.32	0.61
MARYLAND	1.13	0.96	0.66	0.54	0.51	0.47	0.42	0.42	0.35	0.33	0.33	0.28	0.27	0.53
MASSACHUSETTS	2.28	1.51	1.52	1.30	1.30	1.08	0.99	0.90	0.82	0.72	0.67	0.73	0.66	1.51
MICHIGAN	1.50	0.97	0.82	0.67	0.64	0.71	0.55	0.51	0.44	0.40	0.39	0.41	0.37	0.80
MINNESOTA	1.60	0.98	1.06	0.84	0.71	0.68	0.65	0.58	0.51	0.43	0.46	0.45	0.44	0.92
MISSISSIPPI	0.52	0.32	0.28	0.25	0.28	0.22	0.23	0.19	0.18	0.16	0.18	0.15	0.18	0.41
MISSOURI	1.05	0.62	0.56	0.53	0.45	0.44	0.41	0.37	0.33	0.29	0.29	0.27	0.28	0.69
MONTANA	1.37	0.94	0.70	0.64	0.64	0.58	0.52	0.52	0.38	0.37	0.36	0.34	0.43	0.70
NEBRASKA	1.30	0.73	0.54	0.58	0.53	0.46	0.48	0.40	0.35	0.32	0.33	0.37	0.40	0.71
NEVADA	1.70	1.09	0.91	0.76	0.73	0.73	0.63	0.61	0.50	0.48	0.42	0.42	0.42	0.92
NEW HAMPSHIRE	1.91	1.24	1.29	1.24	0.84	0.75	0.80	0.75	0.65	0.57	0.57	0.51	0.56	1.20
NEW JERSEY	1.81	1.20	1.21	1.11	1.00	0.94	1.14	0.82	0.72	0.63	0.60	0.56	0.55	0.97
NEW MEXICO	0.69	0.50	0.38	0.30	0.30	0.29	0.25	0.24	0.23	0.21	0.19	0.18	0.22	0.31
NEW YORK	4.62	2.89	2.62	2.30	2.05	1.97	1.80	1.65	1.49	1.37	1.26	1.23	1.35	2.66
NORTH CAROLINA	0.60	0.35	0.38	0.28	0.25	0.23	0.22	0.20	0.17	0.15	0.17	0.14	0.13	0.35
NORTH DAKOTA	1.23	0.71	0.66	0.57	0.67	0.44	0.43	0.39	0.40	0.35	0.35	0.35	0.43	0.62
OHIO	1.08	0.72	0.61	0.59	0.49	0.52	0.45	0.40	0.35	0.34	0.32	0.34	0.39	0.67
OKLAHOMA	0.74	0.37	0.33	0.31	0.29	0.32	0.24	0.22	0.21	0.19	0.18	0.18	0.18	0.38
OREGON	1.93	1.04	0.86	0.74	0.72	0.66	0.59	0.57	0.46	0.46	0.44	0.47	0.57	0.97
PENNSYLVANIA	1.32	0.82	0.67	0.67	0.70	0.51	0.57	0.46	0.40	0.38	0.34	0.36	0.38	0.75
RHODE ISLAND	1.29	0.87	0.79	0.69	0.75	0.55	0.52	0.52	0.44	0.41	0.37	0.36	0.41	0.72
SOUTH CAROLINA	0.53	0.34	0.30	0.29	0.31	0.29	0.23	0.26	0.20	0.18	0.17	0.19	0.18	0.44
SOUTH DAKOTA	1.04	0.63	0.55	0.47	0.52	0.54	0.44	0.38	0.35	0.32	0.37	0.34	0.39	0.68
TENNESSEE	1.26	0.74	0.66	0.58	0.55	0.50	0.49	0.47	0.39	0.40	0.36	0.37	0.40	1.09
TEXAS	1.14	0.65	0.62	0.51	0.47	0.43	0.40	0.38	0.34	0.32	0.29	0.33	0.33	0.67
UTAH	1.14	0.54	0.52	0.45	0.42	0.37	0.36	0.30	0.27	0.24	0.23	0.22	0.26	0.48
VERMONT	1.38	0.78	0.84	0.71	0.64	0.64	0.58	0.56	0.51	0.45	0.46	0.37	0.62	1.05
VIRGINIA	1.00	0.61	0.48	0.51	0.48	0.40	0.36	0.36	0.28	0.28	0.24	0.26	0.22	0.46
WASHINGTON	0.94	0.56	0.50	0.43	0.40	0.41	0.35	0.30	0.28	0.24	0.22	0.22	0.23	0.50
WEST VIRGINIA	0.35	0.28	0.21	0.17	0.19	0.16	0.13	0.13	0.12	0.11	0.11	0.13	0.18	0.29
WISCONSIN	1.41	0.82	0.84	0.61	0.60	0.62	0.64	0.50	0.40	0.38	0.37	0.39	0.45	0.78
WYOMING	1.40	0.85	0.72	0.63	0.57	0.57	0.62	0.47	0.43	0.41	0.36	0.38	0.39	0.85
AVERAGE	1.25	0.78	0.70	0.62	0.57	0.53	0.49	0.44	0.39	0.36	0.34	0.34	0.37	0.71

* EFFECTIVE TAX RATE EQUALS ZERO BEFORE ROUNDING. AN ENTIRE ROW OF * MEANS THAT THIS TAX IS NOT USED IN THIS STATE.

TABLE A-65

EFFECTIVE TAX RATES: LOCAL REAL PROPERTY TAX-COMMERCIAL PROPERTY (MOST REGRESSIVE)
INCIDENCE: CONSUMERS IN GENERAL
ALLOCATOR: TOTAL CONSUMPTION EXPENDITURES

STATE	UNDER $3,000	$3,000 -3,999	$4,000 -4,999	$5,000 -5,999	$6,000 -6,999	$7,000 -7,999	$8,000 -9,999	$10,000 -11,999	$12,000 -14,999	$15,000 -19,999	$20,000 -24,999	$25,000 -29,999	$30,000 -34,999	OVER $35,000
ALABAMA	0.34	0.21	0.18	0.16	0.14	0.13	0.12	0.11	0.10	0.09	0.08	0.07	0.07	0.03
ALASKA	2.01	1.28	1.11	1.09	1.00	0.88	0.84	0.76	0.69	0.59	0.54	0.51	0.48	0.37
ARIZONA	2.55	1.53	1.18	1.15	1.00	0.87	0.85	0.75	0.68	0.61	0.52	0.47	0.47	0.37
ARKANSAS	0.65	0.40	0.34	0.30	0.29	0.27	0.24	0.22	0.19	0.18	0.17	0.15	0.14	0.09
CALIFORNIA	2.23	1.45	1.19	1.07	0.96	0.89	0.78	0.71	0.64	0.56	0.50	0.46	0.43	0.32
COLORADO	2.78	1.75	1.41	1.27	1.21	1.06	0.92	0.87	0.79	0.69	0.62	0.58	0.49	0.42
CONNECTICUT	1.75	1.26	1.04	1.03	0.93	0.98	0.80	0.73	0.67	0.61	0.57	0.53	0.49	0.35
DELAWARE	0.99	0.60	0.58	0.48	0.45	0.43	0.39	0.34	0.33	0.30	0.27	0.25	0.22	0.16
FLORIDA	1.16	0.72	0.58	0.53	0.51	0.47	0.42	0.38	0.35	0.31	0.29	0.26	0.23	0.11
GEORGIA	1.34	0.77	0.69	0.63	0.58	0.56	0.49	0.44	0.41	0.38	0.34	0.31	0.29	0.20
HAWAII	1.39	0.91	0.89	0.80	0.72	0.68	0.61	0.55	0.50	0.44	0.40	0.38	0.33	0.29
IDAHO	1.26	0.75	0.62	0.59	0.53	0.48	0.45	0.39	0.36	0.31	0.28	0.26	0.23	0.19
ILLINOIS	1.71	1.15	0.99	0.89	0.80	0.77	0.70	0.63	0.59	0.53	0.47	0.45	0.42	0.32
INDIANA	1.13	0.70	0.58	0.55	0.50	0.47	0.41	0.39	0.35	0.31	0.29	0.25	0.25	0.20
IOWA	1.31	0.82	0.76	0.60	0.60	0.56	0.50	0.48	0.42	0.38	0.35	0.33	0.30	0.27
KANSAS	1.02	0.63	0.55	0.45	0.44	0.41	0.40	0.35	0.32	0.28	0.24	0.24	0.23	0.17
KENTUCKY	0.57	0.35	0.31	0.26	0.25	0.23	0.22	0.20	0.17	0.16	0.15	0.14	0.13	0.08
LOUISIANA	0.65	0.38	0.32	0.31	0.28	0.26	0.25	0.22	0.20	0.19	0.17	0.16	0.15	0.12
MAINE	1.27	0.81	0.71	0.56	0.59	0.53	0.49	0.44	0.40	0.36	0.34	0.30	0.29	0.20
MARYLAND	1.48	0.94	0.80	0.66	0.65	0.60	0.56	0.50	0.45	0.40	0.36	0.35	0.29	0.25
MASSACHUSETTS	2.70	2.04	1.67	1.45	1.41	1.31	1.19	1.14	0.97	0.91	0.83	0.82	0.79	0.53
MICHIGAN	1.84	1.18	0.96	0.83	0.75	0.76	0.65	0.61	0.55	0.49	0.45	0.41	0.40	0.30
MINNESOTA	2.02	1.30	1.01	0.97	0.88	0.89	0.74	0.69	0.62	0.55	0.51	0.49	0.45	0.34
MISSISSIPPI	0.69	0.44	0.36	0.32	0.29	0.28	0.26	0.24	0.21	0.19	0.17	0.17	0.16	0.10
MISSOURI	1.40	0.78	0.74	0.64	0.58	0.55	0.50	0.46	0.40	0.35	0.33	0.30	0.25	0.22
MONTANA	1.68	1.06	0.91	0.78	0.74	0.68	0.59	0.53	0.49	0.44	0.40	0.35	0.36	0.29
NEBRASKA	1.48	0.95	0.74	0.68	0.63	0.59	0.54	0.50	0.45	0.42	0.38	0.35	0.34	0.28
NEVADA	2.17	1.44	1.21	1.03	1.02	0.94	0.83	0.73	0.64	0.58	0.51	0.50	0.46	0.30
NEW HAMPSHIRE	2.26	1.48	1.16	1.14	1.02	0.92	0.91	0.82	0.76	0.71	0.64	0.60	0.58	0.42
NEW JERSEY	2.27	1.49	1.32	1.21	1.14	1.09	0.95	0.94	0.84	0.77	0.72	0.68	0.63	0.48
NEW MEXICO	0.89	0.56	0.50	0.42	0.41	0.35	0.32	0.29	0.25	0.23	0.20	0.17	0.14	0.14
NEW YORK	5.92	3.63	3.01	2.64	2.55	2.39	2.17	2.05	1.84	1.68	1.57	1.49	1.41	1.00
NORTH CAROLINA	0.73	0.44	0.38	0.32	0.31	0.28	0.27	0.24	0.22	0.19	0.18	0.16	0.15	0.10
NORTH DAKOTA	1.49	0.89	0.78	0.68	0.63	0.59	0.54	0.51	0.47	0.42	0.39	0.36	0.35	0.31
OHIO	1.35	0.87	0.75	0.65	0.60	0.60	0.53	0.48	0.44	0.41	0.38	0.35	0.32	0.25
OKLAHOMA	0.90	0.51	0.43	0.41	0.38	0.33	0.30	0.29	0.25	0.22	0.21	0.19	0.17	0.15
OREGON	2.24	1.35	1.13	1.04	0.93	0.87	0.78	0.70	0.61	0.54	0.48	0.45	0.39	0.31
PENNSYLVANIA	1.59	0.97	0.85	0.73	0.71	0.66	0.62	0.57	0.51	0.47	0.41	0.39	0.39	0.28
RHODE ISLAND	1.61	0.93	0.92	0.81	0.66	0.64	0.61	0.55	0.52	0.49	0.45	0.43	0.37	0.28
SOUTH CAROLINA	0.72	0.45	0.38	0.35	0.32	0.31	0.28	0.26	0.24	0.22	0.20	0.19	0.16	0.12
SOUTH DAKOTA	1.29	0.80	0.71	0.62	0.59	0.54	0.48	0.46	0.42	0.39	0.36	0.33	0.31	0.26
TENNESSEE	1.59	1.01	0.87	0.79	0.71	0.69	0.61	0.57	0.52	0.47	0.43	0.39	0.38	0.26
TEXAS	1.36	0.86	0.72	0.67	0.61	0.56	0.53	0.48	0.43	0.39	0.36	0.33	0.29	0.22
UTAH	1.21	0.74	0.59	0.52	0.54	0.45	0.41	0.37	0.33	0.29	0.26	0.23	0.23	0.19
VERMONT	1.79	1.08	1.00	0.85	0.80	0.75	0.67	0.64	0.57	0.53	0.49	0.43	0.40	0.30
VIRGINIA	1.28	0.71	0.65	0.58	0.51	0.48	0.46	0.41	0.37	0.33	0.29	0.28	0.23	0.18
WASHINGTON	1.30	0.79	0.63	0.54	0.50	0.48	0.42	0.40	0.34	0.29	0.27	0.25	0.20	0.14
WEST VIRGINIA	0.51	0.31	0.25	0.22	0.21	0.19	0.17	0.17	0.15	0.14	0.12	0.11	0.10	0.08
WISCONSIN	1.78	1.04	0.90	0.81	0.77	0.75	0.61	0.58	0.52	0.47	0.41	0.39	0.37	0.28
WYOMING	1.59	1.06	0.96	0.85	0.77	0.72	0.64	0.60	0.55	0.48	0.44	0.43	0.41	0.33
AVERAGE	1.55	0.97	0.83	0.74	0.69	0.64	0.58	0.53	0.48	0.43	0.40	0.37	0.34	0.26

* EFFECTIVE TAX RATE EQUALS ZERO BEFORE ROUNDING. AN ENTIRE ROW OF * MEANS THAT THIS TAX IS NOT USED IN THIS STATE.

TABLE A-66

EFFECTIVE TAX RATES: LOCAL REAL PROPERTY TAX-COMMERCIAL PROPERTY (MOST PROGRESSIVE)
INCIDENCE: OWNERS OF BUSINESSES-1/2 INCORPORATED, 1/2 UNINCORPORATED
ALLOCATOR: DIVIDEND INCOME, BUSINESS AND PARTNERSHIP PROFIT

STATE	UNDER $3,000	$3,000 -3,999	$4,000 -4,999	$5,000 -5,999	$6,000 -6,999	$7,000 -7,999	$8,000 -9,999	$10,000 -11,999	$12,000 -14,999	$15,000 -19,999	$20,000 -24,999	$25,000 -29,999	$30,000 -34,999	OVER $35,000
ALABAMA	0.10	0.04	0.07	0.06	0.04	0.08	0.03	0.03	0.02	0.03	0.07	0.04	0.12	0.63
ALASKA	0.70	1.59	0.94	0.21	0.57	0.52	0.29	0.26	0.16	0.42	0.37	0.25	0.27	0.85
ARIZONA	0.99	0.99	0.63	0.66	0.60	0.29	0.36	0.37	0.29	0.40	0.43	0.38	0.87	1.87
ARKANSAS	0.32	0.26	0.24	0.30	0.10	0.10	0.13	0.12	0.13	0.08	0.08	0.14	0.22	1.00
CALIFORNIA	0.92	0.39	0.42	0.57	0.35	0.33	0.41	0.37	0.35	0.28	0.28	0.39	0.55	1.64
COLORADO	1.39	0.18	1.55	0.35	0.17	0.97	0.31	0.25	0.31	0.20	0.40	0.28	0.79	2.70
CONNECTICUT	0.57	0.73	1.00	0.76	0.47	0.26	0.43	0.33	0.26	0.41	0.19	0.23	0.21	1.66
DELAWARE	0.43	0.43	0.25	0.36	0.10	0.23	0.14	0.14	0.15	0.11	0.09	0.13	0.16	1.00
FLORIDA	0.51	0.26	0.26	0.29	0.23	0.22	0.18	0.23	0.15	0.20	0.20	0.26	0.42	1.06
GEORGIA	0.59	0.36	0.34	0.44	0.30	0.17	0.17	0.16	0.21	0.17	0.16	0.25	0.59	1.61
HAWAII	1.48	0.39	0.28	0.36	0.78	0.32	0.36	0.20	0.20	0.33	0.15	0.09	0.24	1.15
IDAHO	0.73	0.42	0.25	0.12	0.15	0.29	0.14	0.17	0.10	0.11	0.38	0.28	0.63	1.28
ILLINOIS	0.71	0.42	0.36	0.59	0.33	0.34	0.37	0.39	0.18	0.24	0.20	0.27	0.35	1.78
INDIANA	0.40	0.26	0.17	0.08	0.11	0.20	0.15	0.16	0.12	0.16	0.20	0.32	0.24	1.25
IOWA	0.28	0.29	0.34	0.56	0.17	0.17	0.32	0.36	0.14	0.18	0.16	0.29	0.81	1.30
KANSAS	0.38	0.19	0.14	0.21	0.36	0.19	0.12	0.24	0.10	0.13	0.18	0.24	0.14	1.06
KENTUCKY	0.12	0.12	0.10	0.26	0.03	0.08	0.09	0.03	0.05	0.07	0.07	0.17	0.10	1.12
LOUISIANA	0.17	0.09	0.14	0.08	0.09	0.13	0.08	0.10	0.07	0.08	0.07	0.13	0.21	0.85
MAINE	0.45	0.30	0.33	0.58	0.17	0.22	0.51	0.15	0.20	0.28	0.21	0.55	0.39	1.44
MARYLAND	0.42	1.02	0.38	0.31	0.23	0.21	0.14	0.25	0.15	0.19	0.26	0.12	0.23	1.09
MASSACHUSETTS	1.44	0.42	1.21	0.99	1.09	0.63	0.60	0.42	0.51	0.33	0.35	0.55	0.41	3.48
MICHIGAN	0.81	0.53	0.54	0.37	0.41	0.61	0.36	0.30	0.21	0.20	0.26	0.41	0.31	1.81
MINNESOTA	0.76	0.35	1.17	0.59	0.36	0.26	0.47	0.36	0.29	0.20	0.38	0.36	0.44	2.11
MISSISSIPPI	0.16	0.09	0.13	0.12	0.27	0.09	0.17	0.10	0.12	0.11	0.18	0.12	0.22	1.04
MISSOURI	0.33	0.30	0.18	0.33	0.19	0.21	0.22	0.19	0.18	0.17	0.22	0.21	0.32	1.65
MONTANA	0.73	0.69	0.27	0.36	0.42	0.38	0.40	0.50	0.15	0.22	0.27	0.31	0.56	1.55
NEBRASKA	0.91	0.28	0.14	0.39	0.34	0.19	0.36	0.18	0.14	0.13	0.23	0.39	0.52	1.59
NEVADA	0.74	0.38	0.29	0.20	0.15	0.31	0.23	0.36	0.20	0.27	0.22	0.27	0.35	2.18
NEW HAMPSHIRE	1.21	0.75	1.57	1.46	0.46	0.40	0.58	0.62	0.43	0.28	0.44	0.33	0.53	2.78
NEW JERSEY	0.89	0.61	0.99	0.91	0.73	0.62	1.52	0.58	0.45	0.34	0.35	0.31	0.39	1.94
NEW MEXICO	0.28	0.37	0.12	0.07	0.09	0.15	0.10	0.15	0.18	0.18	0.17	0.19	0.38	0.64
NEW YORK	1.97	1.40	1.83	1.61	1.05	1.09	1.07	0.83	0.79	0.73	0.62	0.71	1.23	6.02
NORTH CAROLINA	0.35	0.16	0.39	0.18	0.13	0.13	0.14	0.11	0.07	0.07	0.16	0.09	0.11	0.87
NORTH DAKOTA	0.71	0.34	0.43	0.33	0.74	0.11	0.23	0.14	0.25	0.21	0.29	0.34	0.59	1.25
OHIO	0.53	0.42	0.33	0.48	0.28	0.38	0.29	0.23	0.16	0.19	0.19	0.31	0.52	1.52
OKLAHOMA	0.42	0.09	0.12	0.10	0.12	0.28	0.11	0.09	0.13	0.11	0.11	0.16	0.20	0.86
OREGON	1.30	0.42	0.31	0.11	0.28	0.22	0.22	0.31	0.16	0.31	0.37	0.50	0.93	2.33
PENNSYLVANIA	0.77	0.52	0.30	0.55	0.69	0.21	0.48	0.24	0.18	0.21	0.20	0.31	0.36	1.71
RHODE ISLAND	0.65	0.76	0.52	0.45	0.93	0.38	0.34	0.46	0.28	0.24	0.20	0.21	0.50	1.61
SOUTH CAROLINA	0.13	0.10	0.14	0.16	0.29	0.25	0.14	0.24	0.13	0.10	0.10	0.18	0.21	1.08
SOUTH DAKOTA	0.52	0.30	0.24	0.17	0.37	0.54	0.34	0.20	0.22	0.20	0.39	0.36	0.54	1.55
TENNESSEE	0.57	0.20	0.23	0.16	0.22	0.11	0.25	0.26	0.11	0.26	0.22	0.32	0.45	2.76
TEXAS	0.67	0.23	0.41	0.20	0.20	0.17	0.14	0.16	0.16	0.18	0.14	0.33	0.42	1.60
UTAH	0.99	0.13	0.37	0.30	0.18	0.20	0.25	0.15	0.13	0.14	0.18	0.20	0.31	1.06
VERMONT	0.54	0.19	0.52	0.41	0.32	0.41	0.39	0.42	0.38	0.28	0.40	0.25	1.07	2.57
VIRGINIA	0.43	0.41	0.14	0.36	0.43	0.23	0.17	0.26	0.10	0.18	0.15	0.21	0.20	1.03
WASHINGTON	0.21	0.11	0.23	0.21	0.21	0.25	0.23	0.10	0.15	0.13	0.13	0.15	0.31	1.22
WEST VIRGINIA	0.03	0.20	0.11	0.07	0.14	0.08	0.04	0.07	0.07	0.05	0.09	0.17	0.34	0.72
WISCONSIN	0.67	0.38	0.73	0.20	0.26	0.37	0.72	0.32	0.16	0.21	0.29	0.37	0.60	1.80
WYOMING	1.02	0.42	0.24	0.18	0.16	0.26	0.57	0.20	0.19	0.26	0.17	0.27	0.35	1.89
AVERAGE	0.65	0.41	0.45	0.38	0.34	0.30	0.32	0.26	0.20	0.21	0.23	0.27	0.42	1.61

* EFFECTIVE TAX RATE EQUALS ZERO BEFORE ROUNDING. AN ENTIRE ROW OF * MEANS THAT THIS TAX IS NOT USED IN THIS STATE.

TABLE A-67

EFFECTIVE TAX RATES: LOCAL REAL PROPERTY TAX-INDUSTRIAL PROPERTY (BENCHMARK)
INCIDENCE: 2/3 CONSUMERS, 2/9 INCORPORATED BUSINESSES, 1/9 UNINCORPORATED BUSINESSES
ALLOCATOR: CONSUMPTION, DIVIDEND INCOME, BUSINESS AND PARTNERSHIP PROFIT

STATE	UNDER $3,000	$3,000 -3,999	$4,000 -4,999	$5,000 -5,999	$6,000 -6,999	$7,000 -7,999	$8,000 -9,999	$10,000 -11,999	$12,000 -14,999	$15,000 -19,999	$20,000 -24,999	$25,000 -29,999	$30,000 -34,999	OVER $35,000
ALABAMA	0.08	0.05	0.04	0.04	0.03	0.03	0.03	0.02	0.02	0.02	0.02	0.02	0.02	0.07
ALASKA	0.20	0.19	0.14	0.10	0.10	0.09	0.08	0.07	0.06	0.07	0.06	0.05	0.05	0.06
ARIZONA	0.45	0.30	0.23	0.22	0.20	0.14	0.15	0.13	0.12	0.12	0.10	0.09	0.12	0.19
ARKANSAS	0.08	0.05	0.04	0.05	0.03	0.03	0.03	0.03	0.02	0.02	0.02	0.02	0.02	0.05
CALIFORNIA	0.70	0.43	0.36	0.35	0.29	0.26	0.25	0.22	0.20	0.17	0.15	0.15	0.16	0.27
COLORADO	0.40	0.21	0.27	0.16	0.14	0.18	0.11	0.10	0.10	0.08	0.08	0.07	0.09	0.20
CONNECTICUT	0.41	0.34	0.32	0.29	0.23	0.21	0.18	0.16	0.15	0.15	0.11	0.11	0.09	0.21
DELAWARE	0.24	0.15	0.13	0.12	0.09	0.11	0.08	0.07	0.07	0.06	0.05	0.05	0.04	0.11
FLORIDA	0.15	0.09	0.07	0.07	0.07	0.06	0.05	0.05	0.04	0.04	0.04	0.04	0.04	0.06
GEORGIA	0.13	0.07	0.06	0.06	0.06	0.05	0.04	0.04	0.04	0.03	0.03	0.03	0.04	0.07
HAWAII	0.33	0.16	0.15	0.15	0.17	0.12	0.11	0.09	0.08	0.08	0.06	0.06	0.06	0.12
IDAHO	0.24	0.14	0.11	0.09	0.09	0.09	0.07	0.07	0.06	0.05	0.07	0.05	0.08	0.12
ILLINOIS	0.62	0.41	0.34	0.35	0.28	0.27	0.25	0.23	0.19	0.17	0.15	0.15	0.15	0.33
INDIANA	0.31	0.19	0.15	0.13	0.13	0.13	0.10	0.11	0.09	0.09	0.09	0.09	0.08	0.18
IOWA	0.21	0.15	0.14	0.13	0.10	0.09	0.10	0.10	0.07	0.07	0.06	0.06	0.11	0.13
KANSAS	0.13	0.08	0.06	0.06	0.07	0.05	0.05	0.05	0.04	0.03	0.03	0.03	0.03	0.07
KENTUCKY	0.08	0.05	0.04	0.05	0.03	0.03	0.03	0.03	0.02	0.02	0.02	0.03	0.02	0.08
LOUISIANA	0.07	0.04	0.04	0.03	0.03	0.03	0.03	0.02	0.02	0.02	0.02	0.02	0.02	0.05
MAINE	0.37	0.24	0.21	0.21	0.16	0.15	0.18	0.12	0.12	0.12	0.10	0.14	0.10	0.21
MARYLAND	0.22	0.21	0.13	0.11	0.10	0.09	0.08	0.08	0.06	0.06	0.06	0.05	0.04	0.09
MASSACHUSETTS	0.63	0.41	0.41	0.35	0.35	0.28	0.25	0.24	0.20	0.18	0.16	0.19	0.16	0.38
MICHIGAN	0.73	0.48	0.41	0.32	0.30	0.34	0.26	0.23	0.20	0.18	0.17	0.19	0.15	0.36
MINNESOTA	0.49	0.28	0.34	0.24	0.21	0.20	0.20	0.17	0.14	0.12	0.12	0.13	0.11	0.28
MISSISSIPPI	0.05	0.03	0.03	0.02	0.03	0.02	0.02	0.02	0.02	0.01	0.02	0.01	0.02	0.04
MISSOURI	0.23	0.14	0.12	0.12	0.10	0.10	0.09	0.08	0.07	0.06	0.06	0.05	0.05	0.15
MONTANA	0.39	0.28	0.20	0.18	0.18	0.17	0.14	0.15	0.10	0.10	0.10	0.08	0.11	0.20
NEBRASKA	0.20	0.11	0.08	0.09	0.08	0.07	0.07	0.06	0.05	0.05	0.05	0.05	0.06	0.11
NEVADA	0.17	0.11	0.09	0.07	0.07	0.07	0.06	0.06	0.04	0.05	0.04	0.04	0.03	0.09
NEW HAMPSHIRE	0.95	0.59	0.68	0.65	0.38	0.34	0.37	0.36	0.30	0.26	0.25	0.22	0.25	0.57
NEW JERSEY	0.85	0.54	0.58	0.53	0.47	0.42	0.55	0.37	0.30	0.27	0.25	0.23	0.22	0.39
NEW MEXICO	0.12	0.09	0.06	0.05	0.05	0.05	0.04	0.04	0.04	0.03	0.03	0.03	0.03	0.05
NEW YORK	0.66	0.41	0.37	0.32	0.28	0.27	0.24	0.22	0.20	0.18	0.16	0.16	0.18	0.34
NORTH CAROLINA	0.20	0.11	0.13	0.09	0.08	0.07	0.07	0.06	0.05	0.05	0.05	0.04	0.04	0.11
NORTH DAKOTA	0.06	0.03	0.03	0.03	0.03	0.02	0.02	0.02	0.02	0.02	0.02	0.02	0.02	0.03
OHIO	0.36	0.24	0.20	0.20	0.15	0.16	0.15	0.13	0.11	0.10	0.10	0.10	0.12	0.21
OKLAHOMA	0.08	0.04	0.04	0.03	0.03	0.03	0.03	0.02	0.02	0.02	0.02	0.02	0.02	0.04
OREGON	0.85	0.42	0.36	0.30	0.29	0.26	0.23	0.23	0.18	0.18	0.17	0.17	0.23	0.39
PENNSYLVANIA	0.37	0.23	0.18	0.18	0.19	0.13	0.15	0.12	0.10	0.10	0.08	0.09	0.09	0.19
RHODE ISLAND	0.45	0.32	0.27	0.24	0.27	0.17	0.17	0.16	0.14	0.13	0.11	0.11	0.12	0.21
SOUTH CAROLINA	0.29	0.18	0.16	0.15	0.18	0.16	0.13	0.14	0.11	0.09	0.08	0.09	0.08	0.24
SOUTH DAKOTA	0.06	0.04	0.03	0.03	0.03	0.03	0.03	0.02	0.02	0.02	0.02	0.02	0.02	0.04
TENNESSEE	0.28	0.16	0.14	0.12	0.12	0.10	0.10	0.10	0.08	0.08	0.07	0.07	0.08	0.23
TEXAS	0.49	0.27	0.26	0.22	0.20	0.18	0.16	0.15	0.14	0.13	0.11	0.13	0.12	0.27
UTAH	0.27	0.12	0.12	0.10	0.09	0.08	0.08	0.06	0.05	0.05	0.05	0.04	0.05	0.11
VERMONT	0.78	0.43	0.45	0.41	0.36	0.35	0.32	0.30	0.28	0.23	0.25	0.18	0.36	0.56
VIRGINIA	0.19	0.12	0.09	0.10	0.10	0.07	0.07	0.07	0.05	0.05	0.04	0.04	0.03	0.08
WASHINGTON	0.23	0.13	0.12	0.10	0.09	0.09	0.08	0.07	0.06	0.05	0.04	0.04	0.04	0.11
WEST VIRGINIA	0.10	0.08	0.06	0.05	0.05	0.04	0.03	0.03	0.03	0.03	0.03	0.03	0.05	0.08
WISCONSIN	0.29	0.16	0.17	0.12	0.12	0.13	0.13	0.10	0.07	0.07	0.07	0.07	0.08	0.15
WYOMING	0.18	0.12	0.10	0.08	0.07	0.08	0.08	0.06	0.05	0.05	0.05	0.05	0.05	0.11
AVERAGE	0.33	0.20	0.19	0.17	0.15	0.13	0.13	0.11	0.10	0.09	0.08	0.08	0.09	0.18

* EFFECTIVE TAX RATE EQUALS ZERO BEFORE ROUNDING. AN ENTIRE ROW OF * MEANS THAT THIS TAX IS NOT USED IN THIS STATE.

TABLE A-68
EFFECTIVE TAX RATES: LOCAL REAL PROPERTY TAX-INDUSTRIAL PROPERTY (MOST REGRESSIVE)
INCIDENCE: CONSUMERS IN GENERAL
ALLOCATOR: TOTAL CONSUMPTION EXPENDITURES

STATE	UNDER $3,000	$3,000 -3,999	$4,000 -4,999	$5,000 -5,999	$6,000 -6,999	$7,000 -7,999	$8,000 -9,999	$10,000 -11,999	$12,000 -14,999	$15,000 -19,999	$20,000 -24,999	$25,000 -29,999	$30,000 -34,999	OVER $35,000
ALABAMA	0.10	0.06	0.05	0.05	0.04	0.04	0.04	0.03	0.03	0.02	0.02	0.02	0.02	0.00
ALASKA	0.26	0.17	0.14	0.14	0.13	0.11	0.11	0.10	0.09	0.07	0.07	0.06	0.06	0.04
ARIZONA	0.56	0.34	0.26	0.25	0.22	0.19	0.18	0.16	0.15	0.13	0.11	0.10	0.10	0.07
ARKANSAS	0.09	0.06	0.05	0.04	0.04	0.04	0.03	0.03	0.03	0.02	0.02	0.02	0.02	0.01
CALIFORNIA	0.86	0.56	0.46	0.41	0.36	0.34	0.29	0.27	0.24	0.20	0.18	0.16	0.15	0.10
COLORADO	0.47	0.30	0.24	0.22	0.21	0.18	0.15	0.14	0.13	0.11	0.10	0.09	0.07	0.06
CONNECTICUT	0.52	0.37	0.30	0.31	0.27	0.29	0.23	0.21	0.19	0.17	0.16	0.14	0.12	0.07
DELAWARE	0.29	0.17	0.17	0.14	0.13	0.12	0.11	0.09	0.09	0.08	0.07	0.06	0.05	0.03
FLORIDA	0.18	0.11	0.09	0.08	0.08	0.07	0.06	0.06	0.05	0.05	0.04	0.04	0.03	0.01
GEORGIA	0.15	0.09	0.08	0.07	0.07	0.06	0.06	0.05	0.05	0.04	0.04	0.03	0.03	0.01
HAWAII	0.30	0.20	0.19	0.17	0.16	0.15	0.13	0.12	0.10	0.09	0.08	0.08	0.06	0.05
IDAHO	0.27	0.16	0.14	0.13	0.12	0.10	0.10	0.08	0.08	0.06	0.06	0.05	0.04	0.03
ILLINOIS	0.76	0.51	0.44	0.39	0.35	0.34	0.30	0.27	0.25	0.22	0.19	0.18	0.17	0.11
INDIANA	0.39	0.24	0.20	0.19	0.17	0.16	0.14	0.13	0.12	0.10	0.10	0.08	0.08	0.06
IOWA	0.29	0.19	0.17	0.13	0.13	0.12	0.11	0.11	0.09	0.08	0.07	0.07	0.06	0.05
KANSAS	0.16	0.10	0.09	0.07	0.07	0.06	0.06	0.05	0.05	0.04	0.03	0.03	0.03	0.02
KENTUCKY	0.11	0.07	0.06	0.05	0.05	0.04	0.04	0.04	0.03	0.03	0.03	0.02	0.02	0.01
LOUISIANA	0.09	0.05	0.05	0.04	0.04	0.04	0.04	0.03	0.03	0.03	0.02	0.02	0.02	0.01
MAINE	0.48	0.30	0.27	0.20	0.22	0.19	0.18	0.16	0.14	0.13	0.12	0.10	0.09	0.05
MARYLAND	0.30	0.19	0.16	0.13	0.13	0.12	0.11	0.10	0.08	0.07	0.06	0.06	0.05	0.04
MASSACHUSETTS	0.74	0.56	0.46	0.39	0.38	0.35	0.31	0.30	0.25	0.23	0.21	0.21	0.20	0.10
MICHIGAN	0.89	0.57	0.47	0.40	0.35	0.36	0.30	0.29	0.26	0.22	0.20	0.18	0.17	0.10
MINNESOTA	0.61	0.39	0.30	0.29	0.26	0.27	0.22	0.20	0.18	0.16	0.14	0.14	0.12	0.08
MISSISSIPPI	0.07	0.04	0.03	0.03	0.03	0.03	0.02	0.02	0.02	0.02	0.02	0.02	0.01	0.01
MISSOURI	0.32	0.18	0.17	0.14	0.13	0.12	0.11	0.10	0.09	0.07	0.07	0.06	0.05	0.04
MONTANA	0.48	0.30	0.26	0.22	0.21	0.20	0.16	0.15	0.13	0.12	0.11	0.09	0.10	0.07
NEBRASKA	0.23	0.15	0.11	0.10	0.09	0.09	0.08	0.08	0.07	0.06	0.06	0.05	0.05	0.04
NEVADA	0.21	0.14	0.12	0.10	0.10	0.09	0.08	0.07	0.06	0.05	0.05	0.05	0.04	0.02
NEW HAMPSHIRE	1.12	0.73	0.56	0.56	0.49	0.44	0.44	0.39	0.36	0.33	0.29	0.27	0.26	0.15
NEW JERSEY	1.07	0.69	0.60	0.56	0.53	0.50	0.42	0.43	0.37	0.34	0.31	0.29	0.26	0.16
NEW MEXICO	0.15	0.10	0.09	0.07	0.07	0.06	0.06	0.05	0.04	0.04	0.03	0.03	0.02	0.02
NEW YORK	0.83	0.51	0.42	0.36	0.35	0.33	0.30	0.28	0.25	0.22	0.21	0.19	0.18	0.10
NORTH CAROLINA	0.24	0.15	0.12	0.11	0.10	0.09	0.09	0.07	0.07	0.06	0.05	0.05	0.04	0.02
NORTH DAKOTA	0.07	0.04	0.04	0.03	0.03	0.03	0.03	0.02	0.02	0.02	0.02	0.02	0.02	0.01
OHIO	0.45	0.29	0.25	0.21	0.19	0.19	0.17	0.15	0.14	0.13	0.12	0.11	0.10	0.07
OKLAHOMA	0.10	0.06	0.05	0.05	0.04	0.04	0.03	0.03	0.03	0.02	0.02	0.02	0.02	0.01
OREGON	0.94	0.56	0.48	0.44	0.39	0.36	0.32	0.28	0.24	0.21	0.19	0.17	0.14	0.10
PENNSYLVANIA	0.43	0.26	0.23	0.20	0.19	0.17	0.16	0.15	0.13	0.12	0.10	0.10	0.10	0.06
RHODE ISLAND	0.55	0.32	0.31	0.28	0.21	0.21	0.20	0.17	0.17	0.16	0.14	0.14	0.11	0.06
SOUTH CAROLINA	0.39	0.25	0.21	0.19	0.17	0.17	0.15	0.14	0.13	0.11	0.10	0.10	0.07	0.05
SOUTH DAKOTA	0.08	0.05	0.04	0.04	0.03	0.03	0.03	0.03	0.02	0.02	0.02	0.02	0.02	0.01
TENNESSEE	0.35	0.22	0.19	0.17	0.15	0.15	0.13	0.12	0.11	0.10	0.09	0.08	0.08	0.04
TEXAS	0.58	0.37	0.31	0.28	0.26	0.24	0.22	0.20	0.18	0.16	0.14	0.13	0.11	0.07
UTAH	0.27	0.16	0.13	0.12	0.12	0.10	0.09	0.08	0.07	0.06	0.05	0.05	0.05	0.04
VERMONT	1.02	0.61	0.57	0.48	0.45	0.42	0.37	0.35	0.31	0.28	0.26	0.22	0.19	0.11
VIRGINIA	0.25	0.14	0.13	0.11	0.10	0.09	0.09	0.08	0.07	0.06	0.05	0.05	0.04	0.02
WASHINGTON	0.31	0.19	0.15	0.13	0.12	0.11	0.09	0.09	0.07	0.06	0.05	0.05	0.03	0.02
WEST VIRGINIA	0.14	0.09	0.07	0.06	0.06	0.05	0.05	0.05	0.04	0.04	0.03	0.03	0.03	0.02
WISCONSIN	0.37	0.21	0.18	0.16	0.16	0.15	0.12	0.12	0.10	0.09	0.07	0.07	0.07	0.04
WYOMING	0.21	0.14	0.13	0.11	0.10	0.09	0.08	0.08	0.07	0.06	0.06	0.06	0.05	0.04
AVERAGE	0.40	0.25	0.22	0.19	0.18	0.17	0.15	0.14	0.12	0.11	0.10	0.09	0.08	0.05

* EFFECTIVE TAX RATE EQUALS ZERO BEFORE ROUNDING. AN ENTIRE ROW OF * MEANS THAT THIS TAX IS NOT USED IN THIS STATE.

TABLE A-69

EFFECTIVE TAX RATES: LOCAL REAL PROPERTY TAX-INDUSTRIAL PROPERTY (MOST PROGRESSIVE)
INCIDENCE: OWNERS OF BUSINESSES-2/3 INCORPORATED, 1/3 UNINCORPORATED
ALLOCATOR: DIVIDEND INCOME, BUSINESS AND PARTNERSHIP PROFIT

STATE	UNDER $3,000	$3,000 -3,999	$4,000 -4,999	$5,000 -5,999	$6,000 -6,999	$7,000 -7,999	$8,000 -9,999	$10,000 -11,999	$12,000 -14,999	$15,000 -19,999	$20,000 -24,999	$25,000 -29,999	$30,000 -34,999	OVER $35,000
ALABAMA	0.03	0.01	0.02	0.01	0.01	0.02	0.01	0.01	0.00	0.00	0.02	0.01	0.03	0.20
ALASKA	0.08	0.24	0.13	0.02	0.05	0.05	0.03	0.03	0.02	0.06	0.04	0.03	0.03	0.10
ARIZONA	0.20	0.22	0.17	0.14	0.15	0.04	0.07	0.08	0.06	0.09	0.08	0.08	0.16	0.42
ARKANSAS	0.05	0.03	0.03	0.05	0.01	0.01	0.02	0.02	0.02	0.01	0.01	0.02	0.02	0.15
CALIFORNIA	0.38	0.16	0.16	0.23	0.13	0.11	0.15	0.13	0.13	0.09	0.09	0.14	0.18	0.62
COLORADO	0.26	0.02	0.32	0.06	0.02	0.19	0.04	0.02	0.04	0.02	0.05	0.04	0.13	0.47
CONNECTICUT	0.16	0.26	0.34	0.27	0.14	0.05	0.08	0.06	0.07	0.11	0.03	0.04	0.02	0.49
DELAWARE	0.14	0.10	0.06	0.07	0.02	0.08	0.03	0.03	0.04	0.03	0.02	0.03	0.02	0.28
FLORIDA	0.09	0.03	0.04	0.04	0.04	0.03	0.02	0.04	0.02	0.03	0.03	0.04	0.06	0.15
GEORGIA	0.08	0.04	0.03	0.05	0.03	0.01	0.02	0.01	0.02	0.02	0.01	0.02	0.07	0.19
HAWAII	0.37	0.08	0.06	0.09	0.19	0.07	0.08	0.04	0.03	0.07	0.02	0.01	0.04	0.25
IDAHO	0.16	0.08	0.05	0.02	0.02	0.06	0.02	0.03	0.01	0.02	0.08	0.06	0.14	0.29
ILLINOIS	0.33	0.21	0.16	0.27	0.14	0.14	0.15	0.17	0.07	0.08	0.07	0.09	0.12	0.78
INDIANA	0.14	0.09	0.05	0.02	0.03	0.06	0.04	0.05	0.03	0.05	0.07	0.10	0.07	0.44
IOWA	0.05	0.07	0.08	0.13	0.04	0.03	0.08	0.09	0.02	0.03	0.03	0.05	0.19	0.29
KANSAS	0.06	0.03	0.02	0.03	0.06	0.03	0.02	0.04	0.01	0.02	0.03	0.03	0.02	0.16
KENTUCKY	0.02	0.02	0.02	0.05	0.01	0.01	0.01	0.00	0.00	0.01	0.01	0.03	0.01	0.22
LOUISIANA	0.02	0.01	0.02	0.01	0.01	0.02	0.01	0.01	0.01	0.01	0.01	0.01	0.03	0.13
MAINE	0.17	0.10	0.11	0.22	0.05	0.06	0.20	0.03	0.06	0.11	0.05	0.20	0.12	0.53
MARYLAND	0.07	0.24	0.08	0.06	0.03	0.03	0.02	0.05	0.02	0.03	0.05	0.02	0.03	0.21
MASSACHUSETTS	0.40	0.10	0.33	0.26	0.28	0.12	0.12	0.10	0.11	0.06	0.07	0.15	0.08	0.95
MICHIGAN	0.40	0.29	0.28	0.17	0.18	0.29	0.16	0.11	0.08	0.08	0.11	0.20	0.11	0.86
MINNESOTA	0.22	0.08	0.43	0.13	0.09	0.06	0.15	0.09	0.07	0.04	0.09	0.10	0.10	0.68
MISSISSIPPI	0.01	0.01	0.01	0.01	0.03	0.01	0.01	0.01	0.01	0.01	0.02	0.01	0.02	0.10
MISSOURI	0.06	0.05	0.03	0.07	0.04	0.05	0.05	0.04	0.04	0.03	0.04	0.04	0.05	0.39
MONTANA	0.21	0.24	0.07	0.10	0.11	0.12	0.09	0.15	0.03	0.05	0.07	0.07	0.14	0.47
NEBRASKA	0.14	0.04	0.02	0.05	0.06	0.02	0.06	0.02	0.02	0.01	0.03	0.05	0.07	0.25
NEVADA	0.07	0.03	0.02	0.01	0.01	0.02	0.02	0.04	0.01	0.03	0.01	0.02	0.02	0.23
NEW HAMPSHIRE	0.62	0.31	0.90	0.83	0.15	0.13	0.23	0.30	0.17	0.12	0.17	0.11	0.23	1.41
NEW JERSEY	0.40	0.25	0.51	0.48	0.34	0.27	0.80	0.26	0.16	0.12	0.14	0.11	0.15	0.85
NEW MEXICO	0.05	0.06	0.01	0.01	0.01	0.03	0.01	0.02	0.03	0.03	0.03	0.04	0.06	0.11
NEW YORK	0.29	0.21	0.26	0.23	0.12	0.14	0.13	0.10	0.09	0.09	0.08	0.09	0.16	0.82
NORTH CAROLINA	0.12	0.04	0.13	0.05	0.04	0.03	0.04	0.03	0.02	0.02	0.05	0.03	0.03	0.29
NORTH DAKOTA	0.04	0.02	0.02	0.02	0.04	0.01	0.01	0.01	0.01	0.01	0.01	0.02	0.03	0.06
OHIO	0.18	0.15	0.11	0.16	0.06	0.10	0.09	0.07	0.04	0.05	0.06	0.09	0.16	0.51
OKLAHOMA	0.04	0.01	0.01	0.01	0.01	0.03	0.01	0.01	0.01	0.01	0.01	0.02	0.01	0.11
OREGON	0.66	0.12	0.14	0.03	0.09	0.06	0.06	0.12	0.04	0.11	0.14	0.16	0.42	0.99
PENNSYLVANIA	0.24	0.16	0.08	0.16	0.20	0.04	0.13	0.05	0.04	0.05	0.04	0.06	0.09	0.45
RHODE ISLAND	0.25	0.31	0.19	0.16	0.37	0.09	0.10	0.14	0.08	0.07	0.05	0.05	0.15	0.52
SOUTH CAROLINA	0.07	0.04	0.07	0.07	0.18	0.14	0.07	0.14	0.07	0.04	0.04	0.07	0.09	0.61
SOUTH DAKOTA	0.03	0.02	0.01	0.01	0.02	0.04	0.02	0.01	0.01	0.01	0.02	0.02	0.03	0.09
TENNESSEE	0.13	0.03	0.04	0.02	0.04	0.02	0.05	0.06	0.02	0.06	0.04	0.06	0.08	0.61
TEXAS	0.32	0.08	0.18	0.08	0.07	0.06	0.05	0.06	0.06	0.07	0.05	0.13	0.16	0.68
UTAH	0.27	0.02	0.09	0.07	0.03	0.04	0.05	0.03	0.02	0.02	0.03	0.03	0.06	0.25
VERMONT	0.27	0.07	0.21	0.25	0.16	0.22	0.22	0.20	0.20	0.12	0.24	0.10	0.68	1.44
VIRGINIA	0.08	0.08	0.02	0.07	0.09	0.04	0.03	0.05	0.01	0.03	0.02	0.04	0.03	0.19
WASHINGTON	0.05	0.02	0.06	0.05	0.05	0.05	0.04	0.01	0.03	0.02	0.02	0.02	0.06	0.29
WEST VIRGINIA	0.01	0.07	0.03	0.02	0.03	0.02	0.01	0.01	0.02	0.01	0.02	0.04	0.10	0.20
WISCONSIN	0.13	0.06	0.15	0.03	0.03	0.08	0.16	0.06	0.02	0.03	0.05	0.05	0.11	0.37
WYOMING	0.13	0.07	0.03	0.02	0.02	0.04	0.07	0.02	0.02	0.03	0.02	0.03	0.04	0.26
AVERAGE	0.17	0.10	0.13	0.11	0.08	0.07	0.08	0.06	0.04	0.05	0.05	0.06	0.10	0.43

* EFFECTIVE TAX RATE EQUALS ZERO BEFORE ROUNDING. AN ENTIRE ROW OF * MEANS THAT THIS TAX IS NOT USED IN THIS STATE.

TABLE A-70
EFFECTIVE TAX RATES: LOCAL REAL PROPERTY TAX-VACANT LOTS (BENCHMARK)
INCIDENCE: OWNERS OF LAND
ALLOCATOR: DIVIDEND INCOME AND RENT NET INCOME

STATE	UNDER $3,000	$3,000 -3,999	$4,000 -4,999	$5,000 -5,999	$6,000 -6,999	$7,000 -7,999	$8,000 -9,999	$10,000 -11,999	$12,000 -14,999	$15,000 -19,999	$20,000 -24,999	$25,000 -29,999	$30,000 -34,999	OVER $35,000
ALABAMA	0.02	0.00	0.00	0.02	0.03	0.01	*	0.01	0.00	0.00	0.00	0.00	0.00	0.06
ALASKA	0.58	0.65	0.31	0.03	0.00	0.13	0.06	0.05	0.08	0.29	0.17	0.13	0.11	0.51
ARIZONA	0.29	0.22	0.32	1.10	0.23	0.06	0.58	0.18	0.06	0.14	0.08	0.26	0.31	0.66
ARKANSAS	0.14	0.06	0.02	0.05	0.01	0.00	0.02	0.03	0.03	0.01	0.04	0.02	0.02	0.17
CALIFORNIA	0.48	0.27	0.21	0.20	0.11	0.11	0.23	0.10	0.10	0.09	0.08	0.11	0.14	0.55
COLORADO	0.43	0.01	0.24	0.03	0.02	0.15	0.02	0.07	0.06	0.03	0.09	0.06	0.14	0.41
CONNECTICUT	0.11	0.26	0.58	0.21	0.04	0.00	0.01	0.03	0.05	0.06	0.01	0.02	0.01	0.25
DELAWARE	0.09	0.04	0.02	0.01	0.02	0.24	0.01	0.04	0.05	0.04	0.02	0.06	0.02	0.15
FLORIDA	0.47	0.06	0.28	0.18	0.09	0.08	0.10	0.19	0.08	0.11	0.10	0.14	0.35	0.59
GEORGIA	0.31	0.23	0.03	0.17	0.04	0.00	0.01	0.03	0.04	0.03	0.05	0.04	0.12	0.34
HAWAII	1.01	0.11	0.10	0.15	0.90	0.12	0.22	0.08	0.33	0.17	0.11	0.05	0.11	0.55
IDAHO	0.25	0.05	0.09	0.01	0.01	0.17	0.01	0.07	0.01	0.05	0.08	0.07	0.15	0.40
ILLINOIS	0.19	0.12	0.14	0.19	0.05	0.08	0.07	0.07	0.02	0.06	0.02	0.06	0.09	0.27
INDIANA	0.14	0.12	0.06	0.02	0.04	0.03	0.11	0.04	0.02	0.03	0.03	0.06	0.02	0.17
IOWA	0.03	0.06	0.04	0.05	0.02	0.03	0.03	0.03	0.02	0.02	0.01	0.01	0.05	0.07
KANSAS	0.07	0.04	0.05	0.02	0.04	0.05	0.03	0.04	0.00	0.01	0.02	0.03	0.02	0.08
KENTUCKY	0.07	0.01	0.04	0.07	0.01	0.01	0.01	*	0.01	0.01	0.01	0.01	0.01	0.11
LOUISIANA	0.04	0.05	0.07	0.04	0.02	0.01	0.01	0.01	0.02	0.02	0.01	0.01	0.07	0.13
MAINE	0.06	0.13	0.04	0.08	0.02	0.03	0.07	0.02	0.03	0.06	0.03	0.07	0.06	0.23
MARYLAND	0.47	0.25	0.15	0.42	0.14	0.01	0.03	0.06	0.06	0.07	0.06	0.05	0.05	0.29
MASSACHUSETTS	0.94	0.04	0.22	0.27	0.26	0.04	0.25	0.07	0.07	0.06	0.07	0.11	0.05	0.47
MICHIGAN	0.38	0.18	0.11	0.17	0.16	0.09	0.04	0.06	0.04	0.04	0.07	0.08	0.04	0.30
MINNESOTA	0.14	0.01	0.23	0.11	0.03	0.00	0.04	0.02	0.03	0.02	0.02	0.04	0.05	0.21
MISSISSIPPI	0.08	0.14	0.01	0.00	0.06	0.01	0.02	0.02	0.03	0.03	0.09	0.04	0.04	0.24
MISSOURI	0.14	0.11	0.06	0.18	0.05	0.05	0.04	0.05	0.04	0.06	0.03	0.02	0.08	0.36
MONTANA	0.23	0.17	0.05	0.12	0.04	0.06	0.09	0.09	0.09	0.03	0.04	0.06	0.12	0.24
NEBRASKA	0.07	0.09	0.07	0.05	0.03	0.04	0.03	0.00	0.05	0.02	0.03	0.02	0.09	0.14
NEVADA	0.28	0.03	0.10	0.01	0.01	0.02	0.02	0.20	0.04	0.07	0.02	0.04	0.02	0.44
NEW HAMPSHIRE	0.31	0.06	0.12	0.16	0.01	0.17	0.07	0.04	0.04	0.02	0.03	0.01	0.02	0.28
NEW JERSEY	0.54	0.59	0.26	0.62	0.31	0.24	0.37	0.21	0.15	0.07	0.07	0.07	0.18	0.59
NEW MEXICO	0.27	0.21	0.04	0.01	0.06	0.20	0.05	0.16	0.14	0.13	0.12	0.11	0.19	0.35
NEW YORK	0.51	0.18	0.14	0.33	0.16	0.13	0.11	0.09	0.05	0.05	0.07	0.08	0.13	0.40
NORTH CAROLINA	0.21	0.04	0.11	0.27	0.03	0.04	0.06	0.05	0.02	0.03	0.04	0.04	0.07	0.28
NORTH DAKOTA	0.06	0.03	0.05	0.06	0.09	0.03	0.03	0.03	0.02	0.02	0.02	0.03	0.04	0.06
OHIO	0.21	0.10	0.09	0.31	0.26	0.07	0.07	0.07	0.05	0.05	0.05	0.05	0.10	0.33
OKLAHOMA	0.05	0.04	0.03	0.02	0.02	0.07	0.01	0.00	0.02	0.03	0.05	0.02	0.02	0.11
OREGON	0.80	0.45	0.27	0.14	0.14	0.20	0.07	0.07	0.04	0.06	0.10	0.08	0.27	0.55
PENNSYLVANIA	0.18	0.07	0.05	0.16	0.11	0.02	0.05	0.02	0.03	0.03	0.02	0.01	0.02	0.13
RHODE ISLAND	0.19	0.26	0.65	0.09	0.30	0.19	0.07	0.09	0.09	0.08	0.10	0.09	0.10	0.43
SOUTH CAROLINA	0.16	0.12	0.08	0.01	0.09	0.18	0.04	0.10	0.04	0.04	0.03	0.04	0.05	0.36
SOUTH DAKOTA	0.08	0.09	0.08	0.06	0.10	0.16	0.05	0.05	0.04	0.03	0.04	0.05	0.09	0.18
TENNESSEE	0.16	0.04	0.07	0.07	0.05	0.00	0.07	0.04	0.01	0.04	0.03	0.02	0.05	0.26
TEXAS	0.21	0.12	0.07	0.03	0.03	0.05	0.02	0.04	0.05	0.02	0.02	0.07	0.07	0.27
UTAH	0.43	0.03	0.30	0.11	0.02	0.08	0.06	0.10	0.10	0.06	0.05	0.04	0.11	0.38
VERMONT	0.01	0.00	0.02	0.00	0.00	0.00	0.01	0.00	0.01	0.00	0.00	0.00	0.01	0.01
VIRGINIA	0.13	0.16	0.13	0.09	0.20	0.03	0.03	0.13	0.03	0.02	0.02	0.03	0.06	0.25
WASHINGTON	0.26	0.03	0.11	0.11	0.06	0.05	0.06	0.01	0.04	0.04	0.02	0.01	0.15	0.33
WEST VIRGINIA	0.04	0.04	0.02	0.02	0.01	0.03	0.02	0.00	0.02	0.02	0.01	0.06	0.05	0.10
WISCONSIN	0.21	0.12	0.22	0.02	0.06	0.06	0.18	0.04	0.02	0.04	0.07	0.13	0.10	0.28
WYOMING	0.15	0.16	0.03	0.06	0.02	0.06	0.04	0.00	0.01	0.02	0.01	0.03	0.03	0.19
AVERAGE	0.25	0.13	0.13	0.13	0.09	0.07	0.07	0.06	0.05	0.05	0.05	0.06	0.08	0.29

* EFFECTIVE TAX RATE EQUALS ZERO BEFORE ROUNDING. AN ENTIRE ROW OF * MEANS THAT THIS TAX IS NOT USED IN THIS STATE.

TABLE A-71
EFFECTIVE TAX RATES: LOCAL REAL PROPERTY TAX-VACANT LOTS
INCIDENCE: HOUSEHOLDS
ALLOCATOR: HOUSEHOLD INCOME DISTRIBUTION

STATE	UNDER $3,000	$3,000 -3,999	$4,000 -4,999	$5,000 -5,999	$6,000 -6,999	$7,000 -7,999	$8,000 -9,999	$10,000 -11,999	$12,000 -14,999	$15,000 -19,999	$20,000 -24,999	$25,000 -29,999	$30,000 -34,999	OVER $35,000
ALABAMA	0.01	0.01	0.01	0.01	0.01	0.01	0.01	0.01	0.01	0.01	0.01	0.01	0.01	0.01
ALASKA	0.21	0.26	0.26	0.31	0.31	0.30	0.32	0.32	0.32	0.30	0.30	0.30	0.30	0.27
ARIZONA	0.22	0.27	0.25	0.28	0.27	0.26	0.29	0.28	0.29	0.30	0.28	0.28	0.29	0.27
ARKANSAS	0.03	0.04	0.04	0.04	0.04	0.04	0.04	0.04	0.04	0.04	0.04	0.04	0.04	0.03
CALIFORNIA	0.15	0.19	0.19	0.20	0.20	0.20	0.20	0.20	0.20	0.20	0.20	0.20	0.20	0.18
COLORADO	0.09	0.12	0.12	0.12	0.13	0.13	0.12	0.13	0.13	0.13	0.13	0.13	0.12	0.12
CONNECTICUT	0.06	0.08	0.08	0.09	0.09	0.11	0.09	0.09	0.09	0.09	0.10	0.10	0.09	0.08
DELAWARE	0.05	0.05	0.06	0.06	0.06	0.06	0.06	0.06	0.06	0.06	0.06	0.06	0.06	0.05
FLORIDA	0.17	0.20	0.19	0.20	0.21	0.21	0.21	0.21	0.22	0.21	0.21	0.21	0.19	0.15
GEORGIA	0.07	0.08	0.09	0.09	0.09	0.10	0.09	0.09	0.09	0.10	0.09	0.09	0.09	0.08
HAWAII	0.15	0.20	0.23	0.24	0.24	0.25	0.25	0.25	0.25	0.25	0.25	0.26	0.24	0.24
IDAHO	0.07	0.09	0.09	0.10	0.10	0.10	0.10	0.10	0.10	0.10	0.10	0.10	0.10	0.10
ILLINOIS	0.07	0.09	0.09	0.09	0.09	0.10	0.10	0.10	0.10	0.10	0.10	0.10	0.10	0.09
INDIANA	0.04	0.05	0.05	0.06	0.06	0.06	0.06	0.06	0.06	0.06	0.06	0.05	0.06	0.05
IOWA	0.02	0.03	0.03	0.03	0.03	0.03	0.03	0.03	0.03	0.03	0.03	0.03	0.03	0.03
KANSAS	0.02	0.03	0.03	0.03	0.03	0.03	0.03	0.03	0.03	0.03	0.03	0.03	0.03	0.03
KENTUCKY	0.02	0.02	0.02	0.02	0.02	0.02	0.02	0.02	0.02	0.02	0.02	0.02	0.02	0.02
LOUISIANA	0.03	0.03	0.03	0.04	0.04	0.04	0.04	0.04	0.04	0.04	0.04	0.04	0.04	0.03
MAINE	0.05	0.06	0.07	0.06	0.07	0.07	0.07	0.07	0.07	0.07	0.07	0.06	0.06	0.06
MARYLAND	0.09	0.12	0.12	0.11	0.12	0.12	0.13	0.12	0.12	0.12	0.12	0.12	0.11	0.11
MASSACHUSETTS	0.10	0.16	0.15	0.15	0.16	0.16	0.16	0.17	0.16	0.17	0.17	0.17	0.18	0.14
MICHIGAN	0.08	0.10	0.10	0.09	0.09	0.10	0.10	0.10	0.10	0.10	0.10	0.10	0.10	0.09
MINNESOTA	0.04	0.05	0.05	0.06	0.06	0.06	0.06	0.06	0.06	0.06	0.06	0.06	0.06	0.05
MISSISSIPPI	0.05	0.06	0.06	0.06	0.06	0.06	0.06	0.07	0.06	0.06	0.06	0.07	0.06	0.05
MISSOURI	0.07	0.08	0.09	0.09	0.09	0.10	0.10	0.10	0.09	0.09	0.09	0.09	0.09	0.08
MONTANA	0.07	0.09	0.09	0.09	0.09	0.09	0.09	0.09	0.09	0.10	0.10	0.09	0.10	0.09
NEBRASKA	0.04	0.05	0.04	0.05	0.05	0.05	0.05	0.05	0.05	0.05	0.05	0.05	0.05	0.05
NEVADA	0.09	0.12	0.12	0.11	0.13	0.13	0.13	0.13	0.12	0.13	0.12	0.13	0.13	0.11
NEW HAMPSHIRE	0.05	0.06	0.06	0.07	0.07	0.06	0.07	0.07	0.07	0.07	0.07	0.07	0.07	0.06
NEW JERSEY	0.16	0.20	0.21	0.22	0.23	0.24	0.23	0.25	0.24	0.24	0.25	0.25	0.24	0.21
NEW MEXICO	0.12	0.15	0.17	0.16	0.17	0.16	0.17	0.17	0.16	0.17	0.17	0.16	0.15	0.16
NEW YORK	0.12	0.14	0.14	0.13	0.14	0.15	0.15	0.15	0.15	0.15	0.15	0.15	0.15	0.13
NORTH CAROLINA	0.07	0.08	0.08	0.08	0.08	0.08	0.08	0.08	0.08	0.08	0.08	0.08	0.08	0.06
NORTH DAKOTA	0.03	0.03	0.03	0.03	0.03	0.03	0.03	0.03	0.04	0.04	0.04	0.03	0.04	0.03
OHIO	0.07	0.09	0.10	0.10	0.10	0.11	0.11	0.11	0.11	0.11	0.11	0.11	0.11	0.10
OKLAHOMA	0.03	0.04	0.04	0.04	0.04	0.04	0.04	0.04	0.04	0.04	0.04	0.04	0.04	0.04
OREGON	0.13	0.16	0.16	0.18	0.18	0.18	0.18	0.18	0.18	0.18	0.18	0.18	0.17	0.16
PENNSYLVANIA	0.04	0.05	0.05	0.05	0.05	0.05	0.05	0.05	0.05	0.05	0.05	0.05	0.05	0.04
RHODE ISLAND	0.12	0.14	0.16	0.16	0.14	0.15	0.16	0.16	0.16	0.17	0.17	0.17	0.16	0.14
SOUTH CAROLINA	0.07	0.08	0.08	0.08	0.08	0.09	0.09	0.09	0.09	0.09	0.09	0.09	0.08	0.07
SOUTH DAKOTA	0.05	0.06	0.06	0.06	0.07	0.06	0.06	0.07	0.07	0.07	0.07	0.07	0.07	0.06
TENNESSEE	0.05	0.06	0.06	0.06	0.06	0.07	0.06	0.07	0.07	0.07	0.07	0.06	0.06	0.05
TEXAS	0.06	0.08	0.08	0.08	0.08	0.08	0.08	0.08	0.08	0.08	0.08	0.08	0.07	0.07
UTAH	0.09	0.11	0.11	0.11	0.13	0.12	0.12	0.13	0.13	0.13	0.13	0.12	0.13	0.12
VERMONT	0.00	0.00	0.00	0.00	0.00	0.00	0.00	0.00	0.00	0.00	0.00	0.00	0.00	0.00
VIRGINIA	0.07	0.08	0.08	0.09	0.08	0.09	0.09	0.09	0.09	0.09	0.08	0.09	0.08	0.07
WASHINGTON	0.08	0.09	0.09	0.09	0.09	0.10	0.09	0.10	0.10	0.09	0.09	0.10	0.08	0.08
WEST VIRGINIA	0.02	0.03	0.03	0.03	0.03	0.03	0.03	0.03	0.03	0.03	0.03	0.03	0.03	0.03
WISCONSIN	0.08	0.09	0.09	0.09	0.10	0.10	0.09	0.10	0.10	0.10	0.10	0.10	0.10	0.09
WYOMING	0.03	0.04	0.05	0.05	0.05	0.05	0.05	0.05	0.05	0.05	0.05	0.06	0.06	0.05
AVERAGE	0.07	0.09	0.09	0.10	0.10	0.10	0.10	0.10	0.10	0.10	0.10	0.10	0.10	0.09

* EFFECTIVE TAX RATE EQUALS ZERO BEFORE ROUNDING. AN ENTIRE ROW OF * MEANS THAT THIS TAX IS NOT USED IN THIS STATE.

TABLE A-72
EFFECTIVE TAX RATES: LOCAL REAL PROPERTY TAX-OTHER N.E.C. (BENCHMARK)
INCIDENCE: 1/2 OWNERS OF CAPITAL, 1/2 CONSUMERS IN GENERAL
ALLOCATOR: DIVIDEND INCOME AND CONSUMPTION

STATE	UNDER $3,000	$3,000 -3,999	$4,000 -4,999	$5,000 -5,999	$6,000 -6,999	$7,000 -7,999	$8,000 -9,999	$10,000 -11,999	$12,000 -14,999	$15,000 -19,999	$20,000 -24,999	$25,000 -29,999	$30,000 -34,999	OVER $35,000
ALABAMA	0.00	0.00	0.00	0.00	0.00	0.00	0.00	0.00	0.00	0.00	0.00	0.00	0.00	0.01
ALASKA	0.00	0.00	0.00	0.00	0.00	0.00	0.00	0.00	0.00	0.00	0.00	0.00	0.00	0.00
ARIZONA	*	*	*	*	*	*	*	*	*	*	*	*	*	*
ARKANSAS	0.00	0.00	0.00	0.00	0.00	0.00	0.00	0.00	0.00	0.00	0.00	0.00	0.00	0.00
CALIFORNIA	0.16	0.09	0.08	0.08	0.06	0.05	0.06	0.05	0.05	0.04	0.03	0.04	0.04	0.10
COLORADO	0.27	0.11	0.23	0.09	0.07	0.14	0.06	0.05	0.05	0.04	0.05	0.04	0.08	0.20
CONNECTICUT	0.00	0.00	0.00	0.00	0.00	0.00	0.00	0.00	0.00	0.00	0.00	0.00	0.00	0.00
DELAWARE	0.00	0.00	0.00	0.00	0.00	0.00	0.00	0.00	0.00	0.00	0.00	0.00	0.00	0.00
FLORIDA	0.03	0.01	0.01	0.01	0.01	0.01	0.01	0.01	0.01	0.01	0.01	0.01	0.01	0.02
GEORGIA	0.00	0.00	0.00	0.00	0.00	0.00	0.00	0.00	0.00	0.00	0.00	0.00	0.00	0.00
HAWAII	*	*	*	*	*	*	*	*	*	*	*	*	*	*
IDAHO	0.00	0.00	0.00	0.00	0.00	0.00	0.00	0.00	0.00	0.00	0.00	0.00	0.00	0.00
ILLINOIS	0.01	0.01	0.00	0.00	0.00	0.00	0.00	0.00	0.00	0.00	0.00	0.00	0.00	0.01
INDIANA	0.00	0.00	0.00	0.00	0.00	0.00	0.00	0.00	0.00	0.00	0.00	0.00	0.00	0.00
IOWA	0.00	0.00	0.00	0.00	0.00	0.00	0.00	0.00	0.00	0.00	0.00	0.00	0.00	0.00
KANSAS	0.01	0.00	0.00	0.00	0.01	0.00	0.00	0.00	0.00	0.00	0.00	0.00	0.00	0.01
KENTUCKY	0.01	0.00	0.00	0.01	0.00	0.00	0.00	0.00	0.00	0.00	0.00	0.00	0.00	0.02
LOUISIANA	0.00	0.00	0.00	0.00	0.00	0.00	0.00	0.00	0.00	0.00	0.00	0.00	0.00	0.00
MAINE	0.02	0.01	0.01	0.01	0.01	0.01	0.01	0.00	0.00	0.01	0.00	0.01	0.00	0.02
MARYLAND	0.00	0.00	0.00	0.00	0.00	0.00	0.00	0.00	0.00	0.00	0.00	0.00	0.00	0.00
MASSACHUSETTS	*	*	*	*	*	*	*	*	*	*	*	*	*	*
MICHIGAN	0.08	0.06	0.05	0.04	0.03	0.04	0.03	0.02	0.02	0.02	0.02	0.03	0.02	0.07
MINNESOTA	0.00	0.00	0.00	0.00	0.00	0.00	0.00	0.00	0.00	0.00	0.00	0.00	0.00	0.00
MISSISSIPPI	*	*	*	*	*	*	*	*	*	*	*	*	*	*
MISSOURI	*	*	*	*	*	*	*	*	*	*	*	*	*	*
MONTANA	0.02	0.02	0.01	0.01	0.01	0.01	0.01	0.01	0.00	0.00	0.01	0.00	0.01	0.02
NEBRASKA	*	*	*	*	*	*	*	*	*	*	*	*	*	*
NEVADA	0.02	0.01	0.01	0.01	0.01	0.01	0.01	0.01	0.01	0.01	0.00	0.01	0.00	0.02
NEW HAMPSHIRE	0.00	0.00	0.00	0.00	0.00	0.00	0.00	0.00	0.00	0.00	0.00	0.00	0.00	0.00
NEW JERSEY	0.01	0.00	0.01	0.00	0.00	0.00	0.01	0.00	0.00	0.00	0.00	0.00	0.00	0.00
NEW MEXICO	0.07	0.05	0.03	0.03	0.03	0.03	0.02	0.03	0.03	0.02	0.02	0.03	0.03	0.05
NEW YORK	0.01	0.01	0.01	0.01	0.00	0.00	0.00	0.00	0.00	0.00	0.00	0.00	0.00	0.01
NORTH CAROLINA	0.00	0.00	0.00	0.00	0.00	0.00	0.00	0.00	0.00	0.00	0.00	0.00	0.00	0.00
NORTH DAKOTA	*	*	*	*	*	*	*	*	*	*	*	*	*	*
OHIO	0.00	0.00	0.00	0.00	0.00	0.00	0.00	0.00	0.00	0.00	0.00	0.00	0.00	0.00
OKLAHOMA	0.01	0.01	0.00	0.00	0.01	0.01	0.00	0.00	0.00	0.00	0.00	0.00	0.00	0.01
OREGON	0.05	0.02	0.02	0.01	0.01	0.01	0.01	0.01	0.01	0.01	0.01	0.01	0.02	0.03
PENNSYLVANIA	0.04	0.03	0.02	0.02	0.02	0.01	0.02	0.01	0.01	0.01	0.01	0.01	0.01	0.03
RHODE ISLAND	0.01	0.01	0.01	0.00	0.01	0.00	0.00	0.00	0.00	0.00	0.00	0.00	0.00	0.01
SOUTH CAROLINA	*	*	*	*	*	*	*	*	*	*	*	*	*	*
SOUTH DAKOTA	0.13	0.08	0.07	0.05	0.07	0.10	0.06	0.05	0.04	0.04	0.05	0.05	0.05	0.14
TENNESSEE	0.01	0.00	0.00	0.00	0.00	0.00	0.00	0.00	0.00	0.00	0.00	0.00	0.00	0.01
TEXAS	0.73	0.31	0.37	0.28	0.22	0.21	0.19	0.19	0.19	0.16	0.13	0.19	0.18	0.59
UTAH	*	*	*	*	*	*	*	*	*	*	*	*	*	*
VERMONT	*	*	*	*	*	*	*	*	*	*	*	*	*	*
VIRGINIA	0.00	0.00	0.00	0.00	0.00	0.00	0.00	0.00	0.00	0.00	0.00	0.00	0.00	0.00
WASHINGTON	0.00	0.00	0.00	0.00	0.00	0.00	0.00	0.00	0.00	0.00	0.00	0.00	0.00	0.00
WEST VIRGINIA	0.03	0.04	0.02	0.01	0.01	0.02	0.01	0.01	0.01	0.01	0.01	0.01	0.03	0.05
WISCONSIN	*	*	*	*	*	*	*	*	*	*	*	*	*	*
WYOMING	0.15	0.11	0.07	0.06	0.05	0.07	0.07	0.04	0.04	0.04	0.03	0.03	0.04	0.15
AVERAGE	0.05	0.03	0.03	0.02	0.02	0.02	0.02	0.01	0.01	0.01	0.01	0.01	0.01	0.04

* EFFECTIVE TAX RATE EQUALS ZERO BEFORE ROUNDING. AN ENTIRE ROW OF * MEANS THAT THIS TAX IS NOT USED IN THIS STATE.

TABLE A-73
EFFECTIVE TAX RATES: LOCAL REAL PROPERTY TAX-OTHER N.E.C. (MOST REGRESSIVE)
INCIDENCE: CONSUMERS IN GENERAL
ALLOCATOR: TOTAL CONSUMPTION EXPENDITURES

STATE	UNDER $3,000	$3,000 -3,999	$4,000 -4,999	$5,000 -5,999	$6,000 -6,999	$7,000 -7,999	$8,000 -9,999	$10,000 -11,999	$12,000 -14,999	$15,000 -19,999	$20,000 -24,999	$25,000 -29,999	$30,000 -34,999	OVER $35,000
ALABAMA	0.01	0.00	0.00	0.00	0.00	0.00	0.00	0.00	0.00	0.00	0.00	0.00	0.00	0.00
ALASKA	0.00	0.00	0.00	0.00	0.00	0.00	0.00	0.00	0.00	0.00	0.00	0.00	0.00	0.00
ARIZONA	*	*	*	*	*	*	*	*	*	*	*	*	*	*
ARKANSAS	0.00	0.00	0.00	0.00	0.00	0.00	0.00	0.00	0.00	0.00	0.00	0.00	0.00	0.00
CALIFORNIA	0.22	0.14	0.12	0.10	0.09	0.09	0.08	0.07	0.06	0.05	0.05	0.04	0.04	0.03
COLORADO	0.32	0.20	0.17	0.15	0.14	0.12	0.11	0.10	0.09	0.08	0.07	0.07	0.05	0.04
CONNECTICUT	0.00	0.00	0.00	0.00	0.00	0.00	0.00	0.00	0.00	0.00	0.00	0.00	0.00	0.00
DELAWARE	0.00	0.00	0.00	0.00	0.00	0.00	0.00	0.00	0.00	0.00	0.00	0.00	0.00	0.00
FLORIDA	0.03	0.02	0.02	0.02	0.01	0.01	0.01	0.01	0.01	0.01	0.01	0.01	0.01	0.00
GEORGIA	0.00	0.00	0.00	0.00	0.00	0.00	0.00	0.00	0.00	0.00	0.00	0.00	0.00	0.00
HAWAII	*	*	*	*	*	*	*	*	*	*	*	*	*	*
IDAHO	0.01	0.00	0.00	0.00	0.00	0.00	0.00	0.00	0.00	0.00	0.00	0.00	0.00	0.00
ILLINOIS	0.01	0.01	0.01	0.01	0.00	0.00	0.00	0.00	0.00	0.00	0.00	0.00	0.00	0.00
INDIANA	0.00	0.00	0.00	0.00	0.00	0.00	0.00	0.00	0.00	0.00	0.00	0.00	0.00	0.00
IOWA	0.00	0.00	0.00	0.00	0.00	0.00	0.00	0.00	0.00	0.00	0.00	0.00	0.00	0.00
KANSAS	0.01	0.01	0.01	0.00	0.00	0.00	0.00	0.00	0.00	0.00	0.00	0.00	0.00	0.00
KENTUCKY	0.01	0.01	0.01	0.01	0.01	0.00	0.00	0.00	0.00	0.00	0.00	0.00	0.00	0.00
LOUISIANA	0.00	0.00	0.00	0.00	0.00	0.00	0.00	0.00	0.00	0.00	0.00	0.00	0.00	0.00
MAINE	0.02	0.01	0.01	0.01	0.01	0.01	0.01	0.01	0.01	0.01	0.01	0.01	0.00	0.00
MARYLAND	0.00	0.00	0.00	0.00	0.00	0.00	0.00	0.00	0.00	0.00	0.00	0.00	0.00	0.00
MASSACHUSETTS	*	*	*	*	*	*	*	*	*	*	*	*	*	*
MICHIGAN	0.11	0.07	0.06	0.05	0.05	0.05	0.04	0.04	0.03	0.03	0.03	0.02	0.02	0.02
MINNESOTA	0.01	0.00	0.00	0.00	0.00	0.00	0.00	0.00	0.00	0.00	0.00	0.00	0.00	0.00
MISSISSIPPI	*	*	*	*	*	*	*	*	*	*	*	*	*	*
MISSOURI	*	*	*	*	*	*	*	*	*	*	*	*	*	*
MONTANA	0.03	0.02	0.02	0.01	0.01	0.01	0.01	0.01	0.01	0.01	0.01	0.01	0.01	0.00
NEBRASKA	*	*	*	*	*	*	*	*	*	*	*	*	*	*
NEVADA	0.03	0.02	0.02	0.02	0.02	0.01	0.01	0.01	0.01	0.01	0.01	0.01	0.01	0.00
NEW HAMPSHIRE	0.00	0.00	0.00	0.00	0.00	0.00	0.00	0.00	0.00	0.00	0.00	0.00	0.00	0.00
NEW JERSEY	0.01	0.01	0.00	0.00	0.00	0.00	0.00	0.00	0.00	0.00	0.00	0.00	0.00	0.00
NEW MEXICO	0.11	0.07	0.06	0.05	0.05	0.04	0.04	0.03	0.03	0.03	0.02	0.02	0.02	0.02
NEW YORK	0.01	0.01	0.01	0.01	0.01	0.01	0.01	0.01	0.00	0.00	0.00	0.00	0.00	0.00
NORTH CAROLINA	0.00	0.00	0.00	0.00	0.00	0.00	0.00	0.00	0.00	0.00	0.00	0.00	0.00	0.00
NORTH DAKOTA	*	*	*	*	*	*	*	*	*	*	*	*	*	*
OHIO	0.01	0.00	0.00	0.00	0.00	0.00	0.00	0.00	0.00	0.00	0.00	0.00	0.00	0.00
OKLAHOMA	0.02	0.01	0.01	0.01	0.01	0.01	0.01	0.01	0.01	0.01	0.00	0.00	0.00	0.00
OREGON	0.05	0.03	0.03	0.02	0.02	0.02	0.02	0.02	0.01	0.01	0.01	0.01	0.01	0.01
PENNSYLVANIA	0.05	0.03	0.03	0.02	0.02	0.02	0.02	0.02	0.02	0.01	0.01	0.01	0.01	0.01
RHODE ISLAND	0.01	0.01	0.01	0.01	0.00	0.00	0.00	0.00	0.00	0.00	0.00	0.00	0.00	0.00
SOUTH CAROLINA	*	*	*	*	*	*	*	*	*	*	*	*	*	*
SOUTH DAKOTA	0.18	0.11	0.10	0.09	0.08	0.08	0.07	0.07	0.06	0.05	0.05	0.05	0.04	0.03
TENNESSEE	0.01	0.00	0.00	0.00	0.00	0.00	0.00	0.00	0.00	0.00	0.00	0.00	0.00	0.00
TEXAS	0.89	0.56	0.47	0.43	0.40	0.36	0.34	0.31	0.27	0.24	0.22	0.19	0.15	0.08
UTAH	*	*	*	*	*	*	*	*	*	*	*	*	*	*
VERMONT	*	*	*	*	*	*	*	*	*	*	*	*	*	*
VIRGINIA	0.00	0.00	0.00	0.00	0.00	0.00	0.00	0.00	0.00	0.00	0.00	0.00	0.00	0.00
WASHINGTON	0.01	0.00	0.00	0.00	0.00	0.00	0.00	0.00	0.00	0.00	0.00	0.00	0.00	0.00
WEST VIRGINIA	0.06	0.04	0.03	0.03	0.02	0.02	0.02	0.02	0.02	0.02	0.01	0.01	0.01	0.01
WISCONSIN	*	*	*	*	*	*	*	*	*	*	*	*	*	*
WYOMING	0.19	0.13	0.11	0.10	0.09	0.09	0.08	0.07	0.06	0.06	0.05	0.05	0.05	0.04
AVERAGE	0.06	0.04	0.03	0.03	0.03	0.03	0.02	0.02	0.02	0.02	0.02	0.01	0.01	0.01

* EFFECTIVE TAX RATE EQUALS ZERO BEFORE ROUNDING. AN ENTIRE ROW OF * MEANS THAT THIS TAX IS NOT USED IN THIS STATE.

TABLE A-74

EFFECTIVE TAX RATES: LOCAL REAL PROPERTY TAX-OTHER N.E.C. (MOST PROGRESSIVE)
INCIDENCE: OWNERS OF CAPITAL
ALLOCATOR: DIVIDEND INCOME

STATE	UNDER $3,000	$3,000 -3,999	$4,000 -4,999	$5,000 -5,999	$6,000 -6,999	$7,000 -7,999	$8,000 -9,999	$10,000 -11,999	$12,000 -14,999	$15,000 -19,999	$20,000 -24,999	$25,000 -29,999	$30,000 -34,999	OVER $35,000
ALABAMA	0.00	0.00	0.00	0.00	0.00	0.00	*	0.00	0.00	0.00	0.00	0.00	0.00	0.01
ALASKA	0.00	0.00	0.00	0.00	*	0.00	0.00	0.00	0.00	0.00	0.00	0.00	0.00	0.00
ARIZONA	*	*	*	*	*	*	*	*	*	*	*	*	*	*
ARKANSAS	0.00	0.00	0.00	0.00	0.00	*	0.00	0.00	0.00	0.00	0.00	0.00	0.00	0.00
CALIFORNIA	0.11	0.04	0.04	0.07	0.03	0.02	0.04	0.03	0.04	0.02	0.02	0.03	0.04	0.17
COLORADO	0.21	0.01	0.29	0.04	0.00	0.16	0.02	0.00	0.01	0.01	0.03	0.02	0.10	0.36
CONNECTICUT	0.00	0.00	0.00	0.00	0.00	0.00	0.00	0.00	0.00	0.00	0.00	0.00	*	0.00
DELAWARE	0.00	0.00	0.00	0.00	*	0.00	0.00	0.00	0.00	0.00	0.00	0.00	0.00	0.00
FLORIDA	0.02	0.00	0.01	0.01	0.01	0.01	0.00	0.01	0.00	0.01	0.00	0.01	0.01	0.03
GEORGIA	0.00	0.00	0.00	0.00	0.00	0.00	0.00	*	0.00	0.00	0.00	0.00	0.00	0.00
HAWAII	*	*	*	*	*	*	*	*	*	*	*	*	*	*
IDAHO	0.00	0.00	0.00	0.00	0.00	0.00	0.00	0.00	0.00	0.00	0.00	0.00	0.00	0.01
ILLINOIS	0.00	0.00	0.00	0.00	0.00	0.00	0.00	0.00	0.00	0.00	0.00	0.00	0.00	0.01
INDIANA	0.00	0.00	0.00	0.00	0.00	0.00	0.00	0.00	0.00	0.00	0.00	0.00	0.00	0.00
IOWA	0.00	0.00	0.00	0.00	0.00	*	0.00	0.00	0.00	0.00	0.00	0.00	0.00	0.00
KANSAS	0.00	0.00	0.00	0.00	0.01	0.00	0.00	0.00	0.00	0.00	0.00	0.00	0.00	0.01
KENTUCKY	0.00	0.00	0.00	0.01	0.00	*	0.00	*	0.00	0.00	0.00	0.00	0.00	0.03
LOUISIANA	0.00	0.00	0.00	0.00	0.00	0.00	0.00	0.00	0.00	0.00	0.00	0.00	0.00	0.01
MAINE	0.01	0.00	0.00	0.01	0.00	0.00	0.01	0.00	0.00	0.01	0.00	0.01	0.00	0.03
MARYLAND	0.00	0.00	0.00	0.00	0.00	0.00	0.00	0.00	0.00	0.00	0.00	0.00	0.00	0.00
MASSACHUSETTS	*	*	*	*	*	*	*	*	*	*	*	*	*	*
MICHIGAN	0.05	0.04	0.04	0.02	0.02	0.04	0.02	0.01	0.01	0.01	0.01	0.03	0.01	0.12
MINNESOTA	0.00	0.00	0.01	0.00	0.00	0.00	0.00	0.00	0.00	0.00	0.00	0.00	0.00	0.01
MISSISSIPPI	*	*	*	*	*	*	*	*	*	*	*	*	*	*
MISSOURI	*	*	*	*	*	*	*	*	*	*	*	*	*	*
MONTANA	0.01	0.02	0.00	0.01	0.01	0.01	0.00	0.01	0.00	0.00	0.00	0.00	0.01	0.03
NEBRASKA	*	*	*	*	*	*	*	*	*	*	*	*	*	*
NEVADA	0.01	0.00	0.00	0.00	*	0.00	0.00	0.01	0.00	0.00	0.00	0.00	*	0.04
NEW HAMPSHIRE	0.00	0.00	0.00	0.00	0.00	0.00	0.00	0.00	0.00	0.00	0.00	0.00	0.00	0.00
NEW JERSEY	0.00	0.00	0.01	0.00	0.00	0.00	0.01	0.00	0.00	0.00	0.00	0.00	0.00	0.01
NEW MEXICO	0.03	0.04	0.00	*	0.00	0.02	0.01	0.02	0.02	0.02	0.02	0.03	0.04	0.08
NEW YORK	0.01	0.00	0.00	0.00	0.00	0.00	0.00	0.00	0.00	0.00	0.00	0.00	0.00	0.02
NORTH CAROLINA	0.00	0.00	0.00	0.00	0.00	0.00	0.00	0.00	0.00	0.00	0.00	0.00	0.00	0.00
NORTH DAKOTA	*	*	*	*	*	*	*	*	*	*	*	*	*	*
OHIO	0.00	0.00	0.00	0.00	0.00	0.00	0.00	0.00	0.00	0.00	0.00	0.00	0.00	0.01
OKLAHOMA	0.01	0.00	*	0.00	0.00	0.00	0.00	*	0.00	0.00	0.00	0.00	0.00	0.03
OREGON	0.05	0.00	0.01	*	0.00	*	0.00	0.01	0.00	0.01	0.01	0.01	0.03	0.06
PENNSYLVANIA	0.03	0.02	0.01	0.02	0.03	0.00	0.02	0.00	0.00	0.01	0.00	0.01	0.01	0.05
RHODE ISLAND	0.01	0.01	0.00	0.00	0.01	0.00	0.00	0.00	0.00	0.00	0.00	0.00	0.00	0.01
SOUTH CAROLINA	*	*	*	*	*	*	*	*	*	*	*	*	*	*
SOUTH DAKOTA	0.07	0.05	0.04	0.02	0.05	0.13	0.06	0.04	0.02	0.02	0.05	0.04	0.06	0.25
TENNESSEE	0.00	0.00	0.00	*	0.00	0.00	0.00	0.00	0.00	0.00	0.00	0.00	0.00	0.01
TEXAS	0.58	0.06	0.28	0.13	0.05	0.06	0.04	0.06	0.10	0.08	0.04	0.19	0.21	1.09
UTAH	*	*	*	*	*	*	*	*	*	*	*	*	*	*
VERMONT	*	*	*	*	*	*	*	*	*	*	*	*	*	*
VIRGINIA	0.00	0.00	0.00	0.00	0.00	0.00	0.00	0.00	0.00	0.00	0.00	0.00	0.00	0.00
WASHINGTON	0.00	0.00	0.00	0.00	0.00	0.00	0.00	0.00	0.00	0.00	0.00	0.00	0.00	0.01
WEST VIRGINIA	0.00	0.04	0.01	0.00	0.00	0.01	0.00	0.00	0.00	0.01	0.01	0.02	0.05	0.09
WISCONSIN	*	*	*	*	*	*	*	*	*	*	*	*	*	*
WYOMING	0.10	0.09	0.03	0.02	0.01	0.05	0.06	0.01	0.01	0.03	0.01	0.02	0.03	0.27
AVERAGE	0.03	0.01	0.02	0.01	0.01	0.01	0.01	0.01	0.01	0.01	0.01	0.01	0.02	0.07

* EFFECTIVE TAX RATE EQUALS ZERO BEFORE ROUNDING. AN ENTIRE ROW OF * MEANS THAT THIS TAX IS NOT USED IN THIS STATE.

TABLE A-75

EFFECTIVE TAX RATES: LOCAL REAL PROPERTY TAX-SINGLE FAMILY RESIDENTIAL (BENCHMARK)
INCIDENCE: HOUSEHOLDS
ALLOCATOR: HOUSING VALUES

STATE	UNDER $3,000	$3,000 -3,999	$4,000 -4,999	$5,000 -5,999	$6,000 -6,999	$7,000 -7,999	$8,000 -9,999	$10,000 -11,999	$12,000 -14,999	$15,000 -19,999	$20,000 -24,999	$25,000 -29,999	$30,000 -34,999	OVER $35,000
ALABAMA	1.06	0.65	0.56	0.50	0.45	0.43	0.40	0.36	0.32	0.29	0.26	0.24	0.23	0.11
ALASKA	4.02	2.42	2.07	2.00	1.80	1.55	1.46	1.29	1.15	0.96	0.85	0.78	0.72	0.53
ARIZONA	6.88	3.96	2.99	2.88	2.47	2.13	2.03	1.76	1.56	1.36	1.12	0.99	0.97	0.72
ARKANSAS	2.12	1.31	1.14	1.01	0.98	0.89	0.82	0.74	0.66	0.60	0.56	0.51	0.49	0.31
CALIFORNIA	11.05	6.89	5.55	4.90	4.32	3.96	3.44	3.05	2.68	2.26	1.97	1.78	1.64	1.15
COLORADO	7.74	4.66	3.71	3.27	3.08	2.67	2.28	2.09	1.87	1.57	1.37	1.25	1.04	0.83
CONNECTICUT	11.05	7.12	5.68	5.37	4.67	4.76	3.71	3.24	2.82	2.38	2.09	1.84	1.60	0.94
DELAWARE	3.45	2.10	2.03	1.70	1.58	1.51	1.40	1.21	1.18	1.07	0.98	0.89	0.80	0.59
FLORIDA	4.07	2.53	2.07	1.88	1.82	1.68	1.52	1.37	1.28	1.13	1.05	0.97	0.84	0.47
GEORGIA	3.75	2.16	1.96	1.78	1.67	1.60	1.41	1.27	1.18	1.09	0.98	0.90	0.84	0.60
HAWAII	3.89	2.42	2.33	2.05	1.82	1.70	1.51	1.33	1.18	1.02	0.90	0.85	0.71	0.60
IDAHO	5.09	2.92	2.36	2.23	1.97	1.75	1.61	1.37	1.22	1.04	0.90	0.82	0.71	0.55
ILLINOIS	6.19	3.86	3.25	2.84	2.49	2.35	2.06	1.80	1.65	1.40	1.21	1.11	1.01	0.70
INDIANA	6.09	3.56	2.85	2.62	2.37	2.15	1.82	1.68	1.47	1.25	1.11	0.91	0.92	0.66
IOWA	6.30	3.68	3.34	2.57	2.48	2.26	1.99	1.84	1.56	1.37	1.18	1.09	0.96	0.80
KANSAS	4.87	2.80	2.39	1.91	1.83	1.66	1.57	1.31	1.18	0.97	0.81	0.79	0.73	0.48
KENTUCKY	2.19	1.36	1.20	1.01	0.96	0.90	0.86	0.78	0.67	0.63	0.59	0.55	0.51	0.32
LOUISIANA	1.85	1.09	0.93	0.90	0.82	0.77	0.73	0.65	0.60	0.55	0.52	0.48	0.45	0.35
MAINE	7.29	4.18	3.51	2.67	2.69	2.33	2.08	1.77	1.54	1.29	1.14	0.94	0.85	0.45
MARYLAND	6.71	4.28	3.70	3.02	2.99	2.79	2.61	2.33	2.08	1.87	1.69	1.66	1.39	1.19
MASSACHUSETTS	15.47	10.46	8.23	6.87	6.42	5.77	5.05	4.58	3.70	3.25	2.76	2.57	2.36	1.27
MICHIGAN	10.19	6.13	4.86	4.09	3.64	3.56	2.99	2.73	2.38	2.02	1.76	1.57	1.46	0.98
MINNESOTA	8.90	5.34	4.05	3.77	3.36	3.33	2.68	2.43	2.11	1.79	1.57	1.46	1.30	0.89
MISSISSIPPI	2.53	1.61	1.32	1.19	1.06	1.06	0.96	0.89	0.79	0.71	0.66	0.65	0.59	0.40
MISSOURI	5.56	2.89	2.67	2.23	2.00	1.84	1.63	1.46	1.22	1.03	0.91	0.82	0.65	0.51
MONTANA	5.62	3.40	2.85	2.43	2.27	2.06	1.74	1.53	1.38	1.21	1.06	0.92	0.91	0.69
NEBRASKA	4.98	2.97	2.26	2.01	1.81	1.68	1.49	1.35	1.17	1.03	0.91	0.81	0.76	0.57
NEVADA	5.42	3.45	2.85	2.40	2.34	2.12	1.84	1.59	1.37	1.21	1.04	0.98	0.90	0.55
NEW HAMPSHIRE	14.79	8.75	6.54	6.18	5.42	4.68	4.44	3.78	3.33	2.90	2.44	2.17	2.01	1.19
NEW JERSEY	16.31	9.68	8.18	7.19	6.49	6.05	5.09	4.71	4.02	3.41	2.97	2.66	2.35	1.52
NEW MEXICO	3.10	1.87	1.64	1.36	1.29	1.10	1.00	0.87	0.73	0.65	0.57	0.47	0.37	0.35
NEW YORK	9.66	5.33	4.23	3.59	3.31	3.02	2.62	2.35	2.00	1.71	1.48	1.34	1.21	0.71
NORTH CAROLINA	2.62	1.60	1.39	1.17	1.15	1.03	0.98	0.87	0.81	0.71	0.66	0.62	0.55	0.38
NORTH DAKOTA	4.45	2.48	2.10	1.79	1.61	1.49	1.31	1.20	1.07	0.92	0.81	0.73	0.70	0.56
OHIO	7.27	4.36	3.66	3.10	2.80	2.72	2.37	2.07	1.83	1.62	1.44	1.29	1.16	0.81
OKLAHOMA	2.90	1.65	1.41	1.33	1.25	1.10	1.00	0.95	0.84	0.74	0.70	0.63	0.58	0.50
OREGON	8.91	5.13	4.24	3.84	3.37	3.13	2.73	2.40	2.04	1.74	1.52	1.40	1.16	0.86
PENNSYLVANIA	7.84	4.30	3.59	2.99	2.79	2.51	2.25	1.97	1.65	1.43	1.16	1.05	0.99	0.57
RHODE ISLAND	10.00	5.22	4.91	4.13	3.30	3.09	2.82	2.41	2.17	1.88	1.62	1.48	1.19	0.71
SOUTH CAROLINA	2.74	1.73	1.47	1.35	1.24	1.19	1.09	1.02	0.93	0.85	0.80	0.76	0.63	0.50
SOUTH DAKOTA	5.09	2.92	2.52	2.17	2.00	1.78	1.56	1.45	1.27	1.12	0.99	0.90	0.82	0.62
TENNESSEE	2.92	1.87	1.62	1.47	1.33	1.28	1.15	1.07	0.99	0.88	0.82	0.74	0.73	0.51
TEXAS	2.98	1.89	1.59	1.48	1.36	1.25	1.19	1.09	0.98	0.89	0.81	0.75	0.66	0.50
UTAH	6.44	3.77	2.96	2.57	2.59	2.15	1.93	1.71	1.51	1.27	1.10	0.95	0.93	0.72
VERMONT	13.11	7.12	6.34	5.19	4.68	4.25	3.64	3.29	2.80	2.40	2.08	1.73	1.49	0.89
VIRGINIA	4.15	2.32	2.12	1.93	1.67	1.59	1.52	1.37	1.24	1.11	0.99	0.94	0.80	0.62
WASHINGTON	4.24	2.46	1.94	1.64	1.48	1.42	1.21	1.12	0.93	0.79	0.68	0.63	0.48	0.31
WEST VIRGINIA	2.01	1.26	1.01	0.90	0.85	0.79	0.70	0.68	0.61	0.56	0.51	0.45	0.43	0.35
WISCONSIN	9.04	4.96	4.17	3.65	3.41	3.22	2.56	2.36	2.06	1.75	1.48	1.36	1.25	0.85
WYOMING	6.04	3.84	3.43	2.96	2.64	2.45	2.13	1.95	1.74	1.49	1.34	1.27	1.18	0.91
AVERAGE	6.22	3.70	3.08	2.68	2.44	2.25	1.98	1.77	1.55	1.34	1.18	1.07	0.96	0.66

* EFFECTIVE TAX RATE EQUALS ZERO BEFORE ROUNDING. AN ENTIRE ROW OF * MEANS THAT THIS TAX IS NOT USED IN THIS STATE.

TABLE A-76
EFFECTIVE TAX RATES: LOCAL REAL PROPERTY TAX-SINGLE FAMILY RESIDENTIAL (MOST REGRESSIVE)
INCIDENCE: HOUSEHOLDS
ALLOCATOR: HOUSING EXPENDITURES

STATE	UNDER $3,000	$3,000 -3,999	$4,000 -4,999	$5,000 -5,999	$6,000 -6,999	$7,000 -7,999	$8,000 -9,999	$10,000 -11,999	$12,000 -14,999	$15,000 -19,999	$20,000 -24,999	$25,000 -29,999	$30,000 -34,999	OVER $35,000
ALABAMA	0.83	0.56	0.49	0.45	0.41	0.40	0.38	0.35	0.33	0.30	0.29	0.27	0.26	0.15
ALASKA	2.40	1.65	1.45	1.47	1.37	1.23	1.20	1.11	1.04	0.91	0.85	0.83	0.79	0.64
ARIZONA	4.72	3.01	2.37	2.37	2.09	1.85	1.85	1.68	1.56	1.45	1.28	1.19	1.20	1.01
ARKANSAS	1.68	1.13	1.02	0.93	0.92	0.85	0.80	0.74	0.68	0.64	0.61	0.57	0.56	0.38
CALIFORNIA	7.37	5.10	4.30	3.95	3.60	3.41	3.07	2.85	2.63	2.37	2.20	2.08	2.00	1.61
COLORADO	5.21	3.48	2.90	2.66	2.58	2.31	2.04	1.97	1.85	1.66	1.53	1.47	1.29	1.15
CONNECTICUT	5.61	4.30	3.65	3.68	3.37	3.63	2.99	2.80	2.62	2.45	2.36	2.24	2.08	1.60
DELAWARE	2.61	1.74	1.73	1.48	1.41	1.37	1.31	1.16	1.16	1.08	1.02	0.95	0.87	0.68
FLORIDA	3.17	2.15	1.81	1.69	1.68	1.57	1.46	1.36	1.30	1.18	1.13	1.06	0.95	0.60
GEORGIA	2.92	1.83	1.71	1.60	1.53	1.50	1.35	1.25	1.20	1.14	1.06	0.99	0.94	0.71
HAWAII	2.48	1.73	1.74	1.60	1.47	1.42	1.30	1.21	1.12	1.03	0.96	0.95	0.83	0.77
IDAHO	3.50	2.24	1.88	1.85	1.69	1.54	1.48	1.32	1.24	1.11	1.03	0.98	0.90	0.78
ILLINOIS	4.44	3.02	2.63	2.37	2.13	2.07	1.86	1.69	1.61	1.44	1.30	1.25	1.17	0.91
INDIANA	4.50	2.84	2.34	2.23	2.06	1.91	1.67	1.61	1.45	1.30	1.22	1.04	1.08	0.86
IOWA	4.65	2.94	2.76	2.18	2.17	2.02	1.84	1.76	1.55	1.43	1.29	1.24	1.13	1.03
KANSAS	3.60	2.25	1.97	1.63	1.60	1.48	1.45	1.26	1.18	1.02	0.90	0.90	0.86	0.64
KENTUCKY	1.72	1.16	1.06	0.91	0.89	0.85	0.84	0.78	0.69	0.66	0.64	0.61	0.57	0.39
LOUISIANA	1.44	0.93	0.81	0.81	0.76	0.72	0.70	0.64	0.60	0.57	0.55	0.52	0.50	0.41
MAINE	4.19	2.84	2.56	2.03	2.20	1.99	1.89	1.72	1.63	1.50	1.45	1.32	1.28	0.96
MARYLAND	5.04	3.51	3.11	2.62	2.65	2.52	2.41	2.21	2.03	1.88	1.75	1.75	1.50	1.35
MASSACHUSETTS	8.10	6.53	5.49	4.85	4.80	4.53	4.19	4.10	3.57	3.46	3.23	3.22	3.15	2.27
MICHIGAN	7.42	4.84	3.96	3.41	3.12	3.14	2.71	2.57	2.33	2.08	1.91	1.78	1.70	1.30
MINNESOTA	6.57	4.25	3.34	3.21	2.93	2.98	2.47	2.33	2.10	1.87	1.73	1.67	1.54	1.19
MISSISSIPPI	2.00	1.40	1.18	1.09	1.00	1.01	0.94	0.90	0.81	0.75	0.72	0.72	0.67	0.48
MISSOURI	4.17	2.35	2.23	1.93	1.77	1.68	1.53	1.42	1.23	1.10	1.02	0.96	0.80	0.69
MONTANA	3.84	2.58	2.27	2.00	1.94	1.81	1.59	1.47	1.39	1.30	1.21	1.10	1.13	0.95
NEBRASKA	3.69	2.38	1.87	1.72	1.59	1.51	1.38	1.30	1.17	1.08	1.01	0.93	0.90	0.74
NEVADA	3.61	2.56	2.21	1.93	1.94	1.82	1.64	1.49	1.35	1.26	1.15	1.13	1.08	0.79
NEW HAMPSHIRE	8.09	5.68	4.51	4.54	4.15	3.78	3.82	3.49	3.31	3.18	2.94	2.82	2.77	2.11
NEW JERSEY	8.20	5.75	5.18	4.89	4.65	4.54	4.04	4.07	3.74	3.49	3.33	3.21	3.02	2.44
NEW MEXICO	2.14	1.43	1.31	1.13	1.11	0.98	0.92	0.84	0.74	0.70	0.65	0.58	0.49	0.50
NEW YORK	5.08	3.32	2.82	2.53	2.47	2.37	2.19	2.11	1.94	1.82	1.73	1.68	1.61	1.21
NORTH CAROLINA	2.04	1.36	1.21	1.06	1.05	0.96	0.94	0.86	0.82	0.75	0.71	0.68	0.62	0.46
NORTH DAKOTA	3.27	1.98	1.73	1.53	1.41	1.34	1.21	1.15	1.07	0.97	0.89	0.84	0.82	0.71
OHIO	5.33	3.46	3.02	2.62	2.43	2.42	2.17	1.96	1.81	1.68	1.57	1.46	1.36	1.07
OKLAHOMA	2.25	1.40	1.23	1.19	1.15	1.02	0.96	0.93	0.85	0.77	0.75	0.69	0.65	0.58
OREGON	6.09	3.91	3.37	3.17	2.89	2.75	2.51	2.31	2.06	1.88	1.75	1.68	1.47	1.26
PENNSYLVANIA	4.20	2.74	2.45	2.17	2.14	2.02	1.92	1.81	1.64	1.56	1.40	1.36	1.36	1.04
RHODE ISLAND	5.39	3.33	3.36	3.02	2.50	2.46	2.41	2.21	2.16	2.05	1.95	1.90	1.67	1.31
SOUTH CAROLINA	2.13	1.47	1.28	1.21	1.14	1.12	1.05	1.00	0.94	0.88	0.85	0.82	0.71	0.59
SOUTH DAKOTA	3.84	2.39	2.13	1.90	1.79	1.64	1.47	1.42	1.30	1.20	1.11	1.05	0.98	0.82
TENNESSEE	2.28	1.60	1.43	1.33	1.23	1.21	1.11	1.06	1.00	0.93	0.88	0.82	0.81	0.61
TEXAS	2.30	1.60	1.39	1.33	1.24	1.17	1.13	1.06	0.98	0.92	0.87	0.82	0.74	0.59
UTAH	4.35	2.82	2.31	2.09	2.18	1.85	1.74	1.61	1.49	1.34	1.24	1.13	1.14	0.99
VERMONT	7.46	4.79	4.59	3.98	3.78	3.60	3.28	3.19	2.93	2.77	2.64	2.38	2.22	1.79
VIRGINIA	3.17	1.94	1.81	1.69	1.50	1.46	1.43	1.32	1.23	1.13	1.04	1.01	0.88	0.73
WASHINGTON	2.83	1.84	1.51	1.32	1.23	1.22	1.08	1.05	0.92	0.83	0.77	0.75	0.61	0.48
WEST VIRGINIA	1.57	1.07	0.89	0.81	0.79	0.74	0.67	0.68	0.62	0.59	0.55	0.50	0.48	0.42
WISCONSIN	6.69	3.96	3.43	3.08	2.97	2.87	2.35	2.26	2.04	1.83	1.64	1.56	1.49	1.15
WYOMING	4.00	2.85	2.65	2.38	2.20	2.11	1.91	1.83	1.71	1.55	1.48	1.46	1.41	1.19
AVERAGE	4.08	2.72	2.37	2.15	2.03	1.94	1.77	1.67	1.53	1.42	1.32	1.26	1.18	0.94

* EFFECTIVE TAX RATE EQUALS ZERO BEFORE ROUNDING. AN ENTIRE ROW OF * MEANS THAT THIS TAX IS NOT USED IN THIS STATE.

TABLE A-77
EFFECTIVE TAX RATES: LOCAL REAL PROPERTY TAX-SINGLE FAMILY RESIDENTIAL (MOST PROGRESSIVE)
INCIDENCE: OWNERS OF CAPITAL
ALLOCATOR: DIVIDEND INCOME

STATE	UNDER $3,000	$3,000 -3,999	$4,000 -4,999	$5,000 -5,999	$6,000 -6,999	$7,000 -7,999	$8,000 -9,999	$10,000 -11,999	$12,000 -14,999	$15,000 -19,999	$20,000 -24,999	$25,000 -29,999	$30,000 -34,999	OVER $35,000
ALABAMA	0.24	0.07	0.13	0.02	0.12	0.07	*	0.10	0.04	0.02	0.20	0.07	0.16	2.63
ALASKA	0.58	3.73	1.86	0.14	*	0.24	0.33	0.17	0.14	0.82	0.35	0.33	0.36	1.48
ARIZONA	1.83	2.46	2.35	1.37	1.89	0.21	0.66	0.92	0.59	1.02	0.74	0.91	1.25	4.66
ARKANSAS	1.13	0.40	0.58	1.41	0.17	*	0.58	0.52	0.50	0.14	0.33	0.27	0.21	3.79
CALIFORNIA	4.64	1.92	1.80	2.80	1.32	1.06	1.59	1.39	1.64	0.99	0.94	1.58	1.77	7.37
COLORADO	4.19	0.14	5.76	0.73	0.03	3.28	0.51	0.08	0.31	0.21	0.55	0.49	2.10	7.21
CONNECTICUT	2.03	4.61	5.95	4.72	2.17	0.06	0.15	0.26	1.29	1.58	0.36	0.48	0.10	7.75
DELAWARE	1.99	0.67	0.42	0.17	*	1.26	0.05	0.23	0.61	0.37	0.43	0.46	0.22	4.01
FLORIDA	2.27	0.56	1.20	1.00	0.93	0.74	0.54	1.01	0.59	0.72	0.56	1.12	1.57	3.77
GEORGIA	2.27	1.08	0.46	1.07	0.90	0.03	0.25	0.00	0.31	0.37	0.39	0.56	2.00	5.64
HAWAII	4.80	0.81	0.70	1.17	2.57	0.76	0.87	0.40	0.25	0.81	0.17	0.11	0.51	2.80
IDAHO	2.52	0.84	0.46	0.20	0.14	0.86	0.19	0.40	0.09	0.28	1.43	0.97	2.77	5.09
ILLINOIS	2.13	1.67	0.99	1.79	0.95	0.75	0.83	1.13	0.39	0.45	0.51	0.60	0.69	5.33
INDIANA	1.58	1.03	0.58	0.01	0.11	0.55	0.23	0.61	0.31	0.53	0.82	1.43	0.85	5.92
IOWA	0.42	1.14	1.44	2.28	0.70	*	1.52	1.66	0.18	0.51	0.54	0.67	3.76	5.15
KANSAS	1.44	0.64	0.57	0.69	1.93	0.78	0.40	0.84	0.21	0.32	0.75	0.82	0.39	4.17
KENTUCKY	0.23	0.09	0.27	1.30	0.10	*	0.21	*	0.04	0.23	0.13	0.70	0.26	5.33
LOUISIANA	0.54	0.19	0.45	0.12	0.13	0.24	0.13	0.20	0.12	0.22	0.13	0.21	0.58	2.92
MAINE	1.80	0.96	0.79	2.68	0.28	0.44	2.46	0.17	0.55	1.46	0.40	2.43	1.16	6.28
MARYLAND	1.34	7.19	1.86	1.38	0.29	0.47	0.30	1.23	0.38	0.92	1.40	0.58	0.98	5.26
MASSACHUSETTS	5.76	1.07	4.47	3.43	3.67	0.67	1.30	1.25	1.60	0.73	0.95	2.73	0.97	14.61
MICHIGAN	3.50	2.95	2.78	1.46	1.49	2.64	1.60	0.72	0.52	0.68	1.02	2.30	0.93	8.14
MINNESOTA	2.27	0.45	6.64	0.47	0.80	0.12	1.92	0.72	0.63	0.30	0.74	1.38	0.87	9.04
MISSISSIPPI	0.41	0.01	0.41	0.00	1.11	0.11	0.45	0.43	0.31	0.29	0.94	0.47	0.63	4.46
MISSOURI	0.63	0.36	0.17	1.02	0.35	0.63	0.58	0.56	0.50	0.26	0.65	0.54	0.55	6.12
MONTANA	2.00	3.36	0.57	0.94	1.05	1.36	0.60	1.80	0.30	0.34	0.64	0.49	1.09	5.38
NEBRASKA	2.29	0.54	0.09	0.38	1.22	0.23	1.05	0.15	0.31	0.13	0.64	0.46	1.25	4.96
NEVADA	1.25	0.62	0.33	0.15	*	0.14	0.17	0.99	0.10	0.63	0.13	0.44	*	5.67
NEW HAMPSHIRE	5.92	1.63	10.29	9.41	0.60	0.21	1.45	3.01	1.31	1.17	1.26	0.60	2.17	14.69
NEW JERSEY	3.36	2.09	6.32	5.98	3.57	2.56	9.97	2.80	1.19	1.18	1.54	1.30	1.80	8.64
NEW MEXICO	0.70	1.01	0.04	*	0.10	0.62	0.17	0.43	0.61	0.47	0.53	0.82	1.01	2.00
NEW YORK	2.36	1.87	2.14	2.03	0.72	0.93	0.83	0.60	0.68	0.72	0.73	0.78	1.43	6.64
NORTH CAROLINA	1.57	0.27	1.68	0.38	0.40	0.19	0.31	0.27	0.22	0.27	0.49	0.48	0.37	3.69
NORTH DAKOTA	2.20	0.59	1.31	0.57	2.23	0.26	0.38	0.23	0.62	0.25	0.75	0.87	1.12	2.94
OHIO	2.54	2.06	1.52	2.26	0.17	0.79	1.05	0.85	0.44	0.62	0.87	1.03	2.13	7.05
OKLAHOMA	0.98	0.05	*	0.01	0.32	0.48	0.13	*	0.21	0.26	0.42	0.57	0.18	3.73
OREGON	7.11	0.23	1.29	*	0.25	*	0.11	1.16	0.30	0.91	1.25	0.86	4.29	8.77
PENNSYLVANIA	3.49	2.38	1.13	2.21	2.93	0.23	1.73	0.51	0.45	0.75	0.46	0.62	1.18	5.81
RHODE ISLAND	3.65	5.12	2.62	1.96	6.07	0.40	1.07	1.77	1.14	0.93	0.48	0.57	2.16	6.86
SOUTH CAROLINA	0.48	*	0.32	0.22	1.61	1.04	0.59	1.08	0.59	0.31	0.16	0.21	0.56	5.11
SOUTH DAKOTA	1.52	1.10	0.82	0.40	1.02	2.86	1.31	0.79	0.38	0.37	1.06	0.96	1.31	5.39
TENNESSEE	1.14	0.03	0.17	*	0.34	0.02	0.34	0.56	0.08	0.55	0.35	0.50	0.49	5.81
TEXAS	2.00	0.22	0.96	0.47	0.18	0.23	0.15	0.24	0.38	0.33	0.22	0.73	0.84	3.98
UTAH	7.36	0.03	2.14	1.68	0.26	0.96	0.87	0.47	0.19	0.44	0.72	0.51	1.07	5.71
VERMONT	1.61	0.10	0.32	2.56	1.26	1.89	2.29	1.43	1.83	0.91	2.65	0.88	8.10	13.71
VIRGINIA	1.07	1.37	0.15	1.33	2.05	0.31	0.62	0.96	0.21	0.53	0.39	0.73	0.52	3.72
WASHINGTON	0.52	0.10	0.88	0.61	0.57	0.64	0.40	0.03	0.42	0.35	0.25	0.25	0.84	3.71
WEST VIRGINIA	0.06	1.42	0.45	0.17	0.16	0.42	0.14	0.01	0.15	0.21	0.39	0.58	1.78	3.23
WISCONSIN	2.25	0.82	2.89	0.28	*	1.52	3.75	0.96	0.27	0.80	1.29	0.72	2.17	8.00
WYOMING	2.70	2.29	0.81	0.61	0.30	1.30	1.56	0.20	0.22	0.68	0.40	0.48	0.85	7.16
AVERAGE	2.21	1.29	1.65	1.32	0.99	0.71	0.97	0.73	0.49	0.57	0.67	0.77	1.29	5.83

* EFFECTIVE TAX RATE EQUALS ZERO BEFORE ROUNDING. AN ENTIRE ROW OF * MEANS THAT THIS TAX IS NOT USED IN THIS STATE.

TABLE A-78
EFFECTIVE TAX RATES: LOCAL REAL PROPERTY TAX-SINGLE FAMILY RESIDENTIAL
INCIDENCE: HOUSEHOLDS
ALLOCATOR: REAL ESTATE TAX PAYMENTS

STATE	UNDER $3,000	$3,000 -3,999	$4,000 -4,999	$5,000 -5,999	$6,000 -6,999	$7,000 -7,999	$8,000 -9,999	$10,000 -11,999	$12,000 -14,999	$15,000 -19,999	$20,000 -24,999	$25,000 -29,999	$30,000 -34,999	OVER $35,000
ALABAMA	0.13	0.01	0.08	0.07	0.10	0.27	0.16	0.21	0.34	0.38	0.37	0.37	0.39	0.62
ALASKA	0.15	*	2.01	0.23	0.53	0.19	0.20	0.62	0.48	0.70	0.88	0.79	0.75	1.06
ARIZONA	0.12	0.66	0.76	0.49	0.85	2.21	1.18	1.92	1.74	1.35	2.01	1.92	1.43	1.43
ARKANSAS	*	0.25	0.33	0.36	0.26	0.20	0.43	0.38	0.93	0.86	0.73	1.03	0.90	1.49
CALIFORNIA	0.90	0.95	1.20	0.96	1.79	1.38	2.23	2.22	2.54	2.86	2.83	2.65	2.51	2.70
COLORADO	0.28	0.47	0.66	0.55	0.65	0.85	2.34	2.18	1.68	1.96	1.96	1.76	2.23	1.59
CONNECTICUT	*	0.72	2.52	0.70	1.82	0.55	1.85	2.81	2.35	2.42	2.40	2.51	2.70	2.80
DELAWARE	*	0.19	0.56	0.06	0.84	0.53	0.43	0.99	1.03	0.96	1.15	1.11	1.34	1.44
FLORIDA	0.15	0.29	1.44	0.97	0.46	0.81	1.01	1.03	1.02	1.19	1.13	1.23	1.62	2.32
GEORGIA	0.09	0.30	0.68	0.64	0.79	0.47	0.86	0.94	1.19	1.03	1.29	1.53	1.55	1.96
HAWAII	0.11	0.05	0.14	0.13	0.40	0.21	0.66	0.58	1.00	1.12	1.29	1.08	1.53	1.04
IDAHO	0.21	0.01	0.21	0.19	0.39	0.44	0.72	1.10	1.26	1.55	1.52	1.34	1.87	1.39
ILLINOIS	0.11	0.62	0.49	1.11	0.92	0.57	1.13	1.48	1.10	1.54	1.76	1.65	1.64	1.66
INDIANA	0.06	0.44	0.81	0.53	0.44	0.74	1.29	0.76	1.16	1.42	1.37	2.25	1.59	1.95
IOWA	0.17	0.11	0.20	1.14	0.35	0.60	0.48	0.88	1.85	1.64	2.21	1.82	2.10	1.58
KANSAS	0.01	0.20	0.68	0.75	0.93	0.80	0.47	0.69	0.83	1.40	1.67	1.19	1.01	1.37
KENTUCKY	0.02	0.31	0.15	0.75	0.16	0.50	0.30	0.53	0.97	0.84	0.79	0.76	0.82	1.16
LOUISIANA	*	*	0.04	0.03	0.26	0.57	0.48	0.58	0.28	0.46	0.66	0.96	0.81	1.21
MAINE	0.11	0.72	0.09	3.05	0.37	0.81	1.48	1.99	1.59	1.85	1.66	1.99	1.74	2.31
MARYLAND	1.55	0.21	0.14	1.80	0.26	0.17	1.09	1.80	1.85	2.15	2.19	1.71	2.54	1.78
MASSACHUSETTS	2.37	1.61	2.03	3.10	2.01	2.28	4.13	2.56	4:31	3.64	3.86	3.00	2.81	4.21
MICHIGAN	0.60	0.61	0.69	1.58	2.69	1.46	2.46	1.97	1.98	2.22	2.32	2.50	2.19	2.30
MINNESOTA	*	2.66	2.51	0.74	1.15	0.17	1.42	1.64	1.95	2.42	2.35	1.84	2.29	2.34
MISSISSIPPI	0.36	*	*	0.20	0.42	0.25	0.50	0.49	0.86	1.19	1.07	0.82	1.06	1.67
MISSOURI	0.07	0.36	0.98	0.38	0.83	0.46	0.56	0.63	1.23	1.60	1.49	1.48	2.11	1.36
MONTANA	0.48	0.46	0.30	0.85	0.61	0.39	1.38	2.05	1.50	1.43	1.52	2.06	1.08	1.41
NEBRASKA	*	*	0.16	*	0.85	0.91	1.11	0.88	1.40	1.21	1.21	1.62	1.13	1.40
NEVADA	0.13	0.13	0.42	1.17	0.90	0.59	1.04	1.39	1.72	1.43	1.42	1.04	1.01	1.55
NEW HAMPSHIRE	0.25	0.32	1.84	1.23	5.49	2.63	2.23	3.32	3.25	2.97	3.71	3.73	2.80	4.59
NEW JERSEY	0.46	4.13	4.27	3.10	2.53	3.28	5.23	2.92	3.32	3.71	3.37	3.29	3.25	3.36
NEW MEXICO	0.05	0.20	0.05	0.45	0.07	0.74	0.59	0.62	0.98	0.76	0.84	1.15	1.42	0.69
NEW YORK	0.24	1.10	1.04	2.13	1.81	1.42	1.28	1.59	1.77	1.92	1.92	1.79	1.71	2.44
NORTH CAROLINA	0.04	0.19	0.56	0.03	0.33	0.48	0.50	0.76	0.70	0.96	0.87	0.94	1.08	1.26
NORTH DAKOTA	*	0.48	0.35	0.15	0.31	0.63	0.86	0.92	1.08	1.20	1.30	1.34	1.00	1.11
OHIO	0.21	0.24	0.55	0.98	1.65	1.15	1.28	1.57	1.87	1.72	1.71	1.96	2.10	2.45
OKLAHOMA	0.41	0.09	0.83	0.24	0.20	0.94	0.85	0.44	0.70	1.06	0.97	1.12	1.11	0.91
OREGON	1.82	1.32	0.94	0.61	0.07	0.89	1.72	2.04	2.50	2.40	2.28	2.07	2.62	2.21
PENNSYLVANIA	0.12	0.73	0.64	0.67	0.88	1.18	1.11	1.24	1.64	1.58	2.10	1.99	1.60	1.91
RHODE ISLAND	0.08	1.00	0.91	0.16	3.08	3.05	2.20	3.08	2.14	1.92	1.93	1.55	2.52	2.54
SOUTH CAROLINA	*	*	0.05	0.50	0.24	0.51	0.59	0.91	0.95	0.99	0.91	0.94	1.89	1.71
SOUTH DAKOTA	1.11	0.14	0.24	0.69	0.50	0.62	1.63	1.17	1.26	1.46	1.59	1.50	1.47	1.83
TENNESSEE	0.10	0.03	*	0.67	0.65	0.51	0.68	0.80	0.74	0.99	1.21	1.48	1.36	1.84
TEXAS	0.37	0.12	0.26	0.20	0.30	0.50	0.54	0.55	0.77	0.89	1.12	1.22	1.53	1.62
UTAH	0.66	0.75	1.31	0.25	0.38	1.75	1.27	1.50	1.57	1.72	1.62	1.91	1.09	1.01
VERMONT	0.15	2.38	0.58	1.79	1.52	2.24	2.84	2.71	2.57	3.31	2.98	3.74	3.92	4.68
VIRGINIA	0.14	0.12	0.17	0.41	1.03	0.47	0.50	0.83	0.77	1.14	1.42	1.18	1.75	1.50
WASHINGTON	0.11	0.07	0.34	1.06	0.67	0.63	1.02	0.57	0.92	1.03	0.99	0.68	0.99	0.96
WEST VIRGINIA	*	*	0.45	0.10	*	1.14	0.38	0.25	0.26	0.52	0.73	1.48	1.08	1.37
WISCONSIN	0.30	1.03	0.77	1.65	0.86	0.83	1.94	1.42	1.93	2.22	2.51	2.10	2.05	1.90
WYOMING	*	0.11	0.48	*	1.84	0.77	2.05	1.59	1.51	1.81	1.63	1.51	1.81	2.14
AVERAGE	0.30	0.54	0.74	0.79	0.93	0.91	1.25	1.32	1.47	1.58	1.66	1.65	1.70	1.86

* EFFECTIVE TAX RATE EQUALS ZERO BEFORE ROUNDING. AN ENTIRE ROW OF * MEANS THAT THIS TAX IS NOT USED IN THIS STATE.

TABLE A-79
EFFECTIVE TAX RATES: LOCAL REAL PROPERTY TAX-MULTIFAMILY RESIDENTIAL (BENCHMARK)
INCIDENCE: 1/2 TENANTS, 1/4 INCORPORATED LANDLORDS, 1/4 UNINCORPORATED LANDLORDS
ALLOCATOR: RENT PAYMENTS, RENT NET INCOME, AND DIVIDEND INCOME

STATE	UNDER $3,000	$3,000 -3,999	$4,000 -4,999	$5,000 -5,999	$6,000 -6,999	$7,000 -7,999	$8,000 -9,999	$10,000 -11,999	$12,000 -14,999	$15,000 -19,999	$20,000 -24,999	$25,000 -29,999	$30,000 -34,999	OVER $35,000
ALABAMA	0.05	0.02	0.02	0.04	0.05	0.02	0.01	0.02	0.01	0.01	0.01	0.01	0.01	0.07
ALASKA	0.51	0.37	0.26	0.18	0.16	0.16	0.14	0.12	0.11	0.14	0.10	0.09	0.08	0.15
ARIZONA	0.91	0.54	0.48	0.88	0.38	0.25	0.51	0.27	0.18	0.20	0.14	0.22	0.24	0.40
ARKANSAS	0.18	0.09	0.06	0.07	0.05	0.03	0.04	0.05	0.04	0.03	0.04	0.03	0.03	0.12
CALIFORNIA	2.09	1.24	0.97	0.87	0.67	0.62	0.73	0.49	0.44	0.37	0.31	0.34	0.36	0.87
COLORADO	0.87	0.31	0.44	0.23	0.21	0.29	0.16	0.18	0.16	0.12	0.15	0.12	0.17	0.38
CONNECTICUT	1.15	1.13	1.71	0.89	0.47	0.39	0.33	0.32	0.34	0.33	0.19	0.19	0.14	0.61
DELAWARE	0.30	0.16	0.14	0.11	0.11	0.33	0.09	0.11	0.11	0.09	0.07	0.11	0.06	0.18
FLORIDA	0.81	0.33	0.43	0.34	0.27	0.25	0.24	0.28	0.20	0.20	0.18	0.20	0.33	0.45
GEORGIA	0.49	0.32	0.15	0.24	0.13	0.10	0.10	0.10	0.10	0.09	0.10	0.08	0.14	0.30
HAWAII	2.15	0.80	0.75	0.72	1.40	0.58	0.62	0.43	0.64	0.42	0.33	0.25	0.27	0.69
IDAHO	0.14	0.06	0.06	0.04	0.03	0.06	0.03	0.03	0.02	0.02	0.03	0.02	0.04	0.08
ILLINOIS	1.26	0.78	0.73	0.78	0.44	0.48	0.43	0.38	0.26	0.30	0.21	0.26	0.30	0.63
INDIANA	0.29	0.20	0.13	0.09	0.10	0.09	0.13	0.08	0.06	0.05	0.05	0.07	0.04	0.14
IOWA	0.17	0.14	0.11	0.10	0.07	0.08	0.07	0.07	0.05	0.04	0.04	0.03	0.07	0.09
KANSAS	0.34	0.19	0.18	0.11	0.15	0.15	0.12	0.11	0.06	0.06	0.07	0.08	0.06	0.15
KENTUCKY	0.10	0.04	0.06	0.07	0.03	0.03	0.03	0.02	0.02	0.02	0.02	0.02	0.02	0.09
LOUISIANA	0.21	0.15	0.16	0.13	0.10	0.08	0.07	0.06	0.07	0.07	0.05	0.04	0.12	0.19
MAINE	0.56	0.47	0.28	0.29	0.19	0.19	0.24	0.14	0.14	0.17	0.11	0.17	0.15	0.39
MARYLAND	1.01	0.58	0.43	0.67	0.36	0.21	0.22	0.23	0.20	0.21	0.17	0.16	0.15	0.38
MASSACHUSETTS	3.73	1.20	1.35	1.32	1.26	0.70	1.07	0.63	0.54	0.48	0.44	0.50	0.34	1.19
MICHIGAN	0.97	0.53	0.38	0.40	0.36	0.28	0.20	0.21	0.16	0.15	0.16	0.17	0.12	0.38
MINNESOTA	0.74	0.31	0.64	0.40	0.23	0.18	0.21	0.16	0.16	0.12	0.12	0.15	0.16	0.42
MISSISSIPPI	0.14	0.13	0.05	0.04	0.07	0.04	0.04	0.04	0.04	0.04	0.07	0.04	0.04	0.13
MISSOURI	0.53	0.30	0.24	0.32	0.18	0.18	0.15	0.15	0.12	0.12	0.09	0.07	0.12	0.36
MONTANA	0.29	0.18	0.11	0.13	0.09	0.09	0.09	0.08	0.08	0.05	0.05	0.05	0.08	0.12
NEBRASKA	0.36	0.26	0.20	0.17	0.13	0.14	0.11	0.08	0.12	0.07	0.08	0.07	0.15	0.19
NEVADA	0.50	0.23	0.23	0.15	0.14	0.14	0.11	0.20	0.10	0.10	0.06	0.07	0.05	0.28
NEW HAMPSHIRE	2.02	0.81	0.85	0.95	0.41	0.86	0.52	0.38	0.34	0.25	0.26	0.18	0.21	0.99
NEW JERSEY	2.26	1.71	1.12	1.52	1.03	0.90	0.97	0.72	0.58	0.41	0.36	0.34	0.46	0.94
NEW MEXICO	0.21	0.13	0.08	0.06	0.07	0.09	0.05	0.07	0.06	0.05	0.05	0.04	0.05	0.08
NEW YORK	6.43	3.02	2.39	3.08	2.11	1.83	1.61	1.39	1.04	0.93	0.91	0.94	1.14	2.28
NORTH CAROLINA	0.18	0.08	0.10	0.15	0.05	0.05	0.06	0.05	0.04	0.04	0.04	0.04	0.05	0.12
NORTH DAKOTA	0.40	0.22	0.22	0.23	0.26	0.14	0.13	0.12	0.11	0.09	0.09	0.10	0.11	0.14
OHIO	0.57	0.32	0.27	0.42	0.36	0.20	0.18	0.17	0.14	0.12	0.11	0.11	0.14	0.32
OKLAHOMA	0.19	0.11	0.09	0.08	0.08	0.11	0.05	0.05	0.06	0.06	0.07	0.04	0.04	0.12
OREGON	0.96	0.54	0.38	0.28	0.26	0.28	0.18	0.16	0.12	0.12	0.13	0.11	0.21	0.36
PENNSYLVANIA	0.87	0.42	0.33	0.52	0.39	0.20	0.25	0.16	0.16	0.15	0.12	0.09	0.10	0.30
RHODE ISLAND	1.38	0.95	1.47	0.58	0.79	0.61	0.41	0.39	0.37	0.32	0.31	0.29	0.27	0.69
SOUTH CAROLINA	0.25	0.17	0.12	0.08	0.12	0.16	0.08	0.11	0.07	0.07	0.06	0.06	0.06	0.23
SOUTH DAKOTA	0.28	0.19	0.16	0.14	0.16	0.20	0.10	0.10	0.08	0.07	0.07	0.07	0.10	0.17
TENNESSEE	0.24	0.11	0.12	0.11	0.09	0.06	0.10	0.07	0.05	0.06	0.05	0.04	0.06	0.20
TEXAS	0.31	0.18	0.13	0.10	0.10	0.10	0.08	0.09	0.08	0.06	0.06	0.08	0.07	0.20
UTAH	0.27	0.10	0.15	0.09	0.07	0.07	0.06	0.06	0.06	0.04	0.04	0.03	0.05	0.11
VERMONT	0.50	0.22	0.36	0.18	0.14	0.12	0.15	0.09	0.13	0.07	0.08	0.05	0.14	0.22
VIRGINIA	0.62	0.46	0.39	0.31	0.43	0.20	0.19	0.30	0.16	0.14	0.13	0.13	0.15	0.39
WASHINGTON	0.50	0.21	0.21	0.19	0.14	0.13	0.13	0.08	0.09	0.08	0.06	0.05	0.12	0.23
WEST VIRGINIA	0.07	0.05	0.03	0.03	0.02	0.03	0.02	0.01	0.02	0.02	0.02	0.04	0.03	0.05
WISCONSIN	0.83	0.46	0.53	0.25	0.29	0.27	0.37	0.19	0.14	0.15	0.17	0.24	0.19	0.38
WYOMING	0.31	0.24	0.12	0.14	0.10	0.12	0.10	0.06	0.06	0.06	0.05	0.06	0.06	0.18
AVERAGE	0.81	0.44	0.41	0.39	0.31	0.26	0.24	0.20	0.17	0.15	0.13	0.14	0.15	0.36

* EFFECTIVE TAX RATE EQUALS ZERO BEFORE ROUNDING. AN ENTIRE ROW OF * MEANS THAT THIS TAX IS NOT USED IN THIS STATE.

TABLE A-80

EFFECTIVE TAX RATES: LOCAL REAL PROPERTY TAX-MULTIFAMILY RESIDENTIAL (MOST REGRESSIVE)
INCIDENCE: TENANTS
ALLOCATOR: RENT PAYMENTS

STATE	UNDER $3,000	$3,000 -3,999	$4,000 -4,999	$5,000 -5,999	$6,000 -6,999	$7,000 -7,999	$8,000 -9,999	$10,000 -11,999	$12,000 -14,999	$15,000 -19,999	$20,000 -24,999	$25,000 -29,999	$30,000 -34,999	OVER $35,000
ALABAMA	0.07	0.04	0.04	0.03	0.03	0.03	0.03	0.02	0.02	0.02	0.02	0.01	0.01	0.01
ALASKA	0.76	0.44	0.38	0.35	0.32	0.27	0.25	0.22	0.19	0.15	0.13	0.12	0.11	0.07
ARIZONA	1.51	0.85	0.63	0.60	0.51	0.43	0.41	0.35	0.30	0.26	0.20	0.17	0.17	0.11
ARKANSAS	0.17	0.10	0.09	0.08	0.07	0.07	0.06	0.05	0.05	0.04	0.04	0.04	0.03	0.02
CALIFORNIA	2.83	1.71	1.36	1.19	1.04	0.94	0.80	0.70	0.60	0.49	0.42	0.37	0.33	0.21
COLORADO	1.04	0.61	0.48	0.42	0.39	0.33	0.28	0.25	0.22	0.18	0.15	0.14	0.11	0.08
CONNECTICUT	1.82	1.17	0.93	0.87	0.76	0.77	0.60	0.53	0.45	0.38	0.33	0.29	0.25	0.15
DELAWARE	0.42	0.25	0.24	0.20	0.18	0.17	0.16	0.14	0.13	0.12	0.11	0.10	0.09	0.06
FLORIDA	0.98	0.59	0.48	0.43	0.42	0.38	0.34	0.31	0.28	0.24	0.22	0.20	0.18	0.09
GEORGIA	0.50	0.28	0.25	0.23	0.21	0.20	0.17	0.16	0.14	0.13	0.12	0.10	0.10	0.07
HAWAII	2.27	1.37	1.30	1.12	0.99	0.91	0.80	0.69	0.60	0.50	0.43	0.39	0.32	0.25
IDAHO	0.18	0.10	0.08	0.07	0.06	0.06	0.05	0.04	0.04	0.03	0.03	0.02	0.02	0.01
ILLINOIS	1.74	1.07	0.90	0.78	0.68	0.64	0.56	0.48	0.44	0.37	0.31	0.28	0.26	0.17
INDIANA	0.38	0.22	0.17	0.16	0.14	0.13	0.11	0.10	0.09	0.07	0.06	0.05	0.05	0.04
IOWA	0.27	0.15	0.14	0.11	0.10	0.09	0.08	0.07	0.06	0.05	0.05	0.04	0.04	0.03
KANSAS	0.46	0.26	0.22	0.17	0.17	0.15	0.14	0.12	0.10	0.08	0.07	0.07	0.06	0.04
KENTUCKY	0.11	0.07	0.06	0.05	0.05	0.04	0.04	0.04	0.03	0.03	0.03	0.02	0.02	0.01
LOUISIANA	0.31	0.18	0.15	0.15	0.13	0.12	0.11	0.10	0.09	0.08	0.08	0.07	0.07	0.05
MAINE	0.92	0.53	0.44	0.33	0.34	0.29	0.26	0.22	0.19	0.16	0.14	0.12	0.10	0.05
MARYLAND	1.01	0.63	0.53	0.44	0.42	0.39	0.36	0.32	0.29	0.25	0.23	0.22	0.18	0.15
MASSACHUSETTS	3.26	2.20	1.73	1.44	1.34	1.21	1.05	0.95	0.77	0.67	0.57	0.53	0.48	0.26
MICHIGAN	1.10	0.65	0.52	0.43	0.38	0.37	0.31	0.28	0.24	0.20	0.18	0.15	0.14	0.09
MINNESOTA	0.98	0.58	0.44	0.41	0.36	0.36	0.28	0.26	0.22	0.18	0.16	0.15	0.13	0.09
MISSISSIPPI	0.19	0.12	0.10	0.09	0.08	0.07	0.07	0.06	0.05	0.05	0.04	0.04	0.04	0.03
MISSOURI	0.80	0.41	0.38	0.31	0.28	0.26	0.23	0.20	0.17	0.14	0.12	0.11	0.08	0.06
MONTANA	0.38	0.22	0.18	0.15	0.14	0.13	0.11	0.09	0.08	0.07	0.06	0.05	0.05	0.03
NEBRASKA	0.54	0.32	0.24	0.21	0.19	0.18	0.16	0.14	0.12	0.10	0.09	0.08	0.08	0.05
NEVADA	0.68	0.42	0.34	0.29	0.27	0.25	0.21	0.18	0.15	0.13	0.11	0.10	0.09	0.05
NEW HAMPSHIRE	2.06	1.21	0.90	0.86	0.75	0.64	0.61	0.52	0.46	0.40	0.33	0.29	0.27	0.16
NEW JERSEY	3.08	1.82	1.54	1.35	1.22	1.13	0.95	0.88	0.75	0.63	0.55	0.49	0.43	0.27
NEW MEXICO	0.30	0.18	0.15	0.13	0.12	0.10	0.09	0.08	0.06	0.05	0.05	0.04	0.03	0.02
NEW YORK	7.77	4.27	3.38	2.86	2.65	2.40	2.08	1.87	1.58	1.34	1.16	1.05	0.94	0.55
NORTH CAROLINA	0.21	0.13	0.11	0.09	0.09	0.08	0.07	0.06	0.06	0.05	0.05	0.04	0.04	0.03
NORTH DAKOTA	0.57	0.32	0.27	0.22	0.20	0.19	0.16	0.15	0.13	0.11	0.10	0.09	0.08	0.06
OHIO	0.78	0.46	0.39	0.33	0.29	0.28	0.25	0.21	0.19	0.16	0.14	0.13	0.11	0.08
OKLAHOMA	0.28	0.15	0.13	0.12	0.11	0.10	0.09	0.08	0.07	0.06	0.06	0.05	0.05	0.04
OREGON	0.99	0.55	0.45	0.40	0.35	0.32	0.28	0.24	0.20	0.16	0.14	0.12	0.10	0.07
PENNSYLVANIA	1.00	0.55	0.46	0.38	0.35	0.32	0.28	0.25	0.21	0.18	0.15	0.13	0.12	0.07
RHODE ISLAND	2.21	1.15	1.08	0.91	0.72	0.67	0.62	0.53	0.47	0.41	0.35	0.32	0.25	0.15
SOUTH CAROLINA	0.31	0.19	0.16	0.15	0.13	0.13	0.12	0.11	0.10	0.09	0.08	0.08	0.06	0.05
SOUTH DAKOTA	0.42	0.24	0.20	0.18	0.16	0.14	0.12	0.11	0.10	0.09	0.08	0.07	0.06	0.05
TENNESSEE	0.27	0.17	0.15	0.13	0.12	0.11	0.10	0.09	0.08	0.07	0.07	0.06	0.06	0.04
TEXAS	0.34	0.21	0.18	0.16	0.15	0.14	0.13	0.11	0.10	0.09	0.08	0.08	0.07	0.05
UTAH	0.32	0.18	0.14	0.12	0.12	0.10	0.09	0.08	0.07	0.05	0.05	0.04	0.04	0.03
VERMONT	0.58	0.31	0.28	0.23	0.20	0.19	0.16	0.14	0.12	0.10	0.09	0.07	0.06	0.04
VIRGINIA	0.89	0.49	0.44	0.40	0.34	0.32	0.30	0.27	0.24	0.21	0.19	0.18	0.15	0.11
WASHINGTON	0.66	0.37	0.29	0.24	0.21	0.20	0.17	0.15	0.13	0.10	0.09	0.08	0.06	0.03
WEST VIRGINIA	0.09	0.06	0.05	0.04	0.04	0.03	0.03	0.03	0.03	0.02	0.02	0.02	0.02	0.01
WISCONSIN	1.15	0.62	0.52	0.45	0.42	0.39	0.31	0.29	0.25	0.21	0.17	0.16	0.14	0.09
WYOMING	0.38	0.23	0.20	0.17	0.15	0.14	0.12	0.11	0.09	0.08	0.07	0.06	0.06	0.04
AVERAGE	1.01	0.59	0.48	0.42	0.38	0.35	0.30	0.27	0.23	0.20	0.17	0.15	0.14	0.09

* EFFECTIVE TAX RATE EQUALS ZERO BEFORE ROUNDING. AN ENTIRE ROW OF * MEANS THAT THIS TAX IS NOT USED IN THIS STATE.

TABLE A-81

EFFECTIVE TAX RATES: LOCAL REAL PROPERTY TAX-MULTIFAMILY RESIDENTIAL (MOST PROGRESSIVE)
INCIDENCE: OWNERS OF CAPITAL
ALLOCATOR: DIVIDEND INCOME

STATE	UNDER $3,000	$3,000 -3,999	$4,000 -4,999	$5,000 -5,999	$6,000 -6,999	$7,000 -7,999	$8,000 -9,999	$10,000 -11,999	$12,000 -14,999	$15,000 -19,999	$20,000 -24,999	$25,000 -29,999	$30,000 -34,999	OVER $35,000
ALABAMA	0.02	0.00	0.01	0.00	0.01	0.00	*	0.01	0.00	0.00	0.01	0.00	0.01	0.17
ALASKA	0.09	0.58	0.29	0.02	*	0.04	0.05	0.03	0.02	0.13	0.06	0.05	0.06	0.23
ARIZONA	0.35	0.48	0.45	0.26	0.37	0.04	0.13	0.18	0.11	0.20	0.14	0.18	0.24	0.90
ARKANSAS	0.08	0.03	0.04	0.11	0.01	*	0.04	0.04	0.04	0.01	0.02	0.02	0.02	0.28
CALIFORNIA	1.03	0.43	0.40	0.62	0.29	0.24	0.35	0.31	0.36	0.22	0.21	0.35	0.39	1.64
COLORADO	0.49	0.02	0.68	0.09	0.00	0.39	0.06	0.01	0.04	0.02	0.07	0.06	0.25	0.85
CONNECTICUT	0.33	0.74	0.96	0.76	0.35	0.01	0.02	0.04	0.21	0.25	0.06	0.08	0.02	1.25
DELAWARE	0.22	0.07	0.05	0.02	*	0.14	0.00	0.03	0.07	0.04	0.05	0.05	0.02	0.44
FLORIDA	0.50	0.12	0.26	0.22	0.20	0.16	0.12	0.22	0.13	0.16	0.12	0.25	0.35	0.83
GEORGIA	0.28	0.13	0.06	0.13	0.11	0.00	0.03	0.00	0.04	0.04	0.05	0.07	0.24	0.68
HAWAII	2.37	0.40	0.35	0.58	1.27	0.37	0.43	0.20	0.12	0.40	0.08	0.05	0.25	1.39
IDAHO	0.08	0.03	0.01	0.01	0.00	0.03	0.01	0.01	0.00	0.01	0.04	0.03	0.09	0.16
ILLINOIS	0.56	0.44	0.26	0.47	0.25	0.20	0.22	0.30	0.10	0.12	0.13	0.16	0.18	1.41
INDIANA	0.09	0.06	0.03	0.00	0.01	0.03	0.01	0.04	0.02	0.03	0.05	0.08	0.05	0.35
IOWA	0.02	0.05	0.06	0.09	0.03	*	0.06	0.07	0.01	0.02	0.02	0.03	0.15	0.20
KANSAS	0.13	0.06	0.05	0.06	0.17	0.07	0.03	0.07	0.02	0.03	0.07	0.07	0.03	0.37
KENTUCKY	0.01	0.00	0.01	0.06	0.00	*	0.01	*	0.00	0.01	0.01	0.03	0.01	0.25
LOUISIANA	0.08	0.03	0.07	0.02	0.02	0.04	0.02	0.03	0.02	0.03	0.02	0.03	0.09	0.45
MAINE	0.22	0.12	0.10	0.33	0.04	0.05	0.31	0.02	0.07	0.18	0.05	0.30	0.14	0.78
MARYLAND	0.18	0.97	0.25	0.19	0.04	0.06	0.04	0.17	0.05	0.12	0.19	0.08	0.13	0.71
MASSACHUSETTS	1.19	0.22	0.93	0.71	0.76	0.14	0.27	0.26	0.33	0.15	0.20	0.57	0.20	3.03
MICHIGAN	0.36	0.30	0.28	0.15	0.15	0.27	0.16	0.07	0.05	0.07	0.10	0.23	0.09	0.83
MINNESOTA	0.24	0.05	0.69	0.05	0.08	0.01	0.20	0.08	0.07	0.03	0.08	0.14	0.09	0.94
MISSISSIPPI	0.03	0.00	0.03	0.00	0.08	0.01	0.03	0.03	0.02	0.02	0.07	0.03	0.04	0.31
MISSOURI	0.09	0.05	0.02	0.14	0.05	0.09	0.08	0.08	0.07	0.04	0.09	0.07	0.07	0.83
MONTANA	0.12	0.20	0.03	0.06	0.06	0.08	0.04	0.11	0.02	0.02	0.04	0.03	0.06	0.32
NEBRASKA	0.24	0.06	0.01	0.04	0.13	0.02	0.11	0.01	0.03	0.01	0.07	0.05	0.13	0.51
NEVADA	0.14	0.07	0.04	0.02	*	0.01	0.02	0.11	0.01	0.07	0.01	0.05	*	0.62
NEW HAMPSHIRE	0.81	0.22	1.41	1.29	0.08	0.03	0.20	0.41	0.18	0.16	0.17	0.08	0.30	2.01
NEW JERSEY	0.62	0.39	1.17	1.11	0.66	0.47	1.85	0.52	0.22	0.22	0.28	0.24	0.33	1.60
NEW MEXICO	0.06	0.09	0.00	*	0.01	0.05	0.01	0.04	0.05	0.04	0.05	0.07	0.09	0.17
NEW YORK	1.86	1.48	1.69	1.61	0.57	0.74	0.66	0.47	0.54	0.57	0.57	0.62	1.13	5.24
NORTH CAROLINA	0.12	0.02	0.12	0.03	0.03	0.01	0.02	0.02	0.02	0.02	0.04	0.04	0.03	0.27
NORTH DAKOTA	0.27	0.07	0.16	0.07	0.27	0.03	0.05	0.03	0.08	0.03	0.09	0.11	0.14	0.36
OHIO	0.26	0.21	0.15	0.23	0.02	0.08	0.11	0.09	0.04	0.06	0.09	0.10	0.22	0.72
OKLAHOMA	0.09	0.00	*	0.00	0.03	0.04	0.01	*	0.02	0.02	0.04	0.05	0.02	0.33
OREGON	0.69	0.02	0.13	*	0.02	*	0.01	0.11	0.03	0.09	0.12	0.08	0.42	0.86
PENNSYLVANIA	0.44	0.30	0.14	0.28	0.37	0.03	0.22	0.06	0.06	0.09	0.06	0.08	0.15	0.73
RHODE ISLAND	0.79	1.11	0.57	0.43	1.32	0.09	0.23	0.38	0.25	0.20	0.10	0.12	0.47	1.49
SOUTH CAROLINA	0.05	*	0.03	0.02	0.17	0.11	0.06	0.11	0.06	0.03	0.02	0.02	0.06	0.53
SOUTH DAKOTA	0.12	0.09	0.06	0.03	0.08	0.22	0.10	0.06	0.03	0.03	0.08	0.08	0.10	0.42
TENNESSEE	0.10	0.00	0.02	*	0.03	0.00	0.03	0.05	0.01	0.05	0.03	0.04	0.04	0.50
TEXAS	0.21	0.02	0.10	0.05	0.02	0.02	0.02	0.02	0.04	0.03	0.02	0.08	0.09	0.42
UTAH	0.32	0.00	0.09	0.07	0.01	0.04	0.04	0.02	0.01	0.02	0.03	0.02	0.05	0.25
VERMONT	0.07	0.00	0.01	0.11	0.05	0.08	0.10	0.06	0.08	0.04	0.12	0.04	0.35	0.60
VIRGINIA	0.21	0.27	0.03	0.26	0.40	0.06	0.12	0.19	0.04	0.10	0.08	0.14	0.10	0.73
WASHINGTON	0.07	0.01	0.12	0.08	0.08	0.09	0.05	0.00	0.06	0.05	0.03	0.03	0.11	0.50
WEST VIRGINIA	0.00	0.06	0.02	0.01	0.01	0.02	0.01	0.00	0.01	0.01	0.02	0.02	0.08	0.14
WISCONSIN	0.27	0.10	0.35	0.03	*	0.18	0.45	0.12	0.03	0.10	0.15	0.09	0.26	0.96
WYOMING	0.15	0.12	0.04	0.03	0.02	0.07	0.08	0.01	0.01	0.04	0.02	0.03	0.05	0.38
AVERAGE	0.34	0.21	0.26	0.22	0.17	0.10	0.15	0.11	0.08	0.09	0.09	0.11	0.16	0.80

* EFFECTIVE TAX RATE EQUALS ZERO BEFORE ROUNDING. AN ENTIRE ROW OF * MEANS THAT THIS TAX IS NOT USED IN THIS STATE.

TABLE A-82
EFFECTIVE TAX RATES: LOCAL REAL PROPERTY TAX-MULTIFAMILY RESIDENTIAL
INCIDENCE: LANDLORDS-1/2 INCORPORATED, 1/2 UNINCORPORATED
ALLOCATOR: DIVIDEND INCOME AND RENT NET INCOME

STATE	UNDER $3,000	$3,000 -3,999	$4,000 -4,999	$5,000 -5,999	$6,000 -6,999	$7,000 -7,999	$8,000 -9,999	$10,000 -11,999	$12,000 -14,999	$15,000 -19,999	$20,000 -24,999	$25,000 -29,999	$30,000 -34,999	OVER $35,000
ALABAMA	0.03	0.00	0.01	0.05	0.07	0.01	*	0.01	0.00	0.00	0.01	0.00	0.01	0.12
ALASKA	0.26	0.29	0.14	0.01	0.00	0.06	0.03	0.02	0.04	0.13	0.07	0.06	0.05	0.23
ARIZONA	0.30	0.24	0.33	1.15	0.25	0.06	0.60	0.19	0.06	0.15	0.08	0.27	0.32	0.69
ARKANSAS	0.18	0.07	0.03	0.06	0.02	0.00	0.03	0.04	0.03	0.02	0.05	0.02	0.02	0.21
CALIFORNIA	1.35	0.76	0.58	0.55	0.31	0.30	0.65	0.29	0.27	0.25	0.21	0.31	0.38	1.53
COLORADO	0.70	0.01	0.39	0.05	0.04	0.24	0.03	0.11	0.10	0.05	0.15	0.10	0.23	0.67
CONNECTICUT	0.48	1.09	2.49	0.91	0.18	0.01	0.06	0.11	0.23	0.27	0.05	0.09	0.03	1.07
DELAWARE	0.18	0.08	0.04	0.02	0.04	0.48	0.01	0.08	0.10	0.07	0.03	0.12	0.03	0.30
FLORIDA	0.65	0.08	0.38	0.25	0.12	0.11	0.14	0.25	0.11	0.15	0.14	0.19	0.48	0.80
GEORGIA	0.49	0.36	0.05	0.26	0.06	0.00	0.02	0.05	0.06	0.04	0.08	0.06	0.19	0.54
HAWAII	2.04	0.23	0.20	0.31	1.82	0.25	0.44	0.17	0.67	0.34	0.23	0.10	0.22	1.12
IDAHO	0.09	0.02	0.03	0.01	0.01	0.06	0.00	0.02	0.01	0.02	0.03	0.02	0.06	0.15
ILLINOIS	0.78	0.49	0.56	0.77	0.21	0.33	0.30	0.28	0.09	0.23	0.10	0.23	0.35	1.10
INDIANA	0.20	0.18	0.08	0.02	0.05	0.05	0.16	0.05	0.03	0.04	0.04	0.08	0.03	0.24
IOWA	0.07	0.12	0.08	0.09	0.05	0.06	0.07	0.07	0.03	0.03	0.03	0.02	0.10	0.15
KANSAS	0.23	0.13	0.14	0.05	0.14	0.15	0.10	0.11	0.01	0.03	0.07	0.10	0.06	0.25
KENTUCKY	0.10	0.02	0.06	0.10	0.02	0.02	0.01	*	0.01	0.01	0.02	0.02	0.01	0.16
LOUISIANA	0.10	0.12	0.17	0.11	0.06	0.03	0.03	0.03	0.04	0.06	0.03	0.02	0.17	0.32
MAINE	0.19	0.42	0.12	0.24	0.05	0.09	0.23	0.06	0.08	0.18	0.08	0.23	0.19	0.73
MARYLAND	1.01	0.54	0.32	0.90	0.30	0.03	0.07	0.13	0.12	0.16	0.12	0.10	0.12	0.62
MASSACHUSETTS	4.20	0.20	0.98	1.20	1.18	0.20	1.10	0.31	0.32	0.29	0.32	0.48	0.20	2.12
MICHIGAN	0.83	0.41	0.24	0.37	0.35	0.19	0.08	0.13	0.09	0.09	0.15	0.19	0.09	0.66
MINNESOTA	0.50	0.03	0.84	0.39	0.10	0.01	0.13	0.07	0.10	0.06	0.08	0.16	0.18	0.75
MISSISSIPPI	0.08	0.13	0.01	0.00	0.05	0.01	0.01	0.02	0.03	0.03	0.09	0.04	0.04	0.23
MISSOURI	0.25	0.19	0.10	0.33	0.09	0.10	0.07	0.10	0.07	0.11	0.06	0.03	0.15	0.66
MONTANA	0.20	0.15	0.04	0.11	0.04	0.06	0.08	0.08	0.08	0.02	0.04	0.05	0.11	0.21
NEBRASKA	0.18	0.21	0.16	0.13	0.08	0.11	0.07	0.01	0.12	0.04	0.07	0.05	0.22	0.33
NEVADA	0.33	0.03	0.11	0.01	0.01	0.02	0.02	0.23	0.04	0.08	0.02	0.04	0.02	0.51
NEW HAMPSHIRE	1.97	0.41	0.79	1.05	0.07	1.08	0.42	0.23	0.23	0.11	0.20	0.07	0.14	1.82
NEW JERSEY	1.45	1.60	0.69	1.68	0.84	0.66	0.99	0.57	0.40	0.20	0.18	0.20	0.50	1.61
NEW MEXICO	0.11	0.08	0.02	0.00	0.02	0.08	0.02	0.07	0.06	0.05	0.05	0.04	0.08	0.14
NEW YORK	5.09	1.77	1.41	3.29	1.57	1.26	1.15	0.91	0.50	0.52	0.66	0.84	1.34	4.02
NORTH CAROLINA	0.16	0.03	0.08	0.21	0.02	0.03	0.05	0.04	0.01	0.02	0.03	0.03	0.05	0.21
NORTH DAKOTA	0.23	0.12	0.17	0.24	0.32	0.10	0.10	0.10	0.08	0.07	0.08	0.12	0.13	0.23
OHIO	0.36	0.17	0.16	0.51	0.43	0.12	0.12	0.12	0.09	0.08	0.08	0.09	0.17	0.56
OKLAHOMA	0.10	0.06	0.05	0.04	0.04	0.12	0.02	0.01	0.04	0.05	0.08	0.04	0.03	0.21
OREGON	0.93	0.52	0.31	0.16	0.17	0.23	0.09	0.08	0.04	0.07	0.11	0.10	0.31	0.65
PENNSYLVANIA	0.74	0.30	0.21	0.66	0.43	0.07	0.21	0.08	0.11	0.13	0.09	0.06	0.08	0.52
RHODE ISLAND	0.55	0.75	1.86	0.25	0.86	0.55	0.20	0.25	0.27	0.24	0.27	0.27	0.28	1.22
SOUTH CAROLINA	0.19	0.14	0.09	0.01	0.11	0.20	0.04	0.11	0.05	0.05	0.04	0.04	0.06	0.41
SOUTH DAKOTA	0.13	0.13	0.12	0.10	0.16	0.25	0.08	0.08	0.06	0.05	0.06	0.08	0.15	0.29
TENNESSEE	0.21	0.05	0.09	0.09	0.06	0.00	0.09	0.05	0.02	0.05	0.04	0.02	0.07	0.35
TEXAS	0.27	0.15	0.09	0.04	0.04	0.06	0.02	0.06	0.06	0.03	0.03	0.09	0.08	0.35
UTAH	0.21	0.02	0.15	0.06	0.01	0.04	0.03	0.05	0.05	0.03	0.03	0.02	0.06	0.19
VERMONT	0.42	0.12	0.45	0.14	0.08	0.06	0.15	0.04	0.15	0.04	0.07	0.02	0.22	0.41
VIRGINIA	0.35	0.44	0.34	0.23	0.52	0.09	0.08	0.34	0.08	0.06	0.06	0.08	0.16	0.67
WASHINGTON	0.34	0.04	0.14	0.14	0.07	0.06	0.08	0.01	0.06	0.06	0.03	0.01	0.19	0.43
WEST VIRGINIA	0.04	0.03	0.01	0.02	0.01	0.03	0.01	0.00	0.01	0.02	0.01	0.06	0.05	0.10
WISCONSIN	0.51	0.30	0.54	0.04	0.16	0.15	0.43	0.10	0.04	0.09	0.17	0.31	0.24	0.67
WYOMING	0.25	0.26	0.04	0.11	0.04	0.10	0.07	0.01	0.02	0.04	0.02	0.05	0.06	0.32
AVERAGE	0.61	0.28	0.33	0.35	0.23	0.17	0.18	0.13	0.11	0.10	0.10	0.12	0.17	0.64

* EFFECTIVE TAX RATE EQUALS ZERO BEFORE ROUNDING. AN ENTIRE ROW OF * MEANS THAT THIS TAX IS NOT USED IN THIS STATE.

TABLE A-83
EFFECTIVE TAX RATES: TOTAL REAL PROPERTY TAXES (BENCHMARK)
INCIDENCE: SUM OF EFFECTIVE TAX RATES FOR INDIVIDUAL TAXES
ALLOCATOR: BASED ON INDIVIDUAL TAXES

STATE	UNDER $3,000	$3,000 -3,999	$4,000 -4,999	$5,000 -5,999	$6,000 -6,999	$7,000 -7,999	$8,000 -9,999	$10,000 -11,999	$12,000 -14,999	$15,000 -19,999	$20,000 -24,999	$25,000 -29,999	$30,000 -34,999	OVER $35,000
ALABAMA	1.64	1.03	0.83	0.78	0.71	0.67	0.57	0.53	0.46	0.42	0.40	0.39	0.42	0.58
ALASKA	7.14	5.18	3.97	3.25	3.06	2.82	2.52	2.22	2.03	2.07	1.73	1.55	1.43	1.94
ARIZONA	11.05	6.66	5.24	6.28	4.44	3.42	4.12	3.11	2.59	2.57	2.04	2.25	2.33	3.15
ARKANSAS	4.01	2.36	1.98	1.96	1.76	1.47	1.39	1.35	1.16	1.03	1.05	1.02	1.13	1.64
CALIFORNIA	17.29	10.59	8.56	7.73	6.67	6.08	5.66	4.77	4.26	3.62	3.20	3.15	2.99	4.20
COLORADO	12.93	6.96	6.81	5.09	5.17	4.92	3.72	3.42	3.13	2.61	2.52	2.31	2.26	3.58
CONNECTICUT	14.20	10.01	9.39	7.77	6.24	6.17	5.06	4.39	3.98	3.55	2.88	2.63	2.27	2.81
DELAWARE	5.32	3.24	3.03	2.81	2.32	2.70	2.06	1.83	1.80	1.62	1.48	1.44	1.48	1.56
FLORIDA	7.52	4.09	3.71	3.40	3.13	2.74	2.50	2.55	2.17	1.91	1.84	1.88	2.35	2.24
GEORGIA	7.29	4.45	3.47	3.63	3.15	2.69	2.44	2.47	2.22	1.89	1.82	1.58	1.72	2.69
HAWAII	9.35	4.37	4.15	3.84	5.16	3.34	3.08	2.46	2.72	2.22	1.79	1.56	1.51	2.66
IDAHO	9.17	5.12	4.38	3.84	3.65	3.49	3.02	2.66	2.33	2.19	2.26	2.03	2.33	3.09
ILLINOIS	10.87	6.84	5.98	5.61	4.45	4.42	4.01	3.50	3.09	2.80	2.43	2.39	2.48	3.46
INDIANA	9.06	5.69	4.20	4.07	3.78	3.43	3.06	2.76	2.38	2.09	1.95	1.83	1.85	2.24
IOWA	12.47	7.71	6.97	6.07	5.57	5.37	4.47	4.32	4.02	3.53	3.17	3.62	3.57	4.17
KANSAS	8.77	5.12	4.38	3.67	3.48	3.42	3.27	2.81	2.47	2.05	1.88	2.11	1.88	2.59
KENTUCKY	4.47	2.54	2.51	1.93	1.79	1.53	1.55	1.39	1.09	1.07	0.96	0.96	1.20	1.39
LOUISIANA	2.89	1.74	1.60	1.53	1.28	1.24	1.11	0.99	0.93	0.87	0.85	0.74	0.87	1.22
MAINE	9.97	5.95	5.11	3.98	3.76	3.29	3.33	2.52	2.29	2.08	1.83	1.80	1.59	2.27
MARYLAND	9.99	6.55	5.50	5.40	4.27	3.74	3.51	3.25	3.00	2.71	2.45	2.26	1.96	2.57
MASSACHUSETTS	23.24	13.81	11.79	10.20	9.65	7.92	7.65	6.45	5.37	4.74	4.18	4.12	3.60	4.84
MICHIGAN	14.73	9.45	7.06	6.12	5.64	5.36	4.50	4.09	3.66	3.16	2.79	2.70	2.50	3.26
MINNESOTA	14.18	8.30	7.31	6.22	5.61	5.51	4.58	4.19	3.71	3.16	2.95	2.83	3.09	3.40
MISSISSIPPI	4.35	2.76	2.39	1.97	1.85	1.98	1.76	1.56	1.31	1.15	1.17	1.05	1.04	1.93
MISSOURI	8.71	4.92	4.37	3.80	3.26	2.96	2.83	2.51	2.16	1.94	1.70	1.50	1.73	2.28
MONTANA	10.08	6.53	5.38	4.50	4.47	3.90	3.45	3.09	2.83	2.55	2.30	2.51	2.84	3.33
NEBRASKA	11.41	7.21	5.70	5.66	4.68	4.89	3.69	3.81	3.39	2.90	3.14	2.80	3.27	3.73
NEVADA	8.85	5.42	4.60	3.76	3.67	3.43	2.96	3.07	2.30	2.12	2.15	1.88	1.72	2.62
NEW HAMPSHIRE	22.66	11.88	9.81	9.51	7.33	7.05	6.45	5.72	4.88	4.33	3.77	3.24	3.20	4.49
NEW JERSEY	22.72	13.89	11.48	11.12	9.51	8.67	8.21	7.36	5.85	4.87	4.32	3.93	3.90	4.48
NEW MEXICO	4.86	3.26	2.41	1.96	1.99	1.89	1.61	1.52	1.42	1.21	1.10	0.94	0.95	1.31
NEW YORK	22.20	12.03	9.92	9.77	8.17	7.50	6.54	5.85	5.09	4.32	3.96	3.90	4.07	6.47
NORTH CAROLINA	4.94	2.60	2.52	2.25	2.01	1.68	1.71	1.45	1.31	1.19	1.28	1.07	0.95	1.40
NORTH DAKOTA	10.91	6.52	5.83	5.15	5.04	4.89	4.05	3.82	3.53	3.07	3.12	3.13	3.37	4.11
OHIO	10.32	6.23	5.55	5.17	4.61	4.11	3.57	3.21	2.82	2.53	2.28	2.24	2.33	2.83
OKLAHOMA	5.12	2.70	2.41	2.35	2.03	1.93	1.65	1.49	1.44	1.34	1.25	1.33	0.96	1.46
OREGON	15.53	8.71	7.07	6.24	5.92	5.28	4.97	4.05	3.59	3.07	2.91	3.14	3.28	4.31
PENNSYLVANIA	10.96	6.11	5.03	4.66	4.36	3.47	3.46	2.98	2.49	2.20	1.79	1.68	1.63	2.01
RHODE ISLAND	13.44	7.69	8.15	5.78	5.46	4.65	4.03	3.61	3.26	2.85	2.54	2.37	2.12	2.89
SOUTH CAROLINA	4.75	3.31	2.48	2.33	2.43	2.25	2.08	1.88	1.61	1.40	1.49	1.28	1.10	2.08
SOUTH DAKOTA	12.31	7.26	6.49	5.83	5.66	5.61	4.48	4.25	4.08	3.86	3.47	3.75	4.70	4.18
TENNESSEE	5.90	3.39	3.03	2.75	2.73	2.20	2.33	2.04	1.78	1.64	1.48	1.35	1.43	2.56
TEXAS	7.02	4.12	3.67	3.04	2.82	2.64	2.46	2.22	2.09	1.87	1.64	1.89	1.82	2.87
UTAH	9.17	4.94	4.62	4.10	3.50	2.97	2.78	2.63	2.21	1.87	1.63	1.63	1.53	2.05
VERMONT	18.69	11.69	8.92	8.07	6.54	6.02	5.41	5.18	4.38	3.79	3.72	2.66	2.92	2.98
VIRGINIA	6.69	4.00	4.24	3.18	3.07	2.74	2.42	2.63	1.94	1.72	1.63	1.49	1.34	1.89
WASHINGTON	7.06	3.97	3.27	2.80	2.63	2.55	2.08	1.82	1.62	1.44	1.20	1.17	1.20	2.11
WEST VIRGINIA	3.22	1.90	1.48	1.29	1.25	1.85	1.00	0.96	0.88	0.82	0.74	0.77	0.88	0.99
WISCONSIN	12.83	7.55	6.68	5.26	5.25	4.79	4.35	3.66	3.16	2.83	2.42	2.48	2.27	2.70
WYOMING	10.19	7.10	5.65	5.91	4.41	4.58	3.89	3.45	3.24	2.83	2.76	2.53	3.03	3.72
AVERAGE	10.25	6.11	5.22	4.67	4.19	3.84	3.43	3.08	2.71	2.39	2.19	2.10	2.13	2.79

* EFFECTIVE TAX RATE EQUALS ZERO BEFORE ROUNDING. AN ENTIRE ROW OF * MEANS THAT THIS TAX IS NOT USED IN THIS STATE.

TABLE A-84
EFFECTIVE TAX RATES: TOTAL REAL PROPERTY TAXES (MOST REGRESSIVE)
INCIDENCE: SUM OF EFFECTIVE TAX RATES FOR INDIVIDUAL TAXES
ALLOCATOR: BASED ON INDIVIDUAL TAXES

STATE	UNDER $3,000	$3,000 -3,999	$4,000 -4,999	$5,000 -5,999	$6,000 -6,999	$7,000 -7,999	$8,000 -9,999	$10,000 -11,999	$12,000 -14,999	$15,000 -19,999	$20,000 -24,999	$25,000 -29,999	$30,000 -34,999	OVER $35,000
ALABAMA	1.54	1.03	0.83	0.76	0.70	0.67	0.61	0.57	0.51	0.47	0.43	0.44	0.43	0.29
ALASKA	6.28	4.35	3.53	3.23	2.96	2.74	2.58	2.33	2.19	2.10	1.83	1.72	1.60	1.80
ARIZONA	10.12	6.23	4.98	5.68	4.35	3.56	4.04	3.26	2.87	2.80	2.29	2.43	2.33	2.54
ARKANSAS	3.69	2.25	1.93	1.88	1.81	1.52	1.43	1.40	1.21	1.12	1.13	1.09	1.17	1.27
CALIFORNIA	15.00	9.82	8.08	7.35	6.62	6.13	5.56	4.95	4.52	4.00	3.64	3.52	3.28	3.31
COLORADO	11.17	6.79	5.92	5.07	5.32	4.61	3.89	3.66	3.39	2.98	2.80	2.68	2.31	2.55
CONNECTICUT	9.94	7.44	6.57	6.16	5.43	5.74	4.77	4.33	4.07	3.76	3.46	3.26	2.99	2.44
DELAWARE	4.83	3.04	2.98	2.74	2.37	2.49	2.16	1.90	1.87	1.73	1.63	1.54	1.60	1.16
FLORIDA	7.04	4.15	3.62	3.39	3.24	2.86	2.64	2.62	2.35	2.06	2.00	1.98	2.23	1.64
GEORGIA	6.73	4.23	3.45	3.50	3.20	2.84	2.58	2.61	2.35	2.06	1.98	1.71	1.66	2.05
HAWAII	8.00	4.45	4.36	3.96	4.35	3.53	3.15	2.74	2.74	2.35	2.05	1.92	1.72	2.04
IDAHO	7.84	4.62	4.08	3.68	3.55	3.36	3.04	2.70	2.46	2.36	2.35	2.18	2.33	2.80
ILLINOIS	10.08	6.61	5.83	5.28	4.55	4.50	4.10	3.60	3.42	3.05	2.76	2.64	2.64	2.50
INDIANA	7.88	5.18	3.93	3.96	3.70	3.36	3.00	2.81	2.50	2.23	2.10	1.91	2.03	1.87
IOWA	11.34	7.20	6.59	5.70	5.45	5.31	4.40	4.29	4.14	3.68	3.37	3.80	3.50	3.92
KANSAS	7.86	4.80	4.16	3.54	3.29	3.33	3.29	2.80	2.60	2.18	1.99	2.21	2.05	2.30
KENTUCKY	4.19	2.46	2.45	1.81	1.82	1.55	1.59	1.47	1.16	1.15	1.05	1.01	1.28	0.96
LOUISIANA	2.76	1.71	1.54	1.54	1.32	1.29	1.19	1.07	1.02	0.95	0.95	0.83	0.84	0.85
MAINE	7.61	4.90	4.50	3.37	3.61	3.20	3.15	2.69	2.52	2.31	2.25	1.99	1.94	1.86
MARYLAND	8.73	5.78	5.18	4.90	4.17	3.81	3.63	3.32	3.14	2.85	2.60	2.51	2.13	2.16
MASSACHUSETTS	15.93	11.56	9.63	8.50	8.25	7.48	7.03	6.60	5.66	5.39	4.99	4.91	4.69	3.65
MICHIGAN	12.63	8.61	6.51	5.72	5.32	5.10	4.48	4.18	3.87	3.44	3.06	2.88	2.82	2.49
MINNESOTA	12.64	7.90	6.30	5.85	5.54	5.62	4.56	4.33	3.90	3.46	3.20	3.08	3.32	2.59
MISSISSIPPI	4.07	2.66	2.37	1.99	1.80	2.03	1.80	1.64	1.38	1.23	1.21	1.14	1.09	1.58
MISSOURI	8.03	4.68	4.29	3.61	3.29	3.01	2.92	2.63	2.31	2.10	1.89	1.71	1.83	1.58
MONTANA	8.79	5.89	5.14	4.28	4.33	3.82	3.41	3.05	2.99	2.76	2.51	2.72	2.94	2.95
NEBRASKA	10.51	6.93	5.59	5.52	4.62	4.91	3.69	3.95	3.51	3.09	3.30	2.92	3.26	3.25
NEVADA	7.76	5.12	4.42	3.74	3.73	3.48	3.08	3.08	2.49	2.32	2.42	2.15	1.99	1.91
NEW HAMPSHIRE	16.50	9.60	7.59	7.58	6.70	6.21	6.10	5.67	5.15	4.97	4.44	4.14	4.06	3.37
NEW JERSEY	16.10	10.50	9.04	8.78	8.05	7.62	6.83	7.04	5.94	5.38	5.05	4.80	4.66	4.02
NEW MEXICO	4.27	2.95	2.33	1.95	2.00	1.85	1.67	1.56	1.46	1.28	1.20	1.02	0.94	1.18
NEW YORK	20.44	12.10	9.94	8.88	8.44	7.92	7.00	6.56	5.97	5.21	4.82	4.63	4.34	3.33
NORTH CAROLINA	4.55	2.53	2.35	2.14	2.03	1.71	1.74	1.51	1.41	1.29	1.34	1.17	1.03	1.04
NORTH DAKOTA	10.17	6.31	5.64	5.00	4.74	4.95	4.09	3.93	3.62	3.21	3.24	3.23	3.39	3.86
OHIO	8.95	5.67	5.20	4.67	4.32	3.99	3.54	3.26	2.98	2.73	2.52	2.45	2.42	2.28
OKLAHOMA	4.74	2.66	2.39	2.38	2.06	1.86	1.72	1.59	1.51	1.43	1.32	1.41	1.04	1.18
OREGON	13.14	7.97	6.67	6.15	5.86	5.28	5.11	4.23	3.91	3.36	3.20	3.44	3.21	3.43
PENNSYLVANIA	7.79	4.86	4.25	3.77	3.67	3.30	3.23	3.05	2.67	2.46	2.15	2.07	2.04	1.63
RHODE ISLAND	10.07	6.06	6.38	5.15	4.44	4.21	3.95	3.58	3.45	3.22	3.02	2.92	2.52	2.36
SOUTH CAROLINA	4.50	3.27	2.46	2.36	2.35	2.17	2.14	1.87	1.70	1.52	1.62	1.37	1.15	1.48
SOUTH DAKOTA	11.53	6.98	6.34	5.79	5.55	5.37	4.47	4.34	4.22	4.05	3.59	3.88	4.73	3.70
TENNESSEE	5.70	3.51	3.13	2.88	2.86	2.41	2.45	2.18	2.00	1.78	1.64	1.48	1.49	1.49
TEXAS	6.85	4.41	3.74	3.32	3.13	2.94	2.80	2.51	2.33	2.11	1.91	1.95	1.80	1.64
UTAH	7.21	4.33	4.05	3.74	3.29	2.81	2.67	2.64	2.29	2.01	1.81	1.83	1.69	1.88
VERMONT	13.76	9.92	7.37	7.12	5.95	5.61	5.19	5.25	4.59	4.32	4.33	3.45	3.18	2.50
VIRGINIA	6.32	3.75	4.19	3.12	2.84	2.83	2.55	2.60	2.12	1.87	1.80	1.64	1.43	1.38
WASHINGTON	6.27	3.79	3.07	2.66	2.57	2.53	2.08	1.96	1.73	1.58	1.37	1.36	1.22	1.63
WEST VIRGINIA	3.04	1.78	1.44	1.30	1.25	1.86	1.04	1.02	0.93	0.88	0.80	0.77	0.80	0.70
WISCONSIN	11.25	6.98	6.00	5.14	5.15	4.71	4.03	3.75	3.39	3.07	2.62	2.61	2.37	2.11
WYOMING	8.48	6.34	5.27	5.65	4.30	4.45	3.73	3.56	3.41	3.02	3.04	2.81	3.28	3.15
AVERAGE	8.69	5.53	4.75	4.32	4.01	3.77	3.40	3.16	2.88	2.61	2.44	2.35	2.30	2.19

* EFFECTIVE TAX RATE EQUALS ZERO BEFORE ROUNDING. AN ENTIRE ROW OF * MEANS THAT THIS TAX IS NOT USED IN THIS STATE.

TABLE A-85

EFFECTIVE TAX RATES: TOTAL REAL PROPERTY TAXES (MOST PROGRESSIVE)
INCIDENCE: SUM OF EFFECTIVE TAX RATES FOR INDIVIDUAL TAXES
ALLOCATOR: BASED ON INDIVIDUAL TAXES

STATE	UNDER $3,000	$3,000 -3,999	$4,000 -4,999	$5,000 -5,999	$6,000 -6,999	$7,000 -7,999	$8,000 -9,999	$10,000 -11,999	$12,000 -14,999	$15,000 -19,999	$20,000 -24,999	$25,000 -29,999	$30,000 -34,999	OVER $35,000
ALABAMA	0.57	0.28	0.29	0.17	0.25	0.24	0.08	0.19	0.10	0.08	0.32	0.18	0.39	3.74
ALASKA	2.28	6.97	3.66	0.56	0.76	1.09	0.88	0.64	0.52	1.79	1.06	0.87	0.89	3.33
ARIZONA	4.16	4.66	4.14	3.75	3.54	0.80	1.97	1.87	1.24	2.05	1.58	2.05	2.93	8.83
ARKANSAS	2.68	1.27	1.32	2.39	0.77	0.41	1.06	1.05	0.96	0.48	0.73	0.76	0.89	5.99
CALIFORNIA	8.57	3.79	3.48	4.90	2.69	2.23	3.06	2.59	2.88	1.92	1.84	2.90	3.25	12.49
COLORADO	7.87	0.82	9.30	1.62	1.02	5.58	1.33	0.69	1.02	0.73	1.43	1.23	3.65	12.39
CONNECTICUT	3.33	6.68	8.91	6.79	3.23	0.45	0.84	0.76	1.98	2.51	0.68	0.87	0.39	11.42
DELAWARE	3.29	1.56	1.03	1.06	0.32	2.11	0.40	0.58	1.03	0.70	0.76	0.85	0.79	5.98
FLORIDA	4.90	1.54	2.42	2.22	1.95	1.52	1.21	2.02	1.25	1.37	1.22	2.09	3.24	6.67
GEORGIA	5.02	2.88	1.61	2.67	2.15	0.73	0.98	0.88	1.13	0.97	1.04	1.18	3.22	9.18
HAWAII	10.60	1.94	1.62	2.47	5.84	1.89	2.05	1.01	1.02	1.89	0.61	0.39	1.22	6.27
IDAHO	6.11	2.72	2.13	1.38	1.47	2.40	1.32	1.48	0.96	1.25	2.89	2.20	4.77	8.61
ILLINOIS	5.15	3.61	2.63	3.97	2.27	2.10	2.25	2.54	1.27	1.38	1.39	1.59	1.95	10.29
INDIANA	3.69	2.62	1.47	0.94	1.07	1.53	1.11	1.43	0.97	1.21	1.57	2.43	1.78	8.68
IOWA	5.58	4.63	4.68	5.73	3.39	2.71	3.85	4.04	2.37	2.47	2.37	3.16	6.88	9.48
KANSAS	4.63	2.47	2.11	2.20	3.53	2.29	1.79	2.20	1.28	1.26	1.76	2.13	1.44	7.20
KENTUCKY	2.04	1.04	1.36	2.21	0.72	0.47	0.78	0.45	0.34	0.59	0.42	1.15	0.92	7.42
LOUISIANA	1.09	0.50	0.89	0.47	0.36	0.56	0.32	0.42	0.31	0.43	0.34	0.43	1.02	4.61
MAINE	3.37	1.90	1.84	4.07	0.80	0.96	3.81	0.52	1.03	2.20	0.90	3.65	1.99	9.65
MARYLAND	2.92	9.95	3.13	2.99	0.90	0.96	0.68	1.89	0.89	1.51	2.10	0.92	1.49	7.64
MASSACHUSETTS	9.91	2.05	7.21	5.76	6.12	1.65	2.58	2.13	2.66	1.39	1.72	4.12	1.73	22.56
MICHIGAN	6.39	5.40	4.46	2.77	2.91	4.28	2.78	1.61	1.32	1.44	1.79	3.51	1.85	12.44
MINNESOTA	5.92	2.30	10.14	2.21	2.43	1.56	3.59	2.10	1.83	1.26	1.95	2.63	2.58	13.68
MISSISSIPPI	1.73	0.77	1.29	0.59	1.90	0.85	1.17	0.99	0.74	0.66	1.46	0.83	1.12	6.87
MISSOURI	2.45	1.72	1.18	2.15	1.15	1.38	1.48	1.32	1.22	0.93	1.36	1.13	1.63	9.56
MONTANA	5.47	6.21	2.46	2.57	2.93	2.93	2.09	3.36	1.39	1.46	1.76	2.02	3.17	9.35
NEBRASKA	8.15	4.05	2.87	3.66	3.87	3.01	3.12	2.28	2.21	1.72	2.73	2.46	3.87	9.46
NEVADA	3.26	1.64	1.21	0.76	0.53	0.84	0.74	2.10	0.61	1.28	0.97	1.15	0.67	9.49
NEW HAMPSHIRE	11.54	3.40	14.63	13.47	1.58	1.19	2.77	4.79	2.36	2.08	2.29	1.28	3.38	21.43
NEW JERSEY	6.75	4.09	9.40	9.25	5.82	4.28	14.60	4.89	2.25	2.02	2.44	2.10	2.99	13.71
NEW MEXICO	1.79	2.19	0.40	0.23	0.47	1.20	0.55	0.93	1.25	0.98	1.04	1.34	1.82	3.48
NEW YORK	7.32	5.32	6.22	5.96	2.88	3.32	2.95	2.24	2.46	2.23	2.14	2.42	4.15	19.21
NORTH CAROLINA	3.50	0.95	2.85	1.21	1.08	0.66	0.89	0.71	0.56	0.63	1.10	0.85	0.72	5.57
NORTH DAKOTA	7.97	4.09	4.74	3.52	5.75	3.20	2.82	2.50	2.89	2.18	2.99	3.27	3.99	7.37
OHIO	4.54	3.43	2.91	3.99	1.33	1.84	1.96	1.68	1.09	1.28	1.52	1.94	3.55	10.62
OKLAHOMA	2.72	0.68	0.67	0.71	0.86	1.19	0.59	0.35	0.67	0.74	0.87	1.25	0.55	5.44
OREGON	12.63	2.35	3.09	1.21	1.93	1.23	1.62	2.40	1.32	1.98	2.52	2.60	7.19	14.71
PENNSYLVANIA	5.50	3.70	1.91	3.49	4.48	0.62	2.80	1.13	0.89	1.24	0.84	1.15	1.85	8.93
RHODE ISLAND	5.65	7.63	4.62	3.14	9.04	1.18	1.85	2.87	1.88	1.56	0.95	1.09	3.41	11.06
SOUTH CAROLINA	1.67	1.04	0.99	0.94	2.83	1.99	1.41	1.94	1.15	0.70	0.70	0.67	1.07	8.02
SOUTH DAKOTA	7.97	4.95	4.33	3.59	4.43	6.75	4.14	3.36	2.97	2.91	3.58	3.83	5.36	10.23
TENNESSEE	3.14	0.76	0.96	0.64	1.27	0.40	1.15	1.27	0.49	1.11	0.81	1.06	1.21	10.23
TEXAS	5.16	1.44	2.62	1.38	0.99	1.02	0.84	0.87	1.10	1.00	0.71	1.86	2.16	8.40
UTAH	9.99	0.59	3.57	3.02	0.82	1.55	1.56	1.16	0.67	0.89	1.17	1.16	1.72	7.91
VERMONT	5.40	3.49	1.98	4.92	2.52	3.25	3.72	3.04	3.14	1.99	4.25	1.61	10.52	18.58
VIRGINIA	2.51	2.61	1.50	2.35	3.38	1.11	1.21	1.98	0.56	0.98	0.86	1.25	0.98	6.02
WASHINGTON	2.02	0.85	1.77	1.38	1.41	1.53	1.04	0.40	0.91	0.83	0.63	0.67	1.64	6.68
WEST VIRGINIA	0.77	2.00	0.78	0.40	0.46	1.36	0.30	0.17	0.33	0.38	0.59	0.93	2.50	4.54
WISCONSIN	4.58	2.50	5.08	1.18	1.12	2.69	5.73	1.97	0.96	1.61	2.11	1.67	3.44	11.66
WYOMING	6.20	4.93	2.35	2.90	1.49	3.01	3.24	1.32	1.38	1.82	1.58	1.57	2.63	11.47
AVERAGE	5.01	2.98	3.32	2.84	2.30	1.84	2.10	1.70	1.32	1.36	1.49	1.69	2.53	9.57

* EFFECTIVE TAX RATE EQUALS ZERO BEFORE ROUNDING. AN ENTIRE ROW OF * MEANS THAT THIS TAX IS NOT USED IN THIS STATE.

TABLE A-86
EFFECTIVE TAX RATES: TOTAL LOCAL PROPERTY TAXES (BENCHMARK)
INCIDENCE: SUM OF EFFECTIVE TAX RATES FOR INDIVIDUAL TAXES
ALLOCATOR: BASED ON INDIVIDUAL TAXES

STATE	UNDER $3,000	$3,000 -3,999	$4,000 -4,999	$5,000 -5,999	$6,000 -6,999	$7,000 -7,999	$8,000 -9,999	$10,000 -11,999	$12,000 -14,999	$15,000 -19,999	$20,000 -24,999	$25,000 -29,999	$30,000 -34,999	OVER $35,000
ALABAMA	2.42	1.58	1.34	1.24	1.14	1.10	0.99	0.92	0.83	0.77	0.74	0.73	0.75	0.85
ALASKA	7.47	5.59	4.42	3.74	3.56	3.29	3.02	2.73	2.53	2.56	2.22	2.05	1.92	2.42
ARIZONA	12.13	7.46	5.83	6.88	5.00	3.84	4.55	3.52	2.95	2.96	2.39	2.61	2.78	3.89
ARKANSAS	5.64	3.37	2.86	2.81	2.50	2.11	2.00	1.91	1.68	1.49	1.49	1.48	1.63	2.52
CALIFORNIA	19.06	11.64	9.47	8.66	7.43	6.78	6.35	5.39	4.84	4.13	3.67	3.68	3.58	5.39
COLORADO	14.10	7.52	7.60	5.54	5.69	5.48	4.11	3.75	3.44	2.88	2.82	2.60	2.60	4.41
CONNECTICUT	15.52	11.26	10.70	8.97	7.23	7.16	6.00	5.28	4.82	4.43	3.65	3.42	3.04	4.26
DELAWARE	5.32	3.24	3.03	2.81	2.32	2.70	2.06	1.83	1.80	1.62	1.48	1.44	1.48	1.56
FLORIDA	7.86	4.50	4.12	3.82	3.55	3.19	2.96	3.00	2.63	2.37	2.31	2.34	2.80	2.63
GEORGIA	8.73	5.46	4.46	4.58	4.08	3.61	3.29	3.28	3.02	2.67	2.56	2.30	2.42	3.35
HAWAII	9.35	4.37	4.15	3.84	5.16	3.34	3.08	2.46	2.72	2.22	1.79	1.56	1.51	2.66
IDAHO	10.28	5.78	4.98	4.34	4.18	4.00	3.50	3.08	2.72	2.60	2.74	2.47	2.90	3.89
ILLINOIS	11.70	7.48	6.58	6.24	5.00	4.97	4.55	4.03	3.57	3.28	2.89	2.86	2.98	4.26
INDIANA	9.75	6.54	5.05	4.99	4.72	4.38	3.97	3.72	3.34	3.05	2.92	2.75	2.84	3.19
IOWA	13.08	8.12	7.36	6.47	5.87	5.67	4.76	4.60	4.25	3.74	3.38	3.87	3.91	4.65
KANSAS	10.00	6.63	5.96	5.12	5.09	5.03	5.02	4.48	4.18	3.74	3.55	3.85	3.61	4.21
KENTUCKY	5.45	3.14	3.03	2.45	2.18	1.92	1.91	1.70	1.38	1.33	1.22	1.24	1.45	1.97
LOUISIANA	3.70	2.38	2.24	2.16	1.90	1.88	1.73	1.60	1.51	1.45	1.43	1.35	1.52	2.24
MAINE	10.67	6.41	5.55	4.45	4.08	3.60	3.74	2.77	2.54	2.35	2.07	2.15	1.88	2.96
MARYLAND	10.03	6.60	5.52	5.42	4.29	3.76	3.52	3.27	3.01	2.72	2.46	2.27	1.97	2.60
MASSACHUSETTS	23.83	14.24	12.25	10.63	10.08	8.29	8.00	6.76	5.66	5.02	4.45	4.41	3.87	5.44
MICHIGAN	15.21	10.06	7.66	6.72	6.26	6.02	5.14	4.76	4.32	3.83	3.47	3.39	3.19	3.93
MINNESOTA	14.22	8.33	7.33	6.24	5.62	5.53	4.59	4.19	3.71	3.16	2.95	2.83	3.09	3.41
MISSISSIPPI	6.67	4.17	3.55	2.99	2.86	2.86	2.59	2.28	1.97	1.72	1.75	1.56	1.60	2.91
MISSOURI	10.18	5.93	5.36	4.68	4.10	3.77	3.64	3.26	2.87	2.62	2.38	2.15	2.43	3.19
MONTANA	15.69	10.54	8.75	7.40	7.51	6.57	5.94	5.46	4.92	4.61	4.25	4.72	5.21	6.45
NEBRASKA	14.90	9.48	7.54	7.63	6.41	6.65	5.22	5.30	4.78	4.16	4.53	4.20	4.83	5.89
NEVADA	9.43	5.95	5.10	4.25	4.17	3.93	3.41	3.56	2.75	2.57	2.63	2.34	2.19	3.21
NEW HAMPSHIRE	22.66	11.88	9.82	9.52	7.34	7.06	6.45	5.72	4.88	4.33	3.77	3.24	3.20	4.49
NEW JERSEY	22.96	14.06	11.67	11.28	9.66	8.81	8.42	7.47	5.96	4.96	4.41	4.02	3.98	4.69
NEW MEXICO	5.00	3.42	2.55	2.08	2.13	2.02	1.76	1.65	1.57	1.33	1.23	1.06	1.07	1.45
NEW YORK	22.20	12.03	9.92	9.77	8.17	7.50	6.54	5.85	5.09	4.32	3.96	3.90	4.07	6.47
NORTH CAROLINA	6.96	3.76	3.73	3.14	2.86	2.46	2.46	2.12	1.91	1.73	1.88	1.60	1.45	2.53
NORTH DAKOTA	10.91	6.52	5.83	5.15	5.04	4.89	4.05	3.82	3.53	3.07	3.12	3.13	3.37	4.11
OHIO	10.98	6.68	5.94	5.56	4.92	4.45	3.86	3.47	3.05	2.76	2.49	2.49	2.63	3.32
OKLAHOMA	6.26	3.30	3.00	2.93	2.55	2.50	2.11	1.91	1.88	1.76	1.62	1.76	1.36	2.24
OREGON	17.34	9.65	7.87	6.91	6.62	5.92	5.60	4.64	4.10	3.60	3.45	3.77	4.10	5.77
PENNSYLVANIA	10.96	6.11	5.03	4.66	4.36	3.47	3.46	2.98	2.49	2.20	1.79	1.68	1.63	2.01
RHODE ISLAND	14.19	8.55	9.15	6.77	6.40	5.58	5.05	4.64	4.30	3.91	3.62	3.46	3.19	3.93
SOUTH CAROLINA	6.13	4.17	3.17	2.96	3.01	2.80	2.57	2.33	2.01	1.76	1.82	1.59	1.38	2.34
SOUTH DAKOTA	14.92	8.91	8.03	7.27	7.13	7.11	5.74	5.45	5.30	5.07	4.64	5.00	6.32	5.87
TENNESSEE	6.10	3.64	3.29	3.02	3.00	2.47	2.61	2.32	2.06	1.92	1.77	1.64	1.72	2.84
TEXAS	7.55	4.76	4.31	3.71	3.50	3.33	3.17	2.93	2.79	2.57	2.35	2.60	2.53	3.55
UTAH	11.06	5.96	5.58	4.97	4.30	3.67	3.44	3.24	2.75	2.36	2.10	2.11	2.00	2.78
VERMONT	19.60	12.27	9.50	8.60	6.98	6.49	5.85	5.60	4.78	4.15	4.11	2.97	3.51	4.10
VIRGINIA	7.16	4.43	4.66	3.63	3.52	3.16	2.85	3.04	2.34	2.12	2.02	1.89	1.73	2.35
WASHINGTON	7.84	4.46	3.72	3.23	3.02	2.97	2.44	2.12	1.92	1.72	1.46	1.43	1.52	2.86
WEST VIRGINIA	4.83	3.17	2.59	2.35	2.31	3.07	1.97	1.95	1.82	1.76	1.66	1.66	1.74	1.87
WISCONSIN	14.20	8.47	7.62	5.91	5.94	5.44	5.12	4.23	3.65	3.32	2.89	2.99	2.85	3.82
WYOMING	13.74	9.49	7.53	7.94	5.95	6.26	5.62	4.83	4.57	4.10	3.98	3.76	4.57	6.75
AVERAGE	11.32	6.87	5.93	5.33	4.81	4.46	4.02	3.63	3.23	2.90	2.69	2.61	2.68	3.57

* EFFECTIVE TAX RATE EQUALS ZERO BEFORE ROUNDING. AN ENTIRE ROW OF * MEANS THAT THIS TAX IS NOT USED IN THIS STATE.

TABLE A-87
EFFECTIVE TAX RATES: TOTAL LOCAL TAXES (BENCHMARK)
INCIDENCE: SUM OF EFFECTIVE TAX RATES FOR INDIVIDUAL TAXES
ALLOCATOR: BASED ON INDIVIDUAL TAXES

STATE	UNDER $3,000	$3,000 -3,999	$4,000 -4,999	$5,000 -5,999	$6,000 -6,999	$7,000 -7,999	$8,000 -9,999	$10,000 -11,999	$12,000 -14,999	$15,000 -19,999	$20,000 -24,999	$25,000 -29,999	$30,000 -34,999	OVER $35,000
ALABAMA	6.05	3.87	3.34	3.01	2.75	2.66	2.45	2.25	2.04	1.88	1.79	1.72	1.73	1.52
ALASKA	10.50	7.51	6.18	5.39	5.09	4.58	4.28	3.89	3.58	3.42	3.03	2.79	2.60	2.94
ARIZONA	14.46	8.95	7.01	8.06	6.04	4.79	5.48	4.37	3.74	3.68	3.05	3.23	3.40	4.44
ARKANSAS	6.24	3.72	3.16	3.08	2.75	2.34	2.21	2.10	1.85	1.64	1.63	1.62	1.76	2.63
CALIFORNIA	21.42	13.31	10.89	9.97	8.64	7.92	7.39	6.37	5.76	4.97	4.46	4.44	4.32	6.06
COLORADO	17.42	9.78	9.50	7.27	7.39	6.99	5.48	5.06	4.66	3.99	3.86	3.60	3.48	5.23
CONNECTICUT	15.65	11.36	10.78	9.05	7.30	7.23	6.06	5.33	4.87	4.48	3.70	3.46	3.09	4.30
DELAWARE	5.80	3.61	3.43	3.16	2.68	3.05	2.40	2.14	2.12	1.92	1.77	1.70	1.71	1.65
FLORIDA	9.80	5.64	5.05	4.64	4.32	3.89	3.59	3.56	3.14	2.81	2.71	2.72	3.15	2.94
GEORGIA	10.46	6.50	5.42	5.46	4.92	4.41	4.02	3.94	3.65	3.26	3.12	2.83	2.93	3.81
HAWAII	10.88	5.38	5.14	4.72	5.96	4.10	3.77	3.08	3.30	2.74	2.27	2.04	1.95	3.06
IDAHO	10.58	5.96	5.12	4.48	4.30	4.11	3.60	3.18	2.81	2.67	2.81	2.53	2.96	3.95
ILLINOIS	13.88	9.00	7.91	7.46	6.10	6.04	5.54	4.94	4.44	4.07	3.63	3.58	3.67	4.87
INDIANA	9.88	6.65	5.15	5.10	4.83	4.48	4.07	3.82	3.43	3.13	3.01	2.82	2.92	3.25
IOWA	13.33	8.27	7.51	6.58	5.98	5.77	4.85	4.69	4.33	3.82	3.45	3.94	3.98	4.71
KANSAS	10.71	7.06	6.34	5.43	5.40	5.31	5.29	4.72	4.40	3.93	3.72	4.02	3.78	4.36
KENTUCKY	6.97	4.30	4.11	3.43	3.13	2.86	2.83	2.58	2.17	2.09	1.96	1.95	2.09	2.27
LOUISIANA	7.43	4.82	4.39	4.30	3.90	3.81	3.62	3.30	3.10	2.97	2.92	2.81	2.89	3.45
MAINE	10.75	6.46	5.59	4.49	4.12	3.64	3.77	2.80	2.57	2.37	2.10	2.17	1.90	2.98
MARYLAND	12.59	8.71	7.51	7.23	6.12	5.54	5.29	4.96	4.59	4.23	3.88	3.72	3.21	3.62
MASSACHUSETTS	23.94	14.33	12.33	10.69	10.14	8.35	8.05	6.81	5.71	5.06	4.49	4.45	3.91	5.47
MICHIGAN	15.76	10.54	8.09	7.12	6.65	6.43	5.51	5.13	4.67	4.16	3.79	3.69	3.47	4.12
MINNESOTA	14.72	8.65	7.58	6.47	5.84	5.74	4.76	4.36	3.86	3.30	3.07	2.95	3.21	3.51
MISSISSIPPI	7.12	4.44	3.77	3.19	3.03	3.02	2.75	2.42	2.09	1.83	1.85	1.66	1.69	2.99
MISSOURI	13.51	7.92	7.31	6.36	5.69	5.27	5.04	4.58	4.05	3.71	3.41	3.13	3.30	3.89
MONTANA	16.23	10.89	9.05	7.66	7.75	6.80	6.14	5.65	5.10	4.77	4.40	4.86	5.35	6.57
NEBRASKA	15.98	10.20	8.11	8.16	6.91	7.13	5.67	5.72	5.16	4.52	4.87	4.52	5.14	6.18
NEVADA	13.62	8.78	7.49	6.35	6.24	5.83	5.11	5.10	4.15	3.84	3.78	3.43	3.25	4.12
NEW HAMPSHIRE	23.00	12.10	9.99	9.69	7.50	7.20	6.59	5.85	5.00	4.44	3.87	3.34	3.30	4.57
NEW JERSEY	25.02	15.38	12.82	12.31	10.61	9.72	9.23	8.22	6.64	5.57	4.98	4.55	4.48	5.13
NEW MEXICO	5.90	4.00	3.05	2.52	2.55	2.39	2.10	1.96	1.84	1.58	1.47	1.28	1.27	1.63
NEW YORK	26.87	15.62	13.13	12.82	11.23	10.48	9.34	8.63	7.71	6.84	6.41	6.29	6.38	7.88
NORTH CAROLINA	8.34	4.63	4.50	3.78	3.50	3.04	3.02	2.62	2.38	2.16	2.28	1.99	1.82	2.84
NORTH DAKOTA	11.54	6.90	6.16	5.43	5.30	5.14	4.28	4.04	3.73	3.25	3.29	3.29	3.53	4.25
OHIO	12.04	7.72	6.97	6.55	5.90	5.50	4.86	4.44	4.00	3.71	3.42	3.39	3.45	3.78
OKLAHOMA	8.77	4.73	4.24	4.08	3.63	3.47	2.99	2.73	2.62	2.42	2.25	2.34	1.91	2.74
OREGON	18.24	10.19	8.32	7.32	6.98	6.26	5.91	4.92	4.35	3.83	3.65	3.96	4.28	5.93
PENNSYLVANIA	13.61	8.02	6.79	6.25	5.97	5.02	4.96	4.42	3.83	3.50	2.99	2.86	2.81	2.97
RHODE ISLAND	14.33	8.63	9.23	6.84	6.46	5.64	5.11	4.69	4.35	3.96	3.67	3.50	3.23	3.96
SOUTH CAROLINA	6.66	4.50	3.45	3.22	3.24	3.03	2.78	2.53	2.20	1.92	1.98	1.74	1.52	2.47
SOUTH DAKOTA	16.23	9.75	8.79	7.96	7.79	7.73	6.31	6.00	5.81	5.55	5.10	5.44	6.75	6.26
TENNESSEE	9.00	5.56	4.96	4.57	4.41	3.84	3.84	3.49	3.14	2.91	2.71	2.52	2.60	3.54
TEXAS	8.97	5.69	5.10	4.46	4.19	3.97	3.78	3.51	3.31	3.06	2.81	3.03	2.94	3.90
UTAH	12.76	7.08	6.50	5.78	5.16	4.42	4.13	3.89	3.34	2.90	2.60	2.59	2.46	3.21
VERMONT	19.80	12.40	9.62	8.70	7.08	6.57	5.93	5.68	4.85	4.21	4.18	3.03	3.56	4.15
VIRGINIA	11.57	6.83	6.84	5.60	5.25	4.78	4.38	4.42	3.58	3.24	3.05	2.86	2.64	3.15
WASHINGTON	10.56	6.16	5.11	4.48	4.16	4.08	3.45	3.06	2.77	2.50	2.18	2.12	2.15	3.44
WEST VIRGINIA	6.24	4.04	3.30	2.97	2.90	3.63	2.45	2.43	2.24	2.15	2.02	2.00	2.06	2.18
WISCONSIN	14.42	8.61	7.73	6.02	6.04	5.54	5.20	4.31	3.72	3.39	2.95	3.05	2.91	3.87
WYOMING	14.45	9.99	7.98	8.35	6.33	6.62	5.94	5.14	4.85	4.36	4.22	3.99	4.80	6.95
AVERAGE	12.88	7.90	6.84	6.16	5.60	5.20	4.71	4.28	3.83	3.45	3.21	3.11	3.15	3.95

* EFFECTIVE TAX RATE EQUALS ZERO BEFORE ROUNDING. AN ENTIRE ROW OF * MEANS THAT THIS TAX IS NOT USED IN THIS STATE.

TABLE A-88
EFFECTIVE TAX RATES: TOTAL LOCAL TAXES (MOST REGRESSIVE)
INCIDENCE: SUM OF EFFECTIVE TAX RATES FOR INDIVIDUAL TAXES
ALLOCATOR: BASED ON INDIVIDUAL TAXES

STATE	UNDER $3,000	$3,000 -3,999	$4,000 -4,999	$5,000 -5,999	$6,000 -6,999	$7,000 -7,999	$8,000 -9,999	$10,000 -11,999	$12,000 -14,999	$15,000 -19,999	$20,000 -24,999	$25,000 -29,999	$30,000 -34,999	OVER $35,000
ALABAMA	5.95	3.87	3.33	3.00	2.74	2.67	2.49	2.29	2.09	1.93	1.82	1.76	1.74	1.22
ALASKA	9.64	6.69	5.74	5.36	4.99	4.50	4.34	4.00	3.75	3.45	3.13	2.95	2.77	2.79
ARIZONA	13.53	8.52	6.75	7.47	5.95	4.93	5.40	4.52	4.03	3.91	3.31	3.41	3.40	3.83
ARKANSAS	5.91	3.62	3.11	3.00	2.80	2.40	2.25	2.14	1.90	1.73	1.71	1.69	1.80	2.26
CALIFORNIA	19.13	12.53	10.41	9.59	8.59	7.97	7.29	6.55	6.01	5.34	4.90	4.80	4.61	5.18
COLORADO	15.66	9.61	8.60	7.25	7.54	6.68	5.65	5.30	4.92	4.36	4.13	3.98	3.53	4.21
CONNECTICUT	11.39	8.78	7.96	7.44	6.49	6.80	5.78	5.28	4.96	4.68	4.28	4.09	3.81	3.93
DELAWARE	5.31	3.41	3.37	3.09	2.73	2.84	2.50	2.21	2.19	2.04	1.92	1.79	1.83	1.25
FLORIDA	9.32	5.70	4.97	4.63	4.43	4.02	3.73	3.63	3.33	2.96	2.87	2.82	3.02	2.34
GEORGIA	9.90	6.28	5.41	5.33	4.96	4.56	4.16	4.08	3.78	3.43	3.28	2.96	2.87	3.16
HAWAII	9.53	5.46	5.34	4.85	5.15	4.29	3.84	3.36	3.32	2.88	2.54	2.40	2.16	2.45
IDAHO	9.24	5.45	4.82	4.32	4.20	3.98	3.62	3.22	2.94	2.84	2.90	2.69	2.96	3.66
ILLINOIS	13.09	8.78	7.76	7.14	6.20	6.11	5.63	5.04	4.77	4.32	3.97	3.83	3.82	3.91
INDIANA	8.70	6.15	4.87	4.98	4.74	4.40	4.01	3.87	3.55	3.27	3.16	2.90	3.10	2.87
IOWA	12.19	7.76	7.13	6.22	5.87	5.71	4.78	4.66	4.45	3.98	3.65	4.12	3.91	4.46
KANSAS	9.80	6.74	6.12	5.31	5.20	5.22	5.30	4.71	4.53	4.06	3.83	4.12	3.95	4.07
KENTUCKY	6.69	4.22	4.05	3.31	3.16	2.88	2.87	2.66	2.24	2.17	2.05	2.00	2.17	1.84
LOUISIANA	7.30	4.79	4.33	4.32	3.95	3.86	3.70	3.38	3.19	3.05	3.03	2.89	2.87	3.09
MAINE	8.39	5.41	4.98	3.88	3.97	3.54	3.59	2.98	2.80	2.61	2.51	2.37	2.24	2.57
MARYLAND	11.34	7.94	7.19	6.73	6.01	5.61	5.41	5.03	4.73	4.37	4.03	3.96	3.38	3.21
MASSACHUSETTS	16.64	12.08	10.16	8.99	8.75	7.91	7.43	6.97	6.00	5.71	5.30	5.24	5.00	4.28
MICHIGAN	13.65	9.69	7.54	6.72	6.33	6.17	5.50	5.22	4.89	4.43	4.05	3.87	3.79	3.36
MINNESOTA	13.18	8.25	6.58	6.10	5.77	5.84	4.74	4.50	4.06	3.60	3.33	3.20	3.44	2.69
MISSISSIPPI	6.84	4.34	3.75	3.21	2.98	3.08	2.79	2.49	2.16	1.91	1.89	1.76	1.75	2.63
MISSOURI	12.83	7.68	7.23	6.17	5.72	5.32	5.13	4.70	4.20	3.87	3.59	3.35	3.40	3.19
MONTANA	14.94	10.25	8.81	7.44	7.62	6.72	6.10	5.61	5.26	4.98	4.62	5.07	5.45	6.18
NEBRASKA	15.08	9.92	8.01	8.03	6.85	7.15	5.67	5.86	5.28	4.72	5.04	4.65	5.14	5.70
NEVADA	12.52	8.48	7.31	6.32	6.30	5.88	5.24	5.11	4.35	4.03	4.06	3.70	3.52	3.41
NEW HAMPSHIRE	16.84	9.82	7.76	7.75	6.87	6.35	6.24	5.79	5.27	5.08	4.54	4.24	4.15	3.46
NEW JERSEY	18.40	11.99	10.37	9.96	9.15	8.67	7.85	7.90	6.73	6.09	5.70	5.42	5.24	4.68
NEW MEXICO	5.31	3.69	2.97	2.51	2.56	2.35	2.16	1.99	1.88	1.65	1.56	1.37	1.26	1.50
NEW YORK	25.10	15.70	13.16	11.93	11.50	10.90	9.79	9.33	8.58	7.72	7.26	7.03	6.65	4.74
NORTH CAROLINA	7.95	4.56	4.33	3.67	3.52	3.07	3.05	2.68	2.48	2.26	2.34	2.09	1.90	2.48
NORTH DAKOTA	10.80	6.69	5.96	5.29	5.00	5.20	4.32	4.14	3.82	3.39	3.41	3.39	3.54	4.00
OHIO	10.67	7.16	6.62	6.06	5.61	5.39	4.84	4.49	4.16	3.91	3.66	3.60	3.54	3.22
OKLAHOMA	8.39	4.68	4.22	4.10	3.66	3.41	3.06	2.82	2.69	2.50	2.32	2.42	1.99	2.46
OREGON	15.86	9.45	7.91	7.23	6.92	6.26	6.06	5.09	4.67	4.12	3.94	4.25	4.20	5.05
PENNSYLVANIA	10.44	6.77	6.01	5.37	5.28	4.84	4.73	4.49	4.00	3.76	3.36	3.26	3.22	2.58
RHODE ISLAND	10.96	7.00	7.46	6.21	5.45	5.20	5.03	4.66	4.54	4.32	4.15	4.04	3.63	3.44
SOUTH CAROLINA	6.41	4.45	3.43	3.26	3.17	2.95	2.85	2.52	2.28	2.04	2.11	1.84	1.58	1.87
SOUTH DAKOTA	15.45	9.48	8.65	7.92	7.68	7.49	6.30	6.10	5.95	5.74	5.22	5.58	6.78	5.78
TENNESSEE	8.80	5.68	5.06	4.71	4.53	4.06	3.95	3.62	3.36	3.05	2.87	2.64	2.66	2.46
TEXAS	8.79	5.98	5.18	4.74	4.50	4.26	4.12	3.79	3.55	3.30	3.08	3.09	2.92	2.68
UTAH	10.80	6.46	5.93	5.42	4.95	4.25	4.03	3.89	3.42	3.05	2.78	2.79	2.63	3.04
VERMONT	14.89	10.64	8.07	7.75	6.49	6.16	5.71	5.75	5.06	4.75	4.78	3.82	3.83	3.67
VIRGINIA	11.20	6.59	6.79	5.54	5.01	4.86	4.51	4.40	3.76	3.40	3.23	3.00	2.73	2.64
WASHINGTON	9.76	5.98	4.92	4.35	4.10	4.06	3.44	3.20	2.88	2.63	2.36	2.32	2.17	2.96
WEST VIRGINIA	6.06	3.92	3.26	2.97	2.90	3.64	2.50	2.50	2.30	2.21	2.08	2.01	1.98	1.89
WISCONSIN	12.84	8.03	7.05	5.90	5.94	5.46	4.88	4.40	3.96	3.63	3.16	3.18	3.01	3.28
WYOMING	12.75	9.23	7.60	8.09	6.22	6.49	5.78	5.25	5.02	4.54	4.50	4.27	5.06	6.38
AVERAGE	11.32	7.33	6.37	5.82	5.42	5.13	4.68	4.36	4.00	3.68	3.47	3.36	3.32	3.36

* EFFECTIVE TAX RATE EQUALS ZERO BEFORE ROUNDING. AN ENTIRE ROW OF * MEANS THAT THIS TAX IS NOT USED IN THIS STATE.

TABLE A-89
EFFECTIVE TAX RATES: TOTAL LOCAL TAXES (MOST PROGRESSIVE)
INCIDENCE: SUM OF EFFECTIVE TAX RATES FOR INDIVIDUAL TAXES
ALLOCATOR: BASED ON INDIVIDUAL TAXES

STATE	UNDER $3,000	$3,000 -3,999	$4,000 -4,999	$5,000 -5,999	$6,000 -6,999	$7,000 -7,999	$8,000 -9,999	$10,000 -11,999	$12,000 -14,999	$15,000 -19,999	$20,000 -24,999	$25,000 -29,999	$30,000 -34,999	OVER $35,000
ALABAMA	4.98	3.12	2.79	2.41	2.29	2.24	1.95	1.92	1.68	1.55	1.71	1.50	1.69	4.67
ALASKA	5.64	9.30	5.87	2.69	2.79	2.85	2.65	2.31	2.07	3.14	2.36	2.10	2.05	4.32
ARIZONA	7.57	6.95	5.91	5.53	5.14	2.18	3.33	3.13	2.40	3.16	2.59	3.03	3.99	10.12
ARKANSAS	4.90	2.64	2.50	3.51	1.76	1.28	1.88	1.79	1.65	1.09	1.31	1.36	1.52	6.97
CALIFORNIA	12.70	6.51	5.81	7.14	4.66	4.07	4.80	4.19	4.38	3.26	3.11	4.18	4.58	14.35
COLORADO	12.36	3.64	11.98	3.79	3.24	7.65	3.10	2.33	2.55	2.11	2.76	2.52	4.87	14.04
CONNECTICUT	4.78	8.03	10.30	8.06	4.29	1.50	1.85	1.70	2.86	3.44	1.49	1.71	1.21	12.90
DELAWARE	3.77	1.93	1.43	1.41	0.68	2.46	0.74	0.90	1.35	1.01	1.05	1.11	1.02	6.07
FLORIDA	7.18	3.09	3.76	3.46	3.14	2.68	2.30	3.03	2.22	2.27	2.10	2.92	4.04	7.37
GEORGIA	8.20	4.93	3.56	4.50	3.92	2.45	2.56	2.36	2.56	2.34	2.34	2.42	4.43	10.29
HAWAII	12.12	2.95	2.61	3.36	6.64	2.65	2.74	1.64	1.60	2.41	1.10	0.86	1.66	6.68
IDAHO	7.51	3.56	2.87	2.02	2.12	3.02	1.90	2.00	1.44	1.74	3.44	2.70	5.40	9.47
ILLINOIS	8.16	5.77	4.56	5.82	3.92	3.72	3.78	3.97	2.61	2.65	2.60	2.79	3.14	11.71
INDIANA	4.51	3.58	2.41	1.96	2.11	2.58	2.12	2.50	2.02	2.25	2.63	3.42	2.85	9.68
IOWA	6.44	5.19	5.21	6.25	3.81	3.11	4.22	4.41	2.68	2.77	2.65	3.48	7.29	10.03
KANSAS	6.57	4.42	4.07	3.96	5.45	4.18	3.81	4.11	3.22	3.14	3.61	4.04	3.34	8.97
KENTUCKY	4.54	2.80	2.96	3.72	2.06	1.80	2.06	1.63	1.42	1.61	1.42	2.13	1.81	8.30
LOUISIANA	5.63	3.58	3.68	3.24	2.98	3.13	2.83	2.73	2.48	2.53	2.42	2.49	3.04	6.84
MAINE	4.16	2.41	2.32	4.58	1.15	1.31	4.25	0.81	1.32	2.50	1.16	4.03	2.29	10.36
MARYLAND	5.53	12.11	5.15	4.82	2.75	2.75	2.47	3.59	2.49	3.03	3.52	2.38	2.74	8.70
MASSACHUSETTS	10.62	2.57	7.74	6.25	6.62	2.07	2.98	2.49	2.99	1.71	2.02	4.45	2.04	23.19
MICHIGAN	7.41	6.48	5.48	3.76	3.91	5.35	3.80	2.65	2.34	2.43	2.79	4.50	2.82	13.30
MINNESOTA	6.46	2.65	10.42	2.46	2.66	1.79	3.78	2.27	1.98	1.40	2.07	2.75	2.69	13.78
MISSISSIPPI	4.50	2.45	2.67	1.80	3.08	1.90	2.16	1.85	1.52	1.34	2.14	1.44	1.78	7.92
MISSOURI	7.25	4.72	4.12	4.72	3.58	3.69	3.69	3.39	3.11	2.70	3.06	2.77	3.21	11.17
MONTANA	11.62	10.57	6.13	5.73	6.22	5.83	4.77	5.92	3.66	3.68	3.86	4.36	5.68	12.58
NEBRASKA	12.72	7.04	5.29	6.16	6.10	5.24	5.09	4.20	3.98	3.34	4.46	4.18	5.75	11.91
NEVADA	8.02	5.00	4.10	3.34	3.10	3.24	2.90	4.13	2.47	3.00	2.60	2.70	2.20	10.99
NEW HAMPSHIRE	11.88	3.62	14.80	13.65	1.75	1.33	2.91	4.92	2.47	2.19	2.39	1.38	3.48	21.52
NEW JERSEY	9.04	5.58	10.74	10.44	6.92	5.33	15.62	5.76	3.04	2.72	3.10	2.72	3.57	14.36
NEW MEXICO	2.84	2.93	1.05	0.79	1.03	1.70	1.03	1.36	1.66	1.35	1.40	1.69	2.13	3.80
NEW YORK	11.99	8.92	9.43	9.01	5.93	6.30	5.74	5.01	5.07	4.75	4.59	4.81	6.45	20.62
NORTH CAROLINA	6.90	2.98	4.83	2.74	2.56	2.02	2.20	1.88	1.63	1.60	2.10	1.78	1.59	7.00
NORTH DAKOTA	8.60	4.47	5.07	3.81	6.01	3.45	3.05	2.72	3.09	2.36	3.16	3.42	4.14	7.51
OHIO	6.27	4.92	4.33	5.38	2.62	3.24	3.26	2.91	2.27	2.45	2.66	3.09	4.67	11.57
OKLAHOMA	6.37	2.70	2.50	2.44	2.46	2.73	1.93	1.58	1.86	1.82	1.87	2.26	1.51	6.72
OREGON	15.35	3.84	4.33	2.28	2.98	2.20	2.57	3.27	2.08	2.74	3.26	3.41	8.19	16.32
PENNSYLVANIA	8.16	5.60	3.68	5.09	6.08	2.16	4.30	2.57	2.23	2.54	2.05	2.34	3.03	9.88
RHODE ISLAND	6.54	8.57	5.69	4.20	10.05	2.17	2.93	3.95	2.97	2.66	2.07	2.21	4.52	12.13
SOUTH CAROLINA	3.59	2.22	1.96	1.83	3.65	2.76	2.12	2.58	1.73	1.22	1.19	1.13	1.49	8.41
SOUTH DAKOTA	11.89	7.45	6.63	5.73	6.56	8.87	5.97	5.12	4.70	4.61	5.21	5.52	7.41	12.31
TENNESSEE	6.24	2.92	2.88	2.46	2.95	2.05	2.66	2.71	1.85	2.38	2.04	2.22	2.38	11.20
TEXAS	7.10	3.01	4.05	2.80	2.36	2.35	2.16	2.15	2.33	2.18	1.89	3.00	3.28	9.43
UTAH	13.59	2.73	5.45	4.69	2.47	3.00	2.92	2.42	1.80	1.93	2.14	2.12	2.66	9.06
VERMONT	6.52	4.21	2.68	5.55	3.06	3.81	4.23	3.54	3.61	2.42	4.71	1.97	11.16	19.74
VIRGINIA	7.39	5.45	4.10	4.77	5.55	3.14	3.17	3.78	2.20	2.51	2.29	2.62	2.29	7.28
WASHINGTON	5.51	3.03	3.62	3.07	2.94	3.06	2.41	1.64	2.06	1.89	1.61	1.63	2.59	8.02
WEST VIRGINIA	3.79	4.14	2.61	2.07	2.11	3.15	1.76	1.64	1.69	1.71	1.87	2.17	3.68	5.73
WISCONSIN	6.17	3.55	6.13	1.93	1.90	3.44	6.58	2.62	1.52	2.17	2.65	2.23	4.09	12.84
WYOMING	10.47	7.81	4.69	5.34	3.40	5.04	5.29	3.00	2.99	3.35	3.04	3.03	4.41	14.70
AVERAGE	7.64	4.77	4.94	4.33	3.71	3.20	3.39	2.90	2.44	2.42	2.51	2.70	3.56	10.74

* EFFECTIVE TAX RATE EQUALS ZERO BEFORE ROUNDING. AN ENTIRE ROW OF * MEANS THAT THIS TAX IS NOT USED IN THIS STATE.

TABLE A-90
EFFECTIVE TAX RATES: IMPORTED TAXES
INCIDENCE: CONSUMERS OF TAXED ITEMS
ALLOCATOR: SPECIAL SERIES ON CONSUMPTION OF TAXED ITEMS

STATE	UNDER $3,000	$3,000 -3,999	$4,000 -4,999	$5,000 -5,999	$6,000 -6,999	$7,000 -7,999	$8,000 -9,999	$10,000 -11,999	$12,000 -14,999	$15,000 -19,999	$20,000 -24,999	$25,000 -29,999	$30,000 -34,999	OVER $35,000
ALABAMA	2.56	1.55	1.36	1.18	1.10	1.07	0.96	0.91	0.83	0.76	0.77	0.70	0.71	1.28
ALASKA	2.21	1.64	1.43	1.26	1.17	1.03	1.01	0.94	0.87	0.82	0.75	0.73	0.70	0.71
ARIZONA	2.82	1.93	1.57	1.41	1.35	1.02	1.05	1.01	0.89	0.88	0.79	0.77	0.81	1.23
ARKANSAS	2.69	1.63	1.46	1.48	1.20	1.06	1.10	0.99	0.93	0.80	0.79	0.74	0.71	1.34
CALIFORNIA	2.77	1.77	1.50	1.44	1.23	1.14	1.09	1.00	0.95	0.83	0.78	0.80	0.79	1.16
COLORADO	2.84	1.59	1.85	1.25	1.14	1.33	0.99	0.90	0.85	0.76	0.75	0.71	0.83	1.27
CONNECTICUT	2.16	2.13	2.16	1.95	1.51	1.26	1.11	1.11	1.20	1.18	0.99	1.00	0.93	2.02
DELAWARE	3.04	1.67	1.55	1.21	1.12	1.52	1.00	0.99	1.12	0.95	0.95	0.91	0.82	2.20
FLORIDA	3.09	1.70	1.65	1.46	1.38	1.27	1.13	1.17	1.00	0.97	0.89	1.01	1.12	1.73
GEORGIA	2.73	1.56	1.37	1.32	1.23	1.08	1.00	0.88	0.87	0.82	0.77	0.76	0.91	1.29
HAWAII	2.82	1.48	1.45	1.40	1.55	1.18	1.13	0.97	0.90	0.93	0.78	0.75	0.80	1.14
IDAHO	2.69	1.59	1.30	1.24	1.12	1.09	0.98	0.90	0.82	0.76	0.82	0.74	0.89	1.05
ILLINOIS	2.37	1.68	1.40	1.43	1.19	1.12	1.07	1.05	0.90	0.85	0.82	0.81	0.81	1.46
INDIANA	2.40	1.56	1.29	1.17	1.10	1.08	0.95	0.95	0.86	0.81	0.81	0.83	0.77	1.26
IOWA	2.24	1.53	1.47	1.29	1.14	1.01	1.06	1.05	0.84	0.81	0.78	0.76	1.02	1.10
KANSAS	2.52	1.57	1.41	1.21	1.41	1.15	1.06	1.02	0.88	0.83	0.85	0.85	0.76	1.34
KENTUCKY	2.44	1.52	1.38	1.46	1.09	1.02	1.02	0.90	0.85	0.83	0.77	0.88	0.75	1.93
LOUISIANA	2.53	1.47	1.31	1.21	1.12	1.08	1.01	0.92	0.83	0.80	0.75	0.74	0.77	1.15
MAINE	2.43	1.59	1.39	1.50	1.13	1.06	1.34	0.93	0.93	1.01	0.83	1.10	0.90	1.66
MARYLAND	2.49	2.08	1.45	1.23	1.08	1.03	0.98	0.99	0.85	0.83	0.82	0.73	0.74	1.04
MASSACHUSETTS	2.27	1.54	1.54	1.35	1.32	1.06	1.07	1.01	0.97	0.86	0.84	0.95	0.82	1.72
MICHIGAN	2.47	1.68	1.42	1.18	1.13	1.20	1.02	0.91	0.83	0.78	0.77	0.84	0.72	1.21
MINNESOTA	2.41	1.55	1.77	1.17	1.11	1.06	1.07	0.93	0.86	0.77	0.77	0.80	0.75	1.39
MISSISSIPPI	2.52	1.57	1.34	1.17	1.20	1.06	1.02	0.95	0.85	0.79	0.83	0.75	0.75	1.16
MISSOURI	2.49	1.44	1.37	1.33	1.14	1.12	1.04	0.98	0.89	0.80	0.83	0.79	0.77	1.71
MONTANA	2.66	1.94	1.44	1.32	1.28	1.22	1.03	1.09	0.87	0.81	0.79	0.74	0.78	1.16
NEBRASKA	2.60	1.59	1.22	1.16	1.21	1.04	1.07	0.90	0.87	0.78	0.81	0.76	0.84	1.24
NEVADA	2.49	1.67	1.39	1.21	1.16	1.10	1.01	1.08	0.86	0.88	0.73	0.75	0.66	1.64
NEW HAMPSHIRE	2.64	1.71	2.09	2.03	1.32	1.15	1.27	1.32	1.15	1.11	1.08	1.01	1.12	2.02
NEW JERSEY	2.41	1.88	2.06	1.95	1.74	1.68	2.11	1.59	1.44	1.39	1.39	1.36	1.36	1.79
NEW MEXICO	2.54	1.78	1.41	1.21	1.19	1.19	1.02	0.99	0.94	0.85	0.83	0.86	0.86	1.04
NEW YORK	2.65	1.78	1.59	1.48	1.23	1.20	1.10	1.03	0.99	0.94	0.92	0.90	0.99	1.80
NORTH CAROLINA	2.92	1.63	1.81	1.24	1.23	1.08	1.07	0.98	0.92	0.86	0.87	0.85	0.80	1.63
NORTH DAKOTA	2.70	1.59	1.48	1.25	1.35	1.09	1.02	0.96	0.95	0.84	0.85	0.83	0.85	0.99
OHIO	2.38	1.62	1.39	1.33	1.04	1.11	1.04	0.95	0.85	0.83	0.82	0.81	0.91	1.40
OKLAHOMA	2.80	1.51	1.31	1.22	1.20	1.12	0.98	0.89	0.84	0.79	0.78	0.77	0.69	1.21
OREGON	3.09	1.57	1.43	1.22	1.11	1.05	0.98	0.99	0.84	0.82	0.80	0.74	0.98	1.31
PENNSYLVANIA	2.69	1.75	1.42	1.42	1.51	1.08	1.24	1.01	0.94	0.94	0.86	0.87	0.93	1.54
RHODE ISLAND	2.58	1.93	1.63	1.39	1.77	1.07	1.11	1.14	1.02	0.94	0.85	0.84	1.01	1.55
SOUTH CAROLINA	2.41	1.48	1.31	1.21	1.34	1.22	1.06	1.10	0.94	0.83	0.77	0.75	0.78	1.49
SOUTH DAKOTA	2.49	1.59	1.40	1.22	1.24	1.40	1.12	1.01	0.90	0.84	0.89	0.85	0.87	1.36
TENNESSEE	2.45	1.50	1.31	1.20	1.12	1.05	0.98	0.95	0.83	0.81	0.75	0.73	0.72	1.22
TEXAS	2.74	1.55	1.45	1.28	1.13	1.07	1.00	0.94	0.90	0.82	0.76	0.82	0.83	1.35
UTAH	3.04	1.53	1.44	1.24	1.16	1.09	1.00	0.90	0.81	0.76	0.73	0.68	0.70	1.04
VERMONT	2.31	1.38	1.31	1.39	1.19	1.21	1.18	1.05	1.03	0.90	1.05	0.83	1.56	2.13
VIRGINIA	2.70	1.63	1.33	1.39	1.37	1.05	1.05	1.03	0.85	0.84	0.78	0.79	0.75	1.17
WASHINGTON	2.69	1.65	1.49	1.33	1.21	1.20	1.07	0.93	0.93	0.85	0.79	0.75	0.81	1.25
WEST VIRGINIA	2.61	1.97	1.44	1.21	1.15	1.17	0.96	0.91	0.84	0.81	0.80	0.82	1.07	1.39
WISCONSIN	2.43	1.46	1.46	1.16	1.08	1.18	1.23	0.95	0.86	0.85	0.85	0.77	0.89	1.33
WYOMING	2.42	1.71	1.41	1.24	1.12	1.18	1.12	0.89	0.83	0.81	0.73	0.73	0.76	1.47
AVERAGE	2.59	1.65	1.48	1.33	1.23	1.14	1.08	1.00	0.92	0.86	0.83	0.82	0.86	1.40

* EFFECTIVE TAX RATE EQUALS ZERO BEFORE ROUNDING. AN ENTIRE ROW OF * MEANS THAT THIS TAX IS NOT USED IN THIS STATE.

TABLE A-91
EFFECTIVE TAX RATES: TOTAL STATE AND LOCAL TAXES (BENCHMARK)
INCIDENCE: SUM OF EFFECTIVE TAX RATES FOR INDIVIDUAL TAXES
ALLOCATOR: BASED ON INDIVIDUAL TAXES

STATE	UNDER $3,000	$3,000 -3,999	$4,000 -4,999	$5,000 -5,999	$6,000 -6,999	$7,000 -7,999	$8,000 -9,999	$10,000 -11,999	$12,000 -14,999	$15,000 -19,999	$20,000 -24,999	$25,000 -29,999	$30,000 -34,999	OVER $35,000
ALABAMA	23.04	14.20	12.41	11.22	10.31	10.15	9.61	9.17	8.48	7.92	7.79	7.36	7.51	7.95
ALASKA	53.59	35.98	32.51	29.83	28.17	24.80	24.04	22.47	21.11	19.33	19.03	18.58	18.28	18.54
ARIZONA	33.57	21.57	17.20	17.92	15.09	12.68	13.57	12.09	11.11	10.80	9.57	9.26	9.64	11.07
ARKANSAS	23.42	14.20	12.41	11.75	10.58	9.75	9.39	8.94	8.31	7.84	8.20	8.05	8.34	9.13
CALIFORNIA	34.24	22.14	18.45	17.20	15.08	13.95	13.09	11.95	11.34	10.81	10.96	11.33	11.17	14.08
COLORADO	29.56	17.38	16.90	13.43	13.46	12.97	10.80	10.64	10.26	9.59	9.22	8.84	8.29	10.74
CONNECTICUT	26.09	20.38	19.25	17.13	14.38	14.38	12.19	11.32	10.70	10.08	9.00	8.72	8.04	11.35
DELAWARE	18.35	11.57	11.21	9.69	8.87	9.84	8.89	8.43	9.06	8.24	7.99	7.80	7.96	12.58
FLORIDA	26.41	15.83	14.05	12.74	12.09	11.14	10.16	9.82	8.85	8.08	7.67	7.69	8.10	8.74
GEORGIA	25.91	15.36	13.40	12.84	11.99	11.06	10.24	9.69	9.52	9.49	9.16	8.65	8.96	9.95
HAWAII	27.83	16.48	16.44	15.84	17.09	14.71	13.95	13.08	13.01	12.39	11.57	11.97	11.31	13.35
IDAHO	24.68	14.66	12.64	12.09	11.69	11.29	10.62	10.10	9.60	9.06	9.38	8.91	9.32	10.97
ILLINOIS	25.93	17.83	15.94	15.40	13.42	13.25	12.44	11.59	10.81	10.12	9.43	9.27	9.30	11.40
INDIANA	22.00	15.24	12.77	12.58	12.09	11.54	10.44	10.27	9.54	8.95	8.77	8.10	8.37	9.60
IOWA	24.84	16.17	15.29	13.35	12.61	12.26	11.60	11.47	10.64	10.42	9.86	10.41	11.25	13.15
KANSAS	23.59	15.64	14.20	12.16	12.67	11.72	11.93	10.97	10.24	9.62	9.21	10.18	9.55	10.99
KENTUCKY	22.85	14.47	13.49	12.47	10.79	10.44	10.20	9.92	9.16	9.21	8.95	9.20	8.65	11.70
LOUISIANA	25.35	15.58	13.79	13.30	12.20	11.78	11.24	10.25	9.54	9.15	9.42	9.23	9.19	10.72
MAINE	31.28	20.46	18.18	15.73	14.92	13.60	14.19	11.98	11.35	11.27	10.98	11.30	10.92	14.07
MARYLAND	25.86	18.52	15.45	14.72	13.64	12.97	12.59	12.09	11.16	10.71	10.17	9.96	8.94	9.92
MASSACHUSETTS	32.94	21.08	19.54	17.75	17.46	15.21	15.17	14.13	12.62	11.98	11.32	11.77	11.00	13.72
MICHIGAN	27.78	18.93	15.27	13.69	13.19	13.52	11.85	11.37	10.69	9.95	9.54	9.61	9.08	10.94
MINNESOTA	29.28	18.49	16.70	13.99	12.88	12.72	11.79	11.87	11.60	11.38	11.66	11.86	12.47	13.67
MISSISSIPPI	28.43	17.94	14.95	13.14	12.33	11.95	10.97	10.22	9.41	9.17	9.39	9.14	9.14	11.04
MISSOURI	25.39	14.94	14.22	12.69	11.61	11.03	10.53	10.02	9.15	8.82	8.58	8.21	7.95	9.92
MONTANA	28.60	19.68	16.25	14.48	14.47	13.37	11.96	11.66	10.79	10.61	10.37	10.49	11.38	13.57
NEBRASKA	28.42	18.34	14.54	14.17	12.82	12.88	11.35	11.04	10.24	9.48	10.02	9.49	10.60	12.81
NEVADA	27.59	18.61	15.97	13.87	13.67	12.83	11.51	11.23	9.61	9.09	8.51	8.08	7.71	9.99
NEW HAMPSHIRE	33.45	19.00	16.95	16.27	12.66	11.72	11.23	10.29	9.08	8.17	7.45	6.71	6.85	10.36
NEW JERSEY	34.40	22.50	19.92	18.98	16.79	15.73	15.77	13.85	11.83	10.56	9.86	9.24	9.04	10.87
NEW MEXICO	27.39	18.57	15.92	13.80	13.60	12.55	11.58	10.81	10.02	9.31	9.16	8.82	8.40	10.01
NEW YORK	38.73	23.60	20.16	19.78	17.85	16.95	15.57	14.96	13.96	13.24	13.73	14.29	15.17	17.30
NORTH CAROLINA	24.11	14.22	13.91	11.38	11.11	9.98	10.30	9.66	9.11	8.92	8.87	8.58	7.93	10.60
NORTH DAKOTA	27.95	17.49	15.74	13.87	14.01	12.91	11.74	11.61	11.69	11.25	11.24	10.97	11.60	11.82
OHIO	23.05	15.37	13.77	12.84	11.39	11.31	10.26	9.42	8.94	8.51	8.33	8.41	8.51	9.89
OKLAHOMA	25.11	13.77	12.11	11.46	10.65	9.90	8.73	8.26	7.99	7.71	8.04	7.88	7.19	9.61
OREGON	27.22	15.70	13.65	12.73	12.07	11.25	11.03	9.73	9.22	9.34	9.24	9.44	9.52	13.06
PENNSYLVANIA	26.97	17.02	14.53	13.64	14.82	12.82	13.13	11.85	10.72	10.30	9.30	9.18	9.34	11.98
RHODE ISLAND	27.10	17.40	17.91	14.77	14.55	12.49	12.06	11.54	10.90	10.41	10.02	9.82	9.67	12.05
SOUTH CAROLINA	22.69	14.78	12.37	11.47	11.63	11.08	10.28	10.22	9.46	9.18	9.03	8.69	8.02	9.87
SOUTH DAKOTA	31.25	19.47	17.59	15.91	15.52	15.08	12.92	12.34	11.68	11.11	10.47	10.65	11.85	12.91
TENNESSEE	24.86	15.41	13.55	12.39	11.63	10.61	10.05	9.34	8.34	7.82	7.28	6.94	7.17	10.74
TEXAS	24.31	15.21	13.40	12.08	11.14	10.48	9.93	9.19	8.55	7.86	7.32	7.44	7.18	8.87
UTAH	28.41	16.69	14.96	13.52	13.21	11.89	11.12	10.74	10.04	9.45	8.97	8.73	8.76	10.24
VERMONT	33.85	21.36	18.40	17.24	15.03	14.48	14.12	13.68	12.70	11.99	12.18	10.39	12.34	14.53
VIRGINIA	25.23	14.99	14.09	12.70	11.98	10.74	10.90	10.64	9.20	8.97	8.52	8.20	7.68	8.50
WASHINGTON	32.42	20.17	17.33	15.58	14.20	14.21	12.50	11.39	10.73	9.78	9.07	8.74	8.69	12.70
WEST VIRGINIA	28.59	19.10	15.49	13.76	13.33	13.78	11.26	11.12	10.41	10.11	9.74	9.53	9.83	12.29
WISCONSIN	28.48	17.84	16.43	13.88	13.99	13.85	13.03	11.74	11.44	11.56	11.33	11.21	11.54	13.42
WYOMING	32.73	22.81	19.69	18.79	15.97	15.89	14.40	12.98	12.15	11.01	10.47	10.19	10.94	13.37
AVERAGE	28.10	17.88	15.83	14.44	13.53	12.75	11.96	11.26	10.52	10.00	9.71	9.55	9.59	11.61

* EFFECTIVE TAX RATE EQUALS ZERO BEFORE ROUNDING. AN ENTIRE ROW OF * MEANS THAT THIS TAX IS NOT USED IN THIS STATE.

TABLE A-92

EFFECTIVE TAX RATES: TOTAL STATE AND LOCAL TAXES (MOST REGRESSIVE)
INCIDENCE: SUM OF EFFECTIVE TAX RATES FOR INDIVIDUAL TAXES
ALLOCATOR: BASED ON INDIVIDUAL TAXES

STATE	UNDER $3,000	$3,000 -3,999	$4,000 -4,999	$5,000 -5,999	$6,000 -6,999	$7,000 -7,999	$8,000 -9,999	$10,000 -11,999	$12,000 -14,999	$15,000 -19,999	$20,000 -24,999	$25,000 -29,999	$30,000 -34,999	OVER $35,000
ALABAMA	23.17	14.36	12.53	11.34	10.39	10.25	9.76	9.28	8.60	8.04	7.84	7.46	7.55	6.96
ALASKA	53.41	34.70	32.04	30.23	28.49	25.03	24.36	22.85	21.53	19.40	19.26	18.88	18.56	18.16
ARIZONA	32.88	21.20	16.95	17.41	15.02	12.93	13.56	12.29	11.45	11.05	9.85	9.46	9.63	10.23
ARKANSAS	23.32	14.30	12.49	11.58	10.80	10.01	9.49	9.04	8.39	8.02	8.33	8.18	8.45	7.99
CALIFORNIA	32.38	21.74	18.27	16.97	15.28	14.25	13.15	12.28	11.69	11.31	11.51	11.73	11.46	12.64
COLORADO	27.94	17.46	15.85	13.55	13.78	12.61	11.08	11.00	10.63	10.05	9.55	9.27	8.28	9.33
CONNECTICUT	22.15	17.84	16.31	15.48	13.66	14.20	12.11	11.44	10.88	10.34	9.70	9.46	8.89	10.57
DELAWARE	18.09	11.58	11.40	9.85	9.16	9.67	9.19	8.64	9.21	8.45	8.22	7.95	8.17	11.69
FLORIDA	26.08	16.06	14.04	12.80	12.27	11.34	10.38	9.91	9.09	8.26	7.87	7.77	7.92	7.88
GEORGIA	25.53	15.25	13.56	12.79	12.13	11.38	10.51	9.97	9.74	9.74	9.38	8.82	8.76	8.75
HAWAII	26.23	16.75	16.85	16.06	16.14	15.02	14.10	13.49	13.17	12.56	11.94	12.46	11.55	12.41
IDAHO	23.62	14.43	12.59	12.21	11.85	11.28	10.85	10.29	9.91	9.35	9.39	9.06	9.02	10.01
ILLINOIS	25.32	17.71	15.91	15.12	13.60	13.43	12.61	11.73	11.23	10.44	9.82	9.57	9.49	10.12
INDIANA	20.99	14.84	12.59	12.58	12.12	11.54	10.47	10.37	9.72	9.13	8.94	8.16	8.56	8.95
IOWA	24.08	15.83	15.03	12.99	12.63	12.37	11.55	11.45	10.88	10.66	10.12	10.63	10.95	12.55
KANSAS	23.05	15.59	14.22	12.19	12.43	11.75	12.12	11.04	10.53	9.86	9.34	10.29	9.80	10.11
KENTUCKY	23.16	14.77	13.72	12.27	11.08	10.74	10.43	10.24	9.42	9.41	9.17	9.21	8.80	9.78
LOUISIANA	25.51	15.75	13.83	13.48	12.39	11.95	11.45	10.42	9.72	9.29	9.60	9.37	9.14	9.82
MAINE	29.24	19.63	17.77	15.08	14.96	13.67	13.95	12.31	11.69	11.50	11.49	11.37	11.26	13.13
MARYLAND	24.91	17.60	15.23	14.31	13.69	13.17	12.83	12.22	11.39	10.89	10.34	10.26	9.13	9.29
MASSACHUSETTS	25.92	19.26	17.49	16.18	16.16	15.04	14.75	14.48	13.04	12.80	12.27	12.58	12.22	11.70
MICHIGAN	25.98	18.22	14.81	13.44	12.99	13.30	11.92	11.60	11.03	10.32	9.86	9.75	9.45	9.68
MINNESOTA	28.23	18.52	15.34	13.92	13.05	13.13	11.83	12.18	11.95	11.85	12.02	12.14	12.76	12.00
MISSISSIPPI	28.44	18.06	15.05	13.32	12.28	12.13	11.07	10.35	9.54	9.31	9.39	9.26	9.19	10.15
MISSOURI	24.94	14.83	14.28	12.56	11.73	11.14	10.69	10.20	9.35	9.03	8.79	8.45	8.06	8.88
MONTANA	27.59	19.01	16.22	14.40	14.45	13.35	12.03	11.58	11.07	10.92	10.64	10.75	11.47	12.71
NEBRASKA	27.64	18.21	14.57	14.14	12.79	13.00	11.38	11.26	10.42	9.74	10.21	9.65	10.57	12.02
NEVADA	26.49	18.31	15.78	13.84	13.74	12.88	11.63	11.24	9.80	9.28	8.79	8.35	7.98	9.29
NEW HAMPSHIRE	27.47	16.92	14.50	14.15	12.19	11.03	10.99	10.26	9.43	8.89	8.18	7.69	7.72	8.71
NEW JERSEY	28.00	19.26	17.46	16.62	15.38	14.76	14.20	13.58	12.00	11.15	10.64	10.17	9.82	10.21
NEW MEXICO	27.05	18.35	16.02	13.95	13.76	12.57	11.74	10.90	10.08	9.41	9.27	8.87	8.32	9.68
NEW YORK	37.43	23.92	20.30	18.98	18.36	17.56	16.20	15.85	14.99	14.25	14.70	15.13	15.45	13.50
NORTH CAROLINA	23.91	14.39	13.69	11.41	11.26	10.16	10.44	9.82	9.31	9.10	8.96	8.70	8.03	9.67
NORTH DAKOTA	27.37	17.47	15.61	13.86	13.59	13.11	11.89	11.84	11.85	11.48	11.38	11.05	11.57	11.27
OHIO	21.88	14.91	13.53	12.37	11.25	11.31	10.31	9.55	9.19	8.78	8.62	8.64	8.55	8.93
OKLAHOMA	24.97	13.92	12.27	11.64	10.80	9.91	8.90	8.47	8.14	7.85	8.14	7.97	7.31	8.95
OREGON	24.86	15.20	13.38	12.84	12.17	11.42	11.32	9.97	9.64	9.68	9.55	9.77	9.28	11.74
PENNSYLVANIA	24.06	15.90	14.01	12.78	14.04	12.95	12.94	12.13	11.09	10.69	9.80	9.68	9.75	10.82
RHODE ISLAND	23.94	15.67	16.22	14.24	13.29	12.21	12.08	11.55	11.17	10.85	10.60	10.46	10.03	11.11
SOUTH CAROLINA	22.85	15.04	12.55	11.71	11.49	11.02	10.43	10.20	9.61	9.39	9.27	8.88	8.08	8.47
SOUTH DAKOTA	30.50	19.21	17.46	15.88	15.42	14.84	12.92	12.44	11.83	11.31	10.59	10.79	11.88	12.37
TENNESSEE	24.98	15.85	13.89	12.78	11.92	11.04	10.30	9.56	8.71	8.02	7.53	7.10	7.27	8.77
TEXAS	24.13	15.49	13.47	12.36	11.44	10.77	10.26	9.48	8.79	8.11	7.59	7.50	7.16	7.65
UTAH	26.32	16.30	14.42	13.20	13.15	11.79	11.08	10.82	10.20	9.65	9.18	8.97	8.92	9.75
VERMONT	29.31	19.86	17.08	16.38	14.58	14.16	13.95	13.84	12.97	12.62	12.78	11.25	12.30	13.44
VIRGINIA	25.17	14.84	14.24	12.70	11.71	10.96	11.12	10.65	9.47	9.18	8.75	8.37	7.79	7.69
WASHINGTON	31.62	19.99	17.14	15.44	14.14	14.18	12.50	11.52	10.84	9.92	9.25	8.94	8.71	12.22
WEST VIRGINIA	28.60	18.95	15.51	13.84	13.39	13.83	11.36	11.25	10.52	10.21	9.81	9.52	9.61	11.72
WISCONSIN	27.34	17.56	15.80	14.03	14.17	13.90	12.58	11.95	11.84	11.90	11.57	11.43	11.58	12.19
WYOMING	31.02	22.05	19.31	18.54	15.86	15.76	14.23	13.09	12.32	11.19	10.75	10.46	11.20	12.81
AVERAGE	26.78	17.46	15.45	14.20	13.45	12.80	12.02	11.44	10.78	10.29	10.01	9.83	9.75	10.57

* EFFECTIVE TAX RATE EQUALS ZERO BEFORE ROUNDING. AN ENTIRE ROW OF * MEANS THAT THIS TAX IS NOT USED IN THIS STATE.

TABLE A-93
EFFECTIVE TAX RATES: TOTAL STATE AND LOCAL TAXES (MOST PROGRESSIVE)
INCIDENCE: SUM OF EFFECTIVE TAX RATES FOR INDIVIDUAL TAXES
ALLOCATOR: BASED ON INDIVIDUAL TAXES

STATE	UNDER $3,000	$3,000 -3,999	$4,000 -4,999	$5,000 -5,999	$6,000 -6,999	$7,000 -7,999	$8,000 -9,999	$10,000 -11,999	$12,000 -14,999	$15,000 -19,999	$20,000 -24,999	$25,000 -29,999	$30,000 -34,999	OVER $35,000
ALABAMA	21.73	13.28	11.74	10.48	9.76	9.62	9.00	8.76	8.04	7.51	7.69	7.10	7.46	11.80
ALASKA	48.03	38.23	32.23	26.71	25.44	22.77	22.14	20.61	19.35	19.02	18.23	17.77	17.63	20.16
ARIZONA	26.43	19.51	16.08	15.32	14.17	9.96	11.34	10.81	9.70	10.25	9.08	9.05	10.24	16.98
ARKANSAS	21.85	12.91	11.62	12.27	9.40	8.49	9.01	8.59	8.07	7.18	7.83	7.75	8.04	14.26
CALIFORNIA	25.09	14.95	13.08	14.21	10.85	9.85	10.33	9.63	9.87	8.99	9.50	11.05	11.41	22.94
COLORADO	24.35	10.99	19.54	9.82	9.13	13.68	8.32	7.79	8.06	7.62	8.07	7.71	9.74	19.94
CONNECTICUT	14.90	17.03	18.89	16.19	11.27	8.40	7.78	7.52	8.60	8.98	6.67	6.86	6.04	20.36
DELAWARE	16.10	9.67	8.97	7.71	6.63	9.22	7.03	7.04	8.20	7.22	7.20	7.14	7.19	17.50
FLORIDA	23.65	13.13	12.69	11.49	10.83	9.85	8.79	9.25	7.88	7.51	7.01	7.91	9.05	13.43
GEORGIA	23.47	13.66	11.37	11.79	10.91	8.93	8.65	7.96	8.33	8.49	8.31	8.21	10.58	16.99
HAWAII	29.32	13.85	13.71	14.37	17.92	13.14	12.83	11.50	11.17	12.02	10.27	10.68	10.98	17.29
IDAHO	21.34	12.00	10.13	9.35	9.25	10.08	8.71	8.77	8.06	8.01	10.08	9.09	12.06	17.16
ILLINOIS	20.03	14.50	12.47	13.71	11.14	10.84	10.60	10.58	8.90	8.63	8.34	8.43	8.74	18.56
INDIANA	16.46	12.07	9.93	9.32	9.28	9.56	8.42	8.89	8.06	8.03	8.37	8.72	8.29	16.31
IOWA	17.57	12.93	12.88	13.02	10.31	9.42	10.94	11.18	8.87	9.29	8.99	9.90	14.79	18.82
KANSAS	19.07	12.71	11.69	10.52	12.77	10.47	10.27	10.30	8.89	8.71	9.07	10.18	9.04	16.19
KENTUCKY	19.82	12.59	12.06	12.84	9.46	9.11	9.23	8.74	8.22	8.61	8.28	9.43	8.30	19.21
LOUISIANA	23.27	14.16	12.98	12.07	11.14	10.99	10.33	9.58	8.81	8.64	8.83	8.87	9.37	14.65
MAINE	24.37	16.19	14.72	15.87	11.75	11.11	14.72	9.84	9.99	11.39	9.96	13.27	11.31	21.98
MARYLAND	18.50	22.07	12.98	12.22	10.12	10.06	9.63	10.67	8.97	9.46	9.80	8.56	8.45	15.21
MASSACHUSETTS	19.34	8.89	14.84	13.18	13.83	8.66	9.89	9.61	9.77	8.45	8.71	11.75	8.99	32.27
MICHIGAN	19.13	14.73	12.57	10.19	10.33	12.40	10.05	8.75	8.22	8.12	8.48	10.45	8.37	20.61
MINNESOTA	20.53	12.07	19.88	9.67	9.47	8.45	10.74	9.60	9.56	9.31	10.55	11.63	11.88	24.80
MISSISSIPPI	25.52	15.73	13.73	11.60	12.39	10.70	10.31	9.59	8.77	8.63	9.72	8.91	9.23	16.51
MISSOURI	18.89	11.62	10.90	10.99	9.41	9.38	9.12	8.78	8.17	7.75	8.22	7.83	7.83	17.54
MONTANA	23.70	19.41	13.13	12.42	12.83	12.34	10.48	11.96	9.24	9.42	9.77	9.94	11.72	20.06
NEBRASKA	25.04	15.04	11.58	12.07	11.97	10.89	10.75	9.43	9.00	8.22	9.59	9.11	11.24	18.87
NEVADA	21.99	14.82	12.57	10.87	10.53	10.24	9.30	10.26	7.92	8.24	7.33	7.34	6.66	16.87
NEW HAMPSHIRE	22.17	10.31	21.99	20.41	6.74	5.69	7.44	9.33	6.47	5.83	5.90	4.65	7.01	27.85
NEW JERSEY	18.21	12.55	17.85	17.12	13.05	11.26	22.34	11.34	8.14	7.64	7.93	7.36	8.09	20.31
NEW MEXICO	24.08	17.42	13.73	11.91	11.94	11.81	10.42	10.16	9.83	9.05	9.08	9.26	9.35	12.38
NEW YORK	23.39	16.67	16.33	15.88	12.33	12.58	11.80	11.16	11.17	11.02	11.80	12.72	15.23	30.70
NORTH CAROLINA	22.47	12.34	14.29	10.20	10.05	8.82	9.37	8.82	8.26	8.28	8.66	8.34	7.67	15.33
NORTH DAKOTA	24.86	14.87	14.59	12.12	14.82	11.07	10.40	10.16	11.00	10.26	11.09	11.11	12.25	15.37
OHIO	17.07	12.48	11.03	11.63	7.95	8.94	8.58	7.81	7.12	7.18	7.53	8.07	9.79	18.09
OKLAHOMA	22.49	11.55	10.20	9.66	9.37	9.09	7.57	7.00	7.15	7.06	7.63	7.79	6.73	13.98
OREGON	24.30	9.10	9.52	7.49	7.91	7.03	7.54	8.01	6.85	8.20	8.83	8.86	13.60	23.89
PENNSYLVANIA	21.25	14.49	11.16	12.45	15.04	9.66	12.43	9.79	8.93	9.22	8.21	8.55	9.54	19.68
RHODE ISLAND	19.10	17.43	14.29	12.03	18.37	8.86	9.77	10.77	9.45	9.04	8.33	8.45	11.01	20.62
SOUTH CAROLINA	19.21	12.19	10.67	9.88	12.09	10.78	9.52	10.29	8.93	8.38	8.14	7.99	7.98	16.62
SOUTH DAKOTA	26.88	17.14	15.41	13.65	14.28	16.25	12.58	11.45	10.56	10.15	10.57	10.73	12.52	19.02
TENNESSEE	21.79	12.45	11.22	10.02	10.00	8.60	8.73	8.47	6.89	7.24	6.54	6.60	6.92	19.31
TEXAS	22.44	12.53	12.35	10.42	9.30	8.85	8.30	7.83	7.56	6.99	6.39	7.41	7.52	14.40
UTAH	29.36	12.12	13.87	12.39	10.38	10.40	9.84	9.19	8.40	8.42	8.47	8.23	8.96	16.43
VERMONT	20.20	12.90	11.22	14.00	10.87	11.62	12.37	11.45	11.41	10.11	12.72	9.27	20.24	30.73
VIRGINIA	20.74	13.51	11.16	11.81	12.32	8.98	9.61	9.95	7.71	8.18	7.70	7.94	7.30	12.93
WASHINGTON	27.37	17.05	15.84	14.17	12.99	13.19	11.46	9.97	10.02	9.18	8.50	8.25	9.13	17.28
WEST VIRGINIA	25.94	19.20	14.74	12.80	12.47	13.26	10.51	10.26	9.82	9.64	9.57	9.71	11.58	16.12
WISCONSIN	19.80	12.48	14.76	9.53	9.57	11.63	14.54	9.92	9.07	10.25	11.00	10.32	12.79	23.02
WYOMING	28.74	20.64	16.40	15.79	13.05	14.32	13.75	10.85	10.29	10.00	9.29	9.22	10.55	21.13
AVERAGE	22.63	14.60	13.83	12.51	11.54	10.63	10.55	9.80	9.04	8.90	8.96	9.11	10.01	18.85

* EFFECTIVE TAX RATE EQUALS ZERO BEFORE ROUNDING. AN ENTIRE ROW OF * MEANS THAT THIS TAX IS NOT USED IN THIS STATE.

Appendix B

Supplementary Statistical Information

TABLE B-1
CUMULATIVE PERCENTAGE OF FAMILIES
BY INCOME CLASS*

STATE	UNDER $3,000	$3,000 -3,999	$4,000 -4,999	$5,000 -5,999	$6,000 -6,999	$7,000 -7,999	$8,000 -9,999	$10,000 -11,999	$12,000 -14,999	$15,000 -19,999	$20,000 -24,999	$25,000 -29,999	$30,000 -34,999	OVER $35,000
ALABAMA	16.53	21.80	27.60	32.28	37.17	41.94	51.24	60.07	71.71	84.36	92.43	96.28	97.96	100.00
ALASKA	6.35	9.29	11.85	15.15	18.22	20.98	28.13	34.99	44.21	55.94	65.98	77.60	84.27	100.00
ARIZONA	11.16	16.56	20.83	26.80	32.19	36.68	45.93	54.25	66.62	81.33	89.69	93.83	96.00	100.00
ARKANSAS	16.48	22.64	28.99	35.96	42.68	48.48	58.60	67.20	76.64	87.22	94.21	96.90	98.17	100.00
CALIFORNIA	9.32	15.91	21.20	26.21	31.18	36.04	44.11	51.65	62.31	76.37	85.58	91.87	95.00	100.00
COLORADO	10.30	15.16	19.85	24.30	29.30	34.25	43.12	50.53	62.88	78.68	87.51	93.11	95.84	100.00
CONNECTICUT	7.03	11.47	15.54	19.40	24.10	27.71	35.45	43.64	55.83	71.75	83.23	89.95	93.49	100.00
DELAWARE	9.00	13.22	17.50	21.24	25.30	28.74	36.78	44.16	56.68	73.80	85.48	91.67	94.79	100.00
FLORIDA	12.66	19.67	25.48	31.12	36.94	42.17	52.18	60.26	71.78	83.75	91.37	94.96	96.80	100.00
GEORGIA	14.34	19.75	25.39	31.52	36.57	41.76	50.34	57.68	68.73	82.31	91.01	95.04	96.99	100.00
HAWAII	8.49	12.62	16.67	20.40	24.47	28.32	35.93	43.29	52.67	66.82	78.71	88.38	93.04	100.00
IDAHO	10.90	15.59	20.27	25.41	30.44	35.40	45.33	55.42	68.38	83.43	90.81	94.97	96.98	100.00
ILLINOIS	8.96	14.18	19.11	23.23	27.16	31.40	38.92	46.56	57.59	73.75	84.79	91.62	94.93	100.00
INDIANA	8.96	13.23	17.98	22.57	26.79	31.49	39.15	48.56	62.21	79.30	89.37	93.84	96.12	100.00
IOWA	10.65	15.61	20.58	25.30	29.54	34.27	42.63	51.23	63.69	79.50	89.04	93.64	95.98	100.00
KANSAS	9.77	14.87	19.22	23.32	28.20	33.59	44.15	52.95	66.61	81.11	89.40	93.81	96.07	100.00
KENTUCKY	15.15	22.13	28.07	32.89	37.99	42.99	53.25	61.51	72.31	85.06	92.73	96.27	97.88	100.00
LOUISIANA	17.31	23.39	28.69	33.76	38.59	43.19	51.14	58.25	68.38	81.75	90.97	94.71	96.64	100.00
MAINE	12.70	18.82	24.48	29.27	36.13	41.34	52.09	61.45	73.28	86.51	93.23	96.18	97.64	100.00
MARYLAND	7.87	11.48	15.34	18.54	22.57	26.18	34.27	41.86	52.86	68.18	79.92	88.84	93.21	100.00
MASSACHUSETTS	7.83	14.22	18.77	22.94	27.10	31.19	39.90	48.72	59.72	75.41	85.89	92.55	95.66	100.00
MICHIGAN	8.98	13.94	18.35	22.37	26.28	30.12	37.58	45.64	58.41	75.06	86.24	92.93	95.98	100.00
MINNESOTA	10.10	16.01	20.44	25.18	29.90	34.13	42.61	50.66	63.16	78.91	88.88	93.85	96.28	100.00
MISSISSIPPI	20.36	27.41	32.72	39.08	43.80	48.42	58.56	66.63	75.92	87.00	93.46	96.60	98.05	100.00
MISSOURI	13.13	18.43	24.14	29.29	34.92	39.96	48.53	56.73	68.31	81.59	90.44	94.71	96.79	100.00
MONTANA	12.72	18.50	23.75	28.81	33.02	38.16	46.77	54.80	67.02	82.09	90.40	94.36	96.40	100.00
NEBRASKA	12.30	17.29	21.83	26.70	31.93	35.68	44.56	52.97	65.11	79.90	89.42	93.85	96.11	100.00
NEVADA	8.92	13.49	18.27	23.16	28.20	34.20	43.31	50.98	62.49	76.86	86.53	92.23	95.12	100.00
NEW HAMPSHIRE	8.53	13.74	18.04	22.40	27.15	31.26	41.37	50.71	64.14	81.47	90.41	94.90	97.01	100.00
NEW JERSEY	7.11	11.29	15.25	19.26	23.20	26.86	34.49	42.62	53.89	70.54	82.43	90.11	93.92	100.00
NEW MEXICO	13.26	18.42	24.09	30.53	36.38	41.89	51.28	59.88	70.06	81.23	89.64	93.75	95.92	100.00
NEW YORK	9.72	15.25	19.86	23.95	28.35	33.14	41.42	50.07	60.32	75.10	85.55	92.18	95.34	100.00
NORTH CAROLINA	12.52	18.00	23.12	27.94	34.94	39.39	50.35	59.14	71.76	84.65	91.77	95.27	97.04	100.00
NORTH DAKOTA	11.36	16.56	22.07	27.24	31.69	36.10	44.81	53.65	66.22	79.88	88.40	93.01	95.44	100.00
OHIO	9.39	13.90	18.26	22.36	26.37	30.42	39.46	47.93	60.36	78.38	88.70	93.77	96.24	100.00
OKLAHOMA	14.58	20.38	26.08	31.70	37.32	41.37	51.41	59.52	70.78	82.78	90.50	94.10	96.06	100.00
OREGON	11.79	17.32	22.58	28.09	33.72	38.55	47.89	55.95	67.60	81.40	90.13	94.66	96.83	100.00
PENNSYLVANIA	10.47	15.69	20.52	25.16	29.42	33.88	42.11	51.58	64.15	80.42	88.91	93.67	96.06	100.00
RHODE ISLAND	11.30	15.99	21.04	25.41	30.19	34.40	42.59	50.61	63.03	79.99	89.13	93.93	96.29	100.00
SOUTH CAROLINA	12.24	17.06	22.27	27.68	32.60	38.25	47.89	57.36	69.50	83.87	92.25	95.99	97.71	100.00
SOUTH DAKOTA	12.75	19.36	24.63	30.26	35.91	40.59	50.00	59.42	70.33	85.31	92.33	95.77	97.44	100.00
TENNESSEE	13.00	19.81	25.10	30.30	35.99	42.22	52.22	61.33	72.83	85.56	92.50	95.84	97.47	100.00
TEXAS	12.26	17.37	22.07	27.85	32.80	38.54	48.46	57.50	68.79	82.02	90.33	94.28	96.33	100.00
UTAH	9.96	14.47	18.71	23.07	28.14	32.56	40.89	49.64	62.85	79.54	89.15	93.69	96.01	100.00
VERMONT	12.88	18.83	23.94	29.85	35.44	40.86	50.19	59.76	70.95	84.61	92.59	96.23	97.87	100.00
VIRGINIA	9.33	13.39	17.88	22.44	26.86	31.47	40.65	49.85	60.76	75.29	85.81	92.06	95.14	100.00
WASHINGTON	10.34	15.60	20.52	25.36	29.91	34.35	42.88	50.96	63.06	77.98	87.70	93.27	95.96	100.00
WEST VIRGINIA	14.73	20.38	26.10	30.54	35.40	40.88	50.30	60.36	71.18	85.88	93.47	96.21	97.61	100.00
WISCONSIN	8.85	14.14	18.74	23.45	28.25	32.69	40.96	48.96	61.25	78.40	89.04	94.29	96.71	100.00
WYOMING	9.96	14.77	18.92	22.80	26.83	31.40	40.12	48.46	61.32	76.91	86.80	92.86	95.75	100.00
AVERAGE	11.29	16.57	21.45	26.28	31.15	35.80	44.73	53.16	64.81	79.38	88.49	93.49	95.97	100.00

* BASED ON UNPUBLISHED DATA FROM THE SURVEY OF INCOME AND EDUCATION (REFER TO BUREAU OF THE CENSUS 1978A) ADJUSTED FOR DIFFERENCES IN INCOME CLASS DEFINITIONS.

TABLE B-2
CUMULATIVE PERCENTAGE OF INCOME
BY INCOME CLASS*

STATE	UNDER $3,000	$3,000 -3,999	$4,000 -4,999	$5,000 -5,999	$6,000 -6,999	$7,000 -7,999	$8,000 -9,999	$10,000 -11,999	$12,000 -14,999	$15,000 -19,999	$20,000 -24,999	$25,000 -29,999	$30,000 -34,999	OVER $35,000
ALABAMA	2.74	4.45	6.82	9.14	12.02	15.08	22.16	30.41	43.67	62.27	77.28	86.04	90.46	100.00
ALASKA	0.69	1.29	1.89	2.78	3.73	4.77	7.80	11.31	17.04	26.75	37.19	51.74	61.67	100.00
ARIZONA	1.73	3.31	5.02	7.61	10.43	13.17	19.48	26.32	38.70	57.47	71.25	79.67	84.74	100.00
ARKANSAS	3.08	5.29	8.14	11.92	15.98	20.08	28.47	37.33	49.11	66.16	80.44	87.16	90.89	100.00
CALIFORNIA	1.41	3.16	4.97	6.99	9.33	11.94	17.09	22.88	32.84	49.72	63.77	75.47	82.26	100.00
COLORADO	1.59	2.95	4.65	6.56	8.92	11.71	17.62	23.36	35.05	54.31	68.00	78.49	84.70	100.00
CONNECTICUT	1.10	2.26	3.61	5.03	7.07	8.68	13.17	18.78	29.01	46.22	61.67	72.61	79.43	100.00
DELAWARE	1.25	2.41	3.72	5.22	7.04	8.79	13.59	19.08	29.75	48.79	65.19	76.02	82.47	100.00
FLORIDA	2.08	4.29	6.64	9.37	12.53	15.75	23.13	30.39	42.87	59.81	73.43	81.27	86.11	100.00
GEORGIA	2.31	4.12	6.36	9.24	11.96	15.07	21.37	27.97	39.86	58.46	73.76	82.40	87.39	100.00
HAWAII	1.36	2.52	3.76	5.12	6.85	8.69	12.94	17.94	25.50	40.14	55.60	70.56	79.20	100.00
IDAHO	1.80	3.28	5.19	7.49	10.12	13.16	20.09	28.75	42.13	62.10	74.57	83.18	88.07	100.00
ILLINOIS	1.36	2.75	4.39	6.00	7.83	10.02	14.63	20.30	30.05	48.41	64.35	76.20	82.98	100.00
INDIANA	1.35	2.55	4.28	6.18	8.19	10.74	15.83	23.14	36.04	56.95	72.50	81.12	86.13	100.00
IOWA	1.70	3.18	4.89	7.07	9.20	11.89	17.61	24.38	36.53	56.22	71.29	80.11	85.43	100.00
KANSAS	1.51	3.01	4.57	6.47	8.91	12.02	18.86	26.08	39.40	57.88	71.47	80.01	85.17	100.00
KENTUCKY	2.63	4.97	7.45	9.95	13.00	16.36	24.32	32.04	44.59	63.56	77.86	85.93	90.30	100.00
LOUISIANA	2.77	4.76	6.98	9.34	11.97	14.80	20.45	26.78	37.91	56.61	72.71	80.65	85.57	100.00
MAINE	2.27	4.30	6.65	9.20	13.12	16.62	24.92	33.70	47.21	66.71	79.06	85.82	89.72	100.00
MARYLAND	0.98	1.83	2.98	4.17	5.85	7.58	11.95	16.92	25.77	41.57	57.00	71.02	79.30	100.00
MASSACHUSETTS	1.30	3.00	4.58	6.35	8.31	10.51	15.94	22.48	32.67	51.05	66.60	78.42	84.85	100.00
MICHIGAN	1.28	2.56	4.05	5.72	7.58	9.55	14.23	20.20	31.75	51.26	67.80	79.77	86.16	100.00
MINNESOTA	1.56	3.20	4.87	6.92	9.29	11.54	17.33	23.74	35.83	55.49	71.22	80.74	86.15	100.00
MISSISSIPPI	3.75	6.21	8.67	12.18	15.27	18.54	27.07	35.23	46.98	64.91	78.20	85.96	90.19	100.00
MISSOURI	2.06	3.80	5.90	8.28	11.26	14.30	20.42	27.40	39.75	57.75	72.86	81.68	86.90	100.00
MONTANA	2.15	3.92	5.93	8.28	10.45	13.50	19.74	26.63	39.29	59.21	73.11	81.18	86.08	100.00
NEBRASKA	1.91	3.34	5.12	7.36	10.10	12.29	18.43	25.32	37.46	56.32	71.66	80.28	85.47	100.00
NEVADA	1.43	2.70	4.36	6.42	8.70	11.83	17.53	23.34	33.93	50.92	65.64	76.07	82.23	100.00
NEW HAMPSHIRE	1.39	2.92	4.66	6.59	8.99	11.51	18.35	26.04	39.32	60.96	75.20	83.66	88.62	100.00
NEW JERSEY	1.05	2.15	3.42	4.94	6.65	8.40	12.75	18.26	27.58	45.21	61.13	73.58	80.95	100.00
NEW MEXICO	2.32	3.94	6.08	9.08	12.10	15.45	22.11	29.52	40.44	55.59	69.85	78.42	83.93	100.00
NEW YORK	1.34	2.82	4.42	6.13	8.18	10.73	16.04	22.50	31.93	49.32	64.77	76.61	83.32	100.00
NORTH CAROLINA	2.01	3.74	5.73	8.17	12.01	14.88	22.97	30.90	44.54	62.64	75.45	82.97	87.53	100.00
NORTH DAKOTA	1.70	3.24	5.26	7.59	9.89	12.45	18.49	25.64	37.86	55.03	68.71	77.74	83.26	100.00
OHIO	1.48	2.79	4.35	6.14	8.14	10.32	16.18	22.85	34.66	56.26	71.85	81.16	86.49	100.00
OKLAHOMA	2.17	3.99	6.22	8.76	11.67	14.13	21.41	28.48	40.69	57.43	70.96	78.70	83.63	100.00
OREGON	1.92	3.62	5.67	8.15	11.17	14.02	20.54	27.31	39.45	57.92	72.73	81.99	87.36	100.00
PENNSYLVANIA	1.58	3.12	4.89	7.00	9.13	11.67	17.12	24.66	37.00	57.31	70.95	80.11	85.48	100.00
RHODE ISLAND	1.76	3.26	5.03	6.94	9.48	11.95	17.50	24.01	36.12	57.24	71.61	80.76	86.17	100.00
SOUTH CAROLINA	2.09	3.66	5.84	8.47	11.26	14.80	21.98	30.30	43.39	63.31	78.00	85.92	90.29	100.00
SOUTH DAKOTA	2.28	4.56	6.75	9.58	12.78	15.87	23.23	31.82	43.91	64.93	77.44	84.92	89.23	100.00
TENNESSEE	2.29	4.54	6.74	9.26	12.52	16.50	24.22	32.62	45.50	64.02	76.73	84.30	88.56	100.00
TEXAS	1.92	3.44	5.25	7.81	10.39	13.81	20.63	28.20	39.87	57.56	71.59	79.78	84.83	100.00
UTAH	1.53	2.81	4.40	6.38	8.74	11.23	16.74	23.64	36.24	56.73	71.74	80.37	85.61	100.00
VERMONT	2.26	4.31	6.37	9.34	12.58	16.10	23.36	32.10	44.73	64.05	78.38	86.51	90.89	100.00
VIRGINIA	1.23	2.38	3.88	5.67	7.75	10.22	15.83	22.64	32.58	49.53	65.08	76.39	83.01	100.00
WASHINGTON	1.51	2.96	4.75	6.82	9.12	11.55	17.10	23.40	34.93	53.31	68.41	78.93	85.11	100.00
WEST VIRGINIA	2.34	4.06	6.40	8.62	11.35	14.81	22.31	31.46	43.95	65.41	79.57	85.83	89.65	100.00
WISCONSIN	1.34	2.93	4.65	6.69	9.05	11.44	17.11	23.54	35.34	56.39	72.93	82.84	88.13	100.00
WYOMING	1.68	3.08	4.50	6.10	8.02	10.47	16.09	22.43	34.25	52.99	67.98	78.83	84.87	100.00
AVERAGE	1.81	3.40	5.23	7.41	9.92	12.63	18.77	25.69	37.30	55.80	70.33	79.80	85.34	100.00

* SEE THE TEXT FOR A DISCUSSION OF THE INCOME BASE USED.

Table B-3. Selected State and Local Taxes: Elasticity Estimates[a] (benchmark case)

	State Taxes						Local Taxes		
State	Motor Fuels Selective Sales	Tobacco Selective Sales	Alcohol Selective Sales	Total Selective Sales	Total License Taxes	Corporation Net Income	Total Nonproperty	Total Personal Property	Total Local
Alabama	−0.529	−0.730	−0.125	−0.457	−0.033[b]	+0.192[b]	−0.419	−0.246	−0.352
Alaska	−0.448	−0.675	−0.290	−0.418	−0.284	−0.286[b]	−0.522	+0.032[b]	−0.397
Arizona	−0.507	−0.725	−0.344	−0.505	−0.313	−0.162[b]	−0.381	−0.120[b]	−0.377
Arkansas	−0.502	−0.732	−0.125	−0.488	−0.307	−0.016[b]	−0.459	−0.191[b]	−0.241
California	−0.535	−0.715	−0.338	−0.501	−0.271	−0.116[b]	−0.350	−0.125[b]	−0.408
Colorado	−0.524	−0.720	−0.341	−0.508	−0.241	−0.078[b]	−0.390	−0.142[b]	−0.382
Connecticut	−0.350	−0.548	−0.119	−0.390	−0.156	−0.244[b]	−0.344	−0.095[b]	−0.513
Delaware	−0.517	−0.713	−0.091	−0.486	−0.137[b]	+0.018[b]	−0.408	[d]	−0.351
Florida	−0.540	−0.734	−0.122	−0.452	−0.253	+0.012[b]	−0.506	+0.012[b]	−0.273
Georgia	−0.509	−0.723	−0.103	−0.450	−0.195[c]	+0.108[b]	−0.326	−0.178	−0.282
Hawaii	−0.442	−0.689	−0.276	−0.429	+0.006[b]	+0.210[b]	−0.408	[d]	−0.425
Idaho	−0.497	−0.716	−0.333	−0.477	−0.171[c]	+0.179[b]	−0.467	+0.015[b]	−0.247
Illinois	−0.418	−0.538	−0.216	−0.427	−0.242	−0.099[b]	−0.356	−0.019[b]	−0.342
Indiana	−0.419	−0.567	−0.244	−0.416	−0.242	+0.102[b]	−0.212	+0.039[c]	−0.314
Iowa	−0.398	−0.553	−0.228	−0.406	−0.247	+0.012[b]	−0.390	−0.063[b]	−0.294
Kansas	−0.405	−0.553	−0.232	−0.400	−0.187	−0.045[b]	−0.432	+0.043[c]	−0.228
Kentucky	−0.492	−0.716	−0.103	−0.423	−0.156[b]	+0.169[b]	−0.390	−0.194[b]	−0.304
Louisiana	−0.490	−0.717	−0.100	−0.437	−0.039[b]	+0.112[b]	−0.261	+0.085[b]	−0.185
Maine	−0.328	−0.569	−0.143	−0.347	−0.083[b]	+0.060[b]	−0.369	−0.021[b]	−0.420
Maryland	−0.567	−0.733	−0.104	−0.489	−0.344	−0.169[b]	−0.250	−0.408[c]	−0.383
Massachusetts	−0.351	−0.562	−0.130	−0.348	−0.146[b]	−0.036[b]	−0.359	−0.089[b]	−0.502
Michigan	−0.442	−0.561	−0.239	−0.421	−0.182[c]	−0.107[b]	−0.282	+0.057	−0.406
Minnesota	−0.421	−0.561	−0.240	−0.426	−0.237	−0.040[b]	−0.432	−3.380[b]	−0.427
Mississippi	−0.492	−0.726	−0.118	−0.449	−0.054[b]	+0.179[b]	−0.461	−0.274[c]	−0.288
Missouri	−0.426	−0.565	−0.246	−0.422	−0.215	+0.064[b]	−0.401	−0.112[c]	−0.353
Montana	−0.457	−0.710	−0.327	−0.461	−0.215	−0.143[b]	−0.414	−0.154[c]	−0.257
Nebraska	−0.381	−0.551	−0.225	−0.381	−0.184	+0.080[b]	−0.344	−0.087[b]	−0.252
Nevada	−0.486	−0.714	−0.335	−0.407	−0.233	[d]	−0.441	+0.004[b]	−0.359

Table B-3 (*continued*)

State	State Taxes						Local Taxes		
	Motor Fuels Selective Sales	Tobacco Selective Sales	Alcohol Selective Sales	Total Selective Sales	Total License Taxes	Corporation Net Income	Total Nonproperty	Total Personal Property	Total Local
New Hampshire	−0.327	−0.563	−0.125	−0.363	−0.150[c]	−0.106[b]	−0.357	−6.023	−0.508
New Jersey	−0.320	−0.535	−0.107	−0.361	−0.182	−0.213[b]	−0.443	−0.185[b]	−0.537
New Mexico	−0.484	−0.720	−0.342	−0.478	−0.283	+0.049[b]	−0.456	−0.064[b]	−0.398
New York	−0.384	−0.556	−0.132	−0.389	−0.186	−0.056[b]	−0.273	[d]	−0.347
North Carolina	−0.504	−0.723	−0.106	−0.434	−0.198[c]	+0.016[b]	−0.384	−0.200[b]	−0.311
North Dakota	−0.370	−0.539	−0.215	−0.374	−0.191	−0.040[b]	−0.387	[d]	−0.266
Ohio	−0.411	−0.550	−0.223	−0.434	−0.188[c]	+0.007[b]	−0.218	−0.101[b]	−0.351
Oklahoma	−0.513	−0.732	−0.120	−0.463	−0.323	+0.109[b]	−0.423	−0.056[b]	−0.300
Oregon	−0.507	−0.718	−0.339	−0.512	−0.233	+0.173[b]	−0.482	+0.071[b]	−0.308
Pennsylvania	−0.321	−0.546	−0.119	−0.373	−0.105[b]	−0.106[b]	−0.246	[d]	−0.452
Rhode Island	−0.315	−0.548	−0.115	−0.385	−0.160	−0.175[b]	−0.343	+0.067	−0.408
South Carolina	−0.492	−0.715	−0.090	−0.380	−0.129[b]	+0.061[b]	−0.346	−0.473	−0.333
South Dakota	−0.364	−0.546	−0.220	−0.362	−0.080[b]	+0.018[b]	−0.311	−0.179[b]	−0.196
Tennessee	−0.516	−0.727	−0.115	−0.481	+0.055[b]	+0.195[b]	−0.366	+0.041	−0.266
Texas	−0.506	−0.722	−0.115	−0.467	−0.157[b]	[d]	−0.355	+0.030[c]	−0.207
Utah	−0.499	−0.722	−0.340	−0.489	−0.289	−0.059[b]	−0.376	−0.265	−0.423
Vermont	−0.335	−0.565	−0.137	−0.347	−0.149	+0.222[b]	−0.364	+0.064[b]	−0.490
Virginia	−0.527	−0.732	−0.104	−0.453	−0.284	−0.087[b]	−0.445	−0.022	−0.392
Washington	−0.497	−0.706	−0.326	−0.487	−0.195	[d]	−0.410	−0.048[b]	−0.356
West Virginia	−0.498	−0.731	−0.127	−0.437	−0.312	+0.134[b]	−0.394	−0.138	−0.258
Wisconsin	−0.411	−0.557	−0.228	−0.438	−0.212	+0.036[b]	−0.391	−0.081[b]	−0.425
Wyoming	−0.443	−0.702	−0.314	−0.460	−0.323	[d]	−0.368	−0.045[b]	−0.246[c]
U.S. total	−0.527	−0.669	−0.251	−0.496	−0.284	−0.159	−0.335	−0.163[c]	−0.402

[a]Significant at 0.01 level unless noted otherwise; these are unweighted elasticity estimates.
[b]Coefficient not significant, a proportional burden.
[c]Significant at 0.05 level but not at 0.01 level.
[d]Tax not used in this state.

Table B-4. Suits Index of Tax Progressivity.[a] Selected State-Local Taxes by Type of Tax (benchmark case)

	State Taxes						Local Taxes		
State	Motor Fuels Selective Sales	Tobacco Selective Sales	Alcohol Selective Sales	Total Selective Sales	Total License Taxes	Corporation Net Income	Total Nonproperty	Total Personal Property	Total Local
Alabama	−0.22	−0.31	−0.05	−0.19	0.03	0.25	−0.17	−0.10	−0.15
Alaska	−0.14	−0.23	−0.08	−0.13	−0.03	0.07	−0.19	0.00[b]	−0.08
Arizona	−0.20	−0.29	−0.13	−0.20	−0.11	0.04	−0.15	0.02	−0.12
Arkansas	−0.22	−0.32	−0.05	−0.22	−0.14	0.05	−0.21	−0.09	−0.12
California	−0.20	−0.29	−0.12	−0.19	−0.07	0.07	−0.13	0.05	−0.12
Colorado	−0.19	−0.28	−0.12	−0.19	−0.07	0.12	−0.14	0.06	−0.11
Connecticut	−0.11	−0.19	−0.03	−0.12	−0.02	0.12	−0.11	0.06	−0.13
Delaware	−0.18	−0.26	−0.03	−0.17	0.07	0.16	−0.16	[c]	−0.11
Florida	−0.23	−0.31	−0.05	−0.19	−0.09	0.06	−0.22	0.00[b]	−0.12
Georgia	−0.21	−0.31	−0.04	−0.19	−0.07	0.16	−0.13	−0.07	−0.11
Hawaii	−0.14	−0.24	−0.08	−0.14	0.12	0.05	−0.13	[c]	−0.11
Idaho	−0.19	−0.27	−0.12	−0.18	−0.04	0.16	−0.18	0.04	−0.07
Illinois	−0.14	−0.19	−0.07	−0.15	−0.06	0.13	−0.12	0.05	−0.08
Indiana	−0.14	−0.20	−0.08	−0.14	−0.06	0.18	−0.08	0.00[b]	−0.09
Iowa	−0.14	−0.21	−0.08	−0.15	−0.08	0.11	−0.14	0.04	−0.08
Kansas	−0.15	−0.21	−0.08	−0.15	−0.04	0.11	−0.16	0.00[b]	−0.07
Kentucky	−0.21	−0.30	−0.04	−0.18	−0.05	0.23	−0.13	−0.06	−0.13
Louisiana	−0.21	−0.32	−0.04	−0.19	0.06	0.19	−0.11	0.06	−0.07
Maine	−0.13	−0.23	−0.05	−0.14	−0.02	0.07	−0.15	0.03	−0.17
Maryland	−0.19	−0.27	−0.03	−0.16	−0.08	0.11	−0.10	0.09	−0.11
Massachusetts	−0.11	−0.20	−0.04	−0.11	−0.01	0.15	−0.12	0.05	−0.16
Michigan	−0.15	−0.20	−0.07	−0.14	0.00[b]	0.11	−0.10	−0.01	−0.12
Minnesota	−0.15	−0.21	−0.08	−0.15	−0.07	0.14	−0.16	−0.48	−0.15
Mississippi	−0.23	−0.33	−0.05	−0.21	0.00[b]	0.14	−0.22	−0.13	−0.14
Missouri	−0.17	−0.23	−0.09	−0.17	−0.07	0.16	−0.16	−0.02	−0.14
Montana	−0.18	−0.28	−0.12	−0.18	−0.07	0.06	−0.16	−0.02	−0.07
Nebraska	−0.14	−0.21	−0.08	−0.14	−0.05	0.15	−0.13	0.00[b]	−0.07
Nevada	−0.18	−0.28	−0.12	−0.15	−0.07	[c]	−0.16	0.03	−0.11

Table B-4 (continued)

State	State Taxes						Local Taxes		
	Motor Fuels Selective Sales	Tobacco Selective Sales	Alcohol Selective Sales	Total Selective Sales	Total License Taxes	Corporation Net Income	Total Nonproperty	Total Personal Property	Total Local
New Hampshire	−0.11	−0.20	−0.04	−0.12	−0.03	0.08	−0.12	−0.82	−0.18
New Jersey	−0.10	−0.18	−0.03	−0.11	−0.03	0.03	−0.15	0.04	−0.17
New Mexico	−0.20	−0.30	−0.14	−0.20	−0.10	0.07	−0.19	−0.01	−0.15
New York	−0.13	−0.21	−0.04	−0.14	−0.04	0.13	−0.11	[c]	−0.10
North Carolina	−0.20	−0.29	−0.04	−0.17	−0.04	0.13	−0.15	−0.03	−0.11
North Dakota	−0.14	−0.21	−0.08	−0.14	−0.05	0.08	−0.15	[c]	−0.07
Ohio	−0.14	−0.19	−0.07	−0.15	−0.03	0.14	−0.08	0.03	−0.11
Oklahoma	−0.22	−0.32	−0.05	−0.20	−0.13	0.20	−0.18	0.03	−0.11
Oregon	−0.20	−0.29	−0.13	−0.20	−0.07	0.14	−0.19	0.09	−0.10
Pennsylvania	−0.11	−0.21	−0.04	−0.14	0.01	0.08	−0.09	[c]	−0.16
Rhode Island	−0.11	−0.21	−0.04	−0.14	−0.04	0.03	−0.12	0.01	−0.13
South Carolina	−0.19	−0.28	−0.03	−0.14	−0.03	0.10	−0.14	−0.18	−0.12
South Dakota	−0.14	−0.22	−0.08	−0.14	−0.02	0.07	−0.12	0.00[b]	−0.08
Tennessee	−0.21	−0.30	−0.04	−0.20	0.08	0.20	−0.15	0.01	−0.10
Texas	−0.21	−0.30	−0.04	−0.19	−0.01	[c]	−0.14	0.00[b]	−0.06
Utah	−0.18	−0.27	−0.12	−0.17	−0.09	0.09	−0.13	−0.06	−0.14
Vermont	−0.13	−0.23	−0.05	−0.13	−0.05	0.13	−0.14	0.06	−0.20
Virginia	−0.20	−0.28	−0.03	−0.17	−0.07	0.10	−0.16	0.00[b]	−0.12
Washington	−0.18	−0.28	−0.12	−0.18	−0.04	[c]	−0.15	0.09	−0.10
West Virginia	−0.20	−0.30	−0.04	−0.18	−0.12	0.19	−0.16	−0.05	−0.10
Wisconsin	−0.14	−0.20	−0.07	−0.15	−0.06	0.09	−0.13	0.03	−0.14
Wyoming	−0.15	−0.26	−0.10	−0.16	−0.11	[c]	−0.13	0.07	−0.04
U.S. average	−0.17	−0.26	−0.07	−0.17	−0.05	0.12	−0.15	−0.02	−0.12

[a]For a discussion of this index refer to the text or Suits (1977b).
[b]Rounds to zero.
[c]Tax not used in this state.

References

Aaron, H. (1965). "Some Criticisms of Tax Burden Indices." *National Tax Journal* 18 (September): 313-318.

______ (1970). "Income Taxes and Housing." *American Economic Review* 60 (December): 789-806.

______ (1974). "A New View of Property Tax Incidence." *American Economic Review, Papers and Proceedings* 64 (May): 212-221.

______ (1975). *Who Pays the Property Tax? A New View.* Washington, D.C.: Brookings Institution.

______ (1977). "The 'New View' of the Property Tax: A Caveat." *National Tax Journal* 30 (March): 69-75.

Adler, John H. (1951). "The Fiscal System, the Distribution of Income and Public Welfare." In Kenyon Poole (ed.), *Fiscal Policies and the American Economy.* New York: Prentice-Hall, 359-409.

Advisory Commission on Intergovernmental Relations (1961). *Tax Overlapping in the United States 1961.* Washington, D.C.: Advisory Commission.

______ (1964). *Tax Overlapping in the United States 1964.* Washington, D.C.: Advisory Commission.

______ (1965). *Federal-State Coordination of Personal Income Taxes.* Washington, D.C.: Advisory Commission.

______ (1967). *State-Local Taxation and Industrial Location.* Washington, D.C.: Advisory Commission.

______ (1969). *State and Local Taxes: Significant Features: 1967 to 1970.* Washington, D.C.: Advisory Commission.

______ (1972). *State and Local Finances: Significant Features: 1972.* Washington, D.C.: Advisory Commission.

______ (1977a). *Significant Features of Fiscal Federalism: 1976-77 Edition.* Vols. 1-3. Washington, D.C.: Advisory Commission.

______ (1977b). *State Limitations on Local Taxes and Expenditures.* Washington, D.C.: Advisory Commission.

Allen, H. K., and R. F. Fryman (1964). "Comparison of Revenues and Expenditures in Income and Non-Income Tax States in 1962." *National Tax Journal* 17 (December): 356-364.

Anderson, Martin (1978). "The Roller-Coaster Income Tax." *The Public Interest* (Winter): 17-28.

Bahl, Roy W., and Alan K. Campbell (eds.) (1976). *State and Local Government: The Political Economy of Reform.* New York: Free Press.

Bahl, Roy W., and Walter Vogt (1975). *Fiscal Centralization and Tax Burdens: State and Regional Financing of City Services.* Cambridge, Mass.: Ballinger.

Bahl, Roy, et al. (1975). "Comparative Tax Burdens in Manhattan, Queens and Selected Metropolitan Area Suburbs." Syracuse, N.Y.: Metropolitan Studies Program, Occasional Paper No. 20.

Bannink, R. (1960). "The Incidence of Taxes and Premiums for Social Insurance on Family Budgets." *Public Finance* (No. 1): 72-91.

Beaton, J. R. (1962). "Family Tax Burdens by Income Levels." *National Tax Journal* 15 (March): 14-25.

Billings, R. Bruce (1972). "Income Tax Credits to Reduce the Regressivity of State-Local Tax Systems." *American Journal of Economics and Sociology* 31 (October): 397-411.

Bird, R. A. (1964). "A Note on Tax 'Sacrifice' Comparisons." *National Tax Journal* 17 (September): 303-308.

Bishop, G. A. (1961). "The Tax Burden by Income Class, 1958." *National Tax Journal* 14 (March): 41-57.

______ (1966). "Income Redistribution in the Framework of the National Income Accounts." *National Tax Journal* 19 (December): 378-390.

Black, David E. (1977). "Property Tax Incidence: The Excise-Tax Effect and Assessment Practices." *National Tax Journal* 30 (December): 429-434.

Black, Duncan (1939). *The Incidence of Income Taxes.* London: Macmillan.

Bowie, Norman E. (1971). *Towards a New Theory of Distributive Justice.* Amherst: University of Massachusetts Press.

Bowman, Mary Jean (1951). "A Graphical Analysis of Personal Income Distribution in the United States." In R. A. Musgrave and C. S. Shoup (eds.), *A.E.A. Readings in the Theory of Income Distribution.* Homewood, Ill: Richard D. Irwin, 72-99.

Boyle, Gerald J. (1974). "A Comprehensive Tax Credit for Achieving Proportionality in State and Local Tax Structures." *National Tax Journal* 27 (December): 569-582.

Brazer, Harvey E. (1966). Review of *Essays in Fiscal Federalism,* edited by R. A. Musgrave. *Journal of Political Economy* 74 (December): 637.

Brazer, Harvey E., et al. (1974). Discussion on "The Property Tax: Progressive or Regressive?" *American Economic Review, Papers and Proceedings* 64 (May): 230-235.

Break, George F. (1974). "The Incidence and Economic Effects of Taxation." in *The Economics of Public Finance.* Washington, D.C.: Brookings Institution, 119-237.

Bridges, Benjamin, Jr. (1966). "Deductibility of State and Local Non-Business Taxes under the Federal Individual Income Tax." *National Tax Journal* 19 (March): 1-17.

Brownlee, O. H. (1960). *Estimated Distribution of Minnesota Taxes and Public Expenditure Benefits.* Minneapolis: University of Minnesota Press.

Buchanan, James M. (1960a). "The Methodology of Incidence Theory: A Critical Review of Some Recent Contributions." In *Fiscal Theory and Political Economy.* Chapel Hill: University of North Carolina Press, 125-150.

_____ (1960b). *Fiscal Theory and Political Economy.* Chapel Hill: University of North Carolina Press.

_____ (1969). *Cost and Choice.* Chicago: Markham.

Bureau of the Census (1963). *Census of Governments: 1962.* Vol. 2, *Taxable Property Values.* Washington, D.C.: U.S. Government Printing Office.

_____ (1964a). *Census of Governments: 1962.* Vol. 5, *Local Government in Metropolitan Areas.* Washington, D.C.: U.S. Government Printing Office.

_____ (1964b). *Census of Governments: 1962.* Vol. 4, *Compendium of Government Finances.* Washington, D.C.: U.S. Government Printing Office.

_____ (1974). *Property Values Subject to Local General Property Taxation in the United States: 1973.* Washington, D.C.: U.S. Government Printing Office, GSS No. 69.

_____ (1975). *State and Local Ratio Studies and Property Assessment.* Washington, D.C.: U.S. Government Printing Office, GSS No. 72.

_____ (1977a). *Governmental Finances in 1975-76.* Washington, D.C.: U.S. Government Printing Office, GF76 No. 5.

_____ (1977b). *State Government Finances in 1976.* Washington, D.C.: U.S. Government Printing Office, GF76 No. 3.

_____ (1977c). *Household Money Income in 1975, by Housing Tenure and Residence, for the United States, Regions, Divisions, and States* (Spring, 1976 Survey of Income and Education). Washington, D.C.: U.S. Government Printing Office, P-60, No. 108.

_____ (1978a). *Money Income and Poverty Status in 1975 of Families and Persons in the United States* (Spring, 1976 Survey of Income and Education, reports issued for each of four regions). Washington, D.C.: U.S. Government Printing Office, P-60 No., 110-113.

_____ (1978b). *Household Money Income in 1976 and Selected Social and Economic Characteristics of Households.* Washington, D.C.: U.S. Government Printing Office, P-60, No. 109.

_____ (1978c). *1977 Census of Governments.* Vol. 2, *Taxable Property Values and Assessment/Sales Price Ratios.* Washington, D.C.: U.S. Government Printing Office, GC77 (2).

Bureau of Economic Analysis (1973). "Size Distribution of Family Personal Income: Methodology and Estimates for 1964." Washington, D.C.: BEA-SP73-021.

Bureau of Labor Statistics (1966). *Survey of Consumer Expenditures and Income 1960-61* (Reports 237-89 to 237-92 and supplemental reports). Washington, D.C.: U.S. Government Printing Office.

_____ (1971). *Consumer Expenditures and Income: Survey Guidelines.* Washington, D.C.: U.S. Government Printing Office, Bulletin 1684.

______ (1977). *Consumer Expenditure Survey: Diary Survey, July 1972-June 1974.* Washington, D.C.: U.S. Government Printing Office, Bulletin 1959.

______ (1978). *Consumer Expenditure Survey Series: Interview Survey, 1972-73.* Washington, D.C.: Department of Labor, Bulletin 1985.

Calmus, Thomas W. (1970). "The Burden of Federal Excise Taxes by Income Class," *Quarterly Review of Economics and Business* 10 (Spring): 17-23.

Campbell, Alan K. (1948). "The Tax Burden of Three Hypothetical Detroit Families." Master's thesis, Department of Public Affairs, Wayne University.

Carvalho, M. De (1968). "Distribution of the Tax Burden and Its Empirical Analysis." *Arquivo Institute* 3: 53-84.

Colberg, Marshall R. (1954). "Shifting of a Specific Excise Tax." *Public Finance* 9 (No. 2): 168-173.

Collier, R. P. (1958). "Some Empirical Evidence of Tax Incidence." *National Tax Journal* 11 (March): 35-55.

Colm, G., and H. P. Wald (1952). "Some Comments on Tax Burden Comparisons." *National Tax Journal* 5 (March): 1-14.

Conrad, Alfred (1955). "On the Calculation of Tax Burdens." *Economica* (N.S.) 22 (November): 342-348.

Cowell, F. A. (1977). *Measuring Inequality.* New York: John Wiley.

Cragg, John G.; A. C. Harberger; and Peter Mieszkowski (1957). "Empirical Evidence on the Incidence of the Corporation Income Tax." *Journal of Political Economy* 75 (December): 811-821.

Daicoff, Darwin, and Robert H. Glass (1978). "Who Pays Kansas Taxes? Lawrence: University of Kansas, Institute for Economic and Business Research.

Davies, David G. (1959). "An Empirical Test of Sales Tax Regressivity." *Journal of Political Economy* 67 (February): 72-78.

______ (1960). "Progressiveness of a Sales Tax in Relation to Various Income Bases." *American Economic Review* 50 (December): 987-995.

______ (1969). "The Significance of Taxation of Services for the Pattern of Distribution of Tax Burden by Income Class." *Proceedings of the Sixty-Second Annual Conference, National Tax Association,* Boston, 138-146.

______ (1971). "Clothing Exemptions and Sales Tax Regressivity: Note." *American Economic Review* 61 (March): 187-189.

Davies, David G., and David E. Black (1975). "Equity Effects of Including Housing Services in a Sales Tax Base." *National Tax Journal* 28 (March): 135-137.

Donnahoe, Alan S. (1947). "Measuring State Tax Burden." *Journal of Political Economy* 55 (June): 234-244.

Due, John (1963). "Sales Taxation and the Consumer." *American Economic Review* 53 (December): 1078-1084.

______ (1965). "The Value Added Tax." *Western Economic Journal* 3 (Spring): 165-171.

Eapen, Thomas A., and Ann Navarro Eapen (no date). "Differential Incidence of State and Local Tax Structures: An Empirical Study." (Unpublished paper.)

______ (1970). "Incidence of Taxes and Expenditures of Connecticut State and

Local Governments: Fiscal Year 1967." (Report prepared for the Connecticut State Revenue Task Force.)
Ebel, Robert D., and Robert M. Kamins (1975). "Who Pays Hawaii's Taxes?" Honolulu: Social Sciences and Linguistics Institute, University of Hawaii at Manoa.
Fox, Karl (1968). *Intermediate Economic Statistics.* New York: John Wiley.
Frank, Henry (1959). "Measuring State Tax Burdens." *National Tax Journal* 12 (June): 179-185.
Fredland, John Eric (1972). "An Estimate of the Horizontal Burden of a Retail Sales Tax." *Quarterly Review of Economics and Business* 12 (Winter): 39-44.
Fruchter, B. (1954). *Introduction to Factor Analysis.* Princeton, N.J.: D. Van Nostrand.
Fuchs, Diane, and Steve A. Rabin (1979). "Tax Equity in the Fifty States." Washington, D.C.: Coalition of American Public Employees.
Gaffney, M. Mason (1971). "The Property Tax Is a Progressive Tax." *Proceedings of the Sixty-Fourth Annual Conference, National Tax Association,* Kansas City, Missouri, 408-426.
Garms, Walter I.; James W. Guthrie; and Lawrence C. Pierce *(1978). School Finance: The Economics and Politics of Public Education.* Englewood Cliffs, N.J.: Prentice-Hall.
Garrison, Charles B.; William C. Goolsby; and Kenneth E. Quindry (1977). "Distribution of the Tax Burden Within the 50 States." *Proceedings of the Seventieth Annual Conference, National Tax Association,* Louisville, 132-139.
Ghazanfar, S. M. (1978). "Sales Tax Equity Again: By Income Groups and Income Classes." *Public Finance Quarterly* 6 (July): 343-357.
Gillespie, W. Irwin (1964). *The Incidence of Taxes and Public Expenditures in the Canadian Economy* (Report No. 2. of the Royal Commission on Taxation). Ottawa: Queen's Printer.
______ (1965). "Effect of Public Expenditures on the Distribution of Income." In R. A. Musgrave (ed.), *Essays in Fiscal Federalism.* Washington, D.C.: Brookings Institution, 122-186.
Goode, Richard (1964). *The Individual Income Tax.* Washington, D.C.: Brookings Institution.
Gordon, David M. (1972). "Taxation of the Poor and the Normative Theory of Tax Incidence." *American Economic Review, Papers and Proceedings* 62 (May): 319-328.
Gordon, R. J. (1967). "The Incidence of the Corporation Income Tax in U.S. Manufacturing, 1925-62." *American Economic Review* 57 (September): 731-758.
Gorman, John A. (1970). "The Relationship Between Personal Income and Taxable Income." *Survey of Current Business* 50 (May): 19-21.
Greenwald, William I. (1963). *Statistics for Economics.* Columbus, Ohio: C. E. Merrill Books.
Greytak, David, and Richard McHugh (1978). "Inflation and the Individual Income Tax." *Southern Economic Journal* 45 (July): 168-180.
Guthrie, Robert S. (1979). "Measurement of Relative Tax Progressivity."

National Tax Journal 32 (March): 93-95.

Hady, Thomas F. (1962). "The Incidence of the Personal Property Tax." *National Tax Journal* 15 (December): 368-384.

Halstead, D. Kent (1978). *Tax Wealth in Fifty States.* Washington, D.C.: U.S. Department of Health, Education and Welfare, National Institute of Education.

Hanczaryk, Edwin W., and James H. Thompson (1958). *The Economic Impact of State and Local Taxes in West Virginia.* Morgantown: College of Commerce, West Virginia University.

Hansen, Reed R. (1962). "An Empirical Analysis of the Retail Sales Tax with Policy Recommendations." *National Tax Journal* 15 (March): 1-13.

Harberger, A. C. (1962). "The Incidence of the Corporation Income Tax." *Journal of Political Economy* 70 (June): 215-240.

Harman, Harry S. (1960). *Modern Factor Analysis.* Chicago: University of Chicago Press.

Hendricks, H. G. (1931). "The Incidence of the Gasoline Tax." *American Economic Review* 21 (March): 88-89.

Herber, Bernard P. (1975). *Modern Public Finance.* 3rd ed. Homewood, Ill.: Richard D. Irwin.

Hicks, Ursula K. (1959). "The Terminology of Tax Analysis." In R. A. Musgrave and C. S. Shoup (eds.), *A.E.A. Readings in the Economics of Taxation.* Homewood, Ill., Richard D. Irwin, 214-226.

Hirsch, Werner Z.; Elbert Segelhorst; and Morton Marcus (1969). *Spillover of Public Education Costs and Benefits.* 2nd ed. Los Angeles: University of California, Institute of Government and Public Affairs.

Hoffman, R. F. (1965). "Some Analysis Concerning the Regressivity of Hawaii's General Excise Tax." *National Tax Journal* 18 (June): 219-221.

Internal Revenue Service (1966). *Statistics of Income: Individual Income Tax Returns 1963.* Washington, D.C.: U.S. Government Printing Office.

_____ (1976). *Statistics of Income 1973.* Washington, D.C.: Department of the Treasury, IRS.

_____ (1978). *Statistics of Income 1975.* Washington, D.C.: Department of the Treasury, IRS.

Isbister, John (1968). "On the Theory of Equitable Taxation." *National Tax Journal* 21 (September): 332-339.

Kahn, C. Harry (1960). *Personal Deductions in the Federal Income Tax.* Princeton, N.J.: Princeton University Press.

Kendall, M. G. (1965). *A Course in Multivariate Analysis.* London: Charles Griffin.

Kilpatrick, R. W. (1965). "The Short-Run Forward Shifting of the Corporation Income Tax." *Yale Economic Essays* 5 (No. 2): 355-420.

Kristol, Irving (1974). "Taxes, Poverty, and Equality." *The Public Interest* (Fall): 3-28.

Krzyaniak, Marion (ed.) (1966). *Effects of Corporation Income Tax.* Detroit: Wayne State University Press.

Krzyaniak, Marion, and R. A. Musgrave (1963). *The Shifting of the Corporation Income Tax.* Baltimore: Johns Hopkins University Press.

Ladd, Helen F. (1978). "An Economic Evaluation of State Limitations on

Local Taxing and Spending Powers." *National Tax Journal* 31 (March): 1-18.

Lampman, Robert S., and Aaron, Henry J. (1972). Discussion on "Taxation of the Poor and the Rich." *American Economic Review, Papers and Proceedings* 62 (May): 331-334.

Lawley, D. M., and A. E. Maxwell (1963). *Factor Analysis as a Statistical Method.* London: Butterworth.

Lemale, Helen H. (1965). "Uses of Family Expenditure Data." Paper, annual meeting American Home Economics Association, Atlantic City, N. J.

Liebenberg, J., and J. M. Fitzwilliams (1961). "Size Distribution of Personal Income, 1957-60." *Survey of Current Business* 41 (May): 11-21.

Lile, Stephen E., and Don M. Soule (1969). "Interstate Differences in Family Tax Burdens." *National Tax Journal* 22 (December): 433-445.

Lindholm, Richard, and Hartojo Wignjowijoto (1979). *Financing and Managing State and Local Government.* Lexington, Mass.: Lexington Books.

Lotz, Jørgen R., and Elliot Morss (1967). "Measuring 'Tax Effort' in Developing Countries." *I.M.F. Staff Papers* 14 (November): 478-499.

Maxwell, James A. (1962). *Tax Credits and Intergovernmental Fiscal Relations.* Washington, D.C.: Brookings Institution.

Maxwell, James A., and J. Richard Aronson (1977). *Financing State and Local Governments.* 3rd ed. Washington, D.C.: Brooking Institution.

Mayer, Thomas (1974). "The Distribution of the Tax Burden and Permanent Income." *National Tax Journal* 27 (March): 141-146.

Maynes, E. S., and J. N. Morgan (1957). "The Effective Rate of Real Estate Taxation: An Empirical Investigation." *Review of Economics and Statistics* 39 (February): 14-22.

McLure, Charles (1964). "Commodity Tax Incidence in Open Economies." *National Tax Journal* 17 (June): 187-204.

_____ (1966). "An Analysis of Regional Tax Incidence, with Estimation of Interstate Incidence of State and Local Taxes." Ph.D. dissertation, Department of Economics, Princeton University.

_____ (1967). "Tax Exporting in the United States: Estimates for 1962." *National Tax Journal* 20 (March): 49-77.

_____ (1976). "The Relevance of the New View of the Incidence of the Property Tax in Developing Countries." Prepared for 15th Annual Conference of the Committee on Taxation, Resources, and Economic Development, Cambridge, Mass., October 22-24 (revised April 1977).

_____ (1977). "The 'New View' of the Property Tax: A Caveat." *National Tax Journal* 30 (March): 69-75.

Megee, Mary (1965). "On Economic Growth and the Factor Analysis Method." *Southern Economic Journal* 31 (January): 215-228.

Meinster, David R. (1970). "Property Tax Shifting Assumptions and Effects on Incidence Profiles." *Quarterly Review of Economics and Business* 10 (Winter): 65-83.

Melichar, Emanuel (1963). *State Individual Income Taxes.* Storrs: University of Connecticut.

Mieszkowski, Peter (1967). "On the Theory of Tax Incidence." *Journal of Political Economy* 75 (June): 250-262.

_____ (1969). "Tax Incidence Theory: The Effects of Taxes on the

Distribution of Income." *Journal of Economic Literature* 7 (December): 1103-1124.

______ (1972). "The Property Tax: An Excise Tax or a Profits Tax?" *Journal of Public Economics* 1 (April): 73-96.

Minnesota Tax Study Committee (1956). *Report of the Governor's Minnesota Tax Study.* Minneapolis: Minnesota Tax Study Committee.

Morag, A. (1959). "Is the 'Economic Efficiency' of Taxation Important?" *Economic Journal* 69 (March): 87-94.

Morgan, James N.; Martin H. David; Wilbur J. Cohen; and Harvey E. Brazer (1962). *Income and Welfare in the United States.* New York: McGraw-Hill.

Musgrave, Richard A. (1952). "Distribution of Tax Payments by Income Groups: A Review." *Proceedings of the Forty-Fifth Annual Conference, National Tax Association,* Toronto, 179-195.

______ (1953a). "On Incidence." *Journal of Political Economy* 6 (August): 306-323.

______ (1953b). "General Equilibrium Aspects of Incidence Theory." *American Economic Review, Papers and Proceedings* 43 (May): 504-517.

______ (1959). *The Theory of Public Finance.* New York: McGraw-Hill.

______ (1969). *Fiscal Systems.* New Haven, Conn.: Yale University Press.

______ (1974). "Is a Property Tax on Housing Regressive?" *American Economic Review, Papers and Proceedings* 64 (May): 222-229.

Musgrave, Richard A.; J. J. Carroll; L. D. Cook; and L. Frane (1951). "Distribution of Tax Payments by Income Groups: A Case Study for 1948." *National Tax Journal* 4 (March): 1-53.

Musgrave, Richard A.; Karl E. Case; and Herman Leonard (1974). "The Distribution of Fiscal Burdens and Benefits." *Public Finance Quarterly* 2 (July): 259-311.

Musgrave, Richard A., and Darwin Daicoff (1958). "Who Pays the Michigan Taxes?" *Michigan Tax Study Staff Papers.* Lansing: Secretary of Finance: 131-183.

Musgrave, Richard A., and L. Frane (1952). "Rejoinder to Dr. Tucker." *National Tax Journal* 5 (March): 15-35.

Musgrave, Richard A. and Peggy B. Musgrave (1980). *Public Finance in Theory and Practice.* 3rd ed. New York: McGraw-Hill.

Musgrave, Richard A., and Tun Thin (1948). "Income Tax Progression, 1929-48." *Journal of Political Economy* 56 (December): 498-514.

Mushkin, Selma, and John F. Cotton (1968). *Functional Federalism: Grants-In-Aid and PPB Systems.* Washington, D.C.: State-Local Finances Project of George Washington University.

National Bureau of Economic Research (1972). *Public Expenditures and Taxation.* New York: Columbia University Press.

Neisser, Albert C. (1952). "The Dynamics of Tax Burden Comparisons." *National Tax Journal* 5 (March): 351-364.

Netzer, Dick (1966). *The Economics of the Property Tax.* Washington, D.C.: Brookings Institution.

______ (1973). "The Incidence of the Property Tax Revisited." *National Tax Journal* 26 (December): 515-535.

Newcomer, Mabel (1937). "Estimate of the Tax Burden on Different Income Classes." In *Studies in Current Tax Problems.* New York: Twentieth Century Fund, 1-52.

Odden, Allan R. (no date). "The Incidence of the Property Tax Under Alternative Assumptions and the Effect of a Circuit Breaker: The Case in Minnesota, 1969-71." Denver: Education Finance Center, Education Commission of the States.

Odden, Allan R.; Robert Berne; and Leanna Stiefel (1979). *Equity in School Finance.* Denver; Education Finance Center, Education Commission of the States, Report No. F79-9.

Odden, Allan R., and Phillip E. Vincent (1976). *The Regressivity of the Property Tax.* Denver: Education Finance Center, Education Commission of the States, Report No. F76-4.

Okner, Benjamin (1966). *Income Distribution and the Federal Income Tax.* Ann Arbor: Institute of Public Administration, University of Michigan.

______ (1979). "Distributional Aspects of Tax Reform During the Past Fifteen Years." *National Tax Journal* 32 (March): 11-27.

Okner, Benjamin, and Joseph A. Pechman (1974). "Who Paid the Taxes in 1966?" *American Economic Review, Papers and Proceedings* 64 (May): 168-174.

Paglin, Morton, and Michael Fogarty (1972). "Equity and the Property Tax: A New Conceptual Focus." *National Tax Journal* 24 (December): 557-565.

Paul, Diane B. (1975). *The Politics of the Property Tax.* Lexington, Mass.: Lexington Books.

Pechman, Joseph (1952). "Some Technical Problems in the Measurement of Tax Burdens." *Proceedings of the Forty-Fifth Annual Conference, National Tax Association,* Toronto, 204-212.

______ (1972). "Distribution of Federal and State Income Taxes by Income Classes." *Journal of Finance* 27 (May): 179-191.

______ (1977). *Federal Tax Policy.* 3rd ed. New York: W. W. Norton.

Pechman, Joseph, and Benjamin A. Okner (1972). "Individual Income Tax Erosion by Income Classes." *The Economics of Federal Subsidy Programs,* Joint Economy Committee, 92 Congress, 2nd Session, 13-40.

Pechman, Joseph, and Benjamin A. Okner (1974). *Who Bears the Tax Burden?* Washington, D.C.: Brookings Institution.

Peterson, George E. (1972). "The Regressivity of the Residential Property Tax." Washington, D.C.: Urban Institute Working Paper S1207-10.

Peterson, George E., and Arthur P. Solomon (1973). "Property Taxes and Populist Reform." *The Public Interest* (Winter): 60-75.

Pettengill, Robert B. (1940). "The Tax Burden Among Income Groups in the United States in 1936." *American Economic Review* 30 (March): 60-71.

Phares, Donald (1973). *State-Local Tax Equity: An Empirical Analysis of the Fifty States.* Lexington, Mass.: Lexington Books.

Polinsky, A. Mitchell (1973). "A Note on the Measurement of Tax Incidence. *Public Finance Quarterly* 1 (April): 219-230.

Posner, Richard (1973). "Economic Justice and the Economist." *The Public*

Interest (Fall): 109-119.

Prest, A. R. (1955). "Statistical Calculation of Tax Burdens." *Economica* (N.S.) 22 (August): 234-245.

______ (1956). "On the Calculation of Tax Burdens: A Rejoinder." *Economica* (N.S.) 23 (August): 270-272.

Ratchford, B. U., and P. B. Han (1957). "The Burden of the Corporate Income Tax." *National Tax Journal* 10 (December): 310-324.

Recktenwald, Horst Claus (1971). *Tax Incidence and Income Redistribution.* Translated by Martha V. Stolper. Detroit: Wayne State University Press.

Reischauer, Robert D., and Robert W. Hartman (1973). *Reforming School Finance.* Washington, D.C.: Brookings Institution.

Reynolds, Morgan, and Eugene Smolensky (1974). "The Post Fisc Distribution: 1961 and 1970 Compared." *National Tax Journal* 27 (December): 515-530.

______ (1977). *Public Expenditures, Taxes, and the Distribution of Income: The United States, 1950, 1961, 1970.* New York: Academic Press.

Riggan, William C. (1975). "Incidence of Taxes and Expenditures for Public Lower Education." (Unpublished paper.)

Rummel, R. J. (1957). "Understanding Factor Analysis." *Journal of Conflict Resolution* 11 (December): 444-480.

______ (1970). *Applied Factor Analysis.* Evanston, Ill.: Northwestern University Press.

Sacks, Seymour (1965). "State and Local Finances and Economic Development." In *State and Local Taxes on Business.* Princeton, N.J.: Tax Institute of America, 209-224.

______ (1968). "Metropolitan Fiscal Disparities: Their Nature and Determinants." *The Journal of Finance* 23 (May): 229-250.

Schaefer, Jeffrey M. (1969a). "The Regressivity of State-Local Taxation: A Case Study of New Jersey." *The Quarterly Review of Economics and Business* 9 (Spring): 7-18.

______ (1969b). "Clothing Exemptions and Sales Tax Regressivity." *American Economic Review* 59 (September): 596-599.

______ (1969c). "Sales Tax Regressivity Under Alternative Tax Bases and Income Concepts." *National Tax Journal* 22 (December): 516-527.

Schlesinger, Eugene (1951). "The Statistical Allocation of Taxes and Expenditures in 1938-39 and 1946-47." In K. E. Poole (ed.), *Fiscal Policies and the American Economy.* New York: Prentice-Hall: 410-421.

Schroeder, Larry D., and David L. Sjoquist (1975). *The Property Tax and Alternative Local Taxes: An Economic Analysis.* New York: Praeger.

Seligman, E. R. A. (1959). "Introduction to the Shifting and Incidence of Taxation." In R. A. Musgrave and C. S. Shoup (eds.), *A.E.A. Readings in the Economics of Taxation.* Homewood, Ill.: Richard D. Irwin, 203-213.

Seltzer, Lawrence H. (1968). *The Personal Exemption in the Income Tax.* New York: National Bureau of Economic Research.

Sharkansky, Ira (1969). *The Politics of Taxing and Spending.* New York: Bobbs-Merrill.

Shoup, Carl (1969). *Public Finance.* Chicago: Aldine.

Smelker, Mary W. (1968). "The Impact of Federal Income and Payroll

Taxes on the Distribution of After-Tax Income." *National Tax Journal* 21 (December): 448-456.

Soltow, Lee (ed.) (1969). *Six Papers on the Size Distribution of Wealth and Income.* New York: National Bureau of Economic Research.

Spiro, Michael H. (1974). "On the Tax Incidence of the Pennsylvania Lottery." *National Tax Journal* 27 (March): 57-61.

Steuerie, Eugene; Richard McHugh; and Emil M. Sunley (1978). "Who Benefits from Income Averaging?" *National Tax Journal* 31 (March): 19-32.

Suits, Daniel B. (1977a). "Gambling Taxes: Regressivity and Revenue Potential." *National Tax Journal* 30 (March): 19-35.

_____ (1977b). "Measurement of Tax Progressivity." *American Economic Review* 67 (September): 747-752.

Tarasov, Helen (1942). "Who Does Pay the Taxes?" *Social Research* (Supplement 4).

Tarasov, Helen, and Gerhard Colm (1942). *Who Pays the Taxes?* Monograph No. 3 of the Temporary National Economic Committee.

Tax Foundation (1957). *The Tax Burden in Relation to National Income and Product.* New York: Tax Foundation.

_____ (1960). *Allocation of the Tax Burden by Income Class.* (Project Note No. 45.) New York: Tax Foundation.

_____ (1962). *Retail Sales and Individual Income Taxes in State Tax Structures.* (Project Note No. 48.) New York: Tax Foundation.

_____ (1964). *Allocating the Federal Tax Burden by State.* New York: Tax Foundation.

_____ (1966). "Allocation of the Tax Burden and Expenditure Benefits by Income Class." (Research Bibliography No. 15, revised.) New York: Tax Foundation.

_____ (1967a). *Tax Burdens and Benefits of Government Expenditures by Income Class, 1961 and 1965.* New York: Tax Foundation.

_____ (1967b). *State Tax Studies: 1959-1967.* New York: Tax Foundation.

_____ (1967c). *City Income Taxes.* New York: Tax Foundation.

_____ (1968a). *The Corporation Income Tax.* New York: Tax Foundation.

_____ (1968b). *Property Taxation: Economic Aspects.* (Government Finance Brief No. 13.) New York: Tax Foundation.

_____ (1974). *Federal Tax Burdens in States and Metropolitan Areas.* New York: Tax Foundation.

_____ (annual). *Facts and Figures on Government Finance.* New York: Tax Foundation.

Thurow, Lester C. (1971). *The Impact of Taxes on the American Economy.* New York: Praeger.

_____ (1973a). "Toward a Definition of Economic Justice." *Public Interest* (Spring): 56-80.

_____ (1973b). "A Reply." *The Public Interest* (Fall): 120-127.

_____ (1975). "The Economics of Public Finance." *National Tax Journal* 28 (June): 185-194.

_____ (1976). "The Pursuit of Equity." *Dissent* 23 (Summer): 253-259.

Tiebout, Charles M. (1956). "A Pure Theory of Local Expenditures."

Journal of Political Economy 64 (October): 416-424.

Tucker, Rufus (1951). "The Distribution of Tax Burdens in 1948." *National Tax Journal* 4 (September): 269-285.

_____ (1952a). "Distribution of Tax Burdens in 1948." *Proceedings of the Forty-Fifth Annual Conference, National Tax Association,* Toronto, 195-203.

_____ (1952b). "Rebuttal." *National Tax Journal* 5 (March): 35-38.

_____ (1953). "The Distribution of Government Burdens and Benefits." *American Economic Review, Papers and Proceedings* 43 (May): 518-543.

U.S. Department of Commerce (1977). "State Personal Income Revisions, 1971-76." *Survey of Current Business* 57 (August): 15-32.

U.S. Department of the Treasury (1977). *Blueprints for Basic Tax Reform.* Washington, D.C.: Department of the Treasury.

University of Michigan, Survey Research Center (annual), *Survey Consumer Finances.* Ann Arbor: University of Michigan Press.

University of Wisconsin (1959). *Wisconsin's State and Local Tax Burden.* Madison: University of Wisconsin, School of Commerce.

Vernez, George (1978). "Notes on Alternative Conceptions of Equity." Santa Monica, Calif.: Rand Corporation, P-6223.

Wales, T. J. (1968). "Analysis of the Constancy of the Effective Tax Rate." *Review of Economics and Statistics* 50 (February): 103-110.

Wanniski, Jude (1978). "Taxes, Revenues, and the 'Laffer Curve'." *The Public Interest* (Winter): 3-16.

Weisbrod, Burton A. (1964). *External Benefits of Public Education.* Princeton, N.J.: Department of Economics, Industrial Relations Section, Princeton University.

Williamson, John B. (1976). "Beliefs About the Rich, the Poor and the Taxes they Pay." *American Journal of Economics and Sociology* 35 (January): 9-29.

Worcester, D. A. (1964). "A Graphic General Equilibrium Analysis of the Burden of Taxes." *Western Economic Journal* 2 (Summer): 267-282.

Yaple, Maxine (1936). "The Burden of Direct Taxes as Paid by Income Classes." *American Economic Review* 26 (December): 691-710.

Yntema, Dwight (1933). "Measures of the Inequality in the Personal Distribution of Wealth or Income." *Journal of the American Statistical Association* 28: 423-433.

Index

F

G

H

I

K

L

M

O

P

Q

R

About the Author

Donald Phares is Associate Professor of Economics and Associate Director of the Center for Metropolitan Studies at the University of Missouri-St. Louis. He is author of *State-Local Tax Equity: An Empirical Analysis of the Fifty States,* coauthor of *Municipal Output and Performance in New York City,* and editor of *A Decent Home and Environment: Housing Urban America.* He has also written articles that have appeared in *Social Science Quarterly, Proceedings of the National Tax Association, Annals of Regional Science, Journal of Regional Science, Economic Geography, Journal of Drug Issues, Journal of Psychedelic Drugs, Nation's Cities,* and sections in several books and government reports. Dr. Phares's research deals primarily with housing and neighborhood change and state-local finance and governmental structure. He received his B.A. from Northeastern University and his M.A. and Ph.D from Syracuse University.